JAN CHRISTIAN SMUTS

General J. C. Smuts—Cape Town, 1949

JAN CHRISTIAN
SMUTS

by J. C. SMUTS

with 23 pages of halftone illustrations
and 5 maps

CASSELL & COMPANY LTD

LONDON

CASSELL & CO. LTD

37/38 St Andrew's Hill, Queen Victoria Street
London, E.C.4

and at

210 *Queen Street, Melbourne*
26/30 *Clarence Street, Sydney*
P.O. Box 9, Lower Hutt, N.Z.
263/7 *Adelaide Street West, Toronto*
P.O. Box 275, Cape Town
P.O. Box 1386, Salisbury, S. Rhodesia
122 *East 55th Street, New York 22*
15 *Graham Road, Ballard Estate, Bombay 1*
Islands Brygge 5, Copenhagen
Gartenstrasse 53, Düsseldorf
Avenida 9 de Julho 1138, São Paulo
P.O. Box 959, Accra, Gold Coast
Galeria Güemes, Escritorio 518/520 Florida
165 *Buenos Aires*
Calcada Do Carmo 55–20, Lisbon
25, *Rue Henri Barbusse, Paris 5e*

First published 1952

Set in 12 pt. Bembo type and printed in Great Britain by
Butler & Tanner Ltd., Frome and London
F.552

CONTENTS

v

CONTENTS

vi

CONTENTS

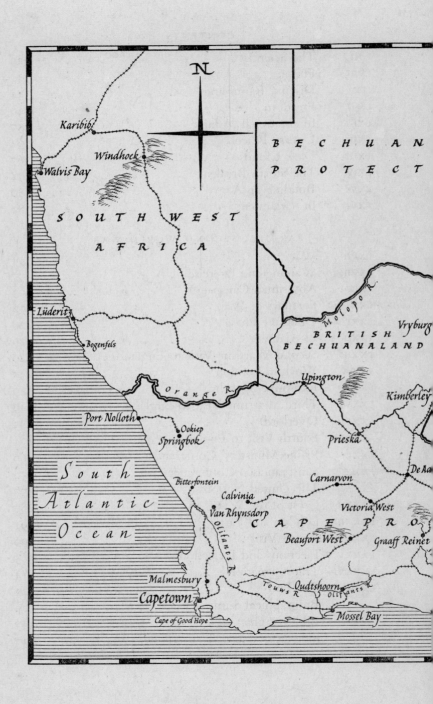

Bulawayo

S O U T H E R N

R H O D E S I A

Tati

Tuli   Beitbridge

AN

ATE

Limpopo

Leydsdorp

erones   Nylstroom

T R A N S V A A L

M
O
Z
A
M
B
I
Q
U
E

Pretoria

Mafeking

Middelburg

Johannesburg

Bethal

SWAZILAND

Lourenço Marques

Vereeniging

Gollel

Vaal R.

Heilbron

Kroonstad

ANGE FREE STATE

MOUNTAINS

Brandfort

Ladysmith

N
A
T
A
L

I n d i a n

oemfontein

BASUTOLAND

Pietermaritzburg

O c e a n

Zastron

Durban

DRAK

orange R

Maclear

Port Shepstone

Dordrecht   Umtata

N C E

Port St. Johns

Bedford

MAP OF
SOUTH AFRICA

East London

Port Alfred

rt Elizabeth

MILES

0   50   100   150   200

LIST OF ILLUSTRATIONS

—————··££ဥ}}··—————

MAPS AND FACSIMILES

INTRODUCTION

IN 1870 a blue-eyed boy was born on a farm in the Cape. Eighty years later, grown to maturity but undimmed by the years, and at heart still a simple child of the veld, he died on a farm in the Transvaal. Between those eighty years and those thousand miles lies a romance of achievement. This simple farm lad was to bring much lustre and fame to the land of his birth. He was, in his time, to become a prophet and interpreter of mankind, a figure loved and revered by peoples far beyond his native land, for he brought to them the breadth of the veld, and the expectation of better things.

Born in the shadow of Riebeeck Kasteel, that mountain buttress rising conspicuously from the plains of Riebeeck West, this boy was himself in years to come to tower like a great mountain above the level plains of humanity. But he never forgot the modest farmhouse where he was born. Throughout his life, though honoured by almost every country of the world, he kept with him that gift of simplicity; it never forsook him and he ended his days in a house as simple as that of his spartan forebears. His memory of the mountain, too, marched with him throughout life and imbued him with those sublime and lofty ideals which he preached so consistently.

When he was twenty his doctor at Cambridge despaired of this youth ever growing old: he was right. At eighty that youth still had not grown old, for the passage of years had touched him lightly.

Greatness never turned his head nor did defeat embitter him. Success was merely an incentive to greater effort and more unselfish service.

This man from Malmesbury was to reintroduce the code of simplicity and higher spiritual and ethical values into the council chambers of the world and to teach men anew the meaning of fairness and magnanimity. This man preached the benign concept of British Imperialism which helped to form a new relationship between the English-speaking elements of the far-flung Empire and led directly to that grand brotherhood which came to be known as the Commonwealth. He was the father of the idea of Commonwealth and also her most illustrious spokesman. It was perhaps the holistic concept of an integrated whole being larger than the sum of its constituent parts that gave him this idea. No less was it this holistic vision that brought about the integration we now know as the Union of South Africa.

Throughout life he carried with him a clear conception of relative values. From his assessment of these values he never turned, even though often criticised and misunderstood. The ultimate greatness of this man lay in the fact that he saw clearly what was right and strove fearlessly and unflinchingly for the attainment of this view. Once he had made up his mind, nothing deterred him, nor was he disillusioned or embittered by obstruction or criticism.

Into the eighty years was crowded great service and achievement, for he was a man of many parts. He was a warrior of three great wars and in all these he attained high distinction, becoming the greatest soldier and strategist South Africa has produced.

As a statesman he attained a unique position in his fatherland and indeed beyond in the great world about him. Britain honoured him with the Order of Merit, the highest civilian award to which South African or Briton can aspire. He came to be known not only as the ambassador of South Africa, but as the Henchman of the Empire and the Founder of the International Peace Organisations.

As a scientist and philosopher he gained supreme honours in many fields. In his treatise on Holism, he suggested a link between the physical and metaphysical and expounded his thesis with a preciseness of reasoning and pureness of prose. His chairmanship at the centenary celebrations of the British Association for the Advancement of Science in 1931 was, he always considered, the supreme honour of his life, for it carried with it the greatest crown that science could offer.

As a politician I think he was the greatest his country has produced, though he never attained this through an eloquence of oratory. He was a great politician, as he had been a great general, both in victory and in defeat. Parliament was indeed graced by the presence of this patient silver-haired sage.

I was privileged to live with this man as a son and friend for many years. I think I can claim to have known him better and more intimately than most men. I have studied him lovingly and carefully. I have seen him in many countries and in many moods, and I would like to put down here my knowledge of him.

I write this account of my father's life with diffidence. I am no journalist, no historian, no scientist, no politician and no military expert. I tackle the task in a sense of duty, of love and admiration. Much of it is written in a mood of eulogy. It would have been too much to expect otherwise of a person who had lived for almost forty years with one of the world's great dreamers and idealists. For this human weakness I make no apologies.

This is not the Official Life of my father. The time is not yet ripe for it. Many aspects still stand too close to history and living personalities. Much is still secret and confidential. Much, in the form of correspondence, still remains to be collected. Documents have to be sorted. So, from many points of view, a weighty Life is not possible for some years.

I write this interim biography merely to give a son's point of view. Perhaps I suffer from the disadvantage of having known him too well to be able to unravel sentiment from fact, or to see my way out of the detail of the history with which I have grown up.

In reviewing the past biographies and books written about my father, I have noticed some deficiencies and distortions. Sometimes the historic setting has been painted with too lavish a brush and the man has been given only a minor role. It is difficult to avoid, in view of my father's intimate, architectural connection with our past.

Unfortunately during most of those years I had been too young to assess properly the moods and highlights of what I saw. Unfortunately, too, with the rest of the family, I failed to keep a diary. All our memories are therefore locked up merely in our heads. It is only during certain of his Second World War visits to England and America, on which I accompanied him, that I kept comprehensive notes.

This is regrettable, for my father was a perfect raconteur of stories and anecdotes on events and people. They covered almost every topic imaginable from the outer spaces of our expanding Universe to the commonplace nonentities of our daily life. On all these topics he was knowledgeable and lucid with a wealth of vision that enthralled both old and young.

These, alas, are now only vague memories, dimmed by the passing of the years. But in the sum total of the complete personality, these minute facets all play their part. For it is by the simplicity of little things almost as much as by his great achievements that my father will be remembered.

If I succeed even in small measure in depicting the simplicity, integrity and consistency of that complex character we all knew as the "Oubaas", I shall be well satisfied. My father was no tight-lipped enigma or hard grey ingot of steel. He was a warm friendly human, with a strongly developed family instinct, living simply and frugally. I trust I shall be able to convey something of this in the pages that follow. He was no bespectacled bookworm, or tight-lipped idealist, or highbrow scientist, or dogmatic politician. He was a generous, kindly and chivalrous man. Greatness never made him too big for the old tin home at Irene or for the narrow confines of his fatherland.

With this great figure I would couple the name of my modest little mother—"Ouma" to many. Her encouragement, understanding, courage and support were an immense help to my father in his career. She too is a great personality, and will rank as one of the most remarkable women produced by South Africa. It was indeed fortunate that these two people should have been privileged to work together.

But one thing is certain as the glorious sun that rises above our limitless veld—the name of Jan Christian Smuts, his deeds, his aspirations, his words and ideals, will live on as long as men take pride in great achievements, and will grow in stature with the passing of the years. To those who follow him he has bequeathed a glorious legacy. It is for history to prove whether we are worthy of this great gift.

PART I

The Boer Leader

B

I THE OLD CAPE

IN the flat wheat-growing area of·Malmesbury, in the south-western Cape, stands the sleepy little hamlet of Riebeeck West, dating back to the early years of European settlement in the eighteenth century. Quiet as is the setting of this rustic village, its bearing on South African history has been profound. For there, within the shadow of the massive rampart of rock known as the Kasteel (Castle), on two farms within a stone's throw of each other, were born, at almost the same time, two men who have had a marked effect on South African history. Close as has been their origin, no paths could later have diverged more sharply. One, Jan Christian Smuts, my father, was essentially of the Herculean mould of nation-builder and statesman, a man of broad-minded tolerance. The other, Daniel François Malan, one-time henchman of General Hertzog, was a man of narrow nationalism. Combine this contrast and there is revealed that strange though colourful part the Boer people have played in the history of South Africa.

Yet essentially these two men are of similar extraction and environment. It is difficult to explain the gulf between them. It has its origin possibly in some distant and obscure genetic back-ground which goes into the composition of the Boer race. Usually the products are a stable type like my father; but not infrequently, by some inexplicable Mendelian mutation, unstable types are initiated with eruptive characteristics, who unfortunately always seem to have a gullible following. Our history abounds with these crusty types. No useful purpose will be served by endeavouring to explain the vagary of the Boer people on an historic basis. For history will show not only deeds of great daring and initiative, but also acts of a suicidal and futile nature. It will show that even under the dire stresses and ever-prevalent dangers from the native hordes during the Great Trek, there was quarrelling rather than co-operation, and serious differences of opinion on questions of leadership and direction.

We must accept the instability in the Boer people as an inherent and indelible trait. And it is in the light of this that we must measure the extent of my father's work and the size of his achievements. At the same time it is also an indication of the dangers and difficulties that lie before us.

The English-speaking element, which constitutes about forty per cent of the population, by contrast to the Afrikaans-speaking element, seems to be over-compensated with stable, passive attributes. One of the most fatal of these is apathy to all matters political, and general disregard of the active side of government. Nothing will induce them to attend meetings or show any enthusiasm, and wild horses can barely drag them to the polling booths.

The political approach to the two sections therefore varies.

*   *   *   *   *

In 1486 the Portuguese explorer Bartholomew Diaz was rudely buffeted past the Cape in a gale. This was the first rounding by European explorers since the days of Pharaoh Necho, seven centuries before Christ. Diaz christened this jutting headland the Cape of Storms. Eleven years later, another Portuguese navigator, da Gama, while on the way to the East, also passed within view of Table Mountain with its cloth of mist. It was calm with a brilliant sun shining. He rechristened it the Cape of Good Hope. This was a more happy augury for the birth of a new country, but the fate of storms predicted by Diaz has been ever close to us.

Thereafter the Cape, with its heavy seas and forbidding coastline, was left in peace for a long while. The few travellers that ventured ashore, or were shipwrecked, were set upon and murdered by the indigenous savages. But trade between Europe and the East was steadily increasing and by the beginning of the seventeenth century the Dutch East India Company had grown into an important concern. In 1652 Jan van Riebeeck was sent out with three ships to establish a revictualling station to provide for the needs of the company on its long and hazardous voyages. And so began the first serious attempt by the white man at settlement in the sub-continent. That foothold, precarious at first and lodged largely in a fort built on the foreshore, grew and expanded steadily, till by the time of van der Stel it had spread inland to Stellenbosch and Paarl and even beyond into the mountains. It was evident that the white man had come to stay.

At about the same time as van Riebeeck's Europeans were establishing their foothold in the Cape, the Bantu tribes were swarming into South Africa from the north. Between them were squeezed the ancient indigenous Bushman and Koranna stock, who because of their pilfering and predatory habits were looked upon as vermin and exterminated on contact by both invaders. Remnants escaped for sanctuary into the arid fastnesses of the Kalahari, where they survive in limited numbers to this day. The Bantu, or Natives, as they are more usually known, are Central African negro migrants with considerable admixtures of Hamitic blood. They moved southwards in a series of separate waves, and between them there was constant raiding and conflict.

So far, the immigrants had been exclusively Dutch, but with the Revocation of the Edict of Nantes and the persecution of the Huguenots, 180 of these stout French folk sought asylum at the Cape in 1688. They brought with them not only ideas on the cultivation of the vine but a measure of culture and enlightenment. Soon their language had been swallowed up by the Dutch and their blood diluted by intermarriage. This blending of the Dutch and French stock resulted in that sturdy race which has come to be known as the Boers. The British first became represented in any numbers in the early years of the nineteenth century, when five thousand 1820 settlers made their homes in the eastern portion of the Cape Province near Port Elizabeth. For geographical reasons, if for no other, intermarriage between Boer and Briton never progressed as had been the case with the French Huguenots. This was a pity.

II RIEBEECK WEST

My father was born on the 24th of May, 1870, in the humble whitewashed homestead on the farm Ongegund, three miles from Riebeeck West. He was the second eldest in a family of four sons and two daughters. The house was situated on the upper section of the farm, and as the lower portion was occupied by another branch of the Smutses this upper part came to be known as Bovenplaats (Upper farm).

His christian names he inherited from his maternal grandfather Jan Christian de Vries. Like his grandfather, he spelt Christian with one "a".

Around, on the undulating plains of Malmesbury, billowed the endless wheat-fields of the great Swartland. Behind the simple, gabled farmhouse, obscuring Table Mountain and the Cape peninsula, rose the three-thousand-foot Kasteel. By contrast to the flatness of its surroundings it formed a conspicuous feature. The homestead on Bovenplaats, or Boplaas as it was more popularly known, was not by any standards a pretentious place, for its thatched roof and narrow construction lent it an almost barnlike appearance. The houses were already many generations old and had always been inhabited by Smutses.

My father was fortunate to be born into the world in an era which offered perhaps more opportunity for an able young man than any previous one. In South Africa the Industrial Revolution was just starting and we were on the threshold of the far-reaching discoveries of diamonds and gold. His life-span was to encompass not only the great age of steel and electricity, of the invention of the internal combustion engine and the aeroplane, but also the golden age of science and the opening phases of the epoch-making atomic age. Each was in itself a world apart—something new the human mind had not previously conceived. Has youth ever before had such an endless abundance of opportunity? He was perhaps fortunate, too, to find himself in South Africa in the formative years of her history.

The farmers of the Swartland did not have the wealth or inclination for the artistic Dutch architectural type of buildings of Constantia or Stellenbosch. They were simpler here, living farther from the centres of civilisation, and wheat farming was a more exacting occupation than the cultivation of the vine of the fertile plains of the Cape proper. So in some ways, though near it geographically, the Swartland formed a world apart from the environs of the mother city. People were judged rather by the fervour with which they embraced the Calvinistic doctrines of the Dutch Reformed Church, and by the pious merits of their deeds. By any standards, the population of the Cape was conservative, and the heavy atmosphere of the coast and the warmth of the sunshine lent a certain self-satisfaction to those who lived there.

Jacobus Abraham Smuts, my paternal grandfather, was a man of some prominence in these parts, for he was member for Malmesbury in the old Cape Legislature or supreme parliament of the province. Photographs show him as a stocky round-faced man, broad of forehead and round of head, a typical Hollander in appearance. His appearance did not belie his extraction, for though the sixth generation of Smutses to be born in the Cape, he was of almost pure Dutch extraction.

The first Smuts to settle in the Cape was Michiel Cornelis, who came out from Zeeland in the service of the Dutch East India Company in 1692.

My father's mother was plump Catharina (Cato) Petronella de Vries, a sister of Bodewyn, the local padre. She was a seventh generation descendant of Jacob Cloete who arrived in 1652 with van Riebeeck's entourage, and in old age was murdered on a farm by natives. In Ouma Cato's veins was about one-sixth French blood, which perhaps accounts for her more mercurial and impressionable temperament. She was a woman of culture and had studied music and French in Cape Town. As a great teller of stories she impressed her young family of four sons and two daughters. At the time of the Boer War my father wrote: "How well I remember the spiritual teaching of my mother."

Boplaas was, in the 1870s, considered quite an attractive farm, lying high up on the sloping ground below the Kasteel, with fine vineyards and lands, and an attractive view across the broad plains below it to the distant, sometimes snow-capped, mountains of the Groot Winterhoek range in the north.

7

In summer, during the height of the dry season the aspect was arid and uninviting, but with the winter rains it became an enchanting panorama of emerald green, which was slowly transformed into a rich gold as the wheat ripened.

Shortly before the Second World War considerable limestone deposits were discovered on Boplaas, which was thereupon taken over by the Cape Portland Cement Company. A descendant, van der Byl Smuts, was at the time living in the old homestead, on the walls of which he had hung photographs of General Hertzog and Dr. Malan. When Sir Alfred Hennessy, Chairman of the old South African Party, mentioned this fact to my father, the latter remarked casually that the main branch in old families was often inclined to degenerate!

The house, which was at that time in a state of neglect, has since been renovated and is now once more being cared for; Mr. van der Byl Smuts, probably still a confirmed Nationalist, lives elsewhere.

In 1945 an old pear tree in the orchard was beginning to show signs of decay, so the hamlet of Malmesbury secured it and had a casket made from the wood, which it presented to my father on his seventy-fifth birthday. It is with me at present for safe keeping. My father well remembered scrambling about in the tree as a boy.

The setting at Boplaas was quiet and peaceful, forming a striking contrast to the seething conditions of the republics beyond the Orange River. Almost three-quarters of a century earlier the British had taken over the Cape after a brief skirmish at Blaauberg, but as annexation was achieved with comparatively little bloodshed, the incident had long since ceased to rankle in the minds of the old colonists. Nor did the problem of mixed European population obtrude itself upon the Smuts environs, for they were here in an exclusively Boer world. Consequently my father grew up in an atmosphere devoid of prejudices and one benevolent towards the British. Though shaken on one occasion, that benign heritage never left him and was to form one of the dominant themes of his life.

In the Boplaas household Afrikaans was spoken exclusively and it was not until my father went to school that he first heard English.

III THE REPUBLICS

IN the north, on the distant frontiers and in the Transvaal and Free State republics, the process of establishing a foothold was still going on apace and there was constant conflict and war, often not without good reason, between white and black. There was equally constant conflict between Boer and Briton, the Boer love of freedom and independence often clashing with the then expansionist phase of British imperialism. There is much to be said either in mitigation or in condemnation of both parties, for the two courses were largely incompatible.

In 1836 the Boers of the frontier, irritated by a series of grievances against the British administration, such as the compensation swindle following the emancipation of the slaves, lack of understanding or sympathetic treatment by Governors of the Cape and misrepresentation by missionaries, decided that the time had come to move on. Whether the decision was based upon the burden of the grievances or whether it was due equally to the inherent restlessness of the Boer people, it is difficult to say. Whatever the reason, they succumbed to their feelings and insatiable wanderlust, and set out on a migration into the unknown interior with their families and belongings, their stock and their wagons, on what is known as the Great Trek. There were various branches to this trek and they encountered varying fortunes in their wanderings. As an epic of bravery and the unflinching facing of great hardships and odds it has few equals in our colourful history, but as a record of organisation and co-operation it gave but a foretaste of the confused future.

Neither the Smutses nor Kriges participated in the migration, for they dwelt in areas far to the south of those which felt the urge of discontent. Piet Retief, the redoubtable trek leader, was, however, closely related to the stock of my mother.

The hardy trekkers, except those who moved into the densely populated Zulu domain of Natal, moved northwards into a country almost devoid of native population. This in no small measure explains much of the success of the trek; for northwards

the country had come into the orbit of the raiding Zulu hordes
and indigenous tribes had been almost completely wiped out.
Only the comeliest marriageable maidens were spared by the
conquerors. In the Transvaal the ruthless Moselekatze, fugitive
lieutenant of Chaka's, whose very name meant "Trail of Blood",
still ravaged the country from end to end in a series of sweeps of
annihilation. Before the Boers finally broke his power at Marico,
it is estimated that he had murdered about a half a million hapless
natives, a record that even Genghis Khan might have envied.
Chaka's own record of over a million is surpassed only by the
liquidations of Adolf Hitler and Josef Stalin.

But the battles for white supremacy were fought out mainly
in Natal, and there, too, only after considerable loss of life was the
Zulu power finally broken at Blood River, and the Royal Kraal
at Umgungundhlovu burnt down.

With the coming of the white man the natives, probably for
the first time in their very ancient tribal history, learned to know
the meaning of peace and freedom from fear; for these blessings
had never existed under the various barbarous and cruel native
potentates. The Bantu are quick to forget this inestimable boon
brought to them by the white man.

With the crushing of the Zulu tyrants a mild form of peace
ensued in the vast hinterland. It was not till 1879 that trouble
once more flared up under Cetawayo, who inflicted a major
defeat upon Lord Chelmsford's forces at Isandhlwana. At Ulundi,
three days later, the Zulu power was finally broken.

By a stroke of fate, the Boers happened to stumble into a
country containing a great wealth of diamonds and gold, and
these were soon not only to attract covetous eyes, but also to
bring pressing problems. At the time the Boers were expanding
their grip in a black empire by a series of skirmishes with the
indigenous populations. These onslaughts upon the black man,
often defensive, ran counter to deep convictions in Britain, where
they were almost invariably misjudged, and British intolerance
of the state of affairs was heightened by the misrepresentations of
certain missionaries of the stamp of van der Kemp and Philip.*

* J. T. van der Kemp was sent out by the London Missionary Society in 1799,
and on his arrival in Cape Colony made his way inland and began work among
the Kafirs and Hottentots. He was prominent in a movement for emancipating

Even that peace-loving missionary David Livingstone did not escape the suspicions of the Boers, being accused of complicity in a gun-smuggling racket to the natives. In actual fact poor Livingstone was quite innocent of gun-running, and it was more likely that the hunter Gordon-Cumming * was dealing in this trade.

The result of all these suspicions mounted up in the end, in many parts, to a strained feeling between the two white sections. Taking all the factors into account, it has nevertheless amazed me how remarkably restrained those feelings have generally been. It says a great deal for the tolerance of both parties that it did not grow into something much deeper.

IV BOYHOOD

B UT in the world of my father's childhood all was peace and quiet. Though not a weak or sickly boy, his constitution was not robust. Furthermore, he was the second son in the family, which in the Dutch hierarchy consigned him to a very much lower status in the house than his brother Michiel. Michiel was the eldest son and on him rested the hopes of the family. He was to be ordained a minister.

So my father was very much of an unspoiled, though not neglected, second fiddle. He was left a fairly free hand to do as he

them from Boer hands. His work was taken up after his death in 1811 by Dr. John Philip, who was sent by the Society to visit their stations in 1819. He remained in Cape Town and devoted his life to the cause of the native peoples. One of his more impractical schemes was to erect independent native states in South Africa.

* R. G. Gordon-Cumming (1820–66) was well known as a hunter. He resigned his commission in the Cape Mounted Rifles in 1843 and spent five years in a senseless slaughter of wild beasts under the guise of big-game shooting. In 1848 he returned to England where he toured the country with his lecture on lion hunting.

wished, providing he carried out the prescribed family duties of tending his father's flocks of geese, goats, horses and cattle. This brought him into contact with that philosophical old farm hand, the wizened Hottentot Adam, who, to my youthful father, was a fount of strange information. It was old Adam who informed him, at a very early age, that the English, though a great people, were as nothing compared to the other people farther across the seas, the Scots. They really were God's chosen race! This little story, suitably embellished, my father told in 1934 as Rector at St. Andrew's University in Scotland during his famous address on Freedom.

Life on the farm, though humdrum in many ways, was never monotonous, for the veld and the farm held so much of interest. The early associations with Boplaas and the mountain formed in my father that indelible love of the veld, farm life and simplicity. Adam gave him an early glimpse into the psychology of the native in which he ever after took an understanding interest. His feelings for these people were always governed more by this practical understanding than by the theorising of books or the sentimentalism of the philanthropist.

As a man of thirty-two he wrote: "How well I remembered the years I spent tending the cattle on the large farm, roaming over all its far expanse of veld, in which every kloof, every valley, every koppie was endeared to me by the most familiar associations. Month after month I had spent there in lonely occupation —alone with the cattle, myself and God. The veld had grown part of me, not only in the sense that my bones were part of it, but in that more vital sense which identifies nature with man. . . . Having no human companion I felt a spirit of comradeship for the objects of nature around me. In my childish way I communed with these as with my own soul; they became the sharers of my confidence."

Throughout life he retained a strong sentimental attachment to his farming forebears. At the age of seventy-seven, when receiving the Freedom of Malmesbury in England, he still claimed with pride: "I am just a son of the veld. Malmesbury in South Africa is a wheat-growing district not far from Cape Town. The whole country is covered with wheat farms. I am a farmer's son, and my people have been farmers throughout the centuries. In 1692 the Smuts family migrated to South Africa from Holland. Last year I went to Middelburg in the Netherlands where the Smutses came from. There I saw the ancient homeland of the Smuts family, where they had been farmers for centuries before coming to South Africa."

That his early life on the farm was never dull was reflected in the stories he used to tell us—and later our children—about the incidents of his youth. There were the disconcerting occasions when he was chased by his father's geese. He used to tell of what he called a miraculous escape from death when he was five. He was playing in the loft above the stables, when something gave way and he crashed through the ceiling amongst the startled mules tethered below. In its panic, one began kicking viciously backwards, but mercifully on each occasion it missed the boy's head by inches. One kick, however, did graze the back of his head and laid him out. It produced a scar, not far from the scar of his 1927 carbuncle operation, which he bore all his life. He described this encounter with the mules as the most dangerous and terrifying he ever met with.

On another occasion, I once heard him tell to my son, aged four, the story of a troop of baboons coming down from the mountain into the orchard behind the house. The three farm dogs soon spotted them and gave chase. The big leader of the baboon pack, whether from arrogance, or to cover the retreat of his troop, refused to be stampeded and climbed into a big fruit tree instead. Here he was bayed by the furious dogs, and he vented his feelings by roaring his defiance even above the din of their barking. Aroused by this noise, old Jacobus Smuts, muzzle-loader in hand and followed by the rest of the family, including my father, rushed out to see what all the noise was about. He took a shot at the baboon which fell badly wounded amongst the hounds, but the poor beast still had some strength left, and before it died, it killed the biggest and finest of the dogs and mauled both the others.

With this self-same gun my father was taught to shoot when he was nine years old. I still have the old weapon in my possession.

Another terrifying incident which my father was fond of relating was an encounter with a fierce dog. It happened during the periodic visit to the farm of a *smous* or pedlar, when he was a lad of four or five. This *smous* had a big dog with his wagons and the great brute broke loose and attacked my father, knocked him down, and stood snarling over him. In this position he was shot by old Jacobus, falling dead on top of the terrified child. Perhaps this incident accounted for my father's life-long aversion to dogs.

Life on the farm was not all fun, for much hard work devolved upon the farm lad of those days. In the ploughing season he had to be up before the first grey signs of dawn, and lead the ox span along the plough furrow all day long till late in the evening. In the mornings it was cold and cheerless and at noontide the sun scorched the earth. But young Jan's constitution, especially after his fourth year, belied his weedy appearance and he came through his strenuous days well.

His grandfather sometimes took pity on him during the coldest mornings and carried him to the fields in his arms.

V STELLENBOSCH

His brother Michiel died of typhoid when my father was twelve. It was now left to this younger boy to carry on the traditions of the family, and it was decided that he should be educated and enter the Church. Not only was this natural, as Dominie A. J. Louw, the Dutch parson, was a close friend of old Jacobus, but it was also reasonable, as my father showed a serious turn of mind for his age. Though he had had some elementary tuition from his mother at home, it was not till the age of twelve that he was sent to school for the first time, and it was with misgiving that he said farewell to the old surroundings and went to board at "Die Ark", which formed part of the school of Mr. T. C. Stofberg in Riebeeck West. "Die Ark", as photographs show, was appropriately named, for it looked rather like the

14

superstructure of a boat. It nestled at the foot of the Kasteel and was well placed for rambles up the mountain slopes.

When my father was eight the family had moved to a new inheritance on Klipfontein which lay fifteen miles on the other side of Riebeeck West. The red-shuttered farmhouse here was a larger and better building than the old homestead at Boplaas and looked out upon the broad valley of the Berg River in the distance.

My father entered school with a mind so empty, yet so craving for knowledge, that he absorbed all the learning Mr. Stofberg had to proffer him. His brain was clear and receptive. He mastered his studies with a photographic faithfulness, readily memorising much of what he read. Stofberg was quick to sense the abilities of his pupil and went out of his way to help him and to put reading matter at his disposal.

Mr. Stofberg later became an Inspector of Schools in the Transvaal and by a queer turn of events, by no means unusual in this country, in 1915 forsook his inspectorship and entered politics to contest, unsuccessfully, the Rustenburg parliamentary seat with a Smuts candidate.

My father's brother, Michiel, when at school in Riebeeck West, had not lodged at "Die Ark" but had boarded with the Malan family on the farm Allesverloren, alongside the village. There was a youngster, Daniel François, about the house whom my father opposed for years in politics in later life. The old Smutses and Malans were very close friends, and eventually when they retired from their farms and went to live in the village at Riebeeck West, they not only saw to it that they occupied adjoining houses, but even went to the extent of leaving a broad gap in the intervening hedge in order that the two houses might be as one.

After a few years at "Die Ark" my father went up for his matric in Stellenbosch. In the four years at Riebeeck West he had gone through the work which took the normal boy eleven years. So he set off to the Victoria College in Stellenbosch, where he lodged with Mr. Ackermann on the Eerste Rivier end of Dorp Street, in the older portion of the town. His ambition was keen, but his heart was filled with forebodings of the worldly distractions that lurked in this great centre of learning. The quaint, naïve, letter he wrote at the time to Professor Charles Murray has been widely quoted, but it is such a pure, old-fashioned creation that I think parts deserve to be quoted here again:

KLIPFONTEIN,
June 12, 1886.

Mr. C. Murray,
Professor, Stellenbosch.

DEAR SIR,

Allow me the honour of your reading and answering these few lines. I intend coming to Stellenbosch in July next, and, having heard that you take an exceptionally great interest in the youth, I trust you will favour me by keeping your eye upon me and helping me with your kindly advice. Moreover, as I shall be a perfect stranger there and, as you know such a place, where a large puerile element exists, affords fair scope for moral, and, what is more important, religious temptation, which, if yielded to, will eclipse alike the expectations of my parents and the intentions of myself, a real friend will prove a lasting blessing for me. For of what use will a mind, enlarged and refined in all possible ways, be to me, if my religion be a deserted pilot and morality a wreck?

To avoid temptation and to make the proper use of my precious time, I purposely refuse entering a public boarding department, as that of Mr. de Kock, but shall board privately (most likely at Mr. W. Ackermann's) which will, in addition, accord with my retired and reserved nature.

[He then makes a few queries about syllabuses and text-books, and concludes:] Sincerely assuring you of my deep gratitude if I may have you for a friend, and also if informed on these points. . . .

Your obedient servant,
J. C. SMUTS.

This letter, so unlike any other he had received, impressed the Professor and he put it to one side. In 1933 he returned it to my father. "After the lapse of many years," the Professor wrote, "I can recollect distinctly that this letter stood out very clearly from the run of such communications—the writer knew what he wanted. . . . The letter tempts me to reminiscences and reflections. . . ."

The letter was written in English, which he had been learning for four years; it was in a thin, timid hand, unlike any I have seen my father use.

My father negotiated the first year at Victoria College with flying colours, matriculating with distinction and coming third

Klipfontein
June 12 - 1886

Mr C. Murray.
    Professor, Stellenbosch

        — " —

Dear Sir,

        Allow me the honour of your
reading and answering these few lines.
I intend coming to Stellenbosch in
July next, and, having heard that you
take an exceptionally great interest
in the youth, I trust you will
favour me by keeping your eye upon
me and helping me with your kindly
advice. Moreover, as I shall be a perfect
stranger there and, as you know such
a place where a large puerile element
exists affords fair scope for moral.
and, what is more important, religious temptation, which, if yielded to will eclipse

        I have the honour, dear Sir, of calling
myself your obedient servant

                            J. C. Smuts

on the lists. My mother, Sybella Margaretha Krige (better known as Isie) came only slightly lower. Her home was in the fine Dutch gabled house "Klein Libertas", alongside the beautiful oak-lined avenue of Dorp Street. Nine years later she was to marry my father. She was the daughter of Japie Krige, a well-known and respected wine and dairy farmer, and their home was a pious one. She was as serious-minded as my father. Photographs show her as a lovely girl, slender and small, with curly brown hair and blue eyes. She was two-thirds French by extraction, and had inherited their daintiness rather than the more ponderous build of the women of purer Dutch descent. My mother's forebears were Huguenots who came to South Africa at the beginning of the eighteenth century.

The Kriges were an able family, many of its members having reached the top of their various professions. They were also noted athletes and Rugby players. But like most people in Stellenbosch they did not love the English.

After matriculating, my mother spent five years at Helderberg, near Stellenbosch, as a school teacher.

On their way to school, my father and mother chatted animatedly as they walked under the massive oaks, some planted in the seventeenth century by Simon van der Stel. Sometimes my father carried her books for her. In this quiet way the friendship ripened and they studied and read books on botany and poetry together.

The Smuts and Krige families did not know each other till these Stellenbosch days. "It was at this stage that I first met the girl, then my class-mate, who was to become my wife ten years afterwards," my father was to write years afterwards in a diary. "Less idealistic than I, but more human . . ., she first like the spirit of poetry in Goethe, recalled me from my intellectual isolation and made me return to my fellows."

There was nothing particularly romantic about the courtship. They were rather reserved and undemonstrative, and from questioning and teasing our mother, we decided that it was rather an odd and old-fashioned courtship. The two young people, though probably not oblivious of the fine surroundings, saw more of the beauties of the classics and the poets than of the fine scenery around them. But what the courtship lacked in impetuosity it gained in depth of friendship and understanding. That friendship, unscathed and undiminished, withstood the test of time, and was the basis of a fruitful and exemplary married life.

Greek formed part of the curriculum. My father tackled it for the first time during the six-day holiday before his final term, and locking himself up in his room memorised the books and mastered Greek to such effect that he not only passed his exams, but actually headed the Cape lists in this subject. He considered that the most remarkable feat of memorising in his life.

In those days he could memorise large portions of books by reading through them. At Stellenbosch his examiners were, till they learned to understand this prodigy, inclined to accuse the youngster of cribbing, for many of his answers were verbatim from the text-books. At Stellenbosch his faculty for memorising was at its peak, he used to say, and by the time he reached Cambridge it had already waned somewhat. Yet at the age of sixty and seventy, while working at his botany he was still memorising the tens of thousands of intricate Latin names of plants with the greatest facility. But as eighty approached I noticed that he often had to fumble for a name. This was partially due, I think, to the pressure of work during World War II, which gave him little time to keep up this hobby. Many might consider prodigious memory a blessing, yet as an old man my father was to remark to my mother how happy he was now that he was losing this gift and growing forgetful.

Cecil Rhodes, Prime Minister of the Cape, paid a visit to Victoria College in 1888. My father was asked to make a speech of welcome on behalf of the students. The substance of this speech was remarkable for a boy of seventeen. He spoke of Pan-Africanism, a theme dear to Rhodes. Rhodes made no effort to meet the boy but remarked to J. H. Hofmeyr, who was sitting next to him: "Keep your eye on the young fellow Smuts." John X. Merriman, that distinguished figure of the old Cape parliament, said to my grandfather Jacobus: "Jan will be the first man in South Africa."

At this stage my father was of a religious frame of mind and regularly attended Sunday services in the Dutch Reformed Church near the Theological College. After services he would hold Bible classes for coloured youths to whom he expounded the truths of the Book. He also belonged to a Bible circle. He never lost his love for the Bible, though his religious feeling for it gradually changed in after life to an interest in it as a panorama of life and a psychological study, and as the supreme classic of the English language.

During the six hectic days in which he was memorising his Greek books for his matriculation examination, he read Shelley as a diversion. He became deeply engrossed in this young poet, and throughout life preferred Shelley, in whom he found more of the philosopher, to other poets. He later went on to Keats, Milton and Shakespeare and other classics, though of these, Shakespeare is the one in whom he sustained the greatest interest. In later life he was to develop a special passion for Shakespeare's tragedies, which as a group, he considered the greatest fictional works in English.

As a youth he read the German poets, especially Goethe and Schiller, but these he appreciated perhaps more as psychological studies than as examples of classical art.

While at Stellenbosch, under Professor Mansveld, he learned Netherlands Dutch; and with his quick and thorough mind became one of the most proficient scholars in the country. In it he wrote a paper on the "Commerce and Prosperity of the Netherlands During the Eighty Years War", which was acclaimed as a fine example of the Dutch language. For its sheer purity of diction, it created a profound impression on Dr. Leyds, a member of Kruger's government. Years later the superb Netherlands Dutch of his *Century of Wrong* was also to draw praise from Dr. Gustav Preller, the South African historian.

At nineteen my father contributed "Homo Sum", a learned dissertation on slavery. His pen was never idle. Dutch and English flowed from it with equal facility, and the newspapers were full of his leaders, letters, articles and reviews. The tremendous energy of the man, which in those days found expression through the pen, was a life-long characteristic.

"The five years I spent at Victoria College, Stellenbosch," he wrote years afterwards, "were probably the happiest of my life. I read much and widely, but especially the poets and philosophical writers. I had not yet any defined channel of thinking or feeling. My mind was simply dazzled and attracted by beauty in all its intellectual forms. . . . My passion for nature made me spend most of my free time in the mountains, along the streams and in the innumerable winding valleys."

VI CAMBRIDGE

IN 1891 my father took his degree in Science as well as Literature and obtained honours in both. This success won for him the Ebdin Scholarship for overseas study, which at that time was worth only £100 a year. He decided to take Law at Cambridge and, selling his farm stock and borrowing an additional £380 from Professor Marais, he set out in the *Roslyn Castle* for England. In 1894 an additional £100 per year was voted to Smuts "in consideration of his distinguished success as a student at Cambridge". His application in 1892 for additional assistance from the Trustees had been withdrawn, as he was told it was inopportune and that its strong wording would create a bad impression.

Many of his contemporaries at Christ's College remembered the serious-faced youth at Cambridge. He preferred to further his studies rather than have a good time. In any case his frugal means did not permit such a course. One can well imagine his fellow students looking upon him as a somewhat anti-social type. He took part in no organised sport, and preferred, as at Stellenbosch, to go walking in the country. On these rambles he would take books with him, books on poetry and philosophy rather than standard works for his studies. Here, in the solitude of the walks alone along the Cam, or in the woods or on the hills farther afield, he would pore over these books and no doubt scheme for the future.

"At Cambridge", he says in his diary, "I read much, walked much and thought much; and when I left the University I had probably drunk as deeply of the well of knowledge as most. . . .

I did not, however, mix much in the social life of the place." For the irresponsible, rollicking type of undergraduate he had little praise.

And so, in the beauties of the English countryside and the atmosphere of the University, the days passed pleasantly and fruitfully. All the time that brilliant brain was active; he not only found time for an immense amount of study, but also in his leisure began, in 1894, a lengthy treatise entitled "Walt Whitman —A Study in the Evolution of Personality." The connection with Whitman is slender, for it is in essentials an abstract study of personality. The angle of approach to the subject is a new one and the concept not dissimilar to that which brought fame later to Sigmund Freud. But this treatise differed from a psycho-analyst text-book in that it did not split personality into the conscious, sub-conscious and other parts, but considered it as one integrated whole. This conception of wholes was to mature slowly in his mind, and thirty years later to appear in his book *Holism and Evolution*. "Walt Whitman" holds the germ of holism; that the whole is something greater than the mere sum total of its parts – that it has gained a new character by this unity. In this earlier work my father says: "Every individual form of life is a unity, a centre of activity dominated by one fundamental property. It is this ultimate internal unity that shapes the innumerable products of life into an orderly and harmonious whole." He says also: "In every individual form of life this fundamental property operates according to its own laws and forms. By studying the mental life as a whole . . . we shall soon get beyond the range of the pure psychologist."

It was unfortunate that my father chose Whitman for his study, for Whitman was a man that attracted little attention at the time. Had he selected Goethe, it is possible that he might have got a publisher for his book, so laboriously copied out in freehand by my mother. Messrs. Chapman & Hall refused it as "not opportune" and "unlikely for the present to win any readers". George Meredith read it for them. Unfortunately the real purpose of the book escaped him, for he considered it as a merely literary study of Whitman.

In a letter to the publishing firm of Longmans Green, written on 18th May, 1895, my father describes his book as "an attempt to apply the method of Evolution *synthetically* to the study of Man". He goes on: "You will perhaps ask why I took Whitman, who is certainly not popular in this country. I took him, not only because he is perhaps the most difficult Personality that could be taken and thus supplies a very severe test of my general theory, but because his life and work raise so many of the great questions which surround personal evolution." He concludes naïvely: "I anticipate a good circulation in America." Longmans Green were not tempted to publish it. Finally, when already back again in South Africa, my father tried to get it published in England in serial form by the *Nineteenth Century*, but they too returned it unpublished.

After this unsympathetic treatment the work reposed quietly on a dusty shelf in my father's study for forty years before he chanced to glance at it again. *Holism* had already appeared some years previously. He was much interested in his early work, remarking, "I have read some of the chapters again, and not without amazement. It is full of puerility, but it has remarkable stuff, as coming from a youngster of twenty-four. Indeed in some respects it is better than *Holism and Evolution* written thirty years later." He said it would never be published now, for it was a "boy's book". Perhaps one day "Walt Whitman" may appear as a study of Smuts's personality.

His studies at Cambridge were a triumph, and though he did both parts of the Law Tripos simultaneously he gained distinction in both, a feat claimed by the *Cape Times* as "quite unparalleled", and described by the *Encyclopædia Britannica* as "unprecedented". Professor Maitland long afterwards described him as the most brilliant law student he had ever taught.

The amazing thing about my father's brain was that it came from a family background that had, so far as we know, never produced anything that might be described as exceptional, far less brilliant.

He won the George Long prize in Roman Law and Jurisprudence, a prize only awarded in cases of exceptional merit. In December, 1894, the Council of Legal Education awarded him a prize of £50 for the best paper on Constitutional Law (English and Colonial) and Legal History. It was indeed "an amazing series of successes"! He entered the Middle Temple after passing the entrance exam with distinction, and practised as a barrister with some success. He was now twenty-five.

Christ's College offered him a fellowship in Law, but he turned it down.

My father never forgot his old University or his debt of gratitude for what it had meant to him in early life. Whenever he was in Britain, in war or in peace, he always made a point of paying Christ's College a visit and seeing the Master. Nor did Cambridge ever forget its protégé, for it appointed him Chancellor in 1948, and with due ceremony inducted him into the post. My brother Japie also spent two very pleasant years at Christ's where he gained a double first in the Engineering Tripos.

Apart from the tedium of study, Smuts's Cambridge days were uneventful. He had not the money to go abroad or to travel. He got about mostly on his own two feet. He took out a life insurance policy which he ceded to Professor Marais as security for his loan. The insurance agents did not want to grant him comprehensive coverage, as they were uncertain about his slender appearance and hereditary background of diabetes. His doctor examined him at Cambridge and said, "Drink beer, my boy. It will do you good!" In 1950 he still drank beer because he enjoyed it.

Perhaps my father's most vivid memory of the University was an incident when they were walking in procession to some ceremony. Out of a clear sky a solitary flash of lightning struck dead a student walking ten feet ahead of him. Throughout his long outdoor life he weathered many a wild African thunderstorm, but he was indifferent to them, beyond admiring the vivid display. Only on one occasion, when wandering alone on the hills at Irene, was he frightened by a storm. It smote the earth with the noise and intensity of an artillery barrage on the Western Front and seeing "fireballs" bowling across the veld, he lay down for protection. Twice, long afterwards, aircraft in which he was flying were struck by lightning.

But my father was a son of the sunshine; the drear skies of Britain depressed him and he yearned for the veld of his homeland and, maybe, for that attractive young lady of Stellenbosch.

So in 1895 he sailed for home and I know with what feeling of delight he saw the dim grey shape of Table Mountain once more looming into view.

Soon he was to hear the Atlantic beating heavily on the familiar shore-line and to feel the impatient south-easter tugging at his clothes as it rushed past, to sense the warm atmosphere of this sunny land, and breathe the fragrance of the wild Cape heath. It was indeed good to be back—with all the prospects and ambitions of a new young life stretching limitlessly before him.

Before we pass on let us pause to take a good look at this youth, Jan Christian Smuts. He has been described by various biographers as gaunt and taciturn, as hollow-faced and serious, as physically feeble and unsociable. It is impossible to refute these descriptions too strenuously. Take a look at this slender youth of five feet nine and see if any of these assertions were true. In appearance he was fair with blue eyes, golden wavy hair and a transparent skin. Photographs show him as attractive in appearance, with certainly no hint of gauntness. Perhaps his high and slightly prominent cheek-bones might suggest that; maybe his over-developed orbital bosses, the forehead bumps above his eyes, would tend to make him look formidable. In build he was slender though the sloping shoulders belied their breadth. His chest was big and deep.

I think my father must have been a presentable and comely youth, fair and clean looking, and serious of countenance. Not for nothing did those blue eyes of his develop the surrounding deep puckers that denote a sense of humour.

Old friends of his, especially my mother, deny that he was unsociable or unfriendly. They did not even notice that he was over-serious, for in the sleepy God-fearing hamlets of the Boland of those days, it was the normal demeanour of the people. The gaiety of Cape Town of the earlier days of the British occupation, so well described by Lady Anne Barnard,★ never touched the more serious hinterland to the north. Farms were too far apart and people too hard-working to indulge in an extravagance of pleasure.

★ Lady Anne Barnard (1750–1825) was a daughter of the Earl of Balcarres and wife of Andrew Barnard, whom she accompanied in 1793 to South Africa on his appointment as colonial secretary to Lord Macartney, Governor of the Cape. On her husband's death in 1807 she returned to England, and settling in London, her Berkeley Square home became the centre of a considerable literary coterie. Her letters from South Africa were published in 1901 as *South Africa a Century Ago.*

From the number of friends my father had and from the full house of visitors he always kept in Pretoria, he must have been a hospitable and agreeable host. The house was not only full, but usually overflowed into the annexe, where young men such as Deneys Reitz, Jimmie Roos, my uncle Tottie Krige, etc., were lodged. A huge tub stood in the garden alongside the annexe, and in summer some embarrassment was caused to other visitors by the naked bathers of the annexe in this tub.

In short, the worst that can be said about my father was that he took life a little too seriously; in every other respect he was a pleasant person and a good companion. At Cambridge he may have lacked a raucous sense of humour or an appreciation of youthful ribaldry, but it could never be said of him that he lacked an extremely well-developed sense of humour, even when a witticism was at his own expense.

In later years, when my father was an old man, I saw him in the company and the councils of the great men of his day. The impression always given was that in appearance, in intellect and in personality he stood above his illustrious contemporaries.

During his time at Stellenbosch, and until he married and left for Pretoria—a period of about eight years—my father was in a romantic frame of mind. Not only did he greedily study the great poets and philosophers, but he began to write poetry and philosophy himself. This is a phase in every young person's life, and my mother played a decisive part in it. She was a girl who knew the great writers, and it was she who provided much of the inspiration, who read and recited to him and encouraged him to do likewise. From all accounts both of them wrote poetry in those days, and it is a pity that my mother some years ago destroyed all she had written. To this day she still has a great knowledge of the older poets and it must be indeed a difficult quotation she cannot place.

VII CAPE TOWN

In 1877, barely half a dozen years after the discovery of diamonds, Joseph Chamberlain, upon the slender pretext of an alleged violation of the Sand River Convention, ordered Sir Theophilus Shepstone to annex the Transvaal. The Boers rose in righteous indignation at this act of aggression, and the result was the First Anglo-Boer War of 1880–81. In a crucial battle at Majuba * on the green border of Natal, the British suffered a reverse in which General Colley was killed; peace was once more restored. But under the terms the British maintained their suzerainty over the Transvaal and the liberties of the Boers were still substantially restricted. The Pretoria Convention of 1881, however, restored the Transvaal to full independence. But if victory was swift, it was equally indecisive, and the British smarted under their solitary defeat. What was significant to subsequent history, however, was the fact that they had not learned their lesson from this episode. Nor were they to learn it from the abortive Jameson Raid scarcely a dozen years later. Britain was in a belligerent mood of expansion. The logical successor to the Raid was the Second Anglo-Boer War, and that set up a chain reaction which still reverberates around the world.

The discovery of diamonds was as nothing to the mad rush that succeeded the discovery of gold, in Barberton in 1883 and on the bleak plateau of the Witwatersrand three years later. The old prospectors never realised what they had stumbled upon when they first struck the gold-bearing outcrops in the tall grass at Langlaagte. Here was wealth beyond the dreams of avarice. Here were problems that would lead to war.

It was into this hectic world that my father returned from the shelter of Cambridge, though as yet he was not aware of the forces about him. He was intent only on making a career in the

* At Majuba Hill Sir George Colley, in command of 650 men, was defeated on 27th February, 1881. The British had climbed the hill in the darkness of the previous night, and had established themselves, but a surprise attack from a superior force of Boers wiped them out.

legal world of the Cape. So he set up in practice in Cape Town, but though a great reputation had preceded him, he lacked experience and his briefs were few. To supplement his income he wrote for the papers, in Afrikaans and English, and his contributions covered many subjects from book reviews and odd scraps of poetry, to descriptive articles on the life of the times, and to politics. He spent some of his spare time in Parliament, reporting the debates and pondering the ways of politicians. His interest in politics grew and he began to feel that his future lay not in the quiet chambers of the Law, but in the rough and tumble of the political world. From the Gallery in the House of Assembly he saw seated in the Legislature the illustrious men of his day. His father was still there, but was known rather for his long silences than for brilliance of repartee. There below him sat Jameson, John X. Merriman, Jan Hendrik Hofmeyr, and many others who later became famous. He marvelled at the superb debating skill of Merriman, standing tall, thin and swaying on his huge feet. Hofmeyr was the Leader of the Afrikaner Bond Party,* which embraced mostly the Dutch element of the electorate. He was a mild and conciliatory man, and co-operated with other parties, not because his majority was indecisive but because he felt that salvation for the country lay only in the welding together of the two great sections. A nephew of his, of similar name, was one day to make an even greater name for himself, and his broader co-operation embraced the non-Europeans as well.

My father, scholar and dreamer that he was, fell under the spell of the House.

The struggle to supplement his income continued and he worked harder than ever. He had little spare time from Parliament and his legal tuition classes, but even in those days Table Mountain became a life-long solace and friend to him and he often struggled up its rugged face for inspiration.

It was a proud day for my father when John X. Merriman told him that J. H. Hofmeyr wanted to see him. He wanted

* The Afrikaner Bond was founded in 1879 with the purpose of removing British power and influence from S. Africa. Its headquarters was at the Cape but it had affiliations throughout S. Africa. J. H. Hofmeyr and J. X. Merriman acquired predominant influence in the Bond, however, and under their guidance it lost its animosity and worked for the cause of a united country.

my father to take up politics openly on the side of Rhodes, who was being severely criticised for his native policy and other matters.

VIII CECIL JOHN RHODES

O N the 5th July, 1853, there was born to the Vicar of Bishop's Stortford a son to become famous as Cecil John Rhodes, a somewhat tubercular lad in a family of five. As a young man he went to South Africa for his health, and was there when the diamond rush to Kimberley started; so he set off with his brother Frank to seek health and fortune in this dusty land of promise. Rhodes has been called an arrogant materialist. He was not a man of abnormal intelligence, but he had a remarkable faculty for business, and a cool and ruthless brain. He saw that the salvation of the chaos at Kimberley lay in the amalgamation of the multitude of struggling small claims and grouping them into larger units. The diggers were in bad straits in those days, and claims could be acquired very cheaply, so his scheme prospered. But Barney Barnato, Solly Joel and others had had similar visions, and ere long Kimberley was split between these big competitors. It was at this stage that Rhodes, aided by Alfred Beit, showed his mettle, and by shrewd business diplomacy swallowed up some of his adversaries. It brought him unlimited wealth, and with wealth went power. He was not satisfied with either, for he had a strange complex that craved the aura of culture, and he decided to take a degree at Oxford. As a sentimentalist and man of means he had big ideas and in his dreams he had sweeping visions. By the grace of God those visions were mostly sound, but even these he was prepared to impair for material gains, as the Jameson Raid revealed.

Rhodes dreamed of an All Red route to Cairo, and in the

memorial above Groote Schuur he is fittingly depicted as gazing to the hinterland in the North.

The mad rush for the partition of Southern Africa was on. Rhodes, having made a success of diamonds failed to grasp the chance the new goldfields of Johannesburg offered and was badly outwitted by some of his old Kimberley adversaries. By the time he saw his error, it was too late. What was more natural, therefore, than that he should turn his attention beyond the Limpopo, to the great empty tract of country that now bears his name, for there, his intuition told him, were to be found fabulous reefs of gold. So by virtue of his wealth, the good services of his friend Dr. L. S. Jameson, who doctored the rheumatic Matabele potentate Lobengula, and by his own very great personal courage in parleying with the natives, he managed to secure this important tract of land from under the very noses of the grabbing Germans. The entry of his pioneer column into this new Chartered Company area was across Providential Pass. For South Africa it was indeed providential to have a friend on her northern frontiers; but the famous hunter, Frederick Courtney Selous,* who acted as guide to the column, did not realise this when he named the road.

It took Rhodes some time to realise how badly his intuition had misled him. Perhaps it was this realisation, perhaps just ruthlessness, that induced him to get embroiled with Kruger on the Rand.

But at this stage Rhodes appeared to my father as a great idealist and his visions were those which my father could himself readily appreciate. How was he to know that Rhodes's co-operation with Jan Hofmeyr was merely a shallow veneer? Even Hofmeyr himself could not see through this ambitious friendship.

⋆　　⋆　　⋆　　⋆　　⋆

In October, 1895, my father paid a hurried visit to the Transvaal to spy out the land. The ways of the sleepy old Cape were too leisurely for him and he saw a greater future in the new Republic in the north.

* F. C. Selous (1851–1917) was a hunter and ivory trader from 1871 to 1881, when he entered the service of the British South Africa Company. He negotiated between Cecil Rhodes and Lobengula in 1890 and was instrumental in securing Mashonaland for Britain. He was killed near Kissaki in German East Africa in World War I.

The "colossal materialism" of the seething gold town of Johannesburg staggered him, with its numerous adventurers, all intent on making quick fortunes. Pretoria, that quiet little town lying warmly in a cup of hills, with its bearded patriarchs and unpretentious houses, was very different. "I was agreeably surprised", he wrote, "by the aristocratic quiet pervading this handsome little town."

On the 29th of that month he addressed his first big political meeting. It was in Kimberley Town Hall, under the chairmanship of the Mayor. The purpose of the address was to rebut certain charges of forced native labour levelled at Rhodes, and to counter the criticism of his native policy by the Cronwright Schreiners.* The charge came about as the result of the Glen Grey Act which persuaded natives to vote by taxing those who did not. At that time certain local negrophilists, of whom the best known was Mr. Saul Solomon, were becoming very active. Mr. Rhodes's championship of the phrase "equal rights for all civilised men south of the Zambesi" did not, however, render him averse to the small measure of discrimination of the Glen Grey Act. My father took this opportunity of reading the Europeans a brief homily: "Unless the white race closes its ranks", he warned, "its position will soon become untenable in the face of the overwhelming majority of prolific barbarism." He dwelt also upon the Bond, diamonds, fair and free trade, Mr. Rhodes's dual position in Rhodesia and the Cape Confederation. "The theory of democracy as currently understood and practised in Europe and America", he declared in one portion of his address, "is inapplicable to the coloured races of South Africa. . . . You cannot safely apply to the barbarous and semi-barbarous natives the advanced political principles and practice of the foremost peoples of civilisation. Too often we make the mistake of looking upon democracy as a deduction from abstract principles, instead of regarding it rather as the outcome of practical politics." The speech received a mixed reception. The Bond organs naturally defended him, but others launched bitter attacks. This was my father's first taste of politics, but he had already come to the

* Mrs. Cronwright Schreiner (1862–1920), wife of S. C. Cronwright Schreiner, was better known as Olive Schreiner, author of *The Story of a South African Farm*. Her husband was a member of the Cape Parliament.

conviction that silence is golden, and he made no attempt to defend himself.

Perhaps I may quote here my father's own impression of this Kimberley speech, written in a diary during the Boer War:

When Mr. Cecil Rhodes appeared on the scene in 1889 as Premier of the Cape Colony under Bond auspices, with a platform of racial conciliation, political consolidation of South Africa and northern expansion, my natural bias as well as the glamour of magnificence which distinguished this policy from the "parish pump" politics of his predecessors, made me a sort of natural convert to his views. I began to dream of a great South Africa in which the English and Boer peoples would dwell together in happy concord.

In 1895, and at the very time when the chief conspirators of the Jameson Raid were most busy hatching and preparing for their criminal schemes, I made a speech at Kimberley, which, while normally a defence of the Bond-Rhodes alliance in Cape politics, was really intended to set forth the general principles of a broader common political platform on a reconciled basis for both the white peoples of the Cape Colony. This speech, although it was called by a hostile daily newspaper of the day the "ablest and clearest exposition yet given of the principles of the Bond-Rhodes alliance" did not attract much attention and was indeed completely overshadowed by a pamphlet written by Olive Schreiner and her husband, in which it was pointed out with prophetic accuracy that the alliance would never last and its influence would in any case be most detrimental to the public welfare, because the motives of Mr. Rhodes were neither honest nor public-spirited. I gave no heed to their warning for I had yet to learn that a politician of such standing and influence as Mr. Rhodes would openly and shamelessly deceive, not his enemies, but his very friends and associates.

Upon the failure of his quest for gold in Rhodesia Rhodes switched his attention to the rich reefs of Johannesburg on which Kruger was now sitting so smugly. At all costs he must now get control of these. His ruthless business brain swept aside his saner political judgment. Perhaps it was the realisation that his days were limited that spurred him on. His fatal illness was on him. He could not wait. In his dying words he identified himself with this urge.

In Paul Kruger he met a rocklike obstinacy.

The House at Boplaas, Riebeeck West, where General Smuts was born in 1870

Sybella Margaretha Krige, 1888, later to become Mrs. J. C. Smuts

Mr. and Mrs. J. A. Smuts, parents of General Smuts—1893

IX KRUGER AND THE JAMESON RAID

THE better to assess the events that followed we must realise how completely Paul Kruger differed from Cecil Rhodes. Kruger as a lad of twelve had moved off with his parents on the Great Trek and in the harsh school of this rough-and-tumble life he grew up. The atmosphere of his surroundings, though a godly one, combined deep distrust of the British and hostility to the natives. His education and code of behaviour he took from the Old Testament; his shrewdness from the school of bitter experience. As a youth he had extraordinary physical strength and to this day the natives of the northern Transvaal have a legend of this remarkable white athlete. The addition of great courage made him a resolute and formidable opponent. Into this solid barnacled mass, now turned into an old and irritable patriarch, Rhodes charged with his impetuous ambition. Kruger was not impressed. In fact, at their one and only meeting the Englishman irritated him. With that went all reasonable hopes of friendly discussion and compromise on the problems which intimately touched them. Kruger had no desire to see the 60,000 alien Uitlanders of the Johannesburg goldfields dominate the policy of his Republic of 30,000 burghers, but he was prepared to permit them franchise rights after fourteen years of residence. When one considers the amorphous nature of the mining fraternity, Kruger's concession was not ungenerous. Under extreme pressure the period of qualification was later reduced to five years.

But Rhodes wanted not the little finger—he wanted the whole hand, and he was not a man to let scruples bar his way. So he not only encouraged, but actively aided and abetted, the growth of elements subversive to Kruger on the goldfield. The Reform Committee was formed and organised on a quasi-military basis, and arms were smuggled by every means into the golden city. The intention was that a rising within the town should correspond with an invasion of 500 sympathisers under Dr. Jameson, from the Bechuanaland border at Pitsani. The organising ability and security measures of the Reform party were, however, inferior to

33 C

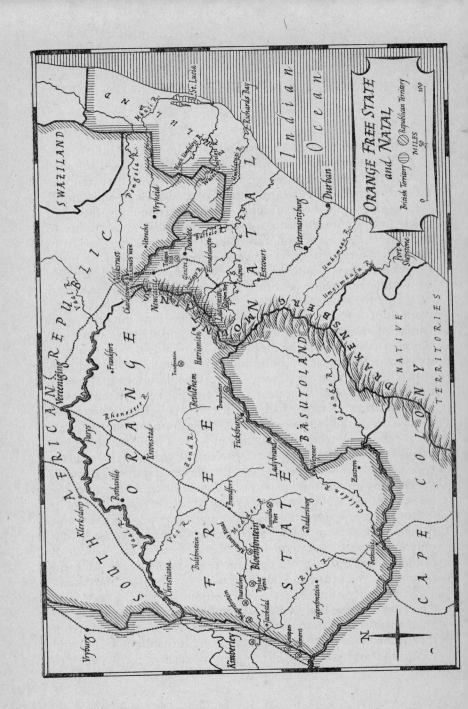

ORANGE FREE STATE and NATAL

British Territory ⬤ Republican Territory ⬤

MILES
0   50   100

their business acumen, and information reached the President of what was happening and in the end the timing of the move also broke down. So when Dr. Jameson approached with his men he was set upon by Piet Cronje at Doornkop, not far from Johannesburg, and well beaten, and members of the Reform Committee of Johannesburg were also taken into custody. This, in essence, was the unhappy incident known as the Jameson Raid.

In spite of its futility, the repercussions of the Raid were serious and far-reaching, for it was established that some of the highest in the Empire were party to it. Sir Henry Lock, British High Commissioner at the Cape, the British Prime Minister, Lord Rosebery, and the Colonial Secretary, Mr. Joseph Chamberlain, were implicated. Europe was staggered by this act of "international brigandage" and Germany adopted a hostile attitude. The Bond denounced Cecil Rhodes in the strongest terms and he was ousted from the premiership of the Cape and from the chairmanship of the De Beers and Chartered Companies. Racialism flamed in the Cape, and the Transvaal and Free State Republics were driven into each other's arms. The Raid was to echo across the world and across the years.

It was on New Year's Day, 1896, exactly two months after my father had made his Kimberley speech, as he was sitting on the stoep of his parents' home at Riebeeck West, that the news of the Raid reached him. He was aghast. This was not only a major breach of faith, but it stung him personally, for Rhodes had made a fool of him. The duplicity of the man left him furious. In one rash move was demolished the good work of friendship and co-operation between the two white races. He did not take solace in the fact that shrewder politicians such as Hofmeyr had been taken in by Rhodes. He had come to his first big crossroads in life, and it turned him towards Kruger.

He wrote bitterly in 1902:

How shall I ever describe the sensations with which I received the news on New Year's Day of 1896 of that fatal and perfidious venture. . . . When during the political storms that arose after the Jameson Raid I quietly asked myself whether I had really been wrong in striving so hard for the national fusion and concord of the white races, I came to the conclusion that I had not been wrong, that my ultimate political lodestar was not a will-o'-the-wisp and was worthy of being followed in the future even more seriously than I had done in the past.

In the course of 1896 it became so clear to me that the British connection was harmful to South Africa's best interest that I feared my future position as a Cape politician would be a false one. I therefore left the old Colony for good and settled in Johannesburg where the next two years were spent in quiet isolation and hard professional work. . . . During these two years I was a silent but intensely interested spectator of the whole South African drama as it was being played in the Golden City where grievances were made quite as systematically as money. . . . My profession brought me behind the scenes. . . . I felt convinced the inevitable struggle was approaching. . . .

I also felt very strongly that I was very young and inexperienced and that it would be far better for me to devote myself for some years purely to my professional work and abstain from all politics and thus allow my mind to mature quietly.

X STATE ATTORNEY

IN September, 1896, *Ons Land* announced that Advocate Smuts would seek admission to the Transvaal Bar. "It would be a cause for regret if the Cape were to lose one of its cleverest, most promising sons." But my father had made up his mind, and the Cape did lose one of its most promising sons, for not long after he left for Johannesburg and set up in chambers in Commissioner Street. The practice, though steady, never really flourished and to assist he also lectured in Law.

At the end of April, 1897, he paid a flying visit to Stellenbosch. Arriving, unexpectedly to all except Isie, at the Krige home on the 29th, he suddenly disclosed his plans for getting married. "I am down here on brief business and Isie and I would like to get married," he told my grandfather. "The day after to-morrow I have to leave for the Transvaal again. We would like to get married to-morrow, failing which Isie will have to come up by train to marry me." The old man said it was all very sudden, but having visions of possibly having to accompany his daughter up to Johannesburg, he decided that the next day it should be, and made arrangements accordingly. On the 30th Isie and Jan were quietly married before Professor J. F. Marais, and on the following day the couple entrained for Johannesburg. They set up house on the spot now occupied by Ingram's Pharmacy at the corner of Twist and Coetzee Streets, on Hospital Hill. Johannesburg was then small, with houses dispersed about the veld, and my mother lived in such mortal fear of natives that when my father was away at his office she carefully locked all the doors. In the Cape she had come across only the Cape Coloureds. Their first visitor in Johannesburg was Daniel François Malan, boyhood friend from Riebeeck West. Later they moved to new apartments in Buxton Street, Doornfontein. Here premature twins were born to them in 1898, but the infants survived but a few weeks.

Meanwhile all was not well in Kruger's house in the Transvaal. He had grouped about him numerous incompetent relatives and friends and there was much criticism of his appointment of Hollanders to high offices. Graft and corruption were considerable, but Kruger, though not personally implicated, shut his eyes to it. For small favours he was in the habit of granting concessions. One was the dynamite concession to Lippert that angered the mining community of Johannesburg so much. Others were connected with the Hatherly Distillery, Selati Railway and mining concessions.

Kruger ruled despotically by "resolution", and few records were kept in government offices. He was now in his seventy-fourth year and the fact that he had the most painful affliction of ingrowing eyelashes did little to improve his humour. His autocratic rule brought him into constant collision with the Supreme Court, and as the resolutions increased in number so did the disagreement. When Mr. Justice Kotze ruled a *grondwet* case, involving over £300,000, in favour of a mining company, Kruger was wrathful. Kotze was dismissed.

The country was scandalised and hardly a supporter for Kruger could be found. My father was just then about to step into the most interesting case he had yet undertaken, the defence of the notorious von Veltheim, who had shot Woolf Joel, nephew of Barney Barnato. He dropped this case at once, for he saw in the Kruger controversy a much more important issue. He stepped in to uphold the President in a very cleverly devised document, quoting at length from the Roman Dutch Law, in which he probably had no peer in the country at the time. The sum of his argument really showed only that the President was not necessarily wrong. The document met with much hostility from the legal fraternity; but it impressed the President. There can be no doubt of my father's sincerity in interfering in this Kotze dispute, for he disapproved strongly of the man's "meddling in politics".

Meanwhile Dr. Leyds,* big, genial, blond, had resigned as State Secretary to take up a diplomatic appointment, to which his charms were eminently suited. Abraham Fischer refused to exchange Bloemfontein for Pretoria, and so for a while, before the appointment of ex-President F. W. Reitz, father of Deneys, the post was vacant. One of the names mentioned in the press for that vacancy had been that of my father. There were, however, obstacles in the way, in that he was still two years too young to sit in the Executive Committee; moreover he was not a burgher of the Republic.

Shortly afterwards Dr. J. Coster, the State Attorney, a Hollander, resigned after serious differences with the President. The name of Jan Smuts was mentioned as a possible successor. Here a friend, Henri Malan, came to my father's help by introducing him to Kruger's young nephew Piet Grobler, who was also his private secretary. Grobler took my father along one morning and introduced him to the President, remarking diplomatically that he would make a good State Attorney. Kruger was taken aback at the boyish looks of the young man before him, but he needed in the Transvaal young men who were both naturally clever and highly educated. Jan Smuts was also a young Afrikaner from the Cape—that was all in his favour.

My father secured the appointment. On the 2nd June the *Star* remarked, "Though he may have all the precociousness of a Pitt,

---

* Dr. W. J. Leyds (1859–1940) was Attorney-General of the South African Republic in 1881. He was later appointed plenipotentiary of the Republic in Europe.

we still consider that twenty-eight is rather too young an age for the State Attorney of the South African Republic."

One of the nicest letters of congratulation upon his appointment was from D. F. Malan.

"I might have hesitated", my father wrote subsequently, "to undertake such a tremendous responsibility as that office entails, for I was conscious, not only of my youth and failings, not only of the temptations of power, but especially of the tempests which the State would have to weather probably during my term of office. I thought that I might yet be able to help the great cause of reconciliation. . . ."

Kruger had given my father his chance in life. He seized it with zest. Though their collaboration was destined to be of limited duration, a firm friendship grew up between these two opposite types, Kruger old, stolid and bigoted, my father youthful, brilliant and idealistic. From the first, Kruger liked this young man, and in the days that followed he saw his value and leaned upon his judgment. The relationship, he said, was as "between a father and his son".

"When long afterwards I asked the President what had induced him to offer so important a post to an inexperienced, unknown youth like me," my father said, "he replied laughingly, because he had heard that my wife was much better than I."

He eulogised my father as "one of the cleverest lawyers in South Africa and a man of versatile attainments besides. He is personally a very simple man and to meet him one would not suspect that he possessed so iron a will or so determined a character. . . . Smuts will yet play a great part in the future of South Africa."

The office of State Attorney was not a political one, for the Attorney was not a member of the Executive Council and only addressed them by request, or in explanation or elucidation of Bills. To legalise my father's appointment, Kruger created him a second-class burgher.

The new job was beset with a hundred and one personal little difficulties, "but these", my father wrote, "were as nothing compared to the intrigue by which I was surrounded, by political and official enemies, by liquor syndicates, scheming concessionaires and powerful evildoers in high places. At times I was so completely worn out by this increasing intrigue and persecution that I would have thrown up the sponge were it not for the unfaltering support of the President, who was aware of the magnitude of the forces arrayed against me."

XI UITLANDERS

My father's position as State Attorney in the Kruger Government was an interesting if peculiar one. All around were corruption and maladministration, these mostly sprouting indirectly from the presidential front. It was, therefore, a matter of delicacy to know just where to tackle matters or how far to go. My father said as much to Sir Percy Fitzpatrick, the leader of the Uitlanders, when the latter came to complain about the state of affairs. One of my father's first actions, in face of considerable opposition in the Volksraad, was to sack Bob Ferguson, the head of the C.I.D., who, he said, was a "particularly smart man, singularly unsuccessful in getting at criminals". He took on the department himself.

"I succeeded", my father wrote, "in clearing out the Augean Stable of the corrupt Detective Administration and established in its stead a system which has worked with admirable results." Strangely enough, Bob Ferguson seemed to bear him no ill-will.

The Raid had done much to bolster Kruger's waning prestige with his countrymen. The young German Emperor William II congratulated him on quelling the Raid without external assistance. Outside interference was further consolidating his position.

My father's recollections of Kruger were vivid, for the old man made a deep impression on him. I have at times heard him describe the President as the "greatest" of all Afrikaners. Clearly he did not really mean the greatest statesman, but the most colourful character or personality. For Kruger was indeed unique in his ancient ruggedness, and might fittingly have stepped back into the days of Abraham or Joshua.

Of his personal integrity my father was never in doubt. True, the old man was not averse to stretching a point, but he was never amenable to professional graft. It was his surroundings that were rotten, but he was too old and weary to deal with the problem.

In June, 1898, my parents went to live in Pretoria, taking a house in Sunnyside on the corner of Walker and Buite (now Bourke) Streets. Here in April of the following year, a son was born to them, who died eighteen months later when my father was fighting in the Western Transvaal.

Meanwhile international relations between the President and Britain were steadily worsening. Rhodes effectively controlled the English-speaking press of South Africa, and the Uitlanders' grievances and countless small points of friction were magnified out of all proportion. Rhodes, like Milner, was determined to force the war issue by any means. The 20,000 Uitlanders petitioned Queen Victoria to come to their assistance in the Transvaal. The papers condemned the "warmongers" Kruger and Smuts. Once and for all the Uitlander Question must be solved. As the English author A. M. S. Methuen wrote, "The South African press became a manufactory of outrages" against the Republic.

That the Uitlanders, many of them no more than gentlemen of adventure, had genuine grievances is only too patent. There was the amazing neglect of the teaching of English in schools, even though the Uitlanders contributed 90 per cent of the fees for education. There was the appalling state of the sanitary arrangements of Johannesburg; and there were the irritating monopolies, more especially the iniquitous dynamite concession granted to Lippert. All this was added to and distorted out of all reason by Rhodes and his clique. Uitlander E. B. Rose condemned the propaganda "as part and parcel of the crusade of calumny upon the Boers, having for its object eventual British intervention and destruction of Boer independence".

The Uitlanders demanded citizenship rights and privileges, yet refused to renounce their nationality and become Transvaal burghers. They declined to serve in the Defence Force or to contribute towards its upkeep. As my father remarked, they were there simply to make money.

41

Meanwhile Kruger was going ahead with his proposed extension of the dynamite concession. The Uitlanders raised their voices in wrath at this half-a-million-pound racket. Milner protested. Conyngham Greene, the British Agent, says that the attitude of my father and others was defiant because they believed that the Imperial Government would threaten but not act.

The arrest of five prominent people in Johannesburg on charges of treason did little to soothe ruffled feelings, even though the charges were later dropped as unfounded. A warrant for the arrest of two British journalists in Johannesburg, Moneypenny of the *Star* and Pakeham of the *Transvaal Leader*, was issued because of the "flagrant and provocative untruths" they were publishing. Little except worsened feelings came of this.

From London Dr. Leyds cabled a word of warning on May 15: "England has now everywhere a free hand. I doubt if anybody will do anything for us." A fortnight later he cabled from Berlin, "Minister of Foreign Affairs says Germany still friendly to South African Republic, but cannot assist in case of war because England is master of the seas. Hope South African Republic will concede as much as is consistent with independence."

In the Cape Milner adopted a firmer attitude towards any show of sympathy with the north. He sent naval units round the coast to Durban. The Cape was not unmindful of the warning of its Governor.

Another unfortunate incident now occurred in Johannesburg when an Uitlander named Edgar was shot dead by a Republic policeman after a brawl. Opinion was divided on the provocation for the use of firearms in this case, and the policeman Jones was fined £300 in a court of law. Such a cry went up that my father ordered a retrial, in which Jones got off. This was nearly the last straw. The people were sick and tired of the bullying methods of the "Zarps" (police). Meetings of protest were held and there was a minor clash in Johannesburg.

XII DARK CLOUDS

ALFRED MILNER appeared on the scene after the Jameson Raid, and as Britain's senior representative was destined to play a decisive part in the storms that followed. He graduated brilliantly from Balliol. From his German father he had inherited a strong streak of ruthlessness, from his Irish mother a certain perversity. He was a determined and capable man. There is reason to believe that he came to South Africa with the fixed idea of forcing the Boer issue. How, did not really matter, for he had little sympathy with the Boers. If he was not contemptuous of them, he certainly distrusted them.

Britain had therefore, either by design or accident, exported to South Africa the most dangerous man she could possibly have chosen. Biographers have generally been kind to the Alfred Milner of this period, but he stands revealed before history by his own Papers. In the worsening conditions that followed, it was not the Boers who were spoiling for a fight, certainly not the Boer Government, but Milner himself, who was determined to bring matters to a head and to crush the Republics. To this same idea he gradually converted Joseph Chamberlain. Though the problems of the day at first appeared to centre round gold and the Uitlander grievances, these merely camouflaged the broader intention of outright annexation. Kruger and my father saw the problem approaching. The attitude they adopted towards Britain was hostile only in the abstract sense. They were not foolish enough to want a war against the greatest Empire in the world, with her almost inexhaustible resources.

I have on numerous occasions heard my father discuss in private conversation the part played by Milner in the months before the war. He always discussed this subject purely as a historian, without any trace of rancour and with complete detachment and absence of bias. He was also, quite obviously, speaking as the greatest living authority on the subject. He never had any doubts that Milner was determined to provoke the war. No compromise would have satisfied him short of complete surrender of sovereignty. Milner was the guilty party; Joseph Chamberlain was only his gullible henchman.

Had Chamberlain himself come out to South Africa in 1899, instead of in 1903, and seen conditions at first hand, instead of through the biased eyes of Milner, my father felt certain that war would have been averted. Contentious topics such as this, however, he always said were better left to the historians. The facts were so well established that there was little he could now add to guide historians. Needless to say, he was an encyclopædia on the inside stories of events of the last fifty years. The failure to write his memoirs, which we all urged him to undertake, was a loss to history.

Sir William Butler, who acted while Milner was away in England for a while, did his best to patch up things. He lost no opportunity of warning his home government that Milner was misleading them. But Chamberlain, under the spell of Milner, turned a deaf ear. Nor did he heed the mounting voice of the Liberal Opposition. Campbell-Bannerman's and Lloyd George's words fell on deaf ears. Catastrophe was fast approaching.

So the two governments availed themselves of the good offers of the Free State Government to hold a Conference in Bloemfontein. This Conference, which lasted a week, started on 30th May, 1899, and was attended by Milner, assisted by his aide Hanbury-Williams and secretary, Lord Belgrave, and three clerical assistants, on the one side, and Kruger, Schalk Burger, Wolmarans and my father on the other. Abraham Fischer acted as interpreter. Sir William Butler did not view the prospects of the Conference with optimism. He distrusted Milner as much as he did Rhodes. Some while earlier he had remarked: "All political questions in South Africa and nearly all information sent from Cape Town to England, are now being worked by . . . a colossal syndicate for the spread of systematic misrepresentation."

Nor did the Conference make an auspicious start, for at a reception given by President Steyn of the Orange Free State, Milner pointedly refused to shake the outstretched hand of Kruger who came to greet him. This little incident typified Milner's attitude at the Conference which followed. He had not come here to bargain, but to dictate. He is said to have greeted my father with civility. Perhaps he thought this might win the young man over and make him more pliable. But as the days progressed he was to find that this spirited young man could not be swayed.

Milner demanded far-reaching franchise rights for the Uit-landers, but Kruger pointed out that this was unreasonable as his burghers would be out-voted by two to one. "If we give them the franchise we may as well give up the Republic," he said. But demand mounted on demand and Kruger, getting more and more harassed, refused each with increasing irritation. My father, however, did not lose his equanimity; he was constantly at Kruger's elbow to restrain and advise. He felt it a grave responsi-bility not to fail Kruger or his friends at this hour, and it was soon apparent that it was my father, and not Kruger, whom Milner had to deal with. The young man kept on bobbing up so frequently to whisper to Kruger, that Milner began to grow exasperated.

Much as he disliked doing so, my father preached compromise at this stage. The odds were too great to permit the Conference to break down before every possible effort at settlement had been explored. The Republic were now prepared to bring the qualify-ing period for complete franchise down to seven years. Milner flatly rejected it. So the haggling went on, Kruger getting more and more weary. At last he could stand it no longer: "It is my country that you want," he cried. "It is our independence you are taking away." He referred with feeling to the stream of British army reinforcements that were pouring into the country. "I am not ready to hand over my country to strangers," he con-cluded. That was his final word, and on this inconclusive, but disturbing, note the Conference broke up. It had been unsatis-factory in every respect, and my father remarked later to Piet Grobler, "It is perfectly clear to me that Milner is planning to make war."

Milner says in his diary that he arrived at the Bloemfontein Conference with the intention of being friendly and co-operative. But as the Conference progressed he grew to dislike Kruger and his henchmen. He did, however, make a note in his diary about "Kruger's brilliant State Attorney".

The Republic was meanwhile thinking things over carefully. On August 19 Kruger wrote that he was prepared to concede the Uitlanders a five years' residential franchise. This was actually what Milner had initially demanded. Joseph Chamberlain rejected the offer.

On his return from Bloemfontein my father saw but one further ray of hope. Perhaps informal discussions with Conyngham Greene, the British Agent in Pretoria, might show a way out. These lasted from 12th July till 28th August and were to end in failure, but a sincere effort had been made by both Greene and my father to explore hopeful channels. These discussions were subsequently the centre of a controversy. Several meetings occurred and there was some correspondence all of which is set out by my father in a Government Green Book.

From this it is clear that there could never have been any doubt in Greene's mind that my father was acting privately without mandate from his Government and that the talks were purely exploratory. Greene, no doubt under diplomatic pressure, after negotiations had broken down denied that he was aware of this. My father said that he was certain that he could obtain from the Volksraad seats for ten Uitlander members for Johannesburg and Barberton in the Government. The Volksraad confirmed their readiness to do this. Greene was friendly and well-disposed towards my father, and it is certain that the breakdown of the negotiations was engineered under instruction from superior authority and did not originate from Greene. In his final note to Greene my father said, "I do not believe that there is the slightest chance that these terms will be altered or amplified. Your decision will therefore have to be arrived at on these terms as they stand."

President M. T. Steyn sent a last desperate message of peace to Britain through the High Commissioner, but to no avail.

On September 22 Chamberlain severed diplomatic relations with the Transvaal. My father drafted an ultimatum to Great Britain on October 9 requesting "Immediate withdrawal of Her Majesty's forces". "Kruger", wrote W. T. Stead in the *Review of Reviews*, "would have been a traitor to his own people if he had not launched the ultimatum."

"God alone knows how deeply I wished, how hard I worked that peace might be maintained," my father wrote in his diary. "In the teeth of the most violent opposition and of the bitterest calumny, I succeeded in inducing the Executive Council and the Volksraad to accept the five years' franchise scheme of Sir A.

46

Milner, with additional clauses as to parliamentary representation which made it even more liberal than the original proposal. . . . I was prepared to sacrifice my position, myself, even to compromise the dignity and honour of the Republic."

XIII BOER WAR

THERE now appeared a Boer manifesto entitled *Century of Wrong*. It was an exhortation to the people on the eve of battle, listing the wrongs perpetrated by the British in South Africa during the past hundred years. It was written by my father in High Dutch, from facts he and Jimmie Roos had collected. The language was said by experts to be superb Netherlands and it abounded in classical idiom. My mother translated it into English. As the manifesto appeared over no name and as it was published by State Secretary Reitz, he was at first thought to be the author.

It is said that in after years my father was ashamed of this hot-headed little manifesto. That is not so, for how can exception be taken to it if the purpose of this document is taken into account. True, he never spoke about it, but that was because he was sick of the political use that was made of it, and of having its anti-English quotations cast at him. It was simply a shrill, clear bugle-call to the nation, and it is unfair to quote it out of its context or historic setting.

Many were subsequently to forget that Britain had made amends for this unhappy century. Politicians in South Africa make the past die hard. My father's message was always for the future. So, in fact, was Kruger's; he had said, "Take only what is good out of the past."

On the way from Irene to our bushveld farm the road passed two spots which never failed to awaken in my father old memories

47

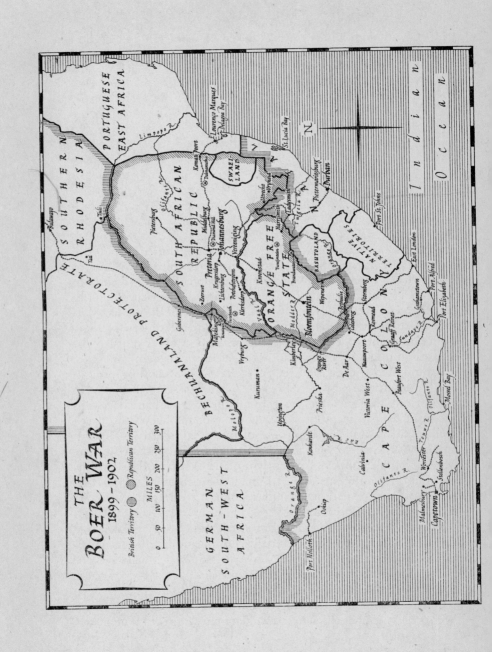

THE BOER WAR
1899-1902

British Territory ⬤ Republican Territory ⬤

MILES
0   50   100   150   200   250   300

SOUTHERN RHODESIA

PORTUGUESE EAST AFRICA

BECHUANALAND PROTECTORATE

GERMAN SOUTH-WEST AFRICA

SOUTH AFRICAN REPUBLIC

ORANGE FREE STATE

SWAZI LAND

NATIVE TERRITORIES

CAPE COLONY

BASUTOLAND

Bulawayo

Tati

Limpopo

Lourenço Marques
Delagoa Bay

Komati Poort

St. Lucia Bay

Pietersburg

Olifants

Pretoria
Johannesburg
Vereeniging

Middelburg

Dalmanutha

Pietermaritzburg
Durban

Pretoria

Ladysmith

Port St. Johns

Krugersdorp
Lichtenburg

Potchefstroom

Zeerust

Kroonstad

Harrismith

Tugela R

East London

Gaberones

Kirksdorp

Vaal

Brandfort

Wepener

Bethulie

Rosmead

Mafeking

Bloemfontein

Colesberg

Stormberg

Grahamstown

Port Alfred

Vryburg

Kimberley

Naauwpoort

Port Elizabeth

Kuruman

Orange River

De Aar

Victoria West

Small Karoo

Sundays R

Mossel Bay

Upington

Prieska

Beaufort West

Olifants R

Kenhardt

Calvinia

Olifants R

Tulbagh

Worcester

Port Nolloth

Okiep

Orange R.

Malmesbury

Stellenbosch

Capetown

of the Boer War, and he would then reminisce about these stirring times. The one spot was where the road crossed the low concrete causeway over the Boekenhout Spruit, the other was the view of the gap through the mountains near Premier Mine, known to the Boers as Donkerhoek and to the British as Diamond Hill. For it was at Diamond Hill that some of the heaviest fighting occurred, and it was the Boekenhout Spruit down which my father passed on his way to the Western Transvaal at the start of the guerrilla phase of the war after the fall of Pretoria. A careful plan for the conduct of the war had been drawn up by the Republic, he told me. The strategy briefly was for the Boers to strike down swiftly at Durban and the other ports upon the outbreak of hostilities, in order to prevent the British landing reinforcements. That phase completed, the mopping up of troops in the country would begin. The Boers felt convinced that in these circumstances Britain would be prepared to make an early peace rather than be involved in a long and costly war. The Transvaal had concluded a mutual assistance pact with the Free State Republic, the general state of arming of the Boers was satisfactory, and they were all well-trained hunters and marksmen. There was also the understanding that their countrymen of the Cape would be sympathetic, if not helpful, and that some reinforcements might come from there.

The Boer commandos of the two Republics were mobilised in good time, and before the ultimatum to Britain expired a vast mounted force was already gathered on the Natal border at Sandspruit, under Commandant-General Piet Joubert.

Well led, this force might, by a lightning stroke, have produced decisive results. The fly in the ointment, however, was the age and decrepitude of this hoary old general, and his conservative and passive outlook on military matters. My father described him as already *passé* at that time, and "hopelessly incompetent". True, the old veteran had in his day had considerable successes in the Kaffir wars, but against resourceful adversaries such as the British he was out of his depth.

The Boers entered Natal in two columns, one under General Lukas Meyer and the other under General Joubert. The war started off with a heartening series of victories for the Boers. Meyer decisively defeated General Penn-Symon's forces at Talana

49

Hill, and Joubert routed Generals White and French at Nicholson's Nek, taking 400 prisoners, but inexplicably failing to pursue
the broken foe. When remonstrated with, he is reported to have
remarked, "It would be barbarous to pursue a beaten Christian
foe." The British forces withdrew into the perimeter of Ladysmith where, instead of by-passing it and pressing on to the coast,
the Boers were delayed by a long and fruitless siege, for it was not
strongly garrisoned and tactically of minor importance. The error
at Ladysmith, my father felt, probably cost the Boers the war.

The concentration of Boer forces on the hills around Ladysmith
left the ports clear and the British rushed in a steady stream of
reinforcements.

General Buller's earlier attempts at the relief of Ladysmith led
to his defeats at Colenso and Spion Kop. Methuen was trounced
by Cronje and de la Rey at Modder River, and Gatacre, sent to
Burghersdorp to check the raiding Free State commandos, was
repulsed by Grobler at Stormberg. Wauchope was defeated by
Cronje at Magersfontein. He himself was killed and a battalion
of the Black Watch virtually wiped out.

The avalanche of reverses shocked and dismayed the British
nation. It was many a year since there had been such a bleak series
of disasters. But reinforcements were pouring in and new hope
was centred in the two crack generals, Lord Roberts of Kandahar,
the Commander-in-Chief, and Lord Kitchener of Khartoum, his
Chief of Staff, who had been sent post-haste to stem the tide and
to take over from Britain's aged Zulu War V.C., General Redvers
Buller.

A British train returning from a reconnaissance was captured
between Frere and Chievely on 15th November, 1899. Amongst
the prisoners was the young correspondent of the *Morning Post*,
Winston Spencer Churchill. His captor was Commandant Louis
Botha. The "defiant young man", my father recounted, was
brought before him looking "dishevelled and most indignant
and claiming immunity as a non-combatant. It was pointed out,
however, that he was carrying a pistol when captured and so he
was sent on detention to Pretoria." The story of Mr. Churchill's
subsequent escape to Lourenço Marques is well known. I heard
him recount it at Chequers forty-five years after the event, and
was amazed at the wealth of place names and detail he still

remembered. Here, too, I heard my father tell Mr. Churchill an aspect of the story of which he had not previously been aware. It appears that my father had developed quite a liking for the high-spirited young man he had interrogated, and so, some days afterwards, he persuaded General Joubert that there was not much point in detaining him, for he was, after all, a newspaper correspondent and his infringement had only been a technical one. His release was, therefore, authorised, but before it could be put into effect he had escaped. Mr. Churchill was delighted to hear this, for he realised that by doing so he had doubly outwitted his adversaries.

Attached to the Boer forces was another British correspondent representing *The Times*, Leo S. Amery, through the long years to become another firm friend of my father's. When things went badly for the Boers they grew suspicious of this correspondent, be it added quite without reason, and sitting one night in his tent Mr. Amery heard himself discussed in unfriendly terms. He took the hint and discreetly departed.

Meanwhile General Joubert had died and Louis Botha had taken over supreme command. The change, though it infused new hope in the Boer forces, came too late to have decisive results.

During these days my father was kept extremely busy not only running the Government in Pretoria and seeing to security measures, but also paying frequent visits to the front. From there he would bring back to the Government first-hand reports of the fighting. He carried out these inspections because he saw the urgent need for hurry, and was forever infusing urgency into the torpid old Boer generals who would not bother about his exhortations.

At last the British were ready. An overpowering mass of men had been assembled on South African soil. Roberts struck, and soon Kimberley, Mafeking and Ladysmith had been relieved. Cronje was encircled at Paardeberg and capitulated with 3,700 men. This was the first big Boer disaster, but was merely a foretaste of what was to follow. On 13th March, 1900, Bloemfontein fell and General French pushed on with his armada of 1,000 wagons on the heels of the retreating commandos. The flat plains of the Free State and the overwhelming nature of the opposition gave the Boers no chance of a stand. President Steyn and General Christian de Wet were slowly rolled backwards towards the

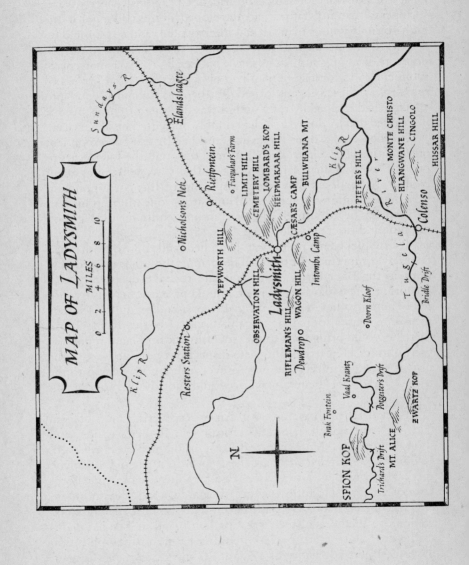

MAP OF LADYSMITH

MILES
0   2   4   6   8   10

N

Sundays R.

Elandslaagte

Klip R.

Nicholson's Nek

Rietfontein

Farquhar's Farm

LIMIT HILL

CEMETERY HILL

LOMBARD'S KOP

HELPMAKAAR HILL

PEPWORTH HILL

OBSERVATION HILL

Resters Station

Klip R.

Ladysmith

RIFLEMAN'S HILL

Dewdrop

WAGON HILL

CÆSAR'S CAMP

Intombi Camp

BULWHANA MT

Klip R.

Doorn Kloof

PIETER'S HILL

MONTE CHRISTO

HLANGWANE HILL

CINGOLO

HUSSAR HILL

Colenso

Tugela River

Bridle Drift

Braak Fontein

Vaal Krantz

Potgieter's Drift

ZWARTZ KOP

SPION KOP

Trichard's Drift

MT. ALICE

Transvaal. From the Natal side, too, Botha and de la Rey were falling back towards Pretoria.

Deneys Reitz says that after the initial Boer successes in Natal, the troops in the field had hoped that Britain might be prepared to call the war off as she had done after her reverse at Majuba in the Anglo-Boer War of 1881 ; but his father, ex-President Reitz of the Free State, told him it was a vain hope. The older man was right: this time Britain had sustained grievous losses, and she was determined, once and for all, to see this struggle through to its bitter end.

Behind the retreating Boers came slowly and relentlessly the long columns from Britain. Even when they were out of view their presence could readily be detected by the great clouds of red dust on the horizon.

The Boers' golden opportunity had come and gone. After Natal it was to be for them, with few exceptions, a long and depressing war of retreat, always vastly outgunned, hopelessly outnumbered, and relentlessly pursued by the massive columns. As an epic of struggle against overwhelming odds this war has few equals, and to many it has always been a source of amazement that any semblance whatever of morale remained. Yet the two years that were to follow proved that it had survived.

XIV PRETORIA FALLS

IT was on the hills to the north of Pretoria that the Boers were to make their final stand. Perhaps it would be appropriate to quote here from a brief account written in English by my father shortly after the war:

This Magaliesberg was destined soon to be the scene of the biggest battle fought by the Boer forces after the great actions on the Tugela and the Modder River, and was thereafter, in consequence of the activity of de la Rey and his lieutenants, to become one of the most famous theatres of the war in South Africa.

It is impossible to contemplate this bleak and uninviting and apparently insignificant mountain range, the silent and grim spectator of so much in the history of Southern Africa, without melancholy emotion.

Rising like a bastion on the lower slopes of the Highveld, it looks on the South at the smiling grassy plains and uplands of the Highveld and on the North at the endless dreary prospect of the lowveld bush. And with the same cold callous look which it wears to-day it has regarded the beautiful valleys North and South along its slopes occupied and cultivated by successive races of men. It saw the nation of the Magatese grow up here in comparative peace until it was the greatest Bantu people in the Transvaal and it took its name from Mamagali, Great Chief of this people. It saw the Magatese power broken and annihilated by the Zulu armies under Moselekatze who cleared the whole country North of the Orange River in order to found on its ruins a kingdom of his own. And where the Magatese bones were bleaching in the sun it saw an endless chain of Zulu kraals and fortifications arising, stretching from a point North of Pretoria to the confines of the Kalahari desert, which can still be seen to-day. It saw in turn the Zulu power smashed in 1837 by the Emigrant Boers in the great actions at Mosega and Maricospoort and this Attila of Central South Africa flee for refuge Northward to the territory of the former glorious kingdom of Monomotapa, where a renewed career of conquest was only to lead to the melancholy fate of his people under his son and successor Lobengula. It saw the country all around converted into one of the most beautiful and fertile parts of South Africa, and Boer and Magatese enjoying the fruits of peace in a land of plenty for more than 80 years. And now it was to see the curtain rise on the most tragic spectacle of all, and a fresh tide of racial war sweep over these fair regions and convert them into ruin and desolation such as even the ruthless barbarians of Moselekatze had failed to effect.

The fall of Pretoria forms in many respects a turning point in the history of the war.

Since the retreat from the Modder River and Tugela, victory had but seldom and then very briefly smiled on the Boer arms. It was everlastingly retreat; retreat—wearying, dispiriting retreat. At every stage of the retreat the Boer cause became more hopeless, the Boer army smaller in numbers, and the Boer resources more exhausted. Pretoria—that holy of holies of the Republic in South Africa—was generally expected to mark a decisive stage of the war; to the British commanders the expected final stand at Pretoria and its capture seemed to be the *coup de grâce* to the Republics; to the Boer rank and file it appeared in advance as the great Armageddon where the Boer force, concentrated from all points of the compass in defence of their central stronghold, would deliver that final united blow from which perhaps the British forces might be sent reeling back to the coast. Perhaps and perhaps not; at any rate the action there would be decisive and thousands of burghers stuck to their commandos in the course of this disastrous retreat simply because they believed that the decisive battle would be fought at Pretoria, and at that battle they were determined to be present.

They did not know that in the inner circle of their Government it had already been decided to abandon Pretoria without a serious resistance and that the hope of those who saw furthest and thought deepers in the Boer cause was not in the fortified town but on the illimitable veld. Paul Kruger and his advisers saw quite clearly that a siege of Pretoria would be of but brief duration and inevitably fatal to the Boer cause. And there is no doubt that they were right; if the Boers had staked their last chance on the defence of Pretoria, the war would have been over in June or July of 1900, at any rate so far as the Transvaal was concerned.

A prolongation of the war was of course undesirable, but it was a better alternative than early and final defeat at Pretoria. And so it happened that, while the Boer forces were still falling back on the forts and fortifications of Pretoria, many with a strange hope born of faith in their cause, the Republican Government had already left the place and had moved on to Middelburg on the Delagoa railway line.

This happened some days before the actual fall of Pretoria. During the day telegrams had arrived to the effect that Boksburg was threatened or taken, that Germiston had been taken, and that a large mounted body of the enemy was moving rapidly on in the direction of Pretoria. In the course of the afternoon driblets of alarmist news came; first one and then another and then yet another station on the road to Pretoria was reported to have been reached by an advanced British force, and it was feared that a forced march would bring the enemy to the capital that same night. The Boer forces were still beyond Johannesburg and nothing could be heard from them. Here evidently was a case for swift decision. The President called a meeting of the Executive at his house late that afternoon where it was decided that he with the State Secretary and some other prominent officials should leave that same night for Middelburg; and to prevent the sudden departure attracting too much attention it was decided that he should go out by cart by the Eastern road and take the train in the direction of Koedoespoort. It was further decided that Schalk Burger and myself should remain behind to represent the Government and maintain order at the capital.

As soon as the Government had left that night and while the alarmist news about the rapid advance of the British was still spreading consternation, we started to take steps to prevent the town from falling bloodlessly into their hands that night. Orders were given for the commandeering of every available burgher in the town and between 9 and 10 that night we left Pretoria with a motley crowd of about 400 or 500 men in the direction of Irene to intercept the advance of the invaders.

Schalk Burger unfortunately became ill that night and could not accompany us but we had the veteran Lukas Meyer to lead us to battle. We held the hills sloping down to Six Mile Spruit with anxious determination and were not a little relieved when morning came without the dreaded foe.

We then returned to town and sent forward scouts to look for the enemy. The alarm proved to have been a false one as the British had not advanced beyond Rietfontein Station and had gone back from there towards evening.

Ridiculous as the whole affair may appear, it must not be forgotten that a night march such as was over and over again performed by the British columns in the later stages of the war would have brought them to Pretoria that night and that but for the show of resistance which would have come from us they might have captured Pretoria without firing a shot.

At that time Pretoria still held all our reserve money and all our reserve ammunition, and the ignominy of such a bloodless capture would have been only equalled by its disastrous effects. . . .

The days that followed were a most anxious time; the Government had left Schalk Burger and myself behind to represent them but had unfortunately omitted to confer on us any special authority.

My colleague immediately thereafter left Pretoria to take his family to Lydenburg and I was left behind alone with such authority as the law confers on the State Attorney in ordinary peaceful times. I had to contradict the wild rumours which the sudden disappearance of the Government had given rise to, and I had to maintain order; while to add to my misfortunes my authority did not remain unquestioned and a rival started up in the shape of a so-called "rust en orde" committee of which the Burgomaster Piet Potgieter and the Chief Justice Gregorowski formed prominent members. This committee consisted of those patriots who had during the course of the war come to conceive a horror of warfare in general and of heavy artillery in particular; as they were not in the know and were under the impression that Pretoria was going to be defended with determination, their principal anxiety was to devise ways and means to prevent the bombardment of the town by an early surrender, so that they acquired the unenviable name of the "surrender committee". Indeed rumour had it that there was a strong rivalry in the committee between the various candidates for the honour of going out in a black coat and with a white flag in order to surrender the town to Lord Roberts.

Another trouble was the absence of the regular police and police officers which compelled us to improvise a force for the maintenance of order. Nor were we quite successful in this, for although there was an unusual absence of crime, we could not prevent the Government stores from being broken into by the populace and looted in broad daylight. The populace at any rate saw no sense in hoarding stores for the invaders; and when the hungry Boer forces arrived at Pretoria some days afterwards they scarcely found anything to eat and thousands passed with sad hearts and empty stomachs through the ungrateful capital.

On the arrival of the Commandant-General military authority was at once resumed over the town, military officers appointed and intriguers and the surrender committee cowed into inactivity.

It was towards the end of that eventful week that a memorable gathering of Boer commanders took place in a room at the telegraph offices for the purpose of laying before the President by telegram the pitiful plight of the Boer cause. There were Botha, de la Rey, Tobias Smuts, Lemmer, Ben Viljoen and most of those who had either become famous or were still to become famous in the following two years. After mature consideration that gathering submitted to the President the tentative suggestion to end the war at Pretoria.

Their motives for doing so were the deplorable state of the Boer army which had melted away so that scarce 7,000 could be mustered at Pretoria; the certainty of an inglorious ending if the war was continued any longer, the strong probability of the complete devastation of the country and the utter hopelessness of achieving any success after the losses and defeats of the past.

I shall never forget the bitter humiliation and despondency of that awful moment when the stoutest hearts and strongest wills in the Transvaal army were, albeit but for a moment, to sink beneath the tide of our misfortune. What all felt so deeply was that the fight had gone out of the Boers, that the heroes who had stood like a stone wall on the Tugela and the Modder River, who had stormed Spion Kop and

Ladysmith and many other forlorn hopes, had lost heart and hope, had gone home and forsaken their officers. It was not Lord Roberts's army that they feared, it was the utter collapse of the Boer rank and file which staggered these great officers. And it staggered the iron-willed old President also, for his reply was that he would consult President Steyn on their suggestion.

This happened on Friday night (1 June) and on Saturday morning a great War Council was to be held to consider what further steps were to be taken for the defence of Pretoria. In the meantime the two Presidents were communicating over the telegraph wires and the suggestion of the Transvaal officers received an answer from the Free State President which was to have momentous effects on the future not only of the war but of the Boer people.

To the despairing cry of the Transvaaler Steyn replied expressing unalterable opposition to peace, practically accused the Transvaalers of cowardice, pointed out that after they had involved the Free State and the Colonial rebels in ruin they were now to conclude a selfish and disgraceful peace as soon as the war had reached their borders, and concluded with the statement that whatever the Transvaalers might do the Free State would fight on even if it stood alone to the bitter end.

The telegrams that passed between President Kruger's Head-quarters and my father at Pretoria, my mother carefully rolled into wads and secreted in the massive brass curtain rods of our house, before the British marched into Pretoria. These she retrieved unharmed after the war and they now form part of my father's documents.

From the siege of Pretoria I still have a dozen heavy fragments of shrapnel picked up by my mother in our garden in Sunnyside, after the British shelling of the railway line.

My mother was in Pretoria at the time it fell. She tells of the feverish activity that went on at our house which more or less became the Boer tactical headquarters as the end approached. She saw the thousands of British troops plod past on their way out. She tells of the numerous officers who had come in search of something to eat. Twice the house was searched, the first time by an officer named Hughes and next by one Silver. They were civil but formal and needless to say found nothing.

My mother had in her possession 200 golden sovereigns which she feared would fall into British hands. When they came on their first search she dropped the money into the hot water boiler of the stove, and all the time the search was on she was on tenter-hooks lest her hoard would melt. As soon as the party left she darted to retrieve the coins and they were subsequently used in the detention camp at Maritzburg.

The fall of Pretoria occurred about a week before the battle that was to follow. There was still much to do in the doomed city as the British approached. I quote here from my father:

So dawned Monday—the eventful 4th of June. Lord Roberts had reached Six Mile Spruit with an enormous force which was more than sufficient to break the show of resistance of less than 7,000 dispirited and demoralised Boers. Between him and Pretoria there was only the low line of hills in which some of the Pretoria toy forts are situated. Meanwhile General French had kept in a Northerly direction from Krugersdorp and after having crossed the Magaliesberg had turned East so that in a day's time he would be behind the Boer lines and would cut off their retreat to the North or attack Pretoria from the rear.

So far as I am aware there was nothing memorable about the fight at Pretoria and I shall therefore leave its details to be dealt with by the historians. All I need say and really the only matter of importance in connection with the fight was that the Boer show of resistance com-pletely succeeded in its object, which was to keep the British out of Pretoria that day and to give the officials time to remove the money and gold belonging to the Government and the vast quantities of reserve ammunition, and some guns that were still at Pretoria.

The removal of the money and gold of the Government, which was lying at the National Bank and in the Mint was my special busi-ness. I had been in friendly negotiations for some days with the directors of the bank in order to obtain peaceable possession of the money and gold of the Government which still remained in their custody to the value of between 400 and 500 thousand pounds sterling. When these negotiations failed nothing remained for me but to issue a warrant for their arrest and to threaten them with criminal proceedings which proved effectual. On the Monday morning the directors informed me that if I employed force they would consent to hand over the gold which was the property of the Government. I therefore got a special body of about 50 police, entered the bank, and obtained delivery of all the gold in question. At the suggestion of General Botha I looked for and found further a special war fund of £25,000 standing to the credit of the Commandant-General. After suitably rewarding the officials of the Mint for their arduous work in coining money for the Government during the war I started for the station, put all the gold on a special train in charge of a reliable force of police and had the train despatched that Monday afternoon while shells were bursting all round the station and a number of howitzers were being vainly used to wreck the railway at Sunnyside going East to Delagoa Bay.

So on the Magaliesberg to the north of Pretoria the 7,000 Boers took up their positions, holding a line mainly to the east of the town. The English were trying vainly to break through the few gaps. For some days a big battle raged at one of these, at Diamond Hill, for here the British launched their major attack. This battle, though critical, at first gradually turned in favour of the Boers, and my father says that after about the fifth day they began to feel distinctly hopeful. The weakness in the position lay in the fact that the Magaliesberg, which here rose 1,000 feet above the Highveld, gradually petered out and merged with the flat country some twenty miles north-east, near Springs. Very heavy fighting went on around Diamond Hill for a week. On the farm Kameelfontein, which my father bought shortly after the war, General Methuen was trapped with a thousand men and in desperate plight. Relief came in the nick of time.

The four forts on the heights surrounding Pretoria, built under contract by Lippert, proved to be, as feared, remnants of an antediluvian concept of strategy and fell without firing a shot.

The British were now turning their attention to the eastern flank held by General Tobias Smuts, a distant relative. One morning at 2 a.m. Koen Brits, his staff officer, burst into the tent my father was sharing with General Botha at Donkerhoek to the east of Pretoria, and told with emotion that the enemy had burst through the Tobias Smuts sector. So the Boer position was outflanked and the whole Magaliesberg line rendered untenable. Pretoria was finished and with it the last hope of large-scale Boer resistance.

In this brief account my father went on as follows:

The history of the Boer War is in many respects the history of grave strategical blunders, which had momentous effects not only on the duration but also on the ultimate issue of the war. From the British point of view the blunder made by Lord Roberts in his march to Pretoria was probably one of the most momentous of the whole war.

The war was nearly ended at Pretoria by the wavering of the officers. However, Lord Roberts could not be supposed to know the intentions of the Boer officers and what he did not know cannot enter into the consideration of any mistake which he did make. But how much did he know at this time and what ought he, as a prudent commander, to have foreseen? He was advancing to Pretoria with an enormous army vastly outnumbering the Boer forces, he knew that the Boer force opposed to his advance was the miserably inadequate one which had been retiring before him ever since the defeat of Cronje, reduced now to a skeleton of its former self by continual defections from the commandos and by the Free State commandos remaining within their borders. The commandos operating on the Western border at Fourteen Streams and Mafeking had been ordered to Pretoria, but most of them never arrived in time and, besides, their numbers were comparatively insignificant. The Natal commandos were still on the Drakensberg to block the advance of Buller, and were so reduced in number that it was impossible for them to spare any reinforcements for Pretoria. Lord Roberts therefore knew that he had only to do with the miserably attenuated forces of Botha and de la Rey in front of him.

It might have been foreseen too that the Boer line of retreat, if there was to be any retreat from Pretoria, was to be towards the East so that the Boer forces might keep in touch with their Government and might continue to utilise the Delagoa Railway for supplies and communication with the outside world. To have retired North towards Pietersburg would have been an altogether foolish undertaking as the unhealthy, sparsely populated and poor Bushveld to the North of Pretoria could offer no inducement whatever for such a step. If the Boer officers who met at the telegraph office at the meeting already described knew that their communications with their Government and their line of retreat towards the East were cut off or to be cut off, and that the only alternative was a retreat to the inhospitable Bushveld of the North, that might have decided their hesitating resolution.

And even if there was to be no retreat from Pretoria Lord Roberts had quite sufficient men at his disposal both for the siege of Pretoria and for cutting off the Boer communications to the East. Springs, on the railway line East of Boksburg, had been occupied shortly after Johannesburg, and, if instead of putting French on the left wing and making him describe the useless detour North of Magaliesberg, he had placed him on his right and sent him from Springs to Middelburg or Balmoral simultaneously with his own advance towards Pretoria, Lord Roberts would have completely upset the Boer plan—which was also the obvious plan—for the further prosecution of the war and would have dealt a staggering if not fatal blow at further resistance by the Transvaal.

If Lord Roberts found it impossible or inexpedient to adopt this strategy with his own forces, Buller, who was still below the Drakensberg should have been ordered to carry it out.

To the Boers the inactivity of Buller in the North of Natal seemed inexplicable except on the theory, at that time generally believed by the Boers, that owing to jealousy between the two principal officers in the British army, Buller's advance had been artificially stayed in order to give his rival a chance of first entry into the Transvaal. This belief, if unfounded, was due to the fact that the dawdling and sulking of Buller after the capture of Ladysmith could not be explained on any other ground known to the Boers. The proper thing for Lord Roberts was to have allowed or ordered Buller to accelerate the snail-like pace of his advance, so that when Lord Roberts arrived at Pretoria, Buller might have been at or far on his way towards the Delagoa railway.

The simultaneous capture of this railway either by Buller or a portion of Lord Roberts's force would have made the fall of Pretoria an event of capital if not decisive importance—as Lord Roberts intended it to be. Its capture, in the manner it was effected by Lord Roberts's short-sighted strategy, was not only an empty event for the British, but turned out to have been a blessing in disguise for the Boer forces, as the inactivity which followed it gave the Boer officers the necessary breathing space for the reorganisation of their forces and consideration of their future plan of campaign.

XV EXPEDITION INTO THE CAPE

WITH the fall of Pretoria yet another phase of the war had come to a close. The Boer leaders forgathered at Balmoral, near Witbank, to take stock of the position, and after deliberation decided that it would be impossible to continue operating as one big army and that they should split up into smaller units and operate independently. My father took this proposal down to President Kruger at Waterval Boven, and with his approval this new scheme, of guerrilla tactics, was set into operation. Botha was now to go to the Eastern Transvaal, de Wet and Hertzog were to take the Free State, de la Rey and my father were to go into the Western Transvaal, while Beyers was to harass the British in the Waterberg. This Waterval Boven meeting was the last occasion on which my father saw the old President.

My father's role as politician had now ceased for a time; he became a man of action in the battlefields. So in June, in the bitter cold of mid-winter, the commandos dispersed to their respective theatres. My father set out with his small forces westwards down the Boekenhout Spruit, past Hamanskraal on the Great North Road, and on to the Magaliesberg beyond. He passed Slagters Nek the day after de la Rey's setback there, and scenes of the encounter were still evident. Rustenburg he found strongly held by General Baden-Powell, and so by-passing it, he made for Zwartruggens. Here he came upon a force of about a thousand Australians, which he immediately attacked, driving them into a small area near the river. A message had, however, been got through to Mafeking and General Corrington set out with reinforcements. Between Zeerust and Zwartruggens, Corrington was intercepted by de la Rey's men and driven back.

As the operation against the Australians unavoidably became drawn out, which was against the settled Boer strategy, my father trekked on again. Wherever possible British forces were attacked, this being part of the hit-and-run tactics to replenish tobacco, sugar and such-like from defeated British units, and also to get fresh stores of ammunition. In these skirmishes the Boers had some successes, but they were exacting in their way and strength was being whittled away in casualties. The British policy of carrying out vast "sweeps" and of destroying Boer potential by burning farm-houses and slaughtering stock was being widely felt by the commandos, whose existence depended on what they could forage from the land. This scorched-earth policy of General French, which Milner did not like, was a sound one from the replenishment aspect, but many of its other virtues were dubious, for though it kept the commandos short of supplies it served to stiffen morale and in the aftermath left a strong taste of bitterness, which even in these days is a weapon of propaganda value.

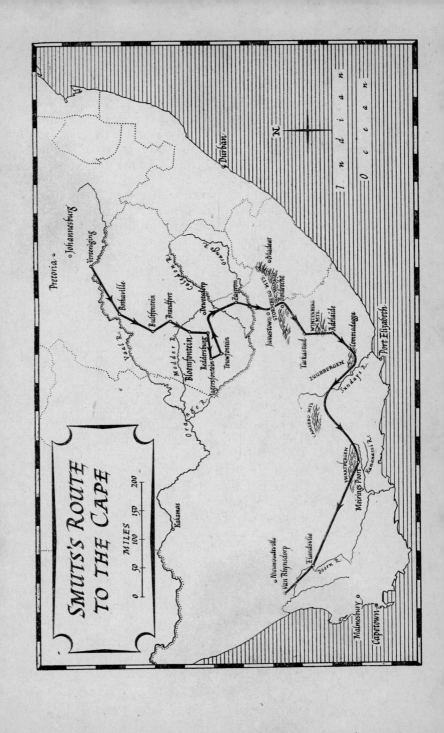

SMUTS'S ROUTE
TO THE CAPE

MILES
0   50   100   150   200

General Smuts with his
Boer War horse "Charlie"
—1901

General Smuts with his
senior Boer War officers,
Van Deventer and Maritz,
O'okiep, Cape—May 1902

J. C. Smuts at Cambridge—November 1892

J. C. Smuts as Student at Stellenbosch—1891

For about two weeks my father operated in the Rustenburg area, but in the Western Transvaal he and de la Rey found it increasingly difficult to move about. From all sides they were beset by the British. So once more they decided to part company, de la Rey remaining in the west while my father went farther south. The whole of this portion of the Transvaal was covered by scattered Boer units, with somewhat larger concentrations at Potchefstroom and Vereeniging. My father's operational strength was about 300, mostly men from the Gatsrand area of Krugersdorp and to the south.

In May, 1901, the picture was grim, and it looked to the British as though results might be achieved by negotiation. Accordingly Kitchener generously allowed my father to contact President Kruger at Utrecht by wire, from Standerton. Needless to say, Kruger, far away and completely out of contact, said "Fight on!"

It was in the Vereeniging and Potchefstroom areas largely that my father operated, continuing his hit-and-run harassing tactics, and keeping considerable British forces locked up. Towards the end of his Transvaal campaign he made plans to retake Johannesburg, and was actually assembling his force at Zuurbekom, about ten miles south of Krugersdorp, when he received orders to start on a sortie into the Cape.

My father had always attached far more importance to the Cape than had any of his colleagues. In fact, he believed that it was almost as much the failure of the Republics to get more active support from here as poor leadership in the first battles of the war, that led to final defeat. At a conference of senior Boer leaders on 20th June, 1901, at Waterval near Standerton, he had once more advocated an expedition into the Cape Midlands.

From the discussions at the conference it was clear that the Free State held out no further prospects of fighting and that the Transvaal had become almost untenable, so it was decided to shift the focus back to Natal, where Louis Botha was to keep the kettle boiling, and to the Cape, into which my father was to lead an exploratory force. The purpose of this latter trip was to see if there was any possibility of getting recruits for the depleted forces (and in this there was a small measure of success) and to cause a tactical diversion. The Cape also happened to offer the only "unscorched" territory in which troops could still subsist.

Affairs in the Free State were at a standstill, and the country had been laid bare by the British. My father was to find de Wet and Hertzog hiding in the Fauresmith hills with a handful of men (Hertzog had only 20) leading a precarious existence. Morale in the civilian population had long since cracked.

My father's sortie into the Cape was not the first of its kind, but it turned out to be the classic of the war. With 1,500 men de Wet had crossed the Orange River in February, 1901, but the effort had not proved a success. General Hertzog had also previously been into the Cape and had penetrated as far as van Rhynsdorp, but he had few men with him and his journey had been precipitate. The people of the Cape spoke disparagingly of Hertzog's sortie. They said he had come down and asked for their support and had then left again as abruptly as he came, leaving them embarrassed and in trouble with the authorities. My father assured them, however, that he had come to stay.

My father's Cape trip has been variously described not only as the most daring manœuvre, but also the most brilliant of the war. With a hand-picked band of 362 men, he set out on a journey which was to carry him 2,000 miles and to keep locked up a British force of fully 35,000. When peace came his force had swelled to between 3,000 and 4,000, though of his original Krugersdorp men only half had survived. My father himself always considered his sally into the Cape the most successful military manœuvre of the war. General French long afterwards told him that it had been one of his most troublesome problems. However, when later summoned to the armistice conference my father was forced to admit that even the Cape held out little promise for the prolongation of the war.

The organisation of the Boer commandos was commendably simple. In charge of a large group would be a Vecht Generaal; under him would be two or three veld cornetcies each of 150–250 men, these in turn being sub-divided into corporalships of 25 men each. My father's two field cornets were Jacobus van Deventer (later one of his generals in the First World War) and Ben Bouwer.

While gathering his men for the Cape trip they were caught one night in a terrible storm near Krugersdorp and six were killed, as they slept, by a single flash of lightning.

The jumping-off place for the Cape sortie was between Vereeniging and Vredefort. In order to elude the British more easily my father divided his forces in two, first taking 250 men under van Deventer a short way on their journey into the Free State. He then returned to Rietpoort near Vredefort to collect the remaining hundred men under Bouwer and left with them a few days later, on the 1st of August, 1901.

On the way back from van Deventer he and some others slept, on the night of the 20th July, near a native kraal at Paardekop, in a small wood, in the Gatsrand Hills. Their boots had got wet in fording the Mooi River that afternoon and against their usual practice they took them off before lying down. But a native had treacherously disclosed their whereabouts to the British. My father, who usually slept a little apart from his snoring men, awoke to the sound of rifle fire and scuffling, and found himself in the midst of the enemy. His native orderly Kleinbooi was shot dead, but in the darkness and confusion, and by dint of speaking English, my father managed to edge away slowly and make off in his bare feet, leaving behind everything, including the saddle-bags containing his confidential documents. A little farther he was challenged in the dark by a person who turned out to be his secretary and brother-in-law, P. S. ("Tottie") Krige, and soon one or two more stragglers joined them. My father's feet were badly lacerated and his friends wrapped towels round them, but progress was slow till they later found mounts again. His saddle-bags, complete with confidential despatches, he later recovered where he had abandoned them.

While in the Vereeniging area one morning while cooking breakfast before setting off on the Cape trip with the second detachment, they were attacked by a large force of mounted Australians, their old friends of the Zwartruggens encounter. After a short sharp skirmish the Australians were beaten off and the Boers went back to finish their meal. My father felt sure that this reverse would rankle and that the enemy would return again later, so he took up position accordingly. Sure enough, they did, and this time the Boers gave them a sound thrashing and took many prisoners. Being in no position to be encumbered with these men, they took from them what they wanted and sent them back in their shirt-tails to Vereeniging, where there were not only concentrations of British troops but also large numbers of Boer women. The embarrassment of the Australians as they rode back into the town never failed to provoke a chuckle of mirth from my father, who I think enjoyed this incident to the full.

On the 2nd August they crossed the Vaal River at Koppies-kraal Drift and thence moved along the Rhenoster River, sleeping the following night at Bothaville. Beyond, they crossed the Vet River and trekked on to Bultfontein. Thirty-five miles farther on, on the night of the 14th, they crossed the Modder River at Brits farm, within a few hundred yards of a British camp where a jolly party was in progress. Then Brandfort, Bloemfontein, Reddersberg and so on southwards, past Jagersfontein towards the Orange.

All along the route was evidence of the scorched-earth policy. Farms were desolate and deserted. In his field diary my father noted (in Afrikaans): "Dams everywhere filled with rotting animals. Water undrinkable. Veld covered with slaughtered herds of sheep and goats, cattle and horses. Hungry lambs run bleating around."

At Touwfontein, where they arrived on the 16th, my father pulled up for a few days. Here he sent for "Rechter * Hertzog", who arrived on the night of the 19th to discuss the situation in the Free State. Hertzog showed my father Kitchener's proclamation of the 15th September, 1901, about the banishment of men and officers, and the confiscation of property. At this point my father notes in his diary: "Nine English columns drawing in around me, so I am trying to cross railway tonight below Jagersfontein Station and Springfontein." On the 25th, near Edenburg, he noted: "Found myself surrounded on all sides and driven on railway line. Had to flee from sun-up to sunset. . . ." Next day the story was the same: "Enemy still in pursuit. . . . My position is precarious; horses much done up; burghers dispirited. Still I shall press on till end."

Thereafter they moved on past Dewetsdorp and crossed the Caledon River near Vechtkop, reaching the Grootrivier, or Orange River, on September 4 at Kafferskop.

The move into the Cape failed to take the British by surprise. In their passage southwards through the Free State my father's

* Judge.

commandos unwittingly moved into the biggest of all sweeps Lord Kitchener had yet staged. This necessitated a considerable amount of dodging and delay, and at the same time revealed the Boer intentions to the British. Accordingly General French was ordered by Kitchener to hold all possible crossings of the Orange River. Four large mounted pursuit columns were also organised, and in the weeks to come they were to stick relentlessly to my father's heels and to harass and chase him unmercifully.

By this time the scorched-earth policy had already been completed and the new block-house and river-line system was nearing perfection. Not only were there now tents and troops everywhere, but along all railway lines were chains of blockhouses linked by tangles of barbed wire. These barriers were formidable and could really only be forced at night, when there was always the hazard of getting lost and blundering into danger.

For the survivors of those who undertook the Cape trip the weather will always be a nightmare memory, for they ran into almost unprecedented wet and cold. Yet though some died of exposure and all were shivering and miserable, the bad weather had its compensations; had it been better it is doubtful if the excursion would have been possible. Not only was visibility reduced and the Boers thus enabled to slip through the narrowest of gaps between the enemy, but the weather equally impeded the enemy's cumbersome movement. The Boers, travelling light, struggled through.

Deneys Reitz graphically describes the trip in his great book *Commando*. He says that at the start he had only four rounds of ammunition for his rifle, and that others were little better off. On their feet they had tattered home-made sandals and they were clad only in ragged trousers and coats. Their shirts and vests had long ceased to exist. As the campaign progressed they were reduced to improvising apparel out of hessian grain bags. Later on they captured British uniforms with which they gladly clothed themselves, and it was only subsequently that they learned that by Kitchener's proclamation all Boers so captured were to be summarily shot. Some unwittingly paid the penalty through being unaware of this British proclamation. Later when they heard of it they speedily retook to their grain bags. But in any case British subjects from the Cape knew only too well that they would be shot upon capture as rebels. Some paid this penalty. The British were most anxious to get hold of my elusive father and put a price of £1,000 on his head, dead or alive.

My father's detachment of a hundred men had now safely joined up at Zastron with van Deventer. This village lies just north of the Orange River, about twenty miles from the Basutoland border. Beyond, the approaches to the river and all its crossings were heavily guarded. Here Louis Wessels, with a party who were conversant with this area, was able to indicate a little-known precipitous path down the escarpment to where the river flowed swiftly down a narrow gorge. This unguarded crossing they negotiated in the dark on September 4th and by daybreak all were safely across the deep swirling waters. The way through the Free State had been arduous. Only 250 men remained to make this crossing. They were now in the British territory of the Cape, on the bare open veld, and hurried southwards to reach the Waschbank Mountains. On the plateau across the river, opposite Herschell, stragglers of the commando were attacked by a force of some 300 mounted Basuto natives. Six men and thirty horses were lost, some of the men being mutilated and dissected for medicine. This hostile attitude of the natives who sympathised with the British brought forth no retaliation from the Boers whose policy it was to concentrate exclusively on the war with the British.

Lady Grey was strongly garrisoned and so they by-passed it and made into the Witteberg Mountains beyond. That night they pressed on, determined to shake the enveloping forces off in the darkness. By daybreak they were looking down on Jamestown, but here again they could see tents and troop columns. So they sought sanctuary in the misty Stormberg Mountains.

The fine weather of recent weeks barely gave them time to cross the Orange before the rains set in and from now on, with little variation, they were to be cold and wet for weeks on end.

To add to their trials they were now continually to find themselves beset by British troops and wherever they looked down from the mountain were white tents.

Near Dordrecht on the 7th September the way out from the mountains led through a narrow defile known as "Moordenaars Poort". The British were known to be at the other side of this poort and the question was whether they had not already taken up positions in the gap itself. My father set out to investigate at four that afternoon with a party of four, including Tottie Krige and Johannes Neethling. Halfway along the poort they met with another reconnoitring party consisting of Japie Neethling, the two Adendorff brothers and another person who had just come back from the British end of the pass, and said the pass was clear but that the British were camped immediately beyond. My father still did not feel happy about the position, so he took with him Johannes Neethling and the two Adendorff brothers and went to investigate. He brought up the rear and in view of the bushy cover in the pass and its ideal setting for an ambush, it was decided that at the first sign of danger it would be a case of every man for himself.

Now it so happened that a British party had entered the poort just as the first reconnoitring party were withdrawing, and they observed the two parties of Boers when they met. So they went into ambush positions in a bush on one shoulder. When the Boers came to within twenty to thirty yards they opened fire, killing one Adendorff and all the horses, and badly wounding Neethling and the other Adendorff. Though my father's horse Charlie was shot from under him, he himself was not hit and was able to make off under a fusilade. By judicious running from cover to cover he eventually reached a donga down which he disappeared. How the British missed him was a mystery, for all this while bullets steadily pinged round him. He told me that in the predicament of the moment he was worried more by the shame of capture than by the fear of being killed. During the half-hour it took him to elude the party he had a lot of rough-and-tumble scrambling, so when he arrived back footsore in camp at midnight he was indeed a sorry sight.

The ambush took place late in the afternoon, and by the time the British had got the two wounded men to the farmhouse of Mrs. Schoeman it was already dark. Both men died shortly after, but before Neethling succumbed he asked Mrs. Schoeman to retrieve the saddle-bags. Next morning she sent out her old native servant girl and the bags were buried. In 1903 they were returned to my father by Mrs. Roodt still intact. She had only taken out a photograph of my mother, which she kept as a memento. The contents of the bags were four books: a Greek New Testament, an English Bible, a Complete Works of Schiller, and a Greek *Anabasis*. This last my father had found at Jagersfontein and it was only partly read when he lost it here. At Parys he had found a *History of Philosophy*, but this he had finished previously. Kant's *Critique of Pure Reason* he was only to find later at Leliefontein near Calvinia. The bags and books now form part of his collection.

It was customary for the Boers to send out senior men on these reconnoitring missions. My father said this was one of the most striking operational differences between the British and the Boers, for the former sent only very junior officers who usually were incompetent to make true assessments of the situation. Many of the British failures he attributed to indifferent reconnoitring. My father made a habit, not only in this war, but also in the two World Wars, of going forward personally to see things for himself. It was a risk, but it paid dividends.

XVI RAIN AND MOUNTAINS

IN the ambushing party of British was an officer named Hughes, the selfsame who had searched our house in Sunnyside at the start of the war. Later he became a firm friend of the family, and as a colonel in the First World War was one of the two staff officers to see my father off at Irene Station when he set out for East Africa. When my mother pulled Colonel Hughes's leg about the poor shooting of the British at Moordenaars Poort, he said it had appeared to all that my father was hit, for he seemed to stumble as he ran and his one arm hung limply at his side. But at all events, he declared, it was providential that their marksmanship had been so poor. My mother was shown a newspaper while she was under detention by the British at 'Maritzburg in which it was reported that my father had been wounded.

It was bitterly cold in the Stormberg Mountains, and the troops, clad mostly only in their grain-bag clothes, were drenched and thoroughly miserable. At Allemanspoort, near Jamestown, conditions were so severe that thirty horses died of exposure during the night. Local sympathisers were to be found everywhere who not only gave what food they had, but also acted as guides.

After marching all night they still were to find no rest on the 10th at Allemanspoort, and that morning they were in action again. In his diary my father noted: "Allemanspoort: enemy repulsed; eleven forces move to surround me." Next day he added: "Enemy surrounds me still further. I retire to Labuschagne's Nek. Marched by Gardiner's bridle path through two English forces half an hour apart. . . . Towards afternoon [of the next day] an enemy force overtook me and an action took place on Stapelberg. . . . Enemy losses 50 or 60."

This happened near Dordrecht in the Stormberg Mountains. They were surrounded on a high plateau by forces under Colonel Monro with little hope of escape. Here a courageous hunchback volunteered to lead them down a remote mountain path, bobbing ahead on a horse in the biting rain and wind, and bringing them out on a route as near the vertical as horses have ever had to negotiate. They gratefully bade the hunchback good-bye and left him hobbling back in the darkness on his crutches. Darkness luckily hid the abysses they negotiated and by daylight they had sprung the trap and for the moment hoped that they had finally eluded the British.

My father often recounted the story of the courageous hunchback, and the six-hour scramble down the mountainside. It was one of his favourite stories of the war.

At the foot of the mountain they came across the railway line from Maclear, and seeing a train approaching the men wanted to roll rocks on to the line. But my father, fearing there might be civilians in it, let it pass unharmed. Little did they realise at the time what they had missed.

On May 15, 1917, at a dinner given by the combined British House of Commons and House of Lords in his honour, over which Lord French presided, my father recalled the incident: "At night I came out of those mountains to the railway. It

73

was a very dark night, and my small force was just on the point of crossing the railway when we heard that a train was coming. I allowed the train to pass, and we stood alongside and looked on. You can imagine my feelings when I heard some time afterwards that the only freight on that train was Lord French, who was moving from one part of the front to the other to find out how I had broken through. If I had not missed that chance Lord French would have been on that occasion my guest. No doubt a very welcome, though a somewhat embarrassing, guest!"

Five miles east of Dordrecht they came upon another train, which this time they captured. In it, amongst other things they found a newspaper with the proclamation by Lord Kitchener to the effect that all burghers caught under arms after 15th September, 1901, would be banished from South Africa. This raised a derisive laugh.

At last, after a gruelling sixty hours of continuous marching, came the first rest. But it was not for long; on the 14th they were on the run again. British forces appeared everywhere and as fast as they shook one column off, they moved into the next. The following night proved the worst of the war, for they were lashed by rain, sleet and wind. The wet grain bags froze solid on their backs as they floundered through the mud, and when daylight came they found that twelve of their number had dropped by the way from exhaustion, presumably to die of cold; though they were leading their weary horses, about sixty of the beasts succumbed. The survivors described it as the worst ordeal of the war, and proudly called themselves "Men of the Great Rains". At one stage it took them six hours to cover three miles in a heavy mist.

On the 17th, at Tarkastad, they were in contact with two columns, one under Colonel Gorringe and the other under Colonel Doran. At Elandsrivierpoort they set upon the camp of the 17th Lancers and after a short sharp skirmish captured it with much booty including an Armstrong gun and Maxim. This success was not perhaps the blessing it appeared to be, for though their tea and food supplies were replenished and they were enabled to get fresh horse mounts and ample stocks of ammunition, they wore the warmer uniforms of the British and not till long after, near Adelaide, did they learn of Kitchener's proclamation.

Maraisburg to the west they found occupied by the enemy and so, skirting it, they made into the Bamboesberg Mountains. Once again they found their paths blocked by troops, and once more they slipped down an obscure steep mountain path into the Bedford district. Here the population, though English, proved not unfriendly, though not co-operative. The Winterberg Mountains into which they now moved were wild and beautiful, with deep valleys of dense primeval woods. From now on, food, for both themselves and their horses, was a problem. In one valley they had to abandon thirty half-starved mounts.

They found Adelaide occupied and so by-passed it, moving into the valley of the Great Fish River. That night, while sleeping in a fold in the ground near the railway line at Commadagga, an armoured train passed, firing shots at random at them in the dark. Next they sought safety in the Zuurbergen where, on the 30th, in a ravenously hungry state, after living sparingly for days on the flesh of mountain tortoise, they came upon an appetising-looking fruit called "Boesmans Brood" (*Encephelartos Altensteinii*) growing on a cycad and looking like a big pineapple. Not knowing that the plant was edible only in certain seasons of the year, at other times being a deadly prussic acid poison, about seventy burghers partook heartily of it. Soon all were overcome by acute abdominal pains and many, including my father, lay retching and writhing on the ground. Being thus incapacitated was most embarrassing, as they were beset from every angle by the British. Many improved during the night, but my father was still in a critical condition when daylight came. He was tied to his horse and by a clever ruse the sick party, who were far behind the main body, managed to slip off at an angle and elude the pursuing British.

That Boesmans Brood left my father with a weakened stomach all his life. This was also one of his favourite Boer War stories.

So they moved swiftly southwards through this rugged mountain mass until eventually, on October 5th, in the distance ahead they could see white sand-dunes and a grey mass which they knew to be the Indian Ocean. They were elated, for they realised now that they had come farther south than any previous commando. After dark the lights of Port Elizabeth shone out in the distance. The men seemed puzzled that my father did not make for the town; but he was content with this distant view, for his mission lay with the Dutch of the Western Cape. Moreover, Port Elizabeth was far too strongly garrisoned. Everywhere were buffalo tracks and wallows, and there were abundant signs of elephant, for they were not far from the present Addo Park. A hunter in the party recognised the area and knew of a path out south through the mountains to the village of Bayville in the Sunday's River valley. There was fighting and skirmishing with the enemy all the way and also in the valley of the Little Sunday's River, where they eluded the enemy by taking an old disused pass down the mountains constructed by Sir Henry Smith during the Kaffir wars of the fifties. So after five hectic days in the mountains they made their way out once more into the Somerset district.

In five weeks they had covered 700 miles under the severest possible conditions. It had been bitterly cold throughout and each man's solitary blanket had offered little comfort at night. They slept, where possible, two in a bed for warmth, and when it was wet they simply lay down on bushes and rocks to keep out of the water. On the march they huddled under their blankets, which afforded little protection against the pelting rain. They had been harassed and chased by the British almost without respite and their horses were too weak to carry on. In the trek they had not only crossed four of the highest mountain ranges of the Cape, but had actually operated extensively in them.

On October 4th Colonel Gorringe, who had been hard on their heels for some time, decided to press home an attack up a steep mountain slope. The Boers, in a strong position, turned round and struck back, driving him down the hillside and inflicting heavy losses. It is said he suffered 200 casualties during the action and lost 900 horses.

It had become increasingly plain to my father that in view of the problems and the harassing tactics of the enemy, it would be better to split his force. So on the 4th October he called the men together and told them that a turning point had been reached by the expeditionary force and that they were now to split into two parties and to move independently westwards to the Atlantic seaboard where they were later to unite again. Van Deventer was to command the second party. My father had great confidence in this commander and it is said that van Deventer was the only man in whom he confided his plans.

My father set off first and after occasional light patrol skirmishes reached the village of Hobsonville, thereafter crossing the Port Elizabeth–Graaff Reinet railway line near Kendrew Siding on the 8th, later passing within seven or eight miles of garrisoned Aberdeen and thence into the Camdebo Mountains. Here the spell of fine weather they had latterly enjoyed once more gave place to bitter cold and drizzle. In the mountains they appeared cornered for a while, but later a bridle-path led them out to safety again. On the plain below they narrowly averted an ambush.

They were now on the flat expanses of the Karroo, but still in constant contact with the enemy. On the 14th, beyond Karega, my father had a narrow escape when an Armstrong shell burst right alongside him, covering him in dust and soil. That same day, due to faulty pickets, they were nearly caught by Colonel Scobell while resting. The next day they moved into the Beaufort West district and marched on all day and the next night. The following day found them at the foot of the Zwartbergen, where they were joined by Commandant Scheepers with a hundred men. Crossing over the mountains they moved on into the Uniondale and Oudtshoorn districts. From valley to valley they moved, in one coming upon a Mr. Guest, who, in the space of a day, had the mortification of being twice visited by the Boers and twice by the British, on each occasion having the pleasure of seeing more of his stock devoured by his guests.

On the 19th they ambushed a British column moving through Meirings Poort and took some booty. Four days later, at Rooikraal, my father had another lucky escape from a shell, again being covered in grit and smoke. Still travelling steadily westwards, they moved into Longkloof the next day.

In the Kamanassi River valley his commando were hotly pursued by a big British mounted column, but he reached the arid plains of the Calvinia district safely and pushed on to Elandsvlei, an oasis complete with waving palm trees. Thence they moved in leisurely fashion to Biddow and Kobbee and so on to van Rhynsdorp, where Manie Maritz had recently been. Maritz was not only a man of courage but a ruthless person of tremendous physical strength, and many years later he was to prove a thorn in my father's side.

* * * * *

Here in the South-Western Cape the commando paused during December, 1901, for the purpose of consolidating into three commandos the small bands of Boers that operated in the district. Many of the troops for the first time saw the sea and they rushed wildly on their horses into the Atlantic surf. On Christmas Day Deneys Reitz, of my father's staff, linked up with van Deventer's commando, and Maritz, too, was found at Tonteldoos, 80 miles to the north. Maritz had been repulsed there the day before and had a gaping wound in his chest, but he made light of it.

Patrolling was carried out from the van Rhynsdorp area to as far afield as beyond Porterville, and within sight of Table Mountain. My uncle Tottie Krige penetrated into the Malmesbury district where he went to visit my grandfather, Jacobus Smuts, from whom he brought back money for my father. He also took a letter, written at Nieuwoudtville, near Calvinia, on 4th January, 1902, from my father to his brother Koos. My father seemed in a depressed frame of mind and worried about my mother's state of health at Pietermaritzburg. He concluded: "I have had numerous narrow escapes in this war, for which I am grateful; but each person has his time. . . . I hold out little hope of seeing you all again: I know you will do your best to help Isie."

My father now made a long reconnaissance with his staff to Kakamas on the Orange River, 300 miles to the north, to organise the commandos there, on the way back pausing at Tonteldoos. On the farm Middelpoort on the Fish River he came upon van Deventer's commando in the midst of an attack on a British camp of 100 wagons, which they took after a sharp skirmish. Meanwhile Bouwer had been left in charge of my father's commando in van Rhynsdorp. Here they were visited by a stocky, middle-aged colonist named Lambert Colyn, who professed a desire to fight the British. After a while, though not quite unnoticed, he slunk off on his horse. The belief that he had come to spy was later confirmed when he stormed the house at the head of a troop of British horsemen, seventeen casualties being inflicted before the Boers escaped.

Later on my father combined his forces again to attack the nearby town of Windhuk where the British had established themselves after being driven from van Rhynsdorp. The town was taken with much booty and 200 persons, amongst whom Colyn was identified. He was brought before my father, who knowing what had happened sent him to be tried by a Court Martial presided over by Commandant L. Boshoff, at Aties, on 25th February, 1902. At this court Colyn handed in a sworn statement in which he admitted his complicity and other witnesses also testified to the same effect. He was found guilty of spying and my father signed the execution order. The documents of this case are also in my father's collection.

"Take him away and shoot him," he said briefly to the guards. Though Colyn collapsed and begged for mercy, and though the women of the van Zyl household fled the house in terror, it made no impression on the precise legalistic mind of my father. When I was young I remember hearing him recount the Colyn incident and he did so in such matter-of-fact terms that I was left without any doubt that he considered it merely a minor incident of the campaign.

Colyn's execution, though based on sound military justice, has not been without subsequent political repercussions, but these may be safely relegated to ignorance or political malice. Biographers have utilised the incident to show a hard streak in my father, but to soldiers in the field such actions are natural, and in cases like this, trivial.

From van Rhynsdorp my father kept in constant touch with his command in the Transvaal and with President Kruger, who had by that time gone to Europe and was living in Holland. Early in 1902 he sent the President an optimistic account of conditions in the Republics and the Cape. He wrote of the dangers threatening the British in the Cape, where there were thousands of disciplined Boer veterans fighting splendidly, all living well by their depredations on the British army.

At Darling, near my father's birthplace, a burgher named Boonzaaier, an adjutant of Maritz, and some of his comrades fired a few rifle shots at a British cruiser lying offshore at Lambert's Bay and then decamped again.

In the beginning of January, at a conference on the farm Soet-water, my father explained to his officers that he had decided to split up his commando into smaller units and to disperse them to many parts of the Cape. This would lock up larger numbers of British troops and would also facilitate their living-off-the-land tactics.

To the north, 150 miles away, lay the copper-mining town of O'okiep with its satellite villages Springbok and Concordia. These were British held, and in order to draw off the attentions of troops in other areas, it was decided to attack them. The commando was to split into small parties and to make for a point in the Kamiesbergen where they were to re-form. Springbok, which lies about three miles from O'okiep, was to be attacked first, then Concordia, and finally O'okiep itself. The defence system was based on blockhouses and the attack therefore resolved itself into a series of experiments with home-made dynamite hand-grenades, some of which eventually breached the defences. Finally, after much bomb-throwing, the last fort was demolished by a mammoth bomb hurled by the herculean Maritz and the outer defences of O'okiep fell into Boer hands. O'okiep itself was, however, a tougher nut and Colonel Shelton was determined to hold out at all costs. My father therefore decided on blockade tactics, as these served his purpose as well as any.

XVII VEREENIGING

ONE morning towards the end of April, 1902, a cart flying a white flag was noticed approaching from the south. The two officers carried a communication from Lord Kitchener to say that a meeting between the British and Boer leaders was to be held at Vereeniging as soon as possible. A safe-conduct was enclosed signed by Colonel D. Haig. This same Douglas Haig, later Field Marshal and Commander-in-Chief of the British forces in the First World War, was to see much of my father during those harrowing years. My father, accompanied by Tottie Krige and Deneys Reitz, was then escorted to Port Nolloth with full military honours and put aboard the troopship *Lake Erie* which then steamed to Cape Town. Here they were to spend a week on board the battleship *Monarch* at Simonstown. Everywhere they were treated with the utmost civility and courtesy by their enemy, and Deneys Reitz was moved to recording: "The British, with all their faults, are a generous nation, and not only on the man-of-war, but throughout the time we were among them, there was no word said that could hurt our feelings or offend our pride, although they knew that we were on an errand of defeat."

On the way up to the Transvaal by train there were frequent guards of honour at various stations; General French came to see them at Matjesfontein, and at Kroonstad Lord Kitchener, on a black charger accompanied by a bodyguard of Pathans, came to meet the train and have discussions with my father. He stressed that he was eager to end the war, and referred repeatedly to the hopelessness of the Boer resistance, pointing out that he had 400,000 troops in South Africa against the Boer 18,000. He would be magnanimous to the enemy if they surrendered. My father made no comment.

Thence, still under escort, my father proceeded first by armoured train and later by cart to the Eastern Transvaal for a conference with General Botha. Here were gathered 300 delegates from every commando in the Eastern Transvaal for the purpose of electing representatives for the Peace Conference at Vereeniging. Deneys Reitz says: "Nothing could have proved more clearly how nearly the Boer cause was spent than these starving, ragged men clad in skins and sacking, their bodies covered in sores. Their appearance was a great shock to us who came from the better-conditioned forces in the Cape. They had reached the limit of physical endurance."

Subsequently delegates from all over the country were brought together in a large tented camp prepared by the British at Vereeniging. Every leader of note was there, including de la Rey,

Christian de Wet, President Steyn, Beyers, Kemp, Hertzog, Botha, my father and others.

The Dutch Premier, Baron Kuyper, had sometime earlier offered the services of the Netherlands Government as an intermediary between the two parties, but Lord Lansdowne had not accepted this. He insisted that negotiations must be direct with Kitchener. Acting-President Burger, of the Transvaal, shortly afterwards approached the British Commander-in-Chief, and later the two Republics held discussions at Klerksdorp with the permission of Kitchener, who also provided facilities for the election of delegates. Thirty of these representatives from each State met therefore at this Vereeniging Peace Conference on 15th May, 1902.

There was considerable divergence of opinion amongst the Boers on the question of surrender. Steyn and de Wet of the Free State were "bitter-enders" and opposed to any idea of surrender. Botha, my father and the Transvaal delegates realised that the game was up and that surrender was unavoidable, though de la Rey, while concurring, was still far from convinced. My father's feelings were that "it was better to negotiate an orderly peace now under the best possible terms than to be crushed later and have ignominious terms thrust upon us".

He put the case clearly to them: "The great danger before this meeting is that it will come to a decision purely from the military point of view. . . . If we consider it only as a military matter, then I must admit we can still go on with the struggle. . . . But we are not here as an army. We are here as a people. . . . Everyone here represents the Afrikander *people*. . . . Burghers, we decided to stand to the bitter end. Let us now, like men, admit that the end has come for us, come in a more bitter shape than we ever thought. . . . We bow to God's will."

After considerable deliberation even de la Rey was forced to exclaim, "Has the bitter end not come?" What was the point in carrying on? Finally a commission consisting of Botha, de Wet, de la Rey, Hertzog and my father was appointed to negotiate with Kitchener and Milner in Pretoria.

At the conference there was considerable difference of opinion between Milner and Kitchener. Kitchener, a kindly understanding man, as a soldier appreciated the feelings of a vanquished foe, and favoured moderation with certain concessions. Milner, businesslike as ever, demanded unconditional surrender and wrote home unflatteringly of Kitchener's bargaining. My father tried vainly for a compromise. Late into the night they argued to break this impasse. Towards morning someone gently touched my father's arm. It was Kitchener. They went outside and walked up and down in earnest discussion. What finally clinched matters was when Kitchener said, "I can only give it to you as my opinion, but my opinion is that in two years' time a Liberal Government will be in power, and if a Liberal Government comes into power, it will grant you a constitution for South Africa." Here, though not a certainty, was a ray of hope. The British Commander's words had turned the scale, though unconditional surrender was in any case inevitable. It sweetened the pill. They returned to Vereeniging with a draft agreement bearing Milner's approval.

The Commission's report was accorded a mixed reception. It was received by the majority without enthusiasm, and it took all President Steyn's efforts to placate de Wet.

To my father with that distant sight of his, the promise of a bright future was already visible. He had statesmanlike visions of a reunited Boer nation dwelling as a peaceful state with its own constitution within the framework of the British Empire.

From the Cape to the Limpopo the map was now red. Rhodes had not lived to see it, for on March 26, several weeks before hostilities ceased, he had died in his small cottage at Muizenberg. "So much to do—so little done!" were said to have been his last words.

My father was now only thirty-two years of age. For almost fifty further years he was to toil in the service of his country. They were a glorious fifty years, in which he was to be both pilot and architect.

There may be some who feel that I have written of the Jameson Raid and the Boer War with a strong pro-Boer bias; this would, however, be an unfair criticism, for in fact, Britain has no stauncher friend and admirer than myself. This period of history was one in which imperialism went berserk, and it is one of which many Britons themselves are far from proud. There is, moreover, a certain justification for writing so critically of British policy of this period, for it serves, by contrast, to indicate the wonderful change of heart that came about after the Boer War. Since then Britain has made ample amends for her sins and South Africa has had no truer friend.

While most of us are quick to appreciate this hand of friendship, there are still misguided countrymen of mine living in the chilly, dead past, who have failed to realise that a new world order has arisen since the Boer War, and still harbour a bitterness in their hearts which time and reason seem incapable of sweetening. They remember only those unpleasant incidents we have long since gladly forgotten. Two World Wars have since shaken civilisation to its foundations, but they have passed unnoticed over the heads of these bitter people.

At present the pendulum, which started at the beginning of the century on the side of imperialism, appears to have passed its mid-point and now moves, strangely, into the area of aggressive Afrikanderism. This, as with all revolutions in the bosoms of men, will run its course, and prove, like its predecessors, a mere fleeting phase. We must not grow impatient. Given time and understanding, sanity will one day prevail.

XVIII THE HARDENED WARRIOR

MY father took as much pride in his exploits of the Boer War as in any other. If the frequency with which he reminisced is any criterion, this certainly is so. I think it was due to the fact that in it he found satisfaction for the first time in physical expression and achievement, in hardships and in really intimate association with his fellow men. It was a return to the veld life of his boyhood, and an opportunity to explore that vast homeland of his. Explore it he certainly did, from the Portuguese border in the east, to the Atlantic at Port Nolloth in the west;

from the Waterberg in the north to the plains near Malmesbury. Exacting conditions tempered and matured him. The experience gave him a respite from his books and administrative duties and time to ponder and to plan. In those long months in the open air he formed a philosophy of life and an understanding of the world which he followed ever after.

There was nothing harsh or artificial about it, for as in nature, all depended upon the beneficent factor of Time. Time was the great Creator, the great healer. Time must not be rushed but given a fair chance to function.

My father also believed that young nations had to pass the fires of testing before they could attain nationhood. Had the war ended tamely at Pretoria, the Boers would have missed those great testing times, and would not have been fused into such a solid mass. Whether this advantage was not over-stressed and whether the subsequent co-operation with the British elements was not jeopardised by this very fact, history alone will be able to tell.

It is said that my father was an embittered man after the Boer War. That I think is an overstatement. Certainly he did pass through a period of depression and despair. It is a known fact that wars produce in all active combatants, whether victors or vanquished, a psychological reaction of cynicism and disillusionment. This has been amply demonstrated by the problem of rehabilitation of ex-Servicemen. In judging my father's reaction one should bear this post-war psychosis in mind. I think it will be agreed that his reactions were remarkably restrained. He had just passed through the most searing fires in life, and had been called upon to make far-reaching decisions. He had seen his companions killed and wounded alongside him in the battlefields, he had seen once-prosperous farms charred and blackened masses, he had seen the work of generations razed to the ground, and the population reduced to the precarious life of wild animals.

My mother felt these tragic events acutely. The kindest, gentlest and most forgiving person I have ever known, she felt bitter towards the British. She says she felt bitter for a long while, and had it not been for the fact that she and my father became close friends with Lord Methuen some years later, falling under the spell of that fine and friendly Englishman, the feeling might have persisted longer. Lord Methuen was fittingly the first visitor to stay at our new house at Irene when he and his daughter Seymour spent New Year there in 1910.

In fairness to my mother I must here add that her bitterness was perhaps not without provocation, for in the years of the war she had lost her baby son, she had seen a price of £1,000 placed on her husband's head, and she herself had been taken from her home in Pretoria and kept in detention in a house in 'Maritzburg from January, 1901, to August, 1902. Her treatment at 'Maritzburg, she has always been quick to add, was scrupulously fair. But perhaps it would have been more generous of the English to have sent her down to her parents at Stellenbosch.

My father emerged from the Boer War with an improved constitution, a great reputation, and considerable experience of leadership. He had tasted power and felt the exhilaration of action. Well did he know the feeling of responsibility, the call of duty. The beard he grew hid the youthful line of his features. When he went to visit his father (his mother had died in February, 1901) the old man failed to recognise this mature son. In conversation, those searching pale blue eyes dominated one's attention. They were remarkable eyes and formed perhaps the most striking feature in his physical personality. In the great ones of the world I have never come across similar eyes. Yet they were understanding and expressive, not without a warmth of friendliness. Their remarkable clearness carried with them a feeling of clarity of soul as well. They never grew frosty or cloudy with his change of mood. It was the tone of voice and general demeanour rather than the eyes that denoted his pleasure or chagrin. There was no mistaking either.

In studying my father at this time one is apt to forget his youth. When he became State Attorney he was only twenty-eight and even now, at Vereeniging, he had barely turned thirty-two. He had become accustomed to moving in the company of experienced men of twice his age, and the respect with which his word and reasoning were treated was all the more remarkable. He must, even then, have had a developed personality. He commanded not only the respect of the public, and the confidence of his troops, but also that of hardened politicians, and diplomats in their council chambers listened to him with attention.

In 1935, at an Imperial Press Conference in Cape Town, my father said: "Only a generation ago this country was locked in a grim and deadly struggle with the old British Empire. We Boers fought for freedom and independence. We found it in a strange way, where we least expected."

In a political speech in Bloemfontein in November, 1939, he observed, "There is talk to-day of the Boer War, of concentration camps, and attempts are being made to make our flesh creep about what happened in the old times. But let us rather think of what has happened since. Let us think also of the fine treatment, the generosity and the helping hand we have experienced from Great Britain ever since. We render the people of this country no service by continually harking back to what happened in the distant past and forgetting what has happened since."

He kept carbon copies of his reports and dispatches during his Boer War sojourn in the South-West Cape. They are mostly still rolled as they had been carried in his saddle-bags. They are written in Dutch and are mostly brief in character and signed J. C. Smuts, Assistant Comdt.-General. The handwriting is unmistakable and little changed. The only difference is that while in the Boer War it was rather angular, it became more rounded and free-flowing. Until people got to know it, strangers found it difficult to read.

These reports and dispatches are as much concerned with such practical matters as fodder for the horses as with the fighting, for they were operating in a semi-desert corner of the arid Karroo, not far from the Port Nolloth diamond fields of Namaqualand. This western Orange River area was not only the driest in the Union but also the hottest. Goodhouse has a record of high temperatures unsurpassed by any other spot in the country.

Here is a translation of a typical field dispatch:

OLIVENHOUTSRIVIER,
27.3.1902.

V. Genl. van Deventer.
DEAR SIR,

I was pleased to receive your report and intend moving north from here as fast as possible. Naude and Bouwer's commandos are already at Arkoep north of Bowesdorp, while Comdt. Bouwer himself has moved on ahead with a detachment to Rietfontein west of Mestklip.

My plan is to move suddenly to between Mestklip and Springbok with the object of cutting off the enemy at Mestklip, and then to attempt to storm Springbok and O'okiep. You must move north with all possible speed to between Springbok and Mestklip, sending out runners to contact me in the vicinity of Rietfontein. I shall also endeavour to establish contact with you.

I have also instructed V. General Maritz to move there. He will leave behind a party to keep watch on the enemy from Garies.

As forage is scarce we must work swiftly to make use of the present favourable position.

Comdt. Wessels reported to me at Leliesfontein. He and Theron drove back some columns from Vischrivier towards Williston.

There is ample fodder at Vischrivier.

(Sgd.) J. C. SMUTS.
Asst. Comdt. Gnl.

The earlier diaries from which I have quoted were written in English. This is a remarkable fact when it is remembered that at the time he was fighting the English. But it does bear out that, even then, he was doing most of his serious thinking in English— a characteristic he retained throughout his life. I often got the impression when he was speaking that he was thinking in English and doing a sub-conscious translation, especially in the way he had sometimes to feel for the Afrikaans idiom.

I might here add, too, that he never lost the queer "Malmesbury" guttural way he had of pronouncing his "r". You could tell without any doubt that it was not an Englishman speaking. After the Boer War, hecklers at political meetings often belittled his pronunciation, forgetting that even at that age he had perhaps as extensive a vocabulary and as wide a reference as any Englishman in the country. "I admit my English is not flawless," he would say. Yet that Malmesbury "r" survived across the generations, and in dark times to come men listened to it gladly as a symbol of hope and optimism.

I might here remark that the guttural "r" is at least infectious, if not hereditary, for only two of us in a family of six have managed to avoid it.

The Boer War was over. South Africa rolled up her sleeves and set about the task of salvaging what remained from the wreckage, while in Europe people sat back to take stock and to ponder the implications of what had occurred. Britain, though victorious, came to feel it was a hollow victory and was shocked and even shamed. She became convinced that her aggressive Imperialism was fraught with grave dangers, and her heart demanded a more ethical approach to relationships. With that realisation began a new era of tolerance and prosperity, which in years to come was to bring her much lustre.

In Germany, much thought had brought that nation to the conclusion that without a navy they were impotent. To become a great power, especially one that spanned the oceans, she had to have a first-class navy. This started Germany off on a building programme which by direct linkage was twelve years later to enable her to plunge the entire world into war.

XIX RECONSTRUCTION

MILNER, newly created a viscount on the strength of his Boer War success, and Governor of the new Transvaal and Orange River Colonies, established his headquarters in Johannesburg and set about the task of reconstructing the shattered country. To his credit it must be noted that he had turned down the attractive offer by Mr. Chamberlain of a Colonial Secretaryship, and had done this in order that he might reconstruct South Africa. His decision to stay on in the country deepened my father's depression.

Lord Milner, undeterred as ever by the feelings of the people about him, was determined to model a new country according to his own ideas. From Oxford he had brought a group of graduates to aid him in this task. Though the idea of bringing out this "Kindergarten" of young experts was a novel one it had much to commend it. In any case the right men were not available in

South Africa. On the whole it worked with great benefit to the country and all its members have since become famous: Geoffrey Dawson was for long to be a distinguished editior of *The Times*; John Buchan became famous as a novelist and historian, and later, as Lord Tweedsmuir, Governor-General of Canada; Philip Kerr, as Marquess of Lothian, became Britain's Ambassador in Washington during World War I; F. B. Smith, a Nobel Prize winner, was to become a famous professor of Agriculture at Cambridge; Patrick Duncan stayed on in South Africa and in years to come was my father's right-hand man and the first Union-domiciled person appointed to the Governor-Generalship; R. H. Brand, economist, served in many capacities with great distinction.

A vast array of problems faced the Milner regime: there was the question of the repatriation of the 32,000 Boer exiles, the return of refugees and 110,000 concentration camp inmates, the restitution of prisoners of war, the transfer from military to civilian government, the establishment of law and order, the revival of trade and industry, reparations, re-establishment of agriculture and a hundred and one other difficulties.

All these tasks were tackled simultaneously with vigour. By March, 1903, all the prisoners of war had been repatriated. The evacuation of British troops was expeditiously carried out, and by March only 30,000 remained. Boer families were brought back from the concentration camps and rehabilitated on their farms. After five years Britain had paid out £9,500,000 in compensation to the Boers—more than three times the amount asked for by my father at Vereeniging. The problem of compensation threatened to become farcical, for the spate of demands from the Boers knew no bounds. People were out to get all they could from Britain.

My father, who returned to his house in Sunnyside, was distressed to find his cherished library of law books wrecked, but he put in no claim. Throughout his life he never put in any claim against governments. It was his conviction that people leading public lives should not do so.

But the manner in which compensation was paid out left much discontent. To give immediate relief Milner decided to give assistance at once and to ask for proof afterwards. He distributed £3,000,000 at the rate of £25 per burgher, regardless of whether the assistance was required or not, and was later to make the adjustments deemed necessary. The "protected burghers", the despised Boer "handsuppers", were granted an additional £1,900,000 and the Uitlanders £2,000,000. This occasioned much bitterness, and the general lack of equity caused much hardship. In addition £3,000,000 was distributed on short-term loan.

To Herbert Baker, another Kindergarten member, was entrusted the design of the new public buildings that were erected throughout the country. Years before, Rhodes had been impressed by the idealism of this young architect and had given him the job, amongst others, of designing his own residence at Groote Schuur, on the slopes of Devil's Peak. By his great gifts of broad vision and sympathetic feeling, Baker created a fine series of buildings. He remained throughout his life a great admirer and firm friend of my father's.

My mother, returned from her nineteen months' sojourn in Pietermaritzburg, looked tired and thin. Under the strain of the war years, her weight had dropped to little over seven stone, but her spirit was undiminished. Her bitterness did not obscure from her the fact that a fresh life had now to be started.

My father returned to the Bar in Pretoria as a junior. He was now well known and he did not have to struggle to make a living as had been the case in Johannesburg. He had friends everywhere and the country was swelled with British money. So his practice prospered and he devoted his time and energies to it.

The most celebrated case that came his way at this time was the defence of a grandson of Paul Kruger, a Mr. S. J. P. Smit, who had murdered an unpopular moneylender named Davis at Swartspruit near Pretoria. My father introduced a defence that was at that time new to this country, that of hereditary insanity. Apparently there was evidence of epilepsy in the family. Much to his surprise, this flimsy defence was accepted; Smit was sent to a mental institution for a year or two and then released. Strange to relate, this same Smit rebelled in 1914 against the man who so narrowly saved him from the gallows.

In June, 1902, General Lyttelton replaced Kitchener.

There were signs that the country was recovering. An indication of this was that land values were rising. This had the effect of placating the farming people. It was unfortunate that a severe drought occurred at the end of 1902, followed later by floods and locusts; the extremely high cost of living was also proving a trial to the people.

In 1903, a deputation of Boers led by Botha went to England to try to obtain financial assistance. They were received most courteously, and were feted and lionised as only Britain can lionise a vanquished foe. But they got nothing beyond goodwill and friendliness; nor did they meet with better luck on the Continent. So they returned to South Africa with the chastened conviction that they would have to settle down and make ends meet as best they could.

In January, 1903, Joseph Chamberlain visited Pretoria at Milner's invitation. He was received by the people at a big reception in the Raadsaal. The Boers were granted permission to put their grievances before him. It was significant that my father, as he was then no politician, was deputed to put their case to Chamberlain in preference to all the other illustrious leaders present. He spoke in Afrikaans, through an interpreter. English was the official language of the land and he now asked that concession be made in respect of the Afrikaans language; he spoke also of the burden of war taxation, and requested an amnesty for the Cape rebels whose crimes had merely been those of the whole Boer race. Chamberlain listened sympathetically but made no immediate concessions. When he departed he told Milner, however, to treat these matters with greater tolerance. He had been favourably impressed by the bearing of the Boers during his visit. My father says their behaviour, which was calm and dignified, made a better impression on Chamberlain than that of his own English countrymen.

This goodwill, spurred on no doubt by the impatience of the Boers, bore fruit, and in 1903 Milner offered seats in his nominated Legislative Council to Botha, de la Rey and my father. Through my father this offer was refused. The time was not ripe yet for popular representative institutions; it would be better to wait till the country was more settled. It was only right that as the government at the moment had all the power, it should also shoulder all the responsibilities.

The refusal was just what Milner wanted. It bore out his contention that the Boers were completely unco-operative.

Long ago, my father was fond of recounting a little incident which went to show how distrustful Milner still was of the Boers and how out of touch with the people. He was to attend a public function at some place in the south-western Transvaal, if I remember rightly Potchefstroom or thereabouts. The town, which was almost completely Boer, decided to give him a rousing welcome and made arrangements accordingly. As Milner's horse-drawn coach entered the village a group of young men were to rush forward, unhitch the animals and themselves draw the cart to the centre of festivities. This little surprise was kept secret from Milner. Imagine, therefore, the poor man's consternation, when, as he got to the boundary, a group of husky young men rushed his entourage trailing wicked ropes. He was convinced that his assassination was imminent, and thinking discretion the better part of valour, jumped to the ground and decamped as fast as he could go. The master of ceremonies, sensing this hitch in the programme, ran after him shouting lustily, "My Lord! My Lord!" but it was some time before they impressed on the King's representative that they were merely acting in a friendly spirit. The picture of Milner doing that desperate sprint, gave my father great pleasure.

He was still very despondent and disillusioned. He wrote to Merriman that he sometimes despaired of the future. "One lives here in an atmosphere which is entirely devoid of culture" and "frankly materialistic".

Much of Milner's scheme of reconstruction was based on funds to be derived from the taxation of profits of a rejuvenated gold-mining industry. But in this he was to be disappointed, for the industry was passing through lean and difficult times. Native labour was almost unobtainable, not only because natives had been spoiled by the readiness with which they made easy money during the war, but also because the wages offered by the mines had dropped from 45 shillings in pre-war days to 30 shillings. Milner failed to appreciate, as Rhodes had done earlier on and had remedied in his Glen Grey Act, that unless a native male is compelled to work by firm persuasion he is very likely to prefer a life of ease, lying happily in the sun.

To Milner, therefore, the only solution lay in indentured Chinese labour and in this he had the full support of George

Farrar, leader of the English party in the House of Assembly. This was not South Africa's first taste of foreign labour. In the 1860s the people of Natal had brought in about six thousand low-caste Madras Indians to help in their sugar-cane fields. The Indians bred prolifically and at the turn of the century presented a formidable problem to Natal and elsewhere. In their easy-going fashion the people of Natal, though perplexed by the problem, had done little to solve it, and instead of raising a clamour to get the coolies repatriated, merely crossed their arms in resignation. Hence the serious problem of the Indian in the Natal of to-day—a people liked by neither whites nor blacks.

My father saw clearly the implications of the proposed importation of Chinese to the Rand. We already had sufficient problems of race and colour in this country. The idea outraged him and his countrymen.

A middle-aged Quaker spinster, Emily Hobhouse, came from England as a welfare worker amongst the Boer families in the concentration camps during the war. She had earned high gratitude and praise for her labours. My parents met her for the first time after the war and thereafter my father was to carry on correspondence with her, somewhat in the form of a diary, for many years. He wrote her a letter in February, 1903, in which he unburdened his bruised feelings. He condemned the intention to import Chinese in the strongest terms; he slated Milner; he castigated the mining industry of which he said that little better than 80 per cent were bogus concerns. We were "merrily spinning to perdition" he wrote in despair.

Kind-hearted and well-meaning Miss Hobhouse, without my father's concurrence, had this long letter published in full in *The Times* of 15th April. It was hard to conceive of a more foolish or damaging act.

The reactions were instantaneous. There was an immediate outcry against my father. He wrote to Miss Hobhouse, "A tremendous sensation was created last week by the cables of my letter which you published. As later letters were hostile to Lord Milner and their publication would have meant my enforced departure from this country, I took the precaution of warning you against further publication.

"On the whole I feel sorry the letter was published, as I would have expressed myself more cautiously had I known it would be published. As it is, it appears exaggerated and unfair. . . . Lord Milner is said to be very pleased, as the letter confirms his view that I am the great Irreconcilable still at large in this blessed satrapy." Later he wrote of "a storm of execration" against him in Johannesburg, especially by the mining houses. In a long poem by Sir Owen Seaman *Punch* caricatured him unflatteringly.

Yet after Miss Hobhouse's unpardonable indiscretion he bore her no ill-will, but wrote as before. His letters were full of the Chinese problem and of queries whether a swing towards a Liberal Government was already discernible, and whether she thought, if the Liberals came into power, they would "stop Chinese importation". He was much depressed: "I see no ray of hope," he wrote in May, 1904.

During the First World War Miss Hobhouse turned as pro-German as she had previously been pro-Boer and denounced my father for his part in the war against Germany. She said some hasty things for which my mother has never forgiven her. But my father remembered only the good work she did amongst the Boer families. He realised that Miss Hobhouse was that earnest type of soul who always championed an underdog. It was through Miss Hobhouse that we were to get to know the Gillett family of Oxford. Mrs. Gillett (née Clark) worked with Miss Hobhouse at one stage out here teaching weaving crafts to Boer women. The Gilletts became my father's lifelong friends.

Milner himself did not like the idea of importing Chinese labour at first. It was only when his reconstruction programme became endangered that he warmed to it. Once he had made up his mind he was inflexible. In June, 1904, the Chinese started to come. By the end of the year there were 23,000 Chinese on the mines and eventually by December, 1908, about 54,000.

The people in South Africa, with the exception of the mine-owners and shareholders, were enraged. Serious crime on the Rand had become disturbing since the arrival of the Orientals. People lived in fear of their safety. The clamour against the Chinese was constant and vehement.

It was to echo all the way across the seas to England, though by the time it reached there, it had assumed a different meaning. In England the by-word became "Slavery". It was the hardship of the Chinese coolies they pitied there, these poor indentured creatures cooped up brutally in mine "prisons"! Campbell-Bannerman cried loudly in protest against the "slave-laws" and the "indentured labour". The British are a kind-hearted, if often misconstruing, people, and they took this propaganda to their hearts. Campbell-Bannerman's protests gathered in force, and the clamour against the Government mounted to such effect that by December, 1905, it sufficed at a general election to unseat them and bring in the Liberals.

Before this, however, Milner's term of office had expired and he was on his way back to England, where now he was to spend ten years in the political wilderness.

On 2nd April, 1905, my father wrote to the departing Governor: "Will you allow me to wish you a bon voyage now that you are leaving South Africa for ever? I am afraid you have not liked us. But I cherish the hope that, as our memories grow mellower, and the nobler features of our respective ideas become clearer, we shall more and more appreciate the contribution of each to the formation of the happier South Africa which is certainly coming, and judge more kindly of each other.

"At any rate it is a consolation to think what is noble in our work will grow to larger issues than we foresaw, and that even our mistakes will be covered up ultimately, not only in merciful oblivion, but also in that unconscious forgiveness which seems to me to be an inherent feature of all historic growth. History writes the word 'reconciliation' over all her quarrels, and will surely write it over the unhappy differences which have agitated us in the past. What is good in our work is not disposed of in the present but can safely appeal to the ear of the future. Our respective contentions will reach a friendly settlement which no one foresees to-day."

My father stigmatised the Milner Administration of 1902–5, "the darkest period in the history of the Transvaal". Milner himself considered his work during this period as the best of his life. My father was to meet him again in the First World War. By that time his period of adversity had had a mellowing effect and he was an easy and pleasant person to work with. They became firm friends.

Lord Selborne succeeded Milner and proved a wise choice.

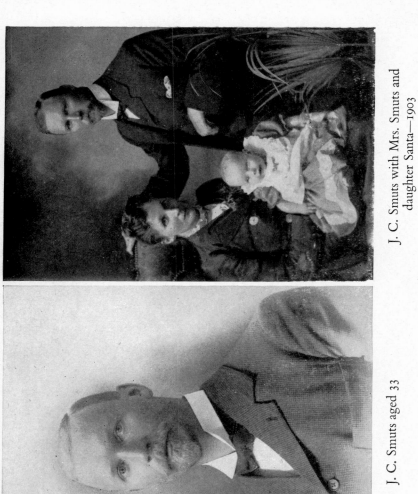

J. C. Smuts with Mrs. Smuts and
daughter Santa—1903

J. C. Smuts aged 33

J. C. Smuts at the wheel of his first car—1911

J. C. Smuts with the Writer—August 1914

He was a quiet, kindly and understanding man, with wide sympathies, keen on farming and affairs of the land, and with his coming there was an instant improvement in the atmosphere. He was a good friend to Botha and my father.

On my father's thirty-fifth birthday Lord Selborne spoke of him as "Mr. Smuts, that brilliant lawyer, the brilliant soldier".

XX RESPONSIBLE GOVERNMENT

MEANWHILE, in the Transvaal the Afrikaans people had founded the Het Volk party under the leadership of Botha, de la Rey and my father. Its objects were responsible government and conciliation between the two white races. The offer of representation under the Lyttelton Constitution was still too near the Crown Colony type of representation to make possible its acceptance by them. They wanted full responsible representation.

With Campbell-Bannerman in power my father was hopeful and active. In 1906 he left for England quietly and unobtrusively, but not so quietly but that the press took notice. In London he stayed at Horrex's Hotel, in the Strand, where Kruger had put up previously. He told reporters that he had come on private business. They were not convinced. The world had begun to realise that his presence always meant something.

His mission was to see the Liberal Government on the question of Responsible Government. But it was difficult to know how to approach them, for of their front-benchers he had so far met only Winston Churchill. So he saw Churchill first, but Churchill was frankly dubious. Morley he saw next, but though he had previously been pro-Boer, he now said there was public opinion to consider.

Campbell-Bannerman asked him why he had refused Milner's

first offer of representation on the Legislative Council. My
father's reply was that it would have led only to friction, for that
government was appointed and not elected. It would have left
the Boer minority on the Council with no power except to talk.
They would have been bitterly criticised by their people. The
Lyttelton Constitution was hardly any better. There was only one
solution, that of self-government.

"I went on explaining," my father said. "I could see Campbell-
Bannerman was listening sympathetically. Without being brilliant he was the sort of personality—large-hearted and honest—
on whom people depended. He reminded me of Botha. Such
men get things done. He told me there was to be a Cabinet
meeting the next day and said, 'Smuts, you have convinced me.'"
That talk settled the future of South Africa.*

Campbell-Bannerman addressed his Cabinet. Lloyd George is
said to have told Lord Riddell: "It was all done in a ten-minute
speech at the Cabinet—the most dramatic, the most important
ten-minute speech delivered in our time. . . . At the outset only
two of us were with him. . . . But his speech convinced the whole
Cabinet. It was the utterance of a plain, kindly, simple man. The
speech moved at least one member of the Cabinet to tears. It
was the most impressive thing I ever saw." Britain extended the
hand of friendship and understanding.

My father returned to South Africa a proud man. He considered this one of the greatest achievements of his life. He said
it was "one of the wisest political settlements ever made in the
history of the English nation".

The Lyttelton Constitution was revoked and in May a Royal
Commission came to Pretoria to settle the details of responsible
government.

A photo of Campbell-Bannerman to this day hangs behind my
father's desk in his study. He felt warmly for the kindness shown
him. At his study door, in an equally commanding position,
hangs a photo of Paul Kruger, the other man to whom he was
eternally grateful.

In December, 1906, the Transvaal was accorded Responsible
Government and the Orange River Colony shortly after. Said
my father: "They gave us back our country in everything but

* Quoted from Sarah Gertrude Millin.

98

name. After four years. Has such a miracle of trust and magnanimity ever happened before? Only people like the English could do it. They may make mistakes, but they are a big people."

In 1906 my father was appointed a King's Counsellor, to the disgust of General Hertzog, who considered it a despised British appendage.

Meanwhile things were going better in the country. The mines once more became prosperous, and with that the prosperity of the whole country took on a new lease. The repatriation of the Chinese now began. They had served their purpose and local natives could take over the work. But the evacuation was not to be complete till March, 1910.

In Het Volk the leadership had now clearly passed into the hands of Botha and my father. They were an ideal partnership: my father provided the brain and drive, Botha the solid personal side in contact with all types of people. They had frequently discussed the future as they sat on the stoep of Botha's house in Sunnyside and had decided to devote their efforts to the rebuilding of a united South African nation. To this purpose they travelled the country making speeches. Their theme was always conciliation and goodwill. The response was gratifying.

In the Orange River Colony General Hertzog had, in 1905, founded the Orangia Unie. It was built on the narrower lines of nationalism and Afrikanderism. Hertzog had not in him that breadth of view or the forgiving nature that stamps the statesman. He was irrevocably ingrained with the hard kernel of Afrikanderism which no reason or argument could shake. It was the obstinate, almost blind, unreasonableness of the Boer race. So far it had not become a major problem, but as the years passed the Orangia Unie was to diverge further and further from the paths of conciliation and to harden to a tone of great bitterness; it was to initiate a two-stream policy from which even her best friends have been unable to save South Africa. Hertzogism was a canker with small beginnings, but it was deep-seated and grew steadily, undermining South African nationhood. It was too big a burden to thrust on to a small, war-ravaged country.

The electioneering campaign of Botha and my father in the Transvaal was designed to counter the Hertzog cult. Nor were their efforts at conciliation unsuccessful, for they gained support from considerable British elements who came forward to join their party.

In February, 1907, elections were held for the Responsible Government. The upper house was appointed by nomination.

On the 28th July, 1906, my father spoke at Ventersdorp of "a new and great nation, neither Boer nor British, but a nation that shall make South Africa into a big, free country".

The Chinese must go, he said repeatedly. At Daspoort near Pretoria he said on the 23rd January, 1907: "The introduction of the Chinese was a crime. We shall not rest until the last Chinaman has left the shores of South Africa." Yet at the same time he was quick to reassure the mines that this would not be done precipitately or to their detriment. "No Chinese will be allowed to leave unless proper substitutes have been previously found."

On the 14th November, 1906, the Johannesburg *Star* praised my father for his consistency, saying there was nothing in his past of which he had reason to be ashamed, but at the same time it remarked that "we happen to regard Mr. Smuts as a particularly dangerous political guide for a young British Colony".

In February, 1907, the elections were held and of the total or 69 seats Het Volk had 37, with the diehard British Progressives securing only 21. Six went to the Affiliated Nationalists (Responsibles) and 5 to Labour and Independents. George Farrar was leader of the Progressives and Christian Beyers Speaker of the House. Sir Lionel Philips was President of the Chamber of Mines.

At about this time the English press for the first time began referring consistently to my father as General Smuts. There was considerable talk at the time of making him Premier, for in ability and intellectual attributes he had no equal in the Government. Wisely, and at the same time with due modesty, he deprecated such a move. He wrote to Merriman, "I think it would be a mistake to take precedence over Botha who is really one of the finest men South Africa has ever produced." To Dr. F. V. Engelenberg he wrote in similar vein: "I agree with you that no one more than General Botha is entitled to appreciation and gratitude. The victory of the people's party at the polls is largely due to his constant labours. . . . These excellent services deserve to be worthily recognised."

Louis Botha was eight years older than my father, and a British subject of Natal by birth. Where my father was light of bone-structure and slender of build, Botha was big-boned and massive, with a frame in later life so heavy that it sapped his vitality. He was of a dark almost swarthy complexion, with prominent black bushy eyebrows and big protruding eyes—a pleasant hand-some face with features suggesting humour and kindness rather than intellectual fire. Botha was by nature and outlook a farmer, with all a farmer's liking for protracted conversation, coffee and tobacco, and always accessible and approachable. At the same time there was in him something solid, which suggested the massive-ness of the mountains of his birthplace.

With the Boer people Botha's stature and popularity were un-surpassed. They could feel he was one of them. Of his transparent honesty and integrity there was never a question. What he lacked in education he made up in human understanding, and he had displayed rare powers of leadership in the old Transvaal Volks-raad, and in the war. His one grave disability was that he spoke little English and his efforts to learn it at this stage of his career were too belated.

My own childhood memories of General Botha are those of a big jovial man, ample of girth and friendly of demeanour. When my father was away on the German East African campaign he came to see how we were all getting on at Irene, and on one occasion found my little sister and myself down with whooping cough and my poor mother worn out with looking after us. Kind soul that he was, he took us each in his arms and carried us around till we were asleep.

My father's association with Louis Botha dated back to the days of the Volksraad in Pretoria. The friendship was formed in the testing days of the war, and it was clinched during those great days of planning the future of the country. It was the closest public friendship my father formed in his life; it was, he said, the intimate friendship of brothers.

In all matters the partnership functioned admirably, for both were selfless men working only for the good of their country. Botha was the solid power, my father the dynamic planner and phenomenal worker. While Botha talked and contacted people, my father sat in his office working, always working, running not only his own portfolios but those of most of the Cabinet as well. Union Cabinets in those days, to a much greater extent than at present, carried a lot of dead-wood, and ministers were as yet inexperienced in the tasks of government. My father did their thinking and their work for them. He also did much of General Botha's, for the General's lack of English often kept him out of the House.

My father said he seldom in life had worked harder than during that period. It is said he was even curt and off-hand with deputations, though I find it hard to credit that.

At the same time he still found time to be cheerful and informal at home. The pleasant old Stellenbosch pastime of reading poetry aloud returned to the house, and my mother says they even sang *volkslieder* and Scottish songs together, she playing the accompaniment on the piano.

In the new Government my father was appointed Colonial Secretary and Minister of Education. His vigour and forcefulness and his administrative ability were plain, and cartoons in the press stressed the multiplicity of the man.

Botha went to England almost immediately after the formation of the Cabinet, leaving my father, the youngest member, in charge. He took an early opportunity to pay an official visit to the Portuguese in Delagoa Bay, and shortly after went to take a look at Beira, travelling via Salisbury.

During this period his work was noteworthy for perhaps four major items of legislation. The first was the Education Bill, which stands in principle to this day. It was in essence one of language equality. All education was put under government control; English was made a compulsory language and Dutch optional. At the same time, to obviate any possible Church interference, all denominational religious education was banned. My father felt "it might have been better if we had only one language, but we must deal with facts and find a solution". Religion was introduced because, "this is a Christian country. Nine-tenths of the population are Christian and wish their children to be educated in the Christian manner. . . . No clergyman will be allowed to come into the schools. . . . There are different opinions. . . . The educational system of the country shall not be run by the Churches." He piloted his Bills skilfully through the House. The *Volkstem* said,

"Oom Jannie has a way of dealing with a complicated matter as if it were the simplest thing on earth."

Next came his stand against Labour. His offer of relief employment at two shillings per day, with keep, was flatly rejected by Labour, whose demands were five shillings plus keep, and relief in forms specific to their own choice. On my father's thirty-seventh birthday three hundred disgruntled men marched from Johannesburg to Pretoria to press their case. It looked as though matters might get out of hand so he called out two British regiments, the Camerons and the Queen's Bays, to patrol the Reef. The trouble subsided, but a cry was raised that foreign troops had been used in a domestic affair. At the time, however, there was no option.

Thirdly came the unpleasantness over the Cullinan diamond. This superb gem of 3,025 carats was discovered near Pretoria on 26th January, 1905. Its value was beyond computation, but it was provisionally insured for £250,000. Botha and my father thought it might be a fine and worthy gesture for this new colony to present the stone to the King.

The Boers supported the motion, but the English members were critical and hostile, pointing out that it scarcely befitted an impoverished small country to be so magnanimous. An acrimonious debate raged for two days before the motion was passed. My father was prompted to remark scathingly that, "When I see the Knight Commanders and D.S.O.'s rise and unblushingly oppose the motion it shows me that although there may be great financial power among them, there is little political insight." And political insight on my father's side there certainly was, for the ink was still drying on the deed of gift when London sanctioned the £5,000,000 Land Bank Loan which was so essential to the Transvaal.

The fourth matter referred to the Indians. My father's trouble with Gandhi began in July, 1907. It never really finished. By the time an Indian assassin's bullet ended Gandhi's life in 1948 the whole Commonwealth had become involved with this diminutive man.

It was almost by accident that he came to be connected with South Africa.

XXI GANDHI

I N 1893 a court case was pending in Pretoria which involved
Indian interests. Gandhi came out to Africa to defend the case.
His journey up from Durban to Pretoria was an eventful one,
for it introduced him drastically to the system of race discrimination, known as the colour bar, which operated in this country. It
did not help him that he had spent five years studying Law in
London and was a man of culture. The colour bar was a hard-
and-fast innovation working regardless of all these things. Gandhi
learned this in the train on the way up. First a European refused to
sit in the same compartment and to save face Gandhi got out of
the train and spent the night on Pietermaritzburg Station. Near
Standerton the following day he had a disagreement with the
conductor of another train which ended in his having his ears
boxed. He changed carriages and proceeded uneventfully to
Johannesburg. There he was told hotels were full, and had to
change into his frock coat and top hat in a cloakroom. Once more
he took a first-class ticket and proceeded to Pretoria, where he
arrived at night. Not being in possession of a "pass", a document
all non-Europeans have to carry at night, he was arrested.

Needless to say this reception did not endear the Transvaal to
him. For all his diminutive size he was a man of moral courage
and tenacity. He spent only a few days in Pretoria before returning to Durban on the way home, but there he learned from a
newspaper that Natal was about to disenfranchise the Indians. It
was, so far as Natal was concerned, a measure of self-protection
to ensure that the country should remain white. The Indian people
were breeding like rabbits and the country was fast becoming
swamped by them. Even a £3 annual head tax had not deterred
them from coming to South Africa.

Gandhi saw there was work for him to do in South Africa.
He drew up a petition of protest against the Bill. For three years
he stayed in Natal, organising the Natal Indian Congress, a fore-
runner of the Congress Party of India he was to initiate later. In
India, where he went for a holiday, he painted such lurid stories

of the brutality of the white man and the disabilities of the non-whites, that people wanted to lynch him on his return to South Africa in s.s. *Courtland*.

During the Boer War he formed a corps of Indian stretcher-bearers which were attached to the British.

In 1903 he decided to return to the Transvaal, but Milner did not want him or any other Indians back again. Eventually a compromise was arrived at whereby such Indians as had their thumb-prints taken might return. Gandhi enrolled as a qualified attorney and practised in the Supreme Court of the Transvaal. In 1904 the Indian cause suffered a severe setback, for after continuous heavy rains, cholera broke out in their community in Johannesburg. The case against having Indians in the Transvaal was now strong. After a further effort at stretcher-bearing in a minor Zulu rebellion in 1906 Gandhi went to England to plead the cause of the Indians. He was told to wait, as the Transvaal was just then about to be granted Responsible Government.

In July, 1907, he organised his first Passive Resistance campaign and was joined by a thousand Chinese under Leong Quinn. In August my father warned him that he would not tolerate breaches of the law "and if the Indians resisted they would only have themselves and their leaders to blame for the consequences". Gandhi's reply was that he was merely striving for the repeal of the Asiatic Land Amendment Act, and for the recognition of the status of educated Indians.

The first Transvaal parliament shortly afterwards passed severe immigration laws which demanded the taking of the finger-prints of the entire hand to obviate forging of documents. A deadline for finger-printing was set at 30th November. Gandhi failed to comply and marched at the head of a crowd into the Central Prison in Pretoria, where he was detained for a year.

While in prison, in an interview with my father, he endeavoured to arrive at a compromise, but my father assured him that only Parliament could alter its own Act. At the next sitting the Asiatic Act and Immigration Act were repealed and Indians already in the Transvaal had their certificates made valid, but no further Asiatic immigration was permitted. Gandhi claimed this was a breach of my father's promise, and he and his followers burned their certificates in protest.

We were not quite finished with Gandhi yet. Some years after, when the Union of the four Provinces had already been completed, he demanded the repeal of the £3 head-tax of Natal. He demonstrated by marching at the head of 3,000 Indians across the Natal border into the Transvaal, where he was promptly arrested and removed to Bloemfontein gaol.

By this time the dark clouds of World War I were already blowing up, and Britain, desirous of maintaining the goodwill of her peoples in India, interceded on India's behalf. Gandhi was released, and just as the war burst upon the world in 1914 he sailed for India, never again to return to these shores.

It is said that once or twice in this tussle Gandhi got the better of my father. This is a distortion of facts. Gandhi's cause had been, as he himself had said, the removal of discriminating immigration laws and the recognition of the educated Indian. He not only achieved neither of these aims, but even failed to make any headway. His only achievement had been to get the repeal of the two Bills in 1907, and this, in effect, had no material bearing on his ambitions. His outwitting by my father had been complete, and it was in this sense of failure that he set out dejectedly to brood and scheme in India.

The 6,000 Indians originally imported had by 1950 multiplied to a quarter of a million. The Indian's tendency to increase prolifically, coupled with his ability to live frugally and undersell the white man, as well as to exploit the African native, has created one of South Africa's most serious problems. The situation is further complicated by the fact that the problems of India and Empire are often projected on to our domestic ones. In 1911 further immigration of Indians into the country was prohibited, but the movement still progresses apace in the remainder of British Africa.

Gandhi had, however, succeeded in stirring up a hornets' nest in the relations between India and South Africa, which to this day grows more acrimonious and dangerous. An ideal platform has been afforded them in the Chambers of the United Nations Organisation. It is a disturbing problem and its end appears more distant than ever. By now it has assumed the guise of the iniquity of discrimination against all non-white races, and to Britain, as a colonial power, it is proving most embarrassing.

Gandhi, though clashing frequently with my father in the old days, was an understanding and forgiving person and bore no grudge. In fact, even when he really had reason to feel sore with my father, at the time when he spent a year in Pretoria Central Gaol, he showed his friendly spirit by making my father a stout pair of leather sandals. These, like Gandhi's friendship, my father kept safely through the years.

At the end of the first session of the new government the Johannesburg *Star* remarked: "Practically the whole of the government business has fallen to Mr. Smuts, who dominates and overshadows his party. Opinions may differ about the value of his achievements in practical legislation . . . but it would be churlish to refuse to recognise the colossal industry and persuasive tact which the Colonial Secretary has almost always brought to his parliamentary duties." The "Mr." denotes that the *Star* was at that time no particular disciple of my father's.

XXII NATIONAL CONVENTION

MEANWHILE a new trend had become discernible in politics. It was an urge for "closer union". That such ideas should arise was perhaps a natural sequel to the constant stream of goodwill, co-operation and conciliation that was being preached, not only by Botha and my father in the Transvaal, but also in the Cape, where Merriman (the Prime Minister), F. S. Malan and Dr. Jameson strongly supported the idea.

Lord Selborne, the Governor, was asked, as Milner had been, to achieve federation. He was convinced from what he saw that the Crown Colony constitution was unsuited to the diverse conditions in South Africa. Strangely enough, by their haggling the railways were a source of division rather than a bond of union. Selborne realised that it was no use waiting, as Milner had done, till the British section in the country were strong enough to write the federal constitution. In fact, by the end of 1906 it was perfectly clear that the Boers were rapidly overtaking the British, and that the latter would never be strong enough to dictate this constitution. It was now clear that the Boers would write this document.

But in the Orange River Colony Steyn and Hertzog displayed scant interest. In a memo Lord Selborne strongly urged the desirability of a closer integration as the best solution to a number of problems that only really arose because of the artificially separate entity of the four Colonies.

Botha had already taken the first step by discussing with the Chief Justice of the Cape★ the desirability of establishing a federal court of appeal. It was most desirable to standardise the legal code.

In May, 1908, a conference was called, ostensibly to adjust customs differences and railway problems. Here my father proposed six resolutions, which were seconded by Mr. Merriman, demanding "a national convention to discuss the closer political and economic union of the South African colonies". These resolutions were passed and later duly ratified by the four Parliaments.

Though the urge for closer relationship was strong, there were no less strong controversial problems in the detail of this move. Many influential people felt the project would be detrimental to their own interests, and the Provinces were one and all chary lest they should lose power and identity through the marriage. The Transvaal and Cape were really the only two that had solid assets to offer. Natal and the Orange River Colony were insignificant by comparison. The Transvaal was fabulously rich. The others were but poor neighbours. It was obvious that the major sacrifices would devolve upon the Transvaal. Much as the other Provinces coveted the wealth of this jewel-box, they had strong reservations on questions of language and of personal prestige. Natal was no lover of the dual language system, and the Orange River Colony had rooted antipathies to English.

Union did not appeal to the Reef. Uitlander pro-British ideas

★ J. Henry de Villiers, first Baron de Villiers (1842–1914), was a South African by birth. He was called to the Bar of the Inner Temple in 1865, became Attorney-General for the Cape of Good Hope in 1872 and the following year was appointed Lord Chief Justice. He was raised to the peerage in 1910.

were running as strongly as ever and there were fears, possibly not unfounded, that an Afrikaner bloc might be set up.

Here was a delicate, almost insuperable problem that would test the best in statesmanship. The only way of tackling it was the long and hard way of patience and persuasion. My father, more than others, was aware of the difficulties and pitfalls that beset the way. On these he touched briefly in a letter to Chief Justice Sir Henry de Villiers on 22nd July, 1907:

. . . from a purely selfish point of view the Transvaal has little to gain from federation. Economically the strongest factor in the South African situation, it is also largely independent of any particular colony, and can therefore view the situation with comparative equanimity. Hence the chief danger and opposition will always come from the Transvaal, where you have a strong section who would prefer to snap their fingers at the rest of British South Africa, and another equally strong section who see in Federation only a consolidation of "Dutch" influence, and therefore an issue to be fought at all hazards. Besides these two you have here a third section who say that federation is near Chauvinism, and that it would be better far to devote our energies to less showy tasks, to repair the losses of the past, to further the material welfare of the people, before we begin a federation policy.

A fourth section (chiefly, I believe, represented by the older and wiser generation of politicians at the Cape) exhorts us to achieve national unity first before we attempt political unity. What with all these views and the real difficulties of the situation, the cause of federation is by no means assured as far as the immediate future is concerned. And I don't think it is really advanced by a one-sided statement such as the memo. attached to Lord Selborne's minute.

But I do not despair. We who love South Africa as a whole, who have our ideal of her, who wish to substitute the idea of a united South Africa for the lost independence, who see in breadth of horizon, in a wider and more embracing statesmanship, the cure for many of our ills and the only escape from the dreary pettiness and bickering of the past—we are prepared to sacrifice much—not to Natal or the Cape, but to South Africa.

Next year, no doubt, Federation Commissions will be appointed from the various South African parliaments to go into the matter. But the real tussle will probably come in February or March of next year when the Railways and Customs Conference will have to take place. That will probably be the most important Conference to be held in South Africa for many a day, and on its issue will largely depend the cause of Union or Federation. I sincerely hope that the various colonies will send their very best men to that Conference, which I hope will be held at Pretoria. If we succeed in establishing an economic union, not on mere patchwork lines but on a broad and permanent policy which will do away with all local friction and irritation, I do not see why we should not soon move further and convert this economic into a political union.

The subject is most difficult and in many ways awkward for a Transvaal politician, but I shall always do my best to keep the larger aspect of the case before me and to contribute something towards the achievement of permanent union. If the end of all our past losses and sufferings is the attainment of a united South Africa in which its people will find peace and satisfaction, that will indeed be a great day. I hope you, who have done so much to keep before South Africans that wider outlook, will live to see that day. I shall do my best to hasten it by all legitimate means, though you much over-rate my influence in this connection. . . .

As regards the Court of Appeal I quite agree with what I gather to be your view—that if federation is at all possible, it should be part and parcel of a federation settlement of South Africa. Should federation be relegated by the developments of the immediate future to a more distant day, then the Appeal Court will have to be considered by itself.

The Transvaal government are doing their best to pave the way for larger things by a policy of conciliation conceived on broad South African lines. The outlook economically is far from bright, but on all hands one notices a desire on the part of the various sections of the population to let bygones be bygones and to draw together in spite of or perhaps because of disappointments and adversity. I hope the same spirit will also prevail in other parts of South Africa and that politicians will recognise that our strength does not lie in isolation, but in union.

In that way Union will come about not as a forced thing but as a ripe fruit fallen from the tree. General Botha's attitude in England will, I hope, have had a beneficial effect all over South Africa. In his profound commonsense I see deeper statesmanship than in all the astuteness and cleverness of smaller men.

The time for a National Convention was now ripe. In order to wean the Transvaal from her independence and isolation my father and Botha toured the country extensively, addressing many public meetings.

"We must have Union," he declared emphatically. "Two such peoples as the Dutch and English must either unite or try to exterminate each other. There is only one road to salvation . . . the road to Union . . . to a South African Nation."

"The Boer has fought for his independence; the Englishman for his Empire; all have fought for what they consider highest. . . . Now the highest is Union. . . . Let us have Union—not of top dog and under dog, but of brothers . . . we are now in for a bigger task than ever before. Let us see it through. . . . Let us make one big South Africa and do our best as wise and prudent sons of South Africa to start a Union here and to rule the country from Table Bay to the Congo and even beyond that. Let us be inventors of a great South Africa."

It was decided to hold the Convention of the four Colonies in Durban.

My father worked on his brief for the conference. The first task was to make a thorough study of all the federal and union constitutions obtainable in order to see which would be most suitable for our rather peculiar conditions in South Africa. He studied especially the American Constitution, of which Walt Whitman had given him an intimate understanding. It was obviously too rigid, however, and it gave the separate federal states too much power and the central authority too little. "We have no right to attempt to hamper and bind ourselves down by any cast-iron system which only a revolution can amend," he decided. There was much to be envied in England's freedom from a binding written constitution, for here there was no document limiting the powers of Parliament. Yet it was obvious that South Africa could not be like that, but it would be advantageous if a constitution with a maximum flexibility could be designed.

He wrote to Lord de Villiers concerning his proposals about Union: "The paper represents merely my personal opinions. If the main ideas are approved, I propose to prepare a draft constitution which might largely expedite the work of the convention: and time is of enormous importance in this matter."

Assisted by experts, including Brand, Curtis and members of the Kindergarten, he had perfected his plans down to the smallest detail. The scheme he had devised he submitted to the four Provinces for criticism and suggestions. With the receipt of these he drew up his final memorandum and left for Durban.

Lord de Villiers, Chief Justice of the Cape, was appointed chairman of this conference. The delegates brought with them a high optimism but no experience in constitution-making. My father had to shepherd them. He had thought out everything, even to the minutest pitfalls.

The work of the conference amounted to a study and watering-down of my father's draft. This was necessary if the whims, fears and sensitiveness of delegates were to be satisfied. Some Natal delegates favoured federation after the Australian model, but my father convinced them that such a loose federation would not suit our conditions. Something closer was desirable.

It is said that he wanted this closeness of union in order that he might wield greater personal power, as he had done in the Transvaal Parliament. This is no more than sensational journalism. My father was never a seeker of power for power's sake. There was nothing personal in his desire for power. Power was obviously required to provide the great cohesive effort which would be necessary to keep the four strange bed-fellows together. Power was merely a means to an ultimate national end. It provided the authority for good legislation and leadership.

Even the sultry summer heat of Durban did not deter him though the majority of the delegates wilted visibly.

In his *Inner History of the South African Convention*, Sir Edgar Walton gives an account of my father's opening address at the Conference:

In his opening sentences at the National Convention which decided on Union and drafted our present constitution, General Smuts appealed to the Convention to fix their minds on great principles and not to allow their work to be spoiled by too much attention to material interests or difficulties of the day. Material interests were evanescent, the problems of the future would not be the problems of to-day, and they were working for the future and were endeavouring to lay down a constitution which the people of South Africa would live under for many generations to come.

There were three points which he thought the delegates should bear in mind. In the first place they must trust the people of South Africa and must trust each other. Distrust and suspicion would be fatal. They must also trust future South Africans, trust their wisdom, and they had no right to hamper them and bind them down by any cast-iron system or constitution which only a revolution could amend. In the second place he urged an open mind on the part of the delegates and hoped they would avoid the danger of following too closely the precedent handed down to them by former constitution framers. They should endeavour to profit by the errors and experiences of other countries and with their own knowledge of South Africa do their best to solve the special problems of this country. In the third place their problem was easier of solution than that of either Canada or Australia. Canada was divided by race, religion and interest, Australia was economically divided, while in South Africa we already had a Customs Union and other close connections.

Turning to the resolution General Smuts pointed out that they had before them three courses. They might adopt federation, or a Union such as that of the United Kingdom, or they might take the middle course suggested by Mr. Merriman of a Legislative Union with a system of provincial government under the authority of the central power. With regard to the first, in his opinion, federation was in-applicable to South Africa. Federation, he took it, was a treaty or a pact, an agreement between independent powers. In South Africa they were not independent powers, but brothers.

Let them study the history of the United States of America, let them see what grave trouble had arisen purely from the nature of the Con-stitution. Such a machinery for legislation would be unworkable in South Africa, for the sovereign power was so dispersed as to be in-effective for the essential purposes of civilised government. In South Africa we already had adopted the British system of responsible government, which worked well and which the people understood; in the United States of America they had a Legislature, one Chamber of which represented the people and the other represented the States, and they found the power of the Upper Chamber or Senate increasing. In those States there was no power responsible for order among the States, no power to punish wrong-doing by a State. In establishing the Commonwealth of Australia they adopted the American principle for forming Parliaments and for investing the individual States with sovereign power, but the British system of responsible government. It would (he believed) be found that in Australia the real power was vested in the Senate and that a deadlock was inevitable.

They could only be altered by unanimous consent. The Constitution of the United States had only twice been altered, for the difficulties in the way of alteration were almost insuperable and the States were

113

now working under a Constitution made in the eighteenth century when the conditions of the country were entirely different from what they were to-day. Machinery for alteration was devised but it was found to be almost unworkable and the experience of the States was an object-lesson for us.

The hands of South Africa should not be so tied and they had no right to shackle future South Africans. He supported Mr. Merriman's contention that corruption was almost inevitable under federation because power was so dispersed that there was no authority able to punish and it was difficult to fix the responsibility. He hoped sincerely that they would avoid a situation in South Africa under which honest men would decline to enter public life.

The alternative to federation was the union as it existed in the British Islands. It was, he believed, the most successful system the world had ever seen and it was a model which all free people could safely copy. It was true that in Great Britain there was a demand for greater local powers and with a sovereign parliament in the United Kingdom it was possible to delegate any powers which it was necessary for localities to exercise. It was now being contemplated to grant such powers to Ireland and to carry that measure would merely require an Act of the Imperial Parliament. They were told that there were exceptional difficulties in South Africa and that under Union the Central Parliament would be overloaded with work and become congested. It was also objected that the interests of the respective Colonies were very divergent and required special attention. There were the wine farmers of the western side of the Cape, the tea and sugar planters of Natal, the gold mines of the Transvaal and the diamond mines, and it was urged that one Central Parliament would be unable to do all the work required of it to the satisfaction of South Africa and that therefore there must be local Parliaments to control and promote local interests.

General Smuts said he had much sympathy with that argument, but in his opinion South Africa required a whipping boy and that whipping boy would be most safely found in the Central Government and Central Parliament. To meet the argument advanced he was in favour of a Central Sovereign Parliament together with local Legislatures (Provincial Councils), with delegated and defined powers and, of course, subject to the Central Parliament. In his opinion that middle course would give the least possible occasion for friction in the future for it could accommodate itself to the needs of the people from time to time and the powers of the local Legislatures could be extended or curtailed as occasion demanded. What was essential was that they must create machinery which "will work" and that they must as far as was humanly possible ensure themselves against future trouble or deadlock.

Finally, and in solemn and impressive words, General Smuts urged the Convention to remember that if they were not successful in drafting a constitution which South Africa would accept, if they were not able to bring about union in South Africa, then there was grave trouble in the future for their common country. Union, he believed, was the only means of averting terrible disaster and he urged upon every delegate present to come to a determination that the Convention should not separate without having come to an agreement.

Thirty-three men forgathered at the Conference—men, Lord Curzon said, "whose names a few years ago were anathema to each other; men who not only would have put each other to death, but were within an ace of doing so; men who had never before been in the same room. . . . And there was not one of them who, while loyal to his colony or his race or his following, was not more loyal to the wider cause of South African Union within the sheltering embrace of the British Empire."

My father had with him nineteen secretaries and advisers, a staff larger by half than the total from all the other Provinces. This comprehensive staff of experts was able to handle all problems expeditiously. There could be no delay which might impair the smooth functioning of the deliberations.

Snags and pitfalls confronted them at every turn. There were questions of the location of the future capital, to which great prestige was attached, and a corresponding sensitiveness. There was the native problem which was much entangled by the question of old rights of the coloured folk of the Cape. There was the Indian problem. There was the highly controversial problem of language rights, and many other difficulties each of which by itself might have been quite capable of wrecking the Conference.

At my father's suggestion it was decided, eventually, to leave the native problem for solution at some future date. He also did his best to steer the Conference clear of details and other sources of deadlocks. "Give us a National Parliament, a national executive and trust to them for a solution of those questions that have troubled us in the past," he pleaded.

Hertzog was on the point of starting his language quarrels in the Free State. Had the Convention been held less than a year later it would have broken down on this. Even now he displayed little enthusiasm at the substance of the Conference, and at times proved somewhat difficult. All his life, in fact, he was to prove difficult. For though a friendly and chivalrous person, a demon seemed to enter his blood once he got to his feet at public meetings, for his passions would run riot with his reasoning, making him say outrageous things. He never mastered these distressing symptoms; in fact, they became aggravated with age. But he was never repentant and never withdrew anything he said. He was, indeed, the stormy petrel of our public life.

But my father remained calm and persuasive, and in the end the Conference accepted his proposals. The convention was later to meet in Cape Town and Bloemfontein, where further amendments were considered, the documents rounded off and the final constitution decided upon. This proposed constitution was thereafter passed by the Parliament of the four Colonies.

"You have probably heard it stated", my father declared when the constitution was published, "that a small number of men, having their own ends to serve, rushed this matter forward in the face of public apathy and public opposition. . . . The constitution is not a man's work. It bears the impress of a Higher Hand." However that may be, the records show much of the constitution to have been written in his own hand.

Sir Roderick Jones writing in *Nineteenth Century*, in November, 1915, wrote thus of the Conference: "Often difficulties sprang up from the inability of delegates, men of different race, of different political parties, and from different provinces, to agree upon fundamental principles which entailed a sacrifice; sentimental or material, perhaps both in one direction or another. Then it was that Smuts, with his nimble brain, his facile pen, came to the rescue. The Convention after hours of earnest exchange and exhausting debate, would adjourn the day's proceedings, face to face apparently with a deadlock. Next morning Smuts would appear on the scene with a formula, simple, lucid and comprehensive, that reconciled what had seemed to be irreconcilable and enabled the Convention to proceed smoothly to the consideration of the next problem. . . . I think all who are acquainted with the proceedings of that momentous conclave are agreed that he, more than any other delegate, was the one to whom, in the last resort, they looked for sagacious and resourceful draughtsmanship."

A deputation of nine members, led by Botha and my father, took the draft document to England where it passed both Houses of Parliament in due course as an Imperial Bill, which, before the year was out, was signed by the King and became law. Balfour described the Bill as "the most wonderful issue out of all those divisions, controversies, battles, bloodshed, devastation and horrors of war, and of the difficulties of peace". It passed the Commons with only a minor amendment concerning Asiatics, and then went on to the Lords where its passage was equally simple.

While in London Botha, my father, Hertzog, Jameson and Steyn were invited to lunch with the King. Queen Alexandra was wearing the superb Cullinan diamonds.

Before the Act of Union took effect, on the 31st May, 1910, the Transvaal Parliament had two more tasks to perform before being dissolved. Both concerned the surplus funds in the Treasury. Whatever ideas the other Provinces might have had about the sharing of this wealth for the common weal, the Transvaal had its own ideas. She was going to deal with them under an old Act which makes provision for such unauthorised expenditure, providing the Governor puts his signature to it. To help introduce a more friendly spirit into the Transvaal members of parliament, to drive out the last germ of isolationism by an act of goodwill, and to remunerate the members for this premature termination of their services, my father decided to give them each a bonus of £250. This involved a mere £20,000. As the idea met with violent opposition, he thought it safest to short-circuit the Upper House and go straight to the Governor for his signature. After a great outcry about questions of an ethical and constitutional nature, Britain finally authorised the embarrassed Governor to sign the document. My father had got his way—not because he wanted to show his power, but because he believed it to be for the ultimate good of the spirit of Union.

The second item was to vote £1,500,000 for the erection of the Union Buildings on Meintje's Kop in Pretoria. These stand as the greatest masterpiece to the credit of Herbert Baker, and the finest modern buildings in the southern hemisphere. The old storm over their erection has turned to unabashed adulation. We take pride in the noble edifice as one of the finest showpieces in our country. But as yet Baker's dream is incomplete, for he drew up plans for additional buildings behind the present one, higher up on the Koppie. which may one day consummate his vision.

XXIII UNION

LORD GLADSTONE was appointed Governor-General on the recommendation of Botha and my father, and arrived in the beginning of May. His first task, the appointment of a Prime Minister, was no easy one. Both Merriman and Botha had claims.

Merriman, "the Premier of the Mother State of South Africa and the Grand Old Man of South African politics", had been a member of Parliament since the year before my father was born. He was a gifted scholar and a skilful debater, with a certain caustic humour, his oratorical skill being unsurpassed by any South African. In 1924 he retired after sitting fifty-five years in Parliament, and was revered alike by Boer and Briton. No one in the Empire has had a longer or more honourable parliamentary career. He died two years after his retirement.

Merriman himself felt strongly about his claims to the Premiership. When Botha was elected, he felt not only hurt but almost betrayed. Botha was his inferior in intellect, in age and in experience. The old man was frankly pessimistic about the future. Some years later my father told Parliament, "Mr. Merriman admitted to me that he had doubted General Botha and myself. He used to think that, in the hour of trial, we should not stand by the policy we preached." He served under Botha only with reluctance and never again became the great figure he had been in the old Cape House. The fire had gone out of him. He ascribed being overlooked to the fact that King Edward did not like him, and the fact also that he had antagonised Lord Selborne by saying he would decline to attend the Convention if Selborne presided. More probably his supercession was due to my father's championship of Botha, for Botha would carry both the Transvaal and the Boers.

Hertzog and Steyn, significantly, backed Merriman. Hertzog was deeply jealous of Botha. Consequently, when the latter came to draw up his Cabinet his chief difficulty lay with Hertzog. Yet he was the Free State's first choice. At the same time Hertzog was also far from *persona grata* with the British, largely because of his quarrel on the language position. The English press opposed him.

My father and Botha were much worried about Hertzog, for they sensed rocks ahead. So my father invited him to breakfast at the Mount Nelson Hotel where he tried to persuade him to take a seat on the Court of Appeal in lieu of a Cabinet portfolio. This was flatly rejected. People were yet to learn that Hertzog could be more stubborn than the proverbial mule. He visited the Mount Nelson again, this time at Botha's invitation. "There", Hertzog wrote afterwards, "I was taken by General Smuts to his room, where I was informed that I should be included in the Cabinet with the Portfolio of Justice. Afterwards I met General Botha, who did not speak a single word to me on the subject. . . . There was no mistaking the reluctance with which the Prime Minister accepted me as a colleague."

There were nine portfolios in the Cabinet. My father was given three, all important ones: Mines, Defence and Interior.

When, some while later, Botha asked a prominent Free Stater, who was later elected to the Legislature, what he thought of the new Cabinet, the latter said: "As far as I can make out they are satisfied with it except, perhaps, for the inclusion of General Smuts." Botha was silent for a while as if stifling a feeling of emotion, and then burst out, "Old chap, you people don't know Jan Smuts yet. Our country is still too young to meddle with brains."

My mother says she has never seen a closer friendship than that between Botha and my father. She said, "They seemed to need each other in their work. They could not stay away from each other for long before one sent for the other, either for help or for advice." Its benefits for the country were numerous and enriching.

My father's efforts during the National Convention he looked upon as his greatest single work for his country. He did so not only because the constitution which he pushed through in the teeth of considerable genuine opposition has since stood the test of time, but also because his energy and drive rushed it through just before it grew too late. I think it was success in this battle against time he relished as much as anything else.

* * * * *

Meanwhile our old home in Sunnyside had settled down happily after its ordeals of the war. My father had not only repaired the damage to his books, but had expanded his collection. The shelves were full of a variety of volumes, but mostly works on Law and travel, Africana and books on poetry and literature. Books on philosophy and science had at this stage not crept on to the shelves in any profusion.

The house became a regular staging post for people coming in from outlying districts, mostly Boer War or Government cronies of my father's. Schalk Burger stayed there for long spells on end, and General Koos de la Rey was also a frequent visitor. They looked upon the place as a second home.

In the middle of 1903 my mother persuaded Deneys Reitz to return from his self-imposed exile on Madagascar, and thereafter he spent some years with us. The draft of his famous book *Commando* had already been scribbled in Madagascar between bouts of malaria and arduous transport journeys. He was the chief plunger in the big tub in the garden. Sometimes Justice de Villiers of the Free State would also stay with us. He was a highly cultured man and would join my parents in their music and singing.

Here my sister Santa was born in 1903, as well as, in their turn, my sister Cato, my brother Japie and my sister Sylma. My youngest sister Louis and myself were born at Irene, ten miles from Pretoria, where my parents had gone to live in 1909. There we all grew up in the carefree ways of the farm. My father lived there till his death in 1950. I mention this merely in passing, for I shall describe Doornkloof, our farm at Irene, in some detail later.

My father's love of farming is reflected in the number of farms he acquired at various times, all bought to satisfy a possessive, not a speculative instinct. After the Boer War he had returned to his legal practice in Pretoria and this brought him in quite a lucrative income, the proceeds of which he invested in land. First he bought himself, in conjunction with his friend Jimmy Roos, two farms outside Pretoria, one Onderstepoort near the Bon Accord dam, and the other Kameelfontein in the hills near Premier Mine. The latter attracted him, I think, because of its associations with the battle of Diamond Hill. Some years later this farm was declared an alluvial diamond diggings and turned upside-down, so he reluctantly sold it.

In the Western Transvaal, upon the advice of his old friend General Koos de la Rey, he bought three farms, Barberspan, Kromdraai and Welgevonden. Though good fertile lands and fine farming propositions, they were nevertheless in a bleak and uninviting flat setting, without trees and hills from horizon to horizon, so here again I think there was an association with the Boer War rather than general attractiveness.

Shortly afterwards followed his acquisition of Buffelspan, in the massive primeval crater of Pilandersberg, near Rustenburg. Though he knew this feature from his operations in this vicinity during the war his attraction to it was a geological one, for it was from this extinct vent that the igneous rocks were spewed forth to form the beds of the Transvaal bushveld. Topographically, too, it was attractive country. Not far away on the Marico River he bought at about the same time two additional farms Wydhoek and Klipdrift. These two latter farms he never exploited, and in about 1930 he sold them when in need of funds.

In 1908 he bought the beautiful farm Doornkloof, a few miles outside Pretoria, and this purchase probably brought him more pleasure and satisfaction than any other of his life. Lastly, while on campaign in East Africa in 1916, during the First World War, he bought two farms, Rooikop and Droogegrond, in the bushveld near Rust der Winter, fifty miles north-east of Pretoria, These two he considered good farms and there he conducted serious farming operations through a manager, with considerable success and pride.

By 1928 he was still in possession of ten of these eleven farms, an area totalling about 25,000 morgen (53,000 acres). After that he was soon to sell Barberspan and the two farms at Groot Marico, but the remainder he kept, in 1945 making them over by deed of donation to his children. Three of these farms he had farmed actively himself through managers, but the remainder he had fenced in and turned over to tenants.

From what I know of my father I am convinced that he acquired these farms purely because he was an inveterate lover of the land. It was a sort of symbolic ritual from which he derived great satisfaction but no pecuniary gain. Financial aspects never obtruded, though he was wont to remark that the possession of land afforded a great element of security. Perhaps he was thinking of his old age. As the years went by the farms appreciated many times in value, and he was then inclined to remark with pride on the bargains he had made. But the pride was abstract, and actual ideas of money never entered his head.

XXIV THE SOUTH AFRICAN PARTY

ONE of the first acts of Botha and my father after Union was to form the South African Party. It was predominantly Afrikaans, comprising elements of the Cape Bond, Het Volk and the Orangia Unie, together with fair numbers of English-speaking people. The tide for unity after the convention was running strongly, and Botha and my father threw themselves whole-heartedly into their work. As before, my father accomplished the lion's share; but he was sorely tried by the large number of incompetent people who cluttered up the Government departments. In his impatience he drove them on mercilessly to get the work done, and this naturally resulted in a certain measure of displeasure. No doubt his ways were inclined to be autocratic, not for personal satisfaction but for the common good. In any case, he himself was working harder than any of his subordinates.

The period of harmony and good feeling was, however, short-lived. It could hardly have been otherwise after all the country had been through. It was now only eight years since the war.

The first general elections were approaching. There was therefore a tendency to gloss over difficulties and to appease where possible. This, in the case of General Hertzog, was a political necessity if unity was to be preserved, though it galled the English section. To them Hertzog was an unpalatable pill.

A major trend at the time was the cumbrous stirrings of the Afrikanders. They were determined to catch up with the world which had outstripped them and to shake off an inferiority complex that weighed down on them. Hertzog early sensed this mood and determined to make use of it. He did not initiate the mood he merely spurred it on in his biting speeches. The language "inequality", which he said my father had purposely introduced into his Education Act in which Afrikaans was made optional whilst English was made compulsory, rankled with him.

He was still further angered when, in November, 1910, Sir C. P. Crewe moved in Parliament that the Free State Education Act was in conflict with the spirit of the Act of Union. Hertzog replied to the charge with customary vigour and sufficient ability to attract some support from the Afrikaans section of the House. By such acts he came gradually to be known as the champion of the Dutch.

But he had to climb down over his pro-Afrikaans education policy in the Free State. He did it with reluctance, and liked Botha none the better for having to do so. This had been General Hertzog's first quarrel with the Government. It was the forerunner of a life of quarrels.

On the 1st March, 1911, my father, as Minister of Defence, drafted a scheme for military organisation which received much favourable comment. In the same month he introduced his Miners' Phthisis Bill. This disease, better known as silicosis, is an occupational disability contracted by those who work in rock dust. It was a real scourge amongst underground workers on the Rand who worked in dusty atmospheres deep down in poorly-ventilated mines. The average life of the miner at the time was eight years of underground work before succumbing to this curse. In the Bill my father initiated the principle of compensation for silicosis in its advanced stages. Though the vast majority of miners always voted consistently against my father, few probably realised that he was the great benefactor of the silicosis legislation.

Nor are many aware that he was the father of our Mining Regulations. They are said to be the best and most comprehensive in existence and have been imitated since by other countries. He was, as is known, also the father of our Education system, and of our Defence Force legislation. There is, in fact, very little in South Africa that did not spring from his fertile brain.

My father gave a hint of impending Cabinet troubles at a meeting in the Rambler's Hall. "The Cabinet is composed of men of high position. Some of them are advanced in years and their hairs have grown grey in the service of the State. But there are younger ones who are perhaps too energetic and excessively prone to act on the inspiration of the moment. Ours is a very mixed team; we have men with strong volition, who press their own views; hence, no absolute unanimity can be asked for. These men are determined to fight for their opinions whenever opportunity offers. There is one test which, however, I hope none of us will fail to pass; I shall call it the South African spirit."

In February, 1912, he introduced his Defence Bill. The *Cape Times*, not given at the time to an over-friendly feeling, said, "If General Smuts had before him a splendid task this afternoon, his severest critics will admit that it was splendidly performed. The General is not exactly an orator in the sense that Mr. Merriman is, but rhetoric was not necessary to his purpose. For two and a half hours he held the House with a masterly review of the principles governing the defence of South Africa. . . . This astonished a House already fully aware of General Smuts's almost terrible ability and genuine eloquence, prompted not by a conscious effort, but by the very nature of the subject. As a physical effort alone it was prodigious. Smuts speaks in a highly-pitched but mellifluous voice, which carries clearly to every part of the House. He hardly paused to consult a note. He never faltered for a moment."

There were few critics of the Bill and few efforts at amendments. General Beyers complained that it was "based on a foreign system" but allowed himself to be persuaded of its virtues when he himself was offered the position of Commandant-General of the Forces.

My father, some while afterwards, addressed Staff Officers at Bloemfontein: "We want a force that will be able to defend South Africa against anyone who may come against us. . . . Things may happen that nobody ever foresaw; therefore it behoves us to look forward. . . . At present the nations all seem to be preparing as if doubtful of each other. . . . We want an organisation that shall not be Boer or English, but a South African army. . . . Do your duty in a broad, national spirit."

The English disliked Hertzog and there was growing dissatisfaction at his place in the Cabinet. It was perhaps an indication of this feeling that caused General Botha's defeat in his Pretoria East seat by Sir Percy Fitzpatrick in the elections. Though Botha was quickly given a safe seat at Losberg, he felt strongly that Hertzog had brought about his fall.

XXV HERTZOGISM

THE liberal views of Botha and my father and the extremist nationalist views of Hertzog resulted in an ever-widening rift between the two elements. The first session of Parliament was full of Hertzog's bickerings. Botha shortly afterwards departed for an Imperial Conference in London, where he not only committed the indiscretion of appearing in knee breeches and silk stockings but also accepted a Privy Councillorship and an honorary Generalship in the British Army. The nationalist cry was that he had become a dupe of Britain. When he later advocated the desirability of making a contribution towards the upkeep of the Royal Navy and stressed the advantages of immigration, the Hertzogite fury knew no bounds. Hertzog suggested that South Africa should start its own navy, which showed a considerable measure of woolly thinking.

When Botha unveiled the magnificent memorial to Rhodes,

designed by Sir Herbert Baker, on the slopes of Devil's Peak behind Groote Schuur, his tribute, with memories of the past still fresh, was too much for the more conservative Boers.

My father was nervous about the future of the Government. At a South African Party congress in Bloemfontein he said, "I do not know how long this Government is going to last; it sometimes happens that Governments disappear sooner than people think." A little more than a year later this did happen, though Hertzog had not been the direct cause of the fall. It had come about after serious differences in the Cabinet between H. C. Hull and J. W. Sauer on matters of railway finance, in consequence of which the former resigned. A Cabinet reshuffle took place. My father gave up Mines and Interior, but retained the important Portfolio of Defence, and he now in addition took over Finance. The *Volkstem* remarked, " . . . we regret the diversion of his unmistakable talents to relatively less important duties".

Mr. Ernest Glanville, in the course of an article in the Johannesburg *Sunday Post*, observed: "It has been said that he is a man of cold intellect, without any personal following, but his streak of humour rejects that verdict, for a man balanced with humour has the weakness, the strength, and the charm of human nature, which means that he does not stand coldly aloof. It may be that he has more influence with the Opposition than with his own back-benchers; and if that is true, it is true not because his intellect is hard, but because it marches ahead of his supporters. His arguments are logical, his style is precise, and his manner disarms opposition, while he can be subtle to obscure."

Hertzog was given Native Affairs in addition to Justice, with the hope that it might placate him. It was a vain hope. He made speeches of marked secessionist flavour most notably at Vrededorp and Nylstroom. In December, 1912, on Louis Esselen's farm at de Wildt, he made his most notorious speech. "South Africa must be governed by pure Afrikanders . . ." he said. "The main object is to keep Dutch and British separated. . . . I have always said I do not know what conciliation means. . . . I believe in Imperialism only so far as it benefits South Africa. Wherever it is at variance with the interests of South Africa I am strongly opposed to it. I am ready to stake my future on this doctrine."

The speech was not only a grave embarrassment to his colleagues, but it roused the British to demand his expulsion even more insistently than before.

In one of his usual tirades Hertzog had made some derogatory reference to my father, involving such terms as "caked dung" and "bastard sheep". When later questioned at a meeting about his colleague's unseemly farmyard homily, my father replied lightly that they were to be regarded simply as "veld similes". Nevertheless he was not happy about Hertzog's many similes and the distinctly unfavourable trends.

At Albany, in the Eastern Province, in a by-election following upon Dr. Jameson's retirement, the Government candidate was beaten on the Hertzog issue.

Unionists at meetings heckled my father mercilessly about the bricks Hertzog was constantly dropping. He managed to parry the blows judiciously and in good taste, often putting up quite a good apology for his colleague, without committing himself or condemning his fellow minister.

A minister from Natal, Sir George Leuchars, resigned. The de Wildt speech had been more than he could bear. He told General Botha that he was going because he "could not endure the anti-imperial and anti-British sentiment—and the speeches of General Hertzog".

Abraham Fischer, Hertzog's close friend, and other Orange Free State members, asked Hertzog to apologise for his de Wildt outburst and to behave in future. Hertzog apparently discerned my father's hand in the document, and pushed it away in disgust, with the suggestion that a person who could write such rubbish should be confined to a lunatic asylum. He stubbornly refused to resign, even under strong pressure. To do so would be to harm the Afrikander cause, he said.

Botha had to be rid of him at all costs. There was only one other course open. Botha himself resigned. When called upon by the Governor-General to form a new Cabinet the names of Hertzog and Leuchars were omitted.

Hertzog was now out of the Cabinet, but he remained in the South African Party for another year.

The final break came in November, 1913, at the annual South African Party congress in Cape Town. After heated exchanges,

Hertzogites, led by Christian de Wet, stamped dramatically out of the hall.

Abraham Fischer dissociated himself from Hertzog in a speech to his constituents at Bethlehem: "He has made impossible demands. He lost the support of the Free State largely through his want of tact. He has the faults of his youth. There are members of his Government who have done for the country ten times as much as he did. They don't deserve to be called traitors and men without principles." The farmers listened attentively and then passed a vote of no confidence in their lifelong leader, by 261 to 152. Broken-hearted, Fischer retired from politics and died a few months later.

Hertzog had now walked out alone into the political wilderness. Only five Orange Free State members out of a House of 121 stood by him. The full fury of the entire press was turned on him. Few would, at that stage, have predicted a political future for him. But they were failing to take into account the dogged obstinacy of the man, his driving fanaticism and spirited courage.

In his manifesto after his expulsion he declared " . . . General Botha, the unconcerned surrenderer of the Dutch people's rights, I, their champion . . ."

It was a long manifesto, running into a full six newspaper columns in his involved and cumbersome style, full of hair-splittings and tedious repetitions. As ever, he kept on losing his thread. One could almost see him gesticulating wildly as he wrote.

He had a son, Albert, who was in high school at the time. Albert followed in his father's footsteps and also became a politician. He was to concentrate on the Mine Workers' Union and cause the Transvaal Chamber of Mines much uneasiness through his attentions to their affairs.

General Hertzog returned to the Free State, dismayed but unchastened, to preach his virulent gospel in every dorp. His attendances were good and his words fell on receptive ears.

Shortly afterwards the Nationalist Party came into existence. Its titular leader was Hertzog. Dr. D. F. Malan was to lead the party in the Cape. He had started life in the Church but found it rather humdrum. He then indulged in considerable social work. This the Dutch Reformed Church did not like. So he dropped

Smuts and Botha—1918

Lieut.-Gen. J. C. Smuts—1917

Groote Schuur, official residence of Union Prime Ministers,
Cape Town

General Smuts's home at Doornkloof, near Pretoria

Holy Orders and took to politics. But he has never succeeded in shaking off the heavy atmosphere of the pulpit.

Tielman Roos was to be the Transvaal leader, and his great roaring was to earn for him the title of "Lion of the North". It rather flattered him. By contrast with Dr. Malan he was of a boisterous and cheerful disposition.

For his private secretary Hertzog had a Dr. Hans van Rensburg, a capable young man, who was later to become Commandant-General of a subversive political organisation known as the Osse-wag Brandwag. In the Boer War Hertzog had had an adjutant by name Nicolaas Havenga, a progressive farmer of the Free State; on Hertzog's eventual political eclipse, he was to follow his leader into the wilderness. Other adherents of Hertzog were ex-President Steyn, de Wet and F. W. Reitz, who had served with my father under Kruger.

There were as yet no English adherents, though Creswell and Labour were to support them later against Botha and my father. It was incongruous to find an Englishman like Creswell in such strange company.

This was the real start of Botha's and my father's troubles. The racial cleavage was now far developed. The vendetta of hate, which was carried on for many years, was levelled chiefly at my father, who to them personified the whole Government. It was a little-desired compliment.

For forty years this struggle was to continue, Malan of Riebeeck West taking over when Hertzog dropped out. We had, in fact, arrived on the threshold of contemporary South African history. From now on the patterns were fixed.

To counter this surge of Afrikanderism my father counselled Botha to take a stronger pro-Boer line and to avoid too obvious contacts with Jameson's Unionist British elements, and also to have less embarrassing contacts with England and the Royal Navy.

XXVI LABOUR UNREST

T HE year 1913 was one of considerable labour unrest, and labour troubles and strikes were to occur acutely over the next nine years. But the 1913 trouble was especially serious in view of the already clear indications of the impending world cataclysm. South Africa could ill afford this phase of unrest, of sabotage and anarchy.

On the 4th of July, 1913, the trouble started on the New Kleinfontein Gold Mine at Benoni. A dispute arose between the General Manager and the men. Trade Unions took up the matter and declared a general strike on the whole Rand. The mine-owners rushed to my father for support, but he refused to intervene in this purely domestic affair. He did, however, prohibit a monster meeting on Market Square, Johannesburg; but the miners disregarded the warning and thousands crowded into the Square. Bain, Morgan and Matthews, their leaders, were there on the platform, as well as the Chief of Police, Colonel Truter, who begged the men to disperse peacefully in compliance with the Government's request. This was greeted with howls of derision. Bain rose and shouted: "We are here for the rights of free speech." The meeting grew out of hand and police rushed the speakers, and general scuffling and fighting ensued.

A woman with a red flag harangued the crowd which surged down the streets bent on trouble. In the afternoon they set on fire the railway station and the *Star* newspaper offices. Looting began and soon became too much for the police. Strikers vainly hunted for the mine bosses, who luckily had fled. My father rushed Imperial troops to Johannesburg to reinforce the police.

Next afternoon the Rand Club was stormed, but the crowd were held back by the troops. A miner, Labuschagne, baring his bosom, defiantly cried "Shoot!" The soldiers did. Labuschagne sank dead to the ground. Twenty others were killed and forty-seven injured, many of them innocent bystanders. The situation was now more dangerous than ever. Botha and my father rushed to the city in an open car, without escort, and at great personal risk. In the Carlton Hotel they held a conference with the four strike leaders. It was an unfavourable atmosphere for a parley, for these ruffians were armed, and outside the crowd looked menacing. Botha and my father were in no position to bargain. They knew the troops would not be able to hold the crowd if trouble arose. So they signed the strikers' document on their own terms. It was capitulation, but temporary capitulation dictated by force of circumstance. My father declared, "We made peace because the Imperial forces informed us that the mob was beyond their control. . . . Anything could happen in Johannesburg that night: the town might be sacked and the mines permanently ruined. . . ." Later he told Parliament the signing of the document was "one of the hardest things I have ever had to do".

Botha and he drove away through the hostile mob. Botha replied to some of their jeers and threats; but my father sat white and mute with anger. Not a word passed his lips, but in his heart he had decided to see that such a state of affairs never again arose. His first step, as Minister of Defence, was to organise the Defence Force.

Times were hard, and with the retrenchments in the railways at the end of the year came fresh resentment. Trade Unions were drunk with their power. The large measure of co-operation between Unions threatened to paralyse almost the whole country. In January, 1914, a strike, involving twenty thousand workers, was called.

This time my father was ready. He had prepared for just such an emergency to the limit of his powers under the Defence Act. He called up the Active Citizen and Burgher Forces and proclaimed Martial Law on the Rand. To the Officers' Commanding the Rand Light Infantry he sent instructions: "Exercise the greatest severity—keep all strikers off the railway line or railway premises. Don't hesitate to shoot if any attempt to enter after warning, or if on apparent malicious intent." The situation was well in hand. The strike leaders in the Drill Hall quickly surrendered when my father ordered de la Rey to train his field guns on the building.

The strike was over.

My father seized the nine leaders, none of whom had been born in the country, and sent them straight to Durban by special train, where they were put on board the *Umgeni* and deported to England. There had been no trial. Just swift decisive action. Unconstitutional, admittedly.

When the news leaked out next day there was consternation, and an appeal was made to the Supreme Court for a writ of habeas corpus. The judges expressed their dismay at my father's precipitate action. But it was too late; the strike leaders were gone and even Creswell's efforts to intercept the *Umgeni* by a specially chartered tug, failed.

In Parliament a Bill was subsequently carried by 95 votes to 11 to indemnify the Government, after long and bitter attacks on my father by Labour members and others. So violent was the Labour denunciation that all the members were suspended in turn by the Speaker. My father spoke for almost six hours in defence of his action. He claimed that the illegality of the act was justified by events. No other course was open. He had to resort, he said, to the "illegal deportations" because he knew that Parliament would never give him "authority in cold blood to expel the men in question. . . . The only crime which fits this state of affairs is high treason but you attempt to indict these people for high treason and see what will be the result. Our law of high treason dates back to the Middle Ages. Our treason law does not fit these new and extraordinary conditions which have arisen in the present case, and if you were to indict these people for a crime they have really committed, you will never obtain a conviction."

During this debate my father made no personal explanations or raised any personal defence. He was concerned purely with the logical development of the facts of the case. The Labour Party gave no credit to the Government for its good intentions. The Unionists disliked the Bill, but were forced to vote for it. Creswell indulged in a series of tirades and scenes; he had brought this dubious gift to perfection.

Of his speech in Parliament in defence of the *Umgeni* deportations the *Cape Argus* said in a leading article, "The Minister made out a much stronger case all round than was generally expected." The same paper's gallery correspondent added: " . . . The speech was a great effort, effortlessly made. For epigram, finish of phrase; for wit, whether in the form of sly humour or biting sarcasm; for the evidence throughout of a scholarly, cultured mind; but, above all, for the power of flinging facts into the right perspective —or, at any rate, for the blending of all these qualities, I have never heard a speech to excel it."

The friendly *Volkstem* spoke in even greater terms of eulogy: "After all that has been said this historical exposition will stand, and we think stand for ever as one of the most marvellous orations of which South Africa can boast."

It was, of course, rather drastic to deport men from a free country without a fair hearing. Much of the world thought so, too. Yet we must not forget what the country was saved from, and in this case few can doubt that the end justified the means.

The matter was referred to in the House of Commons, where the Secretary of State for Colonies reminded the members that South Africa was a self-governing Colony and quite capable of deciding her own actions. The Governor-General's "acquiescence" was also justified in view of the subsequent Parliamentary indemnity.

Merriman spoke of my father as "that ruthless Philosopher".

Though my father's heavy hand had incurred hatred among the workers it nevertheless shook them to their senses and frightened them into a new semblance of stability. The effect had been salutary.

The deportees later returned to South Africa. One became a South African Party organiser under my father; another got an important post in the Chamber of Mines; another joined the Government Service, where he prospered; a fourth became a Member of Parliament.

Racialism had now taken a temporary back seat in favour of industrial and labour problems. But Labour felt compelled to break away from the South African Party, which it had supported for years, and attach itself to Hertzog.

The Government was growing visibly unpopular. The sweeping Labour victories in the Provincial Council elections testified to it. The Government was twice defeated in the House on financial matters. There was a deficit in the Budget, but my father advised Botha to carry on.

In the midst of all these troubles, the roar of great guns convulsed Europe. War had started.

133

XXVII REBELLION

For South Africa, the outbreak of war was a calamity. It came too close upon the heels of her own war. Memories and feelings were still too fresh.

To the Boers, mostly ignorant of the world about them, and somewhat illiterate, the implications of the conflagration were not clear. It was to them of little consequence that it was not a war with Britain but a World War. Rather did it appear as a golden opportunity to throw off the irksome British connection. It did not occur to them to question whether it was right to tackle England in this critical hour. Had not some of their famous Boer War leaders told them that now was the heaven-sent opportunity to reassert themselves? At the same time it would give them a fine chance to teach the traitors Botha and Smuts a lesson.

There was a considerable tide of pro-Boer and anti-British feeling running, but this was more political than racial. It was those Boer elements who supported Botha and my father who came under the lash far more severely than the actual English themselves.

The effect of the war was to transform the superficial political feelings into a deep-seated hatred and bitterness. General Botha and my father saw the implications clearly, but were powerless to avert them. They were, in fact, faced with a dual war; one on their own doorstep against their own people; the other against the German enemy in South-West Africa.

They well understood the feelings of those Boers who did not agree with them. Many had been their comrades in arms in the Boer War. Some were distinguished men of great integrity. Many were their closest personal friends. Yet they did not allow their feelings to obtrude on their sense of duty.

There was, in reality, only one course open; that of going ahead slowly. Tactical reasons also imposed this condition. The German foe was well prepared and a big force had to be assembled if we were to make sure of victory. Recruiting, equipping and training were started expeditiously, but even so, it took time. It is, therefore, incorrect to say that the three months' pause before we marched into South-West Africa was due to the delay caused by internal mopping-up operations. From the military aspect it was almost a blessing that the rebels gave an excuse for not moving prematurely into enemy territory with an insufficient force.

The person who was to come most poorly out of the Rebellion was General Hertzog. He sat resolutely on the fence. While lending vociferous lip-service and much underground moral support to the rebels, he did not take up arms openly in the field. He had numerous apologists; but they voiced an unconvincing series of excuses. When the Rebellion was finally over, Hertzog himself made a long statement of explanation of his conduct; he always stood dead against the unconstitutional overthrow of authority, he declared. The amazing thing was that his followers swallowed these explanations and remained as loyal to him as ever.

As soon as war broke out Botha told Britain that she could safely withdraw her eight thousand troops and that South Africa would take care of her own security. Seven thousand left immediately.

Britain requested the Union on the first possible opportunity to send an expeditionary force to destroy the wireless stations at Luderitzbucht and Swakopmund. But South Africa was not ready for this big task yet; first she had to put her own house in order.

There was considerable opposition throughout the country to the Government's decision to participate in the war and invade South-West Africa. There was wild talk of rebellion in country districts. Disturbances occurred at Potchefstroom, where the magazines were stormed and burned down, and in Pretoria where fire was set to the Imperial Military Stores. Certain diamond mines closed down temporarily in consternation.

Beyers was working quite openly against the Government; so were the other rebel leaders. There was nothing of the cloak and dagger about their activities. Rifles were being collected from the English regiments of the towns who were loyal to the Government and issued to rebel supporters in the platteland.* Maritz collected an army of 600 men and marched across the South-West African border to join the Germans. The majority of his men did not realise what he was up to. Many were loyalists.

* Rural areas.

A pathetic figure of the rebellion was General Koos de la Rey, now grown old and perhaps not so clear of mental perception. Oom Koos was the old Boer type, who had always remained at heart a republican. But he had entered into the spirit of Union because of his great affection for Botha and my father. My mother says three closer friends could not have been imagined. My father venerated de la Rey almost as a parent, and there was nobody, with the exception of Botha, for whom he had a closer feeling. In this confused mental state de la Rey now came strongly under the influence of the prophet Nicholaas van Rensburg. This shrewd seer had served under him in the Boer War where he had done some very creditable "seeing". People knew de la Rey's weakness for van Rensburg. In the national interest his son-in-law Bennie Krige tried unsuccessfully to keep the two apart.

Van Rensburg expounded to the old man a vision of fighting bulls. The significance of the story lay in the prophet's interpretation which was to the effect that Britain would go under and Germany prevail. Botha he could see returning happily to his people, but my father was to disappear overseas and not return. He had seen too, amongst other things, a figure fifteen, with de la Rey, and a carriage, and a cloud dripping blood. These he could not interpret.

De la Rey was impressed. His course was now clear. A meeting was to be held in Lichtenburg on August 15. Trouble was expected. He would here speak out for the rebel cause. On the 14th Botha and my father sent for Oom Koos and spent many hours talking him round. Next day at the meeting, de la Rey, to the amazement of everybody, made a conciliatory speech. Go home quietly, he counselled the gathering. They were dumb-founded, but did as he advised.

Meanwhile Government recruiting was going on apace in Pretoria and on the Rand, and a sizeable force was concentrated at Booysens. The Germans had crossed the border at Nakob and dug in on Union soil. At Schuit Drift, on the Orange River, they attacked a party of Boers and forced them to take refuge on an island.

On August 29 Beyers turned up at Booysens and addressed the troops. Later my father appeared there. "Many people in this country", the latter said, "do not appreciate the tremendous gravity of the crisis in which South Africa, together with the whole Empire, is placed to-day. Although apparently we stand outside, and at some distance from the actual scene of the conflict, yet at any moment we may be drawn into the vortex." The soldiers cheered wildly. They knew the words were directed at Beyers.

Pretoria was the hottest spot. The English were loyal and impatient, but bearded men talked open sedition. Beyers did much talking in coffee houses as well. The Government knew all about it. In the midst of all this subversiveness Hertzog decided to hold a Nationalist Party Congress in the city. Outrageous speeches were made by Senator Wolmarans and others. De la Rey, who had merely attended as a spectator, pleaded for unity in this time of crisis.

On the 4th of September a special ten-day session of Parliament was called. Hertzog vehemently defended Germany, who, he said, had committed no act of aggression. Three days later came the news that the 12th Regiment had departed for an unknown destination.

Meanwhile Maritz was already at Upington, thirty miles from the German border, and from there he sent a secret emissary—P. J. Joubert—to Beyers to say that all was going well and that the German Governor Seitz was expecting him on the 15th.

On the 13th Beyers resigned. My father took over the post of Commander-in-Chief. In accepting Beyers's resignation he declared " . . . I cannot conceive anything more fatal and humiliating than a policy of lip-loyalty in fair weather and a policy of neutrality and pro-German sentiment in days of storm and stress. . . ."

Governor Seitz did not see Beyers on the 15th, for on that day our forces had set sail for Luderitzbucht, and Beyers and de la Rey were on their way to Lichtenburg, where a meeting of protest at our participation in the war was being held. Beyers had come to Pretoria specially to talk de la Rey round.

It was also the day on which all police in Johannesburg had been alerted to be on the look-out for the notorious Foster Gang bandits who were terrorising the town. They believed the gang would attempt a break-out, and had issued instructions to watch all roads for a big black car with three occupants, and to take drastic action if it failed to stop. Beyers and de la Rey were on their way to the Potchefstroom camp where they were to appear at 4 a.m. to start a rising. When called on to stop at a road block, they told the driver to drive on. The sentry took drastic action, but the bullet aimed at the back wheel ricocheted off the road and went through de la Rey's head. His honour was partially saved, but he was dead. My father had no doubts that his old friend was on the wrong path that night. His daughter Polly, who is a very old friend of our family, also feels certain that her father was under the influence of Beyers that night. The shooting was obviously accidental, but a hue and cry was raised that de la Rey had been deliberately murdered.

My father learned of his death at Kimberley, on his way up from Parliament. The funeral took place at Lichtenburg. Botha, my father and Beyers were there. Botha's eyes were filled with tears. My father was not given to outward emotion. Beyers swore loyalty to his cause at the graveside. Van Rensburg had been right about the fifteenth.

On 13th September my father had wired Maritz to come to Pretoria. He refused. My father thereupon ordered Koen Brits, who commanded our forces in the Upington area, to move against Maritz, but the latter became suspicious and moved his men to Van Rooisvlei, near the German border. There a car met him and drove him into German territory. On the 7th October he returned. The English were the enemy, he told his men, and loyalist elements under Major Enslin were arrested and interned. Brits sent Major Bower to Maritz to demand his surrender. Bower found Maritz dressed in a German uniform and was shown German guns and equipment. A safe-conduct for Hertzog, Beyers, Kemp and de Wet was demanded; failing that, he would attack. My father's patience with Maritz was now exhausted; he ordered Brits to attack immediately, and in an action at Kiemoes and Schuit Drift Maritz was defeated and driven into South-West Africa.

Koen Brits was a remarkable character. He was a rough-hewn man standing six foot six inches in his socks, and was said to respect only Botha among man or beast. When Botha wired him to collect troops for South-West Africa, it is said he wired back that he was quite ready to do so, but whom was he to fight, England or Germany? He used to greet friends with a slash of his sjambok in lieu of a more formal military salute, and his propensities for alcohol were a byword. He had also developed to a nicety the ancient art of precision expectoration. British officers who at various times saw him in action, were moved to admiration.

In East Africa he was one of my father's senior gunners, and here again he preferred his own rough estimates of distance to the use of the modern rangefinders. My father tells the story of when they were about twenty miles from Kilimanjaro, and he asked old Koen how far they were from the mountain. Brits viewed the massive land mass through one eye, and not realising the psychological deception of this nineteen-thousand-foot mountain, said quite blandly, "Six miles." No argument would convince him he was wrong. At last my father said, "Well then, lay your gun at six miles and fire a round." Brits did. There was a puff of dust just nearby on the plain. Brits was amazed.

It might here be noted that there was considerable divergence of opinion amongst the rebel leaders on their course of action. Beyers wanted a relatively passive though armed form of resistance—the type that came to be known as a "coup" in the Second World War. He was against civil war. De Wet, more fiery and impetuous, was for vigorous action and pushing through to connect up with Maritz. In his zeal he forgot that he was poorly armed, had no field guns, and was short of ammunition. He also failed to reckon with the mobility afforded the Government by the much-extended railway system, or the advent of the petrol-driven motor-car.

When the rebellion broke, General de la Rey's daughter Polly, and her husband Bennie Krige, manager of the Lichtenburg bank, rushed the money from the bank to Pretoria for safe-keeping from the rebels. They arrived at our house at Irene at midnight, having come much of the way in the complete dark.

My father tells a rather amusing story of Aunt Polly one day in those distant years, when she was motoring with him to a meeting in the Western Transvaal. She was sitting in the back of one of those ancient open cars when it struck both a bad bump and a sandy patch simultaneously, and in the bucking antics that followed she was bounced unceremoniously out into the dust. Everybody rushed back to render assistance, but Aunt Polly was luckily unhurt. My father's secretary, Ernest Lane, was so unnerved that he unwittingly consumed the contents of the first-aid flask of brandy, to the mortification of the patient and upbraiding of the others. Many a laugh has been had at their expense!

During the earlier part of the rebellion my father lived on the farm at Irene. Usually he went in to work by train every day, but during this period of trouble he used his old Napier car. One evening a party of rebels lay in ambush in Fountains Valley to intercept him on the way home. But providentially, he did a thing he seldom did normally; he went home via Roberts Heights. The police got to hear of the affair and thereafter forbade him to travel in the dark, and in future three armed policemen accompanied him in his car.

Trouble was now starting in the Western Transvaal and the Free State. The Dutch Reformed Church Synod warned the people against the folly of civil war and condemned Maritz.

Beyers and de Wet called upon Botha to resign.

My father's reply to that was to call up four mounted and one unmounted regiment, totalling 35,000 men of whom 70 per cent were Dutch. This was a Boer squabble, he said, and he wanted to keep it in the family.

Up to this stage Botha and my father had shown infinite patience with the rebels. They had warned and warned again. They had begged, they had appealed; but they had not acted. There was no deep bitterness in the feelings of the rebels and it was hoped that perhaps they might see reason and disperse of their own accord. My father and Botha were prepared to go to almost any lengths to obviate bloodshed.

Matters were now coming to a head. Beyers in the Western Transvaal and de Wet in the Free State were interfering with recruiting, were holding up trains and looting.

On October 25 Martial Law was declared throughout the Union and rebels were once more called upon to go home, but without result. Twelve days later the order was repeated. By now there were twelve thousand rebels on the rampage. Pretoria was being threatened. My father ordered Transvaal Scottish and Irish regiments to the hills around the city. People were nervous and restive at the delays. There was no news of developments in the papers and there was no hint of action.

Outside South Africa the general situation was extremely grave. The German juggernaut had been stemmed on the Marne and at Ypres, but the position was still insecure. A strong German naval squadron had had successes against British naval units off the coast of Chile; had it come eastward there would have been nothing to stop the bombardment of South African coastal ports or interference with our landings at Luderitzbucht.

At the review of a motor brigade held in Johannesburg on November 7 my father said: "The Dutch people of South Africa feel that their honour is touched. They are determined to do their duty and wipe out this disgrace. . . . Out of the late great war, the Boer people brought little except their good name. That is what they value as their greatest asset in the world. They are not going to allow anyone, no matter how great a part he has played in the past, to drag that good name in the mire. We are going to see this through." The Government had matters well in hand and people "could sleep peacefully".

In the beginning of November fighting started in earnest. At Treurfontein Colonel Alberts defeated the rebel Kemp, who, however, managed personally to get away. Later Kemp gathered eight hundred men about him again and captured Schweizer Reneke, where he foully desecrated the Union Jack. The Natal Light Horse, under Colonel Royston, tried to intercept him at Khies Drift but were tricked with a white flag, and lost many men, while Kemp fled through the Kalahari into South-West Africa.

Botha and my father asked General Hertzog to use his moderating influence. He did not reply. Later they tried to negotiate with Beyers through Meintjes, also without result. Later they tried once more through the magistrate of Wolmaranstad, again without result.

Meanwhile de Wet, after the loss of his son, had gone berserk and was tearing up the Free State. Hertzog made a revolutionary speech in Parliament mourning the poor rebels who were being "murdered".

On November 11 Botha attacked de Wet's 3,500 men at the head of a big army and drove them towards General Lukin at Koraanberg, but owing to sabotage in the signals lines Lukin was too late to intercept. At Mushroom Valley Botha finally cornered his quarry, but again de Wet, together with Harm Oost and two others, managed to escape across the Vaal. Here he collected a new force of 250, and dashed westwards across the desert to the German border. He was pursued by Koen Brits's columns in cars and captured by Colonel Jordaan at Waterbury, in the Kalahari. Botha had used artillery and machine guns and there were heavy casualties.

Meanwhile Beyers had been decisively defeated by Botha near Rustenburg. He seems to have panicked in those latter weeks and his moves lacked purpose. Loyalists disclosed his presence on the Transvaal side of the Vaal near Greylings Request where he was surrounded. Telling Field-Cornet Boshoff that he was going to make a fight of it he sprang on to a strange horse and plunged into the river. The horse grew restive with the shooting, so Beyers slipped off and started to swim for the bank, which was quite near. He turned on his back and appeared to be in difficulties, calling, "I can't keep it up." One of his men tried to help him but was stopped by a bullet. Shooting now ceased and troops from the Transvaal side thrust out branches for him to grasp, but shouting that his coat was entangled with his legs, he disappeared suddenly under the raging brown waters. Rescue attempts were foiled by rebels once more opening fire. Three days later his body was recovered after the floods had subsided. His coat was missing and his bootlaces were tightly entangled. These laces had been his undoing.

Beyers had been a firm friend of my mother's and had been a frequent visitor to us at Irene and in Pretoria. He grew up in Stellenbosch with my Krige uncles, with whom he did much swimming in the local dam. He was said to have been a very good swimmer.

My father was genuinely distressed at the ignominious way in which Beyers had met his end, and himself sat down and drafted his wife a letter of condolence. He also put at her disposal a special train in order that all the relatives might attend the funeral, and helped her in many other ways. There was no bad blood between the two families.

Last to surrender was Commandant Joseph Fourie, a permanent force officer and protégé of Beyers. From a Boer War wound in the knee he had contracted a slight limp. At the start of the rebellion he had treasonably gone over to Beyers in our full military uniform and was therefore in a slightly different category of rebel. On Dingaan's Day, the 16th of December, he was captured by Colonel N. J. Pretorius at Nooitgedacht, near Pretoria. He had acted treacherously and twelve of our troops had lost their lives in the encounter. Now in mufti, and with a huge beard, Jopie Fourie boasted of his crimes and was unrepentant.

At a South African Party congress, held in Bloemfontein in 1915, my father gave this description of Fourie's capture and court martial: "Fourie was called out with the Defence Force Regiment of which he was an officer. He discussed matters with General Botha and myself, giving us the impression that he had no grievance. But he rebelled, and a number of men belonging to his regiment went out with him. He has shed more blood than any other officer. I was obliged to take him seriously. . . . The rebellion was subsiding. Beyers was drowned. General de Wet surrendered when he saw himself hopelessly surrounded. At Reitz, General Botha had taken a large number of prisoners. Only Fourie's band remained contumacious. Twelve of our men were killed at Nooitgedacht. There was no justification for that. Some of them were shot at a range of twelve yards. Fourie was captured by Colonel Pretorius, a grandson of the late President Pretorius and a cousin of Fourie's. . . . A court martial was appointed, strictly according to military law. One of its members told me he felt compunction about serving, because he was a friend of Fourie's. I replied that that was an additional reason why he should be on the tribunal. On Saturday Fourie was unanimously condemned to death. . . . Had I refused to confirm the sentence, I could not have faced the parents of the young men who met their deaths through Fourie's fault. There is something to be said for many a rebel, but in this case I conferred a great benefit on the State by carrying out my most unpleasant duty. . . ."

He had been captured on Dingaan's Day and executed by a firing squad on a Sunday. Frantic last-minute efforts were made by his friends to obtain a reprieve, and delegations tried desperately to see my father. But he was not at home at the time, and in any case, he said, he would not have interfered in the course of justice.

Cheered by the news that Admiral Sturdee's battle-cruisers had destroyed the German Pacific squadron off the Falkland Islands on December 20, Botha was in a position to declare the rebellion over.

Twelve hundred rebels were sent home on parole. When Parliament reassembled four thousand men were still in prison awaiting sentence. A court of three judges was established to try the more important rebels and shortly the remainder were released subject to certain civil disabilities for ten years.

Deneys Reitz summed up the position very clearly when he wrote in *Trekking On*, in 1933: "The rebellion was over. With a great conflict raging in Europe, it passed almost unnoticed in the outside world, but in South Africa the aftermath is with us yet, and the motives and origin are still the subject of fierce controversy.

"I personally have not the slightest doubt that it was a direct outcome of our preceding political warfare. That it was essentially a party quarrel is proved by the fact that every member of the South African Party stood by General Botha, and while not every Nationalist was a rebel, it is literally true that every rebel, without a single exception, was a Nationalist.

"Furthermore, the rebellion was a domestic dispute among the Boers themselves, and hostility towards the British had comparatively little part in it. . . . The rising was crushed by Boer commandos under Boer officers, and to this day the ill-feeling that was engendered lies not between the Dutch and British, but between the two sections of the Boer people in South Africa."

During the necessarily acrimonious debate following my father's introduction of his second Indemnity Bill within a year, he summed up the origins of the rising briefly as follows: "One of the most powerful contributory causes to the rebellion was the campaign of calumny against the Prime Minister. The Dutch people do not draw any fine distinctions, and by a process of reiteration a soil was created into which the fertile seed fell. . . ."

Hertzog said in Parliament: "The Government has done its duty in suppressing disorders and violence in the country. I have never accused the Government of having done anything wrong in so doing." When tackled about his negotiations with Maritz he made the excuse that he could neither have reproached the rebels nor supported the Government without getting into trouble with one or the other. A Unionist member for the Rand, J. W. Quinn, said bluntly: "I would have shot the honourable member for Smithfield."

My father had been tireless during the rebellion and had worked well into every night throughout these trying months. During this time he drove both himself and his subordinates remorselessly. Botha paid him this well-merited tribute: "Nobody can ever appreciate sufficiently the great work General Smuts has done—greater than that of any other man throughout this unhappy period."

The rebels were dealt with liberally on principle, partly as a friendly gesture and partly to avoid creating martyrs. De Wet got six years, but only served eighteen months before being released. Kemp and the prophet van Rensburg, who had escaped into South-West Africa, surrendered when General Botha invaded the colony, and Maritz fled to Europe. All were later allowed to return without penalty.

My father has always felt that the policy of leniency was justified by subsequent history. The one martyr he created, Fourie, gave him quite sufficient trouble.

The weekly *The Cape* wrote in 1915: "From whichever side a criticism of the Government comes, be sure that the odium will fall on General Smuts. There could hardly be any greater tribute than this to the power which he wields in present-day politics. I do not subscribe to the view that General Botha is merely a puppet in the hands of General Smuts, but I do think that, if there had been no Smuts in Union politics, there would have been no Botha. . . . Smuts directs all the machinery of government and oils all the parts. He is always in the background, planning, calculating, plotting. Smuts burrows his way from morning till night through mountains of official documents. . . . When the

Government does anything heroic it is always 'Bravo, Botha!' When it bumps up against public opinion, it is always 'Smuts's slimness'. He never takes a holiday. . . . He alone appears not to feel the need. What a fortunate thing this is for the Botha Ministry!"

PART II
The First World War

XXVIII FIRST WORLD WAR

GERMANY was not a colonising power. Unlike the British, the Portuguese and the Dutch, who acquired their overseas possessions by the courage and enterprise of their pioneers, the Germans were content to get theirs less heroically by annexation or exchange. South-West Africa was virtually a gift from Britain in 1884. The scramble for Africa was just beginning. Previously Germany had been much too busy with her wars on the Continent to have time for colonies. Even now Bismarck was so involved he could barely spare the time. But the lectures of the explorer H. M. Stanley were awakening German interest.

South-West Africa was handed over against the advice of the Cape Government, which itself had been unable to secure it. Dr. Karl Peters and two confederates acquired Tanganyika by going out disguised as artisans and secretly conducting treaties with the native chiefs. The greater part of the Cameroons was gained in similar fashion. The remainder was got from France in 1911 as a favour for keeping her hands off Morocco.

Equally striking is the difference in method of administration between German and English colonies. In the British system a great deal of latitude is permitted the colonies in their own administration. The German possessions were ruled very much from the Fatherland and were exploited for exports and consolidated as military bases.

The German flag was hoisted on 6th August, 1884, at Luderitzbucht, four centuries after Bartholomew Dias had landed there. Nine years later a ruthless series of native wars began which went on till 1908. The German ideal of colonisation was the same as in the old Americas—extermination. Thereafter there was no Red Indian problem. In South-West Africa Germany determined there would be no Herero problem. A British commission estimated the Herero population at 80,000 in 1877. When the punitive efforts had subsided after the 1911 rebellion there were barely 15,130 left. It was not straightforward extermination, but sadistic ill-treatment, flogging, interference with women and brutality.

The Hereros had 150,000 head of cattle in 1892, less than 50,000 at the turn of the century, and none at all five years later.

What had Germany put into the country in return? A few shabby towns, two strategic wireless stations and a raging incidence of venereal disease.

German penetration of Tanganyika also started in 1884. Its advent was marked by continual Arab and native rising, caused by harshness and unsympathetic treatment. Methods of suppression were of the well-known ruthless pattern. Wherever they went they built protective "bomas" or forts. From these they scarce dared venture far. The first rising was the Bushiri rebellion, brought about by the exploitation of the natives by Karl Peters. In two years there was nothing left. The Chagga chiefs of Kilimanjaro were next to revolt. Then followed a two-year war with the Hele of Iringa, farther inland. Rather than be captured the native chiefs committed suicide. Seven years later came the Maji-Maji rebellion. As a punitive measure native crops were burnt, which resulted in widespread starvation. Hundreds of natives were strung up from trees. In all, about 120,000 perished.

The German record in the Cameroons and Togoland is little better.

Her mark upon Africa has not been a happy one.

What was the strategic significance of Germany's possessions in Africa? South-West Africa, a territory 800 miles long and 400 wide, three-quarters the size of the Union of South Africa, runs more than halfway up the west side of the Union. Even though the arid Kalahari intervenes, it nevertheless points a dagger at our very heart. It has two tolerable harbours which might readily be turned into U-boat nests, with incalculable effect on the Atlantic sea routes. Above South-West Africa lies Angola, and on our east coast marches the Mozambique, both territories of our honourable and ancient, but weak, ally Portugal. Between the Rhodesias and Kenya, next to the Belgian Congo, lies Tanganyika. With two fine ports in Tanga and Dar-es-Salaam, she menaces the whole centre part of Africa. She also looks out on a large part of the Indian Ocean. Contrary to general sub-continent practice, Germany trained native levies in military tactics. These askaris we were soon to meet.

The Germans have always been much interested in forming a strategic "bloc" in the heart of Africa. It was part of what they called their "Mittel-Afrika" concept, defined at various times by Leutwein, Zimmerman and Delbrück and including more or less the whole southern half of the continent. If this could not be acquired by peaceful means, perhaps one day she would be strong enough . . .

*　　*　　*　　*　　*

The first Great War was no sudden conflagration stealing stealthily upon the world out of the dark. It did not come silently and unnoticed. The gathering storm had been observed approaching plainly for all to see, but humanity seemed powerless to avert the catastrophe. We have already seen the start of the strained feeling during the Jameson Raid and its worsening during the Boer War, when Germany glowered, impotently, across the screen of warships at the British transports leaving for the front. In 1904 there was to be trouble over Morocco in the so-called Tangier Episode, when the German Emperor steamed there in his private yacht, and made a speech on Morocco's independence which was a distinct challenge to Britain and France. In 1906, in a treaty, the independence of Morocco was guaranteed by all the major powers of Europe. Perhaps all might have been well had the Sultan been a strong man and able to keep his subjects in order. But by 1911 there was so much internal trouble that France felt herself constrained to intervene. This intervention annoyed Germany and she despatched two gunboats to Agadir. Though the move was ostensibly to protect her subjects, it was a hostile display of power by Germany. For a month or two there was suspense, and it was only after the British Chancellor of the Exchequer, Mr. Lloyd George, had made it plain that Britain was quite ready to side with France in this squabble that Germany grew more tractable. France, unimpeded, went on to arrange a treaty with the Sultan for a French protectorate, while Germany was actively spurred on in her naval building programme and was raising an extra £50,000,000 for her army.

France and Germany, though at peace, were in opposite camps, and Britain had professed her love for France. Britain did her best to reduce the tension by despatching Lord Haldane and others on friendly missions to Germany.

Europe had been in an unsettled state over the past few years. In 1908 there had been a revolution in Turkey. In 1912 followed the First Balkan War, initiated by Venizelos of Greece and Ferdinand of Bulgaria. The Turkish army was defeated and the whole of Turkey in Europe was conquered except the outposts of Constantinople and the Peninsula of Gallipoli. The terms of the abortive Treaty of London having failed to be brought into effect, the Second Balkan War ensued a year later in which Bulgaria faced Greece, Serbia and Roumania, till peace was concluded at Constantinople. During this war Turkey had managed to regain her place in south-eastern Europe.

German influence had steadily improved with the Turks to the detriment of that of Britain. It was aggravated by the friendship of Britain with Russia, Turkey's old enemy. On 11th August, 1914, the Turkish Government permitted the German warships *Goeben* and *Breslau* to use the Dardanelles. An endeavour was made to keep the Turks neutral, but on October 29 Turkey threw off the mask and declared war.

In 1911 the Triple Entente Powers, Britain, France and Russia, had shown the Triple Alliance Powers, Germany, Austria and Italy, that none of the Entente powers stood alone, and by sound diplomacy had averted war. In the crisis of July, 1914, it was unable to do so. On 28th June the Archduke Franz Ferdinand, heir to the Austrian throne, had been assassinated at Sarajevo in Bosnia. Austria alleged the foul deed had been due to Serbian intrigues and on July 23 sent an ultimatum to Belgrade. Forty-eight hours of grace were allowed and thereafter Austria began war on Serbia. This it was impossible to limit or confine. Russia began to get her armies ready to help Serbia. On 1st August Germany presented an ultimatum to Russia. When this expired Germany forthwith attacked Russia's ally, France, through neutral Belgium.

On 4th August Britain declared war on Germany.

And so started what was at that time the biggest human up-heaval of all ages. It was indeed a world war in the true sense, for though the major fighting occurred on the Western Front of Europe, it involved bloody struggles with Turkey in the Darda-nelles, in Mesopotamia and North Africa; it involved major naval battles at the Falkland Islands and Jutland; and it involved outpost fighting in South-West Africa and in East Africa; and at the same time there was the continuous and relentless struggle with the U-boat menace over the Seven Seas.

The Allies, in the bloody years that followed, were to realise that they had tackled the most ruthless and efficient military machine the world had ever seen. Not only did Germany at first enjoy a numerical superiority, but man for man the war was to bring the frightening realisation that the German soldier had no equal, and certainly no superior, in the armies of the world. This was amply borne out by casualty figures for the war. Mr. Churchill says: "During the whole war the Germans never lost in any phase of the fighting more than the French whom they fought, and frequently inflicted double casualties upon them . . . in all the British offensives the British casualties were never less than 3 to 2 and often nearly double the corresponding German losses."

The trouble with the war was that it was never fully completed and Germany was never crushingly defeated. Victory came about when the German home front cracked as a result of relentless blockade. When the line on the frontiers was pierced the Germans suddenly capitulated. As an army they were still intact. Their country had not been invaded or treated to the ravages of war. The German population, though starved, never admitted that they had been beaten.

In the half-completed war, and in the half-baked treaty at Versailles, lay the germ for the still bigger war that was to follow in 1939. But that we must leave for later chapters.

Shortly before the outbreak of the revolution in Russia, Lord Milner, together with Sir Samuel Hoare, had been sent there to report on the possibilities of an upheaval. These were the days of a lavish Russian court, of a royal line suffering from the dread bleeders' disease, hæmophilia, and of the scoundrel healer Rasputin, who was murdered just before they left. To Hoare, the imminence of a rising was only too patent, but Milner, out of touch, wrote in his report on board ship that he did not consider a revolution likely. There was wireless silence at the time, and it was only when he landed in England that he heard for the first time that the revolution had already been in progress for some weeks. His report was useless and he tore it up and wrote another.

The major battles of the war were contested grimly on the Western Front, chiefly in the mire of Belgium and France. Hindenburg and Ludendorf had swung round to apply the famed strategy of a right hook on Paris. The French capital was nearly reached. The South African Brigade at Delville Wood, in the vast battles of the Somme, played their small but immortal part in stopping the avalanche.

Germany was finally checked in a muddy world of trenches and barbed wire. Names such as Ypres, the Somme, Verdun, Passchendaele and many others are household words. Millions of young men perished in these battles, the flower of England and France. France had borne the earlier brunt of the juggernaut. Britain took over later, and near the end America also came in to apply the *coup d'état*, but her effort had been too belated to be of crucial value.

In Africa Germany had to be driven from her colonies in South-West Africa and in Tanganyika. South African troops played a dominant part in these campaigns. In the Middle East, Turkey was only subdued after much fighting by Viscount Allenby. The Holy Land had heard the booming of guns and thundering of horses' hoofs. Allied blood lay on the beaches at the Dardanelles. Much of it was Anzac blood. Mr. Churchill bore the brunt of the criticism.

XXIX SOUTH-WEST AFRICAN CAMPAIGN

SOUTH-WEST AFRICA is a vast arid territory of over 317,000 square miles with a thousand-mile-long coast-line. Almost half of it is desert, especially the flat coastal plains which are billowing, sandy, waterless wastes. Well inland the highlands enjoy a better rainfall and form attractive ranching country.

For the defence of this distant outpost of Das Vaterland the Germans had only a little over 8,000 troops. The remainder of the defence was left to the broad belt of surrounding inhospitable desert, which was thought to be impassable to armies encumbered with their water and commissariat problems. Where the Germans, in all their thoroughness, erred, however, was in their under-estimation of the capabilities of the Union troops and their organising skill. For neither Botha nor my father had been idle during the troublous times of the rebellion. They had, rightly, foreseen that the Germans would deem the desert crossings impossible, and they had set about the task of rendering the impossible possible. In the art of desert warfare my father had had considerable experience in the South-West Cape. He saw that with proper organisation a commando-crossing of the desert would be by no means impossible. The first task was to assure a water supply. This was done by putting down a chain of boreholes. Supplies were taken care of by the new-fangled motor-car. In any case, it was going to be a lightning campaign, and the troops would have to travel light, and rough it as best they could. By striking swiftly and decisively he believed he could obtain clear-cut victories, reduce casualties, and shorten the agony. But hard as he drove his men, he drove himself equally relentlessly. His was not a static headquarters days behind the fighting line; he would always be found well up with his troops. In Africa, with its poor communications, this was essential if a general was to remain in touch with his forces. My father could do it because of his frugal way of living, his tremendous fitness and vitality, and his unbounded physical endurance.

This close tactical command paid dividends. It enabled quick decisions and swift moves. Rommel proved it in North Africa in the Second World War, and in those gigantic mobile tank battles it was often decisive. Hitler, sitting back in the Reich Chancellery in Berlin, was out of touch and his poor contact possibly cost Germany the war.

General Botha arrived at Swakopmund on 11th February, 1915. My father did not reach Luderitzbucht till mid-April. This port had previously been taken by British units. In front of the armies lay shifting sands, dust storms, scorching heat and thirst.

South-West Africa was divided into two zones of command. General Botha made Walfish Bay his main base and tackled the enemy in the northern portion of the territory. My father operated in the southern half.

Moving swiftly from Walfish, Botha attacked the Germans at Jakalswater and drove them backwards. Without losing impetus he passed through Otjimbingwe, where the noted African explorer Charles John Andersson had once established himself, and seized Karibib, Friedriksfelde, Wilhelmsthal and Okahanja in turn, entering Windhoek, the capital, on 12th May. Having now driven a wedge across the territory from west to east, Botha divided his force into four columns, for mopping-up operations. The first he put under his trusted Koen Brits, who was to move up northwards on the west side of the railway to Otjivarongo and beyond to Outjo and the Etosha Pan, by so doing severing the German line of retreat to the Cunene and the Kaokoveld. The second column, under Lukin, was to move up along the railway line; the third, under Manie Botha, was to move along east of the line to Tsumeb; the fourth column, under Myburg, was to strike out for the Otavi junction.

The speed of the move, executed in hard forced marches, cut off the 4,000 German troops, who were forced to capitulate. Governor Seitz and Colonel Francke wanted to argue, but Botha demanded unconditional surrender, and the terms were signed on 9th July. One of Botha's columns covered 120 miles of marching in difficult desert conditions.

Meanwhile my father had not been idle. His attack was a three-pronged one. He sent Mackenzie across the desert plains from

Luderitz in the west, van Deventer up from the Orange River in the south across the Kalahari, and Berrange from Kuruman in the east. In a series of gruelling rushed marches he took Keetmanshoop and Gibeon by the beginning of May. There was hardly enough water to keep body and soul together and even the occasional tin of bully beef was a luxury. The supply services had been far outstripped in this land of heat and sand. At first the troops lived on a minimum ration of distilled sea water, and it was not till they reached the highlands after Garus that they came on fresh water.

The Germans had exhibited their characteristic thoroughness in their retreat by poisoning and polluting all water supplies and blowing up or booby-trapping all installations. Along their roads of retreat they planted numerous land mines, and there were constant explosions and casualties as the advancing troops set them off. Some of the wells were filled with fœtid corpses of animals which reeked to high heaven; but the swiftness of our moves enabled us to capture some intact. All around was a "scorched-earth" policy applied in a land that nature had already long ago decided was to be a scorched earth.

My father avoided frontal attacks. He was an inveterate exponent, like all Boers, of the enveloping flanking move. Thus Aus, an important point on the road to Keetmanshoop, though well held and tactically strong, fell without trouble. As ever, my father had the habit of wishing to do his own reconnaissance work wherever possible. Near Keetmanshoop he was returning from one of these trips ahead of his troops when he ran into, and was captured by an outlying screen of our men. He, rather than his subordinates, saw the humour of such situations. They left his senior officers worried but helpless.

The Kalahari column accomplished the almost incredible feat of crossing nearly 700 miles of desert on horses. They made a beeline for Keetmanshoop. It was a brilliant march, and took the enemy by surprise.

Beaten in the south, the Germans swung up towards Windhoek, only to find they had been driven up against General Botha. The campaign was over. It had been a walk-over for the 45,000 Union troops. The casualties—530 dead and wounded—were only half those of the rebellion; this was as much due to superior tactics and good handling as to overwhelming strength. The swiftness and the detailed co-ordination of movements over vast distances was a revelation to students of military history; it was a distinct feather in the caps of General Botha and my father. The cost to the Treasury had only been £15,000,000. It was also the first campaign of the Allies to be brought to a successful conclusion in this war.

After the campaign my father expressed to his troops his pride in their accomplishments: "If you go through the history of wars, you will perhaps only in the Boer War find records like these. . . . If you tell of this march from Nonandas to Karabib people will not believe you; if you tell them how little water you drank and how few biscuits you ate, they will not believe you."

In July, 1915, General Botha and my father returned to the Union as heroes. Botha thanked my father: "South Africa might well be proud of having produced a man of such talents," he said.

In Cape Town, Johannesburg and other towns they were given tumultuous ovations; but in the countryside there was a strong undercurrent of hostility. There they were not heroes returning triumphant from the fields of battles, but just despised tools of Britain. The cry was that they were subordinating South Africa to the interests of the Empire, which at the time was struggling at Gallipoli, gravely threatened by the first U-boat campaign, and helpless to aid a tottering Russia. These opponents were not appeased by victory, or the acquisition of a big slice of new territory. Few people are more difficult to impress than the Boers when they have set their hearts against a thing. Hertzog harped incessantly on imperialism, the blood of brothers that had been shed and the thousands of broken hearts. At Edenburg he said, "South Africa has done enough for the Empire. Personally, I object to any more money being expended on the cause of the Empire."

The five-year term of office of the Government was about to expire as the troops returned from South-West Africa. It was not a propitious time coming so shortly after the rebellion. South African Party prospects at the election were uncertain, though it was known that the Unionists would stand solidly by them on the war issue.

Feelings were running high. The sinking of the *Lusitania* brought about a series of emotional demonstrations which only served to aggravate the cleavage. The sad and disturbing exodus of the Afrikaner from the Botha-Smuts kraal was in full swing. It was one of those baser manifestations of ingratitude that chequered my father's public life.

In August my father cast back at Hertzog his cry that General Botha had become an Englishman. "Since then [the National Convention] others have changed, not we. . . . We want one South Africa, one united people. Five years hence, or fifty years hence, our party will still stand where it now stands. . . . Before the Boer War we had a divided people—the old population and the Uitlanders. The result of that system was blood and tears. . . . Within the past couple of years there has been a reaction against the one-stream policy. Have we not had bloodshed in the past twelve months as a consequence of this? . . ."

On October 15 he remarked: "I am a man of peace. General Hertzog says Botha and Smuts must be got rid of. If it were a personal question, I should like nothing better than to be out of this hell into which I have wandered, and in which I have lived for the last two years . . . the Government will not leave you in the lurch. . . . I shall work with my last breath for the good of South Africa."

In September electioneering started in grim earnest. Meetings were hectic. There was constant heckling and interruption. The case of Jopie Fourie featured prominently, even his widow stepping into the fray. Nationalists accused the Government of having deliberately murdered General de la Rey. A deluge of alleged crimes descended upon the Government. My father had the distinction of being the best-hated and most-maligned man on the Government side. He was also their chief and most indefatigable speaker. There were few dull moments at his meetings. Speeches were drowned by the vociferous, organised, clamour of discontent.

One day when travelling by car in the chilly weather of the highveld, with his coat well up over his ears, between two political meetings, my father said wistfully to Levi, a newspaper correspondent, who was with him: "Do not complain. You have enough to eat. You have no one whose fate depends on you. You have thoughts to call your own, and a certain amount of leisure. Look at me! Thousands, I suppose, envy me my place and power. Yet what are they? My own people curse me; to tens of thousands my name is a by-word. Be satisfied!"

At Brits a questioner asked which came first with him, South Africa or the Empire: "There is no question I could answer more easily," my father said. "The interests of South Africa will always be first with me." But South Africa, he might have added, could only be great if Britain and the Commonwealth were strong and great. At a meeting on 9th September, in Pretoria, he left, after having been refused a hearing, very much the worse for rotten eggs and over-ripe tomatoes.

We must not over-estimate opposition at these meetings, for even in those days the Nationalists had organised roving break-up gangs. They followed principal speakers from meeting to meeting with the express purpose of denying them a hearing. The Nazi thugs of Adolf Hitler used similar tactics.

On September 23, occurred an outrage at Newlands, a poorer suburb of Johannesburg. My father had been warned by friends not to appear there as serious trouble was expected. But he was not one to be deterred by threats of personal violence, for fear formed no part of his physical make-up.

The suppressed hum burst into a full-blooded angry roar as he entered the hall. His chauffeur, George Hodgson, left the Napier parked at the door—just in case. Barely had the official party mounted the platform when Mary Fitzgerald, a Labour agitator, stepped forward with a baby in her arms. "This is the child of Labuschagne whom you murdered," she shouted, referring to the person of 1913 strike fame. Rotten eggs and tomatoes rained on to the platform, as well as objects of more solid composition. "For heaven's sake take the child away," my father said, "or it will get killed." After a brief softening-up process with stones and bottles, some of the crowd rushed the platform and a general mêlée ensued. Sticks and boots were used freely. When the lamps were smashed my father decided it was time to go. It was plain that the most serious personal violence was contemplated. The party had to fight its way out under a hail of brickbats and blows from sticks and clubs. My father was knocked down, but managed to struggle to his feet and got to the door with the rest of them.

Meanwhile Hodgson had started the car, but the mob dragged

him from his seat and switched it off. Twice this happened before my father arrived. Here, as he was boarding the vehicle, a vicious blow aimed at him with a pick-handle missed and felled a hostile miner alongside. A warning shot was fired by a detective and thereafter as the car drove off there were more shots, not fired by the detective. It is presumed that these were the efforts of a would-be assassin.

My father got away with little worse than bruises and ruffled feelings.

The Times, commenting on the Newlands disorder, remarked: "Perhaps South Africans who have hitherto admired, without sympathy, the rather hard brilliancy of General Smuts, may realise, having so nearly lost him, his value to South Africa and the Empire. His enemies may thus have secured for him what, in comparison with other South African public men of less ability, he has curiously lacked hitherto—a popular following."

My earliest recollections are of the appearance of my father's coat the morning after he got back from Newlands. I was three at the time. My mother called us outside to come and look at it, for it was not in a fit state to come indoors. That coat made such a deep impression on me that I decided there and then that the political world was not for me!

The results of the elections were disappointing. In the Free State where in 1910 they had made a clean sweep the South African Party did not win a single seat. Of the entire country 50 per cent of the rural area vote went to Hertzog and three Ministers lost their seats. The Nationalists had polled more than 30 per cent of all votes and had improved their position in the House from five to twenty-seven seats. Labour had four seats, Independents six and the Unionists thirty-nine. The future for the South African Party was therefore insecure and they could only hope to carry on effectively with the help of the Unionists and Independents.

XXX EAST AFRICAN CAMPAIGN

SINCE the outbreak of the war British and German contingents had been skirmishing incessantly on the frontiers of East Africa. The position was unsatisfactory, but Britain had her hands too full in Europe to tackle this outpost campaign seriously. She had merely kept the pot simmering, waiting no doubt till South Africa had cleared up her troubles in the south and was in a position to help. Under von Lettow Vorbeck the Germans had been more enterprising, and his small but efficiently bush-trained army of 2,000 German officers and 20,000 native askaris had crossed the borders of Nyasaland and the Congo and were attacking the Kenya–Uganda railways.

In the second half of 1915, however, Britain was in a position to take the East African war more seriously and began sending out more troops. But even so, Major-General Tighe did not seem able to get going and a naval assault on the port of Tanga proved a failure.

Beyond sending a few troops to Nyasaland and Northern Rhodesia the Union had not been in a position to send men abroad till South-West Africa was cleared up. But now the campaign in East Africa was being freely talked about and volunteers were being called for service there as well as to make up an infantry brigade and five battalions of heavy artillery for service in Europe.

South African troops had been well paid in the South-West African campaign, but in these new campaigns they were to receive only the King's shilling per day. There was considerable pressure, especially from the Unionists and Labour, to bring the pay into line with that of the other Dominions; so the Government decided to make up the difference to three shillings per day, though this was not to apply to the brigade for Europe.

It was an open secret that in the beginning of November my father had been offered the command of all troops in East Africa, but in view of the position in South Africa he had felt constrained to refuse the appointment. Whether this offer had been made as a compliment to his military achievements or in deference to the fact that South Africa would be supplying the major portion of the East African contingent, is not known. Britain might have been more pleased to see Botha in this position, but his absence from the Union was out of the question.

Early in 1916, General Smith-Dorrien was appointed. But on the way to South Africa he was taken seriously ill; at Cape Town he was carried off on a stretcher and taken to Muizenberg, and it soon became apparent that he would need a long convalescence before he would be fit for active duty. Once more the command was offered to my father. By this time he felt he could be spared; in any case he was tired of the bickerings of the political world and yearned for action.

It was with reluctance, however, that he left his friend Botha behind, now burdened in addition with another portfolio.

In Europe the Germans were grimly but slowly bludgeoning their bloody way into Verdun.

On 10th February, 1916, it was officially announced that my father had accepted the command in East Africa with the rank of Lieutenant-General in the British Army—Britain's second youngest general. Brigadier-General J. H. V. Crowe says: "It was a bold stroke to entrust the command of these bodies of troops and the carrying out of these operations to a man who was not a soldier, who had practically no experience in handling any considerable force. Knowing what one does now, one can only say that the Government were wonderfully lucky, for it would have been difficult to have found a more suitable commander than General Smuts proved himself to be." He cannot resist adding the pleasant quip, however, that: "Lest other politicians should attempt a similar role, I would say that General Smuts was successful in spite of being a politician." Concerning the converging movements of my father's three columns on Keetmanshoop Crowe says: "The operations were characterised by peculiarly daring and successful strategy."

Lloyd George summed up the position of a politician becoming a general very succinctly when he says of generals: ". . . there is no profession where experience and training count less in comparison with judgment and flair."

My father left Irene Station on the night of 11th February. As a small boy I had grown weary of the protracted proceedings of the evening, so my father carried me on to the platform in his arms and took me into the train with him. When the time came for the train to depart he kissed my mother good-bye and also the rest of the family, and then with a sigh, Levi says, set me down and gave a last wave as the train clattered into the night.

At Durban he paused for only twenty minutes before boarding a steamer for Kilindini.

The *Pretoria News* remarked, "The appointment is a tribute to his military genius and a compliment to South Africa." Mr. Asquith said in the House of Commons of the new Commander-in-Chief: "We can have the utmost confidence in General Smuts, in view of his varied military experience."

On 19th February he arrived in Mombasa. While on board he had heard that our forces had received a severe check at Salaita Hill. To this position he proceeded with all haste, making a personal reconnaissance to within two miles of the base of the Hill. He then went by car to Kajiado and later to Longido West, whence he had a good view of Meru and Kampfontein, Engare Nanyuki and Ngare Nairobi, all focal points in his immediate strategic position. He then continued on his way to Nairobi, where he arrived on the 23rd. Here he established his headquarters. The settlers and citizens wanted to lionise and entertain him, but he would not have this, for the rains were coming and he had work to do.

The natural strength of the German positions in East Africa was formidable. They started at Kilimanjaro and ran down a series of high mountains and big rivers to the coast. It was a land of dense bush, of mosquito, jigger flea and horse-sickness fly.

His army was an amazingly polyglot one. There were men from the United Kingdom, from South Africa, Cape Corps, Gold Coast, Nigeria and the West Indies; from Kashmir, Jhind, Bhurt-pur and Kaparthalu; Boer settlers from East Africa; Rhodesians, King's African Rifles native troops, Uganda contingents, Arabs, as well as Belgian and Portuguese troops.

His staff he took over almost without change from General Smith-Dorrien. Some were highly-trained regular officers; most were just enthusiastic militant citizens.

I can here do no better than let my father describe the campaign himself, as he did so ably in a long foreword to a book by Briga-dier-General J. H. V. Crowe, his G.O.C. Artillery in East Africa.

I make no apology for quoting thus freely, for I feel that not only does my father speak better for himself than anybody else could, but also that a better study of the man is afforded by this means. This foreword to Crowe's book* is one of the fullest and most lucid of the forewords written by him. It is also the most authoritative summary of the campaign.

Several of the minor side-shows of the world-war [my father says] are not only replete with incident, adventure, and interest to the general reader, but deserve the careful attention of the military student as types of campaigns successfully conducted under very novel conditions. General Botha's South-West African campaign, for instance, will ever remain a model desert campaign in which water and transport difficulties, considered insuperable by the enemy, were successfully overcome, and brilliant and daring strategy resulted in the rapid collapse of the enemy. Our East African campaign of 1916, again, presents a striking instance of a tropical campaign in which within the space of ten months a vast territory was occupied in the face of a resolute and powerful enemy backed up by natural obstacles and climatic difficulties of the most formidable character. These matters are dealt with in considerable detail by General Crowe, but it may be permitted me here to direct attention to some of the more general features of this campaign.

During the nineteen months which had elapsed since the outbreak of the war before my arrival in East Africa, the enemy had on the whole been superior to us both in strategy and effective striking force, and it says much for the tenacity of our defence that during that period British East Africa was not overwhelmed. The enemy, while entrenching himself in our territory and successfully striking minor blows at us in many directions and unceasingly threatening our long railway communications with the coast at many points, wisely foresaw that the real struggle would come later, and devoted his attention mainly to the recruitment and training of a large native army under German officers. The word had gone forth from Berlin that East Africa, the jewel of the German Colonial Empire, was to be held at all costs, and the German commander, Colonel von Lettow Vorbeck, was the man to carry out this order to the bitter end. The initial stocks of guns, machine-guns, rifles, and ammunition were from time to time very largely augmented by several blockade runners, and heavy artillery was supplied by the *Königsberg* and other warships on that coast. When, therefore, I arrived

* *General Smuts's Campaign in East Africa*, with acknowledgement to Mr. ohn Murray.

in February, 1916, with South African reinforcements to take the offensive, I found opposed to me a very large army, in effective strength not much smaller than my own, well trained and ably commanded, formidably equipped with artillery and machine-guns, immune against most tropical diseases, very mobile and able to live on the country, largely untroubled by transport difficulties, and with a morale in some respects higher than that of our troops, who, in inferior strength, had borne the heat and the burden of defence for the last eighteen months.

Powerful as was the enemy's military force, the physical and climatic difficulties of the country added vastly to his power of defence. For 130 miles from the coast to the neighbourhood of the Kilimanjaro Mountain the enemy territory was protected by the high mountain ranges of the Usambara and Pare Mountains. The only practicable gap in this natural rampart was a space about four or five miles wide between the northern extremity of the Pare Mountains and the foothills of the Kilimanjaro, in which Taveta lies and in which the enemy had been entrenching and fortifying himself for the previous eighteen months. This dangerous gap, in which the main enemy force was concentrated, was the gateway—then very much closed—to German East Africa, and towards it my predecessor, Major-General M. J. Tighe, had been building a railway and laying waterpipe lines over the water-less Serengeti Plains. About eight miles in front of the Taveta gap stands like a sentinel Salaita Hill, on which our forces had made a disastrous attack the very day on which I sailed from South Africa.

It must here be interposed that the Salaita Hill setback had been a serious one. This conspicuous hill rises abruptly from flat, dense bush, and owing to faulty intelligence or poor reconnaissance it was believed that only the hill itself was held. When the South African troops attacked they ran into deadly machine-gun and small-arms fire in the bush itself, before reaching the base of the hill. This surprise, combined with the almost completely restricted visibility, made the various formations lose contact and brought about a state of confusion. When, therefore, my father took over after this Salaita Hill disaster he found the troops generally somewhat shaken in morale. It did not take him long to rectify this. The secret was personality, aggressiveness and success. After this initial setback, the South African troops conspicuously distinguished themselves and brought great honour to our arms. Let us turn again to my father's description:

This gap had to be forced at whatever cost. I preferred to manœuvre the enemy out of it, and after spending a week in the most searching reconnaissance of the weak spots of the enemy's dispositions and in misleading movements and ruses, I advanced the bulk of my force by night against the enemy's left flank, took from him the foothills of Kilimanjaro by surprise and without any effort on the morning of March 8th, and within twenty-four hours compelled him to evacuate his practically impregnable Taveta positions. There followed the series of actions at Reata and Latema Hills, at Euphorbia Hill, at Rasthaus, at Massaikraal on the Soko Nassai River, at Kahe Hill and station, and on the Ruwu River which, within the next twelve days, gave us complete possession of the entire Moschi–Aruscha area, and finally drove the enemy army after repeated defeats over the Ruwu into the Pare Mountains and down the Tanga Railway towards the Usambara Mountains. Never had I seen so sudden and complete a transformation in the spirits of opposing forces; our men, who had retreated before the enemy in the confusion at Salaita Hill, now advanced with dauntless élan against the hidden foe in the dense bush of the mountain slopes or the Ruwu swamps.

The enemy, on whom fortune had hitherto almost invariably smiled, now found himself suddenly and repeatedly manœuvred or hurled out of his carefully prepared entrenchments. And this spirit of our men was destined in the following ten months to carry them through the greatest privations and over the most appalling obstacles to the distant valleys of the Rufiji and Ulanga Rivers in the south of German East Africa. The campaign henceforth assumed more and more the character of a campaign against nature, in which climate, geography, and disease fought more effectively against us than the well-trained forces of the enemy.

The pause which followed on the occupation of the Moschi–Aruscha districts gave an opportunity for the full consideration of the strategical problems ahead of us, and the rainy season which set in with extreme violence forced us to consider how the climate and seasons were going to affect our campaign. Our object was not merely the defeat of the enemy, but the effective occupation of his huge territory in the shortest possible time. Merely to follow the enemy in his very mobile retreat might prove an endless game, with the additional danger that the enemy forces might split up into guerilla bands doubling back in all directions and rendering effective occupation of the country impossible. In view of the size of the country it was therefore necessary to invade it from various points with columns strong enough to deal with any combination that could be brought against them, and for these columns as they advanced to clear the country also laterally.

General Northey was operating eastwards and north-eastwards from

Lake Nyassa; a Belgian column was launched eastwards from Lake Kivu (to the north of Lake Tanganyika); in April another Belgian column and a British column were set in motion in a southerly direction from the Uganda border west of Lake Victoria Nyanza; a mounted brigade under van Deventer was launched southwards from Aruscha to Kondoa Irangi, which is the most important strategic point on the interior plateau of the enemy territory; and finally, towards the end of May, three columns advanced south-eastward from the Moschi area against the Pare Mountains and towards the Usambara Mountains.

The combined result of all these movements, as far as possible co-ordinated for mutual assistance into groups according to the anticipated strength of the enemy in the various localities, was that by the beginning of September two-thirds of the enemy country had been effectively occupied up to and including the whole of the Central Railway from Dar-es-Salaam to Lake Tanganyika; and to the south of this railway General Northey had occupied a large territory up to and including Iringa. The successful occupation of so much country in so short a time was largely due to the careful adoption and co-ordination of the various lines of advance, which compelled a general retreat of the enemy without the chance of any other forces remaining behind or doubling back to molest our lines of communication.

It is impossible for those unacquainted with German East Africa to realise the physical, transport, and supply difficulties of the advance over this magnificent country of unrivalled scenery and fertility, consisting of great mountain systems alternating with huge plains; with a great rainfall and wide, unbridged rivers in the regions of the mountains, and insufficient surface water on the plains for the needs of an army; with magnificent bush and primeval forest everywhere, pathless, trackless, except for the spoor of the elephant or the narrow footpaths of the natives; the malaria mosquito everywhere, except on the highest plateaux; everywhere belts infested with the deadly tsetse fly which make an end of all animal transport; the ground almost everywhere, a rich black or red cotton soil, which any transport converts into mud in the rain or dust in the drought. In the rainy seasons which occupy about half the year much of the country becomes a swamp and military movements become impracticable. And everywhere the fierce heat of equatorial Africa, accompanied by a wild luxuriance of parasitic life, breeding tropical diseases in the unacclimatised whites. These conditions make life for the white man in that country far from a pleasure trip; if, in addition, he has to perform real hard work and make long marches on short rations the trial becomes very severe; if, above all, huge masses of men and material have to be moved over hundreds of miles in a great military expedition, against a mobile and alert foe, the strain becomes unendurable. And the chapter of accidents in this region of the unknown! Unseasonable rains cut off expeditions for weeks from their supply bases; animals died by the thousand after passing through an unknown fly belt; mechanical transport got bogged in the marshes, held up by bridges washed away or mountain passes demolished by sudden floods. And the gallant boys, marching far ahead under the pitiless African sun, with fever raging in their blood, pressed ever on after the retreating enemy, often on much reduced rations and without any of the small comforts which in this climate are real necessities. In the story of human endurance this campaign deserves a very special place, and the heroes who went through it uncomplainingly, doggedly, are entitled to all recognition and reverence. Their commander-in-chief will remain eternally proud of them.

Here I would like to add that their proud Commander-in-Chief, my father, was himself a fever-ridden wreck. He had been bitten by an infected anopheles mosquito somewhere in the Pangani region and had been laid up at Luchomo with a bad bout for some days. Like the rest of his men he never quite recovered from his attacks of malaria, and for a long while they were to leave him white, weak, but undaunted. For the rest of his life, whenever he plunged suddenly into a cold climate he would get mild recurrences of this old malady. This was especially so when air travel came into vogue. The attacks were not severe, but for a day he would have shivering fits and be listless and peevish.

Some idea of the ravages of malaria may be gained from the fact that in 1916, of the 58,000 troops, 50,000 went down with attacks. In 1917 the figure rose to 72,000 of whom 499 cases were fatal. The incidence of disease casualties to battle casualties was in the ratio of 31 to 1.

He continues the narrative, giving these reasons for his great hurry:

It may be said that I expected too much of my men, and that I imposed too hard a task on them under the awful conditions of this tropical campaigning. I do not think so. I was sure it was not possible to conduct this campaign successfully in any other way. Hesitation to take risks, slower moves, closer inspection of the auspices, would only have meant the same disappearance of my men from fever and other tropical diseases, without any corresponding compensation to show in the defeat of the enemy and the occupation of his country. Timid Fabian strategy would, of all, have been the most fatal in this country and against this enemy. Besides we had often to hurry to get out of a deadly stretch of country or to cover a wide waterless belt, or because great and rapid moves held the promise of big prizes. The most important centre of Kondoa-Irangi could only have been captured almost bloodlessly after that famous forced march of van Deventer's from Aruscha; Wilhelmstad was occupied bloodlessly after a relentless pursuit of the enemy for 130 miles from the Ruwu River; Dar-es-Salaam, Morogoro, and the Central Railway were captured without opposition after the tremendous march from the Lukigura River north of the Nguru Mountains, in which continuous fighting took place all the way and every man who did not fight was occupied behind in bridge-building, road-making, and bush-cutting. And even when these places had been captured the advance was continued southward without pause for another 100 miles of continuous fighting through the Ulugura Mountains to Kissaki and the Mgeta River in the strong hope that this supreme effort might end the campaign. One hundred and eighty miles of the most difficult mountain and river country had been covered in one month in the face of an enemy who was fighting every inch of the ground of which he was out-manœuvred by wide and difficult turning movements. Simultaneously General van Deventer on my right was making even a longer march from Kondoa-Irangi southwards to Kilimatinde and the Central Railway, and from there eastwards to Kilossa, and from there again southwards to the Great Ruaha River —all in one continuous advance, with fighting most of the way, a march in which some of his units actually covered 800 miles in that awful country and climate. It is true that efforts like these cannot be made without inflicting the greatest hardships on all, but it is equally true that the commander who shrinks from such efforts should stay at home. The transport and supply difficulties which arose from these great efforts were enormous and had to be dealt with mostly by improvised staffs. The way they were dealt with and finally overcome deserves the close attention of the military student.

Yes, here certainly had been no "Timid Fabian Strategy". Here was the same full-blooded dash and élan he had displayed in the Boer War. He took risks, he said, but we can rest assured that those risks had all been carefully weighed and that they had been justified. His moves were all based on meticulous assessment. That is why his men had such blind, a most worshipping, confidence in him.

He goes on:

The problems created by so big a campaign and so rapid an advance in a country which was still virgin soil, practically untouched by the hand of civilisation, without roads or bridges or any communications, except two effectively destroyed railway lines, were very great indeed. The establishment of means of communication, the creation of sea-bases as our advance rapidly progressed southward, were tasks of great magnitude, involving time and prodigious labour, and requiring appliances which could not be secured in those distant parts. I found Mombasa our only sea-base in February, 1915; in the following July the occupation of Tanga and the restoration of that wrecked port and the railway from it enabled us very materially to shorten our lengthy railway communications to the interior; in September Dar-es-Salaam had to be adopted and restored as our sea-base, and as everything there had been effectively destroyed, and such appliances as had existed were never meant for an undertaking of the magnitude of our campaign, it took us several months' unremitting labour to prepare it for our purposes. In October, again, we commenced the preparation of Kilwa as a new sea-base from which big forces could operate south of the Rufiji River; there was a magnificent natural harbour, but absolutely nothing in the way of landing appliances or arrangements. Finally, before I left in January, 1917, I had begun the preparation of Lindi farther south as our final sea-base, in case the enemy forces should escape to the southern frontier of German East Africa. Only those who have had experience of improvising sea-bases for the operations of large forces can appreciate what the preparation of these four bases meant to us in labour and trouble of all kinds. The devotion of our administrative staffs and the work of our pioneer, railway, and labour units in that tropical moist heat of the African coast and low country have been above praise.

While during the months from September to December, 1916, Dar-es-Salaam was being prepared as a base, and the Central Railway from it was being restored, and the sixty or seventy wrecked bridges along it, many of very considerable dimensions, were being rebuilt; while Kilwa harbour was being made ready for the reception of a large force which was being transferred to it, my attention was also preoccupied with the two other tasks; the evacuation of our sick from the country, and the situation which had arisen in the interior on General Northey's front. I believe between October and December we evacuated between 12,000 and 15,000 patients, mostly malaria cases, from our hospitals and ambulances along the Central Railway. Nothing could

show more eloquently the deadly nature of the country into which we
had now moved, and our only consolation was that the Rufiji Valley
into which we had driven our enemy was more deadly still. While
this evacuation was going on, General Northey was, with van
Deventer's assistance, waging a grim struggle in the direction of Iringa
against the enemy forces which had broken away from the Belgian and
British columns in the Tabora area. The retreat of these German forces
from the north impinged violently against Northey's lines of communication and broke them in some places, but by December the
situation had cleared and Northey had given the enemy some staggering blows and reduced him to the defensive.

By the middle of December most of this work on our bases and
communications had been completed, the short rainy season was passing, and I was prepared to resume what I hoped would be our final
advance. By Christmas van Deventer and Northey were on the move
in the interior, and on January 1st, 1917, I moved southwards to the
Rufiji; while General Hoskins, who was based on Kilwa, moved north-
west in order by this converging movement either to enclose the
enemy on the Rufiji or compel his retreat to the southern frontier of
his colony. All our moves were successful, and the great Rufiji River
was, on January 3rd, crossed by General Beves after a flank march
which will remain memorable even in this campaign of fine marching.
Every effort was made, after flinging the enemy across the Rufiji,
to join hands with Hoskins and cut off his retreat. But once again it
was proved to us that in the African bush, with its limited visibility,
it is practically impossible to enclose an enemy determined to escape.

While these operations were going forward, I was, about the middle
of January, ordered to relinquish my command in order that I might,
at the request of the South African Government, represent South
Africa on the forthcoming Imperial Conference, and on January 20th
I sailed from Dar-es-Salaam, with the deepest regret that I had not been
allowed the privilege of finishing my work. After I left the heavy rainy
season set in almost immediately and put a stop to our further moves,
and the enemy was thereby enabled to retreat to the south. The rainy
season lasted till June, when the advance was vigorously resumed by
General van Deventer, with the result that by the beginning of
December the bulk of the enemy's remaining forces had been captured,
and the remnants still in the field had retired over the Rovuma River
into Portuguese East Africa.

Before concluding, he pays tribute to the German commander
and points out the significance of the East African Campaign:

The enemy's stubborn defence of his last colony is not only a great tribute to the military qualities of General von Lettow, but is a proof of the supreme importance attached by the German Imperial Government to this African colony, both as an economic asset and as a strategic point of departure for the establishment of the future Central African Empire which is a cardinal feature in the Pan-Germanic dream. With German East Africa restored to the Kaiser at the end of the war, and a large askari army recruited and trained from its 8,000,000 natives, the conquest or forced acquisition of the Congo Free State, Portuguese East and West Africa, and perhaps even the recovery of the Kameroons may be only a matter of time. In this way this immense tropical territory, with almost unlimited economic and military possibilities, and provided with excellent submarine bases on both the Atlantic and Indian seaboards, might yet become an important milestone on the road to World-Empire. The East African campaign, therefore, while apparently a minor side-show in this great world-war, may yet have important bearings on the future history of the world. And it is to be hoped that our rulers will bear these wider and obscurer issues in mind when terms of peace come to be arranged at the end of this war. I cannot end these few introductory words without expressing the fervent prayer that a land where so many of our heroes lost their lives or their health, where under the most terrible and exacting conditions human loyalty and human service were poured out so lavishly in a great Cause, may never be allowed to become a menace to the future peaceful development of the world. I am sure my gallant boys, dead or living, would wish for no other or greater reward.

The East African campaign, fought over 160,000 square miles of some of the most difficult and unhealthy country on earth, had been not only a lightning stroke but a great success. It might have borne decisive results right at the start had my father's old friend, Jaap van Deventer, not been tardy in coming up to close a gap as arranged. Van Deventer arrived too late and the trap was sprung and Von Lettow lived to tell another tale. However, communications were virtually non-existent, and dense bush shut out the world. My father readily forgave him. For his services van Deventer was knighted after the war.

My father tells this story of an incident of the campaign which shows how completely unwilling he was ever to accept defeat. The retreating German army was streaming down the opposite bank in the bush between the mountains and the broad river.

To head him off before he took up very strong positions in the mountains, we had to get across the swollen river. It was a tactical requirement of great urgency. My father got along his Chief of Engineers and asked how long it would take his sappers, with everybody assisting, to put a bridge across the river for his troops, transport and guns. "Four weeks, sir," the Chief replied. "Can't you do it in less?" my father asked. "No, sir: four weeks is the bare minimum." This was depressing news. But while my father was still on the river a major in the Engineers came along. He put the same question to the major. The officer thought for a while. "Ten days, sir," he said. "Well then, go ahead," my father said, "I will give you all available help." In ten days, true to the major's word, they were across.

In a work by Brigadier-General J. J. Collyer, my father paid this tribute to his "real heroes of the East African campaign—the South African civilian soldiers": "They kept marching and fighting on. From the Lumi to the Rufiji, from the Indian Ocean to the Great Lakes they fought their way through, and in eleven months had mastered a huge stretch of primeval Africa. They stood a test almost beyond human endurance. . . . They have received scant recognition. . . . Let us not begrudge the heroes of the Western Front the glory that is theirs and that is South Africa's. But equally let us not forget that there was no less heroism in East Africa, no less endurance to the utmost limit of human nature, no less a contribution to the heroic record of South Africa. Thousands of them lie there, in the farthest north of our African Trek. . . ."

In his time my father must have written more forewords to books than any other person. They cover every branch of activity and invariably add much to the literary as well as the intrinsic value of the works. All have a distinct character and pleasant flavour. They differ considerably from the more formal forewords that usually adorn books.

This one to Crowe's work is a case in point. It is one of his best. But quite his nicest is the one to Deney's Reitz's *Commando*. No South African volume was considered complete without an introduction by my father. It took up much of his time, but he never grumbled.

XXXI SIDELIGHTS ON THE CAMPAIGN

WHAT my father, as a personality, meant to his troops is ably described by Francis Brett Young, who was a medical officer with the forces, in his *Marching on Tanga*: "I think the thing which most sustained our confidence and made us embark with such high hopes upon the second phase of the East African operations was our absolute confidence in the leadership of Smuts. That he was a fine strategist, the move on Moschi, in spite of the failure of the northern enveloping column, had shown us. Of his personal courage we had been assured by the incidents of the Lumi fight; but there was yet another factor—in this case one might almost have called it a personal attribute—in his success which demanded our confidence, and that was the luck which had followed him throughout his career. Everyone believed in his fortune no less than in his attainments; and it was this belief that sent us so happily on our way. . . . In this war with this General nothing was impossible."

After my father's bout of malaria at Luchomo Brett Young wrote: "Smuts was going back to the front. Again we began to feel as if the campaign were getting under way. The more I think of it the more I realise how the personality of that one man dominated the whole conduct of the war in East Africa. And I sometimes wondered what would have happened if fortune had not carried him safely through the risks he faced daily. . . . We should have lacked the enormous psychical asset which his masterful courage gave us, and I think that we should have endured our privations and our sickness with a less happy confidence."

My father had with him in East Africa the famous Major P. J. Pretorius, one of Africa's greatest elephant hunters. I heard him recount to some friends once how he came across Pretorius. In 1915 a German raider, the cruiser *Königsberg*, disappeared suddenly off the coast of East Africa, and it was suspected that it had taken refuge in the mouth of the Rufiji, but the Navy were unable to locate it. The first my father heard of it was, while he was still in the Union, getting a cable from the Admiralty, "Have you an elephant hunter Pretorius in South Africa? We would like him for a special mission." This was a bit vague and cryptic, but they managed to get hold of Pretorius and sent him up. The Rufiji near its mouth turns into a vast mangrove swamp with huge overhanging trees, large enough to shelter even a cruiser. Pretorius knew the Rufiji well for he had hunted and farmed there before the war. It did not take him long to locate the *Königsberg*, hidden about twenty miles inland. So the monitors *Severn* and *Mersey* were despatched, and from a great distance, with their massive guns, knocked out the raider. After that my father made Pretorius his chief scout. He was an absolutely deadly shot and the natives knew and venerated him. Under him he had about 150 native askaris, and with these he used literally to live well behind the enemy lines and send in valuable reports. My father says he was worth a small army in himself. Once the enemy tried to ambush him in some grass, but in a flash he had coolly shot eight of them and decamped.

I came across Pretorius in 1927, poaching elephants along the then undefined Rhodesian–Mozambique border near Pafuri, and again during the Abyssinian campaign in the Second World War, by which time, however, he had grown rather old for active service.

The *Königsberg* was to be very troublesome for a long while to come, for the enterprise of Lieutenant-Commander Schoenfeld had salvaged her ten 4·1-inch high-velocity guns. These were to be converted into mobile land guns and to outrange our own artillery throughout the campaign and to harass our men incessantly.

In July, 1916, a visit to his troops in East Africa by General Botha did much to cheer up his weary, fever-ridden armies. He had come up primarily to see his men, but also to have discussions with my father on the problems that beset him, as was his wont.

After the Kilimanjaro line fell, my father for a time made his headquarters high up on the mountain slopes in the old German boma at Moschi. From here on clear days he could see the smooth domed head of this most majestic mountain towering with its eternal cap of snow, into the blue heavens above. The prospect of climbing it fascinated him, but time never allowed him the opportunity to conquer Kibo. He spoke with a wistfulness all his life of his ambition to scale this massive old volcano. He never did find time, and it was left to my brother, returning from Cambridge in 1929, to climb to the summit and to put his name with the then dozen others in the little tin at Kaiser Wilhelm Spitze. But the mountain did not quite beat my father, for during the East African campaign in March, 1941, he flew over it in his Lodestar aircraft at a height of 21,000 feet and looked down upon the vast ice-plugged crater and giant glaciers. Of this he took a very fine Kodachrome colour film with his ciné. My wife was with him in the plane, and though she and the others felt dizzy with the altitude, she says my father moved about with his ciné quite unaffected and delighted with events. They had no oxygen apparatus with them, and this last-minute decision to fly over Kilimanjaro was merely a whim developed when he saw the mountain loom alongside in the clear air.

While my father was away in East Africa, and subsequently when he was in England, he never failed regularly to send each of us a brief scribbled postcard. My mother faithfully kept my East African postcards for me. They are as one would expect from a fond parent to a toddler, starting usually "Greetings, Jannie", having some short remark about big rivers or mountains or wild animals and usually ending, "Look well after Mamma, Love, Pappa."

For this touching paternal devotion, I regret my youthful filial affections left much to be desired, for a few months after his departure, I told my mother to write to him that I had now found a new "father" in my uncle, Jimmie Krige, and that he need not bother to return from the war! My mother did, and my father found it a huge joke and never failed to tell the story at my expense.

About this same tender age in life I had been much impressed by the bellowing and dust-pawing antics of a huge Friesland bull, Jan, we had on the farm. In a mood of great confidence I asked my father one day: "Which is the most powerful, God or Jan?" He has frequently quoted this question since as a problem in relative values. Years after, my young son Jan, who had just begun school and was much impressed by his teacher, asked my wife, equally naïvely, whom she thought cleverer, Oupa* or Mrs. Hibbins. This happened during my father's long fatal illness, and when my wife recounted the tale to him he found it most amusing, and had many a laugh over it.

When my father reminisced about East Africa, it was seldom about the war, but rather about the breathtaking beauty of parts of the country or of such homely matters as jigger fleas in one's toes. True, he did mention the building of the bridge across the river or the guns of the *Königsberg*, but he preferred to talk about the vast crater of Ngorongoro, of Kibo and Mawenzi, of the great craters Meru, Longonot, Longido and of the Pare and Usambara mountains. To him the interest and beauty of the country had transcended the horrors of war.

While my father was away in East Africa my mother got me a small khaki uniform, which I wore with great pride. On the shoulder epaulets were elephants sent by my father from East Africa. I called myself the "King of the Elephants". The Nationalist newspapers called me a damn Khaki and were so annoyed that they did me the privilege of putting me in their cartoons. Eventually I grew tired of this prickly uniform, and all the fuss and saluting, and got rid of it.

From East Africa my father brought back his camp stretcher, over which a mosquito-proof canopy of gauze and canvas fitted. To this contraption I took such a liking that I insisted for a long while on sleeping in it next to my father in his room. When I grew tired of it eventually, it was taken over by Fido the Airedale and subsequently by Jackie the monkey. The green Vauxhall car which he had used in the campaign he also brought back, together with George Hodgson, his chauffeur for many years.

My father also used to recount, with a chuckle, stories of his dinner parties on the campaign, when he invited his senior officers to bully beef and hard tack. Their faces could never quite hide the look of surprise as this frugal repast was ushered in.

In the early nineteen-thirties my father attended a dinner in London in honour of von Lettow Vorbeck. It was a pleasant affair at which mutual compliments were paid. The design was also to improve relations with Germany.

My father has always had a high regard for von Lettow, and

* Grandfather.

thereafter they remained friends. After the Second World War my father sent the old man food parcels—which were much appreciated. They corresponded on occasions, and after my father's death von Lettow wrote my mother a most touching letter.

XXXII WAR IN EUROPE

IN mid-January, 1917, while still on the Rufiji, my father was recalled to the Union. Here he was told that he would have to proceed to England immediately to attend the first Imperial Conference, for which Botha himself could not be spared. General Hoskins succeeded my father. Von Lettow was still at large, using the vastness of Africa for his elusive guerilla tactics. He was never captured and surrendered voluntarily upon hearing of the armistice.

Back in the Union my father spoke in glowing terms of the conquest of East Africa: "Through our own efforts and our sacrifice we have secured a voice in the ultimate disposal of this sub-continent. . . . We have followed in the steps of the Voortrekkers and pioneers. . . ." To those well disposed, these were stirring words, but his opponents scoffed at this British imperialist, this reincarnation of Rhodes, who compared himself with the Voortrekkers. He had got too big for his boots. Let him rather go to England, where they liked him so much, and stay there.

To those who jeered that he had grown tired of his own small country he retorted: "I have heard it stated that South Africa is now too small for me. I do not want to speak personally: it is not a time now to speak personally. But let me say this, that South Africa is not too small for me, and that every drop of blood and every bit of courage and determination I have in me will go to the service of my country. Whether it is here in the Union, whether it is away in East Africa, or whether it is in the Council

Chamber of the Empire, I pray that I may have the strength to do my duty with courage and determination, and I trust that nothing I shall ever do will injure the position of South Africa."

In the Union Parliament Merriman condemned the ingratitude of the Nationalists, after all my father had done for the Boer cause in the Boer War and after. "That is what he did for you, his own people, and for that we remember him; for, thank God, we English are men enough to acknowledge the gallant deeds of our enemies."

On March 17 my father arrived in London. He arrived in England's deepest hour of gloom. The revolution in Russia had almost attained its climax; the Tsar and his family had been murdered, and the defeated Russian armies were about to desert the Allies. The unlimited German U-boat menace was in full stride and threatening to beat England to her knees. Serious mutinies were occurring in the exhausted French armies and there had been changes in the Government and the Army. The German forces were as yet unchecked and were slowly battering to a pulp the flower of England and France. German morale was high and her belief in ultimate victory explicit.

The United States was yet to make its belated appearance.

By contrast to his mixed reception in South Africa, England hailed him as the hero of the hour, the conqueror in the first big successes of the war. The propaganda value of this former Boer general, now fighting for Britain, was exploited to the full. England needed cheering news. Into this world of weariness, dejection and disaster my father burst with a new message of hope and encouragement. He was referred to in such eulogistic terms as "the most conspicuous figure in Great Britain . . . a remarkable combination of talents not usually found in the same person, unless, indeed, that person belongs to the small and select class of which the Cæsars and Cromwells, and the Napoleons are the outstanding types".

Mr. Churchill wrote: "At this moment there arrives in England from the outer marches of the Empire a new and altogether extraordinary man. . . . The stormy and hazardous roads he has travelled by would fill all the acts and scenes of a drama. He has warred against us—well we knew it. He has quelled rebellion against our own flag with unswerving loyalty and unfailing

180

shrewdness. He has led raids at desperate odds and conquered provinces by scientific strategy. . . . His astonishing career and his versatile achievements are only the index of a profound sagacity and a cool, far-reaching comprehension. . . ."

My father was overwhelmed by the warmth of the reception and the spontaneous homage of the people. He brushed aside the adulation, protesting that he was only a simple Boer.

On the 20th of March, Lloyd George introduced him to the Imperial War Cabinet as "one of the most brilliant generals in this war". This Cabinet consisted of visiting Dominion Prime Ministers who were attending the Imperial Conference, together with members of the British War Cabinet. It was a large body devoted primarily to an exchange of views, without any direct power. Britain has always believed in the idea that it was sound policy to have Prime Ministers' conferences, where, as my father said, "the Prime Ministers can blow off steam". This safety-valve was an integral part of the Commonwealth system.

In this Imperial War Cabinet my father soon shone forth in his full brilliance.

Lloyd George, the fiery Celt, had succeeded Mr. Asquith in the Premiership only a short while before.

Up to now the war had been far from a series of unbroken triumphs for the Allies. Hardly had hostilities been opened when the French and Belgians were in full retreat, as also the handful of British that had crossed the Channel. The Germans were sitting in Brussels and clamouring at the gates of the French capital. Shortly after, the Russians were decisively defeated at Tannenberg and in October the Belgian Cabinet fled to France. Britain had had her blooding at Ypres. In 1915 she had failed at the Dardanelles, Poland was ravished and countless Allied troops were dying on the Western Front. Italy, after a long delay, made a disastrous entry into the fray. Bulgaria decided the easiest prey was Serbia, and Britain and France left half a million men to languish abortively at Salonika.

1916 brought no better luck. A combined offensive failed. There was Verdun, the Somme, Roumania's failure, huge losses by Russia and Italy, and the inconclusive naval clash at Jutland.

There were strikes and mutinies and changes in the Government and the forces. Kitchener was drowned on the way to

Russia. Churchill paid for the Dardanelles. French and Jellicoe went, and the Chief of Staff, Robertson. So did Austen Chamberlain and Carson. Wilson was talking of war aims. Ludendorf had sanctioned "unlimited" submarine warfare. There was the Irish Rebellion and Roger Casement.

The *Lusitania* had gone to the bottom two years before, and still America was struggling to make up her mind.

Two weeks after his arrival my father was entrusted with a mission to the French Prime Minister Painlevé and to the King of the Belgians. The visits were exploratory to see what the minimum demands on Germany would be. Painlevé was for an early and easy peace. When my father pointed out that South Africa could not be quite so broad-minded over South-West Africa the case fell through. Albert of the Belgians was worried only about Belgium itself. He had been unnerved by events.

At the end of April my father paid a special visit to Headquarters in France. On his return he submitted to the War Cabinet a lengthy survey of the "General Strategic and Military Situation and Particularly that on the Western Front". While stressing here that Germany had to be defeated he stated:

> I repeat here my frank opinion that that will not be merely or even entirely a military defeat. A certain substantial measure of military success will be necessary and must be achieved not only because it is necessary for our ends, but also as a lasting lesson to Prussian militarism.
> But greater forces are fighting for us than our armies. This war will be settled largely by the imponderable—by the forces of public opinion all over the world which have been mobilised by German outrages . . . we should ever strive to keep this world opinion on our side and not be deflected by German methods of barbarism. . . .

> In Salonika, where half a million Allied troops were languishing in what Germany termed her finest internment camp, my father advocated a contraction of the front and the release of all those not required for a small defensive line.

> Possibilities of offensive action which at earlier stages of the War were open to us are no longer possible and several brilliant ideas will not now be put to the test of trial. On the contrary even our present fields of operation may have to be revised and contracted. . . .

Next in importance to the detachment of Bulgaria from Central Europe would be the detachment of Turkey, which might become feasible if the Russian Government would definitely waive their rights under the Bosphorus agreement. The danger, however, of Russia going out of the War on some pretext or other is so serious and would have such far-reaching consequences that I do not think we should moot the question with her at present. . . . I therefore proceed on the assumption that our campaign against the Turkish Empire will continue in full vigour.

As regards Mesopotamia, we have achieved all that we were aiming at and can now consolidate our position and make it impregnable to any future counter-attack. . . .

The Palestine campaign presents very interesting military and even political possibilities. As it progresses to Jerusalem and Damascus, it will threaten the Turkish Empire far more gravely than anything we have so far undertaken except the Dardanelles and Gallipoli campaign. . . .

There remains for consideration the far more important and complicated question of the Western Front. I have always looked upon it as a misfortune, no doubt inevitable under the circumstances, that the British forces have become so entirely absorbed by this front. The result now is that in a theatre mainly of the enemy's choosing, the two most important armies of the Entente are locked up in front of almost impregnable positions. It is essential to our ends that we should keep the initiative and offensive, but both are enormously difficult. . . . I have no confidence that we can break through the enemy lines on any large scale. . . .

We have entered the War in a very small way with a small military force and not as a principal combatant but rather as an auxiliary to France. This fact was reflected in our general military policy, which was of necessity one of great modesty and almost complete subordination to that of France . . . we should, after the present offensive, resume the independence of our military direction. . . . The impressions which I brought from the Front have since been reinforced by the rumour that several important members of the French Government do not approve of General Nivelle's present offensive and consider a defensive policy the wisest one for the French Army to pursue. . . . I feel the danger of a purely defensive policy so gravely that I would make the following suggestions in case the French carry out such a policy.

He suggested that in this contingency we should ask the French to take over a portion of our line and that we should concentrate our forces further to the north and endeavour to "recover the northern coast of Belgium and drive the enemy from Zeebrugge and Ostend. This task will be most formidable. . . . But however difficult the task, something will have to be done to continue our offensive. . . . I see more advantages in an offensive intended to recover the Belgian coast and deprive the enemy of two advanced submarine bases, than in the present offensive. . . ." Sir William Robertson, the Chief of Staff, had said that France appeared unwilling to continue offensive operations. If that was true it would mean a drastic change in the military situation.

Lloyd George had been impressed by my father's advocacy of pushing on with the Palestine campaign. It was perhaps natural that he should have offered my father the command of that theatre. He writes:

In reviewing the course of this [Palestine] campaign on 23rd April, the War Cabinet came to the conclusion that it was desirable to introduce more resolute leadership into the command of the Egyptian Expeditionary Force. . . . In regard to the choice of a successor to Sir Archibald Murray, it was pointed out that General Smuts had expressed very decided views as to the strategical importance of Palestine to the future of the British Empire. He would therefore be likely to prosecute a campaign in that quarter with great determination, and there was a strong feeling that he would be one of the most suitable selections for the Chief Command of the Egyptian Expeditionary Force.

On the other hand, the War Cabinet were aware that there was a growing opinion in favour of the retention of General Smuts in a central position in this country, with a view to the utilisation of his great qualities in the higher conduct of the war.

General Smuts was a standing disproof of the theory tenaciously held by the British War Office (despite the classic example of Oliver Cromwell to the contrary) that no one was competent to hold high military command without long training in the regular army.

The career of General Smuts furnishes a practical demonstration of the absurdity. . . . In East Africa he had shown himself a brilliantly efficient, resourceful and energetic Commander-in-Chief of our forces. Had he consented to take in hand the Palestine campaign, I have not the least doubt that it would, under his charge, have been one of our most successful efforts.

My father thought the matter over carefully and what Sir

William Robertson had to say confirmed his conclusions. It was probable, as the past had so richly proved, that Palestine would merely develop into one of the many forgotten fronts, with too few men to carry out decisive manœuvres and that inevitable stagnation would set in. It might even develop into a defensive retreat. There were perhaps others who could handle such tactics better. He felt he could serve a more useful purpose here in Britain at the nerve centre, where he could watch this campaign and help wherever possible.

To Lloyd George he wrote on 31st May, 1917: "The most careful consideration has merely strengthened my first impression that the Palestine campaign will be a mistake unless at least Jerusalem is made a reasonable certainty, and all the reinforcements necessary for that purpose are assured. A limited advance which stopped short of the capture of Jerusalem, would serve no particular purpose, and might easily be a disappointment to the public and appear as a fresh failure. . . ."

$$\star \qquad \star \qquad \star \qquad \star \qquad \star$$

The time for my father's return to South Africa was approaching. The Prime Minister had, however, decided that England could not, under any circumstances, afford to lose the services of this man.

Lloyd George says: "I retained General Smuts here by making him a member of the War Cabinet—a step which secured general approval, though it called forth some indignant protests from members of my Ministry, who were horrified at the unprecedented step I was taking. Mr. Walter Long deemed it necessary to enter a protest as Colonial Secretary. In his opinion 'it was quite clear that Smuts could only join for Military questions. This appears to raise all sorts of difficulties. . . .' "

The professional soldiers were, however, to complain that my father was merely a politician in the guise of a general and that he was therefore hardly competent to preside over matters of military strategy. Lloyd George quickly silenced them: "That General Smuts should be classed as 'no soldier' is surely a consummate example of the working of the professional military mind. True, he had not devoted all his life to soldiering: neither had Sir Douglas Haig's Chief of the Staff, Sir Herbert Lawrence.

Those who had campaigned against Smuts in the South African War could hardly deny his remarkable military quality. And in the Great War, after a brilliant campaign in German South-West Africa, he commanded during 1916 our forces in East Africa in the fight with von Lettow Vorbeck."

My father took his seat in the British War Cabinet in June. This was a select body of six men who were Britain's brains behind the war. In them was vested the supreme power. Lloyd George was chairman, and the other members were Curzon, Milner, Carson, Bonar Law and Barnes, with Maurice Hankey as Secretary. There was only provision for six members; my father was the seventh, a sort of minister without portfolio, but with powers equal to the others. In truth, it was impossible to legalise or define his position, because he was still Minister of Defence of South Africa and not a British Minister. Both he and Botha had decided that he could not accept a ministership in Britain in view of the political implications. So in the fine informality of the British system he was just a member of the War Cabinet, supreme military tribunal of Britain. He was also the only colonial sitting on that body. In this position he derived no pay and made it clear that he was to deal purely with military matters and not with internal politics.

My father told Colonel Repington after his appointment: "I am going to advise on military matters and will steer clear of politics." Christopher Addison confirms that he "was at all times very scrupulous lest he should become involved in any differences of opinion or controversies that were of a strictly domestic character". Colonel House, Woodrow Wilson's special envoy, wrote on 13th November, 1917: "Nearly everyone I have met has asked me to be certain to meet Smuts. He has grown to be the lion of the hour. . . . He is one of the few men I have met in the Government who does not feel tired. He's alert, energetic and forceful."

Suggesting that Lloyd George would be wise to make my father a member of the Cabinet, Winston Churchill told Lord Riddell that he was "the only unwounded statesman of outstanding ability in the Empire", meaning, as Lord Riddell says, "the only one who is fresh and bright, unwounded mentally and physically".

The majority of my father's colleagues did not really impress. Milner he grew to like and Lloyd George he admired tremendously. "Lloyd George is more than fascinating. He has genius. His mind is brilliant, energetic, resourceful, and courageous without limit. . . History will show him the biggest Englishman of them all."

F. S. Oliver wrote in a letter to his brother: "I regard the taking in of Smuts to the War Cabinet as a most important step. So far as pure intellect goes he is the superior of any member at present on it; and by intellect I don't mean only the power of understanding what is written . . . but a curious and more rare quality of seeing into the very heart of a subject, coupled with the further and still rarer quality, in combination with the foregoing, of being able to state clearly what he has seen. . . ."

Lloyd George in his War Memoirs gives this description of my father: "General Smuts, the gifted and versatile Dutchman, who could be safely trusted to examine into the intricacies of any of our multifarious problems and unravel and smooth them out. . . .

"General Smuts was one of the most remarkable personalities of his time—that fine combination of intellect and human sympathy which constitutes the understanding man. . . . His rare gifts of mind and heart were strengthening elements in this hour of savage temper and pitiless carnage."

Whatever my father's position in the War Cabinet, it worked.

XXXIII THE COMMONWEALTH

ON 15th May, 1917, a banquet was held in the Royal Gallery of the House of Lords in honour of my father. This was a most unusual distinction and the first accorded a Dominion statesman. Lord French, of Boer War days, presided and the guests included the mighty of the land. Milner sat on my father's right. French paid tribute to my father's prowess as a soldier. My father told about Moordenaars Poort and the train with French he had let pass in 1901.

The rest of the speech was devoted to a definition of the Commonwealth and its affairs, which stands to-day as clearly as it did thirty-five years ago.

Speaking of the great convulsion that was shaking the world with its multiplicity of problems he said:

It is inevitable where you have so many difficulties to face that one should forget to keep before oneself the situation as a whole; and yet this is very necessary. It is most essential that even in this struggle, even when Europe is looming so much before our eyes, we should keep before us and see steadily the problem of the whole situation. I would ask you not to forget in these times the British Commonwealth of Nations. . . .

It is apparently a very inopportune moment, but the calling together of the Conference has helped to turn attention once more to that aspect of the whole situation which is so important to us. It is not only Europe we have to consider, but the future of the great Commonwealth to which we all belong. This Commonwealth is peculiarly constituted. It is scattered over the whole world. It is not a compact territory, and it is dependent for its very existence on world-wide communications —communications which must be maintained or this Empire goes to pieces.

In the years of peace behind us we see what has happened. Everywhere on your communications Germany has settled down; everywhere on your communications you will find a German colony or a German settlement, small or large; and the day might come when you would be in jeopardy through your lines of communication being cut. One of the by-products of the war has been that the whole world outside of Europe has been cleared of the enemy. Germany has been swept from all the seas and all the continents except Central Europe. . . . You are now in this position: that once more you can consider the problem of your future as a whole.

When peace comes to be made you have all these cards in your hand, and you can go carefully into the question of what is necessary for your future security and the future safety of the Empire, and can say what you are going to keep and what you are going to give away. I hope that when the time comes—I am speaking for myself and expressing nobody's opinion but my own—when the time comes for peace to be made we shall bear in mind not only Central Europe, but the whole

British Empire. As far as we are concerned, we do not wish this war to have been fought in vain. We have not fought for material gain or for territory, but we have fought for security in the future. If we attach any value to this group of nations which composes the British Empire, then in settling the terms of peace we shall have to look to its future security and safety. . . .

I think that we are inclined to make mistakes in thinking about this group of nations to which we belong, because too often we think about it as one State. We are not a State. The British Empire is much more than a State. I think the very expression "Empire" is misleading, because it makes people think we are one community, to which the word "Empire" can appropriately be applied. Germany is an Empire. Rome was an Empire. India is an Empire. But we are a system of nations. We are not a State, but a community of States and nations. We are far greater than any Empire which has ever existed, and by using this ancient expression we really disguise the main fact that our whole position is different, and that we are not one State or nation or empire, but a whole world by ourselves, consisting of many nations, of many States, and all sorts of communities under one flag.

We are a system of States, and not a stationary system, but a dynamic evolving system, always going forward to new destinies. Take the position of that system to-day. Here you have the United Kingdom with a number of Crown Colonies. Besides that you have a large Protectorate like Egypt, an Empire by itself. Then you have a great Dependency like India, also an Empire by itself, where civilisation has existed from time immemorial, where we are trying to see how East and West can work together.

These are enormous problems, but beyond them we come to the so-called Dominions, independent in their government, which have been evolved on the principles of your free constitutional system into almost independent States, which all belong to this community of nations, and which I prefer to call "the British Commonwealth of Nations".

You can see that no political ideas which have been evolved in the past will apply to this world which is comprised in the British Empire; and any name we have yet found for this group is insufficient. The man who will find a proper name for this system will, I think, do real service to the Empire.

The question is: How are you going to provide for the future government of this Commonwealth? An entirely new problem is presented. If you want to see how great it is, you must indulge in comparison. Look at the United States. There you find what is essentially one nation, not perhaps in the fullest sense, but what is more and more growing into one nation; one big State consisting, no doubt, of separate parts, but all linked up into one big continuous area. The United States had to solve the problem which this presented, and they discovered the federal solution—a solution which provides subordinate treatment for the subordinate parts, but one national Federal Government and Parliament for the whole.

Compare with that State the enormous system which is comprised in the British Empire. You can see at once that a solution which has been found practicable in the case of the United States will never work in the case of a system such as we are comprising a world by itself.

What I feel in regard to all the empires of the past, and even in regard to the United States, is that the effort has always been towards forming one nation. All the empires we have known in the past and that exist to-day are founded on the idea of assimilation, of trying to force human material into one mould. Your whole idea and basis is entirely different. You do not want to standardise the nations of the British Empire; you want to develop them towards greater, fuller nationality. These communities, the offspring of the Mother Country, or territories like my own, which have been annexed after the vicissitudes of war, must not be moulded on any one pattern. You want them to develop freely on the principles of self-government, and therefore your whole idea is different from anything that has ever existed before. That is the fundamental fact we have to bear in mind—that this British Commonwealth of Nations does not stand for standardisation or denationalisation, but for the fuller, richer, and more various life of all the nations comprised in it.

Even the nations which have fought against it, like my own, must feel that their cultural interests, their language, their religion, are as safe and secure under the British flag as those of the children of your own household and your own blood. It is only in proportion as this is realised that you will fulfil the true mission which is yours. Therefore it seems to me that there is only one solution, and that is a solution supplied by our past traditions—the traditions of freedom, self-government, and of the fullest development for all constituent parts of the Empire.

The question arises: How are you going to keep this Commonwealth of Nations together? If there is to be this full development towards a more varied and richer life among our nations, how are you going to keep them together? It seems to me that there are two potent factors that you must rely upon for the future. The first is your hereditary kingship, the other is our Conference system. I have seen some

speculations recently in the newspapers about the position of the kingship in this country—speculations by people who, I am sure, have not
thought of the wider issues that are at stake. You cannot make a
republic of the British Commonwealth of Nations.

In regard to the present system of Imperial Conferences, it will be
necessary to devise better machinery for common consultation than
we have at present. So far, we have relied on Imperial Conferences
which meet once in every four years or thereabouts. However useful
has been the work done at these Conferences, they have not, in my
opinion, been a complete success.

What is necessary is that there shall be called together the most
important rulers of the Empire, say, once a year, to discuss matters
which concern all parts of the Empire in common, in order that causes
of friction and misunderstanding may be prevented or removed. We
also need a meeting like that in order to lay a common policy in
common matters concerning the Empire as a whole, and to determine
the true orientation of our common Imperial policy. There is, for
instance, foreign policy on which the fate of the Empire might from
time to time depend. Some such method of procedure must lead to
very important results and very great changes.

You cannot settle a common foreign policy for the whole of the
British Empire without changing that policy very much from what
it has been in the past, because the policy will have to be, for one thing,
far simpler. In the other parts of the Empire we do not understand
diplomatic finesse. If our foreign policy is going to rest not only on the
basis of our Cabinet here, but, finally, on the whole of the British
Empire, it will have to be a simpler policy, a far more intelligible
policy, and a policy which will in the end lead to less friction and
greater safety.

Far too much stress has been laid in the past on instruments of
government. People are inclined to forget that the world is growing
more democratic, and that public opinion and the forces finding
expression in public opinion are going to be far more powerful than
they have been in the past. Where you build up a common patriotism
and a common ideal, the instrument of government will not be a thing
that matters so much as the spirit which actuates the whole.

XXXIV AFRICAN PROBLEMS

IN the Savoy Hotel on 22nd May, 1917, under the chairman-ship of Lord Selborne, my father delivered a memorable ad-dress on African problems:

When I look around to-night and see all who are sitting here at this table, I feel, and you all feel, that we are lifted out of the world of commonplace into a strange world. We feel that whatever the past has been, whatever mistakes we have made—and we have all made mistakes—whatever services we have been able to render to our South Africa, a kind Providence has intervened and has woven all those mistakes and all those services into a strange and wonderful texture which we call the history of South Africa and of which we are very proud. When we look at that wonderful history we are all cheered and encouraged to move forward in the hope that as our task has not been too difficult for us in the past it may not prove entirely beyond us in the future.

But in South Africa we always feel that there is something more. With us it is never a question of merely material progress and of prosperity, although we are always very eager to have those good things too; we always feel that under our peculiar historical and racial conditions there are very large problems in the background which always press for solution. And that is what gives profound interest to life in South Africa. We have made very great progress in recent years. If you remember that it was within seven years of the Boer War that we had all the British Colonies of South Africa in one great Union you will see how great and rapid that progress has been. But although we have achieved political union, our aim has always been far greater; we have aimed not only at political union, but also at national unity; and when you have to deal with very hard-headed races, such as our people in South Africa, both English and Dutch, you can well under-stand that it takes more than seven years to bring about that con-summation. We have grave difficulties in this respect. We have different racial strains, different political tendencies.

We have people in South Africa who prefer isolation, who prefer to stand aside from the great currents that are carrying South Africa to her new and greater destiny. These are not merely Dutch; many of them are English. We have English fellow-citizens who will always

He loved to play with children. Grandchildren Sibella, Richard
and Petronella Clark

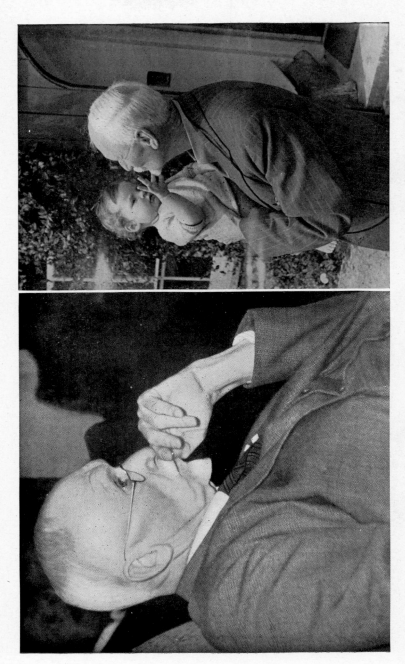

General Smuts in typical attitude listening to a Debate—1941

His beard never failed to intrigue his grand-children. With Sibella Clark—1944

remain English, to whom even the sunshine and the wide spaces of South Africa are not sufficient to bring about the great transformation of soul. We look forward patiently in such cases to the next generation. We have also a large section of my own people, the Dutch people in South Africa, who think that the best policy is for them to stand aside and to remain in isolation. They think that in that way they will be better able to preserve their language, their traditions, and their national type, and that they will in that way not be swallowed up and be submerged by the new currents. They point to the precedent in Canada, where French-Canadians are also standing aside from the general current of Canadian life and national development for the same reasons.

The policy General Botha and his associates have stood for is that we must have national unity in South Africa as the one true basis of future stability and strength—and that national unity is entirely consistent with the preservation of our language, our traditions, our cultural interests, and all that is dear to us in our past. The view we have taken is this, that the different elements in our white populations ought really to be used to build up a stronger and more powerful nation than would have been possible if we had consisted of purely one particular strain. All great Imperial peoples really are a mixture of various stocks. Your own history is one of the completest proofs of that doctrine, and it is only in recent years that this remarkable doctrine of the pure race has come into vogue, and largely in Germany. The man who preached the doctrine most eloquently is a Germanised Englishman, Houston Chamberlain. The doctrine is to the effect that the governing races of the world are pure races, and that they simply debase themselves and become degenerate if mixed with alien blood. They must remain pure, and in so far as they do so they will play a great part in the world. It is more than hinted at that the German race must guide the world because it is one of these pure races. What arrant nonsense!

We do not pretend in South Africa to listen to these siren voices. We want to create a blend out of the various nationalities and to create a new South African nation out of our allied racial stock, and if we succeed in doing that we shall achieve a new nationality embracing and harmonising our various traits and blending them all into a richer national type than could otherwise have been achieved. The ideal of national unity means a continuous effort towards better relations, towards mutual respect and forbearance, towards co-operation, and that breadth of view and character which will be the most potent instrument for dealing with our other problems. Although in South

Africa our national progress is marked by the ox-waggon and not by the train or aeroplane, I am sure in the end we shall achieve success and a new nationhood.

And this is all the more important because in South Africa we are not merely a white man's country. Our problem of white racial unity is being solved in the midst of the black environment in South Africa. Whether we shall succeed in solving that other larger question of the black man's future depends on many factors on which no one could feel very much assurance at present. We know that on the African Continent at various times there have been attempts at civilisation. We read of a great Saracen civilisation in Central Africa, and of the University of Timbuctoo, to which students came from other parts of the world. Rhodesia also shows signs of former civilisation.

Where are those civilisations now? They have all disappeared and barbarism once more rules over the land and makes the thoughtful man nervous about the white man's future in Southern Africa. There are many people in South Africa—and not very foolish people either —who do not feel certain that our white experiment will be a permanent success, or that we shall ever succeed in making a white man's land of Southern Africa; but, at any rate, we mean to press on with the experiment. It has now been in progress for some two hundred and fifty years, as you know, and perhaps the way we have set about it may be the right way. Former civilisations in Africa have existed mostly for the purpose of exploiting the native populations, and in that way, and probably also through inter-mixture of blood, carried in them the seeds of decay.

We have started by creating a new white base in South Africa and to-day we are in a position to move forward towards the North and the civilisation of the African Continent. Our problem is a very difficult one, however; quite unique in its way. In the United States there is a similar problem of black and white with the negro population. But there you have had an overwhelming white population with a smaller negro element in the midst of it. In South Africa the situation is reversed. There you have an overwhelming black population with a small white population which has got a footing there and which has been trying to make that footing secure for more than two centuries.

. . . With us there are certain axioms now in regard to the relations of white and black; and the principal one is "no intermixture of blood between the two colours". It is probably true that earlier civilisations have largely failed because that principle was never recognised, civilising races being rapidly submerged in the quicksands of the African blood. It has now become an accepted axiom in our dealings with the natives that it is dishonourable to mix white and black blood.

We have settled another axiom, and that is that in all our dealings with the natives we must build our practice on what I believe Lord Cromer has called the granite bedrock of the Christian moral code. Honesty, fair-play, justice, and the ordinary Christian virtues must be the basis of all our relations with the natives. We don't always practise them. We don't always practise that exalted doctrine, but the vast bulk of the white population in South Africa believe sincerely in that doctrine as correct and true; they are convinced that they must stick to the fundamental Christian morality if they want to do their duty to the natives and make a success of their great country. Of course, this doctrine applies to other countries besides South Africa.

We were not aware of the great military value of the natives until this war. This war has been an eye-opener in many new directions. It will be a serious question for the statesman of the Empire and Europe whether they are going to allow a state of affairs like that to be possible, and to become a menace not only to Africa, but perhaps to Europe itself. I hope that one of the results of this war will be some arrangement or convention among the nations interested in Central Africa by which the military training of natives in that area will be prevented, as we have prevented it in South Africa. It can well be foreseen that armies may yet be trained there, which under proper leading might prove a danger to civilisation itself. . . .

You will have further questions in regard to the territorial settlement of Central Africa which will follow the war. We are now, after the conquest of the German Colonies, in the happy position of having a through land route from Egypt to the Cape. We are in the secure position of having no danger on the Atlantic seaboard or on the Indian seaboard to our very essential sea communications as an Empire. What will happen to these communications after the settlement will depend on that settlement itself, but I hope it will be borne in mind that East Africa gives us not only this through land communication from one end of the Continent to the other, but that East Africa also ensures to us the safety of the sea route round the Cape and the sea route through the Red Sea to the East. It is a matter of gratification to us South Africans here to-night that South African troops have taken such a large and leading share in securing these extremely valuable results. . .

We shall always have a difficult question not only in Central but in Southern Africa. Unlike other British Dominions, our future as a white civilisation is not assured for the reasons which I have given.

Many thoughtful people are in doubt about our future, and in any case no cheap and easy victory will be scored in South Africa.

We know we have tremendous problems to contend with. We know we have tremendous tasks before us, and in dealing with these problems and in trying to fulfil these tasks one generation of South Africans after another will brace its nerves and strengthen its intellect and broaden its mind and character. Although these difficulties may seem to us, and indeed are, grave perils to our future, I trust that in the long run these difficulties may prove a blessing in disguise and may prove to have afforded the training school for a large-minded, broad-minded, magnanimous race, capable not only of welding together different racial elements into a new and richer national type, but capable of dealing as no other race in history has ever dealt with the question of the relations between black and white. . . .

XXXV THE WESTERN FRONT

ONE of the few bright spots in the dark array that faced the Allies in 1917 was the internal weakness of Austria. War weariness, food shortages, labour troubles and dissension on military matters had made her a progressively more uncertain partner among the Central Powers. Both the Emperor Karl and his Bourbon wife were using their influence in the cause of peace and it looked as though Austria was almost ripe for a break-away.

A preparatory contact had been arranged between Count von Mensdorff and a British Envoy in Copenhagen, but under fear of a suspected leakage the meeting never took place.

In December, in the face of violent opposition from the Foreign Office, Lloyd George decided to hold further talks with Mensdorff and my father was chosen as the British delegate. He did not view the prospects of detaching Austria highly, certainly not unless Italy waived her claims to Austrian territory. But he felt that the talks might serve a useful purpose. Accordingly they met in

Geneva, my father travelling under the name of Mr. Ashworth. Von Weden, the German Ambassador, says Mensdorff's instructions from the Czernin were to find out if peace was possible for both Austria and Germany. My father insisted that he had only come to study the problem of Austria.

Colonel Repington says Briand's version of the talks was that my father put a number of questions to Mensdorff to which he wanted definite "yes" or "no" answers. My father's version was:* "I spent two days with Mensdorff. The mission was afterwards held to be a failure. But the mission was neither a failure nor not a failure. The object was not to make peace, but to find out if there was an opportunity to make peace. Von Mensdorff and I went over the same old ground, and the longer I stayed the clearer I became that von Mensdorff might want to know if I had anything to say to him. But he had nothing to say to me. He never made those proposals he had spoken of in his messages. He was not in a position to negotiate at all. Austria was absolutely held by Germany.

"So I came back and reported to the Prime Minister. I was satisfied no loophole existed for a peace with Austria. That was what we wanted to know. That was what I had gone to find out. . . . There the whole business ended. . . ."

There was afterwards severe criticism of the Government especially by the Socialists, at having sent a simple Boer like my father, unversed in the ways of diplomacy, to cross swords with a trained diplomat like Mensdorff.

That my father was much depressed during these wearying days of the war are revealed in a letter dated 6th August, 1917, to Professor Wolstenholme, an old Cambridge friend. Yet his faith in the future remained unshaken: "I have faith in the ultimate Good of the Universe," he wrote, "in the undercurrents whose drift is in the direction of progress and the slow gradual perfecting of the soul and mechanism of Good.

"But for that Faith I would be of all men most miserable, especially in these sad times, when the human race suffers in a more acute and concentrated form than at any previous time."

By the autumn of 1917 the Allies were weary of the war, France even more so than Britain. America had only just entered. After

* Quoted from Mrs. Sarah Gertrude Millin.

the Nivelle setback the French were despondent and nearly broken. They seemed to be losing countless men without achieving anything. For three years they had borne the heat and burden of the fighting. There had been no more dogged and courageous troops than these Frenchmen. Up to now France had lost nearly two million men. Nivelle was the last straw and there had been mutiny and insubordination. The French had grown tired of dying: tired in fact of the whole war.

The French sectors had grown static and their leaders were set on a costly policy of war by attrition. At a stretch, the mood might turn into outright defeat, or peace at almost any price.

Britain was now shouldering the main burden of the fighting. She had reached the peak of her military potential.

But at sea the submarines were sinking too much shipping and Admiral Jellicoe had warned that these losses could not be faced indefinitely. Something had to be done to the German bases at Zeebrugge and Ostend on the Belgian coast if shipping was to survive during the coming year.

Haig and Robertson, too, on the Army side, decided that something drastic was to be done on the Western Front if France was to be saved from imminent collapse.

To this purpose, Haig, Jellicoe and Robertson put before the War Cabinet plans for an operation to punch a hole through the front and to sweep around and clear the coast of Belgium. The War Cabinet were not impressed by this scheme, but they felt the urgency of immediate action. They had already had sufficient experience of this deeply-defended type of trench warfare to realise that big or quick advances were impossible. My father had gone over the plans carefully with Haig and Robertson and had decided that it was worth an attempt. He put his case to the Cabinet. Lloyd George was cautious; Milner and Bonar Law were sceptical. But at last he convinced them, all agreeing that it was worth a trial. Haig undertook it under these conditions. Lloyd George, possibly influenced by Wilson, insists that Haig and Robertson misled them purposely on many points and withheld much unfavourable information in the knowledge of which the Cabinet would never have sanctioned the plan.

What also facilitated its acceptance was the fact that just at this time Italy had suffered a disastrous defeat at Caporetto, and she, too, had now to be impressed by Allied strength if she was not to drop out of the fight. After the news of the disaster of the Italian armies at Caporetto, Lloyd George invited my father to accompany him to Rome for discussions on future policy. "The Rome Conference saved Italy," says Lloyd George.

One thing is certain, that had the War Cabinet or my father known the true position of weakness in the French army after Nivelle, they would not have risked the Haig plan. The battles came to be known as the Passchendaele Offensive. As a single military manœuvre it was a disaster. But it had broader aspects. Lloyd George spoke scathingly of it. I remember my father doing likewise. They were not criticising the decision to start the offensive, but Haig's failure to call it off once he saw that none of his objectives were being attained.

Lloyd George said: "Passchendaele was indeed one of the greatest disasters of the War, and I never think of it without feeling grateful for the combination of seamanship and luck which enabled us to survive and repair its unutterable folly." ". . . with the Somme and Verdun it will always rank as one of the most gigantic, tenacious, grim, futile and bloody fights ever waged in the history of war. Each of the battles lasted for months. None of them attained the object for which they were fought."

The offensive corresponded with the onset of the rains. The mightiest artillery preparation of the war was laid down on the German positions. Over twenty-five million shells were fired during the first forty days. The result was not to dislodge the Germans, but to turn the front into the most churned-up area of mud of the whole war. A competent observer describes it thus: "After our preliminary bombardment . . . the whole surface of the ground consisted of nothing but a series of over-lapping shell craters, half-full of yellow, slimy water. Through falling into these ponds hundreds upon hundreds of unwounded men, while advancing to the attack, lost their lives by drowning. . . ." Unemotional General Gough sums up the position thus: "Many pens have tried to describe the ghastly expanse of mud which covered the water-logged country, but few men have been able to paint a picture sufficiently intense." This is what Brigadier-General Baker-Carr said about the front which was chosen for the offensive: "To anyone familiar with the terrain in Flanders it was almost inconceivable that this part of the line should have been selected. If a careful search had been made from the English Channel to Switzerland, no more unsuitable spot could have been discovered. . . ."

The battle raged from July to November, not even the first objective, simple by comparison to the rest, was captured. Britain lost 400,000 men, Germany only 270,000, a ratio of 5 to 3. Lloyd George says that short of dismissing Haig and Robertson he could not have called off the offensive. This step for various reasons he could not take. Nothing would prevail on Haig himself to discontinue it. My father never forgave Haig his pig-headed obstinacy. He described him as an "unimaginative man" and was critical of the tactical handling. His dogged courage, too great under the circumstances, no one questioned.

On 3rd November the Canadians took Passchendaele ridge and village. Less than half a dozen miles had been gained in the entire autumn offensive. Was it worth the cost of 400,000 lives?

In 1932 my father answered this question for Mrs. Millin:

I don't think, however—I never did—that the naval objective in itself justified a campaign on the Flanders scale. . . .

There was a second objective: Following the appointment of Nivelle in the place of Joffre, and his initial success, the French had been completely smashed in the Compiègne and Nivelle thrown out. American reinforcements had not appeared in sufficient numbers to stiffen them. There was serious mutiny under Pétain. Paris itself was in danger. Sir Henry Wilson had warned us months ago that the French could do no more. He had turned out to be right. They could not. They had failed us in the summer campaign—had not carried out their undertakings concerning our offensive, had postponed promised attacks on which we relied. It was not their fault. They were the most gallant of people. Their endurance, as a people, living as they were, in the midst of war, had been heroic in the extreme. The circumstances were beyond them.

The Germans, on the other hand, were strengthened by forces released from the Russian campaign. Near as they came to winning the war in the spring of 1918, in the autumn of 1917, with the French so weak, and the Americans so slow, they had an even better chance.

There was, in short, a more urgent reason than the naval demand for the Flanders offensive: nothing less than saving the war. It seemed likely that if we did not succeed in drawing the Germans away from the French, not only would Pétain fail to hold his line, but Paris might be taken and the war lost, before the weight of the American army could be felt. There were only the British to prevent it. I think that by pinning the Germans down in Flanders, they did prevent it. I still think my instinct and reasoning in the awful choice were right.

As it happened the Channel ports were not freed by the offensive, and we lost four hundred thousand men. What there is to put against this terrible cost is that it probably saved the war.

I have stressed Passchendaele because I have wanted to show, how even against their gravest doubts and misgivings about the success of the venture, my father was able to persuade the sanest and most august tribunal in Britain to give it a trial. I have also shown how cool and resolute he could be provided he felt the end justified the means. Not many men would have been able to write with a steady hand "Losses at 100,000 per month = less than half a million whom we can make good." Yet he said to a fellow climber on Sneeuberg in the Cape, who wanted to pick a rare flower for him, "Worship—and pass on"!

At various times much harm was done to the war effort by strikes. It was perhaps a reaction to the long tiring years of the conflict and the austerity of a nation living precariously in the shadow of the submarine. My father had had experience of strikes in the Transvaal. There he had dealt with them with firmness and resolution. He settled a police strike in London without difficulty. The strike by fifty thousand munition workers at Coventry was more serious. But aided by the Labour Leader George Barnes, it was soon over and he was back in London. His colleagues never failed to marvel at his success. In truth it was due to his life-long companions: good nature and friendliness.

In the coal mines of Wales there was more serious trouble. It was brought on largely by trouble-mongers and pacifist agitators. Times were critical. There was no more vital commodity. "A paralysing blow was being struck at us," said my father, "at the very time when we were being told by our navy that they only had reserves of coal for a week, and if the strike went on for another week, we should be paralysed and finished."

Here was work for a Boer rather than a Briton, thought Lloyd George and his Cabinet. As my father was leaving hurriedly for

Wales, Lloyd George gave him a tip: "Remember my fellow countrymen are great singers."

At Cardiff the University honoured him with a doctorate. In the afternoon he moved into the coalfields. There were strikers everywhere, and frequently he stopped his car to address them, much as though on a political tour in South Africa. In the evening he arrived at Tonypandy. Here tens of thousands of miners had gathered, probably out of curiosity; he was a great attraction as the first statesman they were to see from Africa.

Gentlemen, I come from far away, as you know [he said soothingly]. I do not belong to this country. I have come a very long way to do my bit in this war, and I am going to talk to you to-night about this trouble. But I have heard in my country that the Welsh are among the greatest singers in the world, and before I start, I want you first of all to sing me some of the songs of your people.

There was a brief silence, and then a man in the crowd started singing "Land of my Fathers". The rest joined with characteristic fervour, and sang through all the stirring lines. The effect was amazing. Deeply moved, a great silence came over the crowd. Then my father spoke:

Gentlemen, it is not necessary for me to say much here to-night. You know what has happened on the Western Front. You know your comrades in their tens of thousands are risking their lives. You know that the front is just as much here as anywhere else. The trenches are in Tonypandy, and I am sure you are moved by the same spirit as your comrades in France. It is not necessary for me to add anything. You know it as well as I do, and I am sure you are going to defend the Land of your Fathers, of which we have sung here to-night, and that no trouble you may have with the Government about pay or anything else will ever stand in the way of your defence of the Land of your Fathers.

He addressed other meetings in similar fashion that night. There was singing and emphasis on this Land of their Fathers. Their sullen mood left them. My father felt happy and confident.

Back at a Cabinet meeting in London the following afternoon his colleagues said to him in admiration: "What happened? All the men are at work. How did you settle it?" "Well," replied my father, "it is news to me that the men are at work." Long afterwards he said, "The 'Land of my Fathers' saved us."

XXXVI WORK ON COMMITTEES

FAILING a successful campaign on the Western Front, my father advocated a campaign in Turkey. He did not like Lloyd George's idea of attacking Austria through Italy, for there was little chance of detaching Austria while Italy laid strenuous claims to portions of Austrian territory, no matter how tempting it would be to secure a release for the Allied troops locked up in Mesopotamia, Egypt and Salonika. Turkey was attractive because with her elimination it would be possible to use the Dardanelles, to push back Russia and coerce Bulgaria out of the war.

Full use of my father's versatility was made during his stay in England. There was no end to the missions and jobs he was given. Apart from examining and reporting on questions of strategy and visiting the fronts, he was engaged also on social, political and economic activities. Here he was to meet the scientist Dr. Chaim Weizmann, now President of Israel, inventor of a new process for making the explosive TNT, with whom he established a life-long friendship.

Weizmann was a professor of chemistry at the University of Manchester. The Allies were short of this vital explosive. Weizmann devised a new and simplified manufacturing process. For this inestimable service Lloyd George wished to reward him, but Weizmann asked nothing personally but for a home for Jewry in Palestine. Great Britain undertook solemnly to establish such a home. My father says the undertaking was given to "rally Jewish sympathy for the Allied cause in the darkest hour of the war".

By the Balfour Declaration, upon which he and Lord Balfour had worked for a long time, the Jews got their home.

Here also he was to work with the economists J. M. Keynes, Henry Strakosch and Thomas Lamont.

He did so much in such diverse lines that he came to be known as the "Handyman of the Empire". He was appointed to serve on many committees. He became a member of the Middle East Committee, whose purpose it was to help Allenby's campaign against the Turks.

Lloyd George asked him if he was "ready to take on the Russian enterprise", but my father did not like the idea, for he "doubted whether anything could still be done with that country".

In 1917 he worked out the Alexandretta campaign against the Turks and a year later he planned the advance northwards, through Palestine.

In February, 1918, he visited the Middle East, and after holding consultations there with our leaders reported on the 15th in favour of a more defensive disposition by the Mesopotamia forces, and concentrating rather on a thrust by Allenby up towards Aleppo. The Cabinet agreed to this, but it was delayed by the dangerous German break-through on the Western Front.

He was a member of the Northern Neutral Committee, under Curzon, which watched North-Western Europe, and later he became a member of a secret committee to keep an eye on the Netherlands whose neutrality was liable to violation by Germany at any moment.

But perhaps his greatest work was as chairman of the War Priorities Committee. When he got to England my father was forcibly struck by the confusion and lack of co-ordination on questions of production and supply between the various departments in the war. There was rivalry to get weapons, over-lapping and inefficiency. To introduce order into this scramble, he conceived the idea of a War Priorities Committee. On it, under my father, were the First Lord of the Admiralty, the Secretary of State for War, the Minister of Munitions, the Secretary for Air, and the Minister of National Service. My father, as a member of the War Cabinet, presided. The arrangement worked with efficiency and expedition. Mr. Churchill was the Minister of Munitions. It was the start of a long and great friendship.

To maintain the peace amidst these warring factions was not easy. "Never, I suspect," wrote Mr. Churchill, "in all the vicissitudes of his career has General Smuts stood more in need of . . . tact and adroitness."

My father's next great work was in connection with the Air Force. At the start of hostilities, flying was in its infancy and the machines and their armaments were crude and elementary, with little bearing on the course of military warfare. But this new fledgling made rapid strides, and with the increase of speed and performance came refinements of offensive armament. Machine-guns took the place of pistols, and aerial bombs were carried. The aeroplane became a formidable weapon. The conservative army and naval chiefs had not, however, perceived the significant development and were not prepared to recognise its importance. They brushed aside its urgent requests for assistance in men and equipment.

Milner had noticed this great change stealing over the situation. "Say what you like," he wrote to my father, "the soldiers and sailors at the War Office and Admiralty do not yet grasp the fact that there is a new kind of warfare before us and that, besides the help they have to give the army and navy, the airmen will have to fight battles of their own.

"If you were Air Minister with an Air Council of your own selection under you, I should feel easy in my mind on this point. But I recognise the difficulty of this and I see that it may be an even better arrangement to have you in the Cabinet with a special obligation to keep, as Minister, the supervision of Air Departments."

When my father first became interested in the flying services the army and navy each had their own separate and exclusive air components and competed with one another for personnel and materials. Lord Derby, and later Curzon, had failed to make the peace between these ardent rivals. Fundamental differences made collaboration difficult.

With air attacks on Britain the Ministry of Munitions was quick to supply aircraft in such numbers that the air force soon justified its independent existence. It looked as though unification at this stage would be of great benefit.

In July the Germans had grown sufficiently bold to attack

London not only at night with their Zeppelins but even to send over squadrons of bomber aircraft in daylight hours. There were casualties. People grew restive. Something must be done. Parliament in a secret session endorsed this. Lloyd George and my father were to tackle the problem, but Lloyd George backed out and left the matter in the hands of my father, who held consultations with representatives of the Home Forces, the Admiralty and the General Staff.

My father had previously pointed out that the enemy was superior in the air. We must devise an air weapon not only to serve in a defensive role to check these raids, but also an offensive one that could carry the fight into the industrial and munition centres of Germany. He had been alarmed at the backwardness of matters relating to the air weapon.

Now that women and children were being killed in raids on London, the people were clamouring for bombing reprisals against Germany. My father's conclusion was that "we can only defend this island effectively against air attack by offensive measures, by attacking the enemy in his air bases on the Continent and in that way destroying his power of attacking us across the Channel". He ended up by not only dealing with the defences of London, but also with the unification of the air services. This he did so subtly that even Jellicoe and Winston Churchill were placated.

Upon the acceptance of his suggestion that a committee should go into the question of establishing an Air Ministry, he himself was appointed chairman to that committee. This body, between August and October, drafted a Bill for a new Air Ministry which was passed by Parliament a month later without opposition. The First Air Minister was Lord Rothermere. And so by his unification of the various branches of the air services, my father justly came to be known as the Father of the Royal Air Force.

The air raids were gradually mastered and switched to Paris. My father's work had borne fruit.

At Biggin Hill, near London, a young air ace Pierre van Ryneveld was stationed who had made a name for himself. He was later to become my father's Chief of Staff in the Second World War. In 1920, in the *Silver Queen*, with Quentin Brand, he made the first flight from England to the Union.

In London my father occupied a luxurious suite of rooms in the

Savoy Hotel, overlooking the Thames. While he enjoyed the comfort of his surroundings, he was a man of simple tastes and would have been equally at home with less ostentation. But he had little time to consider his own likes and dislikes, for he was constantly working. The same zeal and energy he had displayed at the National Convention he now exercised again, though here it was of necessity much more prolonged. "I had no time for anything but work," he used to remark. "There was no end to the work they wanted me to do. I have never worked so hard in my life. My hair became white." There was little time for relaxation. Whenever possible he would escape into the country or to the Gilletts at Oxford, where he would go for long walks and enjoy a few brief moments of simple life. In London his alert figure could often be seen striding briskly, as was his wont, through the many lovely parks. In winter the sombre skies depressed him and he longed for the warm cheer of Irene. My mother sent him biltong to recall days spent on the sunny veld.

Towards the end of March, 1918, the German army was crashing forward in spectacular fashion. Already they were closing on Amiens. The road to Paris seemed wide open. Only a miracle could save the British lines, declared my father, after a tour of inspection. In March and April there were dangerous breaches in the line and penetrations of up to forty miles. Americans and young lads were hurled in to plug the gaps. At that critical hour Foch was given supreme command of all the Allied Armies.

America's slowness in entering the war was most disconcerting to Britain and France. Her preparations began a year before she entered the war and much enthusiasm had been displayed in New York. By the spring of 1918 they had promised seventeen divisions, each of a size almost twice that of their British counterparts. During the critical days of this March offensive there was actually only a single American division in the line, with three others preparing to move up. The thousand aeroplanes promised per month transpired to be a mere handful, and Americans themselves were using what they had previously described as "unsuitable" British and French guns.

Woodrow Wilson had entertained hopes that the American entrance into the war might persuade the Germans to request an armistice. He had made plain his peace manifesto of Fourteen Points.

By June the position had improved and Americans were pour-ing into the front at thirty thousand per month, and proving themselves worthy soldiers.

On July 15 the Germans launched an all-out attack on this uni-fied line, but it stood firm. The enemy army had spent itself. On August 8 it was clear even to the Kaiser that Germany could not hope to win the war. This day, Ludendorff said, "was the blackest day of the German Army in the history of the war".

The collapse of the Central Powers was sudden. The German army wanted to continue the fight, but their navy had mutinied, and Austria, Turkey and Bulgaria had surrendered. Hungary and parts of Germany were in a state of revolution, and the Kaiser and Crown Prince fled in panic to Holland. The Germans invoked the aid of President Wilson in restoring peace.

On the terms of the Fourteen Points, an armistice was signed in Foch's carriage in the Forest of Compiègne at 5 a.m. on November 11.

The war was over.

XXXVII IDEAS ON PEACE

AFTER the Armistice the pent-up floods or emotion burst. There was great revulsion of feeling against Germany. "Hang the Kaiser", Lloyd George's election cry, echoed throughout the country. The Allies had won the war. My father was determined to see that they won the peace as well. His stand-point, unlike that of Lloyd George, Clemenceau, Orlando and others, was entirely objective. He remained calm, detached and supremely rational. He was shocked and dismayed by the hysteria of his colleagues, but powerless to intervene.

In the middle of May, 1918, my father made a speech at Glasgow in which he said:

I am persuaded this war will end in decisive results one way or the other and not merely in stalemate. But when you talk about victory —victory is a vague term—you must know what you mean. There are people who mean by an Allied victory that we must smash Germany, that we must march to Berlin, occupy the capital of the enemy and dictate terms there. . . . I don't think an out-and-out victory is possible for any group of nations in this war because it will mean an interminable campaign. It will mean that decimated nations will be called upon to wage war for many years to come and what would the results be? . . . The results may be that the civilisation we are out to save may be jeopardised itself. . . .

But at least victory was our goal [he explained years after].* Only what sort of victory? Lloyd George wanted a knock-out blow. I felt that if a decent peace could be achieved—something short, as I said, of marching to Berlin, not something short of retreating to Paris—it would be wrong to sacrifice the human lives and the world's future chances for a knock-out blow. Some of our best soldiers were convinced that if we fought on to 1919 such exhaustion might result as to make recovery impossible. What was there in winning the war if we were ruined ourselves? I am not a believer in barren revenge. We might not even get to that knock-out blow. By God's mercy the Germans broke down internally. As I said in my first month in England, other forces were fighting for us than man and machine. What finished Germany was mutiny in the fleet and at home—the revolution of the people. It was on account of the mutiny and revolution that the Kaiser fled. The army stood firm and fought a magnificent rearguard action back to the Rhine. The Germans never failed as a war machine. My line was right. Everything shows it to-day. I was for a peace that would give the world a chance. Not absolute victors and absolute defeated. We are ruined to-day because the world is divided into victors and defeated.

My father was right. The war was inconclusive. There were no victors and no vanquished—not in the military, nor in the material, sense. In the circumstances the imposing of peace terms that were indecisive—neither harsh nor lenient—was a tragedy from which the world has not recovered.

* Quoted from Mrs. Millin, *General Smuts*, by courtesy of Messrs. Faber & Faber Ltd.

In the flush of victory, and the "emotions of the moment", my father said, "it is not merely that thrones and empires are falling, and ancient institutions suddenly collapsing. A world order is visibly passing before our eyes, and the danger is that things may go too far and a setback be given to Europe from which she does not recover for generations. . . . What a doom has come over Germany! What a price she has paid for her ambitions and crimes. . . . Now as we organise the world for victory, let us organise it against hunger and unemployment. Not only the liberated territories of our Allies, not only our small neutral neighbours, but the enemy countries themselves, require our helping hand. Let us extend it in all generosity and magnanimity."

The claim for Allied magnanimity was a strong one. It had paid Britain handsomely after the Boer War. We were to find, however, that the Prussian spirit was not as amenable as that of the Boer, though no one could foretell it at the time. They thought that the harsh feelings of Clemenceau and others were just a misplaced mania.

At an early stage in the war my father's thoughts had already turned to the machinery of peace. In a speech in Central Hall, Westminster, on 14th May, 1917, he moved the following resolution:

That it is expedient in the interests of mankind that some machinery should be set up after the present war for the purpose of maintaining international rights and general peace, and this meeting welcomes the suggestion put forward for this purpose by the President of the United States and other influential statesmen in America and commends to the sympathetic consideration of the British peoples the idea of forming a union of free nations for the preservation of permanent peace.

He went on:

. . . progress has been made, and the subject is no longer merely academic, no longer merely Utopian. If the war has done nothing more, it has at any rate done this—it has stamped into the hearts of millions of men and women an intense desire for a better order of things . . . Well—it is high time that something were done.

The losses and sufferings of this war truly baffle description; one cannot contemplate without the profoundest emotion this horror that has come over Christendom, this spirit of self-destruction which has overtaken our so-called civilisation. After all the fair promises, all the fair hopes, all the fine enthusiasm of the nineteenth century, this is what we have come to. It is computed that nearly 8,000,000 people have already been killed in this war—not the old and decrepit, not the unfit, but the best—the very best, those who should have been the natural creators of the new world, they lie buried on the battlefields of civilisation, while larger numbers have been maimed and rendered unfit for the rest of their lives. It is probable that the number of killed and wounded in this war is not far short of that of the total white population of the British Empire. Is that not a matter to stir humanity to its depths? I think the time has come for very, very serious consideration of this matter. You see the most criminal disregard of all laws, human and divine. You see civilisation itself almost crumbling to pieces, and I am sure if some means were not provided by which such calamities could be prevented in future, and the repetition of wars like this was still possible in the future, then the whole fabric of our civilisation will be in danger, people will become filled with universal despair, and you will find the nations of the world saying, as the poet said in his despair, "From the world's bitter wind seek shelter in the shadow of the grave." For what would be the use of life, or what would be the use of civilisation, if those are the fruits of all our efforts and all our endeavours?

The scale of the disaster is so vast that the whole matter seems to be uncontrollable. Our nineteenth-century science taught us how to mobilise the forces of nature, but it did not strengthen our social conscience correspondingly, and the result is that all these forces have been collected into some horrible engine of destruction which now moves like the cursed thing it is, like some blind destiny which is treading over our civilisation. . . . This is a time for action: this tragedy that has come over us calls for action. What the human intelligence has done the human intelligence can undo again. And I feel sure that if one-hundredth part of the consideration and the thought that have been given to the war is given to schemes of peace, then you will never see any war again. . . .

Now at first blush it does seem as if the end of this war would be about the most hopeless time imaginable to talk of schemes of lasting peace. For at the end of this war you will find the world divided into two hostile camps, with a chasm of hatred between them such as probably has never been seen in the world before. You will find an atmosphere of hatred and ill-will and of international estrangement such as has never been seen before in the history of the world. And when you come to think of creating machinery for lasting peace, you will have to bear in mind that the time, in a certain sense, will be the most unpropitious possible for the effort you are trying to make.

On the other hand, I have also this feeling, and I am sure it is the right feeling, that deeper than that has been the good work that the war has done—the creation of a better feeling in the hearts of men. . . . And when Europe rises from her sick bed in a long period of convalescence, as no doubt she will have to do, the germs of many good ideas will be able to develop in her, and let it be our effort to see that among those germs none will develop more strongly and more vigorously than this idea of peace which we are here this afternoon to foster. . . .

Now I mention what occurs to me as the second condition, also very important, and that is that at the end of this war we must conclude a good peace, because I do not see how you are going to have a perpetual peace, or the chance of perpetual peace, in future if this war is going to be ended like so many other wars as mere patchwork compromise between various conflicting interests. . . .

The third condition of lasting peace is that in some form or other we must bring about a league or a union of nations with some common organ of consultation on all vital issues. Of course the matter is extremely difficult, and I am not, as I have said, in a position to dogmatise, and in my own mind I am not clear as to the best course to pursue. I can quite well see that we may fail in our object if we start with too elaborate or too ambitious a scheme. The subject is enormously difficult, and you can by trying to achieve too much fail in achieving anything at all, and I must honestly confess that all the schemes that I have heard of so far have failed to carry conviction to my mind that they are practical and that they will achieve the objects we have in view. I would favour something more elastic, something more flexible, something which will be capable of adapting itself to the very complex circumstances which arise from time to time in our complex European relations, and it is perhaps possible in that way to achieve more real good. . . .

There remains another condition—the condition, namely, that in any arrangement for future peace there should be at the back of it some sanction, some force—otherwise it remains merely talk, otherwise it remains simply a vision. . . .

There remains the question of disarmament. It is a very difficult question—more difficult than any other aspect of the subject, but from many points of view the most important. It is no use trying to prevent war when nations are armed to the teeth. . . .

One more consideration—and it is this. I do not refer to this as a condition of any future peace treaty, but I think it is most important and essential that the fundamental provisions to safeguard peace in future should be included in the peace treaty itself which is made after this war. This war has not been fought, at any rate as far as we are concerned, for the purpose of gain or material interests. Millions of men have given their lives in this war, millions more are prepared to give their lives in this war in order to achieve a good peace and to ensure it for the future, and I think it would be the proper course that the peace treaty which is concluded after this war shall contain as an integral part of it the fundamental provision, not in detail, but in principle, which will safeguard the future peace of the world. If that is done, then this war will not have been fought in vain. . . .

In January, 1918, Woodrow Wilson published a treatise on the League of Nations. It bristled with the idealism of which he was such an unrivalled exponent. Unfortunately his was not the rugged type of personality that held the masses, and tragically he soon lost American political support. His plans and aspirations simply became engulfed in the oblivion of isolationism. But he represented a great power and it was essential to maintain his enthusiasm.

A month after the collapse of the Central Powers, on 14th December, 1918, my father resigned from the War Cabinet. His task was done. On that day he wrote to Lloyd George:

Now that the Elections are over I must ask you to release me from further service on the War Cabinet. I would have taken this step earlier, but while other Ministers were preoccupied with the Election I thought it necessary to carry on my work, especially as Chairman of the Cabinet Committee on Demobilisation. Now, however, that will no longer be necessary.

When in May, 1917, you did me the honour to invite me to join the War Cabinet, I agreed in the end to accept your offer as I thought that was perhaps the best way in which I could do the war service which I was anxious to render. Since then we have been through a tremendous period, and I am glad to think that during all its ups and downs I have had the privilege to work in close collaboration with you for that victory which has finally crowned the Allied cause.

For the invariable courtesy and consideration which I have received from you and all my other colleagues during that trying time

I am indeed grateful, and it is with warm feelings that I part from you now.

My father was under no illusions about the difficulties that faced statesmen at the peace table. As early as September, 1917, he had written Lord Loreburn :

. . . Difficult as it has been to wage this terrible war, I am not sure that the making of peace will not be an even more difficult business, requiring greater courage and statesmanship and farsightedness.

Germany is manœuvring in order to get the belligerent Government round a conference table, as she knows that that motley crowd is sure to disagree among themselves and perhaps break up, and that she will win at the Conference Table more than she has lost in the field. . . .

XXXVIII A PRACTICAL SUGGESTION

O N the 15th, the day on which General Botha arrived for the Peace Conference, my father published a comprehensive pamphlet on "The League of Nations—A Practical Suggestion". This "short sketch", which, he says, "was hastily written at the last moment, and amid other pressing duties, in view of the early meeting of the Peace Conference," was to become famous, for it embodied the major portion of ideas that were subsequently incorporated into the constitution of the League. He says in his foreword:

My reflections have convinced me that the ordinary conception of the League of Nations is not a fruitful one, nor is it the right one, and that a radical transformation of it is necessary. If the League is ever to be a success it will have to occupy a much greater position, and perform many other functions besides those ordinarily assigned to it. Peace and War are resultants of many complex forces, and those forces will have to be gripped at an earlier stage of their growth, if peace is to be effectively maintained. To enable it to do so, the League will have to occupy the great position which has been rendered vacant by the destruction of so many of the old European Empires, and the passing away of the old European order. The League should be put into the very forefront of the programme of the Peace Conference, and be made the point of departure for the solution of many of the grave problems with which it will be confronted.

He goes on in this "Practical Suggestion" to view the League

not only as a possible means for preventing future wars, but much more as a great organ of the ordinary peaceful life of civilisation, as the foundation of the new international system which will be erected on the ruins of this war, and as the starting point from which the peace arrangements of the forthcoming Conference should be made. Such an orientation of the idea seems to me necessary if the League is to become a permanent part of our international machinery. It is not sufficient for the League merely to be a sort of *deus ex machina* called in in very grave emergencies when the spectre of war appears; if it is to last, it must be much more. It must become part and parcel of the common international life of States, it must be an ever-visible, living, working organ of the policy of civilisation. It must function so strongly in the ordinary peaceful intercourse of States that it becomes irresistible in their disputes; its peace activity must be the foundation and guarantee of its war power. . . .

The attempt to form empires or leagues of nations on the basis of inequality and the bondage and oppression of the smaller national units has failed, and the work has to be done all over again on a new basis and an enormous scale. The vast elemental forces liberated by this war, even more than the war itself, have been responsible for this great change. In the place of the great Empires we find the map of Europe now dotted with small nations, embryo states, derelict territories. Europe has been reduced to its original atoms. For the moment its political structure, the costly result of so many centuries of effort, has disappeared. But that state of affairs must be looked upon as temporary. The creative process in the political movement of humanity cannot be paralysed; the materials lie ready for a new reconstructive task, to which, let us hope, the courage and genius of Western civilisation will prove equal. . . .

As a programme for the forthcoming Peace Conference I would therefore begin by making two recommendations:

(1) . . . the Conference should regard itself as the first or preliminary meeting of the League, intended to work out its organisation, functions, and programme. . . .

. . . The case of Germany stands on a different footing which is clearly distinguishable in principle. In the first place, if Alsace-Lorraine is annexed to France, that would be a case of disannexation, as it has been put; that is to say, it is a case of restoring to France what was violently and wrongfully taken from her in 1871 against the protests not only of France, but of the population of Alsace-Lorraine speaking through their elected representatives. . . . Its restitution to France would therefore satisfy, instead of violating, the moral sense of the world.

In the second place, the German colonies in the Pacific and Africa are inhabited by barbarians, who not only cannot possibly govern themselves, but to whom it would be impracticable to apply any ideas of political self-determination in the European sense. They might be consulted as to whether they want their German masters back, but the result would be so much a foregone conclusion that the consultation would be quite superfluous. The disposal of these Colonies should be decided on the principles which President Wilson has laid down in the fifth of his celebrated Fourteen Points. . . .

[Next he comes to Mandates, where he commends:]

(4) That any authority, control, or administration which may be necessary in respect of these territories and peoples, other than their own self-determined autonomy, shall be the exclusive function of and shall be vested in the League of Nations and exercised by or on behalf of it.

Now in discussing a problem like the Constitution of the League of Nations we must be careful not to set too much store on precedents. Our problem is gigantic and entirely novel; its solution will depend, not so much on following precedents never meant for such a novel and complex situation, but in boldly facing the situation and, if need be, creating a new precedent to meet it. The grand success of the British Empire depends not on its having followed any constitutional precedent of the past but on having met a new situation in history with a new creation in law; and as a matter of fact the new constitutional system grew empirically and organically out of the practical necessities of the colonial situation. So it will have to be here. And above all let us avoid cut-and-dried schemes meant as complete, definitive, and final solutions of our problem. Let us remember that we are only asked to make a beginning. . . .

. . . we must be equally careful to avoid the mere ineffective debating society at the other end. The new situation does not call for a new talking shop. We want an instrument of government which, however much talk is put into it at the one end, will grind out decisions at the other end. . . .

The League will never be a great success until there is formed as its main support a powerful international public opinion. . . .

After peace there will be a new and most important group of matters calling for the study or control of the permanent Staff. Thus the due execution of the provisions of the Peace Treaty will have to be carefully watched. New conditions of free transit by land, water, and air will become necessary, and require regulation and control by the League. . . .

. . . Then, again, there is the vast subject of industrial conditions, involving international labour conditions, which will call for expert inquiry and statesmanlike handling by the League. All these thorny subjects will call for the appointment of expert committees or commissions on the Staff of the League which could prepare the material for a final expression of opinion by the League.

Now it seems to me that some people expect too much from the new machinery of international Arbitration and Conciliation which emerges as the chief proposal for preventing future wars. War is a symptom of deep-seated evils: it is a disease or growth out of social and political conditions. While these conditions remain unaltered, it is vain to expect any good from new institutions superimposed on those conditions. . . . The new institution of peace must not be something additional, something external, superimposed on the pre-existing structure. It must be an organic change; it must be woven into the very texture of our political system. . . .

There follows a long section on disarmament and disarmament problems. Of these he considers the abolition of conscription the most important.

Thereafter he proceeds to sanctions:

. . . No declaration of war should be necessary, as the state of war arises automatically on the law-breaker proceeding to hostilities, and the boycott follows automatically from the obligation of the League without further resolutions or formalities on the part of the League.

The effect of such a complete automatic trade and financial boycott will necessarily be enormous. The experience of this war has shown how such a boycott, effectively maintained chiefly through sea power, has in the end availed to break completely the most powerful military Power that the world has ever seen; and the lesson is not likely to be lost on future intending evildoers. It is because of this power of the economic and financial weapons that many writers are of opinion that the obligation for action by members of the League should not go beyond the use of these weapons. My view, however, is that they will not be enough if unsupported by military and naval action. A powerful military State may think that a sudden military blow will achieve its object in spite of boycotts, provided that no greater military reaction from the rest of the League need be feared. This fear may under certain circumstances be a more effective deterrent than even the boycott; and I do not think the League is likely to prove a success unless in the last resort the maintenance of the *moratorium* is guaranteed by force. The obligation on the members of the League to use force for this purpose should therefore be absolute, but the amount of the force and the contribution from the members should be left to the recommendation of the Council to the respective Governments in each case. . . .

Finally he draws to an end:

. . . mankind is once more on the move. The very foundations have been shaken and loosened, and things are again fluid. The tents have been struck, and the great caravan of humanity is once more on the march. Vast social and industrial changes are coming, perhaps upheavals which may, in their magnitude and effects, be comparable to war itself. A steadying, controlling, regulating influence will be required to give stability to progress, and to remove that wasteful friction which has dissipated so much social force in the past, and in this war more than ever before. These great functions could only be adequately fulfilled by the League of Nations. Responding to such vital needs and coming at such a unique opportunity in history, it may well be destined to mark a new era in the Government of Man, and become to the peoples the guarantee of Peace, to the workers of all races the great International, and to all the embodiment and living expression of the moral and spiritual unity of the human race.

XXXIX PEACE CONFERENCE

WOODROW WILSON was captivated by the phrase "Europe is being liquidated and the League of Nations must be heir to this great estate". Lansing says he kept on repeating it over and over. He had been equally struck by the rest of my father's treatise. It crystallised his thoughts on many points which so far had been only vague ideas.

He therefore proceeded to redraft his scheme, in which he incorporated virtually all my father's suggestions. There is no controversy on the point of how much of the drafting of the Covenant is Wilson's work. Colonel House and most authorities declare that not a single idea of Wilson's league plan was original. He merely edited and compiled. At a preliminary meeting of the Peace Conference he admitted that he "was unable to foresee the variety of circumstances with which the League would have to deal. I was unable, therefore, to plan all the machinery necessary to meet differing and unexpected contingencies."

The answers to many of these differing and unexpected contingencies were supplied to him, as often as not, by my father. He told the American Senate that he had rewritten his draft on the League "in the light of a paper by General Smuts, who seemed to have done some very clear thinking in regard to what was to be done to pieces of the dismembered Empires".

At Versailles my father was elected to the Commission of the League of Nations, over which Wilson presided. Other members were Lord Cecil for Britain, Leon Bourgeois for France, Roman Dmowski for Poland and Venizelos for Greece.

On 19th January, 1919, it was felt to be high time that agreement was reached between the views of Britain and the United States, so that a united front could be put up to the other countries, who talked interminably. A meeting was arranged. Wilson was accompanied by Colonel House. My father was strangely silent and left Cecil to do the major portion of the talking. Several important decisions resulted from this small meeting, among others the plan for a Permanent Court of International Justice.

From the 3rd to the 13th of February the big Commission held three-hour meetings every day. Orlando of Italy and Dr. Kramarsch the Czech were very loquacious. Wellington Koo of China spoke but seldom. My father again said little and left to Cecil the task of explaining the important problem of protection of minorities, published as Article 22 in my father's treatise of 15th December, 1918.

The conduct of the delegates at the Peace Conference was hardly edifying. All ideas of restraint and reason appeared to have snapped, and greed and rapaciousness prevailed. There was an undisguised and sordid scramble for booty and material gains. With the bare exception of Wilson and my father, all seem to have succumbed. Lloyd George threw himself into the fray with all his Celtic frenzy; on occasion he even clashed with my father. The French ardour turned into a burning fever. The jackals, hyenas and lesser fry all danced around and yapped impatiently for their portions.

It was not only the passion of greed, but also of revenge and vindictiveness. It was inevitable after a great war.

Wilson, the man of the hour, was pained by what he saw. For a while he was almost disillusioned. Yet he never ceased to conduct himself like the great idealist and gentleman. The greedy did not have an easy passage with him. My father saw it was not the time to press for the incorporation of South-West Africa into the Union. He did the next best thing. In his Mandate System, he had devised various categories of mandates. He saw to it that the Union took over South-West Africa under a "C" Mandate, which was almost tantamount to annexation and left the future incorporation open for decision by plebiscite. Virtually South Africa's only obligation was to send annual reports to Geneva.

Wilson dealt firmly with others who wished to annex conquered territory. The best they got was a Mandate. Such were his scruples that he even turned down all the mandates offered to America. Of his integrity at Versailles there can be no question. When America herself clamoured for the sole right to the Panama Canal, he alone insisted that it should be a world gateway.

My father had a very high regard for Wilson's idealism. He was not quite so eulogistic about his leadership at Versailles. He was too much of a dreamer and too little of a practical man. The rough and tumble of the Conference diplomacy was rather beyond his control. Moreover he had about him a group of advisers that left much to be desired.

But for all that he thought him a greater man than Lincoln. Lincoln, he said, was a luckier man, however, for after four years of a poorly-directed war against the South all censure of him was averted by the bullet of an assassin, and his memory has grown ever greater at the expense of poor Grant on whom all the opprobrium has fallen. There was no assassin in Wilson's case. He had to bear the mistakes of the Conference himself, and it broke him and perhaps shattered a great name in the eyes of posterity.

It was [my father says] Wilson's reputation that was murdered. They murdered it with ridicule. Nobody remembered that he was a man with the hand of death on him, standing alone against his country's betrayal of principles to which it was pledged.

I don't say Wilson made no mistakes. He made a mistake in coming to Europe with a poor staff, and a worse mistake in coming without his opponents. He should have included some of his opponents—for instance, Elihu Root and Taft—among the delegates he brought with him, and it would have become a non-political affair and gone through, and all history would have been different.

Instead, he left his opponents in America to conspire against him, and they used the tragedy of Europe for their own political ends. They made it a party business to turn down the Treaty and the League in order to throw out the Democrats.

There are some who think Wilson should not have come to Paris at all. I don't agree with them. Only Wilson could have put through the League. The other statesmen weren't concerned about the League except as an instrument for their own ends—that is to say, their country's ends: Wilson put the League above this greedy squabbling. It was for the League he compromised on other things; whereupon everyone fastened on his small surrenders.

Believe me, the trouble did not lie in the small surrenders, or in the fact that Wilson did not bring home what he called "the fabric" intact. He was not a practical man. He had this vast structure of a plan, which needed to be adapted to varying facts and circumstances and filled in with details, and as he got little help or understanding from his staff, he looked to others for these facts and details.

He was not, as Keynes says in *Economic Consequences*—I saw him a great deal and you can take it from me—so bamboozled that he could not even be de-bamboozled. If, for instance, he yielded his point about the Freedom of the Seas, it wasn't simply because the other Allies insisted on it, or because of bamboozlement. He had to yield it because it could not be squared with the fundamental conception of the League. Freedom of the Seas implies neutrality on the seas. If the League was to be effective—to be able to act in time of war—there could be no neutrality, no freedom of the seas. . . .

The truth is, America wanted a reason for repudiating Wilson. The world wanted a scapegoat. At that opportune moment Keynes brought out his *Economic Consequences of the Peace*. There were a few pages about Wilson in it which exactly suited the politics of America and the world's mood. When I encouraged Keynes to write that book, I knew his views about the statesmen at Paris. But I did not expect a personal note in his book, I did not expect him to turn Wilson into a figure of fun.

These few pages about Wilson in Keynes's book made an Aunt Sally of the noblest figure—perhaps the only noble figure—in the history of the war, and they led a fashion against Wilson that was adopted by the intelligentsia of the day and is not yet past—the intelligentsia (not the intellectuals)—the people who, admiring only their own cleverness, despise real goodness, real thought, real wisdom. . . .

But for Keynes's description of Wilson, nothing worse might have been fairly said of him than that he handled Congress ineptly when he took the League back to America or that he did not understand party politics. I remember saying to him, "*Can* you carry the treaty? *Can* you get your two-thirds majority?" "I absolutely can," he said; and he was struck down in the middle of his single-handed fight for it.

He had no disciples. Perhaps it was a deficiency in him that he found none. I can't help remembering that if it depended on the intelligentsia of the day, our knowledge of Christ would be a casual and contemptuous remark in Tacitus. A few fishermen in Galilee prevented it.*

The failure of Wilson to carry America was more than a disaster, for it meant not only that America did not come into the League, but also that she remained undivorced from her ancient path of isolationism. To the League this was a crippling blow, for it signified that from its very inception it was bereft of its chief member and the only one that could really have enabled it to be a force to be reckoned with. Those who later came to judge the League by its failures and shortcomings would do well to consider what might have been the case had the United States not left it in the lurch.

* Quoted from Mrs. Millin, *op. cit.*

The question of reparations, or as Woodrow Wilson preferred to call them, "indemnities", caused one of the major controversies of the Conference. It raged for months. While my father pleaded that unnecessarily heavy tribute should not be exacted from Germany, committees were deliberating to see how much they could squeeze out of the vanquished. Wilson and my father disagreed fundamentally on the question of reparations. Wilson maintained that indemnities should be limited to material war damage. My father felt they should be used as compensation for damage to civilians.

Meanwhile a British committee under Hughes of Australia had agreed that compensations should be paid to civilians, and provisionally assessed the damage at over twenty-four thousand million pounds. The French had worked out even more far-fetched ideas on compensation to civilians, including pensions to widows and disabled soldiers. Germany must be made to pay for her sins and to restore the world to its pristine condition.

The Americans were more moderate and realistic. They suggested something like two thousand million pounds during the first two years and then interest and capital repayment of twelve thousand million pounds over thirty-five years.

Wilson stuck to his point for months. Then, to break the impasse, he called on my father to "establish a compromise between Lloyd George's election pledge to the British people to demand the entire costs of the war, and the assurance to the contrary given to the enemy by the Allies at the time of the Armistice". Wilson held my father in high esteem both because of his ability and for his championship of the League.

My father prepared a memorandum which "was the final argument" and convinced the President. When Wilson's legal advisers told him that they were strongly opposed to the pension scheme as "all logic was against it", he flew into a frenzy and said he did not "care a damn for logic" and was going to include pensions.

My father's point in insisting on the inclusion of allowances and pensions was to ensure that the war-ravished countries of Europe did not get the lion's share, while financially exhausted England was left in the cold. It was only later, when France swelled her reparation amount to fantastic proportions, my father said, that it became not only a farce but "one of those things that are responsible for the Germany of to-day . . ."

The idea of having the delegates from the Dominions sign the Peace terms independently of the United Kingdom did not appeal to Lloyd George and other British statesmen, but my father pressed the point that it might stress the unique partnership of the Commonwealth.

General Botha had joined my father in London. He was tired and far from well, and had lost much weight. The family liver disease was upon him and already it had gone to his heart and legs, and he himself had a premonition that he would not see the year out. In South Africa he had found the burden since my father had left almost more than he could bear. For the past three years he had had to bear alone the taunts and jeers of the Opposition, as well as the vast responsibilities of a nation at war.

To my father his period in Paris was akin to purgatory. The prodigies of work he had been performing for the past months, and was still performing, had left him somewhat jaded, though Colonel House says that of all the delegates my father appeared the only one not tired. He lived only for the work of the Conference and shunned the distractions of Paris, in which other delegates found a pleasant outlet. Always it was just his suite in the Hotel Majestic and the Conference tables. Nothing could have been more depressing than those committee rooms, with their interminable wrangles, unabashed greed, and inevitable deadlocks. Nobody was in a mood for seeing the broader picture or for planning for posterity. They were out simply to get all they could —and to leave the future to take care of itself. It cut across the idealism of my father and shook his faith—though only momentarily—in human nature. It was not that he was out of his element here; it was just that he despaired of good and sanity prevailing. He has described it as the "unhappiest time" of his life. At times he wondered whether ten million lives had not been shed in vain.

Clemenceau had seen Paris in flames in 1871 and never forgot it. He hated Germany with a deep and implacable hatred. He was for France only. He was ancient, determined and eloquent. With this crusty, often openly contemptuous, veteran Woodrow Wilson had to compete. Unfortunately it was beyond his powers or his nature. Often he found the stormy eloquence of Lloyd George equally difficult to cope with. This gift in the great Welshman must have been phenomenally highly developed, for it made an

General Smuts—1930

General Smuts broadcasting a New Year Message to the Empire from
his home—1939

Mountaineer Smuts on Table Mountain, overlooking Cape
Town—1940

impression on my father unsurpassed even by the immortal orations of Winston Churchill during the Second World War. It was not till 1943 that he was prepared to put Mr. Churchill on an equal footing with the Welshman. Lloyd George must have been a great and wonderful personality; but like Wilson, he was eventually killed by a political system.

*   *   *   *   *

Hungary was in the clutches of a Red revolution. At the head was an unscrupulous Jew named Bela Kun, who had deposed Count Karolyi and established his brigand clique in power. In Paris the Big Four were perturbed at this revolutionary manifestation, for they felt it endangered their European reconstruction programme, and might well spread to Germany and other countries.

At first they decided to send General Mangim to restore authority, but later they changed their minds and asked my father to go instead. With him he had his aide Captain Ernest Lane, R. Leeper, Colonel Heywood, Cyril Butler and Harold Nicolson of the Foreign Office. Nicolson wrote: "The ostensible purpose of our mission is to fix an armistice line between the Hungarians and Roumanians, yet the real idea at the back is to see whether Bela Kun is worth using as a vehicle for getting into touch with Moscow." They travelled at slow speed through Austria, and my father could not help noticing the pinched, starved look of the people. Vienna was littered with rubbish, and in a much neglected state. For Sir Thomas Cunninghame, Head of the British Military Mission, the visit started off badly, for at Sachers he got into disfavour with my father for taking the delegation to a sumptuous meal costing 1,200 kronen, in this land of starvation. My father said it was a "gross error in taste" and that henceforth they were to feed only on their own army rations.

Hungary had been looted and plundered and this terror was continuing daily. When the news of my father's impending visit got about, the plundering was temporarily suspended and people breathed freely once more after weeks of terror. At the same time, the importance of a visit by my father lent considerable support to Kun, who was merely one brigand among many.

On the morning of 4th April they arrived at Budapest station. Bela Kun arrived later, a small insignificant figure in a frock coat

I

and top hat. At midday he left, seemingly pleased with his visit. My father declined his invitation to stay in the Hungaria, which was specially beflagged and decorated for the purpose, saying he would remain in his train. So they continued living frugally in the train where, Nicolson says, "Smuts presides over our trench meals as if giving us a banquet at the Savoy." Nor would my father consent to attend a banquet in the Ritz, whereupon Kun, much affronted, also stayed at home.

On the evening of the next day Kun and retinue paid a visit to my father in the train and handed him a note. Having read it he said: "No, gentlemen, this is not a note which I can accept. There must be no reservations." So briefly bidding them good-bye he got into the train and gave the order to depart, leaving Kun and company standing bewildered on the platform. He had decided that Kun really had no authority and was of no use to them.

"We then dine," Nicolson writes in his diary. "Smuts is delightful, telling us stories of the veld with a ring of deep homesickness in his voice. A lovely man. . . ."

On the 7th in Prague, he drove to the palace to visit Masaryk, with whom he conversed for an hour.

Back in Paris later, they found that the press had described their mission as a "fiasco". It was not that, nor even unfruitful, for it had revealed that Kun was a mere puppet and Hungary in a hopeless condition. To my father the trip had been a pleasant interlude from the depression of Paris.

XL CONTROVERSY

AT Paris my father spared no effort to support the Covenant and to save the peace. He never wearied of the struggle. R. S. Baker says that he, "more than any other man, typified British Liberal opinion at Paris".

At the opening of the Conference in his simple language and forceful logic he begged that the enemy be treated with "pity and restraint", pointing out that "civilisation is one body and we are all members of one another". He pressed doggedly for the "generous treatment of Germany as a vital factor in the restoration of human civilisation".

In 1919 E. T. Raymond wrote ". . . he, above all other statesmen, realises that this is no dynastic struggle to be patched up by another Berlin or Vienna conference".

He kept on complaining that we were insisting on impossible peace terms. Frequently he protested vigorously to Lloyd George and Wilson on the way the treaty was being drafted. "We cannot destroy Germany without destroying Europe. . . . We cannot save Europe without the co-operation of Germany. . . . My fear is that the Paris Conference may prove one of the historic failures of the world.

"You may strip Germany of her colonies, reduce her armaments to a mere police force and her navy to that of a fifth-rate power; all the same, in the end, if she feels that she has been unjustly treated in the peace of 1919 she will find means of exacting retribution from her conquerors."

He never wearied of speaking and writing about the evils of the Peace Treaty. He worked on the various delegates and his associates. He wrote to Lloyd George and to Wilson. He wrote to them again and again, even at the cost of tediousness, of his deep pride, for he felt it was his duty.

He condemned the wisdom and doubted the practicability of some of the terms in the strongest fashion. In May he said to the British Delegation,

They are such that I personally would hesitate before I subscribed my name to them, even if the Germans are willing to submit under duress. . . . If the Germans are prepared to swallow this Treaty, I still consider its provisions such as to make future peace and goodwill in Europe unlikely; an international atmosphere will be created which will make the beneficent operation of the League of Nations impossible; the fires will be kept burning and the pot be kept boiling until it again boils over, either in a new war, or in the breakdown of the European system under the onslaught of social and industrial anarchy. . . . I would urge . . . even at this twelfth hour, and even at the risk of our losing some diplomatic credit, that we remove the most objectionable features from the Peace Treaty. Unfortunately the wrong procedure we have hitherto followed in the dramatic publication and presentation to the Germans makes the course I propose very difficult for us and almost humiliating. But that surely is a minor consideration where so much is at stake for the world. . . .

My proposal is as follows: Germans have been invited to state their objections to provisions of the Draft Treaty. They are now pouring forth a great volume of ponderous notes embodying their views. These views we should be prepared to consider fairly and sincerely on their merits, and where we find a good case made out against our draft we should be prepared to modify our proposals.

In the middle of May he wrote to Lloyd George and Wilson:

The more I have studied the Peace Treaty as a whole, the more I dislike it. The combined effect of the territorial and reparation clauses is to make it practically impossible for Germany to carry out the provisions of the Treaty. And then the Occupation Clauses come in to plant the French on the Rhine indefinitely, even beyond the already far-too-long period of fifteen years, under an undefined régime of martial law. East and West, blocks of Germans are put under their historic enemies. Under this Treaty Europe will know no peace; and the undertaking to defend Europe against aggression may at any time bring the British Empire also into the fire.

I am grieved beyond words that such should be the result of our statesmanship. I admit it was hard to appear to fight for the German cause with our other Allies, especially with devastated France. But now that the Germans can state their own case, I pray you will use your power and influence to make the final Treaty a more moderate and reasonable document.

Wilson replied: "I feel the terrible responsibility of the whole business, but inevitably my thought goes back to the very great offence against civilisation which the German State committed, and the necessity for making it evident once and for all that such things can lead only to the most severe punishment."

My father wrote to Wilson again:

Even at the risk of wearying you I venture to address you once more. The German answer to our draft Peace Terms seems to me to strike the fundamental note which is most dangerous to us and which we are bound to consider most carefully. They say in effect that we are under solemn obligation to them to make a Wilson Peace, a peace in accordance with your Fourteen Points and other Principles enunciated in 1918. To my mind there is absolutely no doubt that this is so. Subject to the two reservations made by the Allies before the Armistice, we are bound to make a peace within the four corners of your Points and Principles, and any provisions of the Treaty which go either *contrary* to or *beyond* their general scope and intent would constitute a breach of agreement. . . .

There will be a terrible disillusionment if the peoples come to think we are not concluding a Wilson Peace, that we are not keeping our promises to the world or faith with the public. But, if in so doing, we appear also to break a formal agreement deliberately entered into (as I think we do), we shall be overwhelmed with the gravest discredit, and this Peace may become an even greater disaster to the world than the war was.

Forgive me for troubling you with this matter, but I believe it goes to the root of the whole case. . . .

There was also heated correspondence between Lloyd George and my father. In a mood of exasperation Lloyd George taunted my father on the question of reparations and South-West Africa. My father replied calmly:

I am sorry to involve you in any correspondence at a time like this, when you are preoccupied with the gravest difficulties. I write to you in no polemical sense. . . .

Whatever view one holds of these [Wilson's] formulas, I should say that our proposed disposal of the Saar Basin, of Danzig, and of Memel violated them. They are indisputably German territories with German populations, which we have no right under these formulas to tear off Germany. . . . And it is not necessary for the future Poland that there should be a free Danzig under Polish suzerainty, any more than it is necessary to have a free Hamburg as an outlet for future Czecho-slovakia. . . .

With regard to the German colonies, I do not for a moment con-template their return to Germany as one of the concessions we should make. No doubt in future, when a new atmosphere has grown up, the German claims to colonial mandates will come to be viewed in a different light and that contingency has to be kept in view of whatever arrangements we make now. But please do not have the impression that I would be generous at the expense of others, so long as the Union gets South-West Africa. In this great business South-West Africa is as dust compared to the burdens now hanging over the civilised world. And that is how the matter will be viewed in the Union also. People who have been under the harrow have been in the greatest of all schools. And believe me the percussion of this Peace Treaty in South Africa is going to be tremendous. Events may soon prove that it has made the position of men like General Botha and myself very difficult, if not impossible. The strength of our position has been the belief of a large section of the Dutch population in the spirit of fair play and moderation as characteristic of British policy. Whether that belief will survive this Peace Treaty time alone can show, but the signs are ominous. And when the sense of fair play of people is outraged and their faith is destroyed and a stain is put on their conscience, they will not stop to look at a bit of desert. No, even as regards South Africa, I view the situation created by the Peace Treaty with the gravest concern. . . .

Prime Minister! do not for a moment imagine that I write in any other but a most friendly and sympathetic spirit which I am sure you will not resent. Perhaps the main difference between us is that you are struggling in the water, while I shout advice from the shore! But I feel deeply this is no time to mince matters. When you are up against a position so terrible in its possibilities for good and evil, you can only do one thing, even if you fail utterly. And that is the right thing, the thing you can justify to your conscience and that of all other reasonable fair-minded people. This Treaty breathes a poisonous spirit of revenge, which may yet scorch the fair face—not of a corner of Europe, but of Europe.

Elsewhere he remarked in regard to Poland: "Poland is an historic failure and will always be a failure, and in this Treaty we are trying to reverse the verdict of history. . . ."

How true these prophecies have unfortunately become!

When Lloyd George invited my father to become a member of a commission on Austrian reparations he turned it down; he had had more than enough of reparations already, and wrote in reply to Mr. Lloyd George: "While I am willing, and indeed anxious, to help with the work I do not think . . . that my going on the commission will serve any useful purpose, and my opposition to what seems your policy will only waste time where speed is right. For the imposition of reparations on a broken, bankrupt, economically impossible state like Austria, or a new, friendly allied state like Czechoslovakia . . . seems to be a hopeless policy which could only lead to the most mischievous results. I am against payment of all reparation of these countries for damage done by the dead and dismembered Austro-Hungarian Empire. And if it is (as it appears) your policy to exact reparation in these cases . . . I hope you will excuse me from serving on the commission. . . ."

From such wranglings and cross-currents and indecision at the Conference dangerous new moods rose. On 23rd June Foch threatened to reopen the war and to cross the Rhine.

Finally the terms of the surrender were agreed upon.

On the 28th June, 1919, the fifth anniversary of Sarajevo, the Peace Treaty was signed.

My father and Botha signed under protest. America did not sign at all.

XLI SIGNING OF THE PEACE

PARIS was a happy hunting ground for delegations of small disgruntled and discontented groups. There had been much talk of sacred rights and the equality of partnership within the Commonwealth. Hertzog brought a delegation to seek a republican constitution for South Africa. When they embarked on their mission at Cape Town the crew of the Union-Castle liner refused to man the vessel. The British admiral's offer of H.M.S. *Minerva* at Simonstown was refused by Hertzog, who preferred to board a Dutch ship and reach Europe via New York. At Paris he was courteously received by Lloyd George, who firmly explained to him that Botha and my father were the official representatives and that he was afraid he could not consider representations from a minority group. Hertzog's mission was a failure, but he returned to the Union with the happy conviction that the

Interphase Not Peace —

Another weakness last hour was Economic

Revolutionised world position : 4 Powers pre

3 remain — America — economically dominant

Russia — colossus very big pre" Japan

Britain — honour & prestige, but weak in

                    trade.

Empire & Com. entire ...

Imbalance in trade

(a) Anglo-American Axis — ...

(b) British branch strengthened in trade

    by Western Democracies in close ...

    on Commonwealth model.

    For them to choose . Position intrinsically

                         precarious

Not Anglo-American — Too narrow a basis

Signal Three Powers in Cooperation

    Stabilising factor in coming age.

    Wall of Peace behind which institutions

    of freedom might be built up.

Portion of notes used in the "Explosive Speech" to the British Parliamentary
Association.   See page 440.

B.E. and Commonwealth

1. Position calls for review.

Two systems — Empire & Com: — one based on decentralization, other on Centralisation in trade

~~Empire~~ ~~Not criticising~~

2. ~~Latter~~ In particular:

Decentralisation must come, and could best keep in ~~tune~~ with branching, having local larger powers such E.G. & Council &c.

3. e.g. Too many units — either haphazard branch regionally & amalgamate smaller units

3 Doms e.g. in Africa / Over simplify?

4 Linking up Empire with Commonwealth by Conference system

to bring in Dominions in their areas and establish

cooperation between Empire & Com.

in larger regions.

Canada in West, Austr. in S.E.
S.A. in Africa.
India in Asia?

Settlements after this war may provide fresh occasion for British resettlement &c

Nationalists would treat this as a personal rebuff, and that it would fan their anti-British feelings.

Woodrow Wilson returned home and toured America to gain support for the Treaty and the League. The American people were not in a mood to be moved. Wilson was rapidly going to pieces himself. His failing health was aggravated by insomnia, and sometimes he would break down and weep in public. In the end his efforts were defeated, and a stroke at the conclusion of his tour left him paralysed.

In the Hall of Mirrors, in the historic palace at Versailles, where Germany had once dictated peace terms to France, the nations forgathered on June 28 to sign the Peace. Of the many delegates assembled who signed, only Foch, Botha and my father had borne active arms against the enemy.

Some days before the signing of the terms, my father told General Botha that he was not prepared to sign this document, and that he had decided to leave shortly for South Africa. Botha cabled the Governor-General, "while I share his difficulties against the Treaty, I have decided to sign because my position as Prime Minister is different from his, and my signature is necessary to make the Union a member of the League of Nations and secure for her the new status in the world". Lloyd George's advice to my father was to sign under protest and to record his objections afterwards. This advice he accepted and forthwith sat down to draft his criticism of the Treaty.

Even as the bells in Britain were pealing the joyous tidings of the peace, this lengthy protest appeared in the British press, where it was regarded as one of the most striking events of the day.

I have signed the Peace Treaty [he recorded], not because I consider it a satisfactory document, but because it is imperatively necessary to close the war; because the world needs peace above all, and nothing could be more fatal than the continuance of the state of suspense between war and peace. The six months since the armistice was signed have perhaps been as upsetting, unsettling, and ruinous to Europe as the previous four years of war. I look upon the Peace Treaty as the close of those two chapters of war and armistice, and only on that ground do I agree to it.

I say this now, not in criticism but in faith; not because I wish to find fault with the work done, but rather because I feel that in the Treaty we have not yet achieved the real peace to which our peoples were looking, and because I feel that the real work of making peace will only begin after this Treaty has been signed, and a definite halt has thereby been called to the destructive passions that have been desolating Europe for nearly five years. This Treaty is simply the liquidation of the war situation in the world.

The promise of the new life, the victory of the great human ideals, for which the peoples have shed their blood and their treasure without stint, the fulfilment of their aspirations towards a new international order, and a fairer, better world, are not written in this Treaty, and will not be written in Treaties. "Not in this Mountain, nor in Jerusalem, but in spirit and in truth," as the Great Master said, must the foundations of the new order be laid. A new heart must be given, not only to our enemies, but also to us; a contrite spirit for the woes which have overwhelmed the world; a spirit of pity, mercy, and forgiveness for the sins and wrongs which we have suffered. A new spirit of generosity and humanity, born in the hearts of the peoples in this great hour of common suffering and sorrow, can alone heal the wounds which have been inflicted on the body of Christendom.

And this new spirit among the peoples will be the solvent for the problems which the statesmen have found too hard at the Conference.

There are territorial settlements which in my humble judgment will need revision.

There are guarantees laid down, which we all hope will soon be found out of harmony with the new peaceful temper and unarmed state of our former enemies.

There are punishments foreshadowed, over most of which a calmer mood may yet prefer to pass the sponge of oblivion.

There are indemnities stipulated, which cannot be enacted without grave injury to the industrial revival of Europe, and which it will be in the interests of all to render more tolerable and moderate.

There are numerous pin-pricks, which will cease to pain under the healing influences of the new international atmosphere.

The real peace of the peoples ought to follow, complete, and amend the peace of the statesmen.

In this Treaty, however, two achievements of far-reaching importance for the world are definitely recorded. The one is the destruction of Prussian militarism; the other is the institution of the League of Nations. I am confident that the League of Nations will yet prove the path of escape for Europe out of the ruin brought about by this war.

But the League is as yet only a form. It still requires the quickening life, which can only come from the active interest and the vitalising contact of the peoples themselves. The new creative spirit, which is once more moving among the peoples in their anguish, must fill the institution with life, and with inspiration for the specific ideals born of this war, and so convert it into a real instrument of progress. In that way the abolition of militarism, in this Treaty unfortunately confined to the enemy, may soon come as a blessing and relief to the Allied peoples as well.

And the enemy peoples should at the earliest possible date join the League, and in collaboration with the Allied peoples learn to practise the great lesson of this war, that not in separate ambitions or in selfish domination, but in common service for the great human causes, lies the true path of national progress.

This joint collaboration is especially necessary to-day for the reconstruction of a ruined and broken world.

The war has resulted, not only in the utter defeat of the enemy armies, but has gone immeasurably further. We witness the collapse of the whole political and economic fabric of Central and Eastern Europe. Unemployment, starvation, anarchy, war, disease, despair stalk through the land. Unless the victors can effectively extend a helping hand to the defeated and broken peoples, a large part of Europe is threatened with exhaustion and decay. Russia has already walked into the night, and the risk that the rest may follow is very grave indeed.

The effects of this disaster would not be confined to Central and Eastern Europe. For civilisation is one body, and we are all members of one another.

A supreme necessity is laid on all to grapple with this situation. And in the joint work of beneficence, the old feuds will tend to be forgotten, the roots of reconciliation among the peoples will begin to grow again, and ultimately flower into active, fruitful, lasting Peace.

To the peoples of the United States and the British Empire, who have been exceptionally blessed with the good things of life, I would make a special appeal. Let them exert themselves to the utmost in this great work of saving the wreckage of life and industry on the Continent of Europe. They have a great mission, and in fulfilling it they will be as much blessed as blessing.

All this is possible, and I hope capable of accomplishment; but only on two conditions.

In the first place, the Germans must convince our peoples of their good faith, of their complete sincerity through a real honest effort to fulfil their obligations under the Treaty to the extent of their ability. They will find the British people disposed to meet them halfway in their unexampled difficulties and perplexities. But any resort to subterfuges or to underhand means to defeat or evade the Peace Treaty will only revive old suspicions and rouse anger and prove fatal to a good understanding.

And in the second place, our Allied peoples must remember that God gave them overwhelming victory, victory far beyond their greatest dreams, not for small selfish ends, not for financial or economic advantages, but for the attainment of the great human ideals for which our heroes gave their lives, and which are the real victors in this war of ideals.

★   ★   ★   ★   ★

At the Conference my father, as a personality, was possibly surpassed by Lloyd George alone. As an influence in the councils none surpassed him. Lloyd George had more faith in him than in any other member, and paid him this tribute: "He is one of the most remarkable personalities of his time. He is that fine blend of intellect and sympathy which constitutes the understanding man . . . his sympathies were too broad to make him a mere fighting man. . . . He had rare and fine gifts of mind and heart. Of his practical contributions to our councils during these trying years, it is difficult to speak too highly."

Lloyd George's biographer, E. T. Raymond, tells us that the Prime Minister "was particularly susceptible to the influence of the last speaker (Smuts), and from a talk with General Smuts he would go to a meeting of the 'Big Four' with proposals which made M. Clemenceau wonder (sometimes aloud) whether the Allies were to ask Germany's pardon for having taken the liberty of beating her".

Milner's admiration of him and confidence in him was greater than he felt for any of the others. Count Sforza described my father as, "one of the rare original brains at the Peace Conference".

The American journalist, I. F. Marcossan, wrote in 1921, "In that gallery of treaty-makers . . . it was Smuts who contributed largely to the mental powerplant that drove the work. . . . He saw the treaty as a new declaration of war instead of an antidote for discord. His judgment, sadly enough, has been confirmed."

The English people loved him and accorded him an affection undimmed by party or politics.

I myself am of opinion that this was one of the greatest constructive periods of his life. He accomplished greater things in the

Second World War, and his standing in the affections of the peoples of the world attained a more exalted position; but he seldom worked so hard or so persistently and with such result as here in London and Paris.

By the sweat of his brow he carved his niche among the immortal great.

PART III

Uneasy Peace

XLII SUFFER FOOLS GLADLY

IT is sometimes said that my father was not a man to suffer fools gladly. Though he did not always suffer them he almost invariably showed extraordinary kindness and patience with tedious people. He was not only a phenomenally busy person all his life, but also a harassed and lionised one. He had to put up a defensive façade and to turn people away in self-defence. Yet he was quite the most patient, approachable and long-suffering person I have ever known.

It is a strange thing, but I have noticed that many people in the presence of my father, either from fear or awe, lost the faculty of being able to make normal conversation. Even members of his family were prone to this nervousness. Personal contacts of this nature, in consequence, lost much of their attractiveness, and it is perhaps pardonable that my father should on occasion have been inwardly bored. To make up for embarrassment in the presence of greatness people either talked nonsense or asked interminable questions.

The conversation of strangers with my father, however, usually took the form of questions and answers. Answers were naturally governed by whether he thought a serious answer worth while, whether it would be better to shift the emphasis on to some other aspect, whether he was desirous of changing the topic, what use was going to be made of his replies and whether a reply would serve a good purpose.

As often as not he would be asked rhetorical questions. On such occasions he never argued but simply said "Yes", or "Perhaps" or made some non-committal remark. There was no point in arguing with well-meaning, but stupid, humanity. If they found satisfaction in their own particular views there was no point in disillusioning them.

It was the pseudo-clever who really bored him. Their views he could not suffer gladly. A stupid person could be pardoned for stupidity; at least his views were elementary and human. Highly educated people should know better, and here one could not just say yes, politely, and leave it at that.

So, the clever and the pseudo-clever he often avoided. We of the family learned to know his pet aversions, and though we could never fathom the source of incompatibility, we knew that we had to keep these people away from him. Many of them were famous men in public life, not only innocuous but really well-meaning and friendly. My father often seemed to crystallise his likes and dislikes before meeting people. This was one of his most human weaknesses. I don't think he could explain it himself. He would vent his feelings by muttering vaguely "that damn fool" or "tiresome person" or "troublesome old woman" (applied to a man usually), or by just making irritable grunting noises and gestures. A cloud of displeasure would cross his brow. "Tell them I am not here," he would say curtly; and his protectors would then have to say that General Smuts was away on his bush-veld farm or out on a long walk. Sometimes contact was un-avoidable and he would then grow glum and uncommunicative —never really rude; but as time went on he would, as often as not, relent and probably end by being most charming. That was a case of kindness and generosity overcoming distinctly human feelings over which he had little control.

It was noticeable, too, that he was more tolerant of women than of men, and more generous and forgiving. Perhaps it was because he considered them childlike; or maybe it was because he had a surfeit of seeing men and liked a change. But I think the real answer was that women were less nervous in his presence and more natural. At all events, women, with the exception of the really talkative society type, he suffered without demur, though not always with any real gladness.

I must here emphasise the point that my father was quite the most disarmingly astute man I have ever come across. He had a mild, quiet way of talking or answering questions that was most soothing and satisfying, and one left with the feeling that the interview had been entirely satisfactory. Only afterwards, in the cool of night, when you came to analyse the interview, did you realise how confused your impressions were, and how little you had gleaned. In fact, you were often not quite aware of what the general impression had been at all. All you could remember was that he appeared to be talking sound logic and that you had agreed with him.

The secret of all this was a mixture of disarming friendliness and astuteness. I sometimes found myself unable to break through his defences, but here I must emphasise that out of deference to my father we never pressed a point or tried to extract views from him. That would have been unfair and ungenerous.

He exercised his mild, evasive technique by sheer force of personality, whether he was at a public meeting or on a commission. In the War Cabinet people had marvelled, and at San Francisco I saw how good-naturedly he twisted the polyglot medley of delegates of the various nations round his finger. It was a revelation to all privileged to see it.

Knowing my father as well as I did, I would treat with considerable reserve statements attributed to him by interviewers. Many of them, from my personal knowledge, were wide of the mark and reflected more the views of those asking the question than my father's true opinions. This is so, too, of people who have written about him. I do not think they always understood his mood or his meaning.

XLIII RETURNS HOME

IN August my father returned to South Africa. In less than a month General Botha was dead—killed at the age of fifty-eight no less by the bitter and unequal political struggle than by his illness.

"He had no equal as a friend," said my father at his graveside. "We have worked together with a closeness seldom vouchsafed to friends. This entitles me to call him the greatest, cleanest, sweetest soul of all my days. Great in his lifetime, he was happy in his death. To his friend is left the bitter task of burying him and of defending his works, which were almost too heavy for him to perform."

Henceforth my father was left to face the future alone.

After the years overseas it is said that he found the decision to return to South Africa a hard one. In England he had lived in an atmosphere free of bitterness and personalities and had been able to accomplish prodigies of solid work. The people loved and admired him and great pressure was brought to bear on him to accept a Cabinet position and remain. There was talk of him as a successor to Lloyd George and of elevation to the peerage. There was the suggestion of a Vice-royalty of India or Governorship of Palestine. He was much drawn to tasks, such as the League, which he had not yet completed. He is quoted to have remarked that the decision to tear himself away from Britain was the "hardest" of his life. No doubt when he said that he had visions of the dreary front of political bitterness facing him in the Union.

"The world was beginning," he said, "and I had been present at its birth. There was the League—my thoughts were in it. To leave Europe in 1919, meant to give up any intimate share in working for these things—the New Order and the League. It meant coming to a land where too often my countrymen hated my ideas and despised my larger hopes. . . ."

It was an expression of wistfulness and no more. Perhaps it was just a generous comment on the wonderful way the British people had treated him. There was certainly no factual substance in the statement. He did not find it hard to make the decision, for he had, in fact, no decision to make. There was no question of his not returning to South Africa to carry on the incompleted labours there of half a life-time. His home, his family and all the familiar attachments of over fifty years were there. Also the brilliant sunshine and limitless spaces. Nothing could resist that ingrained call.

He arrived in South Africa to run up against a solid phalanx of criticism and vituperation. The position had worsened during his absence and was now aggravated by the inevitable aftermath of the war. While loyal South Africans had been shedding their

blood on the battlefields of the world Hertzog and the Nationalists had not been idle. They had been permitted almost unlimited latitude for subversiveness; now they boldly fastened their
teeth in my father's person. The republican urge was running
strongly, and feelings were high, as my father had predicted,
over the unsatisfactory mandatory position of South-West Africa.
South Africa, they clamoured, had vainly sacrificed her sons and
treasure for that territory, and my father and the Imperialists had
swindled her out of her rightful claim. It was no good arguing
that he had done his best at the Peace Conference; would to
heaven he had remained in England with his miserable Imperialist
friends, they cried.

My father returned to South Africa and to his farm Doornkloof. Here there were now many white men, all called "baas"
or master by the native labourers. The time had come for dis-
criminatory designation. In deference to his now grey hair, my
father was called the "ou baas" or old master; so the name
"Oubaas" gradually crept into conversation and received a
broader use, coming to be used by black and white, by family
and strangers alike. Friends still called him General or Oom
Jannie to his face, but behind his back they spoke of him affec-
tionately as the "Oubaas". As the years passed and feelings mel-
lowed, it came to mean more than old master, for it was transformed into a distinct term of endearment and homage. We all
used it. My father liked it. In one of my early visits to Chequers
during the Second World War I spoke of him to Mr. Churchill
as the "Old Man"—I could not very well use the unintelligible
Afrikaans "Oubaas" nor could I say "Old Master". Mr. Churchill
was clearly annoyed and upbraided me for lack of filial deference;
I found it difficult to explain to him that I was merely making
a far from disrespectful translation from the Afrikaans idiom.
Needless to say, I never tried it in that quarter again!

* * * * *

The policy of extracting reparations, as my father had warned,
never worked. The more the Allies tried to extort payment from
Germany the less co-operative she became, and the more good
feelings deteriorated. France was proving specially insistent in
exacting her pound of flesh. Germany was being driven into a

245

sullen and resentful mood. Finally, in ill-conceived, exasperation, France occupied the rich Ruhr area in January, 1923. This precipitate action startled the world, and the Germans in the occupied territory decided on a damaging go-slow work policy.

Bernard Baruch, of the United States, supported by Woodrow Wilson, wanted to enforce demands for payment upon Germany. Baruch solicited my father's support. He cabled: "Your voice is one of high authority because your motives are unquestioned and your character and attainments eminent in your time. If anyone can bring about a realisation of the facts it is you . . .". This brought forth a retort from my father which must have startled Baruch.

Four or five years ago [he declared] we were singing our own songs of victory. To-day we are all marching to certain and inevitable defeat —victor and vanquished alike. The international chaos is growing. The economic and industrial structure of Europe is cracking in all directions. . . . Military hysteria is sapping their depleted financial resources. Everywhere you see armed men, everywhere gigantic armies, even among the small new States which cannot possibly afford them. . . . Famine for large numbers is not far off. . . .

I call for a gallant attempt now to save Europe from the dangers that threaten. . . . The time has come for the convocation of a great conference of the Powers who are mainly interested in the Reparation question. . . . The United States should be there as an active member and bear her full weight. . . .

. . . It is now universally recognised that this amount fixed by the Reparations Commission in May, 1921 (£6,600,000,000) was too high and could not be paid. . . . The amount has to be reduced to a reasonable figure. . . .

Unless the Reparation issue is speedily got out of the way, Europe may soon be faced with a situation in which the Reparation issue will be swallowed up and disappear in far more grave issues. . . .

The British people will no doubt be invited to share in the sports of the Ruhr. . . . My advice is to have nothing to do with the Ruhr. . . . We should make it perfectly clear, in friendly but unmistakable language, that in certain circumstances this country (Britain) will have regard to its own interests and take whatever steps necessary to that end. . . .There is a serious danger lest a policy o f excessive generosity on our part, or on the part of America, may simply enable France still more effectively to subsidise and foster militarism on the Continent.

I sympathise with France. But I am equally moved by profound pity for Europe. Let France in the day of her victory and greatness not forget her noble historic mission as the great bearer of liberal tradition in Europe. . . .

The Liberals in England were delighted. "If we had at the head of affairs in England to-day a statesman of the moral and intellectual calibre of General Smuts the European outlook would be transformed." The Conservatives were not so well pleased and laid the blame at the feet of Germany for "defaulting even to the length of ruining her own currency". France was furious.

By 1931 not only had Germany persistently defaulted, but even Britain herself, and the other powers, were failing in their payments to the United States. South Africa alone of all countries paid off her war debt in full.

It is interesting to note, as Mr. Churchill points out, that while reparations were being dragged out of a reluctant Germany, Britain and the United States found it incumbent to assist her with considerable loans. Thus while the Allies extracted only about a thousand million pounds from Germany, they actually put into her an amount exceeding that figure by two thousand million pounds. There can be no more damning evidence against the policy of reparations.

XLIV POLITICAL TROUBLES

Now that General Botha was gone there was more work than ever for my father to do. Botha's loss was more than that of a friend of twenty years' standing, or of a wise and soothing counsellor. It was the loss of an important bridge between the Government and the conservative masses of Afrikanderdom.

My father wasted no time with formalities. At forty-nine he was still in the fullest flush of physical vigour. He galvanised his ministers, by a little necessary prodding, into a spate of greater activity, and thereafter ruled them with an almost undemocratic firmness. He found it the best way of getting work out of them.

The effect of his return to the Union did not take long to make itself felt. "The new Smuts", it was remarked, "was more than the head of the Government. He *was* the Government. He was the Cabinet—all the departments of the state—the party caucus —the civil service—the Army—Parliament." Much as the Nationalists fumed and ranted, they had grudgingly to admit that the personality of this man controlled the destiny of the country. Though he had not come back with South-West Africa in his pocket, he had come back with something near it. He had considered the annexation of the Belgian Congo and Portuguese East Africa with such seriousness that strongly-worded protests followed from the two governments. The question of incorporation of Southern Rhodesia was also revolving in his mind. There was much to be said for it—and, beyond prejudice, little against it.

He tried to counsel his opponents at home into more constructive channels of reasoning by suggesting that they would do better to concentrate on the present and future than everlastingly casting back their memories to the past. "It is dangerous: it paralyses a people to live in the past."

On the 10th March, 1920, there was a general election. The results were disturbing. The Nationalists headed the poll with forty-four seats. They had taken eleven rural constituencies from my father and were ten thousand votes and three elected members ahead. Under Creswell, Labour staged a come-back by winning twenty-one seats, and the Unionists secured twenty-five. My father's only course was to seek Unionist assistance. "Now that the National Party is firmly resolved", he said, "to continue the propaganda of fanning the fires of secession and of driving the European races apart from each other, the moderate elements of our population have no other alternative than to draw closer to one another in order to fight that policy. A new appeal must, therefore, be made to all right-minded South Africans, irrespective of party or race, to join the new party, which will be strong enough to safeguard the permanent interests of the Union against the disruptive and destructive policy of the Nationalists."

Sir Thomas Smartt and the Unionists, in a spirit of great generosity, responded to my father's appeal for assistance. It was not to be a case of coalition for the Unionists, but of actually giving up their identity in this merger with the South African Party. The Nationalists jeeringly said that my father had now definitely allowed himself to be swallowed up by the Rand capitalists.

With Parliament in such a precarious position he had to tread warily, to do a lot of adjusting of differences and of pleading, and to forestall dangerous Opposition manœuvres. It was a busy and exciting time. One division was carried by a majority of only two votes. But not once during the long session did he allow a decisive division to materialise. In a world of fluid events he was playing for time.

But at the end of the Session in July, despite all efforts, the position was as menacing as ever.

The impasse had to be broken. This was achieved by calling the electorate to the polls again, early in 1921, after a lightning campaign. In the few intervening months there had been a marked change for the better, when stories of Russian atrocities and the corruption of the Bolshevik régime began to filter through. There was a marked swing away from General Hertzog because of his wooing of the Reds. My father got seventy-nine seats, Hertzog forty-five and Labour succeeded in winning only nine, even Colonel Creswell losing his seat. The South African Party now had a safe majority of twenty-four in the House. Three Unionist ministers were brought into the Cabinet. Sir Thomas Smartt became Minister of Agriculture, a position he filled with distinction; J. W. Jagger accomplished wonders with the Railways; and Patrick Duncan, one-time chief secretary to Milner, took over the portfolio of the Interior.

My father himself held the portfolios of Defence and Native Affairs, in addition to being Prime Minister.

In South Africa conditions were daily growing more difficult and the political situation more boisterous. The financial position of the Government was embarrassing, and the resulting increases in taxation and retrenchment were answers to Hertzog's prayers. In the rural areas the Nationalists vehemently denounced the Government as Imperialists, while in the towns they sympathised with the public because of the unbearable burdens of taxation and poor handling of the financial position. My father was personally blamed for the economic illness of the country.

By now it was becoming plain that the Nationalists were wooing Labour, an act inspired by Tielman Roos, their leader in the Transvaal. The object of all the Nationalist efforts was to unseat my father. No trouble was too great, no device too low. They spared neither effort nor decency. Personal vituperation became their accepted order of the day. Labour at the time seemed to understand this type of talk; it was still in its wild and woolly days. Moreover, the agitators of foreign countries were abroad, sowing the poisonous Red doctrines of Trotsky.

In 1919 there were native strikes in Johannesburg, Pretoria and Bloemfontein. A year later, mine natives on the Rand struck for more pay. My father drove them back unceremoniously. In Port Elizabeth a crowd gathered before the local gaol to protest against the imprisonment of their Native Labour Union leader. When the fire hoses were turned on them they retaliated with sticks and stones. A stray shot started a panic, after which the police opened fire; there were six European and sixty-eight native casualties. The country was shocked. My father had to shoulder the blame.

Soon there was an even more serious clash with natives at Bulhoek near Queenstown. The followers of Enoch, the high priest of a religious sect, camped as usual during their festival on some Crown Land. When it was over they refused to move. They refused to leave at the behest of a posse of police; only God was their Master. The Government decided on action. Colonel Truter with a strong force of police was sent to disperse them. The Israelites, with God on their side, charged down on the representatives of the law with assegais, shouting "The hour for the black man is at hand!" At thirty yards the police opened fire. There were close on three hundred native casualties.

Though the Nationalists cared little for the loss of native lives, Hertzog attacked my father violently for the incident. There was some defection from the ranks of the South African Party. Some said my father had been too slow in action, that he should have stepped in earlier.

While this storm was on, he had to leave for an Imperial Conference in London in June. It was a rushed visit. He concentrated on the problem of Japan and the Pacific, which he declared were "the world problems of the next fifty years. There Europe and Asia and America meet. . . .

"If we look to world peace, we must do nothing to alienate Japan. . . . The only path of safety for the British Empire is a path which she can walk together with America. In a certain number of years we shall be in a great crisis in Europe, and not all the time in a position of independence, but involved with France and all the odium which her policy may bring upon us, and not really strong and independent to act according to our interests. That is why I am looking more and more in other directions—that is, to America."

During this visit, while he was spending a quiet week-end with the Gilletts at Oxford, where he had attended a Rhodes dinner, the King sent for him. His Majesty was preoccupied with the problem of opening the Ulster Parliament and wanted advice about the opening address. My father assured him that it was a wonderful opportunity for some quiet elaborating on the Commonwealth theme. Though the official speech drafted for the King was a "blood-thirsty document", His Majesty was so impressed with my father's conciliatory ideas that he asked him to jot down headings for a draft speech. So that evening my father drafted a speech which he handed to the King.

Next day Lloyd George invited my father to a special Cabinet meeting to consider the King's speech. The draft produced there, though nobody knew it, was a typed copy of the one my father had written out the evening before. After discussion, it was passed with minor modifications. The results were historic, and the tone a pattern for Britain's future relations.

Next Tom Casement called on my father in London with an invitation from de Valera and other leaders to meet them in Ireland. De Valera was obsessed with the problems of Northern Ireland and of neutrality. Sir Horace Plunkett wrote to my father: "From my pretty full knowledge of my countrymen at home and abroad I can truthfully say that no living statesman would be more acceptable to the majority of the Irish people as a political adviser than yourself." He sent an invitation for an informal meeting at his home. When told about it, "Lloyd George", my father said, "was delighted. He said it was the very thing to follow the King's speech, and also, he said, I was the very man to do the job—no Englishman, an outsider, a Boer." As an outsider and Boer, he went, not as a representative of the British Government. "No one else knew. Not another member of the Cabinet. We kept it an absolute secret." He went as Mr. Smith. At Kingstown he slipped unnoticed from the ship and took a taxi to Dublin. The driver protested about dangers ahead, but my father said cheerfully "carry on".

In Dublin he joined De Valera, Erskine Childers, Arthur Griffith and others. He was glad to see Griffith there, for he had been a journalist in Johannesburg before the Boer War and would be able to confirm what my father said. My father took the line that it was pointless to go on with the rebellion. It would get them nowhere and England was bound sooner or later to crush it. No one would come to their help. He referred to the King's speech saying it was obvious that England would welcome a settlement. They wanted a republic, they said. England would want facilities for her Navy, my father said. They quite understood that.

He told them the story of the South African Republic and how their vain struggles led almost to their annihilation. But later they were saved and regained their complete independence under the new Dominion Status. He described the virtues of this new status in glowing terms. "Make no mistake about it; you have more privilege, more power, more peace, more security in such a sisterhood of equal nations than in a small, nervous republic having all the time to rely on goodwill, and perhaps the assistance, of foreigners.

"I asked them if they would agree to an immediate armistice with the military now in Ireland, and a conference with the British Government. . . . They agreed before I left."

Before my father left London De Valera, and later a mission, came to discuss details. My father put on record his ideas for Dominion status for Ireland before returning to the turmoil of South Africa. "I pray God that you may be wisely guided and that peace may now be concluded before tempers again change and perhaps another generation of strife ensues."

If the effort transpired to be a partial failure to some, my father was not a party to such a view. "It has not been a failure, and in the end I feel persuaded success will come to the movement that has been set going."

The armistice came in the nick of time, for a massacre was narrowly averted. A large number of gunmen had been detailed to shoot down, at an appointed time, all uniformed people and British agents in Dublin.

XLV THE GREAT STRIKE

As my father disembarked at Cape Town the unemployed booed him; the Nationalists cried that he had brought the country to the verge of ruin. He had been gallivanting in Britain and neglecting his own country. Deputations of every nature flocked to see him. All came with grievances. All sought assistance. There were ominous rumblings on the goldfields.

By 1922 the mines were in straits. Miners' wages stood at a high level, while high-grade ore was running out and working costs were mounting. The industry had to rectify the position, if it was to survive. It was also set on breaking, once and for all, the stranglehold of the Trade Unions. At the same time there were disturbing signs of an impending slump.

The actual trouble arose over the terms of the September Agreement, which laid down that whites would not be replaced by blacks and that the present ratio of Europeans to natives would be maintained. Economic conditions necessitated a deviation. The Trade Unions were confident of their power to break the Chamber of Mines.

On January 1st, 1922, wages on coal mines were reduced by

five shillings per shift and the miners went on strike. The mine-owners flatly refused to take the dispute to arbitration. A few days later the *status quo* on the colour bar was abrogated on the gold mines, and twenty thousand miners went on strike. All attempts at arbitration were bluntly refused. The great struggle between the magnates and the miners was on.

My father looked upon this as a domestic affair and refused to intervene. Apart from his democratic outlook on the rights of individuals, he had other reasons for refusing. It was clear to him that a real show-down was imperative to break the present *impasse*. Those who attribute his tardiness in taking control to indecision and dilatoriness, would do well to bear this in mind. Half-measures at this stage would not have succeeded decisively in bringing Trade Unionism to its senses.

The strikers said that my father was a "paid agent of the Chamber of Mines". The Chamber itself was hardly more complimentary. This was no surprise to my father, who said the Chamber was always quick to run to the Government for help but slow in doing anything for itself. He had begged them for years (and he went on doing so for another twenty years) to take a more intelligent interest in their political welfare and to do something by way of influencing their workmen, by propaganda methods, to a more amenable attitude of mind. The magnates' answer was always the same. They were not prepared to meddle in "politics". So obsessed were they in their fear of the body politic that they complacently allowed the Mine Workers' Union and Dr. Albert Hertzog to move in with that same weapon and to undermine the industry from one end to the other.

By now the strikers had marshalled themselves into commandos and were patrolling the mines to ward off "scabs" from slinking back to work. There were frequent clashes with the police; there were other more disturbing incidents, and feelings were mounting. My father advised the miners to return to work—on the terms of the Chamber. This shattered the last hopes of an amicable settlement.

Disturbances were now occurring all over the Rand. On February 27th there was a clash outside the Boksburg gaol, and three strikers were shot by the police. In Parliament, Tielman Roos demanded an instant enquiry. My father turned down the suggestion flatly: "I think we shall allow things to develop," he said. They developed swiftly. On 4th March the Chamber refused a request from the Industrial Federation for a round-table conference. After that the tempo of events became too much for the leaders of the Industrial Federation to control, and they made way for a group of five revolutionaries who called themselves the Council of Action. Under these the strike soon assumed grave proportions, and striker commandos were active all over the Reef. Their trail was marked by violence and even murder. Mine officials and some natives were clubbed or shot in cold blood. There were acts of pagan brutality.

Up to this stage my father had let matters develop. Now he took swift action. All available police were called up and Active Citizen Force commandos were mobilised. Martial law was proclaimed.

During the earlier phases of the strike my father remained at his office in Pretoria. I remember these times vividly. Threats on his life were pouring in by every post. Once more he was the focal point of all hatred. Our home at Irene was turned into a small fortress, with police guards, bloodhounds and machine-gun posts. The security authorities were well prepared. A wild peach tree now grows in a derelict machine-gun pit on the bend in the road near the white gates at Doornkloof.

When my father eventually decided to go down to Parliament in Cape Town, for security reasons he took with him my mother, my sister Louis and myself. The other children were safely at boarding school. We went in a special train consisting of two coaches and two trucks with our cars. The journey took twenty-seven hours which was a record that stood for many years. There were many unavoidable delays at stations, but when we moved we travelled at great speed. At one station, marks on the ground showed that part of the train had left the tracks, only to be deflected back a little farther along by a guard rail.

My father's business with Parliament was brief. In declaring martial law he said, "The Government was very reluctant to declare martial law, knowing the temper of the people and that in the end there would be serious bloodshed . . . the choice had been taken away from the Government. This morning from practically one side of the Reef to the other the commandos attacked, and fighting has been going on over a large part of the Rand, and is still going on, and there have been heavy casualties. . . . All essential services have been brought to a standstill, and from one end of the Reef to the other the natives are in a state of wild turmoil. . . ."

Having completed his business he prepared to return to Johannesburg. He took with him his party secretary Louis Esselen and Hodgson, his chauffeur, and his car. At Potchefstroom Esselen tried to persuade him to leave the train and proceed by car, as it was not certain that the line ahead had not been blown up. My father would not hear of it. Finally, after Esselen had exhorted him repeatedly to "reconsider" the matter, my father, who appeared to be listening attentively, said suddenly: "Louis, I have thought it out carefully and I am now absolutely convinced that we need six more bulls for Rooikop."* Louis was beaten.

They left the train near Randfontein, untrucked the Cadillac, and Hodgson drove them in to Johannesburg where they made for headquarters at the Drill Hall. Frequently they came under heavy rifle fire. Hodgson drove furiously. They had rifles with them in the car. Louis Esselen returned the fire for all he was worth. In his excitement he said to my father, "Shoot, Oom Jannie, shoot!" But my father just sat impassively. Later on a striker's bullet punctured the back tyre and a little farther on they pulled up to change the wheel. Then my father said to Esselen: "You have kept on telling me to shoot, now how many bullets have you left?" Oom Louis replied that he had used up all his. "A fine fix we might now be in," my father retorted, "if I had also used up all my ammunition."

It appears that during the shooting one of the occupants ducked low behind the bodywork for shelter. Though this seemed to me a wise precaution, my father spoke very scornfully of it. He was, as has so often been repeated, a man without physical fear. I am uncertain whether it was a vice or a virtue.

Louis Esselen was like his uncle Ewald, a great friend of my father's and the family. He was a person of very cheerful disposition and was on intimate terms with friend and foe alike. Consequently, as a source of contact and listening post, he was invaluable. But to say that he was a "backroom boy" whose advice

* His bushveld farm.

swayed my father's judgment would be an over-statement. My father took advice from nobody. He always listened carefully, but preferred to make his own assessments and decisions. Louis Esselen fared no better than others in his efforts to sway my father. It was Louis, in himself, who was such an asset to the Party.

Once in the Drill Hall that evening my father listened briefly to the latest reports and then set briskly about counter-measures. Everything was in a state of chaos. The police were thinly scattered over the Reef guarding mine shafts and crucial points, but beyond this the strikers were in possession of practically the whole Rand. Government troops had been timidly and poorly handled and had suffered heavy casualties. By dawn his plans had been put into operation. The crackle of heavy rifle fire was plainly audible from all directions. Troops everywhere had gone into action. The strikers were swiftly driven out of their strongholds along the ridges at Brixton and Langlaagte and from the Reef towns of Benoni and Boksburg. Sniping and dirty methods of fighting took a heavy toll of Government troops, but they pushed on briskly. In Fordsburg, not far from the heart of the city, the strikers made their last stand. Aircraft dropped on the insurgents warning pamphlets and an ultimatum. At 11 a.m. artillery opened a bombardment of the strikers' headquarters. At noon the white flag was run up. It was all over. Two of the extremist leaders, Fischer and Spendiff, committed suicide.

In the course of a few days my father had quelled this full-blooded revolution. Once he had assumed personal command matters sped to a swift conclusion. Once more he had revealed his brilliance as a military tactician. In all other respects, however, the strike was a disaster of the first magnitude for the Government, and it drove Labour straight into the arms of Hertzog. It had also engendered a bitterness of feeling that was eventually to drive my father's party from power.

The general feeling was that he had delayed too long before taking drastic measures. For myself, I keep an open mind on the matter. As a long-term policy, however, it has paid ample dividends, for it served to break and crush the too-powerful Mine Workers' Union and cleared the atmosphere, in difficult times, for a fresh start by the mines. It also taught the miners a salutary, if bloody, lesson which they have not yet forgotten, and put a fear of strikes into them. So much so, that though the workers of the industry are preponderantly Nationalist, they made no attempt to hold up my father's war effort during the Second World War. I think, therefore, that his handling of the strike has been justified by the test of time.

But unfortunately time and popularity do not necessarily go together.

The mines, which were in dire straits before the revolt, turned into flourishing concerns within a few months of the conclusion of the trouble. Some dividends improved by over a hundred per cent.

In lives the cost had been heavy, being double that of the South-West African campaign. There had been 535 European and 152 native casualties.

My father knew he would suffer, for the spilling of blood by a politician is always a mortal sin. He returned to Parliament. His first action was to ask the House to indemnify the Government. The Nationalists howled and jeered. All this expense and bloodshed could have been avoided, they shouted, had my father chosen it. Hertzog opposed the motion with a characteristic speech. He paraded my father's long sequence of bloody events from the 1913 strike to the present one, ending on a high shrieking note: "The Prime Minister's footsteps drip with blood! His footsteps go down history in that manner!" In ten years my father had declared martial law three times, and on each occasion Parliament had been asked to indemnify the Government.

For three full days derision and scorn were poured upon him. He sat silent and impassive.

After the strike several strikers were executed for murder. The two Hanekom brothers were shot out of hand when caught sniping red-handed. Stassen was hanged for killing two natives. There was a considerable delay in carrying out Stassen's sentence, and as in the case of Jopie Fourie, the Opposition made the best of the position. A white man hanged for the murder of natives! It outraged the feeling of the negrophobes.

A commission of enquiry also revealed how deeply implicated the Nationalist Party had been in the strike. It had, in fact, hoped to turn it into something akin to a rebellion, with Free State and Western Transvaal burghers coming to assist the strikers. It had also done its best to fan the fires of discontent in order to bring additional hatred to bear on the Government. Hertzog, as before in the rebellion, steered clear of personal implication, but he can certainly be said to have been a very interested spectator. There was also strong evidence of a Red hand.

My father was fated to be born into a turbulent period of history. South Africa can thank God he was there to cope with events. Hardly had the shouting over the Johannesburg strike died down when there was fresh serious trouble. This time it was in South-West Africa. The Bondelswarts, a mixed Hottentot race of the Warmbad district, refused to pay a certain tax and were openly defiant. After persuasion had failed, they were briskly bombed into submission by aircraft, a small number being killed in the process.

Serious charges were made against the authorities concerned, and later the Permanent Mandates Commission of the League declined to accept the Administrator's version of the incident and demanded a more authoritative account of the operations. Though they accepted this, and a reassurance and explanation by my father, the Bondelswarts affair nevertheless left a bad taste. Britain later adopted a similar punitive bombing technique in the Middle East against Arab rebels and on the North-West Frontiers of India against the wild tribesmen. It proved effective in result and light in casualties.

In Parliament, the Bondelswarts affair was fought bitterly all over again. As before the trouble was all laid at my father's door.

XLVI GROOTE SCHUUR

IN the seventeenth century the Dutch East India Company built three granaries on the slopes of Devil's Peak above Rondebosch, a few miles outside Cape Town. One of these was known as de Groote Schuur or Big Barn. Groote Schuur frequently changed hands and was rebuilt many times. In 1893 Cecil Rhodes bought it and considerable areas of surrounding land from a Mrs. A. J. van der Byl of "Fairfield", Caledon.

Rhodes had met Herbert Baker, the architect, a year previously and had been fascinated by the young man's idealism; so he commissioned him to remodel Groote Schuur and to collect antique furniture. In 1896 the thatched roof caught alight and the house burned down with all its old furniture, glassware, silver, books and manuscripts. Little was saved. Whereupon Baker designed a new Groote Schuur, slightly bigger, but conforming generally to the old foundations. Once more it was stocked with valuable furniture and relics.

The style was old Cape Dutch, with the characteristic curved gables and twisted chimneys. The windows were teak-shuttered and the doors and all other woodwork heavy and massive. The front of the house looked out upon terraced lawns and ancient oaks. The view was pleasant but restricted. Baker did not like it. He had begged Rhodes to build the house a few hundred yards farther up the slopes, directly above the impressive hydrangea crescent. For sentimental reasons Rhodes wanted it on the site of the former granary.

As an architectural conception Groote Schuur is beautiful. But as a house to live in it left much to be desired. It was more a museum than a home. The heavily-panelled walls and beamed ceilings gave it a dark and gloomy atmosphere. It lacked warmth. With its twelve bedrooms and many other halls and chambers it was a large house. A long marble verandah ran along the back, which was warm and sunny in the afternoons and looked upon the mountains. Rhodes's bedroom, together with the others, was on the upper floor. His had a lovely view on to the wooded slopes of Table Mountain and Devil's Peak, but most of the other bedrooms faced forward on Rondebosch, and did not enjoy the enchantment.

Everywhere were massive chests and on the verandah stood huge green vases. The dining-room was adorned with two Gobelin tapestries. Two more were presented to my father during the Second World War to complete the set. One of these he gave to Libertas, the official residence of the Prime Ministers in Pretoria, the second now hangs with the others in Groote Schuur.

In his will Rhodes bequeathed Groote Schuur to the Prime Ministers of the United South Africa, a dream that was at the time still eight years distant. General Botha was the first to occupy the house. My father took over in 1919 when he became Premier, and during the parliamentary sessions he used to live there. The rest of the family came down in relays to keep him company, for we always considered Irene as our home.

My mother did not like the place, with its darkness and heavy atmosphere. But we as children enjoyed its vast spaces. My father appreciated its privacy and its wonderful views of the mountains. He took a small, plain bedroom for himself looking out on Devil's Peak. He liked it in summer, but in winter the heavy drip-drip of the rain from the enveloping oaks depressed him.

In Rhodes's den, called the Smoking Room, are about three hundred books, many typed and bound in red leather. This collection never failed to amuse my father. It appears that Gibbon had been a great favourite of Rhodes, and so he gave Hatchard of London instructions to translate all the authorities used in the *Decline and Fall*. Half the books consisted of these typed translated volumes which cost Rhodes £8,000. The works were already available in translations, my father said, and in his ignorance Rhodes was simply wasting his money.

In May, 1923, my father scrambled briskly up Skeleton Ravine to the summit of Table Mountain, where he unveiled a memorial at Maclear's Beacon to those who fell in the First World War. He was in a buoyant mood, as he always was on the mountain tops, with the distant panoramas stretching away into the hazy hinterland and the mists swirling in the crags below, and the crisp air of the lofty spaces fanning the heated brow. Here, to a group of hardy climbers squatted on the grey rocks around him, he delivered the greatest and most inspired oration of his life. It has been compared to Lincoln's oration at Gettysburg. I shall quote this speech fully. It came to be known as the "Spirit of the Mountains".

Those whose memory we honour to-day lie buried on the battlefields of the Great War, where they fell. But this is undoubtedly the place to commemorate them.

Nothing could be more fitting and appropriate than this memorial which the Mountain Club of South Africa has erected to the memory of their members who fell in the Great War. And this, the highest point on Table Mountain, is the place to put the memorial. The sons of the cities are remembered and recorded in the streets and squares of their cities and by memorials placed in their churches and cathedrals. But the mountaineers deserve a loftier pedestal and a more appropriate memorial. To them the true church where they worshipped was Table Mountain. Table Mountain was their cathedral where they heard a subtler music and saw wider visions and were inspired with a loftier spirit.

Here in life they breathed the great air; here in death their memory will fill the upper spaces. And it is fitting that in this cathedral of Table Mountain the lasting memorial of their great sacrifice should be placed. Not down there in the glowing and rich plains, but up here on the bleak and cold mountain tops. As Browning put it:

> Here, here's their place,
> Where meteors shoot,
> Clouds form,
> Lightnings are loosened,
> Stars come and go.

Here for a thousand years their memory shall blend with these great rock masses and humanise them. The men and women of the coming centuries, who will in ever-increasing numbers seek health and inspiration on this great mountain summit, will find here not only the spirit of Nature, but also the spirit of man blending with it, the spirit of joy in Nature deepened and intensified by the memory of the great sacrifice here recorded.

Geologists tell us that in the abyss of time Table Mountain was much more of a mountain than it is to-day. Then it was more than 18,000 feet high, of which barely one-fifth remains to-day. And in another million years no trace may be left of it. Here there is no abiding city, neither is there an abiding mountain. Human life itself may be but a passing phase of the history of this great globe. But as long as human memory lasts, as long as men and women will remember and be interested in the history of their storied past, so long the Great War —perhaps the greatest in human history—will be remembered, and the memory of the great sacrifice here recorded will endure as part of it.

Standing here to-day as we do on the summit of Table Mountain, may I add a few words in reference to the spirit of the place?

The attraction of the mountains for us points to something very significant and deep in our natures. May I illustrate the matter by a little story which is not quite true, but neither is it entirely mythical, as it finds some support in the testimony of science.

Once upon a time, in the far-off beginning of things, the ancestors of the present human race lived far down in deep blue pools of the ocean, amid the slimy ooze from which they had themselves sprung. There they lived and developed a long time, and in the sounds of the sea, in the rhythm of the waters, and of the rising and falling tides they learnt that sense of music which is so mysterious a faculty in us, and which is in a much smaller degree shared by so many marine animals.

The music in a sea shell pressed to our ears carries us back to the very beginnings of life on this planet. It is a far-off echo of our most ancient experience as living things. As our ancestors thrived and developed they gradually found the pressure of the waters too much for them. They felt stifled and longed for more freedom to breathe. And so they rose slowly on to the beaches, and finally emerged into the air on the seashore. What a blessed relief was there, what an unconscious sense of lightness and exaltation! No longer submerged in the stifling depths, but with full lungs expanding in the invigorating air. The rising from the sea was the most glorious advance in the forward march of terrestrial life. But it was not enough.

The same process of development and advance continued on the seashore. In the course of time the heavy air of the sea levels became too much for the ever-forward movement of the forms of life. The pressure on the lungs was too great, and the forward movement seemed to be arrested in a sort of atmospheric morass, in which a great heaviness hung on the spirit of life. At this stage a new great advance was registered. The rise to higher levels took place. Some animals developed wings with which they could fly upward and for longer or shorter periods remain in the high places and breathe a keener air. And in this rise they shook off their ancient sluggishness and lethargy, and developed a spirit of joy which had hitherto been unknown to them. The skylark, rising in an ecstasy of song high up into the air, is an illustration of the new great advance.

Other forms of life developed other means of locomotion and of ascent from the heavy low levels. As the dull, deadweight was removed from the lungs a new sense of lightness, of progress, of joy and gladness dawned on the ever higher rising forms of life. The great relief was not only of a physical character, but had the most far-reaching and spiritual values. And so it has come about that finally in man all mortal and spiritual values are expressed in terms of altitude. The low expresses degradation, both physical and moral. If we wish to express great intellectual or moral or spiritual attainments we use the language of the altitudes. We speak of men who have risen, of aims and ideals that are lofty, we place the seat of our highest religious ideals in high heaven, and we consign all that is morally base to nethermost hell. Thus the metaphors embedded in language reflect but the realities of the progress of terrestrial life.

The Mountain is not merely something externally sublime. It has a great historic and spiritual meaning for us. It stands for us as the ladder of life. Nay, more, it is the great ladder of the soul, and in a curious way the source of religion. From it came the Law, from it came the Gospel in the Sermon on the Mount. We may truly say that the highest religion is the Religion of the Mountain.

What is that religion? When we reach the mountain summits we leave behind us all the things that weigh heavily down below on our body and our spirit. We leave behind a feeling of weakness and depression; we feel a new freedom, a great exhilaration, an exaltation of the body no less than of the spirit. We feel a great joy. The Religion of the Mountain is in reality the religion of joy, of the release of the soul from the things that weigh it down and fill it with a sense of weariness, sorrow and defeat. The religion of joy realises the freedom of the soul, the soul's kinship to the great creative spirit and its dominance over all the things of sense. As the body has escaped from the over-weight and depression of the sea, so the soul must be released from all sense of weariness, weakness and depression arising from the fret, worry and friction of our daily lives. We must feel that we are above it all, that the soul is essentially free, and in freedom realises the joy of living. And when the feeling of lassitude and depression and the sense of defeat advances upon us, we must repel it, and maintain an equal and cheerful temper.

We must fill our daily lives with the spirit of joy and delight. We must carry this spirit into our daily lives and tasks. We must perform our work not grudgingly and as a burden imposed on us, but in a spirit of cheerfulness, goodwill and delight in it. Not only on the mountain summits of life, not only on the heights of success and achievement, but down in the deep valleys of drudgery, of anxiety and defeat, we must cultivate this great spirit of joyous freedom and uplift of the soul. We must practise the religion of the mountain down in the valleys also.

This may sound a hard doctrine, and it may be that only after years of practice are we able to triumph in spirit over the things that weigh and drag us down. But it is the nature of the soul, as of all life, to rise, to overcome, and finally to attain complete freedom and happiness. And if we consistently practise the religion of the mountain we must succeed in the end. To this great end Nature will co-operate with the soul.

The mountains uphold us and the stars beckon to us. The mountains of our lovely land will make a constant appeal to us to live the higher life of joy and freedom. Table Mountain, in particular, will preach this great gospel to the myriads of toilers in the valley below. And those who, whether members of the Mountain Club or not, make a habit of ascending her beautiful slopes in their free moments, will reap a rich reward not only in bodily health and strength but also in an inner freedom and purity in an habitual spirit of delight, which will be the crowning glory of their lives.

May I express a hope that in the years to come this memorial will draw myriads who live down below to breathe the purer air and become better men and women. Their spirits will join with those up here, and it will make us all purer and nobler in spirit and better citizens of the country. . . .

XLVII ECLIPSE

A T this time the Chartered Company's contract in Southern Rhodesia was about to expire and the people were given the choice between self-government and incorporation by the Union. Naturally my father wanted Rhodesia to join us in the south, for we had much in common. Little more than the sandy bed of the Limpopo divided us. In order to facilitate discussions he decided to pay the colony a visit. By some it is said it was a political manoeuvre to enhance the Government's voting strength. But in truth the visit was planned because the hour for amalgamation seemed propitious.

Rhodesians will perhaps forgive me for saying that their country, though a fine one, is a poor one so far as earning-capacity is concerned. Rhodesia's livelihood was based largely on her mineral wealth, and more specifically on her gold mines, which were situated on small ore bodies and very much of the nature of wasting assets. Her farming potential, like that of all southern Africa, was distinctly limited and not sufficient to sustain a country dependent largely on imports. Geographically she was a land-locked country, living at the mercy of her neighbours for outlets to the sea. Strategically she was a satellite. Against all this were arrayed only two factors; one was the Rhodesian distrust of the Boers and the Afrikaans language, for the Rhodesians were at that time largely English; the other was Rhodesia's somewhat inflated idea of her own importance. She did not relish the idea of coming in merely as a fifth province of the Union.

Negotiations went on for some while, the Union offering very generous terms to both the Chartered Company and the settlers. Financial authorities in Britain praised the magnanimity of the Union Government, and Lord Milner said that Rhodesia could hardly hope for better terms. Considerable pressure by the Imperial Government was brought to bear on Rhodesia to accept. The publication of the Smuts-Malcolm agreement caused a great boom in Chartered Company shares.

While my father's visit was in progress it looked as though the merger might be successful, but after he left, the Rhodesians had second thoughts and all their old misgivings returned. So, when the plebiscite was held, a majority of 2,785 of the 15,000 voted against incorporation. A golden opportunity had been lost by both countries.

At the time of the Second World War, when my father was once more in power, discussion again took place on the question of a merger. Times were very favourable: we had fought for a common cause—Rhodesian soldiers with Springboks in the Union Defence Force, under the overall command of my father. Mutual regard was good and South African terms attractive. Rhodesia was feeling her financial straits and was looking for a way out. What more natural for her than to look towards her wealthy southern neighbour. But once again the question of prestige dragged out the negotiations, and in the end my father's government was ousted from power and the project died a natural death.

Since then, Rhodesia has had to cast covetous eyes on the

wealthy Northern Rhodesian Copperbelt mines, and to concoct the unwieldy idea of a federation of Central African States. Britain has had misgivings about this ambitious scheme, pointing out that she fails to see what Southern Rhodesia has in common with native-saturated Nyasaland. My father's views were that Rhodesia's incorporation in the Union was inevitable, but that there was no point in endeavouring to hurry the matter; it would come in its own good time. Responsible opinion in Rhodesia, I believe, shares these views.

The Rand strike opened an ever-widening rift between the Government and the Labour Party. Though Labour had little in common with Hertzog, their deep hatred of the South African Party was sufficient to blind them to the many defects of the Nationalists. The Government, which a short while before had a majority of twenty-four, could now muster a lead of only fourteen.

Merriman and many other supporters of my father were now old and in indifferent health; they could not be counted upon to be present in the House during voting. So the majority was in effect considerably smaller. It was clear that the days of the Government were numbered. Tielman Roos was working to bring Hertzog and Creswell together. On 23rd April, 1923, his efforts were rewarded when a coalition between the two parties was formally agreed to. It was a black day for South Africa. It is hard to forgive Labour for this unprincipled act. My father called it an "unholy alliance".

Events now occurred swiftly. His majority had by now been reduced to eight and the first of the post-war slumps had reached its peak. A by-election occurred at Wakkerstroom, a rural constituency in the Eastern Transvaal. The Government had held the seat for three successive general elections and staked all on winning again. They persuaded the well-liked A. G. Robertson, Administrator of the Transvaal, to stand. It came, therefore, as a great shock when the Nationalists won the seat.

Without consulting his Cabinet, or the Party caucus, my father decided to resign and to test the feeling of the country in a general election. A few hours after the result of the by-election became known he told the House of his decision. It was a bombshell. The

House was startled. His friends were angry and resentful, as well they might be. But truth to tell he had decided on this precipitate action because he feared his Party might decide to struggle on as before. He felt the House could not do constructive work with such a slender majority.

The election was notable for the bitterness of the attacks levelled at my father and for the parading of all the old bogeys. Such attacks never failed to form rallying points for the Nationalists. On June 17, 1924, it proved so once again. Hertzog won sixty-three seats against my father's fifty-three, and Labour increased the majority by an additional eighteen.

My father resigned before the House met. Hertzog became Prime Minister. He remained Prime Minister for fourteen years.

It was the end of an era—Part One of the Smuts Era.

XLVIII DOORNKLOOF

MY father moved out into what is known as the "political wilderness". In reality, apart from the affront to his personal feelings, he merely moved out to the quiet of his farm at Irene. Here, in the peacefulness of these congenial surroundings, he was at last able to take a well-earned rest after twenty exacting and crowded years of political and public labours. Doornkloof has been through the years a wonderful refuge and inspiration to him. When my father returned home to Irene after his public trips he would sigh contentedly as he crossed the threshold and say: "Isn't this wonderful!" For he never forgot the irresistible call he first heard at Riebeeck West. The passing of the years had, in fact, merely served to strengthen and mature his deep-rooted love for the veld and the wide unspoiled spaces of nature.

At the time of the National Convention Britain decided to

withdraw her garrison from the Transvaal and evacuate the various cantonments. In 1908 my father bought for £300 a large wood-and-iron officers' mess hut from the camp at Middelburg and this he re-erected on Doornkloof. On the 24th November, 1909, he moved into this house with his four elder children. My youngest sister (named Louis after General Botha) and I were subsequently born in this old tin shanty, and we all grew up on the farm.

Doornkloof is one of the oldest farms in the Transvaal, the first title deeds having been taken out by General Erasmus in 1844. His modest grave is now almost obliterated near the Irene Golf Club.

We were no newcomers to Doornkloof, for in the 1880s two uncles of my mother, Petrus and Jan Schabort, had farmed here for some years. It was on the advice of Jimmie Roos that my father bought the farm from Mr. Erasmus, the price being £6,000.

The first manager of the farm was Jan Krige, my mother's uncle, and one-time market master of Johannesburg. He took over in 1910. Before the Boer War, when my parents lived in Johannesburg, Oom Jan lived with them. When my father took my mother to Johannesburg, in 1897, the old man did not realise that they were married, and being of pious disposition, was much worried that they should be living in sin, and seriously counselled friends to speak to them. He remained at Doornkloof till Andries Weyers, subsequently to marry my eldest sister Santa, took over as manager after the First World War.

Doornkloof lies in the rolling Dolomite country, with its rocky hills and tall grass. Here the Hennops River, the headwaters of the Limpopo, which flows round the northern boundary of the Union, breaks picturesquely through the hills and meanders quietly down a rich loamy valley. This, when my parents first arrived, was a dense virgin wood of thorns, which had given the name of Thorn Valley to the farm. The woods were cleared to make way for the broad strip of land bordering the stream. Along its banks was left a narrow margin of the original trees, and it now has as well a fine façade of tall ashes and oaks, planted by my parents.

In the upper reaches of the farm, above the Rietvlei Dam, where Kaalspruit pierces the hills, rises a conspicuous conical feature known as Bays Hill, which is surmounted by a derelict blockhouse that had been manned by a Derbyshire Regiment during the Boer War. Across the valley, immediately in front of the house, rises a further low rocky koppie, the grey of the dolomite blending attractively with the green grass and wild kippersol bushes. On it are the ruins of another blockhouse, now almost overgrown by a cluster of tall gums.

At the back of the house, and in fact on all sides, rise rocky ridges, dotted here and there with indigenous trees, bristling with jagged outcrops of chert which, inter-bedded with the dolomite, form the most grotesque rockery shapes. Everywhere is the tall, waving canopy of highveld grasses.

Lying at an altitude of 4,800 feet above sea level, the atmosphere is exhilarating, making one feel it is good to be alive. No country on earth boasts a finer climate than the Transvaal highveld. Small wonder my father always took a deep breath whenever he got back from his long journeys.

Though the setting and climate were idyllic, Doornkloof was not a farming proposition, for the profusion of rock considerably curtailed cultivation. Realising that, my father was quite content to do his best, to see the development grow under his eyes and to foot the inevitable annual bill of deficit.

There was nothing on the farm when we arrived excepting its attractive wildness and the prospect of much satisfying development. The only discordant feature was the twelve Boer *bywoner* families sprawled along the rivers. White "squatters" and progressive farming are quite incompatible, and so from the first, my father set about their slow displacement. It took many years, and signs of their humble habitations are still evidenced by the tumbled heaps of stone and neglected fruit trees, the latter now a source of joy to the native piccanins.

The house was erected on the sloping ground overlooking the centre of the valley and a pleasant sweep of the river. From the front could be seen the two blockhouse koppies, and in the trees in the distance, smoke from the little village of Irene. In the crinkle of the river immediately in front of the house is a cluster of wild yellow peach trees, remains of a large British camp here during the 1880 war. At Irene itself there had been a big concentration camp during the Boer War. A railway line runs through

Irene and past the front of the farm. I grew up with the noise of the trains clattering noisily over the bridge. It was a distant friendly sound in the night. In the daytime there was the cooing of the turtle doves in the trees.

Though the house has no architectural beauty it nevertheless has the virtue of spaciousness and pliability. Three-quarters of the way round runs a broad stoep. This was most useful to us as children, and as we grew up parts were partitioned off as additional rooms.

The house, as befitted a good officers' mess, was a large sprawling one, with big mess rooms and numerous smaller apartments. These, by suitable manipulation, we turned into ten quite comfortable bedrooms. It was a corrugated-iron structure, lined with wood, perched well off the ground on tall foundations. In summer it was hot, and in winter bitterly cold, with water freezing in the bedroom jugs, and chilly draughts filtering through the walls. It was an ideal refuge for stoics. The original idea was that this house would be temporary and that a permanent home would be built higher up on the hillside one day. Needless to say the family grew so attached to this old "Groothuis" (big house) that the other idea gradually fell away. The Groothuis was like a big meccano set, for it was easy to dismantle the internal walls and alter its shape at will. Besides, my mother loved it and would not hear of a change.

Its size came in useful not only to store the constant stream of books that flowed in, but also to accommodate the number of visitors inseparable from a public life. The hillside was bare at the time, but my parents set about tree-planting with vigour, and later also found time to put in half a million blue gums for mine-prop timber farther afield. With the establishment of the trees, the wild bees discovered the virtues of the house, and numerous swarms made hives in the partitions between the wood and iron. We have, for as long as I can remember, harboured about a dozen permanent swarms and though docile in winter, the inhabitants were apt to grow irritable as the hot sun beat on the tin in summer. So, at the cost of occasional painful stings, we have had an inexhaustible supply of honey within our walls.

My father grew very attached to his birds and bees, and he made it, to the last, a special duty to see that the hollow stone bird baths had a constant supply of water. In some strange way the bees sensed his sympathy, for he was almost immune to their wrath. But we, as well as many a visitor, were not always so fortunate.

To my father Doornkloof was not only a farm and a home, it was a refuge. Here, away from the bustle of the cities, and far from clamouring humanity, he could relax and live a natural life. Without this quiet contrast, existence would have been quite intolerable. For the life of a public man in South Africa is more exacting than in the Old World. Here people feel that they have a distinct right to call on their public men, and on the slightest provocation come along to see them, whether it be a business call or an excuse for a chat. Some come from distant parts with greetings and messages of goodwill; some come with grievances; some merely come to talk; they arrive in an endless stream. They leave one no time for privacy and little for work. For this reason it is absolutely essential with us in South Africa to have a secluded refuge, some inviolable castle in the wilds. Doornkloof was that, and my father took full advantage of it.

He had always taken an intimate interest in farming, but time pressed too heavily to permit active farming himself. Instead, he employed managers, and to these he gave an almost free hand. They had the pleasure of pouring money into the farm, and my father, disregarding his personal financial affairs, enjoyed seeing the farms grow. On Doornkloof his interest was centred largely on his pedigree Friesland dairy herd, but in the bushveld he took great pride in his red Afrikander cattle and his wheat crops, while in the Western Transvaal his interest was mealies (maize). The bushveld farms satisfied a botanical interest in the tree and shrub line and the other farms afforded an interest in grass types. Nearby, in Irene, was his botanical friend and mentor, Dr. Pole Evans, onetime head of the Government Departments of Botany and Horticulture.

My father's farming efforts were not always free from malicious meddling. A fine Friesland bull, Bloemhof Sondag, for which he paid £1,200, had its tail cut off by some maniac one night, and a few months later was fatally poisoned. Since then quite a few cows have succumbed to arsenical poisoning. With such crude feelings running wild, it was obvious that the owner of the farm himself might not always be clear of hostile attentions, so in times of crises the State provided guards. Though my father found being guarded most irksome, the authorities nevertheless insisted. On some dangerous occasions I remember him going off alone at nightfall wrapped in his greatcoat to the safety of the hill behind the house. In his bedroom cupboard was always a loaded revolver, though I doubt whether he would have known how to use it. Rifles he understood well and was quite a good shot. When my brother and I grew up, he gladly passed on to us all his firearms and wartime souvenirs.

The dolomite area of Irene is honeycombed with caves, which we children loved to explore. My father never showed any desire to go down them, though he took an active interest in their associations. He told us of the last lions that were shot here, about 1850, by General Erasmus. A male and female were encountered at the big white stinkwood tree near the house, and the male being wounded, both made off into the big cave on the river below Bays Hill. They never reappeared.

When we were children he used to tell how, in the days of the ruthless Matabele Chief, Moselekatze, in the 1820s and '30s, natives had sought refuge in the caves. Moselekatze heard of this and by lighting huge fires in the entrances, asphyxiated his hapless victims. We often came upon their skulls and bones in our fossickings.

But perhaps the biggest service Doornkloof rendered my father was the scope it offered for walking, riding and other forms of exercise. He greatly enjoyed walking, and there was no corner for many miles around he did not know from tramping and re-tramping repeatedly. If Table Mountain afforded him the religion of the lofty spaces, in Doornkloof assuredly was centred his worship of the veld. It was his favourite farm, and I feel convinced that his decision to buy it in 1908 was one of his most satisfying and beneficial decisions.

On the northern shoulder of the low koppie behind the house rises a conspicuous cluster of rocks. Here, in this picturesque corner of our sunny veld, with familiar views all around, we scattered his ashes. He had made no request about what was to be done with his mortal remains, for the matter was one of indifference to him; but we all felt that this was a fitting resting-place.

Doornkloof was much like a menagerie, for we always had wild animal pets roaming about. In the days before the First World War we started off with elands, largest of African antelopes, but one after another these had accidents and the experiment petered out. Later on, we had an ill-tempered leopard, Spice, and at various times two lions. The first, Sally, was almost fully grown at fourteen months before we returned her to the Pretoria Zoo. She was a good-natured and playful animal, and like the rest, roamed about at will. We had two stately kudu antelopes, numerous frolicsome copper-coloured impala, many prancing springbuck and lesser duiker and steenbuck. A second attempt at establishing elands proved no more successful, but we were more successful with our blesbuck, and a herd of some hundreds of these roam happily on the hills.

We have also had some large birds as pets, such as ostriches, various cranes and wild geese, canaries and budgerigars. Some of these, like many of the other animals that had grown too tame and familiar, lost their fear of man and grew aggressive. None could be said to have the docile habits of our ordinary domestic friends. They were purely elements to stimulate the eye and interest.

Still wilder and more restful was the bushveld farm. It was warm there and unspoiled, and about the nearest spot of untamed Africa to Pretoria. In that peaceful atmosphere one could feel the ties with the primeval past. It had an irresistible attraction for my father. He went out there frequently whenever he had a chance. In the old days, before we had a house, we used to camp out in small bivouac tents, which got waterlogged or blew away during storms. The journeys there along old ox-wagon roads in the unreliable motor-cars of the past were veritable adventures, and I have vivid memories of pushing through patches of mud or stretches of sand.

In 1930 we had an emergency landing strip prepared in the bush and my father used sometimes to fly down from Pretoria for week-ends. On one occasion his Wapiti only just cleared the trees on its take-off.

Here, as elsewhere, he went for long walks, and from these rambles he sometimes returned hot and covered in minute ticks. For the next few days he would carefully pick these tiny pests from his person. On one occasion I came across him walking back home in the road, minus his trousers, which had become too heavily infested with these parasites.

XLIX HOME

THE attractions of the old shanty at Irene lie in its associations, rather than appearance. The approach to the house along the narrow dirt road is winding and informal and the house is obscured by a haphazard jumble of trees. There is no garden, the rectangle of Kikuyu grass being merely enclosed by indigenous white stinkwood trees, where formerly there had been a hedge. The first impression of the building is of a tall red iron roof and white wooden palings enclosing a broad verandah. The red granolithic steps have an impression of age and rough usage. As a boy I did much hammering on them to test their hardness.

Inside, in the hall which is dark because the stoep shuts out light, one sees first the gong-stand given to my father by his Imperial Staff after the East African campaign of the First World War. On an ebony base stands an arch of elephant tusks from which are suspended two shell-cases of the 4·1-inch guns of the *Königsberg*. On the left and right are the doors to the sitting- and dining-rooms. Ahead stretches a long dark passage, lined all the way with high shelves of books. At the end of this passage is a big mess room with high beamed roof with glass ceiling fittings to admit more light. For this was once the billiards room. My father made it his study. Another door going off to the right at the end of the passage is my father's bedroom.

The rest of the house does not really warrant description except that my father's side was separate. There is one thing common throughout the house, however, and that is that all rooms everywhere are crammed with overflowing bookshelves.

My father's bedroom was as plain and unpretentious as any in the house. It was in fact little better than a broad passage, eleven feet wide and fifteen feet long. A door and window faced on to a fly-screened stoep. Beyond that one looked abruptly on to walls. Until 1928 he used to sleep regularly on a hard iron bed on this stoep, but thereafter he sought refuge from the cold in his room and later surrendered himself to the luxury of a spring mattress. The furniture was plain, consisting of a three-quarter bed, washstand, wardrobe, cupboard and chairs. Clothing overflowed into a curtained bracket screwed on the walls. There are numerous photographs on the walls, mostly of members of the family in their youth, and of grandchildren. Crude little sketches made by various grandchildren in their earlier years of infancy, were thumb-tacked on to the walls. My father was a homely man with a keen family sense, and these intimate little knick-knacks gave him great pleasure, and at times, I think, solace.

The room was extremely tidy. My father was a careful and fastidious person. He would neatly fold his clothes before putting them away and there was no disorder.

In this room he kept a tin of biscuits and a tin of peppermints. These he used sparingly himself on occasion, but really they were there as a lure for his grandchildren. These small folk were to be found there with their Oupa at all times, both parties obviously enjoying the exchange of credentials. Though their parents often felt they were proving a nuisance, their grandfather obviously felt differently, no matter how unorthodox their entertainment. As he lay on his bed reading they would pile their toys and his boots on top of him, or clamber all over him and sit on his tummy. His beard never failed to intrigue them and he had to answer endless questions. We have sometimes arrived on the scene to find them shining his torch into his mouth, the fond patient goodnaturedly submitting to their attentions.

When we remonstrated, he assured us that they were all having a good time. They often had equally good times when out on walks along the farm roads, for the youngsters usually came back looking like dishevelled tramps and their Oupa on such occasions looked guilty as he handed them back to their mothers.

There can be no doubt that my father derived great joy from the presence of little children. They seemed to denote to him the wild, unspoiled, basic human animal from which we have drifted on our devious ways in life, often without any distinct credit to our simple origins. They seemed to rest his mind and at the same time to restore his faith in human nature. They were a wonderful tonic. The younger they were the more fuss he made of them. And at the same time they were also a protection to him when very talkative visitors arrived, for by drawing attention to the children he usually succeeded in diverting the conversation.

Below the house, near the lands, was a dam, and here we all used to swim and canoe in summer. As toddlers the water was too deep for us and my father used to carry us in his arms. He was a strong swimmer, and as in walking, he covered long distances and loved the exercise, swimming quietly with a breast-stroke action. Physical exercise in one form or another formed quite a fetish in his life. After the Boer War he kept in trim by doing physical culture exercises under the eyes of Arthur Collard, preferring the brisk Swedish methods to the other more ponderous muscle-building ones. Another secret of his amazing physical fitness was his perfection of the idea of relaxation. When he really sat in comfort, he always put his feet up on a stool, and even on long journeys in aircraft he did this where possible.

The chill of water never worried him and when at the Cape he bathed in the cold Atlantic at Hout Bay and Witsands quite as readily as in the warm waters of the Indian Ocean at Melkbos Strand or Christian Beach. After one of his climbs of Table Mountain in 1933 he came down via Constantia Nek and before cooling down took a plunge in the frigid waters of Hout Bay. The result was a bad chill and an admonition from Dr. Moffat.

While walking and climbing he bathed where he wished, in the clear pools in the mountains or in the tropical stream of Central Africa. Crocodiles he avoided by venturing only into extensive shallows, and bilharzia, a microbic schistosoma hazard of all African rivers, he outwitted by bathing only in swiftly running waters. Needless to remark the question of bathing costumes seldom obtruded. On one occasion while out walking with a party which included a young woman he suggested they all take a dip in an attractive stream, saying "take my costume". This happened to be one of the cut-away male type and when the young lady protested he said, "Good heavens, child. A woman has nothing to be ashamed of in exposing her bosom!" Convention, however, thought otherwise! He undressed next to his car on public beaches with complete nonchalance.

My father's habit of swimming far out to sea was always a matter of concern to us, for both sharks and angry backwashes lurked beyond the breakers. During the war his guards took the precaution of having a life-saving apparatus handy in the back of the car. The fact that my father had been swept out to sea at Hermanus by the powerful backwash as a youth, and had succeeded in getting back only by dint of keeping cool and casting himself upon the incoming waves, had not deterred him. At the treacherous beach at Witsands he expected us, too, as children to swim in the powerful undertow. It was a streak of abandon in him, rather than the reckless. It was an imp which appeared whenever he drove an automobile as well. But here, too, by skill and cool judgment, his luck held.

Up to 1923 we had worked on the candle and paraffin principle as far as lighting went, but as a surprise, when he was away in England, my mother had had a small electric plant installed. She was disappointed when upon his return my father, not even noticing the change, criticised the darkness of the wall paint, though he had complained about the lights when he got back from the Peace Conference in 1919.

To our intense joy he also brought a radio back with him in 1923, but it crackled so and reception in those days was so poor that we had to turn it off whenever he was about as the noise irritated him. With the advent later of better sets, and as the standard of news services improved, he became inclined to listen to this portion of the programmes. During the hectic years of the rise of Nazism, he liked to listen to the radio news services, and during the war itself he insisted on hearing his radio news. No matter how often he had already read the same reports in the press, he always listened in, not only to the local but also to the Daventry service from England. The 7 a.m. service he listened to while shaving in his bedroom, but the midday service and the 7 p.m. one corresponded with meal times, and all present then had to sit hushed and patient while this item dragged on. Frequently we said to him, "But, Pappa, you have already heard all this before!" To which he would always retort, "Yes, but you never

278

know. You might just pick up something new!" At Irene, with only the family present, these hushed meals were not so bad, but at Groote Schuur, no matter what guests were being entertained, everybody would be hushed and the same ritual gone through. I remember him glancing at his watch and saying to the Queen at Windsor Castle during the war after a late tea, "Would it be possible, Mam, for us to listen to the wireless news?" whereupon Her Majesty obligingly took us off to her sitting-room. Mr. Churchill too, I noticed, always had his small portable brought in to the dinner table at Chequers.

As parents, the two in our family left little to be desired, though at times my father was away so frequently and so long that he became almost a stranger to us. My mother did not usually accompany him on his travels, but stayed at home to look after her large family, which she did good-naturedly, giving us great freedom. She saw to the comforts of the house and left the public duties to my father.

The dual system in the Union of having our Parliamentary seat in Cape Town and Administrative capital in Pretoria is a relic of the days of the National Convention, and a compromise to satisfy the prestige of the two provinces, but it is troublesome in every other respect. For it means that up-country parliamentarians, like ourselves, had to have two homes, one in the Cape during the four months annual sessions of Parliament, and one in the Transvaal for the rest of the year. With families at school, the move down to the Cape became quite impossible for us, and we had to evolve some form of compromise. We felt it our duty for somebody always to be at the Cape with my father.

There is no garden in front of the house at Doornkloof now. My mother was a keen gardener when we first came to live here, but my father preferred his wild, indigenous plants and scorned the exotic varieties of gardens. So gradually my mother was prevailed upon to let nature take its course. The rectangular row of wild Transvaal white stinkwoods marks the position of an erstwhile hawthorn hedge and had their origins in bird droppings. In about 1920, the young trees started coming up through the hedge and my father decided to take the hawthorns away to make room for them. And the flower-beds slowly made room for lawns.

So gradually the colour disappeared from the front of the house, but in its place grew up a wilderness with a character of its own. But the view from the front verandah was sufficiently pleasant, especially in summer, to need no garnishings. And in the evenings the gorgeous Transvaal sunsets painted enchanting pictures in the western skies. But now the trees have hemmed in the garden so effectively that it is difficult to see even the sunsets.

In the old days my father used to go to his office by train, walking the mile and a half to the station. There was no bridge till the First World War (when my mother had one built as a surprise) and when the river came down in spate after heavy thunderstorms, we were sometimes cut off for a while. When the floods were not too high, we were still able to scramble across the trunks of two huge fallen willows. On the way to the station my father would escort his elder children to the local school in the village.

In times of crises, he took, however, to his car, and after the First World War he went regularly to office by this means. He learned to drive an old Buick in 1911 and thereafter he drove many cars, always preferring to do the driving himself. In the open he drove with skill, but he never quite mastered traffic, robots or stop streets. Consequently his driving was at times a bit nerve-racking. My wife tells of a trip round the precipitous Marine Drive of the Cape with the Montagu Normans. Lord Norman had been warned about my father's driving and insisted that my wife should sit in front as a restraining influence. This made matters worse because my father now not only found it necessary to point things out with his hands, but faced backwards when talking. The result was a winding and uncertain course— with a drop of a thousand feet, sheer, at the side. The Normans were too petrified to appreciate the superb scenery and only prayed for the end of the drive. Even my wife on occasion felt moved to draw my father's attention to his driving.

Much as my father had to commend his driving, he had little to boast of as a mechanic. Beyond being able to change a wheel, he was quite helpless with the machine. He was really not good with his hands at all. Their slender shape and long tapering fingers truthfully indicated the artist. They were expressive rather than strong. Hence, as a handyman about the house, he left much to be desired. I don't think I ever saw him using a screwdriver, and I never saw him using a hammer.

But I will say this for his motoring efforts, that when stuck in sand or mud, he pushed and pulled with the best of us, in preference to sitting behind the wheel. He once spent all day pushing his car through the mud of the Game Reserve. When he got to the hotel at Louis Trichardt he chanced to look at the hands of the young man who had been driving. These were white and unsoiled. The contrast spoke for itself. He just gave an eloquent grunt!

In the earlier days, in Johannesburg and Pretoria, he had been a keen cyclist and on week-ends used to ride out for miles into the countryside. I have never seen him on a bicycle, but my mother remembers quite clearly the Raleigh he bought for £31, which gave him so much fun. From his lone cycling jaunts he used to return badly sunburnt and exhausted, but having enjoyed his outing.

As a father of a large family he was absolutely ideal, for he had the unbounded physical energy to join in our vigorous games, and the only complaints were from the smaller ones who said that he was too rough. The big house on Doornkloof was well suited to these vigorous indoor games at night, and after supper there would be absolute pandemonium, with everybody rushing about wildly, followed by my father with a stick. The idea was not to be caught with your feet on the ground, or a painful smack from the stick would result. My mother says he played this self-conceived game with her young brothers and sisters at Stellenbosch, he played it with us, his children, and later he played it with his numerous grandchildren. Even my mother was not always proof against the penalties of the game.

L LIBRARY

M Y father's library of books showed his range of interests.
His collection was not large, numbering a mere 6,000, but
it can truthfully be said that he had read them all and
knew their contents, as the marginal notes in many will show.
Some of the books are valuable, many are authors' inscribed
copies, and some are of considerable age.

In the passage leading up to the Study are his books on travel,
native study, Africana and wars. There are about 70 volumes of
the wars in Africa, chiefly the World Wars. On the World Wars
in Europe there are 250 volumes. There are also in these shelves
numerous books on South African history, South African reminiscences, native folk-lore, anthropology and ethnology.

There is a good Africana collection of about 400 volumes.

In this same passage, in gaps, and above the level of the bookshelves, hang photographs of J. H. Brand, Kruger, Emily Hobhouse, de la Rey and Botha leaving the Houses of Parliament just
before the Rebellion, the First Union Cabinet and the 1919–20
Cabinet.

Also in this passage, at the lower end, are many hundreds of
books on fiction which my mother considered her preserve. They
range from the Walter Scott classics to present-day light Afrikaans
reading.

The Study houses the main collection. Here in this 30-by-20-
foot room there are seven-layer shelves round the entire perimeter
except for the 28 feet taken up by doors and desks. On the two
end walls used to hang the German flags of South-West and of
East Africa. These are now stored elsewhere for safety. There used
also to be numerous Zulu shields and clusters of assegais, East
African bows and arrows, guns and other articles which I removed
elsewhere some years ago. Now there remain only the bronze
emblem of a German train at Keetmanshoop, sawfish teeth, my
father's Boer War sjambok, cartoons and pictures. Over the door
is a large signed photo of the delegates of the National Convention, and just alongside a large autographed one of the Imperial

282

War Cabinet of the First World War. There are smaller photos of Botha, Merriman, Schalk Burger, Campbell-Bannerman, J. H. Hofmeyr and my father at forty. There are also four original cartoons by Ward of *Punch*.

The furniture consists of two large desks, a safe, two settees, chairs, club-easies and my father's leg rest. Legal books form the largest and best part of the collection, filling one complete wall. Of these there are forty large very old Law books in English, French and Dutch, as well as 125 old volumes in various languages. There is a large collection of Gluck's German *Pandecten* and other German books: there is the French *Causes Célèbres* and *Codes Français* and other French works: there are considerable numbers of English Law books, including Maritime Law; there are the Grotius Society books and many others in Dutch.

About 300 of these references are still used in present-day legal practice.

Elsewhere there is an old Dutch Bible from Antwerp dating back to 1534, but otherwise all the books are modern. They include works on Relativity and Evolution; the Quantum theory, Physics and Chemistry; the atom, Biology and Genetics; Cytology, Biochemistry, Heredity, Geology, Darwinism and Evolution; Anthropology and Palæontology; Metallurgy; The Nature of Matter; Agriculture and Ecology; Psychology and Ethics and many others of scientific and philosophical interest. The authors cover the famous scientists of our time: Einstein, Eddington, Jeans, Tutin, Aston, Gregory, Blaikie, Huxley, Lindemann, Millikan, Younge, Russell, Perry, Poulton, Bews, Keith, Infeld, Wagner, Kayser, Passarge, Soddy, Milne, Bragg, Haldane, Hogben, Max Planck, Bohr, Rutherford, Lodge, Faraday, du Toit and numerous others. These more or less fill one wall.

The rest of the shelves are crammed with books of every conceivable character, as well as numerous pamphlets, publications by various societies and government publications. The books cover such topics as history (of many countries), travel, poetry, education, sociology, ethics, international affairs, wars, eugenics, philosophy, government, military operations, Commonwealth affairs, League of Nations, political problems, exploration, Poor White problems, farming, psychology, finance, numerous biographies and autobiographies, constitutional histories, mining, religion,

German books on Foreign Policy, encyclopædias, dictionaries, versions of the Bible, Shakespeare's plays, poetry, Keats, Goethe and the Brontës, Walt Whitman, and much else besides.

In the north stoep annexe, just outside the Study, are his 300 botany books containing such works as Dr. Marloth's complete series of the Flora Capensis; Flowering Plants, Natal Plants, Orchids of the Cape; books by Engler on African botany; Portuguese botany books, general botany, Californian and Pacific plants, volumes on the Stapeliæ, Euphorbiæ and Lithops, Flora Græcæ, Das Kaapland, British botany, Andrew's Heaths, Ferns of Great Britain and Ireland, Forest Flora of the Cape, American Wild Flowers; books on palæo-botany by Seward and Marie Stopes, books by Pole Evans and Hutchinson; and various additional books and journals. Some of the older books are rare and precious. Some represent the only copies in this country. By and large, therefore, it is probably the best private collection in the Union.

Then there is an additional southern annexe on the other side of the study containing mostly books on foreign and international affairs, education and such-like, as well as books on the First World War.

It was throughout a modest collection, neatly stored and all arranged and stacked by my father personally. The family seldom interfered with his books, except periodically to dust them, whereafter he would complain that they had been mixed up.

The rest of the books in the house belonged to my mother and overflowed to every room. They were mostly books on fiction and the classics, and to suit taste, even detective thrillers were included.

*   *   *   *   *

After dinner it was the habit of my father to retire to his study to read or work, and here no one dared disturb him. At 9.30 he would return to the dining-room, which we used as a living-room, and here he would join in family chatter while drinking his nightcap cup of scalding, weak tea. At ten, he would go to bed where he would tune in first of all to the late radio news, and after that he would read till about eleven, when he would turn out the light and drop off to sleep. He was a very light sleeper, but usually he slept soundly till about 4 a.m., when having slept his fill he would switch on his light and read till daybreak. The 7 a.m. news he usually listened to while shaving, and depending on the time of arrival of the morning paper, he might then already be almost through it. Breakfast was at 8, my father standing up and walking about during much of this meal. Yet it was a contented impatience, and after a boiling cup of tea he would go outside into the sunshine to finish the paper.

This completed, he would prepare to leave for his office in Pretoria. At Groote Schuur in Cape Town his ritual was the same. There was never any fuss or bother or ill-humour. My father invariably started off the day fresh and cheerful. The worries with which he had gone to bed, he had long since solved during the night. Once having come to a decision he never worried. His mind was absolutely decisive.

There were always grandchildren around him while he was eating, and for these he would prepare a special plate of bread and honey cut into small squares. They were usually rather noisy and when the news service came on we had to shoo them away.

Work he did in prodigious quantities. He was never idle like a normal person. He never took time off just to sit and ponder. When he wanted to do a little heavy thinking, he often went for a long walk and did both together. He was always either reading, writing or talking. Ordinary novels he virtually never found time to read. We once, for the fun of it, prevailed upon him to read a detective story by Dorothy L. Sayers and he grew so engrossed in the plot that he did not turn out the light till he got to the end. Thereafter he never read another.

In 1923 the Earl of Athlone brought Lord and Lady Milner out to the farm for lunch. Lady Milner mentions this visit in a publication of her diaries in 1950. She refers to my mother as a "plump Boer woman", though at the time my mother weighed only 107 pounds. She says we seemed awed by the presence of a great man (Milner). Doornkloof has seen many great men, and we are not easily awed. And the "scrub cattle" she saw were prize studbook Frieslands. However, my father was very pleased to see Milner and to show him hospitality. It was an informal, enjoyable occasion.

LI HOLISM AND EVOLUTION

IN the quiet of this rambling home my father now found himself in the summer of 1924. The electorate had decided to put him on the shelf. George Hay, a Labour candidate, had ousted him from his seat in Pretoria West. As Leader of the Opposition it was essential that my father should have a seat. Numerous successful South African Party candidates immediately offered him their seats. He chose to accept Gert Wessels's one at Standerton.

Now for the first time he was free to do as he wished. At home he did not go round moping like a defeated man. He seemed buoyant, and almost glad to be out. There was not going to be an idle moment, for he had already long ago planned what he would do one day when he had leisure.

For many years he had been reading, studying and arranging his ideas on a book on philosophy he intended writing. He therefore now sat down, and with little additional preparation, set about writing feverishly. He had read all the philosophers and his ideas were so clear that he had seldom to refer to them again. In laborious longhand, he wrote on and on. It was all done so unobtrusively and with so little fuss and bother that we barely realised he had tackled his great work. There were no stenographers about and no experts in consultation. In eight months the task was completed. *Holism and Evolution* was in manuscript form. To his secretary, Jan Dommisse, fell the difficult task of deciphering the handwriting and typing it all out. Only at this stage did we assess the extent of the activity that was afoot.

In many respects *Holism* is a remarkable book, quite apart from the fact that it is a link between the physical and metaphysical. It is remarkable for the speed in which it was written. It is remarkable because my father wrote it as a relaxation when he must have been suffering considerable mental depression after his rough political drubbing. Nor was he able to devote his time exclusively to writing, for at the same time he was busy with the domestic affairs of his Party, which was threatening to crumble.

Yet under all these varied circumstances he set out his ideas in a clarity of prose that is arresting and almost poetic in parts.

It is not a book for light or casual reading.

Holism will stand out as a message of perfection, building up and leading to still greater perfection, of fragments leading to wholes which are superior to the mere sum total of their constituent parts. It is a doctrine of optimism and elevation.

Yet these great ideas my father had carried modestly in his head all these years. He never spoke of them in the family, and even after the book had been published, he could seldom be drawn into discussion. It was part of his life-long reticence. He often spoke more openly on the public platform than in the small private circle.

Holism ran into three editions in England and a special edition was also printed in America. The Germans were much interested in the work, and a German edition is also available.

On the fly-leaf to the Second Edition, on which he had done extensive corrections, he scribbled:

"To see a world in a grain of sand,
And a heaven in a wild flower—
Hold infinity in the palm of the hand
And eternity in an hour."

Holism, like the theory of the build-up of wholes it propounds, is itself a child of complex creation. It was as a youth when he was fond of poetry that the germ of holistic concept occurred to him, for to him poetry brought the fundamentals of reality. In studying the works of Goethe and Walt Whitman, he said in a lecture at the Witwatersrand University on 21st September, 1927, it seemed to him that there was something greater in them than in their works and in their personalities than in their mere words. It was in studying their personalities that he came upon the conception of the whole. When he returned to South Africa from Cambridge just before the Jameson Raid, he found the country torn by racial strife. After the Raid came years of friction which culminated in the Boer War. The Boer War had left him his first big problem in holism. "We were left fragments out of which we were to make a whole, and it was the problem of South African statesmen to follow up the ideal in the solution of our

287

political problems. We did so and I think not without some success. Gradually we have seen emerging out of these discordant elements the lineaments of a new South Africa. We have not yet the whole, we have not yet a really *united* South Africa, we have not yet attained to the unity which was an ideal. There is still too much of the old division and separation in our national elements, but still the effort has been made, and to-day you see in South Africa the biggest problem facing us being solved along holistic lines."

In the vast complexity of the world around him my father was groping for some solution—some key to the amazing pattern of events around him. As a scientist he was disinclined to the belief that the world was a mere haphazard jumble of disconnected factors. There must be guiding laws in nature and science, if only one could find them.

We all feel we have to be guided by some light through the maze of life. What I have done in philosophy is more from a general standpoint, without any technical thought. I have simply tried to hammer out some rule of thought to carry my action along.

In our day it is all the more necessary for us to hammer out a new point of view. There is no doubt that we are living in a most extraordinary era, and I think the words of the poet apply here:

"The old world is dead,
and the new unready to be born!"

We have left behind us a great era in the history of the world. We do not see it yet, and we are in the transition period between the two. It is one of the most interesting and one of the most difficult periods for any generation to pass through.

What we want is some larger synthesis, some concepts that will bring together the vast details with which we have to deal. There has been an immense movement forward in thought, science, philosophy and all forms of human development. We are now running the risk of getting lost, becoming submerged in the details, and it is all-important for us to get some larger view of all this vast mass. We want what Professor Hoernle would call after Plato, the "synoptic vision" over all these details.

If we could have that vision much of our present-day perplexities would disappear. I have no "synoptic vision". I have only an idea which

Pausing to talk to friends on the way up Table Mountain—1938

General Smuts with the Writer at Wajir, North Frontier District, Kenya—November 1940

General Smuts addressing troops at Mersa Matruh, Egypt—August 1941

Looking from the window of his Lodestar at Kilimanjaro—1940. Note the informal cap to keep his head warm

occurred to me and which may, to some small extent, help to guide us through the surrounding difficulties.

Holism is an attempt at synthesis, an attempt at bringing together many currents of thought and development such as we have seen in our day. It is not a system of philosophy. I do not believe very much in systems. They are sometimes helpful, but it is most difficult, in matters so complex as life and thought, to take any one concept that might embrace adequately the whole. Holism—the theory of the whole—tries to emphasise one aspect of thought that has been hitherto a neglected factor. I am trying to hammer out this neglected factor, which is, to my mind, all important in getting the "synoptic vision"!

After the First World War there was, even more than in the pre-war years of intense, morbid nationalism, the same problem in holism. "I think the League of Nations is a genuine effort in reconstructing the broken front of European civilisation, of once more reforming unity out of division and discord. The American word 'league' was hardly the correct one. I prefer the French word 'society'. The phrase 'Society of Nations' seems to me to bring out the points essential to the unity of spirit which that 'Society of Nations' seeks to produce.

"In the years to come when people look back on the changes in our human attitude, they will probably say the greatest change has been wrought, not by these events, but by science. Science has proved the greatest constructive force in the world, but it had also proved the greatest destructive agent. Our world of ideas had been practically shattered by the changes in science. What was needed was the elaboration of ideas to help the world to get back once more to a sane and wise road."

He thought the most notable change science had made in the world of ideas was the idea of creative evolution. It meant a fundamental change in our outlook. We had all been brought up to look upon the world as something ready-made and completed and moving forward as a fixed, rigid entity. Science had shattered that idea and shown that the world was far from rigid. It was a growing, creative universe, a world in a state of flux with increases in all directions.

The realisation of that concept would mean a complete metamorphosis in our outlook in life. That change was embracing the world in all its many details. There was nothing constant about its components. The Universe changed and grew and developed, just like a human being. You realised that the world at bottom was not substance but flexible changing patterns.

Time and space had changed their character and become flexible. Only ratios still appeared to be constant. Matter had gone by transformation into energy. Only patterns and structures remained.

"If you take patterns as the ultimate structure of the world, if it is arrangements and not stuff that make up the world, the new concept leads you to the concept of wholes. Wholes have no stuff; they are arrangements. Science has come round to the view that the world consists of patterns, and I construe that to be that the world consists of wholes."

The wholes and parts formed and shaped each other. Yet the whole was greater than the sum of its parts. Human personality was the highest whole. A man shaped all his thoughts, all his actions by the whole in him, his personality. At the same time the parts had influenced the whole in him by mutual service and adaptation.

Switching the argument from man to dead things the same principle must apply. The idea that matter was determined by its elements must be abandoned.

The effect of this change in point of view is far reaching. In philosophy it is difficult to estimate values: the beauty, the truth, the goodness of things. They seem to be additional to the substance of things. On the other hand, if you adopt the idea of patterns, you get away from substance and get patterns in which truth, goodness, beauty and value become bound up in the nature of things. To be a whole is to be real. . . .

The world consists of a rising series of wholes. You start with matter, which is the simplest of wholes. You then rise to plants and animals, to mind, to human beings, to personality and the spiritual world. This progression of wholes, rising tier upon tier, makes up the structure of the universe.

This reasoning must effect the concept of causality. The present theory was that there was equality between cause and effect. If that were so the world would now be just as simple as in the beginning. Holism postulated that slightly more was produced in the effect than was contained in the antecedent causes. If this were so, it would necessitate a re-writing of the laws of logic. The universe of to-day was bigger than that of long ago. By an infinity of increments this additional building and creation was continuing.

Wholes are the very basis of reality. Matter is more than it appears, for in it there is a pattern, a whole which is its very inmost nature. "That explains how it is possible for matter to blossom into such forms as mind and life."

He spoke also of the peace of mind his theory produced:

We find, instead of the hostility which is felt in life, that this is a friendly universe. We are all inter-related. The one helps the other. It is an idea that gives strength and peace and is bound to give a more wholesome view of life and nature than we have had so far.

Wholeness is the key to thought, and when we take that view we shall be able to read much more of the riddle of the universe.

In July, 1948, my father replied to Professor Adolf Meyer-Abich, the well-known German philosopher of Hamburg, who had written to him at length about Holism:

At the present moment I can do nothing about Holism. My political responsibilities at my age [78] are so heavy that I cannot find time for the revision of the old book, nor the writing of the new book which has been simmering in my mind for some years. When I look at the world unrest to-day and the confusion which prevails in science, in philosophy, in religion and in our whole human outlook and set-up, I feel more and more that in the concept of Holism we have the key to many a door, and the way to ultimate solutions. Something holistic is at the heart of things and in the nature of this universe, which is not a mere chance or random assemblement of items. The detailed things derive most of their meaning, significance and functioning from the whole of which they are but the parts. They are not mere parts but really members of wholes. Both as a metaphysical and as a scientific concept the whole is basic to an understanding of the world. And in sociology and religion this is more clearly the case. Relativity is only a halfway house to this more fundamental concept.

This being my conviction, you will realise how much importance I attach to Holism, and how anxious I am to give the concept a further push forward. But at present I can do nothing about it. . . . My political position in South Africa, and to a less extent in the world, is such that I cannot say goodbye to that aspect of my work. But I still hope against hope to return to Holism at the end. . . .

Please give no further thought to a degree for me from the Hamburg University. I thank you for the kind thought, but I have already so many honours, and do not wish for more at my time of life.

I feel deeply concerned about the world position, and not least about Germany, which is at the heart of the European, and indeed the human problems facing us to-day. No more critical situation has faced the world in all history.

Questions on the private religious feelings of people are always difficult, for the simple reason that we often find it hard to analyse our own beliefs. To fathom my father's ideas on religion and a Superior Being has always been a problem. If one were to judge by the extent he read the Bible, one might assume that he was of a pious disposition, in the lay sense of the word. But that would be an over-simplification, for he read the Bible as a gem of literature and wisdom and as a saga of family life of distant days.

Whether he believed in God depends on the implications of the question. He certainly did not believe in a supernatural being in the form of a man, or the narrow definition of the Jehovah of the Israelites. But he did believe in some deity, some overall holistic personality, some supreme law that controls the destiny of all in the realms of space. In essence this is a broader interpretation than that of the Old Testament, but is it in reality, not just the same idea grown more comprehensive?

The New Testament he preferred to read in Greek, again as a classic of language and a study of people. That Christ had actually lived he had no doubt, but he thought of him as a very remarkably gifted young man, rather than as the Immaculate Son of God. Few people have studied the New Testament more meticulously, and hence few, he said, realise just how short the active phase of Christ's career was. It must be a difficult study, for it took him years to unravel the details to his satisfaction. He was always thinking of the problem of Personality and of Christ as the Greatest Personality. The world could only advance through the efforts of the Greatest Personality and he pondered over the genius of Christ continually.

As a person who prized the intellectual qualities of man well above his more bovine attributes, it goes without saying that my father placed great store on education. It was this factor, he said, which distinguished man, the pinnacle product of evolution, from the beasts of the fields. Education should have as broad a base as possible, with considerable leavenings of the humanities, arts and classics. It was the function of education to teach people how to think, not what to think. It should not consist of a parrot-like cramming of facts and figures. Rather should it emphasise the appreciation of these facts and figures. And it should include a training on how to seek detail from works of reference. History should be studied not in the narrow national sense, but as a study of past events from which we might learn lessons and avoid pitfalls. Mathematics should introduce an idea of orderliness as well as proportion and perspective. Latin should envisage life in the Roman times rather than declensions and conjugations. Geography should stress the oneness of the human race and science a poetry of the Universe. All are inseparably intermixed. Education is universal.

And with education, he grouped the need to foster hobbies. They were not only a great source of interest and education, but kept off the deadening hand of boredom which seemed to overtake so many old people.

LII HERTZOG GOVERNMENT

IN Hertzog's 1924 Cabinet the Labour Party got two portfolios, Creswell taking on Labour and Defence, and Boydell Posts and Telegraphs and Public Works. The other Cabinet positions were filled by Tielman Roos who took over Justice; Charlie Malan, Railways; Beyers, Mines; the two gentlemen of the 1913 Rebellion, Kemp and Piet Grobler, took on Agriculture and

Lands respectively. Dr. Malan administered Education, Public Health and Interior. All the old friends were now rewarded.

If my father had been great in victory, there are many who now conceded that he was at least as great in eclipse. As the years went by, even his opponents had, grudgingly, to admit that he had that divine spark.

He had now moved across the floor of the House to the seat of the Leader of the Opposition. His attendance was scrupulous, and early or late, dull or bitter, he was always to be found in his place. In demeanour he did not appear buoyant or happy, giving the impression more of serving a penance. It was no more than an impression, for in fact his thoughts and moods were well controlled and almost inscrutable. He simply sat there, impassive and unruffled, usually alert, but otherwise with his eyes focussed vaguely into the unseeing distance. Never did he show that great hurt and humiliation which he harboured in his bosom. His burning pride would never permit that.

The Government were jubilant at their victory and did their best to rub it in. As usual, they concentrated, in reprehensible manner, on the person of my father. He took it all without complaint or the flicker of an eyelid. Only the impatient drumming of his slender fingers or the way he kept folding and unfolding his hands showed his mental tension. So bitter were the attacks on him that the Speaker had frequently to call honourable members to order. Roos and Hertzog were the chief offenders.

This amateur jobs-for-pals government, my father had predicted, would not last long. But he had, for once, miscalculated, for hardly had they come into power when the dark clouds began to lift. Virtually the best rains for a generation soaked the earth, and the world depression was turning into a time of plenty. New discoveries of platinum in the Transvaal brought a measure of relief. Not only was Hertzog lucky, but his Minister of Finance was also to earn the nickname "Lucky Havenga".

The Prince of Wales, who had arranged to visit the Union during the Premiership of my father, now did a triumphal tour of the country. His treatment by the Nationalists left nothing to be desired and they fêted him everywhere. Quite a major boom was brought about by his visit. The Athlones brought him out to Doornkloof, where he was interested in our pedigree dairy herd.

294

When he left the Union, Arthur Barlow, then a Labourite, suggested in Parliament that the King be requested to refrain from conferring titles on people after the Prince's visit. Hertzog and the Nationalists supported this suggestion and it broadened into the banning of all titles for South Africans. My father did not oppose the idea. It had much to commend it. In Parliament many matters that were controversial and contentious were discussed. In one speech lasting an hour and a quarter Hertzog spent almost all his time attacking my father, and a reporter in the Press Gallery counted at least twenty different uncomplimentary adjectives he had coupled with my father's name.

Oswald Pirow placed a big order for locomotives for the railways with Germany, an act which met with the strongest disapproval from the South African Party. For years Britain had made all our locos.

Next, in 1927, cropped up the Flag Question. The Nationalists had no particular love for the Union Jack and decided that, as an independent dominion, it was time we had our own flag. Now, while this was a seemingly small matter, it cut deep into the sentiments of people, especially as the whole idea was obviously tinged with animus. Feeling mounted during the debates, and irresponsible people were even talking of civil trouble. The difficulty was to arrange an acceptable compromise. The English were firm in demanding a prominent place for the Union Jack in the flag, while at the same time the Nationalists were pressing equally hard for a dominance of the old Republican motifs. Every member of Parliament, and the public, became flag-drafters, but efforts were all too elaborate and complicated. So was my father's effort. At last, just as stalemate was about to overtake the House, the Governor-General initiated a final effort, which proved acceptable.

At the next Imperial Conference General Hertzog decided to press for a clearer recognition of the independence of members of the British Commonwealth. In London these views on Dominion status seemed acceptable, though my father was critical of what he called the weakening of certain bonds that tied this commonwealth of nations together. Statesmanship in Britain was at a low ebb and my father was nervous of what might follow.

At a meeting in Paarl General Hertzog told his audience: "As a result of what the Imperial Conference has done, nothing remains

295

of the Old Empire." He declared in Parliament that in the case of war the right of remaining neutral rested with every individual Dominion. My father did not consider this practicable. "I doubt", he said, "whether such an interpretation would be finally and definitely acceptable." A dozen years later these views were to be put to the practical test.

Next the Government steam-rollered through a very much criticised trade agreement with Germany. The pro-German element was very strong in Government circles. At this stage the Labour Party had domestic trouble, which resulted in a split into Creswellite and National Councilite factions. Walter Madeley became Minister of Posts and Telegraphs. His views were rather far to the Left, and one of his first acts was to raise native wages. Anything of this nature was to the Nationalists like a red rag to a bull. They clamoured for his resignation, but he stubbornly refused. Finally Hertzog himself resigned and was called upon to form a new Cabinet, in which Madeley did not reappear.

The 1929 elections were approaching. My father made a Pan-African type of speech at Ermelo, in which he suggested a great federation of states, extending over a large part of Africa. The Nationalists, as ever on the lookout for something to distort, seized upon this. Tielman Roos, aided by General Hertzog, issued the "Black Manifesto", a piece of evergreen colour propaganda. "Smuts wants a Kaffir State in which we are to be members," he croaked—"a black hegemony in which we are all to be on an equal footing."

At political meetings an element of organised hooliganism prevailed and frequently my father was shouted down without a hearing. Missiles flew freely and rowdyism and unruly behaviour were the order of the day. Often the windows of halls were smashed and chairs battered, resulting in considerable damage. The country grew quite accustomed to these Nationalist methods.

Townspeople were not worried by this warped type of propaganda, but the gullible public of the country districts believed that a vote for the South African Party meant equality with the natives. Consequently, when the election occurred my father's Party took a bad beating. Hertzog secured 78 seats against our 61.

The Pact Cabinet was now reorganised. Roos retired, ostensibly for health reasons, and went overseas for treatment, and Pirow took his place in Justice. We had already had numerous apologists in the Cabinet for Germany before, but now we had a person who was openly pro-Nazi.

LIII THE RHODES LECTURES AT OXFORD

A T the end of 1929, during the Michaelmas term, my father went to Oxford to deliver a series of Rhodes Lectures. He also lectured on David Livingstone. This trip to England was a welcome break from the bitterness and tedium of Parliament. The stipend of £500 also afforded an essential and welcome element of financial relief. He spent two months at the University. In these lectures he set out his ideas on the Native Problem clearly and concisely. It was a faithful and authoritative presentation, but the students, like many people in England, had their own strange ideas about the natives and largely failed to appreciate his lectures. Few were really enthusiastic, while the outright Negrophils were frankly disappointed. Otherwise the visit, like all previous ones, was a triumphal one, for the English hearts never failed to warm to this doughty old Boer. In Edinburgh and Glasgow he lectured to large audiences on David Livingstone.

His work in Britain completed, he accepted an invitation to attend the Tenth Annual Meeting of the League of Nations in New York, and later to travel the States and Canada on a lecture tour on League matters. He had long looked forward to such a trip, but this was the first occasion on which he could spare the time.

The Press showered him with bouquets. By some he was described as the greatest living statesman. He was loaded with civic honours and honorary university degrees. In no time he had endeared himself to the Americans. They were amazed at his

297

intimate knowledge of their country, and even more so by his knowledge of their writers Poe, Irving and Whitman. He received the honours modestly, protesting that he was just a simple Boer farmer.

The severe monolithic architecture of the New York sky-scrapers impressed him more as a form of human ingenuity than an exposition of architectural beauty. It would have been too much to expect the contemplation of a troglodytic mode of living to exercise his enthusiasm. But the farming developments inter-ested him immensely. It was all so well planned and on such a mammoth scale, and quite unlike the mediæval methods of his homeland.

His welcome in New York was a boisterous one and he never forgot the overhead snowstorm of ticker tape and confetti as he drove down the deep ravines of the city. It was different from other experiences.

He travelled through the States and Canada, lecturing about the League. Everywhere he was received with enthusiasm. It was an exacting, non-stop tour, which left him exhausted but happy.

The Hearst papers were critical of his presence in America. "Why should we harbour these foreign 'peace' propagandists?" The Negroes loved him until he indiscreetly, but with the best intentions in the world, happened to remark that they were "the most patient creatures next to the ass". He had offered this remark in sincere praise of that most commendable side of the black man's make-up, but it gave offence.

In the Southern Hotel in Baltimore, on the 16th January, 1930, he made these remarks: ". . . I have passed through many things in my life. I am not a pacifist, and I have not come to the peace movement as a pacifist. I have always believed, and I believe to-day, that there are greater things than peace, that there are ideals of justice, of fair play, of right, for which any decent human being ought to be prepared to give his life at any moment. Certain ideals, certain convictions transcend questions of life and death. . . ."

Regarding the value of round table conferences he had this to say:

. . . Since there is a human family, gather them, with all their troubles, around the family table. I want the disputes of mankind in the future, the troubles that arise and lead to war, to be treated in the family spirit. Gather them around the table. Don't let them look askance at each other. Don't let them frown at each other at a distance. Don't let them negotiate at a distance. Let them gather round the table, members of one family, in the family spirit.

Well, that is what the League of Nations has done. The League of Nations is the family table. You may not like it. I know some of you don't like it at all, and I am not here to convert you. It is for you to decide. I cannot speak to you as freely as Dr. Duggan. He can speak to you as an American, from the fullness of his conviction. I can only speak to you as a world citizen. You have to decide in your own national wisdom as to your national course and policy in the future. I can only bear testimony from the outside as a man who does not wish to indulge in propaganda in a foreign country, but who holds to faith in the human race and points the awful lessons of the Great War. . . .

. . . That we have to-day fifty-four nations of the world, almost all of them sitting around that table, is probably the greatest advance which has been made in the whole course of human history. It is a wonderful thing. Eleven years ago these nations were gripped in the most titanic death struggle in history. They were killing each other by the million. To-day they are sitting around the table. . . .

In the Basil Hicks Lecture delivered to the University of Sheffield in October, 1931, he expounded further on the "disarmed peace":

. . . I do not say that disarmament is the only road to peace. It is not the only step to be taken to ensure world peace. The maintenance of peace is a very complex affair which will depend upon many conditions. You cannot, for instance, have peace in a world in which there is no social justice, no honour and respect and high courtesy among the nations. Nor can you have peace for long in a world of chaos, in which each nation is a law unto itself, in which the supranational interests of mankind are not organised into definite institutions, in which the society of nations is not constitutionally recognised and does not find organised expression. Thus, firstly, there must be a rule of justice and fair play; secondly, there must be a permanent institution continuously controlling its application; and thirdly, the means and temptation to use private force must be carefully limited and controlled. These are the essential conditions of good order within the State; and they are no less essential foundations of international order and peace. Let us see how we stand at present in regard to these three conditions of peace. . . .

[Speaking of disarmament, he went on] . . . This is beyond all doubt the greatest and heaviest task before the League. That task is now confronting it in all its grimness. In February next year, the Disarmament Conference will meet, and it is felt on all hands that it is fraught with fateful issues for the League, if not for the world. If that Conference fails—which God forbid—the whole hopeful international situation which has been arising since the Peace will receive a setback. It is a thousand pities that the League is called to such an ordeal in its very infancy. If it were firmly in the saddle, if it had established its authority beyond question, the case would be different. But it is no more than an infant yet, it has barely begun its long career for the leadership of the world, it may yet take a generation or more before it will be sure of itself. And now at the very beginning, the heaviest task is laid upon it. And the present time and temper appear unfavourable for settling the vast issue of Disarmament. Well might the young League say with Hamlet:

"The time is out of joint; O cursed spite
That ever I was born to set it right."

Personally I take a more hopeful and perhaps longer view of the situation which confronts the League. It would be a cruel and fatal mistake to expect the impossible from the Disarmament Conference, and then, if it fails to realise the highest expectations, to give up all as lost. Disarmament is not going to be carried at one bound, so to say, and it would be foolish to expect such a result of the coming Conference. I do not believe the Armageddon of Peace is going to be fought out at that Conference. That is not the way of history. I believe that a beginning is going to be made, a great first step will be taken, which will be continuously followed up until the ghost of the past, the spectre of war, is finally laid. Disarmament will not be a matter for one conference, but for many conferences, and for continuous unwearied effort, prolonged perhaps for decades to come, until the great vision is realised and swords are finally beaten into ploughshares. Of the final result I feel as confident as I am of the League itself. But it may take many long years before mankind is ripe for that final step. . . .

Why should we disarm? There are several cogent and indeed imperative reasons for this step, which cannot be delayed any longer without the gravest risks. We have, to begin with, the obligations created by the Peace Treaties and the Covenant of the League. The Versailles Treaty, for instance, in imposing compulsory disarmament on Germany, expressly provided in the opening clause of Part V that that was only the first step in a general scheme of disarmament which it would be necessary to carry out in future in the interests of mankind. When the German delegates protested against the drastic measure of disarmament imposed on Germany, the Allied spokesmen renewed the assurance that it was only the preliminary to a great scheme of disarmament which would affect all. These assurances and undertakings constitute an obligation which it is impossible to evade much longer. But that is not all. Even if no assurance had been expressly given to Germany in the Peace Treaty, the inherent anomaly which has been created by her exceptional disarmament would call for early action. Germany, the greatest potential power on the Continent of Europe, sits on the Council of the League as one of the Great Powers. She is disarmed while the others are fully armed. Her status is affected, she is placed in a position of inferiority among her equals. The question raised is thus not merely one of disarmament, but of status, of equality among the Powers. It must be clear that the present position is inherently untenable, and that unless a beginning is made with the policy of disarmament, Germany could and might claim the right to arm herself once more, and might decline to sit among her peers in the League as an inferior. The question of allowing Germany to re-arm would raise even more difficult and dangerous issues than the question of general disarmament, and thus the anomaly of the present untenable position in Europe and in the League is forcing us to take a step, which we are in any case in honour bound to take, in order to carry out our assurances and undertakings under the Peace Treaty. We know what an armed Germany means, and we dare not run that risk again. In this connection, may I express the hope that German statesmen will never succumb to the temptation to renew the race of armaments and thereby to court the dangers of her former position again? . . .

In settling the details of disarmament policy, I think the growing consideration should be the importance of securing the lag to which I have referred earlier. Armaments should be such that the conversion of the fighting forces from a peace to a war footing should definitely involve an interval of time, during which the peace functions of the League could operate, freely and effectively. . . .

To conclude. The generation before us tried the novel experiment of the Armed Peace, the maintenance of peace through super-armaments, coupled with alliances and the balance of power. It proved the most disastrous step in the history of our race. Let us, grown wiser from experience, try the converse experiment of the Disarmed Peace, coupled with a universal organisation in support of it. We could not fare worse, and with reasonably good fortune, we may achieve a measure of success which would justify all the labours and sufferings of the past.

In America in 1929 he made his famous declaration in favour of a Jewish Home in Palestine. There had at the time been some friction between the Jews and Arabs in the Holy Land. He spoke of the wonderful services of Jewry throughout the course of time and of the great debt of humanity to them. He spoke of the promises at Versailles. Palestine was theirs to go back to. Britain had been a party to this solemn vow.

My father had always looked upon the Jewish problem as a great human problem. With his knowledge of the Old Testament, and of the history of the Jews and their historic persecutions he felt a warm sympathy with the Jewish cause. His concept of a home in Palestine was a legalistic and humanitarian one. He thought of the Jews not as a people, or a chosen race, but as a cause. As a people it would be incorrect to say that he liked them more than other peoples, for he was in fact a lover of all humanity. Jewry will long remember the services of this man for them, often in the teeth of the strongest opposition. A rich new settlement, not far from Haifa, Ramat Jochanan, is named after him in recognition of his work.

On board ship on the way back to South Africa he learned that the Quota Bill had been introduced into Parliament during his absence. It was aimed at curbing the rapid influx of Jews into the Union. It seemed a desirable protective measure at the time as many of the immigrants were of a very low type and hardly desirable as citizens. The Jews were specifically named in the Bill, which was also intended to limit immigration from the Central European States.

My father arrived back in Parliament during the Third Reading of the Bill. His Party had given it almost unanimous support. He raged at them and took them so to task, that during the final division they voted to a man against it. Here again, he was supporting a legalistic principle, not a people. It was a case of justice.

LIV NATIVE PROBLEM

THOUGH the problem of mixed populations is not a new one in history, it nevertheless presents certain novel aspects in South Africa and the rest of the continent. Normally it takes the form of a minority living in the midst of an overwhelming mass of other people, often under conditions of some disability. Here in South Africa, however, the small minority of whites live not under the normal conditions of sufferance, but actually rule the majority with an iron hand. They have retained in their possession full initiative in so far as tactical power and intellectual advantage is concerned and they have clung aggressively to what they consider their rights in wealth and leadership. The native, so far, has accepted quite willingly the overlordship of the white man, for he has freely admitted their mental superiority. He has been quite contented in this acceptance, for it has long been the tradition in native custom for him to serve unquestioningly some authority, whether it be a black potentate or a white master. Now that the white man has introduced the poll tax and prohibited the old tribal pastime of pillage and war, he has been forced to forsake his beer and his blanket for the location and the factory. Few people realise what a revolution in custom this has involved, for traditionally the native male is a warrior who does no manual work other than fighting. When not so occupied he was content to laze happily on a kaross outside his hut, to drink his beer and to sleep off his torpor, while his poor wives, like beasts of burden, tilled the fields and kept his home. It was the ingrained custom of the centuries. After all, husbands bought wives with cattle in marriage and it was only reasonable that wives should serve as beasts of burden. The fact that they were often pregnant and always had little piccanins strapped to their backs was quite incidental.

When the white man came to the country he very unreasonably demanded that the lazy warriors should work—the very work they had for millennia forced their wives to do. He brought with him, also, a system of monetary remuneration which did not

303

involve the accepted standard of the cow. He taught them the rudiments of Christianity which said we were all equal under the sun, yet this teaching was scrupulously disregarded by him. He frowned upon the native polygamous system which completely upset the system of the pastoral kraal, and he applied a legal code which seemed to the natives mild and anæmic by comparison to their own. He interfered constantly and broke down the authority of the chief and routine of the home, and yet he was annoyed when the black man, degenerated to the ways of the white, did not show him gratitude for all these not-unmixed blessings.

The white man came out to South Africa not merely to missionise and to settle on a trusteeship basis. He made it clear he had come to stay. For three hundred years he has been here and he is determined to stay indefinitely. But with the advancement of civilisation and gradual evolution of the native the gap between white and black has narrowed alarmingly. It is doubtful if the old master-servant relationship will be tenable for many more years to come. The white man sees a grave danger for his children. The black man thinks he sees the days of emancipation approaching. Both are straining to further their ambitions. Troublemongers and agitators, mostly half-educated natives, some Indians and a few misguided whites, are at work among the native masses. They use persuasive words and draw illuminating, over-simplified comparisons. The gullible native is not proof against this insidious propaganda. He is growing restive and unhappy. It is idle to maintain that this phase of unrest is the result of poor housing conditions. It goes much deeper than that, for it is in fact a national madness, a surging phase of unrest.

Different people read the signs differently. The philanthropist advocates the granting of numerous further concessions. The dour Boer farmer of the Platteland feels that harsher measures and a sterner white front are the only solutions. International bodies from overseas, most notably at UNO, quite ignorant of the true facts of the case, are loud in their condemnation of the white man. But so far South Africa has refused to be browbeaten by this criticism.

The native problem in South Africa differs from that in the United States, for there the whites outnumber the negroes by almost twenty to one. Under those circumstances people can afford to be broad-minded and tolerant. Here the white man, at a four to one disadvantage, has to struggle for his existence, and the future for his children is ever uncertain.

Segregation, both racial and geographical, is a strong urge in both the white, the black and the coloured peoples here. They have studiously abhorred fraternisation and hybridisation and each has faithfully bred his own pure type. This in itself is a unique feature in history, and even more so in colonial history. I am not concerning myself here with the political doctrine of "apartheid". I am referring to the separateness which is inherent in the feelings of all white and black men.

What then are the basic facts of this insoluble Native Problem?

The problem may be viewed from three different angles. There is firstly the ethical approach which purports to show that all men are equal. It is the old philanthropic outlook of the Bible. Apart from displaying an honest though over-easy outlook it has little realism to commend it. Its basis of reciprocity of goodwill is a fictitious one as far as the native is concerned, and anthropologists are quick to point out that the native has no gratitude in his social code. It is a weakness unknown to him. He will take all he can get quite gladly, and then blithely ask for more. There is no convincing argument based on sound fact, so far as I can see, to back up this ethical approach. It is simply a noble white urge to see fair play. The idea of equality is based upon shifting sands, and in fact the native is wise enough not to ask for it. All he asks for is unhampered opportunity.

The second approach is the scientific one in which are automatically visualised grades of evolutionary advancement. It is easy for us to do so in South Africa, for we have had before us that arrested type in anthropological development known as the Bushman, like the Australian aborigine, a freak survival from some primitive age. We have never accorded this small evolutionary enigma an equal status. Nor has the native.

It is therefore not difficult to imagine the Bantu an intermediate form between the European and Bushman. In fact, from the scientific aspect it has much to commend it, for undoubtedly the Bantu has features in his bone structure that we associate with Stone Age races. His very skull, for example, is almost half as thick again as that of the European. Yet, so far, study of his brain-size and convolutions has not shown an inferiority to the European. But certainly the massiveness of the facial bone structure suggests a connection with the old Neanderthaloid group of man.

Thirdly there is the tactical approach. It takes into account that the white man in the Union is outnumbered by four to one. It takes into account the fact that the black man is increasing in numbers more rapidly than the white man. It assumes that two peoples cannot indefinitely go on living side by side without some major future eruption. For this day of reckoning we must prepare. We must see that we have in our power all those things which can ensure tactical and military superiority. We must prohibit non-Europeans from possessing firearms, or the training in their use. Manufacturing industry, wealth and education must be kept in white hands. All these add up to military strength. We must frown upon trade unionism amongst the Bantu or upon the formation of political bodies, for that leads to potentially dangerous consolidation. The emotional fear complex is not to be misconstrued with these military prerequisites.

Lastly we must take into account the divergent views held on the native problem by the English and Boer races. Broadly the British outlook is one of goodwill and tolerance, however misguided and over-emphasised it may seem at times. The Boer, after centuries of fighting for a foothold in this country, takes a sterner view of things. He is far less tolerant or sympathetic.

In arriving at a settlement of the native problem due cognisance must be taken of these divergent views. Some compromise must be reached, and depending upon the government of the day, it may be well-disposed or not so friendly towards the natives.

The native policy of governments in South Africa is not the policy of political parties. It is the actual policy of people, based upon their deep convictions. Parliament cannot change the relationship simply by a stroke of the pen. It has first to convince and convert public opinion. Mostly public opinion has been hard against granting too many concessions.

From old Adam at Riebeeck West my father learned to know and to respect the native. From his scientific knowledge of anthropology he got the idea of gradations in the scale of evolution. His sound reasoning powers never allowed sentimentalism to obtrude. From his Boer forebears he inherited the harder Boer viewpoint and from his legalistic studies ideas of justice and fairness. His general kindly outlook on life broadened that into an outlook of sane tolerance. Yet he looked upon over-liberal views on the colour question as extremely dangerous.

My father had complete confidence in the intellectual and administrative superiority of the white man. He was convinced that, come what will, these would see him safely through all trouble. It would also enable him to live indefinitely in a state of semi-overlordship over the blacks. He considered this mental superiority the white man's greatest asset. He had great faith in the inherent stability and good faith of the Bantu and was a strong advocate of breaking down their local tribal customs as little as possible. He did not favour the artificial half-baked white ideas we are foisting upon them.

Nor was he an advocate of over-hasty artificial advancement. Civilisation he believed to be a slow process which should be over-accelerated only at peril. He preferred to see the natives building slowly but solidly. This is also in line with the tactical concept.

In the Rhodes Memorial lectures at Oxford University in 1929 he gave a lucid exposition of his views on the native problem which is worth quoting in some detail:

We are concerned to-day with these racial reactions in so far as they affect Europe and Africa—a small question, but still a very large human question, fraught with immense possibilities for the future of our civilisation as well as that of Africa. What is wanted in Africa to-day is a wise, far-sighted native policy. If we could evolve and pursue a policy which will promote the cause of civilisation in Africa without injustice to the African, without injury to what is typical and specific in the African, we shall render a great service to the cause of humanity. For there is much that is good in the African which ought to be preserved and developed. . . .

Here in this vast continent, with its wide geographical variety and great climatic difference, this unique human type has been fixing itself for hundreds of years. . . . This type has some wonderful characteristics. It has largely remained a child type, with a child psychology and out-look. A child-like human cannot be a bad human. . . . Perhaps, as a direct result of this temperament the African is the only happy human I have come across. No other race is so easily satisfied, so good-tempered, so carefree. If this had not been the case, it could scarcely have survived the intolerable evils which have weighed on it like a nightmare through the ages. A race which could survive the immemorial practice of the witch doctor and slave trader, and preserve its inherent simplicity and sweetness of disposition, must have some very fine moral qualities. The African easily forgets past troubles and does not anticipate future troubles. This happy-go-lucky disposition is a great asset, but it also has its drawbacks.

There is no inward incentive to improvement, there is no persistent effort in construction, and there is complete absorption in the present, its joys and sorrows. . . . No indigenous religion has been evolved, no literature, no art since the magnificent promise of the cavemen and the South African petroglyphist, no architecture since Zimbabwe (if that is African). . . . They can stand any amount of physical hardships and suffering. . . . These children have not the inner toughness and persistence of the European, nor those social and moral incentives to progress. . . . But they have a temperament which suits mother Africa.

It is clear that a race so unique and so different in its mentality and its cultures from those of Europe, requires a policy very unlike that which would suit Europeans. Nothing could be worse for Africa than the application of a policy, the object or tendency of which would be to destroy the basis of the African type, to de-Africanise the African and turn him either into a beast of the field or into a pseudo-European. And yet in the past we have tried both alternatives in our dealings with the African. First we look upon the African as essentially inferior or sub-human, as having no soul, as being only fit to be a slave. As a slave he became an article of commerce, and the greatest article of export from this continent for centuries. . . .

Then we changed to the opposite extreme. The African now became a man and a brother. Religion and politics combined to shape this new African policy. . . . The political system of the natives was ruthlessly destroyed in order to incorporate them as equals into the white system. . . .

In some of the British possessions in Africa the native just emerging from barbarism was accepted as an equal citizen with full political rights along with the whites. But his native institutions were ruthlessly proscribed and destroyed. This principle of equal rights was applied in its crudest form, and while it gave the natives a semblance of equality with whites, which was little good to him, it destroyed the basis of his African system which was his highest good. These are the two extreme native policies which have prevailed in the past, and the second has been only slightly less harmful than the first. If Africa has to be redeemed, if Africa has to make her own contribution to the world, if Africa is to take her rightful place among the continents, we shall have to proceed on different lines and evolve a policy which will not force her institutions into an alien European world, but which will preserve her unity with her own past, conserve what is precious in her past, and build her future progress and civilisation on specifically African foundations. That should be the new policy. . . .

It is a significant fact that this new orientation of African policy had its origin in South Africa, and that its author was Cecil Rhodes in his celebrated Glen Grey Act. Rhodes's African policy embodied two main ideas: white settlement to supply the steel framework and the stimulus for enduring civilisation, and indigenous native institutions to express the specifically African character of the natives in their future development and civilisation. African policies should arise in Africa, from the experience of the men and women who are in daily contact with the living problems. . . .

Prior to the Glen Grey legislation it had been the practice in South Africa, as it had been the practice in all European-occupied territory in Africa, to rule the natives direct through Government officials—direct rule, as it has been called. . . . The native chiefs were either deposed and deprived of authority, or where use was made of them, they were incorporated into the official system and appointed as officers of the Government, from whom they derived all their authority, and in whose name that authority was exercised. . . . His second innovation was to make it possible for natives in their tribal areas to become possessed of their own separate plots of agricultural land instead of the traditional common holding and working of land which is the universal native system throughout Africa. . . .

A third feature of his system was a labour tax of ten shillings per annum, imposed on all native heads of families who did not go to work beyond their district for three months in the year. The object of the tax was obvious. The whites wanted labourers, and the natives were supposed to require some inducement to go to work instead of sitting on their holdings and seeing their women work. . . . The tax, however, was unpopular with the natives from the start and soon appeared to be an unnecessary irritation. . . . The native, although a slow worker, is not lazy, and does not require any special inducement. . . . His main incentive is his rising scale of needs in food and clothing. . . .

The universal experience in Africa is that, although it takes some time at the beginning for the native to enter white employment, his rapidly-growing economic needs in a white environment, and with a rising scale of living, soon make him take his full share of the burden without any necessity to resort to special measures. . . .

The native system of land socialism is not only primitive but most wasteful in its working. . . . The result is that the communal farms rapidly deteriorate and become exhausted, and have to be abandoned after a few years' use. Then the farm shifts to another area of the tribal domain where the same process of uneconomic exhaustion is repeated. . . . In the course of years this shifting cultivation works havoc with the natural resources . . . the tribal lands become a barren waste.

This sad phenomenon can be seen in one degree or another all over the African continent. . . .

Practical agricultural education must indeed become one of the principal subjects of native education.

The main object of the Glen Grey legislation was, however, to give the native his own institutions for self-development and self-government. . . . The new policy is to foster an indigenous native culture or system of cultures and to cease to force the African into alien European moulds. As a practical policy of native government it has worked most successfully. Gradually the system of native councils has been extended from one native area to another in the Cape Province, until to-day about two-thirds of the Cape natives, or roughly over a million, fall under this system and manage their own local affairs according to their own ideas under the supervision of the European magistrates.

After the new system has worked successfully and with ever-increasing efficiency for twenty-five years, I thought the time ripe in 1920 to extend it to the whole Union. . . .

The new system is far-reaching and has come none too soon. Already the African system is disintegrating everywhere over the whole African continent. . . . Many factors have combined to produce this situation. Missionaries share the blame with governments. . . .

The introduction of the Christian religion meant not only the breakdown of the primitive belief in spirits, in magic and witchcraft, and the abandonment of the practice of polygamy; it meant the breakdown of the entire integral native outlook on life and the world. . . .

If the bonds of native tribal cohesion and authority are dissolved, the African governments will everywhere sit with vast hordes of detribalised natives on their hands, for whom the traditional restraints and discipline of the chiefs and elders will have no force or effect. . . . The results may well be general chaos. . . . Such a breakdown should be prevented at all costs.

This policy of dealing with peoples not yet able to stand by themselves in the colonies and territories taken from the defeated powers in the First World War, is in effect, enshrined in the

Covenant of the League of Nations and its mandates. My father was responsible for this mandate principle and for its inclusion in Article 22 of the Covenant.

In this same lecture my father stressed the need for a certain measure of segregation.

This separation is imperative, not only in the interests of a native culture, and to prevent the native traditions and institutions from being swamped by the more powerful organisation of the whites, but also for other important purposes, such as public health, racial purity and public good order. The mixing up of two such alien elements as white and black leads to unhappy social results—racial miscegenation, moral deterioration of both, racial antipathy and clashes, and to many other forms of social evil. . . . It is, however, evident that the proper place of the educated minority of the natives is with the rest of their people, of whom they are natural leaders, and from whom they should not in any way be dissociated.

Far more difficult questions arise on the industrial plane. It is not practicable to separate black and white in industry. . . .

There remains the big question how far the parallelism of native and white institutions is to go. Is it to be confined to local government, or is it to go all the way up to the level of full political or parliamentary government? Should black and white co-operate in the same parliamentary institutions? Few acquainted with the facts and difficulties can profess to see clear daylight in the tangle of this problem. . . .

I do not think there can be, or at the bottom there is, among those who have given the subject serious attention, any doubt that in the supreme legislature of a country with a mixed population all classes and colours should have representation. . . . There can be only one sovereign body in a country and that body should represent the weaker no less than the stronger. To that extent there should be agreement. As to the mode of representation of colour in the supreme parliament there can be legitimate difference of opinion. . . . In South Africa . . . we started with the older system of mixed constituencies in the Cape Colony, and this system is embodied and entrenched in the Act of Union which forms our Constitution.

The present Government has proposed to scrap this system for the future, and to give separate representation in Parliament to native and non-native voters. A policy which might have been easy and, from certain points of view, even commendable, with a clean slate before us, has become enormously difficult because of what has been done in the past, and the justifiable fervour with which the Cape non-Europeans cling to their vested rights, which they have enjoyed for three-quarters of a century.

If we had to do only with the tribal native voters the question would not be so difficult, and the application of the general segregation principle to the particular case of political rights might be justified. . . . Urbanised natives living among the whites constitute the real crux and it is a difficulty which goes far beyond the political issue. They raise a problem for the whole principle of segregation, as they claim to be civilised and Europeanised, and do not wish to be thrust back into the seclusion of their former tribal associations or to forgo their new place in the sun among the whites. . . . Were it not for this case of the urbanised or detribalised natives, the colour problem, not only in South Africa but elsewhere in Africa, would be shorn of most of its difficulties. . . .

It is only when segregation breaks down, when the whole family migrates from the tribal home and out of the tribal jurisdiction to the white man's farm or the white man's town, that the tribal bond is snapped, and the traditional system falls into decay. And it is this migration of the native family, of the females and children, to the farms and towns, which should be prevented. . . .

At the same time I wish to point out that the prevention of this migration will be no easy task, even where ample funds are guaranteed to the natives. The whites like to have the families of their native servants with them. It means more contentment and less broken periods of labour, and it means more satisfied labourers.

He concludes by suggesting that the system of segregation is perhaps more workable at present than in the past. Women and children are to be left at home to carry on their domestic tasks as they have done from the immemorial past.

The men, instead of lying in the sun, or brawling over their beer, or indulging in the dangerous sport of tribal warfare, will go out to work and supplement the family income. . . . Without breaking down what is good in the native system, it will graft on to it a wholesome economic development, which will yet not disturb too deeply the traditional ways of Mother Africa.

In his own home and on his own farms he always took a kind and patriarchal view of his native wards. To Annie, the old Bantu servant girl who had worked faithfully with our family for many years, he left a small legacy in his will.

He always took a keen interest in the native labourers on his farms, especially in the old ones who had been with him for years. These he took pleasure in greeting cheerfully "more booi", "boy" being an Afrikaans derivation having no connection with youthfulness. The natives, sensing an inherent kindness in their old master, treated him with veneration and worked steadily on the farm for years.

It was the little piccanins, however, he preferred, with their shiny, shaven heads and big, dark eyes, and with their wide, white flashing smile. Their behaviour suggested to him the elemental wild animal of nature of which he was so fond. Their eyes, in fact, held a surprised doe-like look which strengthened this feeling. These wild, colourful people, he was fond of photographing with his ciné whenever he had the opportunity.

At Christmas time he would ask my mother to prepare parcels of sweets for the various native families on his farms. He did this for as long as I can remember. Sometimes he would have a little party for them in the garden, and after listening to their singing or watching their dancing efforts, he would have cool drinks and refreshments dispensed. The little piccanins loved the parties, and I think they really loved their "Oubaas" too.

On the northern boundaries of the bushveld farms are extensive native trust areas. These, here, as elsewhere, are hopelessly overcrowded and the fertile bush tracts are rapidly being transformed into semi-arid wastelands. There is considerable overgrazing, especially by the noxious goats, and the trees have mostly been chopped down for firewood. Consequently these native settlements have grown progressively more parasitical on our property, our fences offering little security from depredations by natives and goats alike. Though this made our managers indignant it did not sour my father's feelings towards his neighbours.

IN 1931 my father was invited to London to preside at the
Centenary Meeting of the British Association for the Advancement of Science. Science held no higher honour, for this was
the greatest meeting of the scientists of the world. He considered
this invitation the crowning honour of his life. Nothing ever
pleased him more.

"No president", says Professor J. B. S. Haldane in a letter to my
father, "in recent (or, indeed, in former) times has had anything
like the same knowledge of philosophy, as well as science, as you
have."

First he delivered the opening speech at the Faraday Exhibition.

At the Centenary Meeting the lecture was on "The Scientific
World Picture of To-day". Five thousand delegates, from all over
the world, including some of the most illustrious scientists of the
day, attended. It was a busy time for my father. He was on many
committees. Some days he delivered several addresses, and on one
particularly busy day no less than thirteen. The topics varied from
farming to philosophy. On all these he spoke with confidence and
authority. He also presided at the Sir James Jeans address, and at
Maxwell's centenary celebrations at Cambridge. Wherever he
went, crowds flocked after him and halls were invariably filled to
overflowing. Never before in his life had he been so lionised—not
only by the people, but by the great scientists as well. These meetings left proud memories with him.

From London the Association went to York, where further
meetings were held.

My old friend, Professor J. A. Wilkinson of Johannesburg, who
was a delegate, wrote to me: "To-day the British Association ends
its centenary meeting, one which will never be forgotten by those
who have had the good fortune to attend it. I am sure that your
father has enjoyed it and for him it has been one long triumph

right from the very beginning. The night before last [28.9.31] the honorary degree of D.Sc. was conferred on him by the University of London, a very great distinction indeed, as in the whole history of the University, which is now almost a century old, only two honorary degrees had previously been conferred, namely on Lord Lister, the father of Aseptic Surgery, and Lord Kelvin the physicist. . . ."

My father's main address, covering a full sweep of the fields of science, was a masterly one. It was free of jarring detail, yet explicit and well proportioned. Here are some extracts from it:

[Science] has been continually changing with the changing knowledge and beliefs of man. Thus, there was the world of magic and animism, which was followed by that of the early nature gods. There was the geocentric world which still survives in the world of commonsense. There is the machine or mechanistic world-view dominant since the time of Galileo and Newton, and now, since the coming of Einstein, being replaced by the mathematician's conception of the universe as a symbolic structure of which no mechanical model is possible. All these world-views have in turn obtained currency according as some well-defined aspect of our advancing knowledge has from time to time been dominant. . . .

Science arose from our ordinary experience and commonsense outlook. The world of commonsense is a world of matter, of material stuff, of real separate things and their properties which act on each other and cause changes in each other. To the various things observable by the senses were added the imperceptible things—space and time, invisible forces, life and the soul. Even these were not enough, and the supernatural was added to the natural world. The original inventory was continually being enlarged, and thus a complex empirical world-view arose, full of latent contradictions, but with a solid basis of actual experience and facts behind it. . . .

But underneath this placid surface, the seeds of the future were germinating. With the coming of the twentieth century, fundamental changes began to set in. The new point of departure was reached when physical science ceased to confine its attention to the things that are observed. It dug down to a deeper level, and below the things that appear to the sense, it found, or invented, at the base of the world, so-called scientific entities, not capable of direct observation, but which are necessary to account for the facts of observations. Thus, below molecules and atoms still more ultimate entities appeared; radiations, electrons and protons emerged as elements which underlie and form our world of matter. Matter itself, the time-honoured mother of all, practically disappeared into electrical energy.

> "The cloud-capp'd towers, the gorgeous palaces,
> The solemn temples, the great globe itself."

Yea, all the material forms of earth and sky and sea were dissolved and spirited away into the blue of energy. . . .

The physical concept or insight of space-time is our first revolutionary innovation, our first complete break with the old world of commonsense. Already it has proved an instrument of amazing power in the newer physics. In the hands of an Einstein it has led beyond Euclid and Newton, to the recasting of the law and the concept of gravitation, and to the new relativity conception of the basis structure of the world. The transformation of the concept of space, owing to the injection into it of time, has destroyed the old passive homogeneous notion of space and has substituted a flexible, variable continuum, the curvatures and unevennesses of which constitute to our senses what we call a material world. The new concept has made it possible to construe matter, mass and energy as but definite measure conditions of curvature in the structure of space-time. . . .

I pass on to an even more revolutionary recent advance of physics. The space-time world, however novel, however shattering to commonsense, is not in conflict with reason. Indeed, the space-time world is largely a discovery of the mathematical reason and is an entirely rational world. It is a world where reason, as it were, dissolves the refractoriness of the old material substance and smoothes it out into forms of space-time. Science, which began with empirical brute facts, seems to be heading for the reign of pure reason. But wait a bit; another fundamental discovery of our age has apparently taken us beyond the bounds of rationality, and is thus even more revolutionary than that of space-time. I refer to the Quantum theory, Max Planck's discovery at the end of the nineteenth century, according to which energy is granular, consisting of discrete grains or quanta. The world in space-time is a continuum; the quantum action is a negation of continuity. Thus arises the contradiction, not only of commonsense, but apparently of reason itself. The quantum appears to behave like a particle, but a particle out of space or time. . . .

From the brilliant discoveries of physical science we pass on to the advances in biological science which, although far less revolutionary, have been scarcely less important for our world-outlook. The most important biological discovery of the last century was the great fact of organic evolution; and for this fact the space-time concept has at last come to provide the necessary physical basis. It is unnecessary for my purpose to canvass the claims and discuss the views represented by the great names of Lamarck, Darwin and Mendel, beyond saying that they represent a progressive advance in biological discovery, the end of which has by no means been reached yet. Whatever doubts and differences of opinion there may be about the methods, the mechanism, or the causes, there is no doubt about the reality of organic evolution, which is one of the most firmly-established results in the whole range of science. . . .

The general trend of the recent advances in physics has thus been towards the recognition of the fundamental organic character of the material world. Physics and biology are beginning to look not so utterly unlike each other. Hitherto the great gulf in nature has lain between the material and the vital, between inorganic matter and life. This gulf is now in process of being bridged. The new physics, in dissolving the material world of commonsense and discovering the finer structure of physical nature, has at the same time disclosed certain fundamental features which it has in common with the organic world. Stuff-like entities have disappeared and have been replaced by space-time configurations whose very nature depends on their principle of organisation. And this principle, which I have ventured to call holism, appears to be at the bottom identical with that which pervades the organic structures of the world of life. The quantum and space-time have brought physics closer to biology. As I have pointed out, the quantum anticipates some of the fundamental characters of life, while space-time forms the physical basis for organic evolution. Physics and biology are thus recognised as respectively simpler and more advanced forms of the same fundamental pattern in world-structure. . . .

A living individual is a physiological whole, in which the parts or organs are but differentiations of this whole for purposes of greater efficiency, and remain in organic continuity throughout. They are parts of the individual, and not independent or self-contained units which compose the individual. It is only this conception of the individual as a dynamic organic whole which will make intelligible the extraordinary unity which characterises the multiplicity of functions in an organism, the mobile, ever-changing balance and interdependence of the numerous regulatory processes in it, as well as the operation of all the mechanisms by which organic evolution is brought about. . . .

. . . From matter, as now transformed by space-time and the quantum, we pass step by step through organic nature to conscious mind. Gone is the time when Descartes could divide the world into only two substances—extended substance or matter and thinking substance or mind. There is a whole world of gradations between these two limits. On Descartes' false dichotomy the separate provinces of modern science and philosophy were demarcated. But it is as dead as the epicycles of Ptolemy, and ultimately the Cartesian frontiers between physics and philosophy must largely disappear, and philosophy once more become metaphysic in the original sense. In the meantime, under its harmful influence, the paths of matter and mind, of science and philosophy, were made to diverge farther and farther, so that only the revolution now taking place in thought could bring them together again. I believe, however, their reunion is coming fast. We have seen matter and life indefinitely approaching each other in the ultimate constituents of the world. . . .

The highest reach of this creative process is seen in the realm of values, which is the product of the human mind. Great as is the physical universe which confronts us as a given fact, no less great is our reading and evaluation of it in the world of values, as seen in language, literature, culture, civilisation, society and the state, law, architecture, art, science, morals and religion. Without this revelation of inner meaning and significance the external physical universe would be but an immense empty shell or crumpled surface. The brute fact here receives its meaning, and a new world arises which gives to nature whatever significance it has. As against the physical configurations of nature we see here the ideal patterns or wholes freely created by the human spirit as a home and an environment for itself.

Among the human values thus created science ranks with art and religion. In its selfless pursuit of truth, in its vision of order and beauty, it partakes of the quality of both. More and more it is beginning to make a profound æsthetic and religious appeal to thinking people. Indeed, it may fairly be said that science is perhaps the clearest revelation of God to our age. Science is at last coming into its own as one of the supreme goods of the human race.

While religion, art and science are still separate values they may not always remain such. Indeed, one of the greatest tasks before the human race will be to link up science with ethical values, and thus to remove grave dangers threatening our future. . . .

I have now finished my rapid and necessarily superficial survey of the more prominent recent tendencies in science, and I proceed to summarise the results and draw my conclusions, in so far as they bear on our world-picture.

In the first place we have seen that in the ultimate physical analysis science reaches a microscopic world of scientific entities, very different in character and behaviour from the microscopic world of matter, space and time. The world of atoms, electrons, protons, radiations and quanta does not seem to be space-time, or to conform to natural law in the ordinary sense. The behaviour of these entities cannot be understood without the most abstruse mathematics, nor, apparently, without resort to epistemological considerations. We seem to have passed beyond the definitely physical world into a twilight where pro-physics and metaphysics meet, where space-time does not exist, and where strictly causal law in the old sense does not apply. From this uncertain nebulous underworld there seems to crystallise out, or literally to materialise, the macroscopic world which is the proper sphere of sensuous observation and of natural laws. The pre-material entities or units condense and cohere into constellations, which increase in size and structure until they reach the macroscopic stage of observation. As the macroscopic entities emerge, their space-time field and appropriate natural laws (mostly of a statistical character) emerge *pari passu*. We seem to pass from one level to another in the evolution of the universe, with different units, different behaviours and calling for different concepts and laws. Similarly, we rise to new levels as later on we pass from the physical to the biological level, and again from the latter to the level of conscious mind. But—and this is the significant fact—all these levels are genetically related and form an evolutionary series; and underlying the differences of the successive levels, there remains a fundamental unity of plan or organisation which binds them together as members of a genetic series, as a growing, evolving, creative universe. . . .

But . . . another dualism of a wider reach has appeared, which makes the universe itself appear to be a house divided against itself. For a while the stream of physical tendency throughout the universe is on the whole downward, towards disintegration and dissipation, the organic movement, on this planet at least, is upward, and life structures are on the whole becoming more complex throughout the course of organic evolution. From the viewpoint of physics, life and mind are thus singular and exceptional phenomena, not in line with the movement of the universe as a whole. Recent astronomical theory has come to strengthen this view of life as an exceptional feature off the main track of the universe. For the origin of our planetary system is attributed to an unusual accident, and planets such as ours with favourable environment for life are taken to be rare in the universe. Perhaps we may even say that at the present epoch there is no other globe where life is at the level manifested on the earth. Our origin is thus accidental, our position is exceptional, and our fate is sealed, with the inevitable running down of the solar system. Life and mind, instead of being the natural flowering of the universe, are thus reduced to a very casual and inferior status in the cosmic order. A new meaning and a far deeper poignancy are given to Shakespeare's immortal lines:

> "We are such stuff
> As dreams are made of; our little life
> Is rounded with a sleep."

According to astronomy, life is indeed a lonely and pathetic thing in this physical universe—a transient and embarrassed phantom in an alien, if not hostile, universe.

Such are some of the depressing speculations of recent astronomical theory. But in some respects they have already been discounted in the foregoing. For even if life be merely a terrestrial phenomenon, it is by no means in an alien environment if, as we have seen reason to think, this is an essentially organic universe. In its organic aspects the universe is on the way to life and mind, even if the goal has been actually reached at only one insignificant point in the universe. The potencies of the universe are fundamentally the same order as its actualities. The universe might say, in the words of Rabbi Ben Ezra—

> "All I could never be
> All man ignored in me,
> This I was worth to God."

Then, again, the very possibility of perception, of knowledge and science depends on an intimate relation between mind and the physical universe. Only thus can the concepts of mind come to be a measure for the facts of the universe, and the laws of nature come to be revealed and interpreted by nature's own organ of the human mind. Besides science we have other forms of this inner relation between the mind and the universe, such as poetry, music, art and religion. The human spirit is not a pathetic wandering phantom of the universe, but is at home, and meets with spiritual hospitality and response everywhere. Our deepest thoughts and emotions and endeavours are but responses to stimuli which come to us, not from an alien, but from an essentially friendly and kindred, universe. So far from the cosmic status of life and mind being degraded by the newer astronomy and physics, I would suggest an alternative interpretation of the facts more in accord with the trend of evolutionary science. We have seen a macroscopic universe born or revealed to consciousness out of a prior microscopic order of a very different character. Are we not, in the emergence of life and mind, witnessing the birth or revelation of a new world out of the macroscopic physical universe? I suggest that at the present

Field Marshal Smuts.   A fine photographic study—October 1942

General Smuts writing at his desk—1943

General Smuts with Mr. Churchill, Cairo—1942

cosmic epoch we are the spectators of what is perhaps the grandest event in the immeasurable history of our universe, and that we must interpret the present phase of the universe as a mother and child universe, still joined together by a placenta which science, in its divorce from the other great values, has hitherto failed to unravel.

Piecing together these clues and conclusions we arrive at a world-picture fuller of mystery than ever. In a way it is closer to common-sense and kinder to human nature than was the science of the nineteenth century. Materialism has practically disappeared, and the despotic rule of necessity has been greatly relaxed. In ever-varying degree the universe is organic and holistic through and through. Not only organic concepts, but also, and even more so, psychological viewpoints are becoming necessary to elucidate the facts of science. And while the purely human concepts, such as emotion and value, purpose and will, do not apply in the natural sciences, they retain their unimpaired force in the human sciences. The ancient spiritual goods and heirlooms of our race need not be ruthlessly scrapped. The great values and ideals retain their unfading glory and derive new interest and force from a cosmic setting. But in other respects it is a strange new universe, impalpable, immaterial, consisting not of material or stuff, but of organisation, of patterns or wholes which are unceasingly being woven to more complex or simpler designs. In the large it appears to be a decaying, simplifying universe which attained to its perfection of organisation in the far-distant past and is now regressing to simpler forms—perhaps for good, perhaps only to restart another cycle of organisation. But inside this cosmic process of decline we notice a smaller but far more significant movement—a streaming, protoplasmic tendency; an embryonic infant world emerging, throbbing with passionate life, and striving towards rational and spiritual self-realisation. We see the mysterious creative rise of the higher out of the lower, the more from the less, the picture within its framework, the spiritual kernel inside the phenomenal integuments of the universe. Instead of the animistic, or the mechanistic, or the mathematical universe, we see the genetic, organic, holistic universe, in which the decline of the earlier physical patterns provide the opportunity for the emergence of the more advanced vital and rational patterns.

In this holistic universe man is in very truth the offspring of the stars. The world consists not only of electrons and radiations but also of souls and aspirations. Beauty and holiness are as much aspects of nature as energy and entropy. Thus "in eternal lines to time it grows". An adequate world-view would find them all in their proper context in the framework of the whole. And evolution is perhaps the only way of approach to the framing of a consistent world-picture which would do justice to the immensity, the profundity and the unutterable mystery of the universe.

Such in vague outline is the world-picture to which science seems to me to be pointing. We may not all agree with my rendering of it, which indeed does not claim to be more than a mere sketch. And even if it were generally accepted, we have still to bear in mind that the world-picture of to-morrow will in all probability be very different from any which could be sketched to-day.

It was a memorable address on a memorable occasion.

Sir Alfred Ewing in his presidential address before the Association the following year paid this tribute to his predecessor: "We had long known General Smuts as soldier and statesman: to some it may have come as a surprise when they found him also a philosopher, a student of ideas no less than a maker of history and a leader of men. It would be an impertinence for any successor in this chair to praise General Smuts: to follow him is perforce to follow far behind. . . . His occupancy of the chair not only added to the lustre of our rejoicings; I like to think it also has a deeper significance. May we not regard it as a harbinger of the spirit of goodwill and sanity which civilisation longs for but does not yet see?"

LVI THE GOLD STANDARD

AT the end of 1929 the bottom dropped suddenly out of Wall Street. There was a bad slump in diamonds, wool, maize and other things in general, and South Africa soon found itself, with the rest of the world, drifting to an economic collapse.

Meanwhile other ideas, quite apart from his activities at the Centenary, were revolving in my father's head. For, while the conference was on, Britain suddenly decided to go off the gold standard. He took the opportunity of discussing the implications of the move with some of the leading economists. So far as Britain was concerned the advantages of devaluation were readily discernible, but the question of its effects on a country like South Africa were more controversial. The conclusions they came to was that it would be greatly to our advantage to follow Britain.

So he forthwith sent a cable to South Africa advocating that we should go off gold immediately. The Nationalist Government treated everything done by Britain or my father with suspicion and did so in this case. They obstinately decided to remain on gold. Minister of Finance Havenga had said it was the best thing, and he had some support from the public, commerce, and a few university professors.

Meanwhile the financial position of South Africa was steadily growing more precarious. Lucky Havenga's luck seemed to have turned against him. The exchange rate was playing queer pranks, and trade had dropped alarmingly. There were many bankruptcies. Our Reserve Bank was in difficulties. But the more my father pleaded that we should go off gold, the more obstinately the Government clung to it.

Under the pressure of these events there was a rapid change in the political situation. At Colesberg in the Cape, a Nationalist stronghold, the Government narrowly scraped home in a by-election. In December, 1932, at Germiston, near Johannesburg, Mr. J. G. N. Strauss, against all Government predictions, won the seat for the South African Party. People said that this, like Wolmaransstad, was a straw in the wind. The Government's days were numbered.

The Budget Debate in Parliament lasted twelve days. Tempers were ruffled, and Hertzog in one speech was four times called to order by the Speaker for uncomplimentary references to my father. It was during this debate that my father surprised the House by objecting to an insulting personal reference—only the second time he had ever done so. He had been called a "political trickster". The Minister of Finance showed an estimated budget deficit of £200,000. In the debate my father produced a budget, calculated on an "off gold" basis, which showed, on a conservative estimate, a surplus of three-quarters of a million pounds. The Nationalists laughed.

But the depression was steadily worsening, and to aggravate matters a bad drought hit the farming community.

It was at this stage of stalemate that attention was dramatically drawn to Tielman Roos. I have already explained how he fell out with General Hertzog and how he had retired for health reasons to the Bench. But Roos had now grown tired of the quiet life of the law courts and wanted to return to politics. He had asked Piet Grobler to sound General Hertzog on the possibilities of his return, but the General had said no. Roos was deeply hurt at this brusque rebuff, but awaited his opportunity.

On 22nd December, 1932, he resigned from the Bench and stormed the country with the cry of "off gold". It was no new cry, but his loud roaring seemed to awaken the country. There was a landslide in opinion. Overnight Roos became the hero of the hour, and gold the bogy.

Meanwhile, as it was Christmas time, my father took the opportunity to snatch a few days' holiday in the Eastern Transvaal. He had gone off, opportunely, just after Roos's dramatic re-entry into the fray. Newspaper reporters frantically scoured the country to find him. We of the family said we thought he was in the bushveld. Eventually a reporter ran him to earth in Schoeman's Kloof, where he was quietly botanising on the Crocodile River. To the reporter's amazement, instead of discussing the new developments, my father simply brushed them aside and expounded on the beauty of the Kloof and mountains. In actual fact, he was waiting for matters to develop on their own. There was no point in blundering in at this stage with pronouncements.

On December 28th the Government said it would perish rather than go off gold. For fifteen months they had obstinately clung to it. The cost to the country of this suicidal policy has been calculated at fifty million pounds.

Now in 1933 they suddenly went off gold. Immediately the price of gold rose from four guineas an ounce fine to six pounds. Shares boomed. Gold mines were rejuvenated and low-grade properties were saved from closing down. There was a new prosperity and confidence everywhere. Lucky, undeserving, Havenga.

In January, 1933, Roos publicly called upon the two political parties to unite under him. He had always been an ambitious man, and now the warmth of his reception by the public seemed to have given him an inflated idea of his own importance. His terms were that he was to be Prime Minister and that each of the parties was to have five ministers under him, with an additional Labour minister.

When my father had lost the use of Groote Schuur in the Cape, a group of overseas friends, to give him the privacy of a home in preference to the Civil Services Club where he normally stayed, bought a home for his use in Bowwood Road, Claremont, a pleasant suburb on the slopes of Table Mountain, ten miles out of Cape Town. "Tsalta" was to find a warmer place in the hearts of the Smuts family than Groote Schuur. It was not far from the lovely Kirstenbosch Botanical Gardens and had a fine view of the mountain slopes. Other good but anonymous friends had made him the gift of a new Hudson car in 1924, though for many years he still retained a soft spot for his old war-time Vauxhall, now somewhat unreliable.

My father got into touch with Roos. He came out to "Tsalta" one evening to discuss his merger ideas. It was rumoured that Roos had the support of eleven Nationalist members of Parliament. Could he count on these, my father asked him, and who, in fact were they? Roos said, frankly, he was not quite certain. This, coupled with a noticeable cooling off in public enthusiasm, convinced my father that Roos was already a spent force. But in the South African Party Caucus strong support was to be found for Roos. It is said that there was even talk of disloyalty to my father.

But by now Roos had run his meteoric course and people were tiring of him. It was the lot of most politicians. The same crowds were not in places to meet and to cheer him. My father offered him only four seats in a coalition government. He was to be one of the four, and only the Deputy Prime Minister. This Roos refused.

At the end of January my father moved in the House what was tantamount to a vote of no confidence in the Government. They had said they would stand or fall on the gold standard issue. We were now off gold and they must honour their obligation. It was an abortive appeal.

The Roos business, however, had set my father thinking. He had long since tired of the political bitterness with which he had been living for over twenty years. Almost anything would be preferable to this. Roos had turned down the plan for coalition.

But was that necessarily the end? Might not a more ambitious plan of coalition with Hertzog now be explored? He turned the proposition over in his mind during his rambles on the mountains one week-end.

When he got back from this walk he found J. H. Hofmeyr awaiting him at "Tsalta". This brilliant scholastic prodigy had already in his twenties been Principal of the Witwatersrand University and later Administrator of the Transvaal. At thirty he had turned down the offer of a High Commissionership in London and come into politics on my father's side. In political leanings he was a liberal, not unlike his famous uncle of similar name in the old Cape Parliament. Already Hofmeyr had helped in the previous negotiations between Roos and my father.

What Hofmeyr had now come to say was that Nationalist contacts had hinted that there might be a chance of a Smuts–Hertzog coalition. My father had only to make the offer in Parliament. It would not be refused.

My father said that he had been turning this possibility over in his mind, and that it had his blessing. Perhaps it would be better and make things easier if he himself dropped out of politics. But the Party would not hear of his retirement. They wanted their old leader. This insistence cheered him. My father said he would like to sleep on it. He weighed up what it would mean to him personally to work under a man who had cursed and maligned him for so long. Yet, if the experiment worked, if he could bear it, think of the glorious future it held out for the country. Regardless of his own feelings, he decided it was worth trying.

Hertzog accepted my father's hand. He was to remain Prime Minister and my father was to be his Deputy. Each was to nominate five ministers. As Minister of Justice my father was now back in the exact position of State Attorney (even to the salary) he occupied thirty-five years ago.

Only my father knew what the extension of the hand of friendship to Hertzog meant to him. He banished all personal ambition and submerged his feelings and emotions. The next elections would have brought certain victory. Of that there was no doubt. The Government were thoroughly beaten and spent.

All that he brushed aside. For the sake of unity he was prepared to go to these lengths—and much more. It saddened him that aspiring young Cabinet Ministers would not get their chance. They, too, had to be sacrificed on the national altar. Nor was he under any illusion about what the years ahead would demand of him.

The May General Elections showed how truly the public endorsed this effort. The Coalition took the country by storm. My father's name was actually cheered in Smithfield, Hertzog's constituency. He spoke, with success, in favour of Dr. Malan's candidature at Calvinia, and he helped a Nationalist to defeat Tielman Roos. He did all this gladly at the time, for who could then tell that these men would turn against him?

This was the end of Roos. Once more he retired from public life, dying not long after, a poor man, filled with worries about his young family. My father unveiled a memorial to him.

Speaking in Cape Town in March, 1933, my father said that Coalition had not been the work of any particular leader. It had been practically forced on the leaders by public opinion. There had been an overwhelming feeling in favour of unity. . . . The people had been wiser than their leaders. They had wanted Coalition, and they had got it. . . . The South African Party was probably making a greater contribution to the future peace and welfare of the country by the action they were taking than they could have done by any victory at the polls. "My prayer is that the people of this country, who have been primarily responsible for this coalition movement, will look upon this work as their own, and will not allow party divisions to act as a wedge between them. See that the experiment is a success. . . . Let peace now percolate from the top to the bottom, and let the spirit of peace pass from the leaders to the hearts of the people. . . . Who knows that by coming together at this time, we have not laid the foundations of something very big for South Africa."

★   ★   ★   ★   ★

It is a strange thing that though my father had at one time been Minister of Finance and played a leading part in the discussions of finances at the time of the gold standard crisis, he took little interest in his personal money matters. The feeling was one of distaste and disinterestedness, not of ignorance.

Consequently, though he had made a good Minister of Finance, he made a poor show of his own financial affairs, and except for the early years when he had a lucrative legal practice, he was almost constantly on the red side of the ledger. But usually he was quite unaware of this, for my mother ran his domestic affairs for him. She paid the accounts and made up his income-tax returns and worried about his bank balances. It took a petty burden off his shoulders. It was typical of my father's philosophy that having decided that there was little he himself could do by worrying about it, he turned it over to capable hands and forgot about it.

Though a comparatively poor man, he never refused assistance to friends. I feel that if any of the family had at any time asked for financial assistance he would certainly not have disappointed us. On numerous occasions during his life he received gifts of money from grateful public bodies or wealthy friends. These he never touched himself but turned straight over to public education purposes and trust funds. He was scrupulous in the extreme about receiving financial gifts, and well-wishers who wanted to ease his burdens were at a loss to know how to help him, for they knew that he would never accept any assistance.

The only exceptions to his general rule occurred late in life, when he accepted a legacy left him by Sir Henry Strakosch, an old friend whom he had helped at the start of his career. He did this only because he felt in old age the need for security, so as not to be a burden on his family.

But if he took no direct interest in money for his own use, he took a lively interest in it in the public sense, and he was constantly striving and contriving to get funds for his Party machine. Here many of his old friends, who all prefer to remain anonymous, some long since departed, came to the Party's assistance and my father always remembered them with gratitude. It was all done modestly and discreetly and the public will never know about the services of these benefactors.

Throughout life he frequently lent friends money. We knew of about a dozen people to whom he lent (for him) large sums of money, but the number must be considerably in excess of this. To a man with a bank overdraft it was an act of considerable generosity to be owed some thousands of pounds. I doubt if he expected to get his money back. We know of only a single instance in which these debts were repaid.

When we twitted him about his money-lending efforts, pointing out that he not only had not got the cash back, but that the recipients had frequently turned his bitterest political enemies, he remarked philosophically that "the best way to make an enemy of a person is to lend him money"!

LVII THE SCIENTIST

DURING the quieter years when my father was out of the Government he found time for many things that had been dear to him for years. Primarily for him it was a period of great international speeches and great scientific activity.

Let us trace the development of my father as a scientist. People are inclined to think of him as a scientist merely in addition to being already a soldier and a politician. Here they are really putting the cart before the horse, for whatever other qualities my father possessed, he was above all a scientist. It was from this attribute he inherited the characteristic of careful analysis—the taking apart of things to discover basic factors and principles. It was from this he inherited a clarity of reasoning and perspective which some have attributed to his legal training.

So, basically, let us look upon my father as a patient and painstaking scientific worker, irrespective of whether he was dealing with abstract factors, or the teeming peoples of the earth. His clarity of thought and method of reasoning never varied.

Rather let us say that he was a good general and good politician because he was a versatile scientist.

At an early age he showed these leanings. But in his youth the study of science was still a comparatively new art, with little literature and little publicity. Consequently my father had to grope for a mode of expression. This he found by his reading of the poets and philosophers and his communion with nature. Crude as these methods were, they helped him to write his novel and far-reaching treatise on Walt Whitman. The analysis of Whitman followed him as an intriguing problem for many years and he was not satisfied until he had expressed himself more maturely in *Holism and Evolution*. Yet *Holism* was only an introduction to the problem, and if he had leisure one day he hoped to complete it in a second volume.

Though dealing with inanimate elements and impersonal laws, my father believed that these laws were in fact expressions of a form of personality, and the very atoms and electrons were no less than basic communities of regulated things. Holism (pronounced as if spelt "Hollism") was an endeavour to postulate a link between life and matter. It involved a process of evolution, which after all is a concept of a living trend.

It is a long time since Newton gazed musingly at the gravitational attraction upon an apple, or Faraday dabbled with the elementary phenomena of electricity, but this was the background in which my father spent his early years. When he was at Cambridge he pursued the course of law and rhetoric and had little tutored experience in scientific matters. All the science he learned he gleaned painstakingly for himself by private reading and study. In chemistry he taught himself about Rutherford's atoms and the symbols and reactions of the various elements. Kelvin taught him about electrical behaviour, Edington and Jeans about the composition of the celestial spaces, Planck and Einstein about the abstract behaviour of matter and space in all its dimensions, and the remainder he filled in from other scientists.

The study of Geology fascinated him from an early age. Born in the rugged mountainland of the Cape, it would have been strange had a study of the crust of the earth not intrigued him. It would have been difficult for a mountaineer to stand upon the top of Table Mountain and gaze northwards across the great jagged buttresses, rising one behind the other into the blue distance, without feeling an ambition to unravel the riddle of the crust.

So my father, by reading and observation, soon had a good working knowledge of the rudiments of crustal behaviour. Joly's hypothesis of isostasy, or rising and falling continental masses, interested him, for it personified the pulsations of a living continent. But the Taylor-Wegener theory of continental drift was his great love in the geological realms. For not only did it solve a large number of formerly inexplicable phenomena, but it had a satisfying purposeful trend about it, and purported to show, too, that Africa was the stable mother continent from which the subsequent disruption and drifting had taken place.

His interest in continental drift was stimulated by the inspiring spectacle of the Great Rift Valley of East Africa he saw during his campaigning there in the First World War. For the Great Rift might well be the manifestation or embryo of a new rift and movement, which in the fullness of geological time, might amount to a new division of the African continent. With Dr. A. L. du Toit he had close ties of friendship and association. Du Toit was our leading geologist, and perhaps the greatest modern protagonist of the continental drift hypothesis. My father spotted his brilliance early on and took an active interest in him till his death shortly after the Second World War. The fact that he had failed to indicate satisfactory water boring sites on my father's bushveld farm did not in any way shake my father's faith in him. When Professor Schwarz was expounding his Kalahari redemption scheme in the early 1920s my father sent du Toit to investigate the matter on behalf of the Government. Though this survey was hurried and not completely conclusive it showed that water would have to be persuaded to flow uphill to fill some of the old desert depressions. Many of Schwarz's other premises did not meet with general acceptance. Du Toit had also been intrigued by the personality of Schwarz, who apparently displayed but scant interest during the trip in the geological and topographical investigations, but was wildly interested in the studies of native life he came across. The impression was, du Toit told my father, that Schwarz had already lost interest in his own grandiose scheme.

As President of the British Association for the Advancement of Science when it met in Cape Town on the 6th July, 1925, my father delivered an address on "Science from the South African Point of View", in which he touched briefly on some of his pet ideas in so far as they concerned us.

In the first place [he said] the South African point of view will liberate us from old preconceived ways of looking at many scientific problems. . . . The Northern Hemisphere, and in particular the European continent, is the home of nineteenth-century science, its birthplace and the great field of its labour and triumphs. . . . No wonder it has come to be considered the centre of the world, perhaps the original seat and centre of all terrestrial evolution. . . .

From many points of view Africa occupies a key position among the continents of the world; it has the most curious affinities with all of them; more than any other continent it has special scientific relationships with all the rest. And the character of these relationships shows that it occupies not only geographically but also scientifically a position among the rest, a position which may yet supply the key and the explanation to many problems that are at present obscure or unexplained by science. . . .

Within the last five years a great impetus has been given to this way of looking at Africa by the Wegener theory, or rather hypothesis, for it is, perhaps, not yet more than an hypothesis. . . . The Wegener hypothesis purports to explain the origin, the past and the present of all continents and oceans of this globe. . . .

For us in this part of the world the most interesting feature of the scheme is that in it Africa assumes a central position among the continents. . . . It appears as the mother continent from which South America on the one side and Madagascar, India, Australia and their surrounding areas on the other, have split off and drifted away. . . . The evidence for all this is strong; . . . It may be right in assigning to the African continent a central determining position in many of the great unsolved problems of Geographical Distribution. . . .

One important line of research which it suggests to us is the East–West aspect, in addition to the hitherto prevalent North–South line of orientation. . . . We have looked to the north for explanations as well as our origins. In future . . . we shall look more to East and West. . . . We shall look upon Southern Africa as the centre of the Southern Hemisphere and correlate all the relative scientific problems of this hemisphere from that new point of view. . . .

Let us first take the case of Geology. . . . Several of our formations at the Cape seem to be continued or paralleled by identical or similar formations in India and South America. . . .

We may be enabled thereby to explain just why they are practically the sole producers of the world's diamonds; why the diamond fields of South-West Africa are situated on the one edge of the Atlantic and those of Brazil on the other; why the coalfields of these three countries and of Australia are confined to the eastern portions of each of these land masses; and why the curious and ancient banded ironstones are so widely spread in South Africa, Brazil, peninsular India and Western Australia, though absent from Europe.

But it is when we came to the biological sciences that such a comparative study promises the most fruitful results. . . . Consider, for instance, the problems affecting our Botany. We have two distinct floras in South Africa; the one, the South African flora, which covers most of sub-tropical Africa and is clearly of tropical origin; the other, a temperate flora, found only in the south-west of the Cape Province on the seaward side of the first great mountain barrier, with outliers extending to the north along the mountain systems into the tropics.

The two floras are, apparently, quite different and distinct and are engaged in a mortal conflict with each other. This Cape flora forms, indeed, a problem of profound and baffling interest. What is its origin, and what is its relation to the South African flora? Northern Europe is the source and the north temperate flora of Europe is the origin of both our South African and Cape floras. The north temperate flora of Europe is supposed to have been driven south by the onset of the last great Ice Age in Europe and . . . to have migrated southwards along the eastern mountain systems of Africa until southern Africa was reached.

This common view of the European origin of our floras will, however, require very careful reconsideration. . . . It may, for instance, yet be found that our floras are not of northern origin, but come from the ancient lands of the Southern Hemisphere which are covered by the Wegener hypothesis . . . Similarly, the Cape flora has peculiar affiliations with the floras of certain countries in the Southern Hemisphere. The current view of the northern origin may therefore not be the last word so far as Botany is concerned. . . .

Here it is necessary to point out that Darwin, while holding to the northern origin, yet continued to be haunted by the idea of a southern continent whose mystery might, perhaps, hold also the secret of the origin of the Angiosperms. . . .

The Cape Province . . . is a narrow corner of the African continent. . . . Its wealth of endemic forms is out of all proportion to its area. . . . Is it not more probable that the south-western corner of Africa is the remains of a land which extended much farther in the Southern Ocean? . . . In other words, this flora points . . . to an origin even farther south than the ancient Gondwanaland is commonly supposed to have extended. May we not venture the suggestion that the Cape temperate flora is the survival of an Antarctic and sub-Antarctic flora which has perished in the climate changes of the past?

[My father then switched to zoology and so on to past climates.]

333

Indisputable evidence of the severe and long-continued convulsions of Africa during the Tertiary times exists. The vast cracks and fissures which rent it from south to north exist to-day still in the chains of great lakes and "rift valleys" which extend across Africa from the Zambesi to the Red Sea, the Dead Sea and the deep valley of the Jordan. Farther north the crust of the earth folded up slowly like a crumpled scroll, and as a result the huge mountain chains of the Atlas and the Alps, the Taurus and the Himalayas were formed. Volcanoes burst forth in Africa in many places along the lines of weakness, while in the south the diamond pipes were formed.

During the closing phase of the Tertiary there occurred elevations of the Scandinavian shield and other land masses in many parts of the world. Conditions grew steadily more frigid, until eventually Europe was in the full grip of the last Ice Age, though in the more temperate climes increased rainfall took the place of the snow and ice. Primitive man, the fore-runner of homo sapiens, made his bow during the Ice Age and is represented by the fossil remains found in caves and river drifts.

Three finds of outstanding importance have in recent years signalled South Africa as a great field of research into the human past. The first was the discovery of the Boskop skull, which, according to Professor Dart, represents a still existing strain among our native peoples. The second was the discovery of Homo rhodesiensis at Broken Hill, which Professor Elliot Smith is reported to have declared to have been one of the most significant finds ever to have been made in human palæontology. Finally we have Australopithecus africanus, which largely breaks new ground in palæontology. . . .

It will be seen at once what a change Professor Dart's discovery brings into the situation. For in Australopithecus africanus we have just such an anticipated transitional form between the ape and the human; we have a creature which is still undisputably an ape, but with certain facial features and a brain development which take it some way towards the human. . . . The deduction has been made that Homo rhodesiensis was living quite out of his proper geological horizon, and was surviving in South Africa long ages after his compeers in Europe had passed away. . . . But there is really nothing singular in such an idea. After all, such a situation is typical of South Africa in more respects than one. Our Bushmen are nothing but living fossils, whose "contemporaries" disappeared from Europe many thousands of years ago. The interest of South Africa as a field for anthropological research is partly just this, that it is possibly ten thousand years behind the times, as measured by the standards of European cultures. . . .

It is not only one of the oldest land surfaces, but since the end of the Mesozoic period it has generally enjoyed a fairly habitable, though on the whole, dry climate. . . . No wonder therefore that it should contain not only some of the most ancient fossil records of the human race, and that among its living races it should include what are "fossils" in other continents. Its little Bushmen are unique; its little pigmy population that hide in the tropical and sub-tropical forests are representatives of the long-vanished human past. Going a little farther back, we find in Africa the home of the great anthropoid apes which are nearest to us in the affinities of life. . . .

The scope for scientific work in South Africa in this department of knowledge is therefore immense; the ground lies literally cumbered with the possibilities of great discoveries.

Our coasts are covered with raised beaches and caves which have never been explored and which probably hold precious secrets. Our limestone and dolomite formations are honeycombed with unexplored grottos. . . .

The guess my father hazarded at the "unexplored grottos" was indeed prophetic, for ten years afterwards, an old friend of his, Dr. Robert Broom, began to make the most important series of ape-man discoveries that have occurred in the age of human palæontology. Here, in the old limestone caves near Krugersdorp, were found a wide range of advanced fossil anthropoids dating back between one and two million years, who showed characteristics far in advance of any living ape and who walked upright. The different types varied in size from small apes weighing perhaps a hundred pounds to giant brutes of six hundred pounds.

These epoch-making finds pleased my father quite as much as they did Dr. Broom, for it was my father who, in the early days, had been impressed by the remarkable work Dr. Broom, then a medical practitioner, was doing on the Karroo fossils, and had persuaded him to take up research work in the Transvaal Museum. Broom, more than any other scientist, has brought lustre to this country.

His belief in the raised beaches was also justified long after during the intensified studies of ocean levels and past climates, which culminated in the remarkable results of the investigations of the noted French anthropologist the Abbé Henri Breuil. Breuil was another old friend of my father's, whom after the collapse of

France he had prevailed upon to come to South Africa to study our prehistory.

These and other illustrious scientists who my father grouped about him and encouraged, were his proud "kindergarten". They were not young men like Milner's entourage, but old well-tried veterans.

Darwin he had already studied and mastered as a young man. At an early age it had made a convert of him to the concept of evolution. Evolution led through palæontology and anthropology to the broad aspect of prehistory. Prehistory brought him into contact with the caves and Stone-Age artifact cultures of this country. He persuaded van Riet Lowe to give up his structural engineering work with the Public Works Department and to start a new Bureau of Archæology at the Witwatersrand University.

For myself I can only say how patiently and painstakingly he encouraged me as a child when he saw that I had a certain flair for prehistory. He never developed any marked proficiency as a practical archæologist, but on the theoretical side his knowledge was enormous. When out fossicking or camping he would spend his time botanising, while I dabbled in the simpler and more mundane pastime of collecting stone implements. Such is the profusion of the handiwork of primitive man in this country, that one can readily assemble collections almost anywhere. On returning from our tramps I would show him my stones, and he would then enthuse over them almost as much as over his own botanical specimens, which I need hardly add, were always very dear to his heart.

In July, 1932, at Durban my father delivered a lecture to the South African Association for the Advancement of Science on "Climate and Man in Africa". This, no less than the address of 1925 I have just quoted, was a remarkable document and even now, almost twenty years later, I still consider it the best of its type produced in this country. I say it is remarkable, for here my father was dealing in great detail with a subject he had not really studied intimately before, but one which was still fluid and controversial and one which the timid experts shrank from tackling. He was dealing with the highly contentious details of man's evolutionary path, he was working on a time scale over which there was as yet no general agreement, and he was attempting correlations between various countries that had not previously been linked. The result was a well-balanced, lucid and well-presented paper which astonished many people who looked upon him as a botanist or philosopher or broad-aspect scientist.

This present paper on man and climate really had its origins on his bushveld farm. Here he had twenty enormous Aapiesdoring (*Acacia galpinii*) thorn trees growing. They are as big as any in the sub-continent and were a source of great pride to him. But they are also an indication of a former wetter climate, for they are moisture-loving trees. They suggested to him the idea of exploring the past climates of our country from the botanical aspect. The idea was fortified by the gnarled camelthorn trees (*Acacia giraffæ*) growing near by, which in turn are remnants of a formerly drier climate. So he turned over in his mind the idea of this climatic paper, but the more he thought of it the more he realised that the botanical aspect had limitations and that prehistory held out much better evidence. So he switched the basis of the study to the Stone Age.

The result was the most specialised scientific paper he ever produced. I shall not try to set out his ideas in this book. He indicated, in detail, the events of the last Ice Age in Europe, in so far as it concerned both climate and primitive man. These results he then correlated with those of the Union, using East Africa as a stepping-stone, showing that the various separate advances of the ice sheets of this period had corresponding phases of rainfall or drought in Africa. It sounds comparatively simple, but it is a highly delicate study, which even now, with the passage of many years, still produces conflicting emotions in the breasts of scientists. He concludes with this tragic reflection on the Bushman:

As they were racially and physically not very different 15,000 years ago, what has caused the immense difference between the European and Bushman to-day? We see in one the leading race of the world, while the other, though still living, has become a mere human fossil, verging on extinction. We see the one crowned with all the intellectual and spiritual glory of the race, while the other still occupies the lowest scale in human existence. If race has not made the difference, what has? Of course the question is far too speculative, and our ignorance of all the essential conditions far too profound, to make any attempt at an answer worth while!

But two points may, perhaps, be usefully stressed in this connection. In the first place, if environment has any influence on human evolution, we may look to the physical conditions under which the Bushman and his ancestors have lived for this last 8,000 years and more as an excuse for his degeneracy. No doubt he has gone backward; his brain capacity is even smaller than that of Fish Hoek man, who, in turn, shows a smaller brain capacity than Boskop Man. The Bushman has been physically dwarfed and shrivelled and mentally stunted by nature. Nobody, who has seen him in his present haunts in the Kalahari, or who knew him a generation or two ago in other parts of the Union, will deny that he has become a desert animal, carved and moulded by the desert, just as much as the rest of our desert animals or plants. His desert nature is inbred in him, and he is an additional proof of the semi-arid environment which South Africa must have presented for many millennia. And now that desert conditions are being ameliorated by the ironic touch of civilisation, there is nothing left for him but to disappear. . . .

Professor M. R. Drennan of Cape Town University described it as ". . . a real landmark in the science of Anthropology and I feel certain it is going to be much sought after as a classic on the subject".

* * * * *

The interesting thing to note about my father's entry on to the scientific stage is that it lasted only eight years, from 1925 to 1932. That does not mean that this was necessarily a period of abnormally intensified effort on his part, for in fact he kept continuously abreast of scientific matters at all times. The explanation is, of course, that this period corresponds with the time he was out of government office. It meant that now, for the first time, he had the leisure to sit down and put his ideas on paper. To lead the masses of his people has meant a loss to contemporary science and philosophy. To him personally, too, it was a sadness that he could not do what he really liked.

Holism he started writing almost immediately his Government was defeated in 1924. His frenzied tackling of the task was perhaps a measure of chagrin and frustration at his treatment by the public, but I think it was more the realisation of a long-pent-up urge to tackle his *magnum opus*. He wrote it hastily, too hastily, he feels, to do the subject real justice. But his intention had always been to finish off his ideas in a final volume.

His great mental activity at this time was by no means confined to his exposition of the holistic concept. At the same time he was delving almost boyishly into the joys of botany, both written and in the field. He had always taken a mild interest in botany, ever since he had wandered about the mountains at Stellenbosch in his college days. But it was a mild, semi-dormant interest always, which never really obtruded forcibly on his daily life and habits.

Now the study of plants burst forth as a full-fledged insatiable hobby. He never proceeded into the veld without his magnifying glass or his clipping shears, and as far as he wandered he paused and examined plants and grasses. This really active phase of collecting and studying corresponded in duration with the same quiet political period 1925 to 1934. Thereafter, though his interest never slackened or cooled off, he simply did not have the leisure to devote to his hobby, though he would still often be found with his books or looking through the collections in his small herbarium. In the active period he planned trips whenever possible into the wilds for botanical research. These trips led him as far afield as Lake Tanganyika, Lake Nyasa, the Victoria Falls, the Zimbabwe Ruins, the Zoutpansberg (which he said was particularly interesting), the Blaauberg, Portuguese East Africa, etc., quite apart from expeditions in the Transvaal bushveld and the mountains of the Cape. Many of these areas had not been seriously touched by collectors before and his collections were therefore of special interest and contained many new species. His mountaineering ability and great energy took him to remote places.

But his virtues as a great botanist lay not only in his field work. He was also a well-read botanist and knew the bibliography and history of botany. He read not only English botanical works, but also those of the famous German writers. He knew not only contemporary botanists but was an authority on the works of the old travellers and naturalists. And he was also well acquainted with the works of the palæo-botanists such as his old friends Professor Seward and Dr. Marie Stopes and others. He knew the botany of Mesozoic Gondwanaland almost as well as the Flora Capensis. And in addition he had considerable knowledge of the botany of other countries.

In botany, as in prehistory, Southern Africa is a country of great interest. The vastness of the geographical areas, the differences in climate and elevation, the profusion of grasses as well as shrubs and trees, and the additional strange flora of the Cape make it a country unsurpassed in number or variety. The Union has about ten thousand different species of grasses, and these with their intricate Latin nomenclature form more than a full-time study. Add to that an additional thirty or forty thousand plants, shrubs and trees and the formidable nature of botanical study in this country will be appreciated. The flora of the tip of the Cape alone is as extensive as that of the whole of Great Britain.

No wonder that in botany my father found a hobby to test his mettle.

To him botany was a study of living things set in indigenous surroundings. The artificials and exotics of our man-made gardens did not interest him. True, he liked a blaze of colour, but that was all. He appreciated only wild plants, growing undisturbed in their wild setting. Once having collected a certain plant he would be satisfied merely to admire it and leave it undisturbed in future. The plants he took home he either put in his presses or studied carefully before discarding them again. When in doubt he consulted experts and collections in herbariums. He often went to great pains to collect certain specimens. Tales are told by friends of hair-raising scrambles along precipices to collect tempting-looking specimens. Sometimes a whole protracted expedition would be planned with the sole object of finding some rare plant collected long before by some of our noted explorers. Travelling with my father by car was often quite an ordeal, for he would stop frequently and wander off into the bush to make his collections, leaving one sitting hot and disconsolate in the car. But though he took our chidings and complaints in good nature, he never mended his ways. He brushed away opposition here, as in public life.

Botany to him was largely an African study and though I have fossicked with him in England and America, I noticed he never took the same active interest in plants there.

LVIII FUSION

UPON the death of Tielman Roos, Dr. Malan became heir-apparent to Hertzog. For various reasons, one of which was that he considered Hertzog too aged for leadership and too moderate, he declined to serve under his old leader and now split off and formed a small group of his own, known as the Purified Nationalist Party. He was not interested in a post in the new Cabinet.

To many people the most remarkable thing about coalition was the complete change of heart it brought about in General Hertzog. It was a really commendable effort. No person could have tried harder than the General to make the partnership work, or to have co-operated more actively. Nor was it a shallow veneer. He saw to it that it was to be the greatest work of his life. For it, he deserves full credit. In private life he had always been a courteous and chivalrous man, and he now brought these attributes to bear in the Coalition. He had no light task, for in his ranks were many who did not agree with him and attacked him whenever possible. He remained loyal to my father, and turned his ferocity on his new critics.

My father added the major share to the success of the Coalition movement. To do so he completely effaced himself. This was not difficult, for personal position and status in life held no great lure for him. He was quite prepared to withdraw quietly into the background and to allow Hertzog the limelight. It was, in fact, a sound policy to follow. But there were times when the Prime Minister wandered off the beaten track, when my father found it almost impossible to remain impassive and to swallow things that went against his principles. He did this for the sake of the country.

The personal side of the association of the two leaders presented no difficulties, for though Hertzog and my father had differed for years on political matters, they had throughout, in private, remained on friendly terms. My father had never taken Hertzog's wild outbursts to heart, and I never once in private heard him complain about his opponent's attacks. General Hertzog, away from politics, was, in fact, a retiring and likeable person.

A brief Session of Parliament followed the elections of 1933. Resolutions were flowing in from Party branches all over the country requesting that the partnership should ripen into something closer, called Fusion. Malan's followers, already sorely annoyed at Coalition, now broke away completely from Hertzog whom from now on they attacked vigorously.

The 1934 Session was notable for the passing of the Status Bills. Malan had been the prime mover in raising the issue with Hertzog. These Bills were introduced to "clarify" the position brought about by the 1932 Statute of Westminster, which accorded the Dominions an equal partnership with Britain, in so far as external affairs were concerned. The actual purpose of Dr. Malan's motion was, however, to whip up the old bogy of complete independence from Britain, an idea which was tied up with republicanism and other factors.

My father did not favour the Status Bills. He did not see the need for them, but saw, instead, a great danger in tampering with the Union's constitution, and felt that it would have been wiser to leave the position as defined in the past. If he had had his way the Bills would never have been introduced. But once having made up his mind, Hertzog insisted. Thereafter my father did his best to moderate and placate the Afrikaans and English sections. The attachment to the King in many was deep-rooted. Colonel Stallard maintained that the Bills undermined the sovereign position of the monarch and weakened the ties of Commonwealth, and resigned to form a strongly pro-British Dominion Party. His few adherents were mostly from Natal.

The implication of the Statute of Westminster, which brought about a natural consummation of the Balfour Declaration of 1926, was to form a major source of contention in later years. In the Act of Union of 1910 there were certain entrenched clauses, and certain other clauses were prescribed to protect them. These safeguarding clauses laid down that the entrenched clauses could only be altered by a two-thirds majority of both Houses sitting together. The Act of Union and the Statute of Westminster are both British parliamentary pacts. The contention, later to be introduced by certain constitutional lawyers and Nationalist politicians, was that as both acts are British, the Statute superseded our Act of Union, and that we were now at liberty to modify our own Act at will, without regard to the old two-thirds majority safeguard.

In 1951 this point was to become one of the biggest issues yet faced by our Parliament, when Dr. Malan's Government introduced a change in the Cape Coloured franchise, which happens to be entrenched in our Act. Coloureds have enjoyed franchise rights in the Cape since 1853.

My father, as the architect of the Act of Union, must have been well aware of the intentions and implications of that Act. In addition he was also an authority on constitutional law. His views, both private and public, were that the entrenched clauses of the Act were in no way affected by the Statute of Westminster.

At the time the Statute became operative in 1931 he foresaw the possibility of future trouble and did his best to get the House to declare that the Act of Union was in no way affected. Members, not so far-sighted, while agreeing on this point, were inclined to regard it as an academic issue and it got little support. General Hertzog, who did not share my father's anxiety, willingly accepted an amendment by my father "that the proposed legislation will in no way derogate from the entrenched provisions of the South Africa Act". He confirmed it still further, by stating that "man to man—it is our view that the protection of Section 152 cannot be taken away".

When the Act of Union was being drafted the question of the incorporation into the Union of the three British Protectorates, Basutoland, Bechuanaland and Swaziland, was considered. The idea met with full approval, but at the time it was felt that the Union would have so much to attend to in the next few years that it should not be burdened at that stage with the incorporation of the Protectorates. The idea was that Britain was to continue their administration for perhaps half a dozen years, whereafter the Union was to take over all responsibilities. It has been a long six years, for in 1951 the transfer was still hanging fire.

The position now is that while South Africa owns the title deeds of the Protectorates, Britain still administers them. The stumbling-block has been largely one of colour prejudice. Britain does not approve of the South African views on the native question, and throughout the years this has been her standpoint for refusal to transfer. My father has for many years, in private, impressed on Britain the need for a timely, but gradual, transfer. Otherwise, he said, Britain would one day find herself in a difficult position and might have to do an over-hasty and undignified withdrawal. With a Nationalist Government in power, the issue might well have its hazards.

Soon after completing the final arrangements of Fusion, my father was on his way to Britain again. He could well afford to leave the Union, for matters were proceeding more smoothly than for many years, and the country was prosperous and booming.

LIX DISTANT RUMBLINGS

IN 1924 the British, having grown tired of Mr. Lloyd George, rejected this great fighter. Thereafter followed Ramsay MacDonald, Stanley Baldwin and Neville Chamberlain. It was not a glorious phase in the history of Britain. It was a period of indecision and vacillation and in the end appeasement: not the appeasement of power and confidence, but humiliating appeasement from weakness. Britain still remained a first-class power on land and at sea only because the rest of the world at the time was luckily also at a low ebb.

This weakness was to have far-reaching repercussions, for evil men in other countries were to see their chance and take their risk. For the League it was also catastrophic that Britain and the other powers had not the strength or the will to enforce its clauses or to impose sanctions.

Manchukuo in 1932 was the first test case. Here Japan in flagrant violation of international law and without any pretext, except self-aggrandisement, invaded helpless Manchukuo and proceeded to conquer it. It was a clear-cut case of aggression. The League met to consider the position. Nothing more happened and the incident was accepted with little more than a shrug of the shoulders.

This conspicuous display of weakness was not lost upon the other would-be aggressors.

In 1936 Franco, grown tired of the corruption in Spain, and intolerant of opposition, and also seeing a great opportunity for an ambitious man, started a long and bloody war which cost a million lives and brought untold misery on the population. The great powers used Spain as a testing laboratory for their new weapons. Here Germany, in support of the Franco regime, for the first time tried out her guns, her tanks and her dive bombers. On their success here she based her assessments of their future effectiveness in a world war.

Russian volunteers supported the Left, as did volunteer men from Ireland and elsewhere. In the end Franco's cause prevailed, and with it once more might over justice.

In Italy Benito Mussolini, a bombastic showman, had visions of making Italy once more great. He had had limited success as a newspaper man, but had ambition and energy. As a platform he championed the underdog and rapidly rose in popularity, his earlier and greatest works being associated with the peasantry and agriculture. In later days, to symbolise their earlier beginnings, he used to help in the harvesting of the wheat during the festivals. With his rise in popularity came a swelling of the head and more pugnacious thrusting out of his massive chin. His oratory impressed the populace and stirred them to renewed activity. But greatness was incomplete unless it was backed by military might. So Mussolini dreamed of a mighty Italian army and the restoration of Nice, Corsica and Jibuti. Later he became fanatical about their return. But meantime there was other work to do. There was the stigma of a distant disaster at Adowa in Abyssinia, in 1896, to wipe out. And so, fully confident that the impotence of the League would preclude any drastic reactions, he attacked this wild African State and Emperor Haile Selassie in 1935. General Grazziani pushed the campaign on with great vigour and ruthlessness, at times not even neglecting the advantage of the use of mustard gas. After hectic League meetings sanctions were agreed upon and a mild form of blockade ensued. It was left to the Royal Navy to apply it in the Mediterranean. Here one of her vessels was mysteriously torpedoed by what everybody knew to be an Italian submarine, but the Fleet was too short of ammunition to risk a showdown.

The issue was never in doubt. Abyssinia succumbed and once more might had prevailed.

In 1934, despite my father's previous advice that everything should be done to remain friendly with Japan, and keep her in the League where her actions could be closely watched, she decided to withdraw. Germany had already done so a few years previously, and henceforth her military preparations were wrapped in dangerous obscurity. Just how dangerous, the world was to find out in 1939.

Let us see what happened in Germany after the war. The peace terms and reparations rankled sorely with her, and all those dangerous complexes, which my father had predicted at Versailles, materialised. She became unco-operative and resentful. The country was poor and exhausted and beset with unemployment and labour difficulties. It proved a fertile ground for discordant elements. All the more so because of the lack of strong leadership. Hindenburg, when he became President of the Reich in 1925, was ancient and *passé*, and unable to cope with the situation. Earlier on my father had hoped that von Lettow Vorbeck might assume control, but a petty indiscretion had put him out of the running.

In a beer cellar in Munich Adolf Hitler and his die-hard supporters were holding rallies and evolving ambitious plans. They organised big demonstrations which the police were powerless to break up. By 1933 it was plain that the fuming fanatic was becoming a leader. In the following year he became Chancellor of the German Reich. He had been a corporal in the First World War. He was a loud and tempestuous speaker with a great power over the masses. His doctrine was the fruitful one of the injustices done to Germany. Germany was not beaten in the last war. She was still unconquered. One day she would again be great. He hypnotised the masses. They grew to believe him. He claimed the former German colonies. While in prison, he wrote a book called

Mein Kampf, which set out his ideas and aspirations, and which was to become the bible of the German people.

While Britain was still preaching and practising disarmament, Hitler began to build up a great war machine. The best scientific brains went into the design of equipment, and production went on apace under the financial wizardry of Dr. Schacht. And so, with the growth of his Wehrmacht and his Luftwaffe and Navy, Hitler became more confident and bellicose. Britain under Baldwin and Neville Chamberlain was still placidly sleeping, naïvely believing that it was a time for butter, not for guns.

Russia made one sign as if to awaken from her obscure Asiatic slumbers and lunged out against Finland; but Finland, under Mannerheim, fought back with such effect that Russia was only too glad to come to terms. This campaign falsely convinced the world of Russian weakness. It was later, providentially, to lead Hitler into his greatest blunder.

France was in a poor plight. Utterly exhausted, impoverished and devastated by the First World War, in which she had borne the brunt of the Prussian might, she was now in no state to settle down. The masses were dispirited and workless, and Leftist ideas were turning to outright Communistic persuasion. Leadership was lacking or of the poorest order, and governments came and went with the phases of the moon. France was drifting. The outlawing of Communism, later, only had the effect of forcing it under-ground where, as my father had predicted, it became far more dangerous and insidious.

France blamed Britain for much. When Hitler marched into the Rhineland she begged that they should drive the Germans out again, for at the time France was still comparatively strong and Germany weak. Britain refused and France liked Britain none the more for it. It was an uneasy partnership.

Hitler said he had no quarrel with Britain beyond the question of colonies. At one time I really think he meant it. But later his feelings changed into something more sinister. Yet many in Britain were still not to doubt Hitler's intentions. They were the appeasers, and there were very large numbers of them.

In vain the voice of Winston Churchill cried out to awaken and to warn. In vain Henry Strakosch sent confidential reports to Britain of what was taking place on the Continent. The mood was one of unshakable complacency. Nothing but the rumble of guns would dissipate it.

Firm in his convictions about the coming storms on the international horizon, my father did his best, like Mr. Churchill, to awaken Britain and to warn the world. This was no easy matter. The people were in no mood to be shaken from their happy-go-lucky air of complacency, even though they had grave misgivings about the trend of events. My father lost no opportunity of pointing out the dangers and the dark forces that were threatening freedom, and the monstrous evils that were abroad undermining the minds of peoples in the totalitarian states. The task was long and difficult. In Britain Prime Minister Neville Chamberlain, a well-meaning and sincere, but out-of-touch idealist, was being outwitted by the Axis and was hoping to gain time by means of concessions to Hitler. From the abortive Munich Conference with the German Fuehrer he came back, confident and elated, with a little slip of paper in his hand. He had concluded an agreement with Hitler, and there would be "peace in our time". Never for a moment did the apostle of appeasement doubt the word of the Fuehrer. The poor Czechoslovak people who were the victims of his betrayal and who had on the flimsiest pretext lost the Sudetenland on the grounds of self-determination to a German minority, felt differently about Mr. Chamberlain and his scrap of paper.

It was this problem of gullibility and complacency and make-believe that the lone voices had to combat. At his rectoral address to St. Andrews University in Scotland in 1934 the theme was "Freedom", and my father's speech here on this occasion, which I rank among one of his most memorable, made a great impression. It was a call to Britain to wake up and to take heed of what was happening on the Continent. It was a timely warning, for already Nazism and Fascism were beginning to swallow up rapaciously all those freedoms that were so dear to us. With the rise of Fascist ideas a great intolerance began to grow in Fascist countries. Personal liberties were one after another curtailed or abolished. They became fear states. The Gestapo were there to see to it. No whisper, no thought, was any longer safe.

The full hatred of the Nazis was poured out upon the hapless Jews. It is not clear what they had done to incur Nazi scorn and envy, and even odium. But the Nazis turned on them with unsuppressed hatred, and as time went on with active persecution. Millions of Jews were to perish before the Nazi machine was curbed. Liberties had gone. Germany became a great hand-raising, heel-clicking "yes" state.

This was the dim pattern of events. My father saw it all clearly.

LX FREEDOM

My father's 1934 visit to Britain was a memorable one, for during his stay he delivered two extremely important speeches on international affairs and many lesser ones.

These two addresses I would unhesitatingly rank among his greatest. His speeches on international affairs are all unique. They were addressed to world audiences and were clarion calls to peoples rather than reviews of events. In all, the trend of events was stressed and remedies proffered to forestall disaster. Often they became the adopted policies of nations. They carried not only warnings, but also messages of hope. The language was simple and the facts and reasoning lucid and straightforward. When he wanted to be explicit no one could state his case more clearly or courageously. What these talks meant to the Empire only history will one day be able to assess.

On the 17th October he delivered his Rectoral Address at St. Andrews University in Scotland. In this time of the awakening of the dark forces of Fascism and Nazism, the title was fittingly "Freedom". And equally fittingly it was addressed to the young people of the oldest University in Scotland. Here, as in all his great addresses, he was in good humour. The mood could never be mistaken and he carried himself and his audiences along in the same good humour. So it was at St. Andrews. I shall quote his speech fairly fully.

Professor Blyth Webster, introducing my father, said: "Skilled in war, no less potent in peace as an administrator and statesman . . . True as only the brave are . . . he is at once our advocate and our example of that peace 'whose name is one with honour born of war'. He showed us the practice and taught us the persistence of our own best ideals."

After expressing thanks for his election and paying tribute to his defeated opponent, my father said:

The principal's remark carried my mind back to the first occasion I had heard mention of the Scots. My people were small farming folk in the old Cape Colony, and when I was a very small boy I used to frequent the company of an old Hottentot shepherd of my father, who used to delight me with stories from his native folklore. He had also been to several Kaffir wars, and could tell me of his own wonderful feats of arms in those border campaigns. I listened enthralled. At that time the first Boer War—the one that ended at Majuba—was going on, and I remember asking him whom he thought would win. From his great military knowledge he had no doubt that the British would win. I asked him whether he thought the English were the greatest nation in the world, and he replied "No"; there was one nation still greater who lived in the farthest land in the world; they were the greatest of all nations and even the British were very much afraid of them. They were called the "Scots". That was my first introduction to the Scots—and such was my introducer! The principal must be right. Now, 54 years after those historic conversations, I find myself the rector of a famous university of this land—of romance, as the principal calls it—of the greatest of peoples, as old Adam, the Hottentot, called it.

I shall not venture to flatter you, and so I am bound to confess that in the sense of greatness meant by old Adam, he was wrong about Scotland. I have subsequently learnt that the Scots are, in fact, one of the small nations, although I do not intend to say so outside Scotland. To me and to us in our small beginnings in South Africa you are all the dearer on that account. We small ones of the earth feel mutually drawn to each other in a world which has largely gone crazy with the problems of size and scale. Both of us have learnt from Athens and Jerusalem that the real values were no respecters of dimensions. There were also other ties which link us together in common interests and sympathies of a more intimate character. There are the ties of kinship in the distant past, of a common religious faith, of common moral ideals. John Calvin and John Knox both belong to our invisible foundations, and there remains a community of spiritual outlook and moral values between our peoples which are among the most precious things we bring from our past.

In particular we both cherish and practise liberty as the fundamental rule of life. . . .

You in Scotland have a great story behind you while we in Africa are only at the beginning of things. The best I could wish for my own young people, now beginning to set up house on its own account, is that its future story may not be so very different in outline from yours. Like you, we have started in trouble and bloodshed. We still have our tribes just as you have had your clans. We are trying to come and grow together in nationhood, just as you have gloriously succeeded in your own union and internal peace-making. But more: you have set us an example how, while living your own life and maintaining and developing your own peculiar characteristics, to join in the larger life of a wider group, and thereby to make your contribution to the upbuilding of human civilisation and the establishment of a Commonwealth which to-day secures peace and opportunities for the good life to one-fourth of the human race. Your success in this wider theatre has gone far to justify old Adam the Hottentot in his high opinion of the Scots. They have overflowed their narrow national boundaries and have reinforced human life and endeavour all over the world, and most of all in undeveloped countries like those on the African continent. . . .

But, as I said, we are still at the beginnings. At this moment we are trying to lay the enduring basis of peace in our national life. Nowhere in the Dominions has more good blood been shed. Nowhere has the political aftermath of war been more unpleasant and bitter. But we believe we are at last approaching the end of that chapter. In our politics and our racial relations we are at present concluding the grand pact of union and of fusion. . . . The young nations of the world have their own contribution to make to the human causes, and they can best begin to do so by setting their house in order and pledging themselves afresh to the great human principles on which our Western civilisation rests.

In the old world—in the motherlands of our European civilisation —those principles are no longer considered sacrosanct and are being widely challenged and even openly defied. The things which Thomas Carlyle in the past century classed with the eternal verities are to-day being relegated to his limbo of old clothes. With the cataclysm of the Great War the whole European order threatens to collapse and in the ruins to involve the most precious treasures along with the accumulated rubbish of the nineteenth century. The catastrophe has been so sudden and unexpected that we have not yet had time to do the necessary sifting, to save the treasures from the waste of the middenheap. There has been no time yet to readjust our viewpoints, to take new bearings.

Mankind stands perplexed and baffled before the new situation and the new problems. There is fear, a sense of insecurity among the nations. The primeval dread of the unknown is once more upon us, and the dark irrational forces of the past are once more stalking forward from their obscure background. We have the paralysing sense of having failed. The fair promise of nineteenth-century progress has ended in defeat and frustration and disillusion. There has been a double failure. There was the failure of the Great War, which seemed to be a negation of the principles on which the comity of our Christian civilisation had been laboriously built up, and there was the no-less deep and poignant failure of the peace, when at a vital moment, a critical occasion for Western civilisation, human goodwill appeared to be unequal to its task, and the great hopes for a better ordering of the future were rudely disappointed. Such a chance comes but once in a whole era of history, and we missed it. The politics which is founded on despair or desperation, which covers many European countries to-day with dangerous political experiments, and in others endangers peace and paralyses disarmament, has sprung largely from this second failure and the slaughter of ideals which it involved—a slaughter no less grievous than that of our millions in the war. There was this double human failure, which has wounded, so to say, the very soul of mankind, and left it with insufficient faith and confidence to sustain the causes and the institutions which are essential to our civilisation.

No wonder there is abroad a spirit of pessimism and even of despair. So many high hopes have been dashed. Science, the proudest product of the human reason, the greatest instrument of human progress, the voice of God to our day and generation, has at the same time become the most dangerous weapon for our self-destruction. Democracy, with its promise of international peace, has been no better guarantee against war than the old dynastic rule of kings. International trade and commerce, which were supposed to pave a sure way to better understanding among the nations and a peaceful world, have instead led to economic nationalism, and thereby opened up new sources of international friction and trouble. One by one the vast expectations born of the progress of the last century have been falsified, and to-day we face a bleak world, bereft of the vast capital destroyed in the war, even doubting the principles on which our civilisation is built, without confidence in ourselves and our destiny, and with no clear vision of the road before us. We console ourselves with the truism that we are living in most interesting times. But the hard truth is that they are the most anxious and critical times that mankind has faced for many centuries.

Speaking here to-day to you, the young people of this university, an old hard-bitten campaigner like myself might be asked how I view the prospect before us. What message I have from my own experience, as one who has gone through the immense experience of our generation to those who now stand on the threshold of this strange new world. . . .

My fundamental impression of life I can give you in words which most of you know from your childhood. They occur on the first page of the greatest book in the world. They come from the youth of the world, and to-day in its maturity they are truer than ever. The world is good. This is a good world. We need not approve of all the items in it, nor of all the individuals in it; but the world itself, which is more than its parts or individuals, which has a soul, a spirit, a pull, a fundamental relation to each of us deeper than all other relations, is a friendly world. It has borne us; it has carried us onward; it has humanised us and guided our faltering footsteps throughout the long and slow advance; it has endowed us with strength and courage; it has proved a real vale of soul-making for us humans, and created for us visions, dreams, ideals which are still further moulding us on eternal lines. It is full of tangles, of ups and downs. There is always enough to bite on, to sharpen wits on, to test our courage and manhood. It is indeed a world built for heroism, but also for beauty, tenderness, mercy. I have passed through pretty rough passages.

I have sampled the world and human nature at many points, and I have learnt that it takes all sorts to make a world. But through it all my conviction has only deepened that there is nothing in the nature of things which is alien to what is best in us. There is no malign fatalism which makes fools of us in our dark striving towards the good. On the contrary, what is highest in us is deepest in the nature of things, and as virtue is its own reward, so life carries its own sanctions and the guarantee of its own highest fulfilments and perfections. That is my ultimate Credo; and it is not founded on hearsay, but on my first-hand experience in that cross-section of the world which I have lived through. . . . I remain at heart an optimist.

In spite of the international friction of to-day there is to-day more real goodwill and good feeling in the world than ever before. Contact with the common people everywhere is sufficient to convince us of that fact. There is no decadence abroad, but everywhere the signs of new life and of new forces on the move. In all our feverish activity I see no spirit of defeatism. Indeed, much in the purely human situation is deeply encouraging. . . .

N

But discounting the serious risk of war in the near future, there still remain other grave dangers facing our civilisation. There is a decay of principles, which is eating at the very vitals of free government, and to me that appears to be a far more serious danger to our future than the risk of war. There is to-day a decay of the individual's responsibility and share in government which seems to strike at the roots of our human advance.

For me the individual is basic to any world order that is worth while. Individual freedom, individual independence of mind, individual participation in the difficult work of government seems to me essential to all true progress. Yet to-day the individual seems more and more at a discount in the new experiments in government which are being tried out. The sturdy individualism which inspired progress in the past, which made Rome, which made Scotland, which has created all our best human values, seems to be decaying in the atmosphere of lassitude and disillusion of our day. Men and women have suffered until they are abdicating their rights as individuals. In their misery and helplessness they are surrendering to the mass will which leads straight to autocracy. The feebleness of Continental democracy, its ineffectiveness in a crisis calling for swift and decisive action, has contributed to this defeatist attitude of the individual. And the result is that with this individualist prop of freedom gone, freedom itself seems to be in danger. A new sort of hero worship is arising, very different from that which Carlyle preached, which saps the very foundations of individuality and makes the individual prostrate himself before his national leader as before a god. That way extreme danger lies.

The disappearance of the sturdy, independent-minded, freedom-loving individual, and his replacement by a servile mass mentality is the greatest human menace of our time. Here we reach what I firmly believe is the heart of the problem, the issue round which the greatest battles of this and the coming generation will be fought—if the cause of our civilisation itself is to be saved. As an old soldier in this cause I hope you will excuse me when I state thus bluntly my views on the dangers ahead as I see them. The issue of freedom, the most fundamental issue of all our civilisation, is once more squarely raised by what is happening in the world, and cannot be evaded.

The danger signals are up in many colours and in many lands. The new tyranny, disguised in attractive patriotic colours, is enticing youth everywhere into its horrid service. Freedom must make a great counter-stroke to save itself and our fair Western civilisation. Once more the heroic call is coming to our youth. The fight for human freedom is indeed the supreme issue of the future, as it has always been in the past.

Although the ancient homelands of constitutional liberty in the West are not yet seriously affected, we have to confess sadly that over large parts of Europe the cult of force—what in the Great War we used to call Prussianism—has for the moment triumphed. Popular self-government and parliament are disappearing. The guarantees for private rights and civil liberties are going. Minorities are trampled upon; dissident views are not tolerated and are forcibly suppressed. For those who do not choose to fall into line there is the concentration camp, the distant labour camp in the wilds or on the islands of the sea.

Intellectual freedom is disappearing with political freedom. Freedom of conscience, of speech, of the Press, of thought and teaching is in extreme danger. One party in the State usurps power, and suppresses its opponents and becomes the State. The Press is made to write to order, and public opinion is manufactured for the support of the autocracy. Even freedom of religion is no longer safe, and religious persecution, after being long considered obsolete, once more shows its head. In many, if not most, European countries the standard of human freedom has already fallen far below that of the nineteenth century.

Perhaps I do not exaggerate when I say that of what we call liberty in its full meaning—freedom of thought, speech, action, self-expression—there is to-day less in Europe than there has been during the last 2,000 years. In ancient Athens, in ancient Rome, there was at any rate freedom of thought and speculation and teaching, and generally of religion. Now in the twentieth century, intolerance threatens once more to become the order of the day. In spite of all our scientific expansion, our essential human rights are contracting.

The new dictatorship is nothing but the old tyranny writ large. I fear the new tyranny more than I fear the danger of another great war. Tyranny is infectious. As Burke said, it is a weed which grows in all soils, and it is its nature to spread. Even in this island home of constitutional freedom, I do not know that you are quite immune. Democracy seems to be going out of favour and out of fashion, and unless its methods can be overhauled, its unpopularity may involve the cause of liberty itself.

Let me state quite clearly that I am not against new experiments in human governments. The extraordinary difficulties and complications of modern government call for revised methods and new experiments. What I am here concerned with is the serious threat to freedom and self-government which is involved in the new experiments now being tried out on the Continent. They are all based on a denial of liberty—not as a temporary expedient, but on principle.

355

The assertion that they aim at the eventual enlargement of liberty is vain in view of the fundamental negation of liberty on which they are based, and the absorption of the individual by a State or group, which is their real objective.

I maintain that such a basis of human government is an anachronism, and a moral impossibility in our Western civilisation. The denial of free human rights must in the long run lead to a cataclysm. . . . Dictatorship can only be tolerated as a temporary expedient, and can never be a permanent substitute for free self-government. Freedom is the most ineradicable craving of human nature. Without it peace, contentment and happiness, even manhood itself, are not possible. The declaration of Pericles in his great funeral oration holds for all time. . . .

" Happiness is freedom, and freedom is courage." That is the fundamental equation of all politics and all human government, and any system which ignores it is built on sand. . . .

In these days of widespread backsliding, of lukewarmness or down-right disloyalty to our fundamental human ideals, the countries which have always been in the forefront of the historic fight for human liberty have a very grave duty imposed on them. They cannot refuse the challenge of the times. They dare not abandon the cause which our forefathers rightly placed along with religion itself as calling for the highest loyalty and the greatest sacrifices. . . .

In the long run only the spirit of international comradeship can solve the problems of freedom and of peace. But in the meantime the supreme cause has to be kept going and to be safeguarded from all danger till the coming of a new renascence of the European spirit. . . .

The inner freedom and harmony of the soul; social freedom and equality before the law as the foundation of the State; international freedom in the rule of peace and justice; these should be the creative ideals of the new age, instead of sterilising the repressions of the past and still more sterilising the tyrannies which are forging new shackles for the human spirit. Creative freedom is the watchword of the new order to the realisation of which we should bend our energies. I have no doubt that the present disquieting phase will pass and a new renascence of the European spirit will follow.

What a glorious opportunity to our youth to-day to live in times when the situation is once more fluid and the world is once more in the re-making. Are we going to leave a free field to those who threaten our fundamental human ideals and our proudest heritage from the past? Or are we going to join in battle—an agelong battle which has been going forward from the dawn of history—for the breaking of our bonds and the enlargement of our range of free choice and free

action? Remembering the great appeal of Pericles which rings through
the ages let us seek our happiness in freedom, and bravely do our part
in hastening the coming of the great day of freedom.

LXI INTERNATIONAL AFFAIRS

THE speech which my father made in November before the
Royal Institute of International Affairs on British foreign
policy was of even greater importance, and was at the time
acclaimed by the British press. He pleaded for a generous recognition and equal status for Germany, for a policy of friendship
with Japan, for a strengthening of the influence of the League of
Nations and for a firm tackling of the problem now facing Manchukuo. Once more I quote fairly freely:

Looking at the European situation to-day, as distinct from the wider
world situation (to which I shall refer later), I am deeply impressed by
the fact that two underlying forces are to-day creating and shaping
policies—the fear complex and the inferiority complex. Both are
dangerous complexes, the symptoms of disease and not of healthy
growth, and unless they are treated on wise lines they may in the long
run produce very serious consequences for the public mind and life
of the world. . . . Fear, the meanest of human motives, is to-day the
master of us all. The victors of the Great War, so far from feeling
secure in their victory, are, in fact, obsessed with this almost neurotic
fear. And the vanquished are reacting in the obvious and inevitable
way by refusing to accept their enforced inferiority and their position
as second-class nations in the comity of civilisation. . . .

If Europe is to get back to the right road again, it seems to me
necessary that the nations, both victors and vanquished, should be cured
of their Freudian obsessions, should recover their commonsense and
sanity, and should once more see things in their right and normal
relations. . . . Once Europeans admit to themselves that they are

perhaps a little mad, the cure would come of itself. . . . There is no doubt that the present spell will pass, but what irreparable mischief is not being done while it is on! Let statesmen become the courageous doctors to their sick peoples, and the spell will soon pass. . . .

The remedy for this fear complex is the Freudian way of dragging it out from its hidden depths, bringing it into the open, and exposing it to the light of day. And this is exactly the method of the League of Nations. The League may not be a satisfactory source of security; it may be wanting in that element of sanctions which many consider so necessary. But, at any rate, it is an open forum for discussion among the nations; it is a round table for the statesmen, around which they can ventilate and debate their grievances and viewpoints. . . .

There are those who say that this is not enough—that as long as the League remains merely a talking shop or debating society, and is not furnished with "teeth" or proper sanctions, the sense of insecurity will remain, and the fear complex will continue to dominate international relations. It is also felt that the inability of the League to guarantee the collective system by means of force, if necessary, is discrediting it and leading to its rapid decay. It is said that the crucial case of Manchukuo has exposed its real weakness and shown that, unless armed with force to carry out its policies, it is doomed. My answer to this is twofold.

In the first place, I cannot visualise the League as a military machine. It was not conceived or built for that purpose; it is not equipped for such functions. And if the attempt were now made to transform it into a military machine, into a system to carry on war for the purpose of preventing or ending war, I think its fate is sealed. I cannot conceive the dominions remaining in such a League and pledging themselves to fight the wars of the Old World, and if the dominions leave it, Great Britain is bound to follow.

I cannot conceive anything more calculated to keep the U.S.A. for ever out of the League than its transformation into a fighting machine, pledged to carry out its decisions by force of arms if necessary. And remember the U.S.A. has still to join the League before it will ever be its real self. Membership of the U.S.A. was the assumption on which the League was founded; defection of the U.S.A. has largely defeated its main objects. And the joining up of the U.S.A. must continue to be the ultimate goal of all true friends of the League and of the cause of peace. . . .

But, in the second place, experience since the inception of the League has in fact taught us the way out. Locarno has been incorporated into the League of the collective peace system. And Locarno establishes the principle of limited sanctions, of a smaller group within the League entering into mutual defensive arrangements under the ægis, and subject to the control, of the League. This does not throw the obligation to use force willy-nilly on all members, but binds only those who on grounds of their special situation and interests, choose to enter into such arrangements. . . .

How can the inferiority complex which is obsessing and, I fear, poisoning the mind, and indeed the very soul of Germany, be removed. There is only one way, and that is to recognise her complete equality of status with her fellows, and to do so frankly, freely and unreservedly. That is the only medicine for her disease. And when we have summoned up sufficient courage to treat her in that human way, as our equal in the comity of nations, then, and not till then, will the old wound cease to fester and poison the life of Europe and the world. . . .

While one understands and sympathises with French fears, one cannot but feel for Germany in the position of inferiority in which she still remains sixteen years after the conclusion of the war. The continuance of her Versailles status is becoming an offence to the conscience of Europe and a danger to future peace. Surely there is sufficient human fellow-feeling left in Europe to see that the position has become intolerable and a public danger. There is no place in international law for second-rate nations, and least of all should Germany be kept in that position half a generation after the end of the Great War. . . .

Some people consider magnanimity out of place in international affairs. I have seen it in my own country change a position of dangerous potentialities into one of everlasting friendship between victor and vanquished. That is the way we humans are built. . . .

Germany's equality of status has already been conceded in principle. This was done in December, 1932, when the Great Powers at the Disarmament Conference agreed to accord Germany "equality of rights in a regime of security". If this declaration had been followed up and acted on in the Conference itself Germany would to-day still be a member of the League, and not a disturbing factor outside it, and we should probably have had an agreement on a far-reaching measure of disarmament. Now she is out of the League, her armament position is wrapped in obscurity and danger, and the opportunity for a general measure of disarmament seems farther off than ever. It is the story of the Sibylline books. . . .

So far I have confined my remarks to the European situation. Europe, like the poor, is always with us. But in the Far East a cloud is appearing which, although it is at present no greater than a man's hand, may come to overshadow the whole international sky in time.

Already on its mere appearance it has severely shaken the League and led to menacing reactions in several directions.

People instinctively realise that here is a phenomenon of first-class order, which may have the most far-reaching effects on the fortunes of peace, and indeed of our civilisation. Manchukuo is perhaps not yet the parting of the ways, but it is the warning that we are coming to the parting of the ways and may soon have to make a very solemn choice in national policy.

I have always looked upon the Washington Treaties of 1922 as probably the greatest step forward yet taken since the peace on the road to a stable future world order. In 1921, at the Imperial Conference of that date, I stated my view that a great change was coming over world politics, and that the scene was shifting from the Atlantic to the Pacific. It was felt, and not by me only, that the future of the world would probably be decided, not in the Atlantic, but the Pacific Ocean and countries. The pot might continue to boil in Europe for perhaps another generation, but in the end it would simmer down. . . . The storm centre will pass away from the countries of Christian civilisation and shift to the Far East. There the hand of destiny is still writing in its unknown script—in a language and in ideas which are scarcely intelligible to the Western mind.

The achievement of the Washington Conference was just this—that in this new danger zone of the future a concert or collective system of the Powers concerned had been built up, a loose conference system, founded on certain vital issues, which might do for the Far East what the Geneva League was attempting to do in the West. Comparative naval power, the integrity of China, the open door in that immense potential market, were agreed in principle, and in case of any differences or danger arising the Conference would meet for discussion. Here was the most promising thing for world peace which had yet taken place since the Covenant. The question which is now being raised is whether the promise of Washington will be fulfilled and not prove to be a mere mirage. Manchukuo, as I said, pointed the danger signal. Now the treaty on naval ratios seems to be in danger; and if that goes the other issues settled at Washington may also be re-opened and the whole Pacific concert may collapse. . . .

. . . Adversity makes strange bedfellows, and those who have in the past talked loudest of the Yellow Peril may in future be tempted to look for friends in that unlikely quarter. . . .

In the second place, I would appeal most earnestly and in the friend-liest spirit to Japan as our old friend and war-time ally, to pause before she puts in motion machinery which will in the end imperil the concert in the Pacific. She has already given notice of withdrawal from the League. If, in addition, she withdraws from the Washington Treaties the whole collective system goes, so far as she is concerned. . . .

In the third place, everything possible in the power of diplomacy should be done to avoid even the appearance of antagonism between the East and West. The potentialities of the situation are inherently serious enough, and should not be rendered worse by one-sided diplomacy. Asia is at a curious phase of her awakening. Complexes there, too, are forming. The old exploitation or ascendancy policies are out of place in such a situation, and should be carefully avoided for the future. The past record of the West in the East is not one to be proud of or to be further copied. . . .

Fourthly, and subject to what I have just said, I wish to make another point which I consider no less important and vital. This is a difficult world, in which we have to walk warily, in which even good will may not be enough, and in which we are called upon to exercise a wise discretion as an insurance for the future. In this spirit I would say that to me the future policy and association of our great British Commonwealth lie more with the U.S.A. than with any other group in the world. If ever there comes a parting of the ways, if ever in the crises of the future we are called upon to make a choice, *that*, it seems to me, should be the company we should prefer to walk with and march with to the unknown future. On that path lie our past affiliations, our common moral outlook, our hopes and fears for the future of our common civilisation. Nobody can forecast the outcome of the stormy era of history on which we are now probably entering. Our best insurance in this unknown territory is to be with those with whom we have an instinctive and historic sympathy.

The British Commonwealth has its feet in both worlds. Through Great Britain its one foot is firmly planted in this old continent. Through the Dominions it has its other foot as firmly planted in the outer newer world, where the U.S.A. already plays so great a part. The Dominions have even stronger affiliations towards the U.S.A. than Great Britain has.

There is a community of outlook, of interests, and perhaps of ultimate destiny between the Dominions and the U.S.A. which in essence is only the first and most important of them. Through the Dominions British policy is ultimately tied up with the U.S.A. in a very profound sense, which goes much deeper than the occasional jars which, perhaps, are more acutely felt at any particular moment. That fundamental affinity, coming from the past, stretching to the future, is, or must be, the real foundation of all British foreign policy.

Any policy which ignores it, or runs counter to it, is calculated to have a disruptive effect on the Commonwealth as a whole. We are here on bedrock, which we ignore at our peril.

. . . More and more we are recognising that, in spite of racial and political barriers, humanity is really a whole.

It is in this steadily-growing mutuality of our relations, in this ever-increasing wholeness of our human relationships, that I see the only possible ultimate solution of our present discords. Here lies the true line of progress for the future. And the more we recognise this whole-ness of mankind, this integral character of all our relationships, the surer our success will be in the great adventure of human government, and the brighter the prospects will be for that world of ordered liberty and peace which we are out to build. The driving force in this human world of ours should be, not morbid fears or other sickly obsessions, but this inner urge towards wholesome integration and co-operation. The drive towards holism, which I have elsewhere pointed to as at the basis of nature and the creative process in this universe, is equally operative in our human society. Unless it is artificially interfered with and thwarted, it will lead us forward to sanity, wholeness and wholesomeness and rid us of the pathological obsessions which are to-day producing so much friction and dislocation at every step of our adventure.

. . . Ever since Versailles, where I entered my first protest, I have felt very deeply that the real peace was still to come, and that it would be a peace not merely of mechanical arrangements of the territorial or economic kind, but something psychological, something in the nature of European reconciliation, something reaching down to and resting on our common human and Christian foundations. In that spirit I have once more pleaded for peace to-night. I hope that our statesmen will yet lead us to that peace before it is too late—that is to say, before new, sinister forces have advanced and taken possession of the field and imperilled what centuries of European effort have accom-plished for our human advance. I feel the hour of action has come, or is rapidly coming, and we all pray that our leadership, for which we feel the profoundest sympathy, will not fail us in this crisis of our fate.

A column writer on the *Daily Sketch* wrote: "I have seen many distinguished gatherings, but never such a mass meeting of dis-tinction as there was at the dinner of the Royal Institute of International Affairs in honour of General Smuts. If all the O.Ms, K.C.Bs, LL.Ds and other alphabetical trimmings of the guests had been placed end to end they would have gone twice round the big banqueting room at the Savoy with a bit to spare. . . ."

The *Manchester Guardian* declared: "The dinner which the Royal Institute of International Affairs gave to-night to General Smuts was a remarkable gathering of talent and experience. Lord Derby, who fittingly presided over it as the greatest non-party politician in England, described it as 'probably the most representative dinner at which any of us has ever been present'." The paper continues, "General Smuts, erect, neat, pink and white, speaking in a high voice with a touch of accent more Latin than Dutch, gave it a speech worthy of his powers. No politician in England for many a day has combined his sweep, his detachment, and his subtlety. What impressed one most was the way in which his mind cuts down to essentials and declares them without circumlocution . . . this clarity of mind enables him to grasp and state what he regards as the essentials of a situation in a way which one wishes that any member of our own Government could emulate."

The *Lancashire Post* said that the speech "is expected to have an important influence upon the course of events in several parts of the world. History, present circumstances and intellectual distinction give the General an entirely unique position in the councils of the Empire, and his unrivalled clarity of utterance sends what he has to say echoing round the globe".

The *South Wales Argus* wrote: "Once more General Smuts has revealed himself as a statesman with the international mind. He is one of the comparatively few great men in international politics, and he is great because his heart is right as well as his head. He is a philosopher and psychologist. He sees the working of men's souls behind their actions. He knows that we find the explanation of the follies and crimes of nations—as of individuals—in the hidden working of these instincts and impulses which are the make-up of human nature."

The *African World* described the speech as the "crowning oration of his visit, and, profuse as it has been with brilliant speeches and accustomed as we have become to the pearls of wisdom falling from the lips of General Smuts, his address on Monday night, in world importance, transcended anything he has said during the crowded month of his stay among us, not even excepting his famous 'Freedom' exhortation at St. Andrews. It was a clarion call to the world at large, the Old and the New, the

Nations and the great Commonwealth of the British Empire. . . .
The farewell banquet in his honour at the Savoy on Monday
evening was one of the most notable tributes ever paid to any
man in this country. What other public man, I wondered, looking
round the crowded tables, could have attracted such a gathering.
It was not the size of the audience but its character that was so
impressive."

The Times published the speech in pamphlet form at the request
of the public. It ran into three editions.

The Johannesburg *Sunday Times* remarked in an editorial:
"There is probably no precise parallel in history for the remarkable enthusiasm aroused by General Smuts during his visit to
Great Britain. So might Hannibal have been welcomed in Rome
as a wise and friendly elder statesman of a Carthaginian dominion.
It is no exaggeration, we think, to say that the speeches delivered
by General Smuts during the six weeks of his visit overseas have
placed a new complexion on the broader aspects of world affairs
and inspired weary nations, over-wrought by distrust of each
other, with fresh hope for the future. . . ."

LXII UNEASY PEACE

IN May, 1936, the following little incident occurred in the
House. It was a sequel to a hunting expedition undertaken by
my brother, myself and party into Portuguese East Africa in
1933. On our way back into the Union it was found that we had
unwittingly contravened a new foot-and-mouth disease regulation promulgated in our absence, and we found ourselves in
trouble with the police. Now in 1936 there was an investigation
going on into alleged irregularities in the Police Force, and a
Dominion Party member, Mr. Marwick, brought this case up as
one of irregularity and claimed that we had run clear of trouble

only because we were the Minister of Justice's sons. An altercation ensued between Mr. Marwick and Mr. Blackwell which grew so heated that the former was expelled from the Chamber, Colonel Stallard following him as he walked out.

My poor father was unaware of what had occurred in 1933, as we had kept it a dead secret from the family. Much taken aback at this new situation, he nevertheless rose to the occasion and passed it off with one of his classic evasions: "The Committee will forgive me," he said, "for saying that I am very proud of my boys." (Cheers.)

Mr. Derbyshire: "Wouldn't you spank them for it? . . . How old are these boys?" My father: "They are quite big now. I would not advise my hon. friend to try to spank them." (Laughter.)

And with little more ado, Parliament proceeded with its business.

In March, 1937, my father was installed as Chancellor of the University of Cape Town. It was a distinction that appealed to him greatly. He took the opportunity of giving the students a pleasant fatherly talk on education:

. . . The bookworm is generally a narrow type, moving in one groove or another, and never reaching the broad daylight and the wide vision which goes with universality. Not seldom the scientific or scholastic expert is singularly devoid of that breadth of outlook and perspective, that sense of proportion which is essential to true culture. Just as you may be rich in earthly possession and yet remain poor in spirit, so you may amass much learning with much weariness without acquiring real poise or intellectual balance, and spiritual sensitiveness. . . .

. . . In other directions again you learn of the vast commotion in the great world, of the political, economic and social experiments to-day being tried out in many countries on a scale such as has never been attempted before in history. You learn at close range of the moral and intellectual unrest which is sapping the basis of the old order and heralding the advent of the coming age. You become alive to that atmosphere of hope and fear, of faith and defeatism, which accompanies the great transition and which shows itself in such development as economic and political nationalism, general rearmament and warlike preparations, alongside of brave and by no means forlorn attempts to organise human co-operation and security on a world-wide basis. In short, you are flung into a world of intellectual and social and moral ferment which carries you far, very far from the simple home environment. In all this upheaval in the contemporary world and in your own experience you have to remain yourself and true to yourself, you have to preserve your personal integrity, and you have to adjust yourself to all this strange new world without damage to your real self. In other words, you have to remain loyal to your individuality and at the same time to adjust yourself to universality. Starting from the simple pieties of the home, you have to assimilate what is best in this larger thought and life of the contemporary world, and of our human record throughout the ages. Here you can in a very real sense get the key, the clue to guide you through all this confusing inrush of experiences which threaten to overwhelm you. Academic training, academic life can disclose to you certain dominant landmarks by which you can steer your course. Let me mention a couple of them.

Here you will begin to see this world, not as matter of chance, a chaos, a mere jumble of different jarring warring things flung together at haphazard, but as a unity, as a whole pervaded by law and order, in which our human life links up with and crowns life universal and forms the climax of activities which pervade all things. This vision of harmony in the universe, of principles of order and beauty which are its very nature and constitution—this vision of truth and beauty once seen—will ever remain with you as the most satisfying and abiding experience of your life. It will give you peace in a world of unrest. Your soul will feed on that vision of order and beauty in the world, and it will continue to grow on you till the end of your days. Science, philosophy, poetry, religion—all will help you to clarify and deepen that great experience for you.

Then again you will learn one of the hardest and most valuable lessons of life—to appreciate and be loyal at all costs to fact, objective impartial fact. We begin life in a childish atmosphere of sentiment and prejudices, and thence as we grow older we move on to a world of opinions and passions. But really to know the world is to get down to a true sense of fact, which remains true in spite of all our opinions and partialities and attitudes. This lesson of the true value of fact is perhaps the greatest lesson that science can teach us. . . .

He warned the students against the slavish acceptance of catchwords and clichés:

. . . Amid the evils of our public world of to-day, where the tendency is to follow slogans, to run after catchwords, to worship ideologies, or to exalt party politics unduly, the sovereign remedy is this disinterested loyalty to fact, this gospel of the sacredness of facts which is the supreme message of science to the world. This is a world of fact. It is based on facts and not on opinions, propaganda or ideologies, which are but the froth on the surface of the deeper movement of facts. . . .

After that he passed on to Fascism:

Whatever may be the ultimate outcome of the rival Fascist and Communist systems now contending for mastery in Europe, I would ask you to believe that their hostility to the principle of toleration, of racial, religious and political toleration, must surely be a passing phase, a symptom of the confusion and unrest of the times. The human spirit having once broken its primeval shackles and emerged from its bondage will never again submit to them for good. Evolution never reverts back to discarded forms or organs. And the light that has dawned on our human horizon can never permanently set again. To believe the contrary would be to despair of human nature and to blaspheme our Maker. There may be temporary eclipse, but never again can there be a return for good to the dark age for the human spirit. Time has one direction and never moves back. . . .

His association in this capacity with the University was a very happy one till his death. This, and his connection with the Mountain Club, were probably amongst his happiest memories of the Cape.

LXIII DARK CLOUDS

MY father was under no illusion about the approach of war. He had seen the same signs before. Here were the signs of intolerance and aggressiveness that marked the fever of war in a nation. Hitler was steadily growing hysterical, ranting and raving and threatening in a way that left no doubt that he was going to act. His beer-hall friends of Munich held high positions and there was no doubt that he would receive the fullest support in all he did. The German Fuehrer believed he was a man of destiny with a mission to perform for his people. This, he gradually came to believe, was to enslave other peoples and to Nazify all Europe. Since 1933 the munitions production machine had been set in full-scale motion. Goering was toying with the idea of a vast air armada, and admirals were dreaming of a revived German navy with myriads of U-boats. Among the army chiefs, ideas of a new tactical concept, the swift, crushing blitzkrieg, were crystallising out.

Opposition within the Reich was not only discouraged but ruthlessly stamped out by a Gestapo system later brought to perfection by Heinrich Himmler. Bloody purges took place of all people thought to be a danger to the Nazi régime. These putsches took in all the senior men of the country without fear or favour. Slowly the streets of the towns and villages were beginning to echo to the hobnailed boot and the goosestep, and the handshake and salute had long since changed to the Nazi heil!

Ribbentrop, suave ambassador and one-time village wine merchant, tried to soothe Britain with honeyed words. The British Government, longing for an excuse to avoid rearmament, reluctantly swallowed his sweetened pills. In vain did Winston Churchill warn of the coming dangers. People were either too disinterested or too afraid to face up to realities. Geneva preached disarmament and Stanley Baldwin and others were only too ready to listen. If Hitler and Mussolini were foolish enough to squander money on armaments that was their business. Britain would not indulge in this madness.

But my father was not a man of such easy persuasion. From his distant vantage-point he saw that those dark clouds approaching were no mere wisps of mist. All the signs of the approaching storm were manifest. Long ago, when von Lettow Vorbeck, the man whom he hoped would save Germany, played his cards badly, he had had misgivings about the future of Germany. Von Lettow was young, strong and able, but Hindenburg was an old and tired figurehead under whom things might slide dangerously. Adolf Hitler saw the weakness of the situation, and his great

368

opportunity, and lost no time in putting his ambitions into effect. Hindenburg was no match for him.

My father recognised that his ranting and raving about the former German colonies were blinds to cover much deeper motives. The return of South-West Africa, Tanganyika and the Cameroons would not appease an insatiable Germany.

At the same time Mussolini set about arms production, turning out weapons of poor quality and obsolete pattern, a navy of ships possessing speed rather than fighting power, and millions of soldiers of poor quality and morale, who should have remained peasants.

In the Chambers at Geneva there was vacillation and disagreement. Litvinov the Russian representative did not agree with Samuel Hoare the British representative, and nobody was prepared to do anything but talk through all these troublous times. This precious international machine, which my father had done so much to set up, was being turned into a mere talking shop.

An informal but fairly effective call-up in Germany began under von Papen in 1932. Three years later conscription was started. Hitler completed the call-up by drafting the 1938 conscripts a year early. The preparation was complete, and Germany was ready for war.

In March, 1936, the German re-militarisation of the Rhineland took place, not only destroying a safeguard of French security, but bringing the great munition centres of Cologne, Dusseldorf, Mannheim and Ludwigshafen under German control and rendering the Ruhr industries barely defensible.

Exactly two years later came the annexation of Austria. Hitler had planned it in 1934, when he had caused the Chancellor Dollfuss to be murdered, but it is said Mussolini had restrained him. With Austria, Hitler acquired seven million more German subjects. Schuschnigg was hurried away into captivity and the position of Czechoslovakia became more vulnerable than ever. But the Czechs were protected by a treaty with Britain and France which, if defied, would mean war. Hitler advanced a claim for self-determination by the Sudetenland German minority. Britain had not started the mass production of the munitions of war till 1937 and was in no position to stand up to him. In September, 1938, Britain and France concluded at Munich one of the great capitulations of history. Militarily the Allies' only gain by this had been time. In every other respect the armaments gap had been widened. Six months later the whole of Czechoslovakia had become Hitler's. He was now ready for full-scale war. Germany had for long been working a sixty-hour week, but Britain was still plodding along quietly on a forty-hour cycle.

Poland's alliance with Britain and France stood her in poor stead. It failed to stay the Nazi war machine; at dawn on the 1st September, 1939, German troops streamed across the Polish frontiers at many points.

The Second World War had begun.

Meanwhile Nazism was gradually growing in South Africa. Agents were widespread and they were indulging in fairly open propaganda methods. They were enabled to do this not only because a portion of the populace sympathised with them, but because, in the very Cabinet itself, there were those who were tolerant of the germ. Our Trade Treaty with Germany also brought about many points of unavoidable contact. There were many German tourists in the country about whose activities we were suspicious.

The Press and the more sober public were crying out against these agents. My father preferred to watch and to keep silent. Suggestions from him would only cause serious dissension and make the situation worse. Weichardt had founded his Greyshirt Movement and active training on a quasi-military scale was going on. Soon too a Fascist Blackshirt Movement sprang up and gained considerable support.

Up to now people had been over-tolerant of these activities in their midst. But with the advent of the Italo-Abyssinian War, they realised that the rest of Africa might not be free of the dictators' ambitions. Under pressure from my father, Hertzog consented to the application of sanctions against Italy. But on the whole the democracies were unimpressive when it came to applying pressure on Mussolini. Small wonder the dictators considered life in these countries to be at a low ebb. By contrast the Fascist doctrines seemed the very epitome of vigour and progress.

Times were still prosperous, but there were signs that the enthusiasm for Fusion was waning and that an element of strain had crept in. True, the most discontented had followed Colonel

Stallard into a new party, but there were many others who felt almost as strongly but stayed behind. They remained on with uneasy feelings, daily growing more convinced that Afrikanderism was rapidly swallowing up the British traditions.

In the Cabinet there was disloyalty and a perceptible lack of harmony. On many fundamental problems the two sections agreed to differ. But my father's genius and influence managed to preserve a perilous peace.

In May, 1938, came a general election. Fear of events that were taking place in the outside world did much to lend an advantage to the United Party, and the election was a triumph for my father. He certainly had worked as hard as any man for it. During the last two months he had covered, in spare moments, 2,000 miles by rail, 6,500 by car and 1,000 by air, on electioneering business, making numerous speeches each day.

Of the 117 seats the United Party retained 111. Their loss had been a Malanite gain. But, significantly, an interesting feature of the United Party vote was the fact that it revealed a distinct swing in favour of my father's group.

By this time criticism of Germany in the daily press had become a feature, much to the annoyance of General Hertzog and friends. So now Hertzog began sending off cables of apology to the Fuehrer, and drafted legislation to curb the press. It might have been not without humour had it occurred in less strained times.

On Union Day, less than a fortnight after the elections, an unhappy incident occurred which did much to annoy the English section. Indignation ran high because of the omission of playing "The King" at military parades throughout the country. Only the Afrikaans "Die Stem" had been played. Rumour had it that both the Prime Minister and Minister of Defence Pirow were implicated. It was one of those unhappy storms that blew up so frequently during those days.

Barely had this crisis subsided when fresh trouble arose over the seat of a Native Representative in the Senate, to which Hertzog, without prior consultation, had appointed a friend, A. P. J. Fourie, who was not particularly suited to the post. This time feeling was so outraged that two of my father's adherents in the Cabinet felt constrained to resign.

371

One was Mr. J. H. Hofmeyr, who tendered his resignation on grounds of principle and conscience. While this may have been a dramatic and spectacular act, it had little else to commend it, and it did nothing to ease my father's difficult position in the Cabinet. My father, I remember, was very critical of Hofmeyr's defection on the occasion. He remarked to me: "It's all very well Hofmeyr talking about principles and conscience and resigning. How does he think I feel about the whole business myself? Where would we be if we all lost our heads and resigned? It's the very thing the Nationalists want." Many hailed Hofmeyr as a hero and looked askance at my father as a person who had been prepared to sell his birthright. Little did they realise how grimly my father was holding on and preparing for the dark day he now saw approaching with such speed. Devoted as he grew to Hofmeyr during the war years, and mindful of the superb work he was performing, I don't think the younger man ever quite regained my father's former esteem.

Again my father had to soothe and placate.

In 1938 came the Czechoslovakian debacle, which brought with it, once more, the question of neutrality. On this occasion, but only as a specific instance, my father agreed that events at that time did not warrant the risk of full-scale military intervention.

Shortly before Hitler's birthday in April, 1939, my father, without the concurrence of the Cabinet, as Minister of Justice sent a force of 300 policemen to South-West Africa. It was one of his characteristic, old-time, lightning strokes. Intelligence had revealed that one of the now standard German "coups" would shortly be attempted in the mandated territory by trained German elements, and he was determined to forestall events. "Austria and other small states," he declared, "have been invaded on the plea that they could not keep internal order, but the Union will never lay itself open to invasion on that ground."

Members of the Cabinet with pro-Nazi feelings, who had been outwitted by my father, fumed in silence. But the rest of the Opposition gave vent in full to its outraged feelings. It was nothing short, they claimed, of an act that might provoke an enemy. And it was perpetrated by the same person who in 1914 had led the Union into war with Germany. Dr. Malan said it reminded him of the Nakob incident of 1914. But for all their feelings, it was subsequently proved that the despatch of the force had been amply justified in avoiding serious trouble.

Now followed Italy's invasion of Abyssinia and the intensification of Germany's propaganda war against Poland. The question of neutrality, which had previously been looked upon purely as an academic issue, briskly assumed a more practical guise. But Hertzog and his followers were still of opinion that neutrality was a practicability in time of war.

My father bided his time. Words were of little avail in times like this.

The British element in Parliament insisted that neutrality in time of war was an impossibility. The Malanites were loud in their denunciation of those who said they would fight by the side of Great Britain. Was not England the only country that had ever attacked South Africa?

Matters were now swiftly moving to a climax. On 1st September Hitler's armies streamed into Poland. Two days later France and Britain were at war with Germany.

In the middle of July, 1939, my father accompanied Sir Ernest Oppenheimer on a flying trip to the Copper Belt in Northern Rhodesia and to the jewelled wonderland of the Western Rift Valley of the Belgian Congo. Here in a fertile land of breathtaking scenic grandeur he spent a few very pleasant days surveying the superb cluster of giant volcanoes that rose thousands of feet from the Rift Floor. Nyamlagira was at the time in action, pouring forth a three-mile wide stream of molten lava from its 10,000-foot-high summit into idyllic Lake Kivu, causing a great cloud of steam to rise into the sky. They flew over the top of this "boiling cauldron" and "the whole spectacle was awe-inspiring—indeed inexplicably so", he said.

The other giants, including Ninagongo and Karisimbi (with the grave of the United States explorer Carl Akeley on its slopes) were dormant, but at any moment might burst forth again. In the dense mountain forests dwelt the minute pigmy and the gorilla, while in the plains below lived the tall nilotic Watussi farmer, noted for his feats of high jumping.

To a friend my father wrote after this inspiring flight over the volcanoes: "For me it has been *the* day of the trip. I can never have a greater experience than a real volcano in full action and now can feel calm at the spectacle of Dictator volcanoes spouting forth on the European stage. How ridiculous our human antics are in comparison with the real business of nature! . . . I closed the day with a fine swim in the lake (Kivu) in front of our hotel."

LXIV THE STORM BREAKS

NEUTRALITY was no longer an academic question. It became, immediately, a burning issue.

Hertzog and his henchmen were determined, at all costs, to remain neutral. Having secretly conducted a poll of adherents in the House, they were convinced of a majority vote on the issue. In a flash General Hertzog had reverted in type to the old pattern. His movements and motives were all hidden under a cloak of secrecy, and not an inkling of what was happening was allowed to reach my father.

My father, in turn, was equally determined that South Africa should lose no time in severing relations with Germany. Hertzog had had a good start and there was much leeway to make up.

Parliament was luckily in session at the time, having been prorogued to extend the term of the Senate which had run to a close.

The House met in a tense atmosphere on September 4 to debate our role in the conflict. Numerically there was little between those for and those against, and the matter hung critically in the balance.

It was at this stage that the long years of tolerance and patience exercised by my father in the Fusion Government bore fruit. His behaviour had been so exemplary that it had won him many friends on the other side. This good will now came to his aid, and was, he always claimed, the factor that carried the day for him.

General Hertzog said to his "regret there appeared to be a serious difference" in the Cabinet, an "unbridgeable division . . . It must not be forgotten that we are concerned here in a war in which the Union has not the slightest interest. We are not interested in the war between Poland and Germany. . . . England has certain obligations towards Poland. We have no such obligations . . . it is urged we should take part in the war because the German Chancellor has demonstrated that he is out to obtain world domination. . . . Where can we find proof?" He went on to justify the German seizure of the Rhineland, Austria, Czechoslovakia and Danzig and spoke of the "monster of the Treaty of Versailles". And finally he moved "that this House approves and accepts as the policy of the Government of the Union that the existing relations between the Union of South Africa and the various belligerent countries will, in so far as the Union is concerned, persist unchanged and continue as if no war is being waged. . . ."

My father rose to reply: "I think it would be right and fair and proper," he said quietly, in a hushed but tense House, "on an occasion like this, when issues are raised which go to the very foundations of our national life, that I should make clear the exact points where I, and some of my colleagues, differ from the policy which the Prime Minister has sketched to the House. I shall move an amendment in due course, but before I do so I should like to say, Sir, that I hope the House will look upon this extraordinary situation which has arisen as being of the most serious character. I am not going to make reproaches; I am not going to introduce debating points. I wish this House and the people of this country to realise as clearly as I see it what really is the position and what is at stake. . . .

"I have never in all these years of our political collaboration made a serious point of differences on small issues. I have always been prepared to give way, to hold the peace, and to see that the young life of this nation is given a chance, and for the people to have an opportunity to grow together." He spoke of the "gravest tangles possible" in regard to the Prime Minister's policy of "modified" neutrality, which Germany certainly will not recognise. Of Germany's demands after Danzig he had no doubt that South-West Africa and the German colonies would come next. "To me it is quite clear", he said, "that we are not dealing with a far-away problem in Eastern Europe. We are dealing with a nation whose policy not only to-day, but to-morrow may touch us most vitally in this country."

He therefore moved "that this House declares that the policy of the Union in this crisis shall be based on the following principles and considerations, viz.:

"(1) It is in the interests of the Union that its relations with the German Reich should be severed and that the Union should refuse to adopt an attitude of neutrality in this conflict.

"(2) The Union should carry out the obligations to which it has agreed, and continue its co-operation with its friends and associates in the British Commonwealth of Nations. . . ."

When the motion was put to the Vote my father's amendment was carried by a majority of 80 votes to 67.

Hertzog tendered his resignation to the Governor-General. Sir Patrick Duncan was in a quandary as to what to do next, but after discussing the matter privately with my father, called upon him to form a new Government. We were all at our radios that evening tensely awaiting the news. I was living in a northern suburb of Johannesburg at the time. When the good news came over, muffled shouting and cheering could be heard all over the neighbourhood.

Our honour had been saved. And once more we had a great helmsman at our head. Now in his seventieth year, my father, still in the prime of life and wonderfully fit and alert, was in a position to tackle the future with the greatest vigour and enthusiasm.

*　　*　　*　　*　　*

The War, in one cruel stroke, sent all the work of conciliation of my father, all his unselfish efforts for Coalition and Fusion, which had held out such glorious prospects for the future of the nation, tumbling down. For the question of the Union's participation in a war was no easier now than it had been in 1914. Perhaps those against our entry into the fray were not so numerous as they had been in former times, but they were, nevertheless, very considerable. The Government itself, as will be seen, was split from top to bottom on the issue.

Let my father himself describe what happened in those confused days. Let him tell us, too, how difficult some of the days of Fusion had been. Let him explain this, as he did at a Party meeting in Bloemfontein on 3rd November, 1939. By that time, General Hertzog had resigned and my father had formed a new Cabinet.

Night by night [he said] this country is being attacked and bombarded with propaganda from Germany, in a way far more dangerous, subtle and insidious than any attack by armies. Night by night the soul of the people of South Africa is being sapped and their convictions undermined by that broadcast from Zeesen. There are other broadcasters going about this country from platform to platform and they are even more dangerous than the announcer from Zeesen. No, we were at the crossroads, but we took the right turning. In the years to come, when the situation has cleared up, the people of South Africa will be grateful to the Parliament of this year for deciding to sever relations with Germany and keep this country moving along the same lines as those upon which we have been progressing so well in recent years.

Now I return to the address which General Hertzog gave here within the last few days, and I shall reply to the accusations he made. Speaking of the happenings which led to Parliament's decision on the 4th of September, when, General Hertzog says, "Smuts lay in wait for a good chance to break," it is not necessary for me to deny that accusation, for the whole history of what actually happened denies it. I must say that I was more than surprised when I read this, but if there was this suspicion, if this was in the heart of General Hertzog, did he really trust me in those six years we worked together?

I am human. I must admit it was a shock to realise this after all the trust I had placed in him from year to year, after the support I gave him, after the blood and sweat I gave to see the United Party through its difficulty. I do not boast when I say that the United Party was, in a great measure, my work—my best work for South Africa, my pride and honour. It was the ideal for which I sacrificed everything, for which I sacrificed my personal interests. After I had done all that, why should I break down my own work? Am I fitted for a lunatic asylum? Again I ask you, why should I look for an opportunity and lie in wait to jump out? It never occurred to me. I did everything I could to ensure long life to the Party. There was only one wish I had for my old age—to see that the party should remain as strong as a rock for South Africa, and after I had disappeared the generation who would follow would have an impregnable foundation on which to build. I prayed God to prevent a break.

General Hertzog talks about small incidents such as flags, anthems and oaths. Everything I did was designed to keep the United Party together. I smoothed those incidents over. General Hertzog said I objected to the singing of "Die Stem". That is false. His memory must have failed him, for if he remembers correctly he will acknowledge that I gave him whole-hearted support in his suggestion to have "Die Stem" and "God Save the King" played at the opening of Parliament.

But the question before us at the beginning of September was not one of flags or anthems. It was a question which went to the very roots of our national life. It was the question of the road South Africa should follow in future. I saw we had now reached a point where I would have to give away everything which I regarded as right for the people of South Africa when General Hertzog came to us with a ready-made plan of neutrality. We had reached down to bed-rock.

General Hertzog had consulted his friends and decided to stay neutral on certain lines. He did more. Before he spoke a word to me or one of my colleagues to find out what we thought, he had an assurance that the Nationalist Party would support him in a policy of neutrality. Here are the facts: General Hertzog spoke to me about this for the first time on Saturday, the 2nd of September. I met him in his Chambers with Mr. Havenga and Mr. Pirow. Their policy of neutrality was laid before me and I immediately said: "Impossible". I told them that I found it impossible to subscribe to it. We argued about it for the rest of the morning, and I tried to show them why I thought it was an impossible policy for South Africa. When we could not arrive at an agreement I asked General Hertzog, in view of the seriousness of the situation, to call the Cabinet together. And so the Cabinet was summoned and the matter laid before them. For the whole of that afternoon and again that night we discussed the matter. And all this time General Hertzog had in his possession the assurance of the "Purifieds" that they would support him. General Hertzog did not tell me or a single one of my colleagues anything about the fact that he would rely on the support of the "Purifieds" in his policy of neutrality.

On Saturday night we agreed to meet again. Parliament had been summoned for Monday morning and there was not much time left. Before the Cabinet meeting on Sunday afternoon, General Hertzog again had the assurance—this time in black and white—that the "Purifieds" would support him. Even at that final meeting he told us nothing about that promise from Dr. Malan and his party. I myself heard about it a week later, and for me it was a great shock. . . .

We asked General Hertzog on the Sunday afternoon why he was in such a hurry and advised him that it would be better to call together the Caucus of the Party. But this was also abruptly refused. It was refused because General Hertzog was assured of his majority in Parliament, because he had the letter from the Nationalists in his pocket. The accusation I make against General Hertzog is that he did not tell his colleagues about this letter and that at this critical moment he went over the heads of his own Party members. It is being said that General Smuts and his friends set a trap. If there was a trap, I ask you, "Who set it?" No, my conscience is clear. There was no intrigue on our side. But General Hertzog had the promise of support from the "Purifieds" in his pocket.

I expected something quite different. I thought when I saw which way things were going, that General Hertzog wanted to get rid of some of his Cabinet colleagues; that he would then reform his Cabinet —a thing which he was quite entitled to do—and then go to the country. He would have had a new Government and he would have consulted the people. But instead of that he went to Parliament because he was assured of a majority. They had counted. But they counted wrongly. General Hertzog told me and other responsible persons that he was assured of a majority. But then came the Monday, the debate in Parliament, and the defence of Hitler, and then came the thunderbolt that smashed General Hertzog's secret plans.

I want to make it clear to the people of South Africa that our hands were clean throughout the entire occurrence. General Hertzog and his advisers made mistake upon mistake. I told you what he could have done, but then I am only a dull fellow. General Hertzog leaned on certain "slim" people in the Cabinet who advised him. There was even an attempt to drag in the Governor-General. But everything went wrong. All these miscalculations came to nothing, and the worst of all is that General Hertzog has given over his faithful followers into the hands of the Malanites, in the same way that he is now giving himself over to Dr. Malan. . . .

. . . I am sorry that I have to talk like this of General Hertzog. I respect him, even though I ask for nothing in return. General Hertzog has rendered great service to this country. It grieves me to see that in his old age he is busy destroying the great work which he did in the past six years, and I deeply regret that he has become a tool in the hands of Dr. Malan. I do not accuse him. He was misled by colleagues about him, and especially by one who gives out to be a hundred per cent Afrikaner. But upon this man the people of South Africa look with the deepest suspicion. This counsellor of General Hertzog was General Hertzog's downfall, and to-day he is busy seeking favour with Dr. Malan. . . .

. . . The charge against me, according to General Hertzog, is this: That a year ago (in September, 1938) when the Sudetenland trouble was afoot, we discussed the matter in the Cabinet and we decided that in this particular matter, the Sudetenland problem, we were certainly not going to take part in any resulting war, but that we were going to remain neutral. You will recall what the Sudetenland question was about. It affected a certain small section of the German population on the fringe of Czechoslovakia, who were dissatisfied and complained of being ill-treated. The peace of Europe seemed to be endangered on this account, and nobody wanted to have Europe plunged into a war because of the demands of the Germans there. We certainly had no interest in the matter. We had no good reason at the time to suspect Hitler of his evil intentions. He alleged that he was trying to right the wrongs of his people and save the German minority in Czechoslovakia. Mr. Chamberlain and the French and British Governments conceded that Hitler had a case, and they did not want war.

At that time and in those circumstances we said that if war should come in Europe over this dispute, South Africa would be neutral. I agreed that this was the right course to take, but I must emphasise that our decision was confined to a particular case. It had nothing to do with any other problem that might arise. We never defined or formulated a policy of neutrality for the future. . . ."

LXV BUILDING AN ARMY

Mr. Oswald Pirow had been Minister of Defence in the Fusion Government for six years. He was a young and active man, believed by many to be capable. His defence plans were on a grand Pan-African scale and he propounded them with eloquence. Foremost among his supporters was a considerable proportion of the English-speaking public, now, as ever, susceptible to the honeyed words of plausible speakers. Pirow, in his able way, took in all these good people. With his £3,000,000 Defence Vote in 1939 he was going to build up a great army, specially adapted for African bush warfare. Yet, when my father took over the portfolio a year later, almost the whole Vote was still intact. Pirow's army was merely in the realms of dreams. The best reflection on his efforts would be to remark that when Hitler heard that the Union had declared war, he laughed.

It would be unfair to attribute Pirow's failure as Minister of Defence to ineptitude. He was too able a man for that. It was just that he was even more determined than General Hertzog that South Africa should not go to war. But at the same time, too, it was patent that as a strategist he completely failed to grasp the situation, for he believed in an out-moded bushcart conception of guerilla warfare. It was based on a thin line of half-trained troops, moving light through the bush and living on the country as far as possible. And all this after he had been to Europe and seen the massive units of the German and Italian armies. Perhaps it would be fairest to say that his term as Minister was notable chiefly for his indiscreet pre-war visits to the Dictators, by whom he had been much impressed.

Apart from our semi-military Boer commandos there was little in the country. The weapons were mostly the now obsolete ones brought back by my father after the First World War. The nearest we had to front-line aircraft were two Blenheim bombers. The rest of the Air Force consisted of twenty-six long-obsolete Hawker Furies and Harts and a few converted Junker airliners, and a few dozen trainers. In the tank line were two old demonstration models of Flanders vintage. Our two armoured cars dated back to the same period and had last been used to quell a native rebellion many years ago. Our artillery had seen honourable service against Kaiser Wilhelm.

Our Permanent Force consisted of only 1,350 men. Beyond the personal equipment of these men there were no uniforms and few rifles. Two of our four chief ports, East London and Port Elizabeth, had not one single gun for their defence.

Our navy was the engineless training ship the *General Botha*, moored permanently at Simonstown.

At the start there was a distinct danger of risings in the Nationalist-dominated rural areas. But thanks to an inventory of firearms compiled by the previous Government, my father was able to forestall trouble by calling in all privately-owned rifles, a measure which also helped considerably in our training requirements.

My father set about his new tasks as Prime Minister, Minister of Defence and Minister of External Affairs with a vigour quite in keeping with any previous effort. From top to bottom he had to overhaul the country, and to build up organisations from scratch. He was concerned not only with the recruitment, equipping and training of his army, but also with initiating a commensurate industrial effort. And at the same time he was actively engaged in dealing with internal security measures necessitated by such subversive organisations as the Ossewa Brandwag and the Broederbond. Investigations into these organisations were comprehensive and went on throughout the war. Many senior Government servants were implicated, as well as numerous Members of Parliament, some of whom now hold the highest positions.

There was no department that did not harbour some of these Broeders. The country was completely honeycombed. Against some it was possible to take action, but the majority managed to shelter smugly behind the Law.

It was in this background of confusion, unpreparedness, opposition and subversiveness that my father's efforts of the war years have to be judged. Yet despite all these troubles our national effort progressed with ever-increasing momentum. By 1942 there were 150,000 European men in full-time units, and before the end of the war this figure had passed the 200,000 mark, of whom, strangely perhaps, two-thirds were of Afrikaans parentage. If one bears in mind that South Africa's total European male population, between the ages of twenty and sixty, was only 570,000, and that all men in our forces were volunteers, the extent of the effort will be more readily appreciated. It is said to be unsurpassed among Allied nations.

Of these, 100,000 men were to see Active service abroad in foreign countries, the majority in the Middle East theatre. And under the able direction of Dr. H. J. van der Bijl we were to become the workshop of the desert armies, and a big manufacturing centre of war materials. The Pretoria Mint turned out vast quantities of small-arms ammunition, while Iscor, our iron and steel works, the railways, the mines and other industrial concerns turned out the heavier bombs, shells, field guns and armoured cars. This industrial effort, in itself, was a considerable achievement for a small population.

Britain was at the time deeply involved in her own rearmament, but by virtue of our good name and credit with the United States, we were able to purchase quantities of war material from them, especially bomber aircraft. Such was our good standing with America that we persuaded her to waive certain clauses of her Cash and Carry declaration, and to transport war materials to South Africa in her own ships, a privilege extended to no other nation. For our seaward defences my father roped in the small craft that plied round our coast, which were swiftly adapted to mine-sweeping and patrol duty. A large Coastal Patrol arm of the Air Force was formed to assist them and these scanned the seas for great distances beyond our 2,500-mile shore-line.

For internal security a force of 30,000 National Reserve Volunteers was recruited and these guarded all our essential points, as well as internment and prisoner-of-war camps.

The Straits of Gibraltar at various times became too hazardous and most of the Middle East traffic went round the Cape. Our ports dealt with huge armadas of ships and many hundreds of thousands of troops in passage. During the first two years of the war 6,500 ships put in for repairs or replenishment.

The inspiration behind these activities was the driving, restless personality of Jan Smuts.

LXVI IN PARLIAMENT

BY Tuesday, the 5th September, my father had formed his Cabinet. It was composed mostly of United Party adherents, with additional members from Labour and the Dominion Party who supported his war effort. So it was that Walter Madeley became Minister of Labour and Social Welfare and Colonel Stallard Minister of Mines.

Our old friend Deneys Reitz was second-in-command to my father. There was Colin Steyn, another ex-President's son. And there was J. H. Hofmeyr, Minister of Finance, the most willing and ablest of his ministers. It would be no exaggeration to say that the Cabinet consisted largely of Hofmeyr and my father, for here were teamed together the two ablest ministers in the long history of South African politics. Though both were giants and men of unsurpassed intellect, they differed radically in many ways. Hofmeyr, the child wonder and brilliant student and professor, was brought up quietly in the seclusion of the academic world. He was undoubtedly one of the greatest contemporary orators in the English language, and almost as fluent in Afrikaans. By nature a serious and deeply religious bachelor, and a man of great resolution and moral courage, he tackled unflinchingly and efficiently the work of half a dozen ministers. But Hofmeyr lacked those tempering fires of war that had hardened my father for the battle of life and made a practical man and a man of action of him. He was too rigidly bound by a puritanical outlook to make a successful diplomat, though he made a wonderful friend. He was too bigotedly unbending, and still too much of the professor. The divine spark of leadership had eluded him and he was destined to follow and to sustain, rather than to lead. Yet, he will undoubtedly go down in history as one of our greatest men. My father was first and most generous in praise of Hofmeyr, for he knew only too well the strain of such an intense and sustained effort as his lieutenant was now enduring.

Some people have endeavoured to compare Hofmeyr's intellect with that of my father. They do not bear comparison either in extensiveness or intensiveness or in any other sense. Hofmeyr's would have fitted comfortably into a corner of my father's, and still have been obscured.

Mr. Hofmeyr was heir-apparent to my father, and as such he drew more than a fair share of the Nationalist vituperation which was normally reserved only for my father. But he attracted criticism also on his own accord, for he belonged to a small but distinguished school of liberals, who wished to see a more moderate attitude adopted towards the non-Europeans. The Nationalists

General Smuts addressing a joint sitting of British Houses of Parliament in 1942.

On his left are Mr. Lloyd George and Mr. Churchill

General Smuts. An informal snap taken on his farm Doornkloof, near Pretoria—1943

Mrs. J. C. Smuts—1941

Three generations of Jan Christian Smuts— Rooikop 1944

critically avowed that he was the greatest "Kaffir boetie" (Negrophile) the country had ever seen. They were probably right, for Hofmeyr never lost an opportunity to champion the native cause, often to the intense embarrassment of his friends and his party. No inducement would prevail upon him to maintain a diplomatic silence.

Nothing in South Africa runs deeper than our age-ingrained feelings on colour. They transcend our Christian feelings. Friends tried to explain away Hofmeyr's liberal native policy by saying he was ahead of his time. But the Nationalists made his ideas the focal point of attack. And in time their attacks bore fruit.

In view of Deneys Reitz's failing health, my father, in 1942, induced him to take over the South African High Commissionership in London, a position he filled with great distinction. His sudden death in South Africa House in October, 1944, was a grievous loss to both countries. My father felt the loss of this life-long friend and disciple keenly. In tribute he spoke of his "dear friend and comrade, a faithful companion through the vicissitudes such as few have passed through. He was true, straight and upright—every inch of him—and he leaves a personal memory which I shall cherish all my days."

The new Government set to work with a will, as befitted one in time of crisis. Now, more than ever in its history, Smuts was South Africa. Nobody—not even his opponents—denied it. I think the eight years that followed were the greatest in the life of my father. They were, also, the greatest in the history of South Africa. At a stage in life when most men were tottering slowly towards the grave, this man was called upon to perform his major task and was striding briskly forward, erect and buoyant, young in heart and undaunted in spirit, and eager to be of service to his country. Mentally and physically he was still at his peak. His doctors said he had the arteries of a man twenty years his junior and he himself said he felt fit to live to a hundred. Had he not overworked himself, this might have been a possibility.

The decision of the House on that fateful 4th of September was the finish of Hertzog. Age and disaster now swiftly overtook him, and later, deserted by most of his fair-weather friends, he retired, broken and saddened, to live out his twilight on his farm Waterval near Pretoria. Only Havenga and a few old stalwarts followed him into the night, the rest losing little time in declaring their allegiance to the dour, unbending Dr. Malan, leader of the Purifieds. My father was out of South Africa at the time of Hertzog's death in 1942, or he would unquestionably have made a point of attending the funeral.

For more than half a lifetime Hertzog had lost no opportunity to slander and to vilify my father. My father forgot and forgave all this after he had defeated him. As a first token he put, much to the annoyance of the public, one of the special ministerial coaches on the railways at the General's disposal. On the ex-Prime Minister's birthday he crossed the floor of the House, and after friendly greeting, sat next to him on his bench and chatted for a long while in most friendly manner. Subsequently, when Hertzog retired, my father secured for him a pension of two thousand pounds per annum in recognition of his past services.

The problems that pressed were not only those connected with the war. There was the problem of those ranged against the war. Once more the old issue of republicanism sprang to life, though it never attained its former proportions. There were mass meetings, but feelings were more academic and subdued. But, nevertheless, they were embarrassing, especially as some of the senior politicians were serious about their preachings.

Certain subversive organisations, too, were serious and active. One was the so-called Ossewa Brandwag which was originally conceived more as a cultural organisation and received much support in 1938 from the symbolism of the Voortrekker Centenary Celebrations. But gradually its aims strayed into turbulent political waters and it developed into one of our two most dangerous Afrikaner organisations. Its leader was Dr. J. H. van Rensburg, one-time Administrator of the Free State and Civil servant under my father, and, strangely, always an admirer of his. In its early stages the Ossewa Brandwag and Dr. Malan's Nationalists worked together, but towards the end of 1941, after sharp differences of opinion, many broke away with Dr. van Rensburg to form a new group. Additional elements with Nazi aims hived off in 1942 from the Nationalists to form the New Order Party under Oswald Pirow, to await, hopefully, successful German developments in the war.

My father tolerated all these, as well as the more dangerous

Broederbond with the aggravating patience born of long experience. His patience was almost more than his followers could bear, for it is difficult to be tolerant in time of war. But he knew full well that nothing was quite so humiliating and killing to these organisations as to ignore them completely. More active interest would only have served to consolidate and to strengthen, and to create unwanted martyrs. So he watched them intently and maintained public security and order. Those who perpetrated acts of terrorism by using explosives were dealt with through police channels. A few hundred of the worst extremists were swiftly rounded up and, together with avowed German nationals, put behind barbed wire.

And so, as my father was fond of quoting, "the dogs may bark, but the caravan moves on".

One of his first acts was to pass Emergency Regulations.

He was determined to rush ahead with the parliamentary work with all possible speed. In order to curb verbosity in the War Measures Bill and to expedite its passage, he introduced the "guillotine" or Closure of Debate, which much incensed the Opposition. And a little later, to ensure that the House would finish its work in May, he introduced sittings in the mornings and at night, in addition to the normal afternoon sittings. During the last ten days he rushed through the House an unprecedented volume of work including the Electoral Laws Amendment Bill, the Advertising and Ribbon Amendment Bill, the Industrial Development Bill, the Unemployment Benefit Amendment Bill, the War Pensions Bill, the Income Tax Bill and the Rents Amendment Bill. The Nationalists complained bitterly at the haste, and even my father's followers appeared a little startled. But time was short, and my father was in his stride. Even the pro-Government *Forum* rebuked my father for his "steam-roller methods".

The Session was stormy and unpleasant, quite as bad as any previous one. But his enthusiasm and the nature of the tasks ahead sustained my father and kept him cheerful.

Since my father had last been Prime Minister a fine new official residence, modelled on the Old Cape Dutch style, had been erected on the ridge near Government House, in Bryntirion, Pretoria. This my mother decided to name "Libertas" after the old family home in Stellenbosch, and also because it seemed an appropriate name in time of war. We never lived in Libertas, preferring to stay on in the old rambling farmhouse at Irene. My father used it only to entertain official guests, and occasionally for a hurried lunch. The setting of the house is attractive with fine views of Pretoria sprawling at its feet in the south, and the massive Magaliesberg rampart on the north.

Groote Schuur still formed my father's place of abode during parliamentary sessions. Such of the rest of the family as were available would take it in turn to keep him company, and my father looked forward to the pleasures and distractions of his grandchildren.

Groote Schuur was little changed since our last visits. Mr. Bennington, the caretaker, we were delighted to find still there. "Mr. Benny", who arrived shortly after the days of Rhodes, was quite an institution. The place will never be the same without him. He knew my father's habits and they got on splendidly. And he spoiled us all when down there.

In discussion with Sir Herbert Baker in London at various times, both had agreed that Groote Schuur was too hemmed in by trees. So now my father had some of the decrepit ones behind the house thinned out. The aspect was improved and the public liked it because it gave a better view of the house from the road near the University.

Another botanical matter, this time decided in collaboration with Dr. Pole Evans, was the clearing of the artificial pine woods from the slopes of Devil's Peak above the Rhodes Memorial, to enable the fine Cape flora once more to re-establish itself. This met with some public criticism, but soon the lovely flora began to establish itself and made the experiment a success.

In Parliament my father again revealed himself as an unsurpassed master and showed his strategic skill. His numerical supremacy in the House was slender, if one considers the great tasks that lay ahead. Some of his adherents, though they had voted with him in the crucial neutrality issue, were only lukewarm adherents and their support could not be counted on at all times. By a great mastery, my father managed to smooth over contentious legislation, and other points of disagreement.

At the same time he lent the Opposition no advantage by

388

attacking them. They were at the time a series of warring factions, each manœuvring for personal power. Any form of attack would merely have tended to consolidate them. My father left them alone with their squabblings. Though they were loud and subversive in the House he did nothing to muzzle them. They were merely quarrelling themselves to destruction. But it was a trying policy to follow, and many of my father's loyal supporters were restive at the latitude permitted them. But my father felt he was right in sticking to this tolerance. He was giving them sufficient rope to hang themselves.

Instead the whole United Party machine was turned full blast against Pirow. Scorn, criticism and ridicule were poured on him to such effect that he was deflated and killed politically. He never succeeded in staging a recovery, though he remained an untiring preacher of anti-war propaganda.

It was a sound strategy to make Pirow a focal point, for it roused little feeling in the Opposition, while at the same time it boosted our war morale considerably.

For once, during the blitz on Pirow on March 15, my father departed from his inflexible habit never to launch a personal attack on an opponent. He attacked Pirow for his failure to carry out his defence plan announced in 1934. "I have no objection to the plan itself," my father declared caustically, "I will fulfil it just as I have fulfilled other promises made and broken by Mr. Pirow. Mr. Pirow's work was more a danger to the country than a protection. His plans were all right, but they were just grandiose plans and talk. It was all something on paper. . . . Mr. Pirow dreamed for five years, publicly and before all the country. . . . Now we are working day and night, not to make a plan, but to make an army. That was Mr. Pirow's duty in those five years. . . . We have to do it to-day."

PART IV
Second World War

LXVII WAR

MEANWHILE events had not gone well for us in Europe.
The Polish campaign lasted only three weeks. The
twenty-five Polish divisions were no match for the fifty-
four German ones, of which seven were armoured; nor was
there serious opposition to the 2,000 front-line aircraft of the
Luftwaffe.

Warsaw was bombed into blazing submission.

It was a blitzkreig pattern of battles to come.

The British and French ultimatum expired, and on 3rd September they were in a state of war with Germany. On 3rd October a
British Expeditionary Force under Lord Gort took over a section
of the Franco-Belgian frontier. As yet they numbered only two
corps of three divisions each. Along the French frontier ran the
Maginot Line, an elaborate bastion of steel and concrete, in which
huddled a huge impassive French army. But along the Belgian
frontier there was no fabulous concrete wall.

With the onset of winter came temporary stagnation.

In December the German pocket battleship, *Graf von Spee*, was
run to earth by three British cruisers and scuttled off Montevideo
in the River Plate.

Russia followed up the partition of Poland by casting her eyes
about for fresh gains. At the end of November she invaded Finland. Sweden and Norway blocked direct French support, and
though the Finns at first had the best of exchanges, Russian
numbers told and by the Treaty of Moscow (13th March, 1940)
Finland capitulated to Russian aggression.

In middle February, following her now standard technique of
simultaneous mass invasion at many points, coupled with adroit
use of internal fifth column elements, Germany fell on Norway
and Denmark. Denmark yielded without resistance. Norway put

393

up a brief but ineffectual defence. Britain came to her aid, but in insufficient numbers to stem the tide.

The shock of Norway unseated the Government in Britain and on 6th May, 1940, Winston Churchill succeeded Mr. Chamberlain. One of Mr. Churchill's first acts was to set up a Ministry of Aircraft Production. It was a wise decision. Britain was going to need aircraft.

Though preoccupied with Europe, my father nevertheless realised clearly that his problems lay in Africa. They lay more specifically with Mussolini, who, he had no doubt, would bring Italy into the war when he thought the moment propitious. That is the nature of the jackal. Britain did not feel quite so strongly about this Dictator, but France, doubting his intentions intensely, kept an army of over half a million men in readiness across the Alps.

Our South African army was designed on the assumption of a campaign in East Africa. It was a land of immense size, located far from the big bases. Emphasis was therefore laid upon transport and mobility. Thanks to Henry Ford we soon built up a large fleet of lorries and troop carriers. With memories of the last war, we saw to it that there were ample Medical units in support, as well as many specialist Engineer units to see to water problems and communications. Lieutenant-General Sir Pierre van Ryneveld was the Chief of Staff, with Headquarters in Pretoria, while at Premier Mine, a few miles outside the city, were vast training camps under canvas. The hard work on the parade grounds and clouds of red dust failed to damp our ardour.

We knew Italy had 200,000 troops in Africa, and though some of these were native askaris (*banda*), there was no question that it was a well established and formidable army. The British force in Kenya at the time consisted of elements of the King's African Rifles, native troops, numbering little more than half a division. A thousand miles of frontier had to be defended. Six hundred miles from this frontier lay the key East African towns of Nairobi and Mombasa.

On the 10th of June, Mussolini, satisfied that Germany had already won the war, struck at Moyale, a small outpost on the northern frontiers of Kenya. That same evening he made an impassioned speech from a balcony of the Palazzo Venezia in Rome:

"Italy has done all she possibly can to arrest this terrible war. . . . This is the hour of irrevocable decisions." Italy was at war. On the South African radio that same night my father delivered a national broadcast. South Africa was at war with Italy. War was on our very doorstep.

That day, as the latest Italian bomber aeroplanes sped to their targets in Kenya, four South African Air Force bombers struck at the same time at Moyale with two tons of high explosive bombs. Thereafter our bombing of Italian targets in Abyssinia, such as Yavello, Kisimayo, Neghelli, Mogadishu, became steadily more frequent and more massive, until finally we had literally swept the Italians from the skies of East Africa.

Numerous factors from time to time occurred which proved favourable to the Government. In April, 1940, by a shrewd stroke my father concluded a wool sales agreement with the British Government whereby they agreed to take over our entire wool clip for the period of the war. At the same time the price was raised by a third over the pre-war one of 8s. 3d. per pound. This induced many wool farmers, who were predominantly Nationalist, to swing to my father.

On the 10th of May Holland was invaded and Rotterdam sacked by the Luftwaffe, the Royal Family fleeing to Britain. Considering our racial origins in South Africa, this had a profound effect on people's feelings, though strange to relate, the feelings were not as deep as one would have expected. Dr. Malan and the other die-hard Nationalists passed it off with a shrug, remarking that the move was no doubt dictated by purely strategic considerations. Their excuses had a somewhat hollow ring, but it seemed to satisfy their unenlightened followers.

"Now you see," said my father in a national broadcast, "that neutrality does not mean protection. Germany stops at nothing."

The rape of the Netherlands did serve, however, to expedite the flow of volunteers to the colours. Our camps were full to overflowing.

In April, 1940, General Sir Archibald Wavell, Commander-in-Chief of the Middle East, came down to South Africa for consultations with my father on questions of strategy and South African participation in the war. Shortly after, a fleet of 300,000 tons of transports anchored in Table Bay, by far the largest armada of troopships ever seen in South African waters. They were bound for the Middle East. The first contingent of Springbok troops left with them.

The main mass of our troops left later for East Africa. At the Premier Mine training camp in July my father, dressed in his First World War uniform, but now wearing the badge of rank of a full general, bade them good-bye in fatherly words:

From personal experience I know what awaits you. I know what war means—seven years of my life have been spent in wars. They were among the hardest years of my life, but they were also full of the richest experience that life can give. I would not exchange my war experiences of the Anglo-Boer War and the last Great War for all the gold of the Rand.

You are going to face danger, hardship and sacrifice—perhaps death itself—in all its fierce forms. But through it all you will gather that experience of life and enrichment of character which is more valuable than gold or precious stones.

You will become better and stronger men. You will not return the same as you went. You will bring back memories which you and yours will treasure for life. Above all, you will have that proud consciousness that you have done your duty by your country and rendered your contribution to its future security and happiness.

You will not be mere items in the population; you will come back as builders of your own nation, of its best traditions, of its lofty national spirit and of its national pride. . . .

Many of you will revisit familiar haunts in the north. But to most of you that will be a new world, full of great interest of all kinds. You will see the vastness of this continent, its immense variety, its richness and grandeur of scenery, its magnificence in every respect. You go to it now as the strategic rampart and defence lines of South Africa. . . .

We have fought for our freedom in the past. We now go forth as crusaders, as children of the Cross to fight for freedom itself, the freedom of the human spirit, the free choice of the human individual to shape his own life according to the light that God has given him. The world cause of freedom is also our cause and we shall wage this war for human freedom until God's victory crowns the end.

This First South African Division, like the rest of our volunteer army, wore the distinctive "orange flash" on their shoulder tabs, signifying that they were prepared to serve anywhere in Africa.

This was necessary as the Union Defence Act limited service to our own country.

Throughout these war years stringent security measures were taken to protect the person of my father, as there were many fanatics about as well as Nazi agents. Wherever he went he was accompanied by guards, and security measures were also taken round his house at Irene and at Groote Schuur. He found it irksome having men about him always, but the authorities over-ruled his objections. Yet it was useful in some respects in that it provided him with energetic walking and climbing companions. It was a matter of routine with him that he always walked new ones completely off their feet.

LXVIII WALKING AND EXERCISE

THROUGHOUT his life my father had an implicit faith in exercise, especially walking and climbing, which he considered most beneficial. Walking was an urge he developed as a boy on the farm at Riebeeck West, when he tramped the veld in company with the old Hottentot Adam.

We in the family have lived and grown up with a father who walked or climbed at every opportunity. We were in after years to come to look upon this urge for exercise as the great doctor. Walking had the same effect on my father as that turbulent "Old Doctor" which sweeps the Cape Peninsula, the south-easter. We had come to look upon it both as a safety-valve and a rejuvenator. It was really a religion—that religion of the mountain he expounded so eloquently at Maclear's Beacon in 1923.

My father was never an ardent supporter of the organised forms of sport. He preferred to accord these a more lowly place as something mechanical and synthetic. He did not in his earlier days combine botany with his walking. About 1921 he first came

into contact with Dr. I. B. Pole Evans and under his guidance
that love for plants finally found its full expression. It followed
him thereafter, without diminution, like a great friend, and no
matter where he went he always took with him some book on
botany, even if it were only the slender volume of Burt Davie.

My earliest memories of my father stretch back almost thirty-
five years, and the most indelible of those memories were undoubtedly of jaunts into the veld, of walking, climbing and riding,
and later of botanising. Never a week-end or spare moment passed
without his taking us on some outing. The walking we somewhat
dreaded, for he always walked too fast for us. The climbs we found
still more difficult. The jaunts by car were more to our taste,
though driving in those early days after the First World War was
very different from the comfortable trouble-free travelling of
to-day. All his life, since 1911, my father was fond of driving his
own car, though a lack of insight into mechanical matters (the
only subject in life in which his knowledge was limited) often
made his trips hazardous. He continued driving to the last, to his
eighty-first year. He drove the seventy-five miles back himself
from his bushveld farm the day before he was stricken down by
his fatal coronary thrombosis, though at the time he was much
fatigued and feeling far from well. He enjoyed driving, for it took
his mind off worries.

During holidays, we went on camping expeditions, which
usually took us northwards from Pretoria. His love for the camp
was a remnant of Boer War days, and he liked to camp in most
spartan fashion. Other than a tarpaulin or some small bivouac
tents we took no shelter with us, and thunderstorms left us be-
draggled. These trips covered the sub-continent as far afield as
Lake Tanganyika (described in Dr. John Hutchinson's book) and
Lake Nyasa, the Zimbabwe Ruins, the Victoria Falls, the Kruger
National Park, and much else in addition, all on separate trips.
The Pilandsberg (where he owned a farm), the Blaauberg (where
he was fond of botanising or seeing the blind old native chief
Malaboch), Wyliespoort and the Sebasa Hills were favourite
haunts of his, and though he never hunted, he often accompanied
us on shooting trips into Portuguese East Africa and elsewhere.
On these trips he collected botanical specimens freely and his
bulky botanical presses always formed a problem of stowage in

our cars. The camp fires drew from him a fund of reminiscences. Sometimes in the chill of a winter's night in camp he would rise from his cold bed and kindle a fire, and before long we shivering youngsters would all join him. He relished camp life to the full. Frequently I have heard him give expression to his satisfaction by that old exclamation of his: "Bountiful Jehovah!" Then you knew he was really enjoying himself!

He inherited from the Boer War, too, a fondness for horseback riding. Until about 1930 a long ride was always part of the week-end ritual. Unfortunately I am not a born horseman and must confess that I found these long rides a trial. The satisfaction my father derived from riding was, however, different from that of walking. He looked upon riding as a good mode of exercise and not as one for communion with the universe. I think that that, as well as his tummy trouble, was why in later years he dropped riding and took only to walking, for it was really only from walking that he derived that true inner satisfaction.

Just exactly how he set about his walking and what part the surroundings played I endeavoured to decide for years. The conclusions I came to are that the actual physical artistry of his surroundings played only a minor part. It was the associations of sentiment with areas in which he walked that he really saw. My father was no artist of landscape form. He loved a scene more for what it symbolised in his mind's eye than for its outlines or colours. Not that he was unattuned to the beauties of landscape. No lover of nature could be that. But he just did not see the vistas and panoramas as an artist or a photographer would compose them. Yet for all that, I am certain he loved what he saw just as much, and probably with a deeper understanding.

When my father walked, he walked with gusto and determination, and at a hot pace, never pausing to rest or to admire. He would maintain a steady three and a half miles per hour, for he loved to feel his lungs expanding to the full and to have the sweat running down in rivulets. He preferred what he called the "ups and down" to walking on the flat. A favourite walk of his at Irene was a ten-mile one which took in seven low hills. Roads he shunned wherever possible, preferring a more difficult way through the veld. Barbed-wire fences he took in his stride. He normally took no water or lunch with him, though sometimes he

JAN CHRISTIAN SMUTS

used to carry an orange or an apple. In later years they gave him indigestion so he stopped. With him in his pocket he always carried an iodine pencil, doctoring cuts and scratches on the spot. Slung on his shoulders he would carry a pair of binoculars, though he very seldom used these. I think it was an old wartime habit. In his hand he carried a stout stick, which he seldom used.

He wore heavy boots and thick socks, for he had tender feet and his ankles had both been broken by treading in holes, in his youth. On his head he would wear his oldest and most battered panama hat, an almost unrecognisable article of headgear. In later years he often wore dark glasses for the glare. For the rest he would be dressed in a khaki shirt and slacks, the shirt sleeves never being rolled up, but unbuttoned when hot. That was because he was rather susceptible to sunburn.

From his walks he would come back sun-tanned and wet with perspiration, not fatigued (for he had amazing stamina) but just nicely tired and contented, and at peace with the world. With the quickening of his pulses during the walking he had been able to get a clearer perspective of things and had solved the problems he had had in mind at the start. He had also found time to talk and to reminisce. In all, he had had a really good and satisfying outing. Then followed a mug of cool beer and a bath or shower, after which he settled down happily to a normal working routine for the remainder of the day, as though he had had no strenuous exercise at all.

In 1926 we tried to get him interested in golf at Irene, but after a few swings he said it was far too mechanical. He was quite a familiar figure on the Irene golf course, however, not as a player, but as a figure crossing the fairways en route on some walk. He was also a familiar figure at the Pretoria Country Club, for this was a terminal point on his cross-country walks between Pretoria and Irene.

Mountaineering, like walking, was in my father's blood.

I have vivid memories of my father on the summit of Table Mountain. Here he would pause for a while and, leaning on his long stick, take in the glorious panoramas around him, his hat in his hand and his white hair blowing in the breeze. His open khaki shirt and his unbuttoned sleeves would flap about and complete the informality of the picture.

400

Of the first thirty-five of the forty years my father spent in the Houses of Parliament, he made an ascent of Table Mountain almost every week-end, climbing always on foot, sometimes alone or sometimes with other parties of climbers. On the mountain he was always friendly and approachable. Many young mountaineers learned to know and to love him on these jaunts. All learned to admire his physical stamina and his enriching philosophy.

In all he must have accomplished over 300 climbs of this mountain before he was finally advised in 1948, because of his age, to stop these strenuous climbs. For the twenty years the cableway was in existence, he never used it to get to the top, and on only one occasion, in company with the King and Queen in 1947, did he make a descent in it. He climbed mostly from the north or Kirstenbosch side, preferring Skeleton Gorge to any other, though in his time he made many ascents up every possible route. He never did the hazardous Alpine form of rock climbing, however, preferring the more normal forms of climbing.

In all the years he climbed he always worked to a time schedule of about three hours from Kirstenbosch to Maclear's Beacon. In 1896 it was three hours, and it was still three hours in 1946. He made a point, where possible, of descending by a different route. The rather different form of exercise occasioned by descent he relished quite as much as that of climbing.

He loved not only Table Mountain, but all mountains. In a long life of climbing he found time to climb virtually all the mountains of the Cape, as far afield as Ceres. He could never resist the lure of the mountain.

Though he preferred a fine day for a climb, he was not deterred by unfavourable conditions. His experiences on the mountain have been numerous, but there was one terrifying one which he never failed to relate. It occurred in August, 1939, when winter was already well advanced in the Cape. Parliament had risen, but he had had to make a special journey to Cape Town, as Deputy Prime Minister, to see the Portuguese President Carmona off at the docks. He arrived at the Civil Service Club a day early, and to pass away the time decided to do a lone climb up Table Mountain. The weather looked distinctly drizzly, for it was well into the Cape rainy season, but he thought he might risk it. My sister, Louis, took him as far as the Cableway Station. Platteklip Gorge was running strongly with water, but he managed to make his way up without much difficulty. Near the top it started to rain and he was soon cold and drenched, but he pressed on to the top. By the time he reached Maclear's Beacon it was raining hard and had turned bitterly cold and windy, so he returned the one and a half miles to the Cable Station, hoping to get a cage down. But the weather was too bad for that, and the lower station was locked and the driver gone. There were now only two courses open; to remain here at the Upper Cable Station, or to attempt the descent. While the caretaker dried his clothes before a fire he made up his mind to return, for there was no phone and friends below would worry.

So he set off back in the swirling mists and rain to Maclear's Beacon, finding great difficulty in this, for not only was visibility almost completely restricted, but the whole mountain top was under water, only rocks and boulders sticking out. He made a cold and laborious way by jumping, as far as possible, from rock to rock. Conditions grew steadily worse and more dangerous, for by now it was well into the afternoon and freezingly cold. Eventually, when near Maclear's Beacon, he slipped as he jumped and fell heavily with his right hip on a rock. For some moments, he said, he lay dead still, too afraid to attempt to move, for he felt certain that he had broken his hip. But he found he could sit up and that his hip, though very painful, was intact. And so he progressed on his weary, cold and painful way down the mountain. Skeleton Gorge was an endless series of roaring waterfalls and quite impassable, but by luck, in the gathering gloom, he managed to skirt the gorge by climbing down the series of steep rocky cliffs at the side. All the time it literally poured.

Almost at the end of his tether from strain and exposure, he came out at the Kirstenbosch Kiosk at 8 p.m., and so set at rest many worried people. He told that story in my presence on three occasions with great pride, looking upon this day as one of his greatest victories over overwhelming forces. But he never omitted to remark that it had been a "terrible day! Really terrible!!"

LXIX ABYSSINIAN CAMPAIGN

DURING the war my mother was no less active than my father. With her deep convictions on political issues and her warm motherly feelings for mankind, she quickly took my father's troops to her heart. She was appointed Chairman of our Gifts and Comforts organisation, which provided small luxuries for our army personnel, and speedily had the organisation flourishing on a nation-wide scale. Her enthusiasm for the cause of "my boys" was infectious and the troops grew to love their "Ouma". Groote Schuur and Libertas became a hive of "work parties", where staid housewives and others knitted and sewed. It was an effort which the troops regarded with affection.

During the First World War my mother had also been Chairman of the Gifts and Comforts Committee, but it was at that time a very much smaller organisation. For her services she had been offered a C.B.E., but she had declined this honour on the grounds that there were other more deserving people.

In October, 1940, my father inaugurated the National Reserve Volunteers for internal security duties, including the guarding of vital installations, internment or prisoner-of-war camps.

At the end of October he paid an eight-day visit to the front in East Africa, going first to Khartoum for a conference with Anthony Eden, British Foreign Secretary, and General Wavell. Thereafter he returned to Nairobi where he visited South African hospitals and troops in forward areas.

Mr. Churchill did not favour a campaign in Abyssinia but advocated coming to grips directly with the Italians in the crucial North African theatre. He wanted to send the South African troops to Wavell in the Western Desert where he felt they would be more usefully employed. While there was much to be said on the tactical side for concentrating on the Mediterranean, my father felt that the need to shield the people of Kenya and Southern Africa from an invader outweighed simple tactical considerations. At the Khartoum Conference with Eden my father pressed this point and Wavell concurred. On the strength of this it was decided to wage a vigorous campaign in East Africa. Events have justified this decision.

The East African visit very nearly had disastrous consequences, for after taking off from Nanyuki one morning for Garba Tula, in the North Frontier District, he heard about the superb camouflage of our main air base at Archer's Post, some miles off his route, and decided to go and see for himself. Archer's Post he knew as the erstwhile headquarters of the famous elephant hunter "Karamoja" Bell. With him in the plane, which was a converted German Junkers Ju. 86, was General van Ryneveld, our C.G.S., Lieutenant-General Alan Cunningham, the new General Officer Commanding, East Africa, and Major-General Godwin-Austin, under whom our South African troops were fighting. All the eggs were in one basket.

By an unfortunate oversight, Archer's Post had not been informed of my father's intentions, and by a further unfortunate oversight the pilot, Captain Raubenheimer, was not instructed in the local recognition signals. So, after approaching the aerodrome at a few thousand feet, he did a right-hand circuit instead of a left-hand one, and omitted to lower his undercarriage or to waggle his wings. To those on the ground the plane and its behaviour appeared hostile and some Hawker Fury fighters took off to intercept.

In order to get a better view, my father was sitting forward with Raubenheimer in the cockpit.

General van Ryneveld noticed streaks of dust on the aerodrome below as some machines took off, but thought no more of it. But a few moments later he saw a Fury fighter making straight for them and heard the staccato bark of machine-gun fire and saw dust rise in the machine. He had been shot down twice in the First World War, and realised with horror that they were actually being attacked. The Hurricane escort was in a quandary: short of shooting down a friend, intervention was impossible. However, when the Fury made a second swoop he got in between and warded it off, and at the same time it also dawned on the attacker, who deserves the fullest credit, that the two Junkers aircraft were friendly.

I saw the aircraft on Wajir landing ground where they came down a short while after. There were eight holes in the fuselage of my father's machine, and one bullet had actually passed between his legs. But nobody was hurt and my father made light of it. At the time I was a humble Second Lieutenant in the South African Engineer Corps working on the defences of this picturesque outpost to the south of Moyale. After a few minutes conversation and the handing over of some parcels from home he was off again on a long reconnaissance flight along the Abyssinian frontier to assess the tactical position.

In little over a week he was back from his 7,500-mile trip looking sunburnt and optimistic. His impressions he recorded on the radio after his return:

Physically, our troops make a most favourable impression, and are probably in advance of any force we have ever sent from this country —fit and well, and in stature and muscular development well above the average. I doubt whether anywhere in the world troops of a finer physical type can be found. In height and breadth they are so striking that I have heard a British General call them tanks among men!

How could it be otherwise when as volunteers, and not conscripts, they represent the flower of our Union manhood. The provision for their health and physical welfare in that exacting climate is the best South Africa can give with her hard experience of the past to guide her. Long training both here and in East Africa has produced a fitness and hardness of a very high standard. . . .

Looking at these sons of the fathers whom I was proud to lead in the same historic field a generation ago, I could not but feel high pride and emotion to see that they were worthy of the rock whence they were hewn. They sometimes brought a lump to my throat—how proud one feels of South Africa when one sees how much people are prepared to give up at home and to do in far-away lands and under hard conditions for the honour of their country and the security of its future.

I have spoken of our boys in East Africa. Let me also add a word about that wonderful country, that wonderland, which so many old warriors, who listen to me to-night, remember so well from their experience of the last war. Two impressions stand out in my mind in reference to this visit—the greatness of that world and the goodness of man.

As I flew hour after hour over those endless forests and great lakes, over the Great Rift Valley studded with a jumble of high mountains and extinct volcanoes more magnificent than any to be found elsewhere, I had an overwhelming impression of the vastness and power of Nature and of the forces that had shaped the past of this continent with unrivalled lavishness and grandeur.

In this gigantic world the human element seems dwarfed to utter insignificance, and one bows one's head in wonder before a sublimity so overwhelming. Indeed, no words can express the impression of the physical grandness which that world of East Africa produces on one's mind.

The other impression comes nearer home, touches our hearts more closely, warming them and raising them as no mere external greatness of Nature can do.

I am free to confess that the sight of our boys in East Africa kindled a deeper emotion in me than even that awe-inspiring natural scenery. How grand is Nature! How good is man!

The sight of those young men, with their happy, eager faces, with the thought of what they had given up to serve their fellows and make this a safer world for the spirit of man to dwell in securely—that sight, that thought, made me realise that their souls were worthy to match this glorious setting of Nature, that the goodness of man was a worthy match for the greatness of Nature.

They are the happy warriors of the New Order, the champions of that spiritual order of the universe which in the end is more deeply founded and more secure than these ancient hills and craters. The New Order will not arise under the swastika, which is the symbol of past tyrannies and the moral enslavement of the human spirit. It can only arise under the sign of the Cross, in the spirit of service and self-sacrifice, which has carried man from his brutal, bestial past to the height of his spiritual vision. Not in mastery, but in service, not in dictatorship, but in freedom lies the secret of man's destiny.

This is what these young South Africans stand for, for what I trust South Africa will stand for till the very end.

It was one of his nicest and friendliest broadcasts.

In South Africa Malan, fearing Pirow's competition, had invited the Ossewa Brandwag to join his party. South African politicians sometimes choose strange bedfellows.

Soldiers were getting tired of the Nationalists and others, and there were minor clashes in Johannesburg and elsewhere, the worst occurring in January and February, 1941, when the soldiers rioted against the non-loyal elements in our Police Force.

On New Year's Day my father delivered his annual broadcast:

We have come, my friends, to the end of the darkest year in modern history. During it seven nations have fallen under the Nazi scourge—a new black plague that sears the souls of men, and withers civilisation at its roots. Seven nations that were free are no longer free. Seven peoples that cherished liberty have been enslaved.

That has been calamity enough: but we cannot measure what it has meant, and what it still means, in the sum of human suffering and in the destruction of the treasured fruits of human endeavour.

It has been a dark year; but there have been great flashes of light—that have illumined the darkness when the night has been blackest. These flashes of light, fitful and spasmodic at first, have now become one broad continuous beam, flowing down the path to victory. This is the spirit of free men; this is the beam of light that flashes through a world of darkness when the flint of human courage is struck. . . .

Elsewhere I have spoken about the probable developments of the war in the year 1941, but to my own countrymen I would say that we have ample grounds for confidence. We see to-day the unrivalled resources of the United States of America being turned to our assistance. The people of that great democracy have realised that we of the British Commonwealth are fighting their battle for them, and that if we fail our defeat will be their defeat and their humiliation. We can rest assured of a steady and increasing flow from America of material help, to supplement the moral sympathy that has always been with our cause. In this and in the growing spiritual and material power of the whole British Commonwealth, lies the assurance of victory. . . .

The call for national unity is clear and insistent. National unity is needed for the war; it is indeed, too, for the victory that is assured. The New Year will bring us close to victory; and it will, I trust, take South Africa far along the path of unity and internal peace, to progress and prosperity.

After my father's visit to East Africa we all realised that something big was in the air. On Dingaan's Day, the 16th December, 1940, South African and Gold Coast units, at divisional strength, launched the first big and successful attack of the war on Italian positions at El Wak. For this action the South African brigade commander Dan Pienaar received the D.S.O. Pienaar was to achieve considerable fame as a soldier before his tragic death in an air crash at Kisumu in 1942.

In October Wavell's big North African offensive had opened with conspicuous success.

After El Wak the offensive in East Africa began in earnest. Under the able leadership of General Cunningham the Allied army of two-divisional strength fell upon the hordes of Mussolini and drove them swiftly backwards. Indian troops had for long been hammering desperately at the tough fortress of Keren in Eritrea. The Italians were no match for the dash of our armies or its first-class troops and swiftly their strong-points crumpled and were overrun. On April the 5th the Transvaal Scottish ceremonially marched into Addis Ababa, Ethiopia's capital, and at Amba Alagi, on the 16th May, the Duke of Aosta surrendered with his Italian troops to Brigadier Pienaar.

In many respects it was one of the most remarkable campaigns in history. Its swiftness was unsurpassed. In fifty-three days 1,725 miles had been covered in some of the wildest, most mountainous country in the world. And we had had the privilege of providing the Allies with the first big victory of the war.

General Cunningham in his report on the operations of the East Africa Force, in 1940–41, remarks: "It would be idle to close without reference to the assistance given by the Union of South Africa, without which the campaign could not have been undertaken. Apart from fighting troops, I was indebted to the Union for much of the mechanical transport which made the supply of troops over such great distances in front of railheads and ports possible, and to them also I owed the provision of a large number of special technical units, without which operations in the type of terrain covered could not have taken place. It was with remarkable forethought that these units had been formed before the war and furnished with the most modern equipment.

"Through the personal interest of Field-Marshal Smuts I was at the start able to knit the Force into a whole, and all the many resources which the Union placed at my disposal were pooled for the common good of the whole Force. . . ."

Lord Wavell makes the interesting disclosure that before the operations to be undertaken in East Africa were decided upon, he was being pressed by the Defence Minister in Britain to move his forces from East Africa, where they were standing idle "with no prospect of successful employment", to Egypt, where, in Mr.

Churchill's opinion, they could be more usefully employed. On the other hand, Lord Wavell was well aware of the feeling of nervousness, not only in Kenya but also in Rhodesia and even in South Africa, that the forces in East Africa were not sufficiently strong to prevent an Italian invasion of Kenya and the countries farther south, and my father frequently impressed on him the danger of reducing the forces in East Africa. Fortunately, the Commander-in-Chief gave heed to the warning, resisted proposals for any weakening or diversion of his forces until the enemy had been driven farther back, and gave his divisional commanders the word to go ahead. . . .

In March, 1941, my father flew up to Nairobi in his Lodestar. He then went on to Cairo where he deliberated with Eden, Wavell and Dill. At this meeting my father stressed the importance of the African theatre in the war. He held a firm conviction throughout that some of the major battles would be fought in this area.

In two broadcasts in 1941 my father gave his views on the New Order that would follow victory. From Cape Town on 26th April he said:

Some people appear to be depressed by the turn of events in the Balkans. The sudden and unexpected collapse of Jugoslavia after a brief resistance, and the overwhelming of Greece after her heroic defence against terrible odds, make them fear for the future of the Allied cause. They also note that British forces have once more retired before the superior force of the enemy. They forget that in the last war the position of the Allies in that quarter of Europe was far worse than it is to-day. . . . There is such a rush of events, the canvas of the world war is so overcrowded with incidents, that people are apt to become confused, to lose their sense of perspective, and fail to put events in their proper values and relations in the vast framework of the war. . . .

This war will not be settled in the Balkans, and the commotion and confusion which Germany has stirred up there will in the end only contribute to her own undoing, whatever present successes she may appear to achieve. . . .

That Britain went to the assistance of Greece and other small countries at whatever cost to herself is to her lasting credit. That she failed in Norway, Holland and Belgium is no blame, no dishonour, for her helping hand stretched to them in the hour of her own sore plight. Britain is investing in friendships as Germany is investing in hatreds in the process of the war, and Britain is thus building up the moral capital with which the real new world order will be floated after the peace. As has often happened before, Germany is thus winning the victories and losing the war.

To keep the developments of this war in a proper perspective, one has always to bear in mind what I consider to be the real crux of the situation. It is this, that Hitler began the war, that he is the aggressor and must continue in his aggression to the very end. The role of Britain is essentially a defensive one. If Hitler fails in his attack on the fortress of Britain itself he will have reached that end—his end—and will have lost the war.

. . . The intrinsic importance of our achievement in East and North Africa and in the Mediterranean basin is very great. For one thing, the bubble of Mussolini has been finally pricked. Most of his fleet is at the bottom of his "mare nostrum". His African Empire lies in ruins and Haile Selassie is marching to reoccupy his throne. One of the two Axis partners is hopelessly bankrupt and becomes a liability to the other. That is the way Austria went last time, and Germany followed in due course. . . .

Hitler has roused the American giant from his slumbers—hence the election of President Roosevelt, hence the Lease and Lend Act, hence the firm and unshakable alignment of all responsible American opinion on the side of the Allies. More will follow. America will yet go all the way. This I have for a long time foreseen. To me it has long been evident that only through America's full participation would the way to victory be clear and assured. I have looked forward to this development, not only for the sake of our victory but also for the sake of the peace that was to follow. I could not see a real fruitful peace without America right in it. I could not see America participating in peace unless she had been through the crucible of the war with us.

A fortnight later he spoke of a new World Order that would arise from out-and-out Allied victory:

. . . It seems to me that the day of the small independent sovereign State has passed. That is the sign of the times. In the absence of a mighty world organisation the sad fate of the small independent States of Europe in our day is likely to be their fate more and more in the future. Hitler's victorious course so far has at least proved that much. Philip of Macedon and Alexander the Great proved the same for the

Hellenic world. The Greek City State of ancient history and the small independent nation State of to-day were and are anachronisms in the circumstances of their respective times.

We are unmistakably in for larger human groupings in that holistic process which fundamentally moulds all life and all history. . . .

In the inner circle, which now forms the heart of the resistance to Hitler, is the British Commonwealth of Nations. I need not dilate on the particular links which associate this world-wide circle freely together, but their association is undoubtedly a precedent and a prototype of the larger World Association now in the process of formation.

Closest to this inner circle of the British group is the United States of America, which has the same ethic of life and the same political philosophy. Both have, in addition, the strong link of a common language and literary culture. The two thus form a very natural group. . . .

This new world society would follow positive and constructive policies for the future, and not concern itself particularly with the past and with penal or revengeful action towards old enemies. And in this way, in due course, the world may forget its bitter wrongs and once more move into paths of peace and friendly economic relations among the nations. The mistake of the League of Nations in attempting too wide and universal membership on too loose and nebulous a basis of organisation and duties would thus be avoided and the Association would grow practically out of existing friendships and affinities, and might expand later into the wider international society of the future. We should not attempt to do at one stroke what could only be accomplished in a long process of time and experience.

The crux of this next great step in the organisation of our world will be the attitude of the United States of America. I wish to speak quite plainly on this point. I feel convinced that the United States of America, in abandoning the League of Nations to its fate, after taking the leading part in its foundation, helped to pave the way for the world war which is now devastating Europe and into which she will herself inevitably be drawn. Great is thus her responsibility for the world situation of to-day, although, of course, I do not deny the great responsibility of others. . . .

First and foremost we shall be called upon to put our own house in our own democratic circle in order, and ensure as far as possible against the sort of dangers which have now twice overwhelmed us in one generation. Leave the rest to time, to the workings of ordinary prudence and sympathy and reviving generosity, and do not let us

411

attempt more than is wisely possible for the immediate future after the war. Time is a real force, a great healer and a great builder. Let us leave it its place and its function in our vision of the future. . . .

LXX FORTUNES OF WAR

IN Europe 1940 was a period of great disasters for the Allies. Holland was overrun in May and Rotterdam bombed into a flattened rubble with considerable loss of life. Soon the Meuse and Albert Canal were forced and the whole Belgian front line crumbled. By mid-month German armoured divisions, quickly traversing the difficult Ardennes, broke through the 9th French Army and crossed the Meuse near Sedan, by so doing outflanking the Maginot Line which stopped farther to the south. The Germans sped on. The Allies had not sufficient tanks or anti-tank guns to stop the massed German panzers.

During these anxious days my father kept trying to reassure himself, muttering: "Now France will throw in her reserves. The Frenchman was a wonderful fighter in the last war." But France never threw in her reserves. She had none. What might have been her reserve was snugly locked up with the million and a quarter men in the bowels of the Maginot Line. This Line never fired a shot. It was the undoing of France, psychologically and tactically.

On the 27th the Belgian king surrendered, exposing the flank of Lord Gort's British Expeditionary Force. Thereafter followed the British withdrawal to Dunkirk and the successful evacuation across the Channel of most of the B.E.F. in one of the epic naval exploits of Britain's long naval history. By stimulating seamanship 224,000 British troops and 112,000 other Allied troops, mostly French, were successfully withdrawn.

Britain had suffered a temporary knock-out blow.

By now Weygand had succeeded General Gamelin in command

of the French Armies and a fresh effort was made to stem the German onrush. The Wehrmacht was luckily in no position to pursue the British across the Channel, or the war might soon have been over. So now Hitler continued in a great right hook on Paris, which was entered on 14th June. The French Government had withdrawn steadily southwards, and Reynaud had made way for the Petain–Weygand combination. They lost no time in seeking peace terms, and these were ratified at Compiègne on the 21st in the same railway carriage used by Foch in the 1918 armistice.

On the 17th, as France was dying, Mr. Churchill made his immortal exhortation and pledged Britain to go on fighting alone, till the end. It was one of those decisive declarations that mould history. It was a call that startled and awakened America.

Germany now controlled the coastline from the northern tip of Norway to the southern tip of France. She was ready to prepare for the invasion of Britain. But before she could cross the Channel she had first to knock out the R.A.F. In the beginning of August the daylight air attacks on Britain began. The crucial Battle of Britain had started. It did not finish till the end of October, by which time British pilots and machines had established a clear superiority. On the worst day in September, R.A.F. pilots claimed to have shot down 185 German machines.

By this time it was clear that Britain had won the battle. Goering fell into considerable disfavour with Hitler and plans for an invasion were more or less indefinitely shelved. With these plans baulked, Goering now turned to a nine months' programme of terror-bombing of British cities by night. London bore the brunt, 1,150,000 houses being damaged, but even in Portsmouth only 7 per cent of houses escaped bomb damage. Up to the end of 1941 190,000 high-explosive bombs had been dropped on Britain, killing 43,700 civilians and injuring an additional 50,000. But Hitler gained nothing except hatred and an intensified resolve to fight on.

American aid was steadily pouring in on the "cash and carry" basis, which meant payment in advance and transportation in Britain's own ships. But as funds ran out it was modified in March, 1941, to Roosevelt's fine conception of Lease Lend, which ensured that monetary difficulties would not hamper supplies. In September, 1941, Britain concluded an agreement with the United States whereby she was given fifty American destroyers in exchange for

413

United States rights to establish naval and air bases in Newfoundland, British Guiana and in the West Indies.

On 27th September, 1940, Germany, Italy and Japan signed a Tripartite Pact of Alliance. Washington intelligence reports twice warned Russia of impending German attack. She slumbered peacefully on.

But Italy moved before Germany.

On 13th September large Italian forces under Grazziani crossed the Egyptian frontier from Libya, and after skirmishes with light British forces, paused for three months at Sidi Barrani. Here, on the eleventh of the following month Wavell, reinforced by Indians, Australians and New Zealanders, launched a surprise attack, which was spectacularly successful. Within two months he had driven the enemy out of Egypt and Cyrenaica, capturing 133,000 prisoners and much booty. Wavell had achieved this daring exploit with only 30,000 men and limited resources.

In October Italy, using Albania as a base, had set upon Greece, but the Greeks fought with surprising stubbornness and threw them back. A month later Admiral Andrew Cunningham secured a notable victory over the Italian fleet in Taranto, carrier-borne torpedo Swordfish putting out of commission a major part of the force as it lay at anchor, and decisively swinging naval supremacy in the Mediterranean in Britain's favour.

So far the war had gone well for us in the Middle East, but Germany now intervened actively and it became a long life-and-death struggle. First came her invasion of Greece and Yugoslavia in April, which were overrun after a brief but tenacious defence. Britain had a treaty with Greece and decided, though she could ill afford it on military grounds, to go to her aid. To do so she drew upon forces from Wavell's Western Desert army, leaving Africa dangerously exposed. At great cost to the Navy, the vanquished forces on the Greek mainland were evacuated to Crete. Here, in May, they were fallen upon by superior German airborne forces, and being deficient in anti-aircraft defences and perplexed by this novel form of parachutist attack, succumbed to the invader.

My father gave the decision to intervene in Greece his fullest support. It was not only a question of honour, but an act of goodwill which would bear fruit in the future. He also had a deep admiration and affection for the Greek people and made it his duty throughout the war to look after their interests. Much of his time in Cairo was usually taken up with their affairs. His affection for Greece had its roots in the classics, and their gallant stand in this war did much to enhance it. He also had close ties of friendship with the Greek Royal Family, who sought sanctuary in the Union during the war.

At this time Germany had also landed her Afrika Korps, a highly armoured and mechanised force under the able direction of Rommel, at Tripoli, and this force moved swiftly eastwards to contact our Desert Army. With little effort they drove our depleted force backwards to Sollum on the Egyptian frontier, where the line was stabilised. A garrison of Australians was left to hang on grimly to the isolated fortress of Tobruk on the coast.

Things having gone wrong, a scapegoat was made of Wavell, who was succeeded by General Claude Auchinleck, while General Cunningham, on my father's recommendation and on the strength of his East African victory, was made Commander of the Western Desert Force. The South African First Division, together with our Air Force and other units, had now moved up to join this hardy desert army, and after marshalling at Amariya near Alexandria, were sent up to Mersa Matruh, which was then a key defence point. Tobruk, bombed heavily and unceasingly from nearby airfields, and frequently heavily attacked by land, hung on grimly.

In August, 1941, my father, accompanied by my mother, made a flying three-day visit to Cairo, my mother on Gifts and Comforts business and my father for troop inspections and discussions. At El Alamein he saw our Second South African Division busy training and preparing defences, and at Mersa Matruh, our First Division, under Major-General George Brink, were holding a forward position. Back in the British Embassy in Cairo, he sent off two long letters to Churchill and Roosevelt once more stressing the dangers of neglecting the vital Middle East theatre at the expense of a great and premature build-up for a cross-Channel assault on Europe. Roosevelt, and possibly British statesmen also, did not always take the African war sufficiently seriously.

In November, 1941, Cunningham launched his big offensive to drive back the Germans and to relieve Tobruk. For many days the battle, fought like some great, mobile naval action on the limitless stony flatness of the desert, hung perilously in the balance, the German armour proving distinctly superior to the British. At Sidi Rezegh, on the 21st, the South African 5th Infantry Brigade, battling to connect up the last few miles with Tobruk, ran into a massed Panzer force and was wiped out. At the same time, not far away, the 1st South African Brigade, under the leadership of Brigadier Pienaar, was set upon by a similar tank force, but due to fine tactical handling and a masterly concentrated use of his artillery, Pienaar drove off the Germans. The significance of this action was that it was the first occasion on which it was demonstrated that well-handled guns could drive off mass tank assaults.

Contact was eventually established with Tobruk and the garrison relieved. The Germans withdrew swiftly to El Agheila beyond Benghazi. Cunningham had meanwhile been superseded by General Ritchie. But we had badly overrun our long lines of communication and our forward armoured units were out of petrol. So when Rommel counter-attacked soon after, we were unable to hold the line and were driven back to a weak defensive position behind minefields, known as the Gazala Line. It ran for thirty miles from the Free-French-held strongpoint of Bir Hacheim to the coast, thirty miles west of Tobruk. Here there was a lull while both sides gathered strength.

In May, 1942, my father flew up to Cairo for discussions and found time to inspect the forces as far afield as Tobruk. He slept at General Ritchie's Headquarters on a bay near Gambut which had been Rommel's tank repair workshops, and bathed pleasantly in the warm Mediterranean.

Addressing his troops from the back of a truck under a palm tree on the dunes at Mersa Matruh on 22nd May he said: ". . . we must hold this Middle East block, and we will hold it. There is the possibility that it will become the base for a great offensive. I have come to the conclusion that we will see a great trial of strength. You may see it here in North Africa, which, I have always felt, is destined to become one of the great battlefields of this war."

A young soldier who had seen my father pass in the desert wrote home to his parents: "Thank God South Africa has such a man and thank God I am a South African. His visit did more good in two seconds than fourteen months of army training. He can rest assured that if we are called upon to carry the Union Colours into

General Smuts looking out over San Francisco Bay—1945   General Smuts addressing the Plenary Session of the United Nations at the San Francisco Conference—1945

General Smuts with King George VI on Table Mountain—1947

the line, we will carry them right round the world and back again."

By now both sides had amassed huge tank forces, the British having acquired, in addition to their Crusaders and Matildas, numerous American Grant and Stuart tanks. Rommel struck on May 26, and after a long and almost disastrous struggle broke through our wide minefields and drove the French out of Bir Hacheim. Once more German tanks proved superior both in fighting power and tactical handling, and soon our scarred but gallant army was falling back towards Alexandria. In the biggest tank battle of the war, near Knightsbridge to the south of Tobruk, we lost hundreds of tanks in a single over-impetuous action and our armoured force was virtually wiped out. Our Second South African Division, which had previously taken Bardia, Halfaya and Sollum, was in Tobruk at the time, but it was common knowledge that we would not again commit the dangerous error of trying to hold this or any other isolated strongpoint. The minefields and other defences of Tobruk were therefore never properly prepared for a siege. Our tank forces, which had just been wiped out, were an integral part of the defences of the fortress. It was therefore obvious to all on the spot that Tobruk could never be held. The last-minute decision by the highest authority to hold it came as a complete surprise to us. This decision must either have come from Mr. Churchill or some very high body. The fact that my father, while opposed to the decision, never pressed the enquiry, may perhaps be significant.

And so on 21st June Tobruk fell, and with it South Africa lost the best part of a first-rate division of 13,000 men. It was a grievous blow to the country and to my father. It gave the Opposition endless grounds for criticism and it made many friendly households resentful. And above all, it cast a quite unwarranted stigma upon the South African soldier, who became the scapegoat of a strategic error. People were apt to make comparisons with the previous occasion when Tobruk was invested, forgetting that from the point of view of weight of attack it was like comparing chalk and cheese. There was some consolation in the fact that it was the Indian lines of the perimeter, not the South African, that had been pierced.

In South Africa my father now launched a renewed effort to

get 7,000 recruits for our depleted army. The recruiting cry was "Avenge Tobruk", and the response was gratifying.

In Egypt, the beaten Allied army, including the reconstituted but unbeaten First South African Division, were driven swiftly back by the famous 90th Light Division and mobile units from the Panzer divisions, until on 1st July they reached the defensible narrow thirty-mile waist between the impassable Qattara Depression and the sea. Here, at Alamein, our army turned and stood. It is a matter of pride to South Africans that the first three German attempts to pierce this thin line were made and repulsed on the South African sector. There were, in fact, during the first few critical days, little beyond Springboks and a few remnants of battered British units in the line. Axis flags were flown in expectation in Alexandria and Cairo.

As the Allies were now close to the main base of Alexandria our build-up was brisk and the line soon stabilised itself.

On June 22, 1941, Germany attacked Russia in the full belief that the campaign would be over in a few weeks. It was Hitler's most fatal decision. On December 8 came Pearl Harbour, a disastrous episode in American history. Three days later the British battleships *Prince of Wales* and *Repulse* were sent to the bottom by aircraft in the Gulf of Siam. Japan now ruled these seas. But Russia, in geographical size, in the inexhaustible masses of man-power and in the frigid cold of her winter, after initial setback, proved more than a match for the Germans. And so Russia, more than any other, slowly wore down the strength of Hitler's armies and gave us a breathing space. By the grace of God she fought on the same side as ourselves against a common foe, but she never really became an ally and was to be a great trial to Mr. Churchill and President Roosevelt.

During these critical years in the Middle East my father never failed to stress the importance of this battleground. It held not only the secret of oil, but was also the wedge that prevented Germany and Japan from a grand link-up. In the long ding-dong and costly struggle here, there was always the danger that Britain and America might despair and concentrate on the invasion of Europe. That would have been a disaster.

On the 30th September, 1941, at a special investiture the Governor-General, Sir Patrick Duncan, bestowed on my father, on behalf of the King, the rank of Field Marshal. The King's letter read:

"MY DEAR FIELD MARSHAL,

"I was hoping to present your field marshal's baton to you personally in England, but I well understand the reasons why you do not want to be away from South Africa for so long at the present time.

"I am therefore asking the Governor-General as my personal representative to hand it to you on my behalf.

"I would like you to know how proud my field marshals are to count you among their number.

"With all good wishes believe me,
"Yours very sincerely,
"GEORGE, R.I."

In his personal appreciation of the honour bestowed on my father Sir Patrick said: "I can tell you from my own experience that there is no one inside or outside South Africa who has to make decisions, whether on military strategy or state policy, who would not seek and follow the advice and council of the General. He is a great rock in a weary world. On the one side General Smuts met flattery and approval, on the other the breezes and blasts of enmity. But he has been neither softened by the one, nor hardened by the other. He has pursued his own way . . . this friend of ours is a man of many parts and of great distinction, a prophet not without honour save in his own country. . . . In spite of many adverse blasts there are few South Africans to-day who are not in the depths of their hearts proud to acknowledge General Smuts as a son of South Africa."

My father treated this birthday present with characteristic modesty: "I trust my friends and those who have known me as General Smuts for the last forty years will not hesitate to use my old title. I am still General Smuts to my friends in South Africa, and I hope that the continuity of many years will not be broken by the new appointment. I am too old now to change names."

LXXI OFFENSIVE PHASE

A RESHUFFLE took place in August, 1942, in the desert. General Alexander took over command of the Middle East from General Auchinleck and General Montgomery succeeded General Ritchie. The Army of the Nile became known for the first time as the Eighth Army. These appointments were decided on personally by Mr. Churchill when he passed through Cairo after the Moscow Conference, in conjunction with what he called "the massive judgment of Field Marshal Smuts who flew from Cape Town to Cairo to meet me".

In November, 1942, a vast armada of six hundred ships landed a British and an American army in French North Africa. These armies, under Generals Anderson and Clark, were to engage the Germans under von Arnim in the west, while Montgomery coped with Rommel in the east. By the personal intervention of Mr. Churchill with President Roosevelt, a large number of the new American Sherman tanks were diverted to the Eighth Army. Now for the first time these men could fight the German Mark III and IV Panzers on equal terms.

In a somewhat prophetic broadcast after the Abyssinian campaign on 14th July, 1941, my father had said: "The definite turn of the tide will probably begin in North Africa and the Springboks will have their share in the crowning glory, just as they have had in the first successes of the war." He went on to define our partnership with Russia: "Nobody can say we are now in league with the Communists and are fighting the battles of Communism. More fitly can the neutralists and the fence sitters be charged with fighting the battle of Nazism. If Hitler in his insane megalomania has driven Russia to fight in self-defence, we bless her arms and wish her all success, without for a moment identifying ourselves with her Communistic creed. Hitler has made Russia his enemy and not us friendly to her creed." Mr. Churchill quoted, and identified himself with, this latter part of the speech in the British House of Commons the following day.

The Nationalists, after the advent of Russia into the war,

switched to an anti-Communist type of propaganda and never failed to attack my father for fighting on the side of the Bolsheviks. But the Nationalists were throughout fighting a losing battle, for people's hearts were not in doctrines, but in the war. And so more and more support in the country swung to my father's side, and in by-elections we were invariably successful.

The advent of Japan into the war did not strike terror into the hearts of the Nationalists, who failed to look beyond their political noses. Rather did they rejoice in the mistaken belief that the inevitable withholding of aid from America might hasten the end of Britain. Now we had not only to cope with the active U-boat menace round our coasts, but had to safeguard our shores against a possible invader. The fall of France had led briskly to the establishment of the pro-Nazi Vichy government of Pétain. Madagascar, lying close to our shores, was French. There was a distinct possibility that it might be used as a U-boat refuge, or worse still, as a stepping stone for an invader. So my father sent a South African brigade to accompany the British landing force which was secretly despatched to the island. It was a smooth and swift conquest, but my father was severely attacked in Parliament for sending South African troops outside the country in contravention of their agreement. But after prolonged debate his explanation that Madagascar was more or less Africa, and that preparations against possible Japanese invasion were imperative, carried the day.

In October, 1942, my father paid his first wartime visit to Britain. After conferences in Cairo he boarded Mr. Churchill's semi-converted Liberator aircraft "Commando" and winged his way in the night deep inland across Rommel's territory to Gibraltar 2,500 miles away. Next night they took off again for Britain, flying far out west to sea as a security measure against marauding German aircraft.

The purpose of the visit was, as he said, "the acceleration of the plans of high strategy in the general conduct of the war". To reporters he said: "More and more Africa is emerging as a dominant feature in our war strategy, on which the future outcome of the war will largely depend. I have therefore continued to emphasise to the best of my ability the importance of the

African theatres of war. The central and vital position they occupy in our world strategy is becoming plainer every day. . . ." The purpose of this visit was also for discussions on general Allied war strategy and more specifically on Eisenhower's big North African landing just then being planned. His repeated stressing of the importance of the Middle East theatre was no idle obsession with him. It was a most vital necessity, for already eyes were turning across the Channel. The Americans, especially, were insistent that no time should be lost in getting going on the assault on Europe. It was a hopelessly premature idea but they seemed greatly set on it. It worried Mr. Churchill and my father considerably.

Another aspect of the war which was to worry these two leaders was that there was a tendency for Americans to want to send too much to the Far East. They were not interested so much in the war against Hitler as against Nippon. It was difficult to get them to see that Europe must come first in a grand strategy. We should do little more in the East than to ensure the safety of Australia and New Zealand. This Far-East complex became especially noticeable later on when assault craft were required for the landings in Normandy, and in the Burma campaign, when badly needed airlift was all employed across the Hump to China. These matters were settled as much by private cable between President Roosevelt and Mr. Churchill as by the Allied War Council. In these matters Mr. Churchill put considerable stock in the support he received from my father.

My father's sojourn in England was a strenuous one. Twice daily he attended meetings of the War Cabinet, a distinction extended him alone, of all Dominion ministers, whenever he was in London. He also attended meetings of the Defence Committee, the Privy Council and the Pacific War Council. Together with Mr. Churchill, he addressed a secret meeting with 3,000 coal miners in Westminster, to exhort them to greater efforts of production. He also had an audience with Queen Wilhelmina and broadcast a message in Dutch to the Netherlands and Belgium. In addition he had audiences with the King and kings of Yugoslavia and Greece, foreign émigré prime ministers, ambassadors and numerous people of importance. He found time to pay Mr. Lloyd George a visit at Churt and to look in at Christ's College, Cambridge.

And on his journey back he stopped at Gibraltar in mid-November for discussions with Admiral Cunningham and others.

But to the public this visit will be remembered more for one solitary speech he made than for all the other hard work. For my father had arrived in England at a "stern and sombre moment". The occasion was an invitation to address the combined Houses of Lords and Commons on 21st October, a distinction never previously accorded a Dominion statesman. As my father entered, the thousand members that crowded the hall rose to their feet and cheered him for fully two minutes. It was an unprecedented ovation from one of the most select audiences in the world. The occasion had been much publicised, and it was estimated by the British Broadcasting Corporation that an audience of fully fifteen millions was listening-in in Britain alone.

Lloyd George introduced my father. "No one in calmness or discernment exceeds him in this age," he said with deep emotion.

Britain had been through much, and a feeling of weariness and depression was creeping in. The object of my father's speech, which came to be known as "The Offensive Phase", was to awaken the people and to stir up a new mood of hope and vigour.

He spoke first of the "distinguished leadership" of Lloyd George and of Winston Churchill, and of their "imperishable service". He then went on:

I have spoken of the two great actors, the two greatest actors, in the drama, the continuing drama of our age. I call this a continuing drama because I view this war as a continuation of the last war, and the whole as perhaps another Thirty Years' War, which began in 1914, was interrupted by an armistice in 1918, improperly called a peace, was resumed with greater ferocity in 1939, and may continue (who knows?) till 1944. . . .

I have referred to two great actors in this drama of our age. There is a third and greater actor to be mentioned. I refer to the British people and the spirit that animates them and the young nations around them in the British Commonwealth of Nations.

One occasionally hears idle words about the decay of this country, about the approaching break-up of the great world group we form. What folly and ignorance, what misreading of the real signs of the times! In some quarters what wishful thinking! . . .

. . . And now I have come back to a country over which the fury
of war has swept, a country whose people have had to face in their
grimmest mood the most terrible onslaught in its history.

Many of its ancient monuments are damaged or gone for ever. The
blitz has passed over cities, ports, churches, temples, humble homes and
palaces, Houses of Parliament and Law Courts. Irreplaceable treasures
of one thousand years of almost uninterrupted progress and culture
and peaceful civilisation have disappeared for ever.

War, the horror people still call war, but in its modern scientific
form something very different from what passed under that name
before, war has come to this favoured land and attempted its worst.
Much has gone which is lost for ever.

But one thing is not lost—one thing, the most precious of all,
remains and has rather increased. For what will it profit a nation if it
wins the world and loses its soul? The soul remains. Glory has not
departed from this land. . . .

Look at the wonderful resurgence of the brave little nations of
Western Europe, whom no adversity, no defeat, dangers or chains can
hold down. . . .

And looking farther afield, watch the young nations of the British
Commonwealth at the job. Last and greatest of all, see America in her
invincible might under one of the greatest of leaders, marching to the
flaming ramparts of the world in East and West.

And shall we forget France, not dead, but like Lazarus only sleeping,
and waiting for the dawn to shake off the torpor which has temporarily
overcome her historic genius? . . .

The light of freedom which has guided our slow and faltering
advance through the ages still shines in the night which has overtaken
us. The glory is still with us, and we shall follow it with all our strength
and devotion to the new dawn which surely awaits our race.

But a rough and terrible passage lies before us, and it will call for
all our combined resources, all our concentrated will and effort, all our
highest leadership to carry us to our goal. There is no place for complacency or wishful thinking. . . .

I, therefore, pass on to the war situation. For the first three years of
the war our role had necessarily to be a defensive one. . . .

These are the steps that have marked our climb out of the abyss into
which the fall of France had all but plunged us:

First, the defeat of the German Luftwaffe over London.

Second, the treacherous attack of Germany on Russia, in spite of the
peace treaty between them.

Third, Pearl Harbour and its sudden and timely effect in carrying

America 100 per cent into the war while Admiral Nomura and Mr. Cordell Hull were talking peace at the conference table. . . .

We have now reached the fourth year of this war, and the defence phase has now ended. The stage is set for the last, the offensive phase. Let me set your minds at rest at once; I am not going to discuss the future offensive strategy of the war.

The amateur strategists can do that with greater freedom and less responsibility in the Press. I only wish to emphasise that one phase has ended and another must now begin. . . .

. . . We are approaching the point when both on the war fronts and on the home fronts in enemy countries the situation is ripening for far-reaching developments. . . .

Once the time has come to take the offensive and to strike while the iron is hot it would be folly to delay, to over-prepare, and perhaps miss our opportunity. Nor are we likely to do so—of that I feel satisfied. . . .

Hitler has tried to kill this spirit and to substitute for it some ersatz thing, something which is really its negation. He has instilled into German youth a new racial fanaticism.

He has sought strength in the ancient discarded forest gods of the Teuton. His faith is a reversion to the pagan past and a denial of the spiritual forces which have carried us forward in the Christian advance which constitutes the essence of European civilisation. . . .

I therefore come to the question: What is the sort of world which we envisage as our objective after the war? What sort of social and international order are we aiming at? These are very important questions, deserving of our most careful attention if we mean not only to win the war but also the peace.

Our ideas on these matters twenty-two years ago were much too vague and crude, and at the same time much too ambitious, with the result that when they came to be tested by hard experience they proved wanting, and their failure helped to contribute to the present conflict. With that experience before us we ought this time to hammer out something more clear, definite and practical. . . .

We do not want a mere League, but something more definite and organic, even if to begin with more limited and less ambitious than the League. "The United Nations" is itself a fruitful conception, and on the basis of that conception practical machinery for the functioning of an international order could be explored. . . .

With honesty and sincerity on our part it is possible to make basic reforms both for national and international life which will give mankind a new chance of survival and of progress.

Let this programme, by no means too ambitious, be our task, and let us now already, even in the midst of war, begin to prepare for it.

And may Heaven's Blessing rest on our work in War and in Peace.

LXXII EL ALAMEIN

PEOPLE had not long to wait for the offensive phase to commence. Montgomery, having completed his preparations, at dawn on 23rd October unleashed his "great thunderbolt of an assault", as Mr. Churchill described it, on the German lines at Alamein. Five hundred guns, standing twenty-three yards apart along a six-mile front, brought down a concentrated barrage on enemy positions and at the same time infantry and sappers surged forward to clear a way through the five-mile deep enemy minefield belt. Though stubbornly contested, all the first objectives were attained. Thereafter the progress was slow for ten days, but then our armour broke through and in a ten-hour tank battle at El Aqqaqir the opposing armour was heavily defeated, and the big pursuit was on. Seventy-three thousand prisoners were taken of whom eight thousand were Germans. They were parched and bewildered. In addition the Axis had lost a thousand guns and five hundred tanks.

It was a great victory.

But fortune favoured Rommel, for in the beginning of November torrential rains turned the desert into a quagmire, bogging down our pursuit armour. Had it not been for this, the enemy would undoubtedly have been rounded up before reaching the Egyptian border.

Rommel got away, and reinforced, was to fight many an additional battle. The biggest of these was at the Mareth Line in Tunisia. This happened just as German armour was teaching the inexperienced Americans a salutary lesson at Kasserine and Fiad.

Having learned the hard way that it was men and sound tactics and not just Sherman tanks that won battles, the Americans knuckled down and were to turn into formidable fighters.

Eventually our forces converged on Tunis and Bizerta, and having forced the strong Enfidaville hill positions, captured the two big towns and cornered von Arnim on the Cape Bon peninsula, where after unceasing bombing and attack, he was forced to capitulate on 13th May, 1943. General Alexander cabled to Mr. Churchill: "It is my duty to report that the Tunisian campaign is over. All enemy resistance is ended. We are masters of North Africa."

The quantities of war materials captured were enormous, including over 1,000 guns, 250 tanks and 520 aeroplanes, plus tremendous stores of ammunition and supplies. 291,000 prisoners were taken and enemy dead were estimated at 50,000, making a total of 341,000. This was well in excess of the numbers captured by Russia at Stalingrad. In all, North Africa had cost the Axis 600,000 men: Germany lost 250,000, including those killed in battle, severely wounded or lost at sea. Italy lost 350,000, and to this figure must be added the 300,000 she lost previously in East Africa (of whom many, however, were natives).

In Africa we had seen hard and strained times. Upon the collapse of France there had loomed large the question of the French fleet. There had been naval actions against French units at Dakar, Casablanca and Toulon. General Giraud, whom we had backed so heavily in our North African Free French plans, had proved a grave disappointment and we had perforce to turn to the Vichyite Admiral Darlan. An assassin soon put an end to him. In Britain there was General de Gaulle, tank expert, and reincarnation of Joan of Arc, a difficult man with a difficult mission.

Now all that was of the past, and we rejoiced in the conclusion of a long and hard phase of the war. From now on the tempo of events was steadily increased. For the first time, there was a definite smell of ultimate victory in the air. It prompted President Roosevelt at the Casablanca Conference in January, 1943, to demand "unconditional surrender".

Even Josef Stalin was impressed.

The Parliamentary session opened at Cape Town on 16th January, 1943. The general temper of the people had improved steadily. In Parliament my father's majority had swelled, through by-elections and resignations from anti-war groups, to twenty. With the close of the Session the present five-year term of Parliament expired. The time seemed propitious, and so my father decided on a General Election. This took place on the 7th of July, special arrangements having been made to enable all soldiers to vote.

The result was that 107 pro-war members were returned against 43 of the anti-war Nationalists, a resounding majority of 64. Never has a Government policy been more clearly endorsed or a South African Premier had better support.

*　　*　　*　　*　　*

My father now introduced some slight changes in his Cabinet: a Minister of Economic Development superseded the Minister of Commerce and Industries; the Ministry of Railways and Harbours was broadened into a Ministry of Transport; and a new Minister of Welfare and Demobilisation was appointed to cope with social security problems. The general criticism of this Cabinet, like all previous ones, was that it contained too much age and dead-wood. My father recognised this weakness, but seemed powerless to change it, for the provinces liked being represented by their senior men, who were, inevitably, their old stalwarts. An additional weakness was that my father so overshadowed his ministers that the Cabinet became positively lop-sided. It was a dictatorship every bit as much as Mr. Churchill's, and it worked just as well.

Emphasis in this new Government was on going full-steam ahead with the war and industrial effort, and at the same time paving the way for the problems of demobilisation after the war. General Brink was appointed as Director of Demobilisation to assist his Minister, Mr. Lawrence.

Two committees were established, a National Supplies Council, and a Cabinet Committee on Reconstruction, with my father as chairman.

The years that followed were ones of unprecedented activity and prosperity. It was truly a Golden Age. Never before had so much been accomplished in this country. Never before had things run so smoothly. Nor had our prestige and honour in the world abroad ever stood higher. The gold mines were going at

428

full blast turning out that precious commodity so urgently needed for payments in India and elsewhere. Everywhere new factories had sprung up to turn out the articles we had previously imported. Large concerns were turning out the heavier implements of war. In Parliament the Opposition seemed swamped and stunned. Subversive activities, under stricter control, were nervous and quiet. Farming was booming and there were no surpluses. Even our normally erratic climate was kind. In our ports there was great activity and hundreds of thousands of soldiers in transit enjoyed our hospitality. In the north our armies fraternised happily with those of the rest of the world. It was an age of broadmindedness and tolerance. For a while it looked as though we had shaken off our legacy of the past.

LXXIII SECOND WARTIME VISIT TO ENGLAND

ABOUT the middle of September, 1943, after the conclusion of the North African campaign, I was attached temporarily to my father as Aide on his second wartime visit to Britain. These duties I always found exacting. On the 27th my father arrived in Cairo, spending some days in discussions on war and diplomacy, reviewing his 6th Armoured Division in training at Khatatba, and going to Alexandria for discussions with Admiral John Cunningham, who took him for a trip round the outer harbour to see units of the newly-surrendered Italian battle fleet.

At Khatatba, while taking the salute as his giant men marched past, eighteen abreast, my father was so overcome with pride at their size and bearing that he could not refrain from exclaiming loudly to General Alan Brooke, Chief of the Imperial General Staff, who was sitting some way off to his left: "Brookie, look—look at those fine boys!"

Italy, tired, well-beaten and dispirited, had capitulated on the 8th. Six weeks earlier Mussolini had resigned, but had been kidnapped by German paratroopers before he could come across to the Allies.

On 1st October my father flew out west along the Mediterranean shores towards Tunis, passing over the old desert battlefields, now forsaken and almost obliterated by the shifting sands, across orderly but deserted Italian "Ente" settlements and the green of Cyrenaica, touching down at Castel Benito, Tripoli, for lunch. Then on again, low across the ancient Roman ruins at Sabratha and El Djem, remnants of days when this part of Africa was still well-watered and the great granary of Rome. At Tunis he was the guest of General Eisenhower in his villa on the hill at Sidi Bu Said, above the plains of ancient Carthage. Here my father met General Eisenhower for the first time, forming a favourable impression of this big, bluff, friendly American. The next day was spent in conferences with Eisenhower, Alexander and Tedder, the latter Commander of the Desert Air Forces and greatest wartime expert on air–army co-operation. These three were to prove a great and winning team in the battles for Italy and Europe that were to follow. Eisenhower was to shine as the great peace-maker between English and Americans, and a wonderful soother of ruffled feelings. Alexander was considered by many the most brilliant soldier of the war.

From Tunis my father made a rapid inspection of Sicily, flying round this rugged volcanic island, dominated by Mount Etna, past Messina, with a view across the two-mile wide straits to the Italian mainland, touching down at Gerbini to inspect South African Air Force personnel. Then he left for Malta, battered survivor of 3,000 Axis bomber sorties, where he lunched with the Governor, Lord Gort.

On the way across the Mediterranean from here to Algiers our Lodestar developed trouble in one engine and a great stream of black oil poured out across the wing, causing us to look apprehensively at the white wind-whipped sea below. Though the engine never faltered, we felt it wisest to set course back to Tunis again. Next morning the trip to Algiers was completed in General Spaatz's private Dakota, and in this dazzling city on a broad crescent of a bay, we delayed till 3 p.m., when we took off in

Mr. Churchill's new four-engined Avro York "Ascalon", specially sent to collect my father. Two hours later we turned left through the narrow Straits of Gibraltar and touched down a little later on an American airstrip at Rabat.

Here we tarried till early the next morning, when we took off along a dim flare-path for England. At 8.15 I saw some balloons sticking through the clouds and enquired of the navigator whether we were passing over a convoy. "No," he said, "that is Exeter." Soon we broke cloud, and there, stretched before me, I saw for the first time the grey villages, the green countryside and the innumerable hedgerows which go to make up the solid soil of England. At Northolt, outside London, we touched down, where a welcoming crowd awaited my father, and soon we were speeding to the Hyde Park Hotel, where my father usually stayed.

The occasion was a meeting of Commonwealth Prime Ministers, but this was only to form a minor portion of my father's business. Britain was now in her fifth year of war. Though the after-taste of the air blitz had not completely gone, a second minor blitz was to start during the visit, and for those in the know, there was the prospect of the use at any moment of new and terrible secret long-range weapons by the Germans against England, and more especially London.

Since the start of the war Britain's air force had grown out of all recognition and Air Chief Marshal Leigh Mallory's Tactical Air Force now totalled about 5,000 first-line machines. Fighter Command, which formed part of it, consisted of 86 squadrons of day fighters and an additional 20 of night fighters, in all about 2,000 machines. Though our old Mark IV Spitfires were inferior in performance to the newer German Messerschmitts and Focke Wulfs, the ones currently in production were vastly superior.

Equally notable strides had been made in Bomber Command, where Air Chief Marshal Harris was rapidly building up a formidable fleet of heavy strategic bombers of the Halifax and Lancaster type. "Bomber" Harris, a Rhodesian by birth, and once an infantry man under General Botha and my father in South-West Africa, had been made to walk such prodigious distances in the blazing sun in this campaign, that he swore he would never walk a yard again if he could help it. So he joined the Royal Flying Corps, where he became a famous night-fighter pilot over

London. A man of singular mind and determination, he made it his task to build for Britain a great bomber fleet, for more than any other man he had unlimited faith in this type of warfare. To these ideas of Harris, as much as to any other, we owe our victory in the war.

At No. 10 Downing Street and at Chequers, Britain's equivalent of Groote Schuur, I was privileged for the first time to see the two great men of the Empire, Mr. Churchill and my father, together. Between these two old friends there existed a warmth of feeling and mutual admiration that was touching to behold. In public it was "Prime Minister" and "Field Marshal", but otherwise it was simply "Winston" and "Jan". Mr. Churchill had in him more than the average gift of kindness and warmth of feeling, to which the inherent friendliness of my father was quick to respond. In each other's company they seemed to cast the cares of the world from their shoulders and to assume a new animation. They were a tonic to each other.

During the first week-end at Chequers I jotted down in my note-book: "Mr. Churchill is very keen that the Oubaas should spend some months in England, especially as Anthony Eden will be away in Russia, and he himself would soon be off to a Three Power Conference (Teheran) as well. He wants the Oubaas to take over his job while he is away and says that the British people will ask for nothing better than this. . . ."

I was to find Mr. Churchill a dynamo of mental action and resolution. This man was no mere figure-head. He ruled his Cabinet and military chiefs with a rod of iron and stern peremptoriness. His personal physician had no more influence over him than his valet Sawyers. My father was the only person he listened to with respect. It was incongruous, but lucky, that Mr. Churchill in a democracy was allowed powers no less than those of the Dictators. His judgment was seldom at fault.

Once again my father regularly attended meetings of the War Cabinet, which at the time was examining closely disturbing reports of terrible new secret German weapons. As much forced foreign labour was being utilised on these projects, our intelligence was unusually complete and this was further substantiated by constant aerial reconnaissance. It appears that various types of weapons were being developed at Peenemunde and Watten, including huge rockets, pilotless aircraft and glider-bombs. The War Cabinet was taking the threat very seriously, for it seemed not impossible that the Germans might drop 2,500 to 10,000 tons of explosives on Britain during November and December. The Germans were boasting openly that these "retribution" weapons would produce a million casualties in London during the first week. Mr. Churchill's technical adviser, Lord Cherwell, put the figure more modestly at 90,000 per month. Launching platforms for these devilish devices were going up along the Dieppe coast and on the Cherbourg Peninsula, but the public of Britain were luckily ignorant of all this.

Perhaps it was the fear of these weapons, perhaps fear of weariness and possible stalemate, that caused my father to stress the need for hurry in his speech on 19th October in the old blitzed Guildhall. Fifteen hundred illustrious people crowded the hall, and an additional three thousand listened in to loud-speaker extensions outside. Here are some of the salient passages from this memorable speech:

... The British people are united to a man behind the greatest leader they have ever had—the leader of whom, it is now amusing to recall, a gentleman prominent in your public life told me only a couple of years before this war that he had no party, no followers, and no hope of future leadership! Such are the ironies of history! I reminded my informant that in the later stages of the last war I had heard from a well-known diplomat exactly the same statement about Clemenceau, the Tiger, and that within a month thereafter he was Prime Minister of France and led his own country to final victory in the war.

You have found a greater man than Clemenceau, and he will lead you to a more conclusive and fruitful victory than that of the last war. ...

Another special reason which makes me feel happier to-day is the immense change which has come over the scene since my visit a year ago. I spoke then in a somewhat optimistic frame of mind. I said the defensive phase of the war was over for us, and we were passing over to the offensive which would lead to final victory. ...

Then, at two points of this vast war front, things happened which transformed the whole course of the war and, perhaps, of history. The battles of Stalingrad and El Alamein marked the real turning points in this war and will rank in history with the other decisive battles of the world. ...

... The Russian contribution to the war is immense and, indeed, has surpassed anything which even the most sanguine had expected of her. We are under no temptation to detract from the credit which is hers—which justly is hers. . . .

Our admiration for all this is unbounded, but our high sense of Russia's service should not make us depreciate our own contribution and make us think less of it in comparison. From El Alamein onwards, we of the British Commonwealth have done things on the battlefronts which will stand comparison with the contributions of any of the Allies. . . .

To this must be added our continuous bombing campaign against the enemy industrial centres and communications both in Germany and the occupied territories. Vast destruction has been wrought to the enemy resources and war effort. . . .

. . . It may be no exaggeration to say that our air bombing offensive against enemy centres has had, and is having the dimensions and effects of a large-scale additional front. . . .

We are now in the autumn of 1943. . . . We have climbed out of the depths and moved far forward. . . . And by the coming winter we shall have closed in upon Hitler's central fortress of Europe and be making our dispositions for the grand assault by our armies next year. . . .

One more concluding remark on the war. The time is short. The time factor in this fifth year of the war has become all-important, and from now on every moment counts. Already the moral and physical conditions, especially in the occupied countries, are indescribable, far worse than at the end of the last war. If Europe is to be saved from immeasurable disaster we must look upon the earliest ending of the war as of the first importance.

The longer this agony lasts and the worse it becomes the more difficult, if not impossible, it will be to restore the continent to normal conditions after this war. For carrying on his war Hitler is draining occupied Europe of all its resources of food, materials, and manpower. Everywhere the enslaved populations are being reduced to destitution and despair with the most brutal ruthlessness. Under threats of starvation they are being conscripted for war service and labour service, regardless of age or sex. They are moved about like dumb cattle, far away from home and friends, shot on the least show of resistance, shot as hostages even without any allegation of guilt, while Jews and Poles and other sections of the population are being systematically exterminated. . . .

And there is another reason of a more military character for avoiding delay. Hitler is no longer fighting for victory, but for time—for something to happen—for the accidents that so often set the run of events.

His only hope now is to prolong the war on the off chance of something happening—some new weapon, perhaps some difference among the Allies, war weariness, some unforeseen development, or what not—coming to his assistance and producing a stalemate or compromise peace.

The answer to all this should be our relentless, ever-increasing pressure exerted, without rest or pause, until the crack in his defences comes, and the whole imposing structure begins to topple. The policy of continuous pressure, begun in the Russian offensive since Stalingrad, and in our own increasing tempo of attack since El Alamein in the Mediterranean basin, should be prosecuted ceaselessly so that the final decision could be forced as soon as possible next year. . . .

But more difficult problems lie ahead in connection with the peace: the problem of aggression, the basic problem before our race, and the future of our civilised society. It is the last obstacle to be overcome in our long upward climb from our primeval savagery. Here we come up at last against the toughest and, let me add, one of the most heroic instincts of the race—the instinct of the animal in us, of the beast, but of the kings of beasts: the lion and the tiger. The Christian gospel still fights in vain against this earlier, more deeply founded gospel of our race, which is still upheld in some countries and circles as the code of honour and virtue for our society. The blond beast, the superman of nature, still hurls defiance at the Christian code with its gentle virtues.

That last battle in the West—for our Western civilisation—our race must win, or die. . . .

Let the greatest war in human history become the prelude to the greatest peace. To make it such will be the greatest glory of our age and its noblest bequest to the generations to come.

LXXIV WORK IN LONDON

WHENEVER possible my father got out of London on trips of inspection. These included visits to Fighter Command Headquarters at Bentley Priory, near London; to a tank experimental ground at Chobham; to Harris and his

Bomber Command at High Wycombe; to a Photographic Interpretation unit near Uxbridge; to a Combined Operations display
off the Needles, Isle of Wight, which my father viewed from
aboard a steam gunboat; to General Pile's Hyde Park anti-aircraft
defences, where he saw some of London's 500 heavy air defence
guns, rocket devices and aircraft detection devices; to the South
African Dr. Basil Schonland's Army Scientific Research Station
at Roehampton; and to the Aircraft and Armament Experimental Establishment at Boscombe Down.

The visit to Bomber Harris he found especially interesting, for
here, in stereoscopic aerial photographs, he was able to see the
terrible damage inflicted on Germany, a truly arresting spectacle
of destruction which greatly impressed him. Harris said that there
were only a hundred big towns in Germany, of which about fifty
contained major military objectives. Knock out those fifty, and
Germany could not continue the war. So far, of this fifty, seventeen had been 80 per cent or more destroyed, and a further
seventeen severely battered. All this had been accomplished in
the new heavy bomber offensive of this year. Had we been able
to double our effort, Harris said, Germany would by now have
been on her last legs. His big complaint was that people in high
places did not appreciate sufficiently the power of the bomber
offensive. He wanted my father's support for future top-line
councils. This he succeeded in doing, and Harris had no weightier
champion than my father. He said the bomber offensive was
keeping three million Germans tied up and an additional three
million had been rendered homeless.

Harris's claim for victory through air bombing alone was an
impressive one, but it proved somewhat over-optimistic, for it
failed to take into account the amazing resilience of the German
people, or their ability to do quick repairs and to transfer factories
underground. But even so, there can be no doubt that it was
bombing that strangled Hitler and brought him to his knees.
Rundstedt, Keitel, Kesselring and Jodl subsequently testified to
this.

The difference between Goering's and Harris's bombing was
that the Luftwaffe used light close-support machines, carrying a
small bomb load, whereas the R.A.F. used specially designed
four-engined heavy bombers carrying a four-ton bomb load,

with crews trained in night flying and using all the most modern radar and other target-locating devices. Accuracy, aided by specialist "Pathfinder" target markers, was of a high order and bombing was done in devastatingly brisk "saturation" raids. And much bigger and better bombs were used. The four-tonner was in regular service and already six-tonners were being used on rein-forced concrete U-boat pens. Official German sources quoted 1,200,000 casualties up to date, and the homes of 6,000,000 people destroyed.

On 4th September, 1943, in a national broadcast, my father told his listeners about the effects of the bomber offensive on Germany: "Air attack is already laying in ruins one after another of the great German industrial and munition centres. With our increasing tempo of bombing, most of the great centres of Germany will in another twelve months be in ruins, if not non-existent. If German internal morale broke in 1918 when Germany was intact and had escaped all ravages of the war which she had inflicted on her neighbours, how long will she endure a devasta-tion worse than that of the Thirty Years' War? Hitler's reliance and banking on night fighters to counter this fury of the air will be another vain hope, like the invasion of Britain, or the secret weapon, or the U-boat. The Fortress of Europe will disappear physically before this air onslaught by night and day. And its effects on civilian morale will be even more devastating than its physical effects. Already a nation-wide wail is going up from this blitz which is more than human nature can bear and which even sears the imagination. . . ."

In Italy the Allies appeared bogged down on a line south of Rome, due to a shortage of men. By the year-end Alexander would have fifteen divisions, whereas the Germans already had twenty-four to twenty-eight at their disposal in this theatre, with the possibility of quickly increasing this to sixty if they so wished it.

The general preparations for war everywhere were going pain-fully slowly. It prompted my father to remark privately: "I doubt if we shall ever finish this war. America is more concerned about money matters than beating Germany." But in the United States matters were brightening up, under the able direction of the Chief of Staff, George Marshall, and the country was ponderously getting geared for war. The one bright spot was what Mr. Churchill called the "mastery of the U-boat", which earlier on appeared to be gaining a stranglehold on Britain's long life-lines.

In a memorandum to President Roosevelt and Mr. Churchill on the war situation my father again stressed the importance of the Mediterranean theatre. Here we had our teeth into solid fighting, he said, whereas the whole of the Channel assault plans were still nebulous. He stressed, too, that he did not favour the idea of putting Europe and Italy under the same commander, for the two theatres were too distant and diversified. And he warned that under no circumstances must fighting be allowed to interfere with Bomber Command's offensive. It must remain quite outside the scope of army commanders. This memo, known as "Grand 17", made a favourable impression.

While in London, the Polish Prime Minister and the Foreign Minister, who were at loggerheads with Stalin, came to seek advice and assistance. "Put your case to President Roosevelt and Mr. Churchill and trust to them," my father said. "If anybody can help you, they will. But don't try to negotiate direct with Russia. Your future will be very hard for you—don't place too much hope upon it." After they had gone, he remarked to me: "Poor devils, there is not much one can do for them!"

Towards the end of the visit to Britain I noted in my diary: "It has been a very great privilege to have been present with the Oubaas at all his principal functions in London, for it has permitted a comprehensive study of public opinion regarding him. . . . And it has also brought me into contact with the leading personalities now in London—English, American and others. In this illustrious company the Oubaas has always shown up sufficiently well to dwarf the others. He stands out head and shoulders above any other person here. His pre-eminence as a statesman no one has disputed, and I daily hear it confirmed with greater emphasis. To people he is both a tonic and an elixir. He is also a symbol of steadfastness and security, and the embodiment of optimism and the higher values of life. They listen to him with bated breath, and I, for one, will admit that he cuts a very handsome and inspiring figure on the public platform, dressed in his military uniform, lavishly adorned with red insignias and bedecked with ribbons of service. His face looks so strong and handsome, with its healthy, rosy colouring, his blue eyes, his trim white beard, and snowy hair. When he talks his face lights up with expression and you cannot help being infected with his goodwill and sincerity. He may not be a great orator—as straightforward oratory goes—but he is a profound orator. He talks thoughts, not words . . . and that is why his utterances are so full of precious substance."

Though my father had probably done as much public speaking as any man, one never failed to gather the impression that he was speaking under some nervous tension. It was not the expression on his face, for that was pleasant, animated and soothing. Rather was it the somewhat jerky way he kept straightening his back and bracing his shoulders, or the abrupt way he kept putting his hand on the back of his hip, or moving his fingers. He seldom waved his arms or gesticulated. He never banged his fist to emphasise a point. Nor was he given to slang or colloquial expressions to obtain greater emphasis.

With the passage of years I thought he was inclined to grow long-winded and he often repeated himself, though admittedly in a diverse phrase.

But for all these little weaknesses, he was undoubtedly the most versatile and greatest, though not the best, speaker South Africa has produced. His speeches, no matter what the topic, were always light, uninvolved and readily understandable and well-laced with good humour and ready wit. There was nothing ponderous or funereal about them.

While spending a week-end with the Royal Family at Windsor Castle, His Majesty asked my father to deliver the Sunday sermon in St. George's Chapel. My father confessed to me the previous night that it was one of the most difficult requests he had ever had to comply with. Yet he delivered a truly amazing sermon. He likened this war to a "great crusade for good . . . There had been many religious wars in the past, but this was undoubtedly the greatest of them all". And so he passed happily from one theme to another. A member of the Household remarked to me afterwards that it was the "most religious sermon" he had ever listened to. And yet the word "God" had been used only twice.

At Leo Amery's private birthday party the conversation turned on India. I heard my father telling friends how fatal it would be if

Britain left India at this stage. It would be like taking the reinforcing steel rods out of concrete. The whole mass would simply crumble, and the good work of the past would lapse into confusion and bloodshed.

On 18th November Bomber Harris dropped 1,600 tons on Berlin. On the 22nd 800 R.A.F. heavies dropped another 2,450 tons in thirty minutes. People in Britain, but not in Berlin, were delighted. On the following night yet a further 1,310 tons were sent down. All this was in addition to the regular efforts of Mosquito intruders who were over every night in a strength of fifty or more. The all-out bombing of Germany was now getting into its stride.

LXXV EXPLOSIVE SPEECH

WHILE in London the Empire Parliamentary Association asked my father to deliver an address. He fittingly chose the theme "Thoughts on a New World". On 25th October, a week before returning to South Africa, he addressed about three hundred parliamentarians who crowded into Room 17 of the House of Commons. In this address he spoke from brief notes, not from a written draft as he almost invariably does on important occasions, and consequently he was able to put much of his personality into his words. A facsimile of a portion of his notes will be found on pages 232 and 233.

Here, in what he liked to term his "Explosive Speech", he said he was merely "thinking aloud". On this day he was at his scintillating best, and delivered what I consider the most thoughtful, far-reaching and profound utterance he had ever made, and the most impressive I have ever listened to.

Viscount Cranborne in introducing him said: "When I read the title of his Address I felt, as I expect most of you gentlemen felt, how typical it was of the Field Marshal, how characteristic it was of the whole of his life. If there is one particular aspect of his character in which he differs from the rest of us I think it is that he never looks back. . . He is always looking forward into the future, and he is always constructively moulding the future. He combines the experience of the old with the vision of the young. That I think is the reason why he has played so great a part in his own country; it is the reason why he occupies such a pre-eminent position to-day among the leaders of the nation."

Then my father rose and mildly and quietly commenced his address:

I intend to have a general informal talk with you this afternoon. I have no set opinions; I have no dogmatic beliefs to place before you; I am going to put before you certain lines of thought which are running through my own mind. I think the times in which we live do not really permit of very rigid fixed opinions, or of any dogmatic outlook on life or on the problems before us. We are facing to-day probably the most perplexing complicated human situation that has confronted the world for many generations, and anybody who thinks he has a panacea at his command to deal with these problems must either be sub-human or super-human. . . .

There are two dangers that face us in a situation such as ours to-day. One is the danger of over-simplification. In a world where the problems are so complex we may feel tempted to over-simplify and thus falsify the real character of the problems before us and miss the real solutions. The other danger is what I may call the danger of following slogans or catchwords, and so missing the real inwardness of the problems before us.

Let us look at these two dangers, which are really the same, though I wish to keep them separate for the moment. Let me refer briefly to the first danger of over-simplification. Where you are faced with a situation and problems such as we are faced with, you dare not over-simplify. In such circumstances you can only proceed towards a solution step by step in the old empirical British way, for if you begin to theorise and rationalise and simplify you are lost. . . .

That is one sort of situation that I consider probable—that we may never come to a peace conference at all, and that we may have to be satisfied with a comprehensive armistice on a basis of unconditional surrender, an armistice which will open the door to a long series of investigations and researches, which may take a long number of years before finality is reached. . . .

Again, take the other danger I have referred to—the danger of following slogans and catchwords. To-day we hear a great deal of democracy. We are fighting the battle of democracy. We are fighting for freedom. Of course we are. But these words become *clichés*, they become catchwords and vague slogans, which in the end do not lead you very far. . . . It must be quite clear to anybody who thinks of the real problems that face us that you will only get to practical solutions in the end if you have a good mixture of both democracy and freedom on the one hand, and of leadership on the other. . . .

. . . This war has taught us not only that idealism is not enough, and that universality is not the solution for our security problem, but it has also taught us that we cannot get away from the problem of power.

That is where this greatest war in history had its origin. We have found that all our idealism, all our high aspirations for a better world and a better human society, stand no ghost of a chance unless we reckon with this fundamental factor, and we keep power well in our minds when we search for the solution of the problem of security. The question of power remains fundamental, and it is, I think, the great lesson of this war. Peace unbacked by power remains a dream.

Therefore, looking at the situation that faces us in the near future, I would say that in arranging for a new world organisation for security, as we shall have to do, we shall have to provide not only for freedom and democracy, which are essential, but we shall also have to provide for leadership and for power. If we leave the future security of the world merely to loose arrangements and to aspirations for a peaceful world, we shall be lost.

We shall have to attend to the lesson we have learned, and see to it that in the new organisation to preserve peace for the future, we give a proper place to leadership and to power. To my mind that can be done much more effectively than in the Covenant of the League of Nations, by giving a proper place to the three great Powers that are now at the head of our United Nations.

Great Britain, the United States and Russia now form the trinity at the head of the United Nations fighting the cause of humanity. And as it is in war, so will it have to be in peace. We shall have to see to it that in the new international organisation the leadership remains in the hands of this great trinity of Powers. . . .

I think it was largely because in the League of Nations as constituted after the last war we did not recognise the importance of leadership and power that everything went wrong in the end. What was everybody's business in the end proved to be nobody's business.

442

Each one looked to the other to take the lead, and the aggressors got away with it. . . .

. . . I think one other flaw or weakness in the League organisation after the last war was the fact that we did not pay sufficient attention, or indeed any particular attention to the economic question. The Covenant much too exclusively followed political lines. We looked too much to political solutions. We have learned our lesson there, too. . . .

. . . We have moved into a strange world, a world such as has not been seen for hundreds of years, perhaps not for a thousand years. Europe is completely changing. The old Europe which we have known, into which we were born, and in which we have taken our vital interest as our Mother-Continent, has gone. The map is being rolled up and a new map is unrolling before us. We shall have to do a great deal of fundamental thinking, and scrapping of old points of view, before we find our way through that new Continent which now opens up before us.

Just look for a moment at what is happening, and what will be the state of affairs, at the end of this war. In Europe three of the Great Powers will have disappeared. That will be quite a unique development. We have never seen such a situation in the modern history of this Continent. Three of the five Great Powers in Europe will have disappeared. France has gone, and if ever she returns it will be a hard and long upward pull for her to emerge again. A nation that has once been overtaken by a catastrophe such as she has suffered, reaching to the foundations of her nationhood, will not easily resume her old place again. We may talk about her as a Great Power, but talking will not help her much. We are dealing with one of the greatest and most far-reaching catastrophes in history the like of which I have not read of. The upward climb will be a bitter and a long one. France has gone, and will be gone in our day, and perhaps for many a day. Italy has completely disappeared, and may never be a Great Power again. Germany will disappear. Germany at the end of this war will have disappeared, perhaps never to emerge again in the old form. The old Bismarckian Germany may perhaps never rise again. Nobody knows. The Germans are a great people, with great qualities, and Germany is inherently a great country, but after the smash that will follow this war Germany will be written off the slate in Europe for long, long years and after that a new world may have arisen.

We are therefore left with Great Britain and with Russia. Russia is the new Colossus in Europe—the new Colossus that bestrides this Continent. When we consider all that has happened to Russia within the

last twenty-five years, and we see Russia's inexplicable and phenomenal rise, we can only call it one of the great phenomena in history.
It is the sort of thing to which there is no parallel in history, but it has
come about. . . .

Then you will have this country of Great Britain, with a glory and
an honour and a prestige such as perhaps no nation has ever enjoyed
in history; recognised as possessing a greatness of soul that has entered
into the very substance of world history. But from a material economic
point of view she will be a poor country. She has put in her all. This
country has held nothing back. There is nothing left in the till. She has
put her body and soul and everything into it to win the battle of
mankind. She will have won it, but she will come out of it poor in
substance.

The British Empire and the British Commonwealth remain as one
of the greatest things of the world and of history, and nothing can
touch that fact. But you must remember that the Empire and the
Commonwealth are mostly extra-European. Those are the overflows
of this great British system to other continents. The purely European
position of Great Britain will be one of enormous prestige and respect, and will carry enormous weight, but she will be poor.

Then outside Europe you have the United States, the other great
World Power. You will therefore have these three Great Powers:
Russia the Colossus of Europe, Great Britain with her feet in all continents, but crippled materially here in Europe; and the United States
of America with enormous assets, with wealth and resources and
potentialities of power beyond measure. The question is how you are
going to deal with that world situation. I am just painting before you
the picture of the new world that we shall have to face, which will be
something quite unlike what we have had to deal with for a century,
or indeed for centuries.

Many people look to a union or closer union between the United
States of America and Great Britain, with her Commonwealth and
Empire, as the new path to be followed in the future, in this world
which I am describing as facing us. I myself am doubtful about that.
I attach the greatest importance to Anglo-American collaboration
for the future. To my mind it is, beyond all doubt, one of the great
hopes of mankind. But I do not think that, as what I might call a
political axis, it will do. It would be a one-sided affair. If you were to
pit the British Commonwealth plus the United States against the rest
of the world, it would be a very lop-sided world. You would stir up
opposition and rouse other lions in the path. You would stir up international strife and enmity which might lead to still more colossal

struggles for world power than we have seen in our day. I do not see human welfare, peace, security along those lines. . . .

But then I am troubled with this thought—and this is the explosive stuff I am coming to. In that trinity you will have two partners of immense power and resources—Russia and America. And you will have this island, the heart of the Empire and of the Commonwealth, weak in her European resources in comparison with the vast resources of the other two. An unequal partnership, I am afraid. The idea has repeatedly floated before my mind, and I am just mentioning it here as something to consider and to ponder—whether Great Britain should not strengthen her European position, apart from her position as the centre of this great Empire and Commonwealth outside Europe, by working closely together with those smaller Democracies in Western Europe which are of our way of thinking, which are entirely with us in their outlook and their way of life, and in all their ideals, and which in many ways are of the same political and spiritual substance as ourselves. Should there not be closer union between us?

Should we not cease as Great Britain to be an island? Should we not work intimately together with these small Democracies in Western Europe which by themselves may be lost, as they are lost to-day, and as they may be lost again? They have learned their lesson, they have been taught by the experience of this war when centuries of argument would not have convinced them. Neutrality is obsolete, is dead. They have learned the lesson that, standing by themselves on the Continent, dominated by one or other Great Power, as will be the future position, they are lost. Surely they must feel that their place is with this member of the trinity. Their way of life is with Great Britain, their outlook and their future is with Great Britain and the next world-wide British system. . . .

Let me say a few words about the Commonwealth and Empire, because after all we remain a very great world community. It is not only the spiritual power which we command as no other group on earth commands. It is not only that we possess that strength of soul, that inner freedom which is greater than all the freedoms of the Atlantic Charter, but we are also a very powerful Group, scattered though we are over the world. And we must look to our own inner strength, our inner coherence, our system, our set-up and pattern, to see that it is on safe lines for the future.

What is the present set-up in our group? We are an Empire and a Commonwealth. We are a dual system. In that dual system we follow two different principles. In the Commonwealth we follow to the limit the principle of decentralisation. In the Commonwealth this group of ours has become wholly decentralised as sovereign States. The members of the group maintain the unbreakable spiritual bonds which are stronger than steel, but in all matters of government and their internal and external concerns they are sovereign States.

In the Colonial Empire, on the other hand, we follow quite a different principle. We follow the opposite principle of centralisation. And the centralisation is focused in this country, in London. The question that arises in my own mind, looking at the situation objectively, is whether such a situation can endure. To have the Empire centralised and the Commonwealth decentralised, to have the two groups developed on two different lines, raises grave questions for the future. Is this quality in our group safe? Should we not give very grave thought to this dualism in our system? . . .

. . . The question is whether there should not be an approach between the two systems so as to eliminate gradually this dualism and have a closer approach between the two, and bring Empire and Commonwealth closer together.

Following that line of thought it has seemed to me that our colonial system consists of too many units. If there is to be decentralisation you will have to decentralise from the Colonial Office in London, and give administrative powers of all sorts, and all degrees, sometimes to very small units, or to some still in a very primitive stage of development, and that might be a risky thing to do.

Our colonial system consists of a very large number of units in all stages of development, and if there is to be decentralisation and devolution of power and authority, it becomes, in my opinion, necessary to simplify the system, to tidy it up, to group smaller units, and, in many cases, to do away with units which have simply arisen as an accident by historic haphazard. They should never have existed as separate units, and in many cases their boundaries are quite indefensible. You know how this great show has grown up historically, by bits of history here and there, without any planning, and, of course, inevitably so. But the time has come, or the time may be coming now, when it is necessary to tidy up the show, to reduce the number of independent colonial units, to abolish a number of these separate administrations scattered pell-mell over the Colonial Empire, and to reduce the consequent expenditure which is a burden on the local peoples, many of them very poor, undeveloped and with very small resources. It is a heavy burden on them, and their slender resources might be devoted to better purpose than carrying on a heavy administrative machine, beyond their capacity. . . .

As you will solve this problem of centralisation in the Colonial

Empire you will also solve another equally important problem. And this brings me to the Commonwealth. In many of these cases of colonial reorganisation where there will be new and larger colonial groups under a Governor-General, you will find that it is quite possible to bring these new groups closer to a neighbouring Dominion and thereby interest the Dominion in the colonial group. In this way, instead of the Dominions being a show apart, so to say, having little or nothing to do with the Empire, and taking very little interest in it, these regional Dominions will become sharers and partners in the Empire. You will tighten up your whole show; you will create fresh links between the Empire and the Commonwealth, and create a new interest and life in the system as a whole. You will create better co-operation, and you will bring to bear on the problems of these colonial groups the experience and resources and leadership of the local Dominions, too. In this way you will tighten up your whole system, and instead of being two separate systems, the one decentralised and looking after its own affairs, and the other centralised and centred in London, you will have a much more logical co-operative and statesmanlike arrangement. . . .

. . . I look upon this Empire and Commonwealth as the best missionary enterprise that has been launched for a thousand years. This is a mission to mankind of good will, good government and human co-operation, a mission of freedom and human helpfulness in the perils that beset our human lot. . . .

I utter no dogmatic conclusions, I have no set ideas, I am simply giving you the lines of thought that run in my mind when I survey the new situation facing us in the world. I want us not only to think about the other countries who are to-day labouring in dire trouble all over the world, but also to pay some attention to our own show, which I think also requires a little looking after, and especially at a time like this, when a new world is in the making.

I noted in my diary on that day: "I listened to him enthralled. The rest of the audience were equally overcome, and there was not a single question at question time. The Chairman, who had been deeply moved, described it as a 'profound and thought-provoking speech . . . probably the most remarkable that most of us have ever heard'. The First Lord of the Admiralty, seconding Lord Woolton, quoted some appropriate lines from Emerson and said: 'He has given us some "explosive" thoughts, as he calls them, but they contain the fundamentals of the problems that lie before us. . . . He can stand before us at his age with a great record, with no turning to the right or to the left from those early great inspirations he had; and he is able to say, as perhaps all of us are not able to say, that he has never forsaken the pursuit of the truth which he set himself to follow.' "

At the time all cheered the address enthusiastically, but France was to take grave exception to her description as a spent force. Mindful of this fact, some Member of Parliament subsequently had second, diplomatic, thoughts on this issue, but time so far has certainly proved my father right in saying that the rise of France to her former position will be a slow and difficult one.

The return journey to Africa was delayed for two days at Portreath, on the attractive coast of Cornwall, while anticyclones made flying conditions in the Bay of Biscay too hazardous. But at 3 a.m. in the dark of the 5th of December, on a slightly more favourable weather report, the York took off. As the weather closed in the aircraft climbed higher and higher and soon we were flying at 16,000 feet, but still there was no break in the towering tumble of clouds. Eventually we flew most of the night, on oxygen, at 22,000 feet, steering down the gigantic valleys between the billowing masses, which were almost continuously lit up by vivid lightning flashes, touching down after 2,400 miles at Tunis at 1.15 p.m. Wing-Commander Slee to this day carries that 'favourable' met. report in his pocket. A Dakota which left on the same route ten minutes after our York was never heard of again.

The following evening in Cairo my father dined quietly with President Roosevelt at Mena. All he would say to reporters was that "we two Dutchmen got on splendidly". He had, however, taken the opportunity of once more stressing the importance of the Middle East and warned that it should not be weakened in any way by diverting troops to the European theatre. He had also pointed out the dangers of trying to tackle Japan at the same time as Germany, which must come first in the grand strategy.

During their stay in Cairo, Mr. Churchill, who had returned with Roosevelt from a conference with Stalin, found time to execute a few oil paintings of the pyramids, two of which he presented to my father. One now hangs in Libertas in Pretoria, while the other has remained with our family.

The Teheran Conference was not an unqualified success. Russia

448

surging forward in massive, bloody assault on a broad front, felt she was bearing the heat of the day alone, and to placate her, the Western Allies made concessions they were later to regret. Here, too, President Roosevelt showed his fateful failing in placing too much trust in Josef Stalin. Mr. Churchill was powerless to avert it.

LXXVI THIRD WARTIME VISIT TO ENGLAND

O N 21st April, 1944, my father left on his third wartime visit to England. The occasion was a Commonwealth Prime Ministers' Conference.

In Cairo, as always, he was strenuously involved in military and diplomatic conferences. The first-hand knowledge he gathered here he took with him to the councils in London. On this occasion almost his entire attention was focused on Greek matters. A wave of Communism had swept through the Greek fighting forces, and there had been mutinies in her naval units in Alexandria harbour and in her infantry brigade at Burg-el-Arab in the desert just outside the town. These had been quelled with minor loss of life by loyal Greek elements and Allied troops.

At Cairo Mr. Churchill's York "Ascalon" was awaiting my father, and at Algiers the journey was broken for discussions with General Jumbo Wilson. Thereafter he flew to Gibraltar and after a night trip across the sea arrived in London on the morning of the 28th.

In the Middle East the Allies now had a million and a half troops, consisting of twenty-seven fighting divisions, against the German twenty-three. Our tank superiority was two-and-a-half to one. It was, from the military point of view, a satisfactory state of affairs, though it was indeed a moot point whether we were creating a diversion for the Germans in Italy, or vice versa. My father was never keen on fighting in Italy, for with its mountains and rivers it was a country ideally suited to defence. He always felt that Yugoslavia held greater possibilities.

Britain we were to find in full gear for the great Overlord assault across the Channel. The preparations were complete and everything was ready. The forces and equipment were considered adequate, but there was some disquiet about an acute shortage of landing craft. America was the chief manufacturer of these, and now, as ever, had a tendency to concentrate too much on the Far East.

We spent the first week-end with Mr. Churchill at Chequers. He was looking none the worse for his recent severe bout of pneumonia. He told my father that Overlord had been postponed from May 8, but the reasons were not then quite clear. There appeared to be some differences of opinion in Army councils.

The preparations for the assault involved the isolation of Normandy from the rest of Europe by a drastic severing of all communications. This meant the heavy bombing of the French rail and bridge systems, a procedure that might unfortunately involve the killing of 40,000 Frenchmen. The implications of such a step were clear, but it was unavoidable if the success of our landings was to be assured against the arrival of German reinforcements from elsewhere in Europe.

Montgomery was to be the General-in-Charge across the water and his opponent was none other than Rommel. He remarked to me that he thought he had more than the measure of this old adversary.

The Prime Ministers' Conference involved two meetings daily. In addition to problems and matters of diplomacy, the general war situation was also reviewed. The German Air Force consisted of 5,700 machines of which half were fighters. Only 16 per cent of these fighters were opposing Russia, while 44 per cent were on the Western Front. The R.A.F. had an air superiority of 5 to 1 on the Western Front and Russia had a 3 to 1 superiority. The Allied bomber force had a total lift of 15,000 tons in the European theatre. Germany had throughout the war dropped only 65,000 tons of bombs on Britain, whereas last month alone we had dropped 66,000 tons. In addition the R.A.F had, since the start of the war, laid 32,000 sea mines in German shipping lanes. Berlin had already absorbed four times the weight of bombs that London had. German operational U-boat strength was 170. So far we had sunk 400. Germany had forty-six divisions in France, twenty-three in Italy and twenty-one in Yugoslavia, where the interests were oil and chrome.

Southern England was one vast military camp. Every bit of open ground was occupied by soldiers, tanks, guns and transport. It was almost impossible for my father to go for his walks on the North Downs at Box Hill and the Dorking Gap or elsewhere. All were ready for embarkation at Portsmouth at a moment's notice.

The bombing tempo was slowly being stepped up. In one raid in April we dropped 4,800 tons, and the United States Air Force dropped 1,163 tons on Berlin in one daylight raid. This month the U.S.A.A.F. exceeded the R.A.F. bomb damage for the first time and from now on their effort was to mount steadily till it was almost twice that of the R.A.F. As all American bombing was done during daylight hours, it meant that Germany for the first time was subjected to round-the-clock devastation. The American Flying Fortresses also took a very heavy toll of German fighter aircraft that came up to intercept.

My father at this time was involved in a personal diplomatic tussle with his old friend Dr. Salazar, Prime Minister of Portugal, over the question of wolfram supplies to Germany. The Foreign Office, too, were hard at Salazar and the struggle was to drag on for a long time, for Portugal was in a difficult position in this matter.

Post-war financial topics were also occupying much time at the Prime Ministers' Conference. My father remarked to me that they were simply chasing shadows, for before the war was over, conditions would have changed so radically that all their present decisions would be completely obsolete. "It was the same in the last war," he said, "when all the lofty ideas and resolutions were proved to be quite worthless."

He addressed the Conference frequently. On one occasion it was on world affairs. The dominant note was his grave distrust of the Russia of the future. Russia would swallow up the Baltic States and part of Finland, "that we could not prevent", and thereafter would insinuate her Communistic doctrines into

Poland, France, the Balkans, possibly Germany, Iraq and Persia, and also China. She would be a colossus without fetters, to roam the world at will. He reiterated his belief that France was sleeping even more deeply than Lazarus and that she would have to be handled with care and understanding.

The Allied production machine was in full swing. Aircraft were coming off the lines at $14\frac{1}{2}$ per hour; guns 8 per hour; shells 100,000 per hour and small arms ammunition at three million rounds per hour. All this was apart from the prodigious ship-building programme.

The U-boat was by now largely mastered. In 1939 we lost eleven ships for every U-boat sunk. Now the figure had dropped below parity. It was one of the most heartening signs in the war.

Russia is fond of belittling the aid given her by the other Allies, but a perusal of figures does not bear this out. Up to this stage, at great cost, along the hazardous Murmansk route, Britain had diverted over eleven million tons of shipping, £39,000,000 worth of raw materials, 6,778 aircraft and 5,031 tanks. American aid amounted to 8,800 aircraft, 190,000 trucks, 36,000 Jeeps, 5,200 tanks and 30,000 other types of military vehicles.

In Egypt King Farouk was at loggerheads with his Prime Minister. Years before Farouk's arrogance had been curbed when a squadron of our armoured cars surrounded the Abdin Palace.

In Italy on May 11 the front roared into life with a barrage three times as heavy as that of El Alamein.

On 16th May the curtain was rung down on the first Common-wealth Prime Ministers' Conference. "In many ways", I noted, "it has been a great success, especially in so far as controversy has been completely avoided, and in the good will of the exchanges. It serves, too, to indicate that we merely differed in detail and not in principle, and that we are moving along the same road to the future. The Conference has been largely exploratory and no real resolutions have been thrashed out, but it does indicate for the future that we can at least get together and discuss contentious subjects in a friendly mood. The range of subjects covered was very comprehensive and most of the delegates will leave with a sound background to current world affairs. . . . There has been much mutual patting on the back. So we are all happy and beaming."

On May 19, Birmingham conferred its Freedom on my father. Former freemen included Lloyd George, the three Chamberlains and Lord Roberts.

Here in the Midlands was Britain's greatest armaments manufacturing centre, and factories stretched solidly for many miles. My father toured a portion of the vast Nuffield Mechanisation group. In the town hall he addressed a crowd of 2,800 leading citizens. Here once more he stressed the urgent need for finishing the war quickly. He reiterated his belief in a federated Europe and a League of Nations backed up with powers sufficient to maintain international peace. "We shall not see the same old world after the war," he said. We were coming to a world of social security for the common man. And finally he ended with a warning to the Leftist political elements: "Let us follow rather the Russia of Tolstoi, not of Karl Marx."

The week-end he spent quietly with his daughter Cato in Somerset, where he had a long walk in the Mendip Hills, overlooking Sedgemoor.

Whatever factors we might have had aiding our cause in the war, none fought with quite such telling effect as the magic device Radar. We were luckily well ahead of the enemy in this field of research. Here is some idea of what radar meant to us: it enabled one day-fighter to do the work for which three to five were required previously; it multiplied the usefulness of night-fighters up to fifty times on dark nights; it improved mass area bombing over fifty times; it made U-boat hunting five to ten times as effective at night; anti-aircraft gunnery was improved five times and searchlights ten times; and U.S.A.A.F. strategic bombing was made seven times as effective.

The Germans were feverishly busy with the launching devices for their secret pilotless weapons. Ninety-six V1 and seven Giant Rocket (V2) sites were observed going up on the French coast in the Pas de Calais and Cherbourg areas. Since last year we had dropped 23,000 tons of bombs on these places, damaging 90 per cent of the installations. But simpler modified launchers were going up, and we were now constantly hammering at these on the so-called "Invasion Coast".

On 24th May the second phase of the Italian offensive commenced, the assault on the powerful Hitler Line. Forty divisions, including our South African 6th Armoured Division, were locked in mortal combat. We were determined to see that Hitler could spare no reinforcements from here for the Channel. Our intention in Italy was not to advance all the way up to the Brenner Pass and enter Germany from that direction. We merely wished to secure the valuable Foggia airfields, to liberate Rome and to establish a firm front on a suitable line between Pisa and Rimini. Italy was a dead-end so far as entry into Germany was concerned. In this respect the "soft under-belly" of the Balkans offered much better possibilities. My father, and indeed Churchill, had always been a great champion of the Balkans.

My father had by now built up his South African Air Force strength in the Middle East to twenty-seven squadrons. We were stronger than the R.A.F. in this theatre and were surpassed only by the U.S. 14th Air Force. Two-thirds of the Sappers in the Middle East were South Africans. It was a fine record for a country which had started under the cloud of neutrality.

Six weeks previously the final "softening" of communications in France had commenced. Vast air armadas were streaming out from England daily. It was an impressive sight. It was plain to all that the big lunge was imminent.

London was taking the prospect of the impending cross-Channel assault very calmly. There was no evidence of panic, hysteria or enthusiasm. The people were just plodding along quietly, in their solid, unruffled way. There were very few soldiers about on the streets, but long lorry convoys would pass through the city daily, and occasionally a few tanks and Bren-gun carriers would lumber noisily down Knightsbridge past our hotel. But those were the only outward signs of war—that is, if one excluded the constant drone of air armadas passing high over the city. Now and then you would catch a glimpse of a flight of Fortresses or Liberators very high up in the grey-blue skies, appearing like tiny bright specks as the sunlight glinted on their silver bodies.

Sometimes, towards evening, squadrons of Marauders would be observed streaking low across the city, heading in the direction of the "Invasion Coast", moving very fast and making a great noise.

LXXVII OVERLORD

M Y father was growing impatient at the delay in launching our Second Front offensive. There seemed to be all sorts of last-minute hitches, which he attributed to over-cautiousness. It was a great pity, for weather conditions had been almost ideal a month ago.

On June 2 he went with Mr. Churchill to Portsmouth to see the troops embarking. Here, on a tour round the harbour, he was to see not only a portion of the myriads of assault craft, but also other strange floating devices. These were huge floating drums with mobile piping wound up in great coils like rope. These were to lay pipelines across the ninety miles of Channel to the beaches. There were the vast floating concrete blocks known as Phœnix which were to be towed across and sunk to form big harbours. They were to be connected to the shore by massive floating bridges known by the code word Mulberry.

All was ready now for the final word from General Eisenhower. The favourable dates, corresponding to the moon cycle, were 2 to 6 June. Failing that there would have to be a postponement of twelve days till the next favourable period. But as all the men were already briefed and on board, this, for security, as well as for physical reasons, would obviously be impossible. In any case this would also throw out of phase the big synchronised Russian offensive.

On the afternoon of the 3rd my father, with Mr. Churchill, attended a meeting at General Eisenhower's forward headquarters in a wood just outside Portsmouth, to consider weather conditions. The meteorological report was most unfavourable, and so the zero hour was put off till 4 a.m. next morning for reconsideration. But the position did not look hopeful. My father seemed as deeply depressed at this news as I have ever seen him. He kept muttering that it was "terrible—terrible".

The beaches of Normandy were defended with elaborate under-water stakes, blocks, explosive devices, hedgehogs and wire tangles. These could only be tackled at low tide. Thousands of

the hedgehogs were old French anti-tank defences newly trans-
planted by the Germans.

Both Mr. Churchill and my father felt that we had based our
landings on too ideal conditions. We demanded a clear sky, a
low tide and a smooth sea all at the same time. My father said:
"We must be more audacious!" We must be prepared to sacrifice
a few thousand additional men at the start, for it would pay
handsomely in the long run.

At 4 a.m. the weather was still foul, so Eisenhower called for
a twenty-four-hour postponement. The present weather conditions were the worst for six years, the experts said, but better
weather was predicted from Wednesday onwards. They were
wrong.

General Eisenhower, the man upon whom the great decision
depended, was a man of iron nerve, and seemed the most unruffled of all. He was sitting unmoved in his caravan enjoying
a game of poker with his staff. My father was filled with admiration. Ike was a "big man", he said.

In the afternoon our entourage could wait no longer and
returned to London. It was a tense period.

Tuesday the 6th of June will long remain a great day in the
hearts of free men. At dawn five divisions streamed ashore on
the flat beaches. During the night 20,000 paratroops had been
dropped far to the rear on strategic points, under conditions of
complete surprise. The whole move, in fact, surprised the Germans, who did not consider invasion possible in such unfavourable
weather. During the night 5,197 tons of bombs had been dropped
on coastal batteries and strongpoints.

Amidst scenes of wild enthusiasm Mr. Churchill announced at
noon, in the House of Commons, that the invasion had commenced, adding that everything appeared to be going according
to plan. He said that over 4,000 ships and thousands of lesser craft
had been involved in the landings and that he had 11,000 aircraft
available to support the operations.

A woman who had a room below our suite in the Hyde Park
Hotel told friends that she had heard my father pacing up and
down all night. This was not true for I know that my father slept
soundly.

I was amazed to see how quietly London took this great day

of retribution for which she had waited so long. It was the greatest display of suppressed emotion, almost complete indifference, I have ever witnessed.

In spite of rapidly deteriorating weather conditions, by the night of the 8th we had moved almost a quarter of a million troops across and vast quantities of stores and equipment. By the end of the second day we had 159,595 men and 16,715 vehicles across. Put in a different way it means that during these two days we had ferried across as many men, and infinitely more equipment, than it took us eight months in the First World War. And we were then using the narrowest part of the Channel and were disembarking in proper ports in a friendly France. This was a hundredfold improvement on our old effort, and it was accomplished during stormy weather.

True to his word, Stalin opened his great offensive on the 11th, in the Karelia sector.

At this stage my father met General Marshall, Chief of the American General Staff, for the first time. He was much impressed by this man who had worked such wonders with the American armed forces. Without Marshall Normandy would not have been possible at this stage.

On the 16th, six days after the invasion, my father accompanied Mr. Churchill to Normandy in the destroyer *Kelvin*, landing at Courseulles in the Canadian sector not far from Dives, whence the Norman Conqueror had set out in the opposite direction nine centuries before. Thereafter they made their way by jeep to Montgomery's headquarters near Bayeux. As the initial German retreat had been precipitate, there was not much sign of damage in this area, though there was evidence of Bomber Harris's work and also extensive inundations of low ground, while open spaces were planted with poles as a precaution against Allied glider landings. The two Phœnix harbours, with their Mulberry bridges, each 3,000 yards long, were each bigger than Dover and working at full pressure. There was also Rhinoceros, a vast floating platform for unloading, and Bombardon, the artificial breakwater. At each of three points along the coast there were other breakwaters formed by sinking ten to twelve ships of 8,000 tons. All these proved indispensable during the stormy weather.

Off the mouth of the Orne Mr. Churchill felt he would like to fire a few shells from the *Kelvin* in anger at the German positions, and a few rounds were accordingly let off in the direction of Caen. They were, however, anti-aircraft shells, set to safe, so would not have exploded on contact.

At 6 p.m. we said good-bye to Normandy, and soon the silvery glint from the 300 beachhead balloons was all that remained of a memorable day. We had gazed with interest on Hitler's much-vaunted Iron Wall and the flat dune-crested beaches up which our men had streamed on the 6th.

The initial assault was over, and we were now in the period of build-up, after which a renewed offensive would follow.

In Italy Rome had fallen and our troops were hot on the heels of Kesselring.

The war chiefs were at this time seriously considering the question of creating a big diversion to Overlord by a major invasion of southern France, up the Rhone. My father, and most of the British planners, did not favour this diversion, for Italy was serving the purpose sufficiently well.

On June 14 the first few VI bombs fell in London. It was not till midnight June 15/16 that operation Crossbow started in earnest. The sky was full of searchlight beams and bursting ack-ack shells and then there was the rumble of a distant big explosion. Two minutes later came the next, its impulse duct motor making a very loud purring noise, like some great motor-cycle bearing down on one. A yellow glow issued from its tail, which turned to red before it cut out and plunged into the earth with a massive, rocking rumble. The hotel shook and trembled. My father foolishly stood before his window watching the display. All night long these diabolical devices kept purring along and dying off with an explosion. All night long the anti-aircraft barrage roared away. The alert never lifted.

This was the start of the flying bomb assault which was to go on for three months and to prove a great trial to London. Each bomb demolished a whole block of houses, but only 4,200 of the 9,250 launched, or 5,900 that crossed the Channel, were able to reach London. Altogether 4,261 were brought down by fighter aircraft, barrage balloons and gunfire. Had they been a hundred miles an hour faster, it would have been a different story.

By the end of the first day people had grown more accustomed to the V1 and the anti-aircraft guns were no longer used. But the bomb was to kill a hundred people daily and injure 400, as well as damaging 20,000 houses. It was much more than a nuisance.

At midnight on the 21st my father set out from the Cornish coast in his own new Avro York, with Piet Nel at the controls, landing at Algiers for discussions with General Jumbo Wilson.

I had come away from England with heavy forebodings about our future relations with France and Russia. In France there was a growing touchiness, and in Russia increasing mistrust and aggressiveness.

In the war councils there was a renewed tendency to divert men from Italy to France. My father felt it would be better to exploit our crushing victory in Italy and to drive on into Austria.

From Algiers we flew across to the broad Bay of Naples, past Vesuvius and along the flooded Pontine Marshes and cratered battlefields of Anzio, landing at Ciampino outside Rome. Here my father had discussions with General Alexander and other service chiefs, and the following day flew to his 6th Armoured Division near Orvieto. Next day he crossed the Apennines to visit South African Air Force personnel at Biferno near Foggia on the Adriatic. Then back past Vesuvius, Naples and the Isle of Capri, past Stromboli and Etna, all great volcanoes, but mere toys compared to my father's favourites of the East African Rift. Cairo was in the throes of a heat wave, so after brief military and diplomatic discussions he left for Pretoria, arriving on the 30th.

The famous Danish atomic physicist Professor Niels Bohr was a frequent visitor to my father in London. I never questioned my father on any of his visits, but during a long walk on the South Downs I was to learn something of Bohr's work. Bohr, who my father grouped with Einstein as the greatest living scientist, was engaged on the most hush-hush work of the war. Mr. Churchill naturally knew of it and also Sir John Anderson, Chancellor of the Exchequer, as he was financing part of the work. But the rest of the War Cabinet were unaware of it. Mr. Churchill put my father in touch with Bohr.

As we tramped along the crests of the Downs, my father told me about it. Briefly Bohr and a team were working in America, on the fission of the atom as a warlike weapon. They had solved this vast problem, and already we had a bomb that could explode. The success of the "explosion" depended upon a newly discovered chain reaction, and pressures were exerted of the order of millions of atmospheres and temperatures a hundred times greater than those in the heart of the sun. One charge of this fissionable material would produce an explosion comparable with that of 20,000 tons of TNT. The material was Uranium 235 which was found associated only in minute quantities with Uranium 238. Separation and production processes were difficult and costly. Plants cost hundreds of millions of pounds, and it was this factor which luckily had deterred Hitler and made him pin his faith to win in TNT. But we were not sure how far Germany had got with her researches. All we knew was that she had worked on the atom and that she had at one stage been ahead of us. One of our big commando raids in Norway had been to destroy supplies of heavy water which were connected with this research.

The bomb was being manufactured in America, but as yet there was no hint of its use.

I mention all this, because it has already previously been disclosed to the public by Sir John Anderson and others.

It certainly put a new complexion on warfare.

This visit, like all others, was a most strenuous one. The days were kept full with interviews and visitors, official business, War Cabinet or Prime Ministers' Meetings, official and private luncheons, inspections of military installations, planning, night meetings of the War Cabinet and dinners. Every luncheon or dinner meant a brief speech. It was all very high pressure and top-line, and withal very exacting and tiring. Late nights, especially, my father did not like. It was the one difficulty in his collaboration with Mr. Churchill, who did most of his work in the small hours of the morning. My father liked to be in bed by ten.

The visitors that came to see him varied from kings and princes of occupied territories (all seeking advice and usually assistance as well), Prime Ministers, Cabinet Ministers, diplomats, professors, business men, rich men, poor men, Britons, foreigners, experts, politicians, financiers, High Commissioners, soldiers and a host of others. Also many old friends. They constituted a complete cross-section of life. All were charmingly and courteously received and left much impressed. To the problems and troubles of all these people he listened with interest and understanding, and to all he gave frank advice and soothing judgment. All were impressed by his infectious optimism and steady philosophy.

When my father was in London, his hotel became a place of pilgrimage for important people. They came, as I have said, to get his views on a variety of topics and events. But they also came to give him first-hand information. By these means, he kept himself well informed of what was going on and abreast of the times.

He was a good listener. When they had finished he would put a few pertinent questions, which left one in no doubt that he had taken in every bit of what he was told. I have never known another person able to get to the crux of matters so quickly or easily.

In 1944, after four years of valiantly endeavouring to keep pace with my father, my mother was finally overtaken by the penalty for overwork and suffered a severe breakdown in health, from which it took her many years to recover. This illness of my mother's was most distressing to my father and was to be a long anxiety. Though still taking an undiminished interest in affairs my mother was unable, thereafter, to take an active part. The rest did her good. My father, unrestricted by his doctors, wore himself out. The result was that my frail mother outlived her restless husband.

LXXVIII FOURTH VISIT TO ENGLAND

O N the night of April 1st, 1945, my father left on his fourth and last wartime visit to England. It was an eventful flight. The take-off from Pretoria was nerve-racking, for the York was a ton over-weight, and the run was only two-thirds that normally required at sea level, though we were here at a height of almost 5,000 feet. This meant a very considerable impairment in lift and engine power, and in addition the aerodrome at Zwartkop was concave, which meant an uphill run and a rise over a low hill at the end. We only just cleared this rise, the big machine wallowing ominously in a stalled condition across the jagged chert outcrops. I subconsciously raised my feet off the floor to clear the rocks.

After that we settled down comfortably for the night. At 3 a.m. we ran into a broad storm front over the Rift Valley south of Lake Tanganyika, and having tried various ways of getting past it for half an hour, decided to go through. We were at the time flying at 14,000 feet, and as the passage was very rough Piet Nel had disengaged the automatic "George" and was flying by hand. The cloud was solid and glowed from the constant flashes of lightning. Suddenly there was a terrific explosion and the plane rocked and plunged about. I thought that a time bomb had gone off. But we had merely been heavily struck by lightning. The trailing aerial was severed completely, the thick erect aerial was badly fused, the wireless set was wrecked and a newspaper on the floor set alight. The bucking was caused by the fact that Nel had been temporarily blinded by the flash. At Northolt, mechanics were later to find considerable additional damage. The rivets in the nose of the machine had all become spot-welded, the highly inflammable de-icing device had been fused into little globules of metal, and considerable damage had resulted to the internal spar systems of the one wing. As at the time we still had over a thousand gallons of aviation fuel on board, it will be realised what a narrow escape it had been.

But that was not quite the end of our troubles, for at Cairo it was found that one of our tail fins had a fatigue crack running three-quarters of the way down it. At any moment the break might have become complete, with disastrous results.

I gave a sigh of relief when we reached Northolt. My father had shown not the slightest sign of nervousness throughout the trip, and during the lightning incident did not even bother to rise from his bunk to investigate.

Six months later, on another trip to England, the York was again struck by lightning while over the Mediterranean, but it was only a mild flash.

To complete the list of my father's narrow escapes in the air I have two further incidents to recount. One occurred early on in the war when he was returning to land at Nairobi late one afternoon. From three o'clock Nairobi skies are usually completely clouded over, and on this occasion there was "cotton-wool" right down to within two hundred feet of the ground. Apart from its radio, his Lodestar had no special blind-landing devices, and considering the mountainous nature of the surrounding country, the operation was hazardous. But Piet Nel brought the machine through the clouds with unerring accuracy right over the landing ground, much to the relief of those in the plane, and the reception party.

The other, and most dangerous flight of all was made towards the end of the war when my father flew to Cape Town in his Lodestar with General van Ryneveld to attend the funeral of General Collyer. It was mid-winter in the Cape and beyond Beaufort West they ran into solid cloud. They climbed to 14,000 feet to get above it without success and became heavily iced up. But at 16,000 they eventually got above the flat white blanket and the icing conditions and flew by dead reckoning towards Cape Town. There was never so much as a solitary rift in the cloud. As they approached the end of their run they were told that all the Cape aerodromes were heavily obscured in mist and that landings were absolutely impossible. Even an approach from the sea would have been out of the question. By now their fuel was very nearly exhausted and there was no possibility of flying halfway back to the Transvaal to land. General van Ryneveld, veteran airman, said he had never been in a more hazardous position in all his experience.

But then, just for a moment, there was a tiny break in the cloud, and they espied below them Kalk Bay. That was all Piet Nel needed, and in a moment he was through this opening, and before the mist could close in again he had landed on an emergency strip nearby. Nothing could be less ideal than the mountainous Cape for a blind landing.

Once while travelling by train to the Cape my father had a nightmare and leapt out of the way of impending disaster. Unfortunately he translated this dream into action and leapt out of his bunk towards the window, luckily striking his head hard on the lintel and falling back again.

★   ★   ★   ★   ★

Since our visit last year at the time of Overlord there had been heartening developments in the war situation. In Normandy, Montgomery, having drawn the main German armoured strength, remained blocked for a long while with his British forces outside Caen. The Americans, in an area which had been heavily inundated on the Cherbourg peninsula, appeared effectively bogged down. But suddenly in the end of July there came a lightning change. U.S. armour broke through west of St. Lo and went tearing into France, with dashing General Patton at their head. Three weeks earlier Caen had fallen and on August 12 a general German retreat from Normandy began. In the Falaise Pocket a large part of the retreating German forces were trapped between the British, American and Canadian armies and almost wiped out. Observers described the carnage as the most terrible of the war. On the 25th Paris was liberated. Eisenhower and Montgomery differed on subsequent strategy, Montgomery advocating a swift spear thrust to the Ruhr. Eisenhower felt that without the use of Antwerp such a stroke could not be maintained and therefore moved up more cautiously on a broad front. The port facilities at Antwerp were afterwards found to have been so methodically wrecked by the Germans that it was three months before the first convoys could enter. Intelligence, too, subsequently revealed that the Germans had taken up dispositions for a spear thrust.

The British and Canadians moved up along the coast. The American armies on the right flank did the more spectacular and dashing fighting. In a bold but justifiable gamble, which General Omar Bradley describes as one of the "most imaginative" plans of the war, Montgomery landed strong airborne forces well ahead of his armies at Arnheim in an endeavour to capture the Rhine bridges and so to outflank the Siegfried Line. But bad weather defeated this very gallant effort. This reverse came as a shock to those who believed that German morale had crumbled and that the closing phases of the war would be a walk-over.

German rocket bomb attacks on Britain had commenced earlier in the month and of the 1,115 V2s launched 517 were to crash into Greater London before attacks terminated at the end of March with the capture of the launching sites. There was no defence against these weapons, other than destroying their sources of origin.

From the beginning of 1944 onwards there were signs that all was not well in Germany. Rommel and others were convinced that Germany had lost the war and were anxious to terminate hostilities. Hitler, more fanatical than ever, had other ideas. In February Rommel was persuaded to join an influential group who conspired to overthrow the Fuehrer. Rommel thought the plan involved nothing worse than kidnapping, but in June the others were to use an assassin's bomb unsuccessfully. Stulpnagel, one of the conspirators, tried to commit suicide but merely shot his eye out, and in his delirium he gave Rommel away. For his role Rommel on the 15th October was compelled to take a phial of cyanide. The drastic purge of senior persons that followed the attempt on Hitler's life was an indication that Germany was near the breaking point.

This premature sense of victory in the air was rudely shattered on December 16 when von Rundstedt launched a very powerful surprise attack on the American lines in the Ardennes sector, with the object of capturing Liége, Brussels and even Antwerp. In his forty-mile penetration in this "Battle of the Bulge" Rundstedt very nearly achieved his objectives, and it took us till February of the next year to retrieve the lost ground and to push on again. The Americans crashed through the Maginot Line with little difficulty, crossed the Rhine at Remagen on March 7 and battered their way through the Siegfried Line during September and October.

From the east the Russians were also closing in swiftly.

The race for Berlin was on. Few people at the time, however, realised that questions of occupation had already been settled at the Big Three Crimea Conference in February. In a time of stagnation we made concessions we were afterwards to regret.

The Battle of the Bulge once more brought to the fore an old-standing difference of view on Allied army strategy. My father was gravely disturbed by this lightning stroke of Rundstedt's. He believed, with many, that Eisenhower, the most able administrator on our side, should be left to administer the political part of the war, whereas Alexander, our most able tactician, should be in charge of military operations. This he meant as no reflection on General Eisenhower's great ability, or his brilliant work as a soother of warring factions and his overall command of Overlord work, which he held in the highest regard.

LXXIX PRIME MINISTERS' CONFERENCE

THE purpose of this visit was to attend a Prime Ministers' Conference intended as a prelude to the San Francisco Conference. It was hoped here, at this London Conference, which commenced on 4th April, to establish an identity of views amongst Commonwealth delegates.

There had been a radical deterioration in Russia's attitude since Yalta, and there remained only a faint glimmer of her wish to co-operate. The belief in Britain was that Stalin was no longer master of his own house and that he was taking instructions from what Mr. Churchill called his "back-room" boys. My father did not subscribe to these views. He did not appear to hold a very exalted opinion of the integrity of Stalin and described him as "out to rule Europe". My father was afraid that matters might deteriorate to a point which might jeopardise Russian participation in the war against Japan. We had in our pocket a promise of help from her.

There was minor friction, too, between Britain and America on war aims in Europe, Britain feeling that Montgomery's future role of mopping up Germans in Northern Holland and sweeping round to the Baltic was not a just reward for his past labours. America appeared to be doing the more spectacular fighting.

During March the Allies had dropped 206,000 tons of bombs. Our attacks on oil plants, which were now given highest priority, had reduced German production of oil to $11\frac{1}{2}$ per cent and petrol to 5 per cent of normal, while synthetic oil, too, was down to 6 per cent.

My father told the Prime Ministers that the League of Nations had functioned well in most respects but had been too idealistic. It failed also because America had left it in the lurch at the start. Otherwise this war might well have been avoided. The Dumbarton Oaks proposals introduced a new concept of security based on the Big Three Powers.

News reached my father of the plight of five million starving people in by-passed Holland. He took the matter up immediately with Mr. Churchill and the War Cabinet, and soon supplies of food were arriving by air and road.

In Italy the Germans sent out peace feelers to General Alexander. Stalin accused Roosevelt and Churchill of negotiating a separate peace behind his back, and both denied this with vigour.

Mr. Churchill no longer appeared quite as confident of our future with Russia as he had been last year, and inclined to my father's less optimistic view. He now said: "Our great hope lies in the Big Three; and if that fails there is always the Big Two." My father expounded to me his views on Russia. "Look back on her history," he said, "and you will see that she has been a country of tremendous ups and downs. No phase has lasted very long. It is therefore possible that this present state will pass as rapidly as it appeared. The indications are that the Kremlin cannot keep the people downtrodden for ever. One day the present regime will be overthrown and Russia will once more plunge into the abyss. I am not pessimistic."

We learned now, too, of the V3 which Hitler had been hoping to use against London. It consisted of 400 foot long stage-boosted cannon barrels which were to fire 6-inch shells into the city at the rate of fifty per minute. Each of these shells was to contain thirty pounds of high explosive. The Invasion Coast had been overrun in the nick of time to save the people from this ordeal.

Poland was a source of constant friction between the Western Allies and Russia. At Yalta it had been agreed that the Polish Government would have a broad base of members both from Lublin (Communists) and from the London émigré government, under the premiership of Mikolajezyk. Russia now insisted on almost exclusive Lublin representation. My father for the sake of the San Francisco Conference counselled the angry Mr. Churchill not, at this stage, to break with Russia on this issue.

467

The Russian pattern was by now becoming clear: she wanted Poland, the Balkans and much else as puppet states. But it did look as though she meant business with Japan. The defeat of 1905 at Port Arthur still rankled.

There was at this time talk of a last fanatical German stand in an Inner Redoubt in the Bavarian mountains, which was being given serious consideration.

This Second World War, fought not by men, but by machines, had not proved nearly as costly in life as the First World War. To date Allied casualties in Europe totalled 697,000 of which only 125,000 were dead. And since D-day we had taken a million and a quarter German prisoners. The total British Commonwealth casualties for the whole war totalled only 1,126,802 of whom less than a third of a million were killed.

At this time, too, a bombshell was dropped in British political circles by Ernest Bevin, who attacked the Conservatives at a Party meeting. This initiated a drastic split between Labour and the Conservatives, and heralded the end of the Coalition Government. The general elections were approaching and the party machines were getting into their stride.

The time did not seem propitious for the holding of the San Francisco Conference. The British felt it was premature, but gave way to the Americans.

My father was dubious of the Conference's chances of success. Though little could be done about it, he viewed with misgiving the veto powers given to the Big Three at Yalta, and the mounting truculence of Russia.

There had been constant trouble in Palestine, and now for the first time my father agreed that partition offered the only solution. Extremism seemed for the moment to have gained the upper hand in the Holy Land and Weizmann's more moderate elements were in eclipse.

In 1947 my father was to advocate the idea of partition with greater emphasis: "To the Jews, partition may be a bitter pill, but ancient Palestine itself was never a wholly Jewish state, as the Philistines always occupied the coastal plains which form the best part of it, and the promise of a national home in Palestine never meant the whole of Palestine," he said.

"Nor will the Arabs like partition, but they have come very

well out of their past subjection to Turkey and their rise into five Arab kingdoms by force of Allied arms. Compromise is necessary to prevent internecine friction and worse. Partition now appears the only way out. . . ."

The war news was daily growing better. On April 12 General Simpson's 9th U.S. Army had reached the Elbe near Magdeburg, less than seventy miles from Berlin. Simpson was determined to beat Zhukov to the German capital. Von Papen had been captured in the Ruhr pocket and next to Rudolf Hess was our biggest prize so far. Count Bernadotte had had an interview with Himmler who said he was convinced the war was lost, but Hitler was determined to fight till the bitter end. The Russian capture of Vienna had by now obviated any possibility of a last German stand in the Harz Mountains redoubt near Hitler's eyrie. Tokyo was being heavily bombed by the Americans, who, after sanguinary fighting, had crept close along the stepping-stones of the Pacific.

On April 13th, the shattering news came through that Roosevelt had died suddenly at Hot Springs from a cerebral hæmorrhage. I told my father the tragic news early in the morning while he was shaving. His face was grey as he put down his razor. "God, how terrible," he exclaimed. "This is a knock-out blow!" He was referring to the chances of the San Francisco Conference and of post-war peace. In South Africa, Dr. Malan turned down Mr. Hofmeyr's suggestion that the House should adjourn as a token of respect. It would be difficult to think of a more ill-conceived act of discourtesy. Yet this man was one day to become Prime Minister of South Africa.

My father originally met Franklin Roosevelt in the First World War, when the latter was a United States official at the Peace Conference. Thereafter there was the long gap to the present war, connected only by what he read of Roosevelt in the press. The impression he formed then, and the one he carried through life, was that Roosevelt was a man of great courage. He admired his long, dogged struggle against adverse public opinion and isolationism, and the way he finally brought America into the war, albeit with the providential help of Pearl Harbour.

He gave him credit for more astute worldly capability than Woodrow Wilson, but he never put him on the same exalted pinnacle as Churchill, either from the point of view of ability or achievement. He felt a very warm admiration for his integrity and sincerity, and for his great humanitarian attributes.

On the 16th we left in a Liberator for America. On the same day Alexander started his big spring offensive in Italy which was to prove the final blow. In New York my father stayed for a day with his old friends the Thomas Lamonts. Tom Lamont, like most wealthy people in America, opposed the Roosevelt administration because of its New Deal legislation. My father was to receive many disparaging letters from New Yorkers criticising his decision to stay with the Lamonts. These I consigned, where they belonged, to the waste-paper basket.

LXXX SAN FRANCISCO CONFERENCE

ON the 20th we touched down at Hamilton Airfield outside San Francisco, having flown for 2,600 miles across the waist of America at the level of the Great Lakes, across some of the most impressively rich and fertile country I have ever seen. Vast industrial areas and huge rail marshalling yards sprawled everywhere, emphasising the almost unlimited war potential of this great country. Near Wichita we skirted one of the mammoth new Atomic Energy Installations, though at the time we did not recognise it as such. The world was as yet unaware of these ultra-secret atomic projects. But soon it was to hit headlines.

Upon arrival my father told the press: "The last great battle of the war is not being fought in Berlin or anywhere else, but right here in San Francisco. . . . We have fought the war for a new type of human society. . . . I think any document which concludes this war and starts the future ought to include a statement of faith—the things we stand for."

At the Prime Ministers' Conference he had warned: "If San

Francisco fails I see nothing but stark disaster before mankind. This war has warned us what new forms of war mean. . . . Scientific discoveries have been made in this war which have not yet been embodied in war weapons, have not yet materialised in a munitions programme—discoveries which if any war were to take place in the future, would make this calamity seem small by comparison . . . might even mean the end of the human race."

President Truman officially opened the San Francisco Conference across the air on the 25th. My father was critical of the fact that he had not made a point of doing the opening in person. There could have been no weightier task needing his attention at that time.

The War Memorial Hall was crowded with 3,300 people. Twelve hundred of these were the delegates of the forty-six nations represented and 200 were press photographers and reporters. The flags of the nations draped the stage and thirty-four searchlights turned the atmosphere into a scorched inferno. To render the occasion still more bizarre almost unlimited latitude was allowed the news-crazy press representatives. Everywhere were stalking cameramen, whirring cameras and exploding flashlight bulbs.

Stocky, bull-necked Molotov, colourless, silent and unsmiling, blinked expressionlessly behind his pince-nez glasses. He seemed indifferent to the bursting of flash bulbs and the frenzied attention.

It amazed me to find how little the American people knew of my father or South Africa. Nothing illustrates this better than a little incident that befell us on the way to the opening ceremony when our car was held up in a traffic jam. Two schoolboys peered in at my father through the window. After some discussion one decided that it must be Smuts. "Oh yes," exclaimed the other joyfully, "King Smuts!"

In the hall itself was gathered about the most cosmopolitan medley of mixed humanity the world had ever seen; there were the Whites of Western Europe; there were the Latins and mixed extractions of the twenty South American States; there were the Negroes of Liberia, the Mongolians of the East, the Arab types of Egypt and the Fuzzy-Wuzzies of Abyssinia; there was Bedouin-like Prince Feisal of Saudi Arabia with his quaint head-dress. A

471

member of Feisal's delegation asked the manager of the Fairmont Hotel if he could buy one of the quaint Japanese lift girls to take home with him. He seemed surprised when told that the customs of this country forbade it.

Young, white-haired Edward Stettinius Junior, Secretary of State and one-time chief of Lease Lend and close friend of Roosevelt, was President of the Conference. England was represented by debonair Anthony Eden and Russia by Molotov (assisted by Ambassador Gromyko and interpreter Pavlov). That completed the Big Three sponsoring powers. In addition there were the Lesser Two; China, represented by T. V. Soong (brother-in-law of Chiang Kai-shek) and Dr. Wellington Koo; and France, represented by the wartime leader of her underground, Georges Bidault.

The remaining delegates consisted of Commonwealth Prime Ministers, senior ministers and diplomats of other countries and hangers-on who had merely come to enjoy the pleasures of San Francisco.

Mr. Mackenzie King, Canada's great Prime Minister, paid my father a handsome compliment early on in the Conference by suggesting in the Steering Committee that as my father had a "standing in the diplomatic world unrivalled by any" and as many people were anxious to hear him, he be granted the special privilege of speaking high up on the list at the Plenary Session. Mr. Eden, in support, referred to my father as the "doyen of the Conference—quite unrivalled in intellectual attributes and unsurpassed in experience and authority".

"This war has not been an ordinary one of the old type," my father said in his address to the Plenary Session. "It has been a war of ideologies, of conflicting philosophies of life . . . let us in this charter . . . proclaim to the world and to posterity that this was no mere brute struggle of force between nations, but that for us, behind the material struggle was the vision of an ideal . . . the resolve to vindicate the fundamental rights of man and on that basis to found a better, freer, world for the future." The Charter must contain "in the Preamble a declaration of human rights and of the common faith which has sustained the Allied peoples in their bitter and prolonged struggle for the vindication of those rights and that faith".

The difference between the Covenant of the League of Nations and the United Nations Charter, my father said, was that this new attempt at peace machinery recognised that force was necessary to maintain peace. Only the combined force of the great powers could guarantee the peace, and unity among them was essential. The other nations as well must agree to supply armed forces against aggression. And regional defence groups must help to maintain peace.

The Conference made little progress. It seemed bogged down on matters of principle and procedure, and swamped by over-loquaciousness. After three days of fruitless haggling my father could restrain his impatience no longer. He addressed the Steering Committee on the question of the duration of the Conference. It was absolutely vital, he said, to conclude the business as soon as possible. To prolong the work would be to endanger the prospects of the Conference seriously, for the Conference was merely an isolated meeting in a world crowding with great events. Soon the leading personalities would be recalled to deal with affairs at home, and the Conference would end in a rump. He therefore proposed a definite timetable which would ensure that the work was concluded in a month, which was the maximum time we could risk. This advice was disregarded.

There were squabbles over chairmanship. There were squabbles over Polish representation. The Ukraine and White Russia had already gained admission by the terms of the Yalta agreement.

On April 27 the American and Russian armies joined hands on the Elbe.

The following day Italian patriots in Milan rose and liberated the town. Amongst those captured in the vicinity was Mussolini. After a summary trial he was executed by a firing squad, together with seventeen of his entourage. This bombastic man, who had flung out his challenge to the world from the balcony of the Palazzo Venezia on the 10th of June, 1940, died like a cringing coward when lined up. Thereafter his body was dumped in the main square of Milan and horribly desecrated by the angry mob. And so passed another sawdust Cæsar, a rascal who had aspired to greatness in the world's supreme hour of trial. A just retribution had overtaken him.

Hitler was a wiser man. He had no intention of being captured alive. His dramatic last days in the Bunker of the Reichs Chancellory in Berlin have been faithfully described. In the smoke and dust of the doomed city, while the Russians were battering their bloody way through the outskirts, he made his final plans. According to eye-witnesses he had become mentally unhinged as the final rounds approached. He had for long partaken heavily of drugs, and, near the end, even as the Goebbels family were drinking their draughts of poison, he married Eva Braun. It was an act not without pathos. As the Russians drew close to the Bunker on April 30, he commanded a member of his personal bodyguard to shoot Eva and himself. The bodies were incinerated in a blaze of petrol in the garden outside. And so the last remains of this monster met its pyral end, just as his homeland was flaming to its final doom. Few paused to mourn the passing of this demon dictator who had brought such untold misery on struggling humanity. His is the responsibility for the fifty million casualties of the war.

On May 1st Admiral Doenitz took over. The war would go on, he declared. Germany was crumbling into total destruction.

Descriptions and photographs of German torture camps at Belsen, Buchenwald, Dachau, Auswitz and elsewhere were now coming in. These centres of liquidation were not for prisoners-of-war, but for the Jews and political prisoners. Here were revealed acts of cruelty and sadism unparalleled in the annals of civilisation. Death in these torture camps was not swift or clean. People died slow, agonising, lingering deaths, half starved, beaten, riddled with deadly bacteria, often flogged or kicked to death, often slowly strangled or gassed. They perished here in their millions. The true numbers will never be known.

The pictures are gruesomely pathetic. Thousands of corpses lie dumped in holes in grotesque postures, all emaciated to a degree beyond comprehension. The faces are drawn and ghost-like, with agonised, staring eyes. The transition from this world to the next had not been swift or merciful. Even death could not wipe the terror from their features. They bore mute testimony to the scourge of Nazism.

As the Conference floundered on, my father grew steadily more impatient. He said it was "drifting badly out of control, and the difference between this and the last Peace Conference at Paris is the absence of such dominating personalities as Wilson, Clemenceau and Lloyd George. We shall miss them badly."

My father was appointed President of the General Assembly, one of the four big commissions of the Conference. It dealt, among other things, with the Preamble and trusteeship.

On 1st May the German army in Italy, over a million strong, capitulated, and signed armistice terms with General Alexander at Caserta. The commander, Kesselring, had been captured some days before. He said it was air power that had beaten him in Italy.

Halfway through the Conference I was to note in my diary: "Delegates have been pleasantly surprised at the brisk and efficient way the Oubaas handles his meetings. He has a mild and benevolent manner which is very deceptive, for under this cloak he hides the firm resolve of a dictator. But he does it so well that people do not realise that they are being dictated to, and submit quite readily to his persuasions. So it was this morning. By deftly steering the meeting, pitfalls were avoided and the meeting broke up in high good humour."

People frequently asked my father what he thought we would do with Germany after the war. He always gave somewhat guarded answers to this question. "Only two things are certain. We will bring the war criminals to book and hang a few. As to Germany herself I cannot see us standing by while the population starve. You will find that humanitarianism will prevail and we will help them again on to their feet." He was in favour of meddling as little as possible in the internal affairs of Germany. We should only be there to supervise and to see that law and order were maintained. Under no circumstances must we allow ourselves to be drawn into their domestic affairs, for that would only bring discredit and odium upon our shoulders.

To those conversant with the cross-currents which raged behind the scenes at the Conference there was little that seemed reassuring. For myself, unversed in the ways of big conferences, the proceedings seemed to verge on the hypocritical. There was much else too that was disturbing. Regarding Russia's future role in the scheme of things I noted this down in my diary: "The future looks far from bright. Russia makes a strange bedfellow to her other partners. Every indication at the moment—and God knows there are ample indications—is that Russia is going to make little attempt to co-operate. In fact, the opposite appears more probable at present. I have already mentioned her part in the Polish dispute: the fact that she has gone against her Yalta word and that she is actively fomenting trouble cannot possibly be doubted. Our request to be permitted to send observers there to see for themselves has been flatly refused. Why? Likewise our wishes to send observers to Czechoslovakia and Vienna (both in the Russian zones) have been firmly turned down. Why? Our Military Mission in Moscow has never yet been permitted to visit the Soviet Front. Is that trust and goodwill?

"A short while ago Russia tried to stir up trouble over the capitulation negotiations with Italy at Berne: Stalin sent Roosevelt and Churchill most provocative cables. He has refused (or pretended to refuse) all explanations. Some months ago the Soviet meddled in the oil question in Persia and was offensive to everybody. She did not want at first to participate actively in the San Francisco Conference. De Gaulle had predicted that she was out to break the Conference. And now she has suddenly accused us of treating liberated Russian prisoners-of-war shockingly, which is an infamous lie. She knows it is.

"What are her reasons for all this?

"As I see it, there is only one explanation. Russia is looking for trouble. Mr. Churchill says it is largely bluff and bluster. My father agrees. Appeasement will never pay with the Russians. They understand only one thing—straight angry talk with military might in the background to back it up if necessary.

"Our only hope is for England and America to maintain very big armed forces in post-war days. The safety of the world lies in arming to the hilt, not disarmament."

These seem strange words to be written during a conference of peace.

MEANWHILE in this atmosphere of fantasy the Conference was complacently plodding on, in a world of breathtaking events. On the 4th of May the Germans in Holland, Denmark and West Germany surrendered to Montgomery and armistice terms were signed by von Friedeberg. It was the biggest mass surrender since 1918, and prisoners taken during the past month now totalled four million. There only remained isolated enemy pockets of resistance in Norway and Bavaria.

Still bigger news broke on Monday the 7th, when the newspapers splashed across their front pages in heaviest type: "Germany Surrenders Unconditionally. War in the West is Over." The German Chief of Staff Jodl signed armistice terms in the presence of General Eisenhower in the little red schoolhouse at Rheims. The great day for which anxious mankind had prayed for five and a half years had come at last. But there was surprisingly little display of elation at San Francisco, for this city looked out on the East, and there was still the nightmare of a long struggle with the suicidal Japanese.

United States casualties in Europe totalled 996,089, of whom a quarter of a million were dead. Yet this was an almost insignificantly small figure in comparison with the Russian twelve to fifteen million casualties, half of whom were civilians. The Russians, unlike ourselves, had fought with men, not machines.

It was fitting that my father's Preamble discussion should coincide with these cataclysmic events. He himself introduced his Preamble. The Charter was a cold legalistic document. But the Preamble was a warmer human document which set out plainly our hopes and aspirations. By it, perhaps more than anything else, the Charter will one day be remembered. On the 3rd my father submitted his draft Preamble. When this is compared to the final Preamble, it will be seen how little his original draft has been modified. His draft read:

PREAMBLE TO THE CHARTER OF THE UNITED NATIONS

THE HIGH CONTRACTING PARTIES:

Determined

TO prevent a recurrence of the fratricidal strife which twice in our generation has brought untold sorrow and loss upon mankind,
and
TO re-establish faith in fundamental human rights, in the sanctity and ultimate value of human personality, in the equal rights of men and women of nations large and small,
and
TO promote social progress and better standards of life in larger freedom,
and for these ends
TO practise tolerance and to live together in peace with one another as good neighbours,
IN order that nations may work together to maintain international peace and security,
BY the acceptance of principles and the institution of methods to ensure that armed force shall not be used save in the common interest,
BY the provision of means by which all disputes that threaten the maintenance of international peace and security shall be settled,
BY the establishment of conditions under which justice and respect for the obligation of international law and treaties and fundamental human rights and freedoms can be maintained,
BY the employment of international machinery for the promotion of economic and social advancement of all peoples,
AGREE TO THIS CHARTER OF THE UNITED NATIONS.

The Churches expressed disappointment that the word God did not appear in the Preamble. Senator Vandenberg remarked to my father that he would never be re-elected if he did not "put God into the Charter"!

On the 10th of May my father again felt constrained to warn

the Conference of the urgency of the time factor. The exodus of delegates had started. If matters were to drag on much longer "there was every chance that it might end in a fiasco". Over 700 amendments to the Dumbarton Oaks Proposals were before the Conference. My father suggested that the delegates started with the twenty-seven amendments of the sponsoring powers and tackled the others later, in groups.

Apart from the Veto, the greatest stumbling block at the meeting appeared to be ideas on Trusteeship. Trusteeship, which superseded the Mandate idea of the League of Nations, was Senator Vandenberg's "grand idea", and was powerfully backed by America. There appeared to be much emotional and woolly thinking, few people at first appreciating its far-reaching implications on strategic and colonial problems. The United States was not quite so broad-minded when it came to sharing certain "strategic Pacific Bases". They grew even more unhappy when Russia said she, too, would like strategic bases. Britain found it would mean meddling in the internal affairs of her colonies, and South Africa held strong reservations on South-West Africa, declining, under pressure, to surrender her old "C" Class Mandate.

Various powers were out to stake their territorial claims. Tito lost little time in marching into Trieste, and we only succeeded in dislodging him after considerable trouble. France tried to grab Aosta, and it needed much persuasion to make de Gaulle change his mind. My father said "it is a good reflection on the morality of the French and what we can expect from her in the future". Barely had he made this prediction when France was causing fresh trouble in Syria and the Lebanon and was shelling Damascus and other cities. I asked whether this was the type of dispute in which UNO might intervene. Theoretically yes, he said, but being one of the Big Five she would invoke the Veto to forestall enforcement action.

On VE-day my father sent Mr. Churchill a cable congratulating him on the successful conclusion of hostilities and the memorable contribution he had made. Mr. Churchill wired back: "Nothing in these past stirring days has brought me greater pleasure than your most kind message. Your presence beside me in the councils of the Empire and at the fronts in those long hard years has been to me a constant source of strength and inspiration for which I am most sincerely grateful. I pray that you may long remain with us a trusty friend and guide in war and peace."

One of my father's most pleasant functions at San Francisco was to unveil a memorial plaque to President Roosevelt in Muir Wood, a 400-acre park of giant sequoia redwoods not far outside the town. Here in a deep valley is the most superb glade of huge trees I have ever seen. This sequoia is the tall coastal type (*semper virens*) which attains a height of over 300 feet and an age in excess of a thousand years.

In these idyllic surroundings we strode briskly up the valley to the "theatre". The ground was springy underfoot and the air filled with the fragrance of pine tar. Presently we came to a small platform in a crescent of mammoth trees, the foliage meeting in a canopy high above. Some were already old trees when Columbus sailed out to the West. Some few might have stood here at the time of Christ.

Small wonder that in this setting, unique in my father's long life of speech-making, he should deliver an oration which can compare with his Table Mountain speech. The speech was a written one, but the glorious surroundings fired in him that spark which raised him above worldly things, and he spoke with emotion. "Here among the giant redwoods this great man will find fitting and congenial company. Here henceforth will be the company of the giants."

It was spring-time in California, and San Francisco, jewelled city of seven hills, was looking its best, nestling in green rolling country on one of the world's finest inland harbours. At the portals to this bay was the Golden Gate, spanned by the 4,200-foot suspension bridge of similar name, greatest bridge on earth and one of man's most spectacular creations. Across the bay to Oaklands stretched another eight-mile bridge, longest of its kind in the world.

The countryside, though fashioned on a more generous scale, had all the lushness and verdure of England, with valleys filled with indigenous oaks and pines, and hillsides ablaze with broad sheets of sweet-smelling blue lupins, yellow Californian poppies and orange eschscholtzias. It was a setting in which my father went for long walks whenever he could. His favourite route was out beyond the Golden Gate, above Muir Woods, and up the

General Smuts with the Royal Family at Mont-aux-Sources, Natal—1947

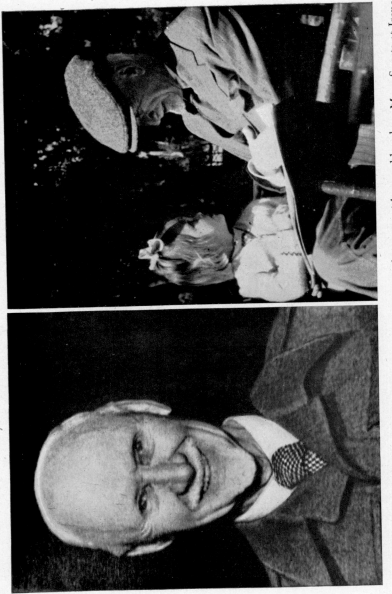

General Smuts on his 80th Birthday at Irene. He was looking thin and far from well

General Smuts with granddaughter Mary Smuts at Irene the day before his death. This was the last photograph taken of him

slopes of Tamalpais, the only mountain feature in the area. By a strange coincidence he was on the summit of Tamalpais at the time the Germans were signing the armistice terms at Rheims.

He found time one Sunday to do a 513-mile round trip to the superb Yosemite National Park in the Sierra Nevadas. Here the Merced River and the glaciers of days gone by have carved out a narrow, lake-studded trough in the mountains, with grey granite sides rising sheer for 4,000 feet in bare vertical faces. From the lip of this chasm plunge a number of exquisite waterfalls, surely unsurpassed anywhere on earth, fed by the snows of the Nevadas. Beyond the imposing granite buttress of El Capitan the Yosemite, one of the world's famous waterfalls, leaped down the cliff. On this side was the slender 1,600-foot Ribbon Falls, while across the valley were the 620-foot Bridal Veil Falls. In the trough, and up the mountain slopes were impressive woods of Douglas firs and the stocky mountain type of sequoia redwoods (*gigantia*). At the Mariposa Grove we gazed upon Grizzly Giant, a tree computed to be about 3,800 years old and still flourishing. It is staggering to reflect that this living object, which was the real reason for my father's visit to Yosemite, was only a thousand years younger than the crumbling pyramids of Egypt.

Then back we came from this dreamland into the battles of the Conference. A severe and prolonged impasse reigned over the veto, which on two occasions threatened to wreck the Conference. This veto had been written into the Dumbarton Oaks proposals to permit the Big Five to veto matters in the Security Council. The initial intention had obviously been for the veto to apply only to drastic enforcement measures, but here it was stretched to mean much more. Britain and the smaller powers were strongly opposed to the veto, which was a child of Roosevelt's. But we had tied our hands in the Polish dispute by insisting on the letter of the Yalta agreement. Now, to alter the veto, it would be necessary to amend Yalta.

My father's solution to the initial deadlock was to cut out the veto from the Charter and to pass the rest. It did not meet with approval. The final compromise adopted after much haggling was that the veto would not apply to preliminary investigations by the Security Council, but only to subsequent serious discussion.

Though in public my father, as was his wont, expressed a fair measure of optimism at the work and achievements of UNO, he was far less enthusiastic in private and much less sanguine of its success. It was only when he considered San Francisco as a mere preliminary, a stepping stone, that he mustered optimism.

In a private appreciation of the work at UNO he wrote: "My reflections and experience of life have led me to question the adequacy of the Marxian view that human conflicts arise solely from material and economic causes, and can be dealt with on that level merely by economic and social reform. There is something else the human spirit wants and craves for its satisfaction. A house swept clean and garnished, but empty of spirit, still remains a place which seven devils may enter and occupy. For instance, I fail to believe that Hitler's war . . . was due merely to economic causes, not to something deeper and more sinister in human outlook and beliefs. There was the Nazi ideology . . . At the heart of our human problem is this issue of ultimate beliefs, of religion, the recession or decay of which has been and may well be again the precursor of untold misfortune to mankind. That great task falls beyond the scope of this Conference, and must be left to other hands, but it cannot be deferred indefinitely by those who have the highest interests of our race and our civilisation at heart."

The best work of UNO my father considered was the regional idea which it introduced, much as in the old Monroe Doctrine.

The intention early on was that my father would be given the honour of making the closing speech on the Conference. He was then to proceed to Washington, where on the 26th June he had been invited by President Truman to address the Senate and House of Representatives. This was later scrapped when the President himself decided to come down to wind up the Conference.

Okinawa fell on the 20th and we were within 325 miles of Japan. 11,260 Americans lost their lives in blotting out the suicidal garrison of 90,401 Japs.

Five days later, at the penultimate Plenary Session, the adoption of the United Nations Charter was unanimously carried. The next day, after nine intensive weeks, the Conference officially ended. President Truman spoke last. My father spoke just before him: "The Charter is a far from perfect document . . ." he said, "but it is a good compromise. . . . We must educate the world to have an abhorrence of war. . . . Let us apply the Charter with goodwill and sincerity—and may God bless our efforts!"

A new Chapter had been written in human relationships.

My own most indelible memories of the Conference are the distrust and live suspicion with which Russia and the Western Powers regarded each other. That had been a major contributing factor to the slowness of the work. The second point that impressed was the solidarity with which the twenty Latin states of South America clung together. Their voting power was out of all proportion to their intrinsic worth. There was also the anæmic attitude adopted by the British delegation, which was inexplicable except on grounds of allowing the United States to steal the limelight. And finally there was the impression that my father, albeit only the representative of a humble nation, was not accorded the merit of his unrivalled position in almost every other respect.

He was also kept on a string by the State Department regarding his appearance before Congress. Though the President had provisionally signified that the 26th June would be convenient, it soon became apparent that all was not in order. First the speech was to be to the combined Houses. Later it was altered to a separate appearance in each. And finally, shortly before the end of the Conference, my father was asked if he would mind standing down, as his appearance in the American parliament might be taken as a partisan effort on the part of the President and hamper the passage of the Charter there.

Apart from his work at the Conference, my father also did more longhand drafting of speeches than ever before. First he did the opening speech for the Conference. Then followed his graduation address at the Berkeley University and his memorial address at Muir Woods. Thereafter he drafted his long closing speech which was to wind up the Conference, which fell through when President Truman decided to do the closing himself. He then, instead, prepared a brief five-minute closing address, which had subsequently to be re-done as he discovered that he would still not be the last man to speak. When he received an invitation to address Congress in Washington he prepared another long speech for the occasion. Subsequently when he learned that he would have to address Congress and the Senate separately, he scrapped his draft and wrote two long new ones. At more or less the same time he wrote another long address for Ottawa. All this was in addition to the numerous semi-brief statements on occasions for the newspapers, as well as one long and two short broadcasts. These were laborious tasks that took him many days. They were not the products of mass production, each being considered separately on its merits.

On June 27 my father left Hamilton Airfield for Ottawa, via the Grand Canyon and Kansas City. His concurrence with my eulogy of America was that it was "too wonderful—too terrific". He preferred the quiet ways of Africa, which he described as a continent "in reserve".

In Ottawa he stayed with his old friends, the Athlones, at Government House. Prime Minister Mackenzie King was delighted to have him in Canada. At the big Canadian Club luncheon in the Chateau Laurier my father delivered a long address.

To the press, the day before he set off on his return journey, he said: "It is a dangerous world in which we live. Let us not disarm again. We must be prepared for any eventuality." The San Francisco Charter is far from perfect. But it is at least a step forward. It takes account of economic and social matters that might endanger world peace. It leaves out, however, the great imponderables, those inexplicable traits of human madness and fanaticism which lie beyond the visible limits of our worldly spectrum. That great task is still left for the future.

At Chequers we found Mr. Churchill in an electioneering mood. He could talk of little else and seemed confident of a majority of a hundred in the House. The country was blowing hot and cold. The chief actors seemed to be Churchill, Attlee and Harold Laski. We left England before the bubble burst. Our stay had been very brief. There was only time for a short visit to see returned South African prisoners-of-war at Brighton.

Our "shuttle service", whereby all Union troops were flown back to South Africa, had already been in operation for some months. It was a great success. It was one of the many little considerations that made South African troops amongst the most pampered (but not always the most appreciative) troops in the world.

On 7 July my father arrived in Milan on a brief tour of inspection in Italy. He reviewed a large parade of Union troops in the Stadium, and the Old Warrior addressing his young warriors warned of difficulties ahead: "I cannot make you any promises for the future. I cannot promise you a new heaven and a new earth. It will be a hard future of hard work and toil, but I shall be with you on the new road of peace, and I think you will be with me."

Thereafter he spent two days at Stresa on Lake Maggiore, where Neville Chamberlain had parleyed with France and Italy during the Abyssinian War. At an official luncheon attended by senior army personnel my father said that the world was continuously passing through cyclic phases of unrest and quiescence. He did not think the present unstable period had yet passed. The world of the future was going to be a dangerous one.

On an inspection of the Gothic Line he traversed, with General Poole, the difficult sector taken by the Springboks, pausing at a dedication ceremony at the picturesque Castiglione Cemetery where five hundred of his troops lie buried. In the fighting in Italy Union troops had regularly suffered only one-third of the casualties of their flanking formations, which is the highest possible tribute to their combat efficiency. At that time the Union had in the Mediterranean theatre 58,000 European troops, of whom 15,500 were Air Force personnel and 10,000 Engineers, in addition to 20,000 non-Europeans.

General Mark Clark, who took over Montgomery's command in Italy when the latter left for Europe, wrote in 1950: "I thought Smuts one of the most remarkable men I met during the war. Smuts's personality was of the magnetic kind, but in addition he impressed me as a 'can do' man—the sort of leader who always has an aggressive and optimistic outlook in tackling a job or problem.

"Just looking at him you knew Smuts was not going to sit back in South Africa and merely do his part. He was going to get out and do things."

After brief business in Rome and Cairo, my father arrived home on the 16th July from this 27,000-mile trip to tackle the problems of demobilisation, rehabilitation and the switch over from a war to a peace-time footing.

Halfway through the Potsdam Big Three Conference, news came through that Mr. Churchill had been defeated by Labour.

To those who had admired the prodigious war effort not only of the Government, but also of Britain's greatest Prime Minister, the result came as a stunning shock. Such is the cruel shape of ingratitude. My father mourned not only the eclipse of one of his closest friends, but was appalled at the implications for the future. He had seen British Labour in action before.

Potsdam also dismayed my father by the extent to which Britain and the United States gave in to Russia. Here it was decided to replace the Peace Conference at the year-end by a Council of Foreign Secretaries, an arrangement which my father described as "hopeless".

On August 6, the first atom bomb was dropped on Hiroshima. It killed not only 100,000 Japanese, but jolted old-world ideas to their very foundations. It was the dawn of a new and terrible era. We had learned to harness the same source of energy as the sun. That four-and-a-half-ton missile was a crude one. A newer version was dropped three days later on Nagasaki. A day previously Russia had declared war on Japan, but it was not this declaration, but the bomb on Nagasaki that finished it.

Those who say it was unethical to use the atom bomb would do well to remember that General Arnold had promised the Japs two million tons of ordinary bombs during the next twelve months. The damage done by these two atom bombs would have been as nothing compared to the effects of this avalanche of old-fashioned ones. It was well in excess of the total tonnage dropped on Germany.

Japan surrendered on the 15th, and Hirohito was succeeded by Douglas MacArthur as unfettered dictator of these islands.

It was peace over all mankind. Twenty million had perished and countless millions dwelt as beasts in burrows. Five and three-quarter millions in the Western Allied Zone of Germany were displaced persons. South Africa had spent £536,000,000. But her debts were paid, and she came out rich, prosperous and booming. All the world lay at our feet.

In a national broadcast my father said: "It is a moment of rejoicing, of deep gratitude, of release and breathing freely again after all the long intolerable strain, all the moral dangers passed, all the harrowing anxieties gone through. These were the years of endurance, of suffering, of the martyrdom of man.

486

"It is also the occasion for silent thought, of reverent and loving remembrance. In this surge of deep emotion we prefer to be silent before an experience so overwhelming, embracing the agonies and exaltations of six of the most terrible years of all history. The release, the escape to an ordinary world of experience, is almost more than one can bear."

LXXXII CREST OF THE WAVE

THE years 1946, 1947 and the first half of 1948 were the most glorious in South Africa's history. Never had there been such prosperity; never had there been greater goodwill; never had our name and affairs stood higher in the eyes of the outside world. It seemed like the golden millennium after the long years of struggle.

True, there was a veneer of discontent at the irksome restrictions and controls, such as the rationing of petrol, shortage of luxury commodities, difficulties in obtaining meat, and such-like, but industry was in full stride, the country was flooded with overseas money and more still kept pouring in.

The overseas boat queues, in both directions, were long ones.

The new Governor-General, the Right Honourable G. Brand van Zyl, had assumed office, my father's first choice, Deneys Reitz, having died some while back.

Mr. Havenga, having vainly waited for his friends to summon him back to politics, decided to stage a come-back on his own.

It was, however, a changed Havenga we were to see from the loyal henchman of General Hertzog of pre-war days. My father soon summed him up and thereafter was under no illusions about the course he would take in the future. In the battle between principles and ambition he had no doubt which would prevail. But few people at that time came to this conclusion. The local

English press, especially an ultra-English paper of Natal, supported him. Like Oswald Pirow, he must have possessed the power to charm to a remarkable degree. He was again to have considerable luck.

Only 30,000 of the 75,000 Italian prisoners-of-war still remained to be repatriated. In view of the shortage of manpower in South Africa it was decided to let out considerable numbers of Italian P.O.W.s towards the end of the war to work on farms. Many farmers were impressed by these labourers and the cheapness of the special service, and when it came to repatriation asked to retain their services. In certain cases the Government agreed to this and numbers were retained as immigrants. Needless to say this did not meet with general favour, for quite sufficient immigrants of a more desirable type could have been obtained from Western Europe.

In personal stature and affection, my father had attained a place in the hearts of the people, yes even with his opponents, unsurpassed by any previous South African. All were proud of our Grand Old Man—our Oubaas.

In his New Year's Day broadcast, 1946, my father said: "The international community has at last come to life. . . . The responsibility for ensuring we have peace in our time and perhaps for ever is really that of the ordinary man and woman, and it depends upon their realisation that only by co-operation as citizens and as nations can peace be guaranteed. One of the things which the war has taught us is the inter-dependence of nations as of individuals on one another."

At the beginning of 1946 he launched the People of Britain Fund: "There was a period of the war when the enemy came within an ace of victory. It was then through the courage and steadfastness of soul of the British people that they saw us through. These people refused to accept setbacks, but with grim confidence saw the situation through—a great people under incomparable leadership! . . ."

In October he presented Prime Minister Attlee with a gold certificate and cheques worth more than a million pounds, for use by the people of Britain.

In March he introduced a White Paper setting out details of a long-range plan to revitalise agriculture in the Union, with emphasis on soil conservation, wool control and the modernisation of methods to raise efficiency and productivity. It also involved a certain measure of education. In five years ten million pounds were to be spent, a figure which was subsequently broadened into a hundred million pounds in twenty-five years.

In February, when replying to a question in Parliament about the intention of UNO to establish its headquarters in New York and not in Geneva, he said: "The site of the new organisation has gone to North America. To my mind, the problem of world defence or peace for a long time will be the European problem. The departure of UNO to North America seems to me like sending the general far away from the field of action." Yet he seemed to find a certain virtue behind this move, for "it is quite possible that this step will increase the force behind the idea that Europe must have a charter to look after her own affairs. . . . A council in Europe might be a great buttress to the whole defence system which we are attempting to erect for the world. I mention Europe because I think it is the most striking case, but the same thing applies to regions in Asia or Africa."

In March Mr. Churchill made a speech at Fulton, Missouri, in which he expressed views on Russia which came very close to those for long entertained by my father. Some papers erroneously interpreted his speech as a call to "get tough with Russia", but it was, in fact, merely a policy of no appeasement and standing up to Russia. Firmness was the only thing the Kremlin understood or appreciated.

Commenting on this Fulton speech in the House my father said: "We are living in a very dangerous world. Peace cannot come automatically. It may take a generation or more. The world is going through the greatest revolution in history. . . ."

The Congress Party of Natal Indians had vainly for three years been clamouring for equal rights with Europeans, full franchise and unrestricted rights to own and occupy property. The European population had equally vehemently implored my father to "save white civilisation in Natal", claiming that Durban was fast becoming an Indian city. My father therefore introduced the Asiatic Representation and Land Tenure Bill. The idea was too much for New Delhi, and the Indian Government severed trade relations with the Union as a counter-measure. The attitude of the Indian community in Natal, supported and encouraged by the nationalist movement in India, was plainly hostile to any solution which would be acceptable to European South Africa.

Nobody was in favour of the existing situation in Natal. Speaking on the Bill in Parliament my father said:

. . . Neither European nor native African culture would be fostered by such a development. We do stand for human rights. We are determined to discharge our human duties in a fair way to all sections of our community and to Indians also, but we are determined that we must preserve the European orientation of our society and not switch to Asiatic culture. That is the fundamental issue in this Bill. . . . The time has come to settle once for all the question of where Indians could live without being the playball of politics.

. . . I am the last person to minimise the importance of this Bill from the international point of view [he went on], but essentially it is an internal measure to provide social peace and the good ordering of our society, and we are not going to be frightened by any movement or propaganda. It was not true that the Bill was an insult or challenge to Asia. . . .

Both in the land tenure clauses and the political clauses of the Bill we are not breaking new ground. We are following well-known South African models. We are following principles and practices which have been adopted in the past and approved by Parliament practically unanimously, and which we look upon as essential to the structure of our complex society in South Africa. Fundamentally the principles of separate land tenure and residence and political representation for Indians are the same in this Bill as for natives in the native legislation already in force. I do not see how Indians can consider that as an insult to them. Rather is the objection an insult to the native population. . . .

South Africa's richest gold strike in a borehole was made in April when a core from a hole on the farm Geduld in the heart of the embryonic Free State goldfield assayed over 68 ounces per ton. This solitary phenomenal result from the area 150 miles to the south of Johannesburg, more than the weighty mass of previous satisfactory geophysical and borehole exploration, convinced the general public that an extensive new minefield had been discovered which bade fair one day to rival the slowly expiring Rand.

LXXXIII LONDON AND PARIS

AT the end of April, 1946, my father left for London to attend Commonwealth Prime Ministers' discussions. In Egypt he paused briefly to talk to the Egyptian Prime Minister about the proposed revision of the 1936 Anglo-Egyptian treaty. Over the Mediterranean his aircraft was struck by lightning.

At the Conference my father stressed that the colonies lost by Italy should not be returned to her and that the trusteeship of Tripolitania should not be entrusted to Russia.

It had originally been the intention that this Conference should be a prelude to the Peace Conference, scheduled to take place on 1st May, but Mr. Byrnes of America suggested that it be postponed till June 15. Before my father's arrival in London the question of the defence of the South and South-West Pacific was under discussion and it was agreed that joint military missions should be established in London, Melbourne and Wellington. Now the subject was re-opened and my father said he considered the opening of such missions would conflict with the freedom of action of the Dominions themselves, a view accepted by the others.

At the same time in South Africa Dr. Malan, Leader of the Opposition, was accused of having dealings with an enemy agent, a Mrs. Denk, during the war, a charge of which he was later exonerated by a Select Committee.

After a brief visit to Berlin my father said to reporters: "It is very different from the last time I arrived in Berlin. That was during the Bruning régime. What a different world it is now."

In an after-dinner address to guests at a function to honour the American Ambassador Averill Harriman, my father, who called himself a "barbarian from the outer marches", told his listeners: ". . . When I look at this world in my simple way—and I am accustomed to simple ways in my small country—it seems to me that the world is shaping on these lines to-day—a vast, powerful, almost impregnable group in the East, and another vast, almost impregnable Power in the far West. In between you have our-selves—you have this British group, not so powerful, not so concentrated, but with immense imponderable assets. We have the experience of human outlook, the knowledge of affairs, of things you learn only by generations of experience. Those things are an enormous asset, and it weighs up against all the hundreds of millions of people in the other groups.

"These are our assets, and very valuable assets, and they are very necessary to the future peace of the world. I look upon the British group as just as essential as UNO. All these vast organisa-tions that we devised for world peace are no greater, no better, than the potentiality for world peace and world security that lies in our group. . . ."

Speaking on the B.B.C. Home Service in early June my father said:

The establishment of UNO and its security system gives a strong ray of hope for the future, but it would be unwise to build our future solely on that hope. . . . The British Commonwealth of Nations has proved itself a worthy worthwhile organisation, and in the day when the storm burst it was for a time the sole refuge of the world in mortal peril. . . . The League broke but the Commonwealth stood, and saved at least its smaller weaker members from extinction. So may it do again if a greater storm should happen to overwhelm UNO—which God forbid."

The problem of what others wanted to do with Germany disturbed him:

. . . What remains of Germany has been cut up into four occupation zones with the unforeseen disappearance of her economic unity, and thus a slow strangulation of the whole economic system. Bad as will be the effects of all these restrictions and curtailments, they will be most severely felt in the British zone, which is not only the most densely populated and most highly industrialised, but at the same time the least food-producing part of Germany, and the part most heavily destroyed by war bombing. Any human and economic collapse will therefore be most severely felt in the British zone, and the inevitable odium, however undeserved, will most severely fall on Britain as the occupying power. The repercussions of all this not only in Germany but here in Britain and in the world generally can be easily imagined.

The situation clearly calls for a revision and reversal of policies which will at least minimise the terrible human and social situation which looms in the not-distant future, and which the conscience neither of this country, nor of the world will long tolerate. It is no use establishing UNO with its elaborate arrangements for security and for maintaining human rights and standards, if in the heart of this mother continent of our civilisation a situation is allowed to arise which will be a reproach to all connected with it.

It would be a case of not merely punishing Germany for her sin against mankind, but of punishing mankind itself and thus adding to the sin and the wrong. Destroy the Germany of Bismarck and Hitler by all means, do away with the highly centralised Germany whose military might proved a menace to the world, decentralise it in a federal system which will be rendered incapable of again becoming a menace, and which might be safely integrated ultimately into UNO. But do not attempt to destroy a great historic people, or their home-land, or their means of livelihood. . . .

The immediate task before us is to save what can still be saved, and thus to preserve the foundations for the future to be built upon. . . .

During this brief visit he found time too to review the South African victory contingent at Kensington Gardens, and was with the King and Queen and other Commonwealth leaders at the saluting base in the great Empire march past.

Back in the Union for a short while he delivered the oration at the unveiling of the monument to Louis Botha below the Union Buildings in Pretoria:

Louis Botha passed away from us twenty-seven years ago, and many of us here to-day still remember that moment of great sorrow and that sense of bitter loss which overwhelmed us when we buried him shortly after his return from the Peace Conference at the end of the last war. Deeply as we felt the loss then, we would have felt it even more, if we had foreseen what lay ahead of us—the ups and downs of a stormy era of history, ending in the greatest tragedy of all history.

I then at his burial called him happy in the moment of his death, in the hour of victory. We would have called him even happier if we could have known what lay ahead, and if we could have guessed the sad fate of the world in the generation that was to follow his going. He was fortunately spared that disillusion which turned our vast hopes after that victory into Dead Sea fruit. . . .

Such was Louis Botha. Of the great South Africans I have known I put Paul Kruger and Louis Botha in a class by themselves, although as types, as personalities, they were poles apart. . . .

At the Transvaal Head Committee of the United Party my father announced his plans for large-scale immigration. "Immigration is the call," he said. "We want men and women. We want our population to increase by leaps and bounds. Let us once more open our doors—we want to make hay while the sun shines. We are going to reshape our machinery both here and overseas to establish an organisation for the selection of immigrants. As we are on the Black Continent we want good Europeans. We can get thousands—hundreds of thousands—millions of them. . . ."

In an official Government statement he amplified his ideas on immigration:

. . . It is recognised that the shift in world forces and the development of new weapons have given South Africa a strategic importance greater than ever possessed in modern times. At the same time she is situated in an exposed geographical position; and in a world still anxiously groping for means of security she dare not neglect any opportunity of building up her resources and defensive strength. The Union Government have, therefore, decided to take whatever vigorous and positive steps are practicable to attract to South Africa promising immigrants from European and other countries.

While the most urgent need is for skilled artisans, it is considered that every effort should also be made to encourage the entry of persons who have experience and means to set up industries, however small, and particularly enterprises that would develop the Union's base minerals and other resources. Indeed, every kind of good and useful immigrant would be welcome. In order, moreover, to balance an increasing industrial population, there would be an increased scope for immigration of professional men, such as engineers of various kinds and architects who are qualified to practise in this country. . . .

. . . Other young countries are taking steps to absorb the best class of immigrants with all speed, and the Union may be left with the leavings if it does not make provision for its requirements without loss of time.

Dr. Malan said the immigration policy was an act of sabotage which must be resisted. He alleged that my father was attempting "to plough the Afrikaner under" and displayed anxiety on the future of the Afrikaner people under the impact of this invasion.

*   *   *   *   *

In mid-August, 1946, my father was off to Europe again to attend the Peace Conference in Paris. He was the only statesman among the twenty-one delegates who had sat at the Versailles tables a quarter of a century before. He held out little hope for the success of the Conference. For the past few years he had been saying that the world was still far too unsettled to permit the success of such a conference. The best they could hope for was a prolonged armistice until such time as stability returned. He had seen enough of Peace Conferences in the troubled time after the First World War. Yet the troubles in those days were as nothing compared to the difficulties that beset the world at present.

These views he emphasised at a luncheon speech in Aberdeen when he referred to the world-wide disappointment at the achievements of the Conference: "The world has been looking to the Paris Conference for some message that might bring hope, but people must have been disappointed with the results so far achieved. They read of the interminable debates, bickerings, quarrellings, and snarlings, and they found it was not what they expected. There were many reasons for this. People had expected too much. They could not expect immediately after a war and catastrophe such as they had passed through that people's minds all over the world would be attuned to the future they had been looking forward to. Human nature did not respond so quickly, and they had still much of the mentality which actuated them during the war. . . ."

Nor did he take a more hopeful line in his speech to the Plenary Session a little later: "While on the whole this conference may fairly be considered a success, one main feature of it has been disappointing and discouraging to those who look beyond the conference. In debate and outlook a cleavage has been revealed which, if not cleared up and removed, may bode ill for the future of this conference and of world peace. Those who scan the debates and votes will be struck by the constancy with which those whom I may call the Slav group on the one hand and the Western group on the other have voted against each other. It has been the revelation of this conference. The importance of it may yet come to over-shadow the conference itself. I therefore think it right to stress this so that it should not be overlooked or hushed up, but openly discussed and ventilated before this conference.

"This is a peace conference, the first of a series of peace confer-ences to mark the final conclusion of this greatest world war. It should not be the overture to bigger struggles to come. If there is one deep longing among the people to-day it is for peace. . . ."

In the Third Programme of the B.B.C. one Sunday evening he gave his listeners what might be considered a contributory cause of the partial failure of the Conference by reminding them that the world was passing through a difficult phase, and appealing to the Great Powers to make a fresh start: "We do not realise," he said, "that our world is passing not through a short- but a long-range cycle of change. We thus become impatient and expect the end almost immediately; we think that the Journey's end is just round the corner and soon we shall enter the promised land. We misunderstand the time factor, so all-important. Great events often unfold slowly, often take a long time to mature and come to pass. Even in physical science the importance of the time factor has come to be recognised as fundamental. . . .

". . . We must look upon world peace not as a mere accom-plishment, or waiting just round the corner, but as a long-range task, calling for a new spirit among the nations and for mighty efforts to achieve it. Of that spirit there is little evidence at present. . . ."

My father did not return quite empty-handed from the Con-ference, for he won us the concession that South Africa would be consulted regarding the disposal of the Italian colonies. He had renounced our claim to reparations from Italy.

*　　*　　*　　*　　*

During mid-October, 1946, he found time to visit Holland and Belgium, addressing the legislatures in both countries and appeal-ing for settlers for the Union. He also spent a few days in Switzerland and London, before leaving for New York on Octo-ber 22 to attend the Assembly of the United Nations, where he was to press our claim for the incorporation of South-West

Africa and to answer the charges brought by India of discrimination against the Indians of Natal, which had prompted her to impose a trade boycott and to recall her High Commissioner.

This charge of discrimination came strangely from an India which had only just completed one of the most savage massacres in modern history in Calcutta and Bengal, where half a million fleeing Moslem refugees were mercilessly butchered. But India felt she had a mission to consolidate the overwhelming non-White mass of the United Nations. It was partly animus and partly ambition.

My father gave South Africa's answer to Mrs. Pandit, Nehru's sister:

South Africa is still a peaceful, well-behaved and well-ordered country free from these violent international antagonisms, and it is the policy of the Union Government to keep it so. It is to prevent such conditions of social clash arising in South Africa, where so many races, cultures and colours come together, that the Union is doing its best on fair, decent and wise lines to keep the different elements, as much as convenient and possible, apart and away from unnecessary intermixture, and so prevent bloody affrays like those in India or pogroms such as we read of in other countries.

We are honestly trying to find a human way of life for a racially, socially and culturally mixed community such as South Africa, where different sections may dwell alongside each other in peace and with comparative goodwill. . . .

Before the first vote was taken my father told the Assembly:

The South African Government has no desire to baulk any inquiry into, or a study of, the position of the Indians in the Union, but must maintain its position as a sovereign state that this matter is one for domestic jurisdiction. My Government, however, has consented to the matter being referred to the International Court. It will agree to that reference being enlarged so as to include facts as well as law. The Court may conduct any inquiry it thinks right on the facts, sending a commission to South Africa if it wishes, so as to establish the true facts and to arrive at the true determination of the law.

We are not able to agree, in the circumstances which have arisen here and in the face of an attack which has included a suggestion that

497

we occupy a position comparable to that of Nazi war criminals, to an inquiry by any outside political body. South Africa is, and will remain, an independent state. . . .

It was of no avail claiming that the treatment of South African national Indians in South Africa was purely a domestic affair. It was of no use warning UNO of the dangerous precedent of meddling it was setting. The warnings of Britain and others went unheeded. The United States did not support us. Dr. Wellington Koo of China described my father as "the greatest living internationalist", but nevertheless failed to support him.

Before Mrs. Pandit left India Gandhi had said to her: "I don't mind whether you come back having won your case or having suffered defeat. But you must come back as a friend of Field Marshal Smuts."

My father had tried unsuccessfully to get it classed as an "Important question", which would have required a two-thirds majority.

Mrs. Pandit won her case, and the two governments were requested to report at the next session.

By the time the South-West African question came up for discussion, it was evident that so much feeling had been aroused against South Africa by the Indian dispute, that it stood little chance of success. And so, despite the strong support of Britain and the Dominions (and the conspicuous absence of support from America), we were again defeated.

In a long broadcast upon his return to the Union my father said: "We found unbelievable misunderstandings about race and colour conditions and their handling in South Africa. We found a solid mass prejudice against the colour policies of South Africa which not even the most efficient publicity could have broken down in the time at our disposal. . . ."

Regarding the incorporation of South-West Africa he remarked firmly: "The Union Government is determined to maintain at least the position given it under the mandate and to discharge the trust it has undertaken to the inhabitants of South-West Africa and to the Union itself, to whose security South-West Africa is essential. . . ." In this my father was to get fullest support from every shade of opinion in South Africa.

498

During his stay in New York he visited the American Museum of Natural History, of which he was an honorary Corresponding Member, where he was introduced to Wendell Phillips, whom he invited to visit South Africa with a team of anthropologists to study our fossil ape-men.

On the way back from America he spent two days in London and a few in Athens.

In South Africa, while resenting our rebuff at UNO, the Nationalists jeered that my father's mission had been a failure and were full of criticism and advice after the event. This had been his first international check in many years, and they exploited it to the full.

My father himself was angry, not to say worried, at his cavalier treatment. What he saw there filled him with forebodings for the organisation's future. If only America had wise and sagacious leadership and could cast off her sentimental immaturity. There it was a case of the blind leading the blind.

LXXXIV ROYAL VISIT

SOUTH AFRICA, too, was resentful of her rough treatment at UNO and feelings were running high at the Indian attitude there. In Natal a boycott of Indian traders was attempted, but nothing came of it.

Immigrants from overseas, and especially Britain, were arriving in a steady stream. Yet many more were held back by shipping bottlenecks, even though two troopship-type Union Castle liners had been set aside especially for them. The passenger waiting list had swelled to thirty thousand. Some in desperation decided to venture along the long overland route to the Union, little realising what tribulations lay along those seven thousand miles of bush and desert. On the way back from Britain my father came across the Macallister family of "overlanders" stranded at Khartoum, and these he gave a lift down in his York.

Immigration my father looked upon as the country's greatest priority if its future as a permanent home for the white man was to be assured. He was determined to see the white man firmly established in the southern end of Africa, where climatic conditions were well suited to the propagation of a sturdy race. The African might well be left to other portions of the continent where he was capable of flourishing under more specialised conditions.

In Parliament my father had to answer interminable criticism of his failure at UNO. Yet Dr. Malan agreed that "it was an attack on our freedom as a nation and our sovereignty". He criticised, however, my father's decision to continue submitting yearly reports to UNO as a measure of courtesy. The Indian problem Malan would solve by transferring them back where they came from. This was a solution that had been tried before but proved a failure. When it came to the vote, my father's work at UNO was approved in the House by a majority of 82 to 46.

Mr. Hofmeyr now stepped in to tell the House that Dr. Malan's proposal for the revision of the Union's colour legislation "on a basis of segregation" could not be justified either morally or ethically, and certainly could not be justified in the light of UNO. It was one of the mild, liberal speeches he often made which gained for him the opprobrious Opposition nickname of "Kaffer boetie" (Negrophilist). Hofmeyr's was a just and fair reflection, but in this country of colour prejudice it did his party no good.

To those who suggested in dudgeon that South Africa should withdraw from UNO, my father said: "South Africa is behind the United Nations if the United Nations plays the game and carries out the Charter. If it does not, it will go the way of the League of Nations. It will fail not because of us, but because it was unfaithful to the Charter. . . . For South Africa at this stage to isolate herself would be disastrous," he warned Parliament. "Though the trend of events may appear disquieting South Africa should not be frightened into pursuing the wrong policy." My father's views always were that it was better to stand inside an organisation, however hostile it might appear, than to stand alone in the cold outside, a target for mud and stones.

In mid-February, 1947, occurred one of the pleasant highlights of our history, when the King and Queen and two Princesses made a two months' triumphant visit to the Union. It was partly a tribute to our fine war effort in the light of much difficulty, but more distinctly, as the press stressed, a personal tribute to my father. He had also been an old friend of King George V and Queen Mary. In fact, as a token of homage, my father throughout the war insisted on sending Queen Mary food parcels, and he made a point of seeing her whenever he was in England. In her letters to my mother Queen Mary addresses her as "Dear Ouma".

When the visit was first mooted a year before, General Kemp was quick in his disapproval: "The position of the Afrikaner and Republican is clear. Those of us who took part in the South African War, or whose forebears took part, and who have since striven and are still striving for a Republic in South Africa, and other pro-Republicans, cannot take part in a festivity which will strengthen the monarchy in the Union." This was a general Nationalist attitude. But the natural friendliness and warmth of the Royal Family were swift to melt the hearts of even the doughtiest Republican, and the tour, though strenuous, was a great success. But strangely, one Nationalist newspaper was so busy sticking its head, ostrich-like, into the sand that it failed to notice that a Royal Visit was on and omitted any mention of it.

During the visit my father made frequent appearances with the Royal party. He had the pleasure, too, of showing them, as he had Prince George before, the breathtaking view from the top of Table Mountain. With an ostrich feather from the Queen's hat stuck in his best panama, he extolled to Their Majesties the virtues of mountaineering. "I could see a glow of enthusiasm, surprise and wonder on the faces of the Royal Family," he said. "I am sure they went back with the feeling that Table Mountain was the grandest in the world."

Later on he was to spend a few days with the Royal Family at the fine Mont-aux-Sources National Park in the Drakensberg of Natal, when they paused for a few days in their endless 10,000-mile tour through the country. Here, in the heart of the highest mountain mass of the Union, they were unfortunate in striking unseasonable drizzly weather, so my father was never able to show the King the view from the summit.

Their Majesties also found time for a hurried visit, one afternoon, to my mother and the rest of us in our old "tin shanty" on Doornkloof. I think this was the most informal visit of the whole tour, and Ouma chatted to the King and Queen as though she had known them all her life.

At the end of the Royal Visit the *Cape Times* said: "We believe we are not rash in hoping that as a consequence of the Royal Visit here there will permanently be something a little sweeter, more sincere, in our public life."

My father was critical of the arrangements for the Royal Tour. He considered them far too strenuous, especially, he said, as he had promised Their Majesties a pleasant holiday when he had initially approached them about the possibilities of the visit. He genuinely intended the tour to be a holiday as much as a welcome from a Dominion.

*   *   *   *   *

Most of the returned soldiers were by now back in civilian occupations. The Directorate of Demobilisation had by the end of November discharged 222,112 volunteers and those still on strength numbered only 17,732. The rate of release had been about 16,000 per month, though it was, naturally, now slowing down. Financial assistance and monetary benefits to ex-volunteers totalled more than forty-seven million pounds, and grants and loans each totalled over nine millions. In addition war gratuities of over thirteen million pounds had been paid out. It was a wonderful achievement.

There was to be trouble during the next few months with the Native Representative Council, which resigned as a body in protest at new legislation, and even when my father announced new concessions in which natives were to be given executive authority, especially in their reserves, they still remained obstinate. The drift of natives to the towns was creating urgent problems, and even to-day we are no nearer their solution. It was the policy of the Government to maintain residential segregation as far as possible. But because of an acute lack of housing, native slum "shanty towns", which were ideal breeding spots for vice, disease and discontent, were springing up on the outskirts of big cities. In one of these, Moroka, there was a serious riot during the year in which three European policemen were stoned to death. White feelings were outraged at this event which did little good to the native cause.

Such was the prosperity of the country that in his Budget Speech in March, 1947, Mr. Hofmeyr was able to announce tax relief of over fifteen and a half million pounds. A few weeks later we handed to America a cheque for twelve and a half million pounds, being half our total lease-lend payment to be made in cash. This was the largest cash payment so far from any lease-lend country.

It was at this time that my father secured for the South African Air Force 136 Spitfires which were to form the nucleus of our post-war air force.

In October he was able to announce an eighty million pound three-year gold loan to Britain, a condition being that she would annually import from South Africa twelve million pounds' worth of fruit, food and wine. The Nationalists naturally supported this loan as it benefited our farmers. They were in two years' time to bless it.

Regarding a peace treaty with Germany my father had advocated an experiment there similar to the fruitful one in this country after the Boer War. Any other basis for a peace treaty, no matter how attractive, would be an idea built on shifting sands. It was dangerous to suggest cutting the Ruhr off from Germany. Germany was the heart of Europe, and by rendering Germany powerless a situation could develop which would steer humanity on the wrong course for years to come. The solution must not be born out of revengefulness.

At the end of May he took the opportunity to review the international situation in the Senate:

There is no doubt that the political situation may be a fruitful source of trouble in the world in the future, but this does not mean that I believe war to be imminent. I cannot believe this sort of danger exists. It is a mistake to think so. The world is tired. I do not believe any of the big nations want war. They are exhausted by the war which has just ended. Their economies are disrupted.

But war is not the only danger. There is a struggle going on between ideologies, and conditions may arise which will make this a great danger. Communism is like a new religion, but it is based on convictions and on hopes for the future of mankind. It is also based on the trouble which has beset mankind.

This movement is going on all over the world, not only in Russia. Russia no doubt looks to these movements in other countries for support and therefore has a grave responsibility in the matter. The danger is that there have been religious wars before with devastating effects. While no Government wants war, these movements, if they continue, if this aggressive propaganda continues, may reach breaking point, resulting in war. . . .

It is not that Britain is no longer a great Power. She is an invalid having been incapacitated by the great effort she had to make in the war. You may be a strong man but nothing will keep you out of hospital if misfortune overtakes you.

I do not like the position of the two super Powers in the world. It is necessary for the peace of the world that Britain shall recover her position and maintain herself as one of the super Powers in the world. That will happen. It is merely a matter of time.

The whole present position has emerged as a result of the war. Take the dollar and sterling position. There is only one cause—the war. It is a position which has arisen simply from the war situation and one which will take time to right itself. To say Britain is down and out, as some say and as some wish, is quite wrong and is wishing for calamity in the world. I go so far as to say I look upon British rule as a safer guarantee of peace in the world than the United Nations itself. I say this not in criticism of UNO, but because UNO is so young and inexperienced.

The squabbling and disagreement in the Security Council had come as a bad blow to all who looked for world peace in the future. The veto right has been abused to such an extent that one does not know whether it will be more of an incubus on the progress of mankind. The General Assembly also has not been very satisfactory. In the atomic council also there had been very sharp disagreement and no progress had been made.

When I am asked to express my opinion on the United Nations I say that wishful thinking will not help us. Judging from indications I have seen so far, I suspend judgment. . . .

LXXXV ELECTIONS AND REJECTION

IN 1947 the Party machines were geared for the elections which were due the middle of the following year. It was plain that it was going to be characteristically fierce and unscrupulous, and that it was going to be fought, as in 1929, on the colour question. Once more the Nationalists were going to appeal to the lower prejudices of the electorate. They were going to point accusing fingers at Hofmeyr and UNO, and scream about a black menace from within as well as without. Dr. Malan had already made this clear. A win for my father, he said, would be a victory for Mr. Hofmeyr, who stood for the removal of the colour bar.

In order to discuss its representation in the Union Parliament, my father visited South-West Africa in July, and in August he was the guest of the Belgian Government during a friendly call on the Congo. "Together we will strive for a new Africa," he told the Belgians.

A month later in Johannesburg, my father had the mortification of having a Party meeting in the City Hall broken up by several hundred striking building workers. He was just telling his audience that the past eight years had been the most brilliant in South Africa's history, and the most stormy, when the noisy mob surged towards the platform.

My father attended the wedding of Princess Elizabeth which took place in London in November. On the way there he had discussions in Athens on Greek matters and in Italy with Count Sforza on the Italian colonies.

While in England he received the Freedom of Malmesbury and of Southampton.

After ten crowded days he was on his way home again. Before leaving he said to the Royal Institute of Philosophy: "We are passing through grave and critical times, times of deep heart searching. Men are hungry, not for bread, but also, and just as much, for things of the spirit. Are they not to be fed? . . . We are starved not only for dollars, but for lack of spiritual currency. . . .

Our danger to-day is surrender, giving in, giving way either to blind submission or blinder revolt."

Back in Pretoria he was to express concern over the relations between Russia and the West. "It is a question whether it is possible to stem this tide before it has gone too far."

Absolute prodigies of work had been accomplished by my father during these years. Not only were there the exacting trips overseas, but on the home front, too, matters were steadily reaching a new tempo as the peace-time change-over progressed. The Opposition, having been dormant for most of the war, especially during the time when the Allies were winning great victories, now became vociferous and aggressive.

There was so much to do, and with the onset of age, so little time left. He now seemed to live only for his work. There was no time for leisure other than an occasional long walk. I felt, and said, that he was rapidly working himself to death. Even a mighty machine needed to pause at times. Yet though my father frequently looked weary, he never displayed this by his actions or his bearing. But I noticed that his hobbies were now almost completely pushed into the background and that in the scientific world he was interested only in the great atomic developments. It was disturbing. I said to people who were planning his political work that they were rapidly burning out our greatest asset, but people kept on calling upon him to open fêtes and bazaars and to cap beauty queens, and he kept flying hither and thither from one end of the country to the other. These were the duties of younger men. It might have been good political policy to display my father to the public in this fashion, but in every other sense it was a short-sighted policy. True, my father could have refused; but he was a gallant and willing horse, and never did.

In a way he must have felt the hand of time slowly stealing over him, for as far back as the last General Elections he had talked about retiring and had said "this old war horse is running its last race".

The year 1948, though it started off full of promise, was to turn to one of great disappointment, disaster and sadness. From the point of view of legislation it was comparatively unproductive, for it was an election year. In January we acquired from Britain two small islands, Marion and Prince Edward, in the Indian

Ocean 1,400 miles south-east of Cape Town, which were to serve as weather stations. The highest peak on Marion was named after my father.

At about this time came the news of the assassination of Mahatma Gandhi. "Gandhi was one of the great men of my time," said my father, "and my acquaintance with him over a period of more than thirty years only deepened my high respect for him, however much we differed in our views and methods."

Yet in 1946 he had not been so eulogistic of the work of Gandhi, when he remarked privately to some of us: "The attitude of Gandhi is anti the material world and as the British personified the material world he is automatically anti-British. Gandhi stressed the spiritual value of things, the religion and the soul of India. The position in India is very complex: Fundamentally it is a battle of religions—the Hindu and the Moslem. It was only the presence and power of Britain that kept India together. Remove it, and you will have the sects once more at each other's throats and India will once more split up into an infinity of small states. The views of Gandhi were aggravating matters and it would perhaps be a good thing if he could pass quietly away into the next world." In May 1948 he remarked to me that matters in India had improved since Gandhi's death and that he now felt more than ever convinced that he had been an "unsettling influence".

At the end of the Mountbatten régime the Socialist Government of Britain could resist the insistent clamour for independence by India no longer and Hindustan and Pakistan were made fellow partners with the older Dominions. And so began a vast new experiment which was fraught with incalculable dangers. Opinion in Britain was divided on the issue of withdrawal from India, and those who, like my father, warned of the dangers of removing the restraining and guiding white hand, have had much to bear out their apprehensions since. My father described our decision to quit as an "awful mistake". We are now faced with a tactical position in which the participation of India on our side in the event of war is not only problematical, but one in which even more disturbing consequences might have to be faced.

A milestone in Commonwealth affairs was passed when it was decided at a Prime Ministers' Conference to permit India to assume a republican status while still remaining a full member of our group. The arrangement delighted only Nehru and the Nationalists of South Africa. My father was filled with grave misgivings and said this would revive the Nationalists' ambitions to obtain a republic for this country.

Speaking on the menace of Communism in the House of Assembly, Cape Town, in March, he said that more and more of Europe was coming under the shadow of Communism:

Czechoslovakia is the last warning . . . a model republic has gone . . . South Africa is not out of danger . . . if the dam breaks I see no point where the danger can be stopped. . . . Dr. Malan has used the word "war" . . . Why declare war if the goal can be reached without it by means of infiltration? I believe the whole world can go down without war. We are keeping watch on the changes going on in the world. There is this new technique, the new method.

Hitler developed a technique which went very far, and this technique is being followed by others to-day. What Hitler did not achieve, others might, by using his technique.

Dangers exist in all countries. . . . The people of the United States also see the danger, and that is why we have the Marshall Plan. . . . From Britain there is another plan—Western Union. It is beginning on a small scale, and if it were a success, it could be extended.

On another occasion when speaking of the menace of Communism he described how it had engulfed Asia, which had now become a Lost Continent. "The prospect of Asia is a pitiable one from the human point of view." If the white man withdrew from Africa the same fate would await it. Though Africans could speak the language of the West, that was not the same thing as leadership or government. There were heavy responsibilities resting on the white communities in Africa: "If Europe is to be saved from Communism and anarchy, the gap between differing native policies will have to be bridged. The Union of South Africa will have to play its part in this co-ordination of policy."

By this time the Nationalists had issued a long statement on their policy of "apartheid" (segregation) and made it clear that they were going to fight the election on colour lines. It was to be the old "black menace" all over again, and the chief target was Mr. Hofmeyr.

My father had reaffirmed that he had no idea of retiring:

"I shall be in the political field as long as I have the strength of to-day and the mind to do so," he told the electorate. He despised the Nationalists for making a "kaffer boetie" and "gogga"* of Hofmeyr.

At a Rotary Club lunch in Johannesburg he declared that "the United Nations itself is becoming a problem. So far from being an effective means of dealing with world problems, the organisation itself is a difficulty". Dealing with Palestine, where the Arab and Jewish populations were in a state of ferment, he said:

In the problem of Palestine there is tragedy at our doorstep. Britain has been trying for twenty years to deal with the problem, but she has failed, and no wonder she is getting sick and tired of it all. Failure in Palestine will not only be a British failure. Other nations have also taken a hand, including America, and they have also failed. Palestine is not a small problem. It is one of the great problems of the world and can have a great effect on the future of the world.

Palestine lies on one of the great highways of history—on the highway between Africa and Asia—and has been a problem through history. We have thought to let the Arabs and Jews fight it out, but we cannot do that. Palestine is closely connected with the big issues in the world. Power is on the move and Palestine lies on that road.

It is a question of oil—one of the instruments of war, of power. But it is not only oil, for Palestine also lies very close to the border which divides the great powers of the world, and some of those great powers are keeping in the background. . . .

Britain had not only given up India. She had withdrawn from the strategic area of Egypt as well, a factor which filled my father with anger. In a B.B.C. broadcast he said:

. . . Our sea power has suffered heavy losses, which can, however, be repaired and even improved by the new scientific discoveries. But our lost communications will never be recovered. I refer to our life line through the Mediterranean and on to the Middle East and to the Far East—from the Commonwealth point of view perhaps the greatest loss we have suffered.

We still hold certain points in the Mediterranean, but Egypt has gone, and with it our position as of right to use it as a base. What such a base meant was proved in the last war. But for it nothing might have

* Frightening insect.

prevented Germany from overrunning the Middle East and linking up with Japan in India. From that base we broke the Italian Empire and Italy itself, so that the final attack on Germany could be made from the West. That line has gone, and other dispositions will have to be made for the Commonwealth to make good that grievous loss. . . .

On his seventy-eighth birthday, the 24th May, 1948, my father announced the Union's *de facto* recognition of the State of Israel. In view of the run of terrorism against British soldiery by the Stern Gang and Irgun, feelings against the Jews were running high in this country, no less than in Britain. To make such an announcement two days before a General Election was therefore an act which I considered unwarranted. I said to my father that I thought he had committed an error of timing and that he would lose many votes. He brushed aside my admonition with words to the effect that I was talking nonsense.

On Wednesday the General Elections were held. In view of the wonderful record of the Government, my father hoped for a considerable majority, though he expected that controls and restrictions would lessen his lead. The result, a Nationalist victory with a majority of five in the House, came as a stunning shock. He had been present in his Standerton constituency during a portion of the voting and had come away with some apprehension about his own position, but he never expected such a complete landslide. It also took nine out of ten Nationalists by surprise, and Dr. Malan himself described it as a "miracle".

But as the night of the counting wore on and one after another of the rural seat results were announced in the Nationalist favour, my father grew more and more gloomy. When the result of the defeat of his first Cabinet Minister, Major Piet van der Byl, came through on the radio he said, "There goes my first Minister!" He did not wait to hear his own result. By this time the issue was a foregone conclusion. W. C. du Plessis defeated him by 224 votes.

One of the first phone calls that came through after this result was announced was from a woman purporting to be the sister of Jopie Fourie. "Now Jopie Fourie is avenged!" she taunted.

The result of these elections, occurring just when the country was at the peak of its development, shocked my father more gravely than any event I have witnessed. It was far worse than a personal slap in the face. He felt, like Churchill, that it was the unjust and ignominious sacking of an old war-horse that had deserved well of its country. Even the superlative self-control of this iron old man could not hide his bitter disappointment. But the thought that it would not be for long cheered him. Their meagre majority would make a long term impossible. But he was not reckoning with their cunning manipulation of numbers, or of Sir Stafford Cripps's heaven-sent succour of devaluation just when Malan's Government seemed down and out.

Three days after the elections, I went with him to the bushveld. Perhaps here he would find solace. We let him drive because we felt it would do him good, but it was plain that his thoughts were very far from the roads, and on one occasion we barely negotiated a fast bend. Near Rooikop he ran over a poor Rhode Island cock standing in the middle of the road. He never noticed the cock nor saw the flurry of feathers. He was alone with his thoughts, looking pale and weary. It was, perhaps, too late now to start the long battle all over again.

After breakfast I went for a long walk with him. I was feeling angry and depressed. He never uttered a word. I thought it might cheer him if I gave him a soliloquy of my thoughts. I remarked to him what wretched and ungrateful creatures I considered his countrymen, what turncoats many of his soldiers must have been in this election, how fickle some of the English, how narrow many of his own Boer stock. What was the use of fighting for these wretches? Let them stew in their own juice—under Dr. Malan! I said again that it was Liberal elements in our midst that had killed him. "Why not do as you so wisely counselled Mr. Churchill," I said. "Why not become an elder statesman and exercise your influence in the background, without getting involved in everyday active politics? Why not retire while you still have strength to do your writing, which you owe to posterity? It is no use fighting all the weary old battles over again. You will never make headway while you have a colleague like Hofmeyr. Let the young men now carry on. Let them for once stand on their own feet and fend for themselves. It's their turn to struggle now. If they want advice they can always come to you."

He listened attentively and now and then appeared to express agreement with my argument, and I came away with the impression that he had definitely decided to retire. He agreed it might be sound advice to retire to an active background. He expressed a low opinion of the integrity of the new Cabinet, whom he described as "a thoroughly bad lot". What he liked least of all about the elections was the opening of a wide rift between town and country.

On Monday 31st Senator Andrew Conroy came to see my father on what he called a "vital point". He had come to persuade my father not to retire from politics. If he retired it would mean the complete break-up, and the end for all time, of the United Party. Conroy must have been eloquent and insistent, and this, combined with the fact that it was Union Day, turned the tide. Next day he announced that he would run again and accepted the offer of Charlie Clark's Pretoria East seat.

This decision acted like a tonic and immediately he began to cheer up and take an active interest in life. "I look forward with confidence to the eventual completion of the task for which fifty years has been all too short a period," he announced. "I hope to continue to take my part and do my duty as leader. We respect the constitutional verdict of the people, although in actual results a minority of electors are in charge of the government of the country.

"Whatever the ultimate effects of this anomalous position may be for South Africa, let us minimise the possible evil and do our best to win it to ultimate good. I know many of you have me in your thoughts at this time—I am now an old man, after fifty years' hard labour for the advance of South Africa. If there is blame for the present failure, let it be mine, as no doubt the heavy punishment will be. I can take it."

Another factor which swayed my father was the fact that the majority of the electorate were still behind him, even though he had a minority in the House. Of the million people who had voted, a hundred thousand more had voted for the United Party than for the Nationalists, a majority of about 20 per cent. We were thus in the anomalous position of being ruled by what was very definitely a minority government.

In January, 1948, my father had been nominated to the office of Chancellor of the University of Cambridge made vacant by the death of Lord Baldwin. Appreciating this very touching honour, he said: "It was well that this Commonwealth aspect should be specially emphasised, as a large number of Dominion students have received and are receiving their highest academic training at the two old British Universities. This recognition therefore comes to the whole Commonwealth. I am naturally very proud and grateful for this high honour," adding: "What I specially appreciate is the great good will behind it which is shown by the nomination having been unanimous."

Three days after his talk with Conroy he flew to England, to his installation at Cambridge. Here he told the students: ". . . My view of the present situation is much influenced by the thought that our perspective of the immediate future is too much influenced by the two world wars, which are but the most prominent feature of something deeper moving in our age. We do not realise that we are in fact passing through one of the great secular revolutions of history, and that deeper forces are at work which—war or no war—may completely reshape our world, and are already in fact transforming our human scene. . . . War is only an incident of this secular change. . . . The fact, however, is that all the Great Powers are anxious to avoid war. None of them are in a position to fight another great war. . . ." He referred to the "aggressive diplomacy" of those "East of the Curtain" and warned of the danger of this: ". . . unpreparedness accentuates this danger. Pacifism, disarmament, unpreparedness, act as direct incentives to this form of aggression. They afford a great temptation to the would-be aggressor. . . ."

Die Burger, a Nationalist newspaper, approved of the speech. "We may differ from him on many issues," it said, "but the honour which he has won for the Afrikaner does not leave us untouched. The thought expressed by General Smuts could in essence have come from Dr. Malan." That was the highest compliment possible.

During this visit, which lasted little over a week, he received a Doctorate of Law from Leyden University, and then returned home to his land of taunts.

LXXXVI TRANSFORMATION

JUST what the name of my father meant to South Africa became evident within the first few days of his eclipse. Overnight, literally, two hundred million pounds, some of it "funk" money, but most of it sound investment, left the country, and we who a week before had been the most flourishing country in the world now became one of the poorer, struggling ones. The efforts of the Minister of Economic Affairs, Eric Louw, to keep down the cost structure were a failure, and Lucky Havenga's Department of Finance struggled to keep afloat and drew heavily on my father's £80,000,000 gold loan to Britain, which they swiftly exhausted, before being compelled to clamp down a rigorous control on imports from England and America. The exploitation of the loan my father described as a disgrace, as it would not help in the development of the country and would merely gain the Government temporary respite.

We were moving into a dark period of totalitarian politics. Gone was the fine national spirit of co-operation; gone the feeling of tolerance; gone the *esprit de corps* in our Army.

General van Ryneveld reached the retiring age. General Poole, his obvious successor, was sent off to Berlin on a flimsy political pretext. General Len Beyers, the new Chief of the General Staff, soon resigned. Throughout the Civil Services bilingualism came before efficiency. The traitors Leibrandt and Holm, who would have been hanged but for the clemency of my father, were pardoned and released, and much was made of them.

There were to be Grievances Commissions to help the "poor people" who had been "victimised" or "unjustly" interned or dismissed by my father during the war. They were reinstated without loss of seniority. It happened in the Railways and Police. It happened everywhere. It was the old story of 1924 of pals helping pals. "South Africa does not deserve a Government like the present one," my father said, "a Government whose policies are leading to constriction and ultimately to depression. South Africa has behaved too grandly, too beautifully, in the years behind us to deserve that fate, to have that sentence inflicted upon it."

In the eyes of the overseas world our stock had fallen so low that the Government felt moved to appoint Mr. Charles te Water, Hertzog's unsuccessful first choice as locally-born Governor-General, as a "roving Ambassador" of goodwill abroad. It had little effect.

These disasters were bad enough in themselves, but towards the close of the year still sadder and more shaking events were to occur.

On the 10th of October, after an illness of only a few hours, my brother Japie died suddenly of an acute attack of cerebral meningitis. We had not even been aware that he was ill. The first news we got was at midnight when I was knocked up and told that my brother had died suddenly at Welgedacht Mine. I had to break this terrible news to my father. He seemed incredulous. But it was true, and it was a staggering blow to him, for Japie was the brilliant one of the family and our cornerstone. The event aged my father and made him work harder than ever.

Barely seven weeks later came the death of the industrial giant, and friend of my father's, Dr. H. J. van der Bijl.

Two days later, on the 3rd of December, followed the still greater blow of the death of Mr. J. H. Hofmeyr. "Within two days of each other these two highly gifted sons of South Africa have left us," my father mourned. "Happy young country which could, within a few years of each other, produce two such brilliant sons! Unhappy country which could, within a couple of days of each other, lose both of them!"

Speaking at Hofmeyr's funeral he said:

Am I the one to complain of what I, too, personally have lost? I who buried my great friend, Louis Botha, at a moment of South Africa's greatest need, and had with my poor strength to continue his work. I, who now lose my right hand who, I had fondly hoped, would have continued my work, if he had been spared. . . . The sense of what South Africa has lost in Jan Hofmeyr remains almost more than one can bear. Once more my thoughts revert to what I personally owe him throughout those years of the great struggle in the Second World War. . . . During my frequent absences he added my heavy burdens in the Cabinet to his own, and carried them all with ability and distinction, with even a gay and buoyant spirit. . . .

Hofmeyr was gone, his ablest Minister and hardest worker. It would mean renewed hard work. That work would devolve largely upon my father's shoulders. His ex-Cabinet colleagues were not men of private means and all were desperately struggling to re-establish themselves in their former occupations. They could spare little time to help with politics.

In August the Ossewa Brandwag had joined hands with Mr. Havenga, Leader of the Afrikaner Party. They had little in common. Dr. van Rensburg continued to live on his island in the Vaal River. But it was a sign that all the old elements were coming together again.

Meanwhile Dr. Malan with his Government of unscrupulous men had not been idle. To improve his majority in the House he had promised South-West Africa six seats in our Assembly, where formerly my father had not been prepared to concede them more than three. Dr. Malan did this because he felt certain the majority of the seats would be Nationalist. It was politics at its lowest ebb. So far from the Union annexing South-West Africa, my father said, it appeared as though the reverse had occurred.

My father declared at a fête that he could not "sit still and keep quiet" when he saw his country "being run on the rocks . . . If I had a voice of thunder, I would speak out in these last years of my life when so much of what we have built up in these last fifty years is being thrown away".

Towards the end of the year he reviewed world affairs on the B.B.C. Third Programme in what he called "The Changing World Picture". I quote briefly:

. . . In 1945 the second world war came to an end, both in the west and east. Simultaneously the San Francisco Conference drafted the Charter of the United Nations. Could any happier conjunction of events have been conceived? To a world that had passed through its greatest tragedy the Charter looked like the rainbow in the sky after the great deluge. And yet it did not take long before disappointment and disillusion once more clouded that prospect. . . . Even before the San Francisco Conference the mistaken assumption that Russia would play and could be trusted to be co-operative among the other Great Powers had led to another serious mistake. In a spirit of trust, and to induce her to make her maximum effort for ending the war, Russia was accorded an exaggerated role, which carried her as an Occupying Power to the Elbe, and enabled her to place much of helpless eastern and central Europe behind her Iron Curtain. . . .

As against the phenomenal and menacing rise of Russia we must, however, now place the even more spectacular rise of North America to a no-less unprecedented position as a great world power. The U.S.A. is the answer of history to the U.S.S.R. But that is not the whole story. For Russian communism is already showing signs of a reaction against itself. It is a disease which creates its own anti-bodies. The menace of communism, both as a Great Power and as a political creed, is already beginning to rouse the west as nothing else could have done. And who knows what is going on among the satellites behind the Curtain or in Russia itself? Tito's case is a flash of light behind the dark Curtain. . . .

In Europe a no-less spectacular change is taking place, which fits into the pattern of the American change. Gone also are the days of President Wilson's self-determination of peoples, which became a disruptive force in Europe and led to its breaking up into many national units, and to changes which, through the new Austria, Czechoslovakia, and Poland, marked out the route which led to the second world war. Now at last Europe is once more resuming the historic movement to greater unity, instead of further disruption. Both European security and European economic prosperity are dependent on closer European unity. That lesson has now at last been burnt into the consciousness of Europe. From this point of view, the possible partition of Germany would be a fatal blot on this picture of unity which is unfolding.

It was not only the security motive which was helping to bring Europe together after the last war. The economic motive was equally urgent. A motley collection of European states—every one of which had been brought to the brink of economic collapse by war damage and exhaustion, and still separated by the old pre-war trade barriers, to which war had added new barriers—was of course an impossible set-up from the point of view of economic recovery. A new set-up had become necessary. Small tentative approaches through the Benelux proposals, followed by the Brussels Pact, in which France and Britain joined Benelux, have swiftly led, through the Marshall Aid Plan, to the new Organisation for European Economic Co-operation. Here again was the insight of a great statesman, backed up by the generosity of a great people. The inspired war-time gesture of Lend-Lease Aid has been followed by the still more impressive peace-time gesture of Marshall Aid, and the O.E.E.C. is in being and already in full operation. Nothing finer has been done in the history of human solidarity. It covers western and southern Europe, with the unfortunate exception of Spain. The fundamental idea was that if the European democracies agreed to combine in a scheme of mutual self-help, the United States of America would supplement their financial needs from its resources. . . .

Independently of this there is another—a political unity movement, of which the world's grand old man, Winston Churchill, has been the foremost advocate. That movement aims at a more ambitious and enduring union of European democracies, which in the long run will build up a United Europe, or United States of Europe, which will form a powerful middle bloc of Powers between the two Great Powers of the U.S.A. and the U.S.S.R. . . .

. . . The success of the Council of Europe will take time. Meanwhile European security has to be safe-guarded. And so a third organisation has been decided upon under the Atlantic Pact. Under this great instrument North America joins with the west European democracies in a regional pact of mutual self-defence. It is now in force and the details are being worked out by the military staffs of the Atlantic Powers. This is the largest and farthest step yet taken towards a peaceful world. With American power and defence resources behind it, stricken Europe can now proceed to build up her security system and render any gamble on aggression unpayable for the future.

. . . There remain other large issues on which I have not touched. There is the immense problem of Asia, from which the European is being extruded and into which communism is marching. It is a bleak and grim prospect which one can only contemplate with grave anxiety. It is all still wrapped in darkness. . . .

. . . The Truman initiative in promoting development of backward areas is another grand insight, like the Marshall Plan, and may help to lift the food and raw materials problem for mankind on to a new plane. Africa, the forgotten continent and the reserve area of this globe, with its vast resources and inexplicable backwardness, will thus also come into the total human picture, and make its contribution towards its own and world progress. Mankind may at last reap the fruits of its immense labours and suffering during this era of history through which we are passing, and World Power may pass to a state of more stable equilibrium.

In South Africa a marked deterioration had occurred in the feelings between black and white. This was partly due to the fact that the moderate Native elements had now decided to withdraw their co-operation from the Government and partly because subversive propagandists saw the moment ripe to press their advantage.

In Durban early in 1949 there was a severe riot between Zulus and Indians in which over a hundred lives were lost. This was no reflection on the white man, for it was an indication merely of the measure of anger of the natives at their exploitation by the unscrupulous Indian merchants. Very similar rioting was later to take place in Newlands in Johannesburg, and though it was on a smaller scale, it had the same basic causes. Once more units of the police and army had to be called out. These riots served to show how near the surface was the old savagery of the Bantu and how unstable the vast volcano of South Africa.

Early in the year South African feelings were outraged at the marriage of Seretse Khama, paramount chief of the Bamangwato of Bechuanaland, to a white English girl. The case was further bungled by the vacillating and belated action of the British authorities. Dr. Malan lost no time in expressing his frank disapproval of the marriage or its probable repercussions on feeling in the subcontinent. Southern Rhodesia did likewise.

This incident also served to draw attention anew to the question of the Protectorates, the Nationalists being quick to point out that Britain was blundering so badly that the time had come for us to assume control of these territories. Dr. Malan even talked of taking our case to the Privy Council. My father did not think the time propitious and said he hoped we would not press our claims, for "a good case can be destroyed by urging it at the wrong time".

At the beginning of the Session Dr. Malan had a "black-out" while speaking and stood distressed and fumbling for words. It was an embarrassing moment for all in the House and the Prime Minister's colleagues seemed paralysed by events. My father was the first to act, going up and talking to the distressed doctor, and at the same time beckoning the ex-Minister of Health, Dr. Gluckman, to come and take a professional look at him.

The Prime Ministers' Conference in London in April was attended by Dr. Malan, and here it was decided to admit India as an independent republic into the Commonwealth group. My father declared that this "violated every concept of the Commonwealth. . . . You are either in the Commonwealth or out of it. If

519

the Commonwealth concept is tampered with or destroyed and it is still proposed to continue the Commonwealth system, there would have to be a new basis of agreement between the member States with a written constitution on the lines of the League of Nations or the organisation of the United Nations," he said. "It is assumed that neither India nor any of the members of the Commonwealth would favour such a plan. What India appears to wish is therefore not compatible with the Commonwealth and cannot be achieved in terms of it."

He went on to warn: "Great care should be taken not to empty the concept of the Commonwealth of all substance and meaning and not to whittle it away until nothing but the word remained with no real meaning or significance. Far better would it be to drop it altogether. . . ."

He said further: " Despite the general chorus of approval wherewith the declaration on the Commonwealth Prime Ministers' Conference on India has been received, I cannot forbear expressing my misgivings about the way wherein India's claim to full membership of the Commonwealth despite its being an independent republic has been dealt with.

"The only satisfactory feature about the declaration is that although the link of allegiance to the King is scrapped for India, it is left intact for other members of the Commonwealth."

The principle which it had introduced was revolutionary and if applied to other cases "may yet come to affect profoundly the future of the Commonwealth". The country he had in mind was South Africa.

My father flew to Cambridge in June to attend the graduation ceremony. It was a very brief visit. To a Press Conference he said: "Something is happening in the East. We are retreating there. The only little people who have stood up to it are the Dutch. They have done a wonderful thing in Indonesia."

If only we had had courage in Egypt and India.

The new Citizenship Bills which were introduced in June caused a storm of protest. The Bills proposed, in place of the existing system under which British citizens qualified after two years' residence, to substitute a waiting period of five years. They were patently anti-British measures. My father attacked them with vigour. "Men and women who came to this country came under

520

the impression—and perhaps it was more than an impression—
that they would be South African citizens and that they would not
be foreigners. We have in a sense broken faith with all those
immigrants who joined us. . . . All I can say is to repeat that our
Party, when it comes back into favour, will see that these injustices
are done away with."

My father had repeatedly declared that he would repeal the
harmful legislation enacted by "this blight that has come over
South Africa—this Broederbond Government".

In October the Minister of Defence suddenly noticed that my
father was still, technically, Commander-in-Chief of the South
African forces. It had for us at home been a standing joke that this
was still so. The Minister wrote my father a letter on October 7
terminating his appointment but omitting to thank him for his
services during the war. This brusque termination caused a storm
of protest from more civil men.

Shortly afterwards my father enunciated a nine-point charter
for the United Party: ". . . The United Party stands by the constitution as framed under the Act of Union; a united South
African nation; freedom and dignity of the individual; European
leadership with justice; the Western way of life; housing, employment and security for the breadwinner and his family; improved
standards of living through the efficient development of all the
nation's resources; a true South African culture, and the restoration of confidence in the Union. . . ."

Having thrown out this new challenge, he flung himself with
renewed energy into the fray. He had been doing far too much as
the spearhead of the so-called action committee, but now he re-
doubled his efforts. He was ageing rapidly, and I personally felt
that the end was approaching. It filled me with indignation that
an old man should be so mercilessly worked.

In one of his walks from Pretoria to Irene across the hills he
had stubbed his toe, and this for some time had been giving
him trouble, often being quite painful. It caused him to walk
with his foot in an unusual position and this put a strain on his
ankle.

Towards the end of the year he developed an acute undiagnosed
pain in his left hip which did not respond to treatment. The correct
treatment would have been rest, but this he refused. It was at

times extremely painful, and disturbed his nights. As time went on it caused him to walk with a decided limp.

But he never complained and never faltered. His even temper and cheerfulness never varied.

In November, 1949, he unwisely flew to London to attend a dinner in honour of Dr. Wiezmann's seventy-fifth birthday. I thought his attendance unnecessary and told him so. But he was determined to go.

On Dingaan's Day, the 16th of December, my father was one of the speakers at the unveiling of the massive £350,000 Voortrekker Monument at Pretoria, where a crowd of 400,000 people were gathered to pay homage to these pioneers. The other speakers dwelt sentimentally on the feats of the past. My father, while praising the achievements of the hardy trekkers, said that one must look to the future and not blindly follow the Voortrekkers, for the history of the Great Trek held many examples of squabblings and bickerings, even in the face of danger and sorrow. "Let us rather be a new order of happy Trekkers," he said.

My father knew his Great Trek as well as anybody, and he admired especially the wonderful record of the Louis Trichardt party who mostly succumbed to malaria in the Zoutpansberg. Many were the pleasant holidays he spent in the mountains trying to trace the path followed by Trichardt in his remarkable crossing of the great Strydpoort range. He was also much interested in trying to find some relics of the van Rensburg party who were murdered on the Limpopo River near our shooting camp in Portuguese East Africa.

And so the year drew to a close with the depressing prospect that the Government was no nearer ejectment than it had been eighteen months before.

For my father, who had for fifty years painstakingly built up greatness and happiness and a co-operative spirit in the Union, it was more than depressing to see his life's work being so swiftly and unscrupulously torn asunder.

LXXXVII THE END

THERE remains little to recount. Many towns were eager to show their affection on the occasion of my father's eightieth birthday and an exacting programme had been planned. There were to be huge public functions, dinners, speeches and freedoms. He would have had to fly backwards and forwards across the country to fit it all in.

At Stellenbosch on 21st April he said at his birthday celebrations: "Safeguard your honour, your integrity, your tolerance, your faith, and look to the future. . . . I do not look to the past, but to the future, and my advice to young South Africans is also —Look to the future!"

Johannesburg, where he had first established himself as a barrister, appropriately, with its massive population, gave him the biggest welcome. Three hundred thousand people cheered him as he drove smilingly down their ranks. At the City Hall he inspected a guard of honour of ex-soldiers, limping perceptibly as he walked straight-backed down the long line. It was a happy day for him.

But he was far from well. Many people remarked on his pale appearance.

The Mayor presented the Freedom of the City in the Council Room. My father replied in a moving little speech which had a distinct note of pathos. It was as if he had suddenly realised that he had grown old and was handing over. It filled me with sadness. "I have served to the best of my ability, with what strength God gave me," he said humbly.

At the banquet in the evening a recorded tribute from Mr. Churchill was played: ". . . I can hardly recall any occasion where we did not reach the same conclusions by simultaneous and independent travail of thought. And now here we have him in our midst, an august octogenarian. Here is the man who raised the name of South Africa in peace and war to the highest rank of respect among the freedom-loving nations of the world. Let us pray that this may not be swept or cast away in the demoralisation which so often follows the greatest human triumphs. Such a melancholy stroke will certainly not fall on South Africa if Smuts's life and strength are prolonged, and that is why we rejoice in his presence here tonight, and why I call upon you to drink his health and wish him from the bottom of all our hearts many, many happy returns of the day."

My father took the opportunity here of once more pleading for Germany to be treated as an equal by the West. If we did this it "may also lead to that equilibrium of world power which will in the long run be the real safeguard of world peace and security".

It was his last earnest plea for a more rational attitude to what he considered the very heart of the European problem.

Pretoria next evening gave him a birthday banquet, and a few days after he was due to fly down to Durban for a similar function, and thereafter he was to leave for Cambridge to attend a graduation ceremony. But the programme never got beyond Pretoria, for on Saturday night, three days after his birthday, he was suddenly stricken down with a coronary thrombosis.

This was the first and last big illness of his life.

I have mentioned recent ailments of the ankle and hip, but this affliction of the heart was the last thing we expected. It was only after he was taken ill that we of the family learned that there had been warning signs during the parliamentary session.

In July, 1949, my father accompanied us on one of our trips into Portuguese East Africa, and I was distressed on this occasion to see how his walking and climbing powers had deteriorated. It came as a very rude shock to me to find, for example, that we had to pause twice while ascending a low steep escarpment, a climb he would not have noticed a year before.

But now, in the 1950 parliamentary session, he wrote casually in his letters to us of a tightness about his chest, which he somehow associated with his throat. He said it sometimes made him uncomfortable. Later he experienced acute pains with this constriction, pains not only of the chest but of the arms as well. Every symptom pointed to heart trouble, yet the almost infallible cardiograph failed to reveal any trouble in this region.

I must here add that we in the Transvaal knew nothing of these extremely painful attacks. My father made light of them, even though each prostrated him in agony for hours. His close friends in the Cape, thinking we knew all about it, did not pass on the information.

And so, with unbelievable fortitude, both mental and physical, he attended to his normal tasks in Parliament and elsewhere.

But the years had at last caught up with him. The end had been hastened by the incredible volume of work he had taken upon himself over the last few years. The aeroplane was as much the cause of his downfall as anything, for it enabled him to dash hither and thither without respite. And even in themselves, these flights were exacting for a man of eighty.

On Sunday morning 28th May the doctors put him to bed, though he still insisted on walking about in his agony for some hours. After that he was on oxygen and drugs for a month and in almost constant delirium. In addition to the extensive area of the heart affected by the thrombosis, he had also his painful hip and swollen ankle. Later, despite the most superb doctoring and nursing and the use of all the most modern drugs, he also developed pneumonia, and on three occasions fragments of clots breaking away caused severe pulmonary embolisms (clots on the lungs).

For a man of his age, or any age for that matter, to survive such a series of mortal afflictions was almost unknown in our medical history. But this hardy old campaigner, with his superb constitution did, and after seven weeks, thin and haggard, he was once more sitting up and going about in a wheel chair. Later he moved about without the aid of a stick and sometimes he was taken into the countryside on long drives.

He did not know the nature of his illness, and we asked that it should not appear in the press, for he still insisted on reading the papers and listening to the radio news.

We were apprehensive too of the effect the knowledge of his crippling illness might have in political circles. The South-West African general elections were at that time about to take place.

We told him that he had merely had a bad bout of pneumonia. It would have been a great unkindness to shake his faith in his indomitable old heart.

He was utterly exhausted. All his reserves were used up, and he was too old to build them up again. At frequent intervals he continued having severe heart attacks without warning, each of which was nearly the finish. We knew that sooner or later the final one would occur.

We allowed him to get up and move about as we found that he got very depressed lying in bed and that his vitality fluctuated with his mood. As there plainly appeared no chance of staging a recovery we all agreed that his remaining days should be made as pleasant as possible and that he should be allowed every freedom. We have never regretted this decision.

In a way I think my father would have welcomed the end, rather than linger on as an invalid. He was much depressed at the Korean affair and the trend of international events. In March he had written to Leo Amery: "Personally I expect very little real response from Russia. Russia is on the march unopposed to virtual occupation of the Far East, which other European Powers have evacuated. This is a conjunction of circumstances which has given her a unique opportunity of which she will avail herself to the limit. It is a fateful prospect, not only for the Far East, but for Europe and the whole world. I sometimes think we do not realise the significance of this moment in world history. The only cheerful possibility is that she may leave the West alone and give it an opportunity to integrate and consolidate itself on a scale which will be worthy of the opportunity."

He was also much worried lest we should be misled by this Russian-sponsored diversion in Korea and concentrate on this distant sideline to the detriment of the real focal point of the danger, which was Europe. It would be absolutely fatal to weaken our already weak position in Europe by waging a major war in the Far East.

He was also distressed to find that he could no longer go for walks. But even this disability he said he hoped to overcome by again taking to horseback riding.

He was constantly asking to have a look at the bushveld farm and no excuse would satisfy him. So we took him there and back one Monday, and he rejoiced in the warm sunshine and the sight of the green wheatfields.

On Sunday the 10th of September he seemed well and cheerful, and I took some pleasant photographs of him on the lawn with the grandchildren.

Next evening, without warning the end came. He had been

remarkably well all day and had gone for two long drives. At dinner that evening he sat at the head of the table as usual and had a good meal. After the meal he rose from the table and walked to his bedroom and sat on his bedside chair for my two sisters Sylma and Louis to take his boots off and to help him to bed.

While they were busy he suddenly slumped forward. The time was 7.40 p.m. There were no dramatic last words.

Louis is a doctor and did all that was possible. But it was beyond mortal powers. A clot had gone to his brain.

The Oubaas had climbed his last Great Mountain.

"A light has gone out from the world of free men," Mr. Attlee aptly remarked.

And so from our scene passed this legendary figure, the last link with so much of our past history—the last member of Kruger's Government; the last senior general of the Boer War; the last Minister of the old Transvaal Colonial Government; the last member of the National Convention; the last, but one, of the Peace of Versailles; the last member of the War Cabinet of the First World War—and almost the last of an age of really great men.

In a cable of sympathy to my mother the King said: "In peace or in war his counsel and his friendship were of inestimable value both to my father and to myself, while the force of his intellect has enriched the wisdom of the whole human race."

Winston Churchill wrote to my mother: "There must be comfort in the proofs of admiration and gratitude that have been evoked all over the world for a warrior-statesman and philosopher who was probably more fitted to guide struggling and blundering humanity through its sufferings and perils towards a better day, than anyone who lived in any country during his epoch."

The Government offered a State funeral. We declined: no Nationalist should have the honour of carrying this great man to his last rest. Instead a deeply impressive military funeral procession took place in Pretoria. Even in a moment of sorrow I could not help being moved to reflection as the coffin, with my mother's wreath of Cape heath, moved past the statue of President Kruger at the railway station before it started on its last train journey.

By far the biggest crowd Johannesburg had ever seen turned out to pay its last respects and stand silently as the hearse wound its way to the Braamfontein Crematorium.

It was the end of a long journey. But what a glorious journey. What a wonderful legacy for a young country.

BIOGRAPHICAL SUMMARY

BORN: 24th May, 1870, on the farm Boplaas at Riebeeck West, Cape.

SCHOOL: 1882–1888 at Riebeeck West, Cape.

UNIVERSITY: 1889–1891 Stellenbosch University College. Graduated B.A. in Science and Literature.

1892–1894 Cambridge University (Ebden Scholarship). Double First Law Tripos.

WROTE "WALT WHITMAN: A STUDY IN THE EVOLUTION OF PERSONALITY": 1895–1896.

PRACTISED AS LAWYER: 1895–1897 (Cape Town and Johannesburg).

MARRIED: 1897—Sybella Margaretha Krige.

STATE ATTORNEY (South African Republic): 1898–1900.

BOER GENERAL: 1901–1902 (Command Boer Forces in Cape).

PRACTISED AS LAWYER: 1903–1906 (Pretoria).

MINISTER OF INTERIOR (Colonial Secretary)
MINISTER OF EDUCATION } (Transvaal Colony 1907–1909).

NATIONAL CONVENTION: 1909–1910. Transvaal delegate and Chief drafter of Constitution of Union of South Africa.

MINISTER OF MINES
MINISTER OF INTERIOR } Union of South Africa 1910–1915.
MINISTER OF DEFENCE

MINISTER OF DEFENCE
MINISTER OF FINANCE } Union of South Africa 1915–1919.

GERMAN SOUTH-WEST AFRICAN CAMPAIGN (Major-General 4.8.1914): 1915.

GERMAN EAST AFRICAN CAMPAIGN (Lieut.-General 10.2.1916): 1916–1917 General Officer Commanding all Forces.

WAR CABINET (Great Britain): 1917–1918.

SIGNED PEACE OF VERSAILLES: 1919. Plenipotentiary for South Africa.

PRIME MINISTER
MINISTER OF DEFENCE } 1919–1924.
MINISTER OF NATIVE AFFAIRS

LEADER OF THE OPPOSITION: 1924–1933.

WROTE "HOLISM AND EVOLUTION": 1924.

PRESIDENT BRITISH ASSOCIATION FOR THE ADVANCEMENT OF SCIENCE: 1931.

DEPUTY PRIME MINISTER
MINISTER OF JUSTICE } 1933–1939.

PRIME MINISTER
MINISTER OF DEFENCE } 1939–1948.
MINISTER OF EXTERNAL AFFAIRS

COMMANDER-IN-CHIEF SOUTH AFRICAN AND RHODESIAN FORCES, Second
    World War: 1940–1945.
FIELD MARSHAL: From 24.5.1941.
LEADER OF THE OPPOSITION: 1948–1950.
DIED: 11th September, 1950 (80 years), on the farm Doornkloof, Irene.

HONOURS—AWARDS—DECORATIONS

COMMONWEALTH APPOINTMENTS AND DECORATIONS:

Privy Councillor	Efficiency Decoration
Order of Merit	King's Counsel
Companion of Honour	Fellow of the Royal Society
Dekoratie voor Trouwe Dienst	Bencher of the Middle Temple

STARS AND MEDALS—COMMONWEALTH AND SOUTH AFRICAN:

Boer War Medal	Africa Star
1914/15 Star	Italy Star
Victory Medal	France and Germany Star
General Service Medal	Defence Medal
King George V's Jubilee Medal	War Medal
King George VI's Coronation Medal	Africa Service Medal

FOREIGN DECORATIONS AND MEDALS:

Order of Merit (U.S.A.)
Service Medal (Mediterranean Area) U.S.A.
Order of the Tower and Sword for Valour, Loyalty and Merit (Portugal)
Grootkruis van die Orde van de Nederlandsche Leeuw (Netherlands)
Grand Cordon of the Order of Mohamed Ali (Egypt)
Grand Cross of the Royal Order of the Saviour (Greece)
Grand Cross of the Order of Leopold (Belgium)
Croix de Guerre (Belgium)
Legion d'Honneur Croix de Commandeur (France)
La Grand Croix de l'Ordre de L'Etoile Africaine (Belgium)
King Christian X Frihedsmedaille (Denmark)
Ariston Andrias (Greece)
Albert Medal of the Royal Society of Arts
Woodrow Wilson Peace Medal

FREEMAN OF THE CITIES OF:

London, 1917	York, 1931
Manchester, 1917	Dundee, 1934
Edinburgh, 1917	Aberdeen, 1942
Glasgow, 1917	Birmingham, 1944
Bath, 1917	Malmesbury, 1945
Cardiff, 1917	Southampton, 1945
Bristol, 1917	Athens, 1947
Sheffield, 1917	Ithaca, 1947
Newcastle-on-Tyne, 1918	Johannesburg, 1950

BIOGRAPHICAL SUMMARY

HONORARY DEGREES:

LL.D. University of Cape of Good Hope, 1915
LL.D. University of South Africa, 1915
LL.D. Cambridge University, 1917
LL.D. Edinburgh University, 1917
F.R.C.P. Edinburgh
LL.D. Glasgow University, 1917
LL.D. University of Wales, 1917
LL.D. Dublin University, 1917
LL.D. Manchester University, 1917
D.C.L. Durham University, 1918
LL.D. Cardiff University, 1921
D.C.L. Oxford University, 1929
LL.D. Witwatersrand University, 1921
LL.D. McGill University, Montreal, 1930
LL.D. Toronto University, 1930
LL.D. Johns Hopkins, Baltimore, 1930
LL.D. Columbia University, New York, 1930
D.Litt. University of Pretoria, 1930
D.Sc. University of Cape Town, 1931
Ph.D. University of Stellenbosch, 1931
D.Sc. London University, 1931
LL.D. Sheffield University, 1931
LL.D. St. Andrews, 1934
LL.D. University of Utrecht, 1936
Ph.D. Berkeley University, California, 1945
LL.D. Leyden University, 1946
F.R.C.O.G. (England), 1947
F.R.C.P. (London), 1948
Ph.D. Athens.

MISCELLANEOUS HONOURS:

Chancellor. University of Cambridge
Clothworkers' Company, 1917
Bencher Middle Temple, June, 1947
Trinity Brethren, September, 1918
Sword of Honour, Pretoria, October, 1919
Skinners' Company, 1929
Great Seal of the State of Massachusetts, January, 1930
President of the S.A. Association for the Advancement of Science, 1925 (Oudtshoorn)
President of the British Association (Centenary Meeting London and York), 1931
Rector of St. Andrews, Scotland, 1931/4
Fellow of the Royal College of Surgeons (Great Britain)
Hon. Fellow Christ's College, Cambridge.

531

SUMMARY

PRIME MINISTER: for 14 years.

DEPUTY PRIME MINISTER: Officially for 5 years: unofficially for 9 years.

MINISTER: for 17 years, during which he held portfolios of Education, Interior, Mines, Defence, Finance, Native Affairs, Justice and External Affairs.

LEADER OF THE OPPOSITION: for 10 years.

MEMBER OF PARLIAMENT: for 45 years, of which 41 years were since Union.

FREEMAN: of 18 Cities.

HONORARY DEGREES: from 29 Universities.

VERY MANY COMMONWEALTH AND FOREIGN DECORATIONS, APPOINTMENTS and MEDALS.

FIELD MARSHAL.

ORDER OF MERIT.

BIBLIOGRAPHY

Amery, L. S., *The Times History of the War in South Africa*. London. S. Low, Marston & Co., Ltd., 1900–09 (7 vols.).

Armstrong, H. C., *Grey Steel*. London. A. Barker, Ltd., 1937.

Baker, Herbert, *Cecil Rhodes*. London. Oxford University Press, 1934.

Baker, Sir Herbert, *Architecture and Personalities*. Country Life, 1944.

Baker, R. S., *Woodrow Wilson and World Settlement*. N.Y. Doubleday, Page & Co., 1922.

Baker, R. S., *Woodrow Wilson. Life and Letters*. N.Y. Doubleday, Page & Co., 1927–39.

Baruch, Bernard, *The Making of the Reparation and Economic Sections of the Treaty*. N.Y. and London. Harper & Bros., 1920.

Birkby, Karl, *Springbok Victory*. Libertas Publications, 1941.

Blackwell, Leslie, *African Occasions*.

Bradley, General Omar, *A Soldier's Story*. Eyre & Spottiswode, 1952.

Brand, Hon. R. H., *The Union of South Africa*. Oxford. The Clarendon Press, 1909.

Brett, B. L. W., *Makers of South Africa*. Nelson & Co., 1944.

Butler, Sir W., *From Naboth's Vineyard*.

Chilvers, Hedley A., *Out of the Crucible*. London. Cassell & Co., Ltd., 1929.

Churchill, Winston S., *The World Crisis, 1911–18*. London. T. Butterworth, Ltd., 1931.

Churchill, Winston S., *The Unrelenting Struggle*. Cassell & Co., 1948.

Churchill, Winston S., *Their Finest Hour*. Cassell & Co., 1950.

Churchill, Winston S., *The Hinge of Fate*. Cassell & Co., 1951.

Collyer, Brig. Gen., *The South Africans with General Smuts in German East Africa*. Pretoria. Government Printer, 1939.

Colvin, Ian. *The Life of Jameson*. London. E. Arnold & Co., 1922.

Crafford, F. S., *Jan Smuts*. Doubleday, Doran & Co., 1944.

Crowe, Brig. Gen. J. H. V., *General Smuts' Campaign in East Africa*. John Murray, 1918.

Cunningham, Admiral of the Fleet, Viscount, *Sailor's Odyssey*, Hutchinson, 1951.

Engelenburg, Dr. F. V., *General Louis Botha*, Pretoria. J. L. van Schaik, 1938.

Fitzpatrick, J. P., *The Transvaal from Within*. W. Heinemann & Co., 1899.

Fort, G. Seymour, *Dr. Jameson*. London. Hurst & Blackett, Ltd., 1918.

Fry, A. Ruth, *Emily Hobhouse*. London. J. Cape, 1929.

Garvin, J. L., *The Life of Joseph Chamberlain*. London. Macmillan & Co., Ltd., 1931–32.

Graumann, Sir Harry, *Rand Riches and South Africa*. Cape Town. Juta & Co., Ltd., 1935.

533

de Guingand, Sir Francis, *Operation Victory*. Hodder & Stoughton, 1947.

Harris, Marshal of the R.A.F., Sir Arthur, *Bomber Offensive*. Collins & Co., 1947.

Hofmeyr, J. H., *Het Leven van J. H. Hofmeyr*.

Hofmeyr, J. H., *South Africa*. London. E. Benn, Ltd., 1931.

Juta, Marjorie, *The Pace of the Ox*. London. Constable & Co., Ltd., 1937.

Keynes, J. M., *A Revision of the Treaty*. Macmillan & Co., 1922.

Keynes, J. M., *The Economic Consequences of the Peace*. Macmillan & Co., 1920.

Kolbe, Monsignor, *A Catholic View of Holism*. N.Y. The Macmillan Co., 1928.

Kraus, Rene, *Old Master*. E. P. Dutton & Co., 1944.

Kruger, Paul, *The Memoirs of Paul Kruger*. N.Y. Century Co., 1902.

Lansing, R., *The Big Four and Others at the Peace Conference*. Boston & N.Y. Houghton Mifflin Co., 1921.

Laurence, Sir Perceval, *The Life of John Xavier Merriman*. London. Constable & Co., Ltd., 1930.

Levi, N., *Jan Smuts*. London. Longmans, Green & Co., 1917.

Lloyd George, D., *War Memoirs of David Lloyd George*. London. I. Nicholson & Watson, 1933–36.

Lucas, Sir Charles P., *The Empire at War*. London. H. Milford, 1921–26.

Macaulay, N., *Mandates*. London. Methuen & Co., Ltd., 1937.

Macdonald, J. Ramsay, *What I Saw in South Africa*. London. "The Echo", 1902.

Mackenzie and Stead, *South Africa, Its History, Heroes, and Wars*. Chicago, Philadelphia. Monarch Book Co., 1899.

Marcossan, I. F., *An African Adventure*. John Lane & Co., 1921.

Marriott, Sir John, *The Evolution of the British Empire, etc*. London. Nicholson, 1939.

Methuen, A. M. S., *Peace or War in South Africa*. London. Methuen & Co., 1901.

Miller, D. H., *The Drafting of the Covenant*. N.Y., London. G. P. Putnam's Sons, 1928.

Millin, S. G., *The South Africans*. London. Constable & Co., Ltd.

Millin, S. G., *General Smuts*. London. Faber & Faber, Ltd., 1936.

Molteno, Sir James Tennant, *South African Recollections*. Methuen, 1926.

Molteno, Sir James Tennant, *Further South African Recollections*. London. Methuen & Co., Ltd., 1926.

Montgomery of Alamein, Field Marshal, Viscount, *Normandy to the Baltic*. Printer and Stationer Series. British Army of the Rhine, 1946.

Montgomery of Alamein, Field Marshal, Viscount, *El Alamein to the Sangro River*. Printer and Stationer Series. British Army of the Rhine, 1946.

Moore-Ritchie, *With Botha in the Field*. London. Longmans, Green & Co., 1915.

Morley, F., *Society of Nations*. Washington. The Brookings Institution, 1932.

Nathan, Manfred, *South Africa from Within*. London. J. Murray, 1926.

Nathan, Manfred, *Paul Kruger*, 4th ed., 1944.

National Review, *Smuts and the Protectorates*.

Neame, L. E., *General Hertzog*. London. Hurst & Blackett, Ltd., 1930.

Nicolson, H., *Peacemaking*. Constable & Co., 1919.

Noble, G. B., *Politics and Opinions at Paris, 1919*. N.Y. The Macmillan Co., 1935.

Oliver, F. S., and Oliver, W. E., *Anvil of War*. London. Macmillan & Co., Ltd., 1936.

Perham and Curtis, *The Protectorates of South Africa*. London. Oxford University Press, 1935.

Phillips, Lionel, *Some Reminiscences*. London. Hutchinson & Co., 1924.

Reed, Douglas, *Disgrace Abounding*. London. J. Cape, 1939.

Reitz, Deneys, *Commando*. Faber & Faber, 1929.

Reitz, Deneys, *No Outspan*. Faber & Faber, 1943.

Reitz, Deneys, *Trekking On*. Faber & Faber, 1933.

Repington, Col., *The First World War, 1914–1918*. London. Constable & Co., Ltd., 1920.

Riddell, Lord, *Lord Riddell's Intimate Diary of the Peace Conference and After*. London. V. Gollancz, Ltd., 1933.

Robertson, Field Marshal Sir William, *Soldiers and Statesmen*. London. Cassell & Co., Ltd., 1926.

Sauer, Dr. Hans, *Ex Africa*. London. Geoffrey Bles, 1937.

Schreiner, Olive, *An English South African's View of the Situation*.

Schreiner, Olive, *Thoughts on South Africa*. London. T. F. Unwin, Ltd., 1923.

Seymour, Charles, *The Intimate Papers of Col. House*. Boston & N.Y. Houghton Mifflin Co., 1926–28.

Sforza, Count C., *Europe and Europeans*. Indianapolis & N.Y. The Bobbs-Merrill Co., 1936.

Simpson, J. S. M., *South Africa Fights*. London. Hodder & Stoughton, Ltd., 1941.

Smuts, J. C., *A Century of Wrong*.

Smuts, J. C., *Holism and Evolution*. N.Y. The Macmillan Co., 1926.

Smuts, J. C., and others, *Our Changing World View*. Johannesburg. University of Witwatersrand Press, 1932.

Smuts, J. C., *Greater South Africa*. (Speeches.)

Smuts, General J. C., *Plans for a Better World*. Hodder & Stoughton, 1942.

Smuts, General J. C., *Towards a Better World*. World Book Co., 1944.

Smuts, General J. C., *Climate and Man in Africa*. South African Journal of Science. October, 1932.

Spender, Harold, *General Botha, the Career and the Man*. Boston & N.Y. Houghton Mifflin Co., 1916.

Stead, W. T., *The Best or Worst of Empires—Which?*

Stead, W. T., *The Review of Reviews* (Jan.–Dec., 1901; Jan.–June, 1902), London.

Tedder, Marshal of the R.A.F., Viscount, *Air Power in War*. Air Ministry Pamphlet, 1947.

Toynbee, A. J., *Study of History*. London. Oxford University Press, 1934–39.

van Hoek, K., *Gesprekke met Dr. W. J. Leyds*. Pretoria, 1939.

von Lettow-Vorbeck, *Reminiscences of East Africa*, 1920.

Walker, Eric A., *A History of South Africa*. London. Longmans, Green & Co., Ltd., 1928.

Walton, Sir Edgar, *The Inner History of the National Convention*. M. Miller.

Webb, H. S., *The Causes of the Rebellion*.

Whittall, Lt.-Commander, *With Botha and Smuts in Africa*. London, N.Y. Cassell & Co., Ltd., 1917.

Williams, Basil, *Botha, Smuts and South Africa*. Hodder & Stoughton, 1946.

Worsfold, W. B., *Lord Milner's Work in South Africa*. New York. Dutton, 1906.

Young, Brett F., *Marching on Tanga*. London. W. Collins Sons & Co., Ltd., 1918.

Young, D., *Rommel*. Collins & Co., 1950.

INDEX

East London, 381

Ebdin Scholarship, 21

Economic Consequences of the Peace (Keynes), 221-2

Economic Developments, Ministry of, 428

Eden, Rt. Hon. Anthony, 403, 409, 432; at San Francisco, 472

Edenburg, 68, 158

Edgar, shooting of, 42

Edinburgh, 297

Education, Smuts's ideas on, 293, 365-7

Education Acts, 102, 123

Edward VII, King, 118; Cullinan diamond given to, 103; gives lunch to S. African delegates, 117

Egypt, troops locked up in, 203; Italy invades, 414; Allied Armies driven back in, 418; revision of British Treaty with, 491; Britain withdraws from, 509

Eighth Army, in Western Desert, 420, 426; tanks for, 420

Einstein, Albert, 316

Eisenhower, General Dwight, N. African campaign of, 422; Smuts confers with, 423, 430; and launching of Overlord, 455-6, 466; and strategy in France, 464-5; Germans surrender to, 477

El Agheila, 416

El Alamein, 415, 426, 433

El Aqqaqir, 426

El Wak, 407-8

Elandsrivierpoort, 74

Elandsvlei, 77

Elizabeth, Princess, 501, 505

Elizabeth, Queen, 493, 501-2

Elliot Smith, Professor, 334

Empire Parliamentary Association, 440-9

Enfidaville, 427

Engare Nanyuki, 164

Engelenberg, Dr. F. V., 100

Enslin, Major, 138

Erasmus, General, 269, 273

Eritrea, 408

Ermelo, 296

Esselen, Louis, 126, 256-7

Etosha Pan, 156

Euphorbia Hill, 167

Europe, unsettled state of, before First World War, 151-2; post-war collapse of Central and Eastern, 236; result of Reparations policy in, 246-7, 346; as origin of Cape flora, 333; Ice Age in, 334, 337; aftermath of war in, 351-2, 357; cult of force in, 355; fear complex in, 357-8; inferiority complex in, 357, 359; need for speed in saving, 434; changes in, 443; Russian domination of Eastern, 468, 517; moves towards unity, 517-18; Council of, 518

Evans, Dr. I. B. Pole, 272, 388, 398

Ewing, Sir Alfred, 322

Falkland Islands, Battle of, 144, 153

Far East, storm centre passing to, 359-60; American bias towards, 422, 450; Russia marching into, 526

Faraday Exhibition, 314

Farouk, King, of Egypt, 452

Farrar, George, and Chinese Labour, 93-4; leader of Progressives, 100

Fascism, rise of, 345-6

Fauresmith hills, 66

Feisal, Prince, of Saudi Arabia, 471-2

Ferdinand, King of Bulgaria, 152

Ferguson, Bob, 40

Fiad, 426

Finland, conquers Russia, 347; conquered by Russia, 393, 451

Fischer, suicide of, 257

Fischer, Abraham, 38, 44, 127-8

Fish Hoek man, 338

Fish River, 78

Fitzgerald, Mary, 160

Fitzpatrick, Sir Percy, 40, 125

Flag Question, 295

Flying bombs (V1), 433, 453, 458-9

Foch, Marshal, 207, 231

Fordsburg, 257

Foreign Secretaries, Council of, 486

Foster Gang, 137-8

stitution of, 111, 113–14; passes S. African help in S. W. Africa, 135; sides with France, 151–2; declares war on Germany, 152, 393; U-boat menace to, 180; appreciates Smuts, 180–1, 237, 244, 314–15, 362–4; war weariness of, 197; shoulders main burden of fighting, 198; air attacks on, 205–6, 413, 424; and reparations, 223; unable to pay war debts, 247; and United States, 251, 444; primitive bombing by, 259; policy of, towards natives, 308; goes off gold standard, 322–3; S. African Protectorates of, 343–344; period of vacillation and appeasement in, 344, 348; France and, 347; fails to take warning of Hitler's intentions, 347–8, 368; helps Norway, 394; S. African wool sales to, 395; American aid to, 407, 413; "invests in friendships", 409–10; threatened invasion of, 413; goes to help of Greece, 414; Smuts on qualities of, 423–4; threatened by secret long-range weapons, 431–3, 453, 467; and India, 439–40, 507; a poor country, 444, 504; and Europe, 445; Colonial system of, 445–7; prepared to invade Continent, 450–1; supplies to Russia from, 452; differs from U.S. as to conduct of European fighting, 464–6; post-war General Election in, 468, 484–6; and Trusteeships, 479; opposed to Veto, 481; weak attitude of, at San Francisco, 483; gives in to Russia, 486; S. African loan to, 503; need for powerful, 504; withdraws from Egypt, 509; joins Benelux, 517

Great Rift Valley, 331, 405–6; Smuts's plane struck by lightning over, 462

Great Ruaha River, 170

Great Trek, 4, 9–10, 522

Greece, in Balkan Wars, 152; in Second World War, 409, 414–5; mutiny among nationals of, in Egypt, 449

Greene, Conyngham, 42, 46

Gregorowski, Chief Justice, 56

Greylings Request, 142

Greyshirt Movement, 370

Grievances Commissions, 514

Griffith, Arthur, 252

Grobler, Piet, introduces Smuts to Kruger,

35; at Stormberg, 50; in Coalition Cabinet, 293; mentioned, 45, 324

Gromyko, M., 472

Groot Winterhock Mountains, 7

Groote Schuur, 259–61; Rhodes's memorial above, 30, 126; building of, 91, 260; Smuts in, 261, 279, 285, 388; thinning trees round, 388; state protection for, 397

Guest, Mr., 77

Haig, Field Marshal Earl, 81, 198–200

Haile Selassie, Emperor, 345, 410

Haldane, Lord, 152

Haldane, Professor J. B. S., 314

Halfaya, 417

Hamanskraal, 63

Hamburg University, 292

Hanbury-Williams, Sir John, 44

Hanekom brothers, 258

Hankey, Maurice, 186

Harriman, Averill, 491

Harris, Air Chief Marshal, 431, 435

Havenga, Nicolaas, follows Hertzog, 129, 385; Minister of Finance, 294, 323–4, 514; and neutrality, 378; returns to public life, 487–8; Ossewa Brandwag joins, 516

Hay, George, 286

Helderberg, 18

Hele rebellion, 150

Hennessy, Sir Alfred, 8

Hennops River, 269

Hereros, extermination of, 150

Hermanus, 278

Herschell, 70

Hertzog, Dr. Albert, 128, 254

Hertzog, General, guerilla campaign of, 63, 66; discusses Free State situation with Smuts, 68; at Vereeniging, 82; and surrender, 82; anti-British feeling of, 99, 158; Afrikanderism of, 99, 123, 126–9; uninterested in Union, 108, 116; at National Convention, 115–16; and language question, 115, 123; political obstreperousness of, 116, 123, 125–8,

INDEX

Kaalsprint, 269

Kafferskop, 68

Kahe Hill, 167

Kajiado, 164

Kakamas, 78

Kalahari Desert, 5, 54, 150; rebels in, 141–142; crossing of, in S.-W. African campaign, 157; Schwarz's redemption scheme for, 331; Bushmen of, 338

Kalk Bay, 463

Kamanassi River, 77

Kameelfontein, 60, 121

Kamiesbergen, 80

Kampfontein, 164

Kaokoveld, 156

Karega, 77

Karibib, 156, 158

Karisimbi, Mount, 373

Karl, Emperor, of Austria-Hungary, 196

Karroo, the, 77, 87

Kasserine, 426

Kasteel, xiii, 3, 6

Keetmanshoop, 157, 163

Keitel, Field Marshal, 436

Kelvin, H.M.S., 457–8

Kemp, General, at Vereeniging, 82; in Rebellion, 138, 141; surrender of, 145; in Coalition Cabinet, 293; and Royal visit, 501

Kemp, J. T. van der, 10

Kendrew Siding, 77

Kenya, British force in, 394; Italy attacks, 394–5; protection for, 403, 409

Kenya-Uganda Railways, 162

Keren, 408

Kerr, Philip, 90

Kesselring, General, 436, 458, 475

Keynes, J. M., 204; *Economic Consequences of the Peace* of, 221–2

Khartoum, conference in, 403; immigrants to S. Africa in, 500

Khatatba, 429

Khies Drift, 141

Kiemoes, 138

Kilimanjaro, Mount, 139; German position near, 164, 166; Smuts's H.Q. on, 176; flying over, 177

Kilimatinde, 170

Kilossa, 170

Kilwa, 171–2

Kimberley, Rhodes gains wealth at, 29; Smuts's speech at (1895), 31–2; relief of, 51

"Kindergarten", Milner's, 89–91, 111

King, Rt. Hon. Mackenzie, 472, 484

King's African Rifles, 394

Kirstenbosch, 401–2

Kisimayo, 395

Kissaki, 170

Kitchener, Earl, of Khartoum, in Boer War, 50, 65; proclamations of, 68–9, 74; Free State sweep of, 69; meets Boers at Vereeniging, 80–2; magnanimity of, 81–83; replaced by Lyttelton, 91; death of, 181

Kivu, Lake, 168, 373–4

Klipdrift, 121

Klipfontein, 15

Knightsbridge, 417

Kobbee, 77

Koedoespoort, 56

Kondoa Irangi, 168, 170

Königsberg, the, in East Africa, 165, 175–6; guns of, 176, 178; trophy from shell-cases of, 275

Koo, Dr. Wellington, 220, 472, 498

Koppieskaal Drift, 68

Koraanberg, 142

Koranna tribes, 5

Korea, 526

Kotze, Mr. Justice, 37–8

Kramarsch, Dr., 220

Krige, Bennie, 136, 139

Krige, Jan, 269

Krige, Japie, 18, 36–7

Krige, Jimmie, 177

Krige, P. S. ("Tottie"), 26; in Boer War, 67, 71, 78; at Vereeniging Conference, 81

Krige, Polly (*née* de la Rey), 138–40

Krige family, 9, 18, 142

550

INDEX

Marshall, General George, 437, 457
Marshall Plan, 508, 517–18
Marwick, Mr., 364–5
Mary, Queen, 279, 501
Masaryk, President, 226
Mashonaland, 30 n.
Massaikraal, 167
Matjesfontein, 81
Mediterranean Theatre, transports bound for, 396; importance of, as theatre of war, 415, 418, 421–2, 448; superiority of forces in, 449; South African strength in, 454, 485
Mein Kampf (Hitler), 347
Meirings Poort, 77
Melkbos Strand, 277
Memel, 229
Mensdorff, Count von, 196–7
Merced River, 481
Meredith, George, 22
Merriman, John X., recognises promise of Smuts, 19; in Parliament, 28; Smuts's letters to, 93, 100; works for Union, 107–8, 113–14; and Premiership, 118–19; on Smuts, 133; on ingratitude of Boers, 180; an old man, 267
Mersa Matruh, 415, 416
Meru, 164
Mesopotamia, campaign in, 153, 183; troops locked up in, 203
Mestklip, 87–8
Methuen, A. M. S., 41
Methuen, Lord, defeated by Boers, 50, 60; Smuts friend, 85–6
Methuen, Seymour, 86
Meyer, General Lukas, 49, 56
Meyer-Abich, Professor Adolf, 291
Mgeta River, 170
Middelburg, 61; Government move to, 55
Middelpoort farm, 78
Middle East Committee, 204
Milan, 473, 484
Milner, Viscount, determined to force war issues, 41, 43–4; protests to Kruger, 42; at Bloemfontein Conference, 44–5; de-

mands unconditional surrender, 82–3; work of, as Governor of Transvaal and Orange River, 89–90, 93; Smuts dislikes administration of, 89, 94–6; Kindergarten of, 89–91; offers Boers seats in Legislative Council, 92, 97–8; distrustful of Boer intentions, 93; inaugurates Chinese labour policy, 93, 95; returns to England, 96; and Russian Revolution, 153–4; in War Cabinet, 186; at banquet to Smuts, 187; on need for separate Air Force, 205; his admiration for Smuts, 237; on S. African terms to Rhodesia, 266; visits Doornkloof, 285; mentioned, 63, 105, 107, 198
Milner, Viscountess, 285
Mine Workers' Union, 254
Miners' Phthisis Bill, 123–4
Minerva, H.M.S., 231
Mines, Chamber of, and Great Strike, 253–5
Mining industry, unrest in, 130–3, 253–8
Mining Regulations, 124
"Mittel-Afrika" concept, 151
Modder River, 68; Battle of, 50, 54, 57
Moffat, Dr., 277
Mogadishu, 395
Molotov, M., at San Francisco Conference, 471–2
Mombasa, 164, 394
Monomotapa, 54
Monro, Colonel, 73
Mont-aux-Sources National Park, 501
Montgomery, General, in Western Desert, 420, 426; in invasion of France, 450, 457, 464, 466; Germans surrender to, 477
Mooi River, 67
Moordenaars Poort, 70, 72, 188
Morley, Lord, 97
Morocco, Germany and, 149, 151
Morogoro, 170
Moroka, 502
Moschi, 167–8, 175–6
Moscow, Treaty of, 393
Mosega, 54
Moselekatze, 10, 54, 273

553   T*

landing craft for, 422, 450; German retreat in, 464

North African Campaign, 420, 422, 426–7

Northern Neutral Committee, 204

Northern Rhodesia, S. African Troops in, 162; question of federation of, 267; Copper Belt of, 267, 373

Northey, General, 167–8, 171–2

Norway, German conquest of, 393, 409; destruction of heavy water plant in, 460

Nyamlagira, Mount, 373

Nyasa, Lake, 168, 339, 398

Nyasaland, 267; German troops in, 162

Nylstroom, 126

Okahanja, 156

Okinawa, 482

Oliver, F. S., 187

Onderstepoort, 121

Ongegund, 6

O'okiep, 80, 88

Oost, Harm, 142

Oppenheimer, Sir Ernest, 373

Orange Free State, white settlers in, 9; effect of Jameson Raid on, 35; Conference in, 44–5; joins Transvaal at war, 49–50; British victories in, 51; refuses to end War, 58; commandos of, remain in their borders, 61; guerilla campaign in, 63; defeat in, 65–6; Smuts's commandos cross, 67–70; representatives of, at Vereeniging, 82; pro-Afrikaans education policy in, 123; Hertzog loses support of, 128–9; election results in, 161; gold strike in, 490

Orange River, 78; crossings of, 66, 69–70; Germans attack Boers on, 136

Orange River Colony, 89; granted self-government, 98; Orangia Unie party in, 99; and Union question, 108; antipathy to Britain in, 108. See also Orange Free State

Orangia Unie Party, 99, 122

Organisation for European Economic Co-operation, 517

Orlando, Signor, 208, 220

Orvieto, 459

Ossewa Brandwag, 129, 382, 386, 406, 516

Ostend, 184, 198

Otavi, 156

Otjimbingwe, 156

Otjivarongo, 156

Ottawa, 484

Oudtshoorn, 77

Outjo, 156

Overlord, Operation, 450, 455–7

Oxford, 207, 251; Smuts delivers Rhodes Lectures in, 297, 307–12

Paardeberg, Battle of, 51

Paardekop, 67

Paarl, 5, 295

Pacific Ocean, future importance of, 251, 360

Painlevé, M., 182

Pakistan, 507

Palestine, campaign in, 183, 204; Smuts offered command in, 184–5; Jews promised home in, 203–4, 302; partition of, 468; Jews and Arabs fight in, 509; terrorism against British soldiers in, 510

Panama Canal, U.S. seek sole right to, 220

Pandit, Mrs., 497–8

Pangani, 169

Papen, Herr von, 369, 469

Pare Mountains, 166–8

Paris, German threat to, 154, 181, 200–1; air raids on, in First World War, 206; Germans take, 413; liberation of, 464; Peace Conference in, 495–6

Parys, 72

Pas de Calais, 453

Patton, General, 464

Pavlov, M., 472

Peace Conference (1919), Smuts proposes programme for, 215–17; preliminary meetings of, 219–20; conduct of delegates to, 220, 224; mandates question, 220; reparations question, 223

306–7, 312–13; his love of veld, 12, 84–5, 268, 273; providential escapes of, 13–14, 67, 71–2, 77–8, 404–5, 448, 461–3; education of, 14–24, 26; memory of, 15, 19–20; courtship of, 18–19; and Rhodes, 19, 30–2, 35; religious feeling of, 19–20, 292; early writings of, 20, 22–3, 26, 28, 330; Netherlands Dutch of, 20, 47; at Cambridge, 21–4, 26; in England, 21–4, 26, 97–8, 117, 180–8, 192, 197–8, 201–10, 213, 244, 251–2, 297, 314, 344, 348–9, 431, 449–56, 458–61, 466–7, 470–1, 491–493, 505, 513, 320, 522; *Holism and Evolution* of, 22–3, 286–92, 330; amazing brain of, 23; practises Law, 23–4, 28, 36–8, 91, 121; returns to S. Africa, 24–5, 27, 27, 243–5, 488; as a youth, 25–6; visits Transvaal, 30–1; speeches of, 31–2, 112–15, 132, 188–96, 209–13, 261–5, 296–302, 306–12, 315–22, 331–8, 348–67, 377–80, 396, 423–6, 433–5, 440–9, 472, 480, 490–8, 503–4, 513; moves to Transvaal, 36; marriage of, 36–7; upholds Kruger, 37–8; State Attorney, 38–40; relations with Kruger, 39–40, 63, 98; on Milner, 43–4, 94–6; at Bloemfontein Conference, 44–5; seeks to prevent war, 45–7; *Century of Wrong* of, 47; and Churchill, 51, 204, 432; work of, in early months of war, 51; left in charge in Pretoria, 56–7; saves Government gold, 59–60; last sees Kruger, 63; guerilla campaigns of, 63 *et seq.*; Cape sortie of, 65 *et seq.*; salvaged saddlebags of, 67, 71–2; price on head of, 70, 86; books of, 72, 90, 120, 282–4; makes own reconnaissances, 72, 157, 164; poisoned by "Boesmans brood", 75; orders execution of spy, 79; at Vereeniging Peace Conference, 80–82; effects of Boer War on, 84–6; depressed spirits of, 85, 93, 197; eyes of, 86; dispatches of, 87–8; diaries of, 88; thinks in English, 88; pronunciation of, 88; defends Smit, 91; puts Boer case to Chamberlain, 92; refuses seat on Legislative Council, 92, 97–8; on Chinese Labour, 94, 100; letter of, in *Times*, 94; unpopularity of, 94–5, 119, 129, 159–160, 244–5, 253–4; gains Responsible Government for Africa, 97–8; appointed King's Counsellor, 99; works for united

S. Africa, 99–100, 107 *et seq.*, 122, 159; his partnership with Botha, 99, 101–2, 145–6; electioneering of, 99–100, 159–161; and Premiership, 100, 248; home life of, 102, 120, 268, 271–85, 397–400; Colonial Secretary and Minister of Education, 102; deals with labour unrest, 103, 131, 201–3, 250, 255–8; and Gandhi, 103, 105–7; letter of, on Union, 109–10; prepares constitution, 111–12, 116; at National Convention, 112–16; 120; and Act of Union, 117, 343; lunches with King, 117; and bonus for Transvaal Members of Parliament, 117; approaches Hertzog, 119; Minister of Mines, Defence and Interior, 119; his friendship with Botha, 119, 243–4; farms of, 120–2, 269–70, 272, 274; a worker and a driver, 122, 145, 248; forms S. African Party, 122; Bills introduced by, 123–4; as a speaker, 124, 126, 132–3, 439; Minister of Defence and Finance, 126; Hertzog's attacks on, 127, 250, 258, 294–5, 323; forced to capitulate to strikers, 131; deports strike leaders, 131–3; loyal to Britain, 134–7; and de la Rey, 136, 138; Commander-in-Chief, 137, 521; attempt to ambush, 140; takes action against rebels, 140, 145; and execution of Fourie, 143–4; odium of unpopular action falls on, 145–6, 250, 254–5, 258–9; S.-W. African campaign of, 155–8; S. Africa comes first with, 160, 179–80; prevented by violence from speaking, 160, 296, 505; offered command in E. Africa, 162–3; leaves his family, 163–4; East African campaign of, 164–74, 175–6, 178–9; forewords of, 164–5, 174; malarial attacks of, 169, 175; qualities of leadership of, 170, 175; relinquishes command, 172; at Imperial Conference, 172, 179, 251; flies over Kilimanjaro, 177; sends postcards home, 177; British tributes to, 180–1, 237, 244; exploratory missions of, 182, 196–7, 225–226; writes survey of "Strategic and Military Position", 182–4; offered command in Palestine, 184–5; member of War Cabinet, 185–7, 243, 422; his admiration for Lloyd George, 187, 225; banquet in honour of, 187–8; on British

30–1, 36; effect of Jameson Raid on, 35, 40; Kruger's rule in, 37–8, 40–1; corrupt Detective Administration of, 40; Uitlanders of, 41–2, 45; ultimatum of, to Britain, 46; strategic plan of, 49; Boers fall back on, 53; despairing suggestion from 57–8, 61; Bushveld of, 61, 339; guerilla campaigns in, 63, 65; gathering of defeated Boers in, 81; representatives of, at Vereeniging, 81–2; Milner the Governor of, 89; Het Volk party in, 97, 99–100; granted self-government, 98; regains prosperity, 99, 108; election in, 99–100; language in, 102; Cullinan diamond disagreement in, 103; British loan to, 103; race discrimination in, 104; immigration laws of, 105; and Union question, 108–10; last tasks of Parliament of, 117; extinct volcano of, 121; Nationalist Party in, 129; platinum found in, 294

Transvaal Leader, 42

Transvaal Scottish, 408

Treurfontein, 141

Trichardt, Louis, 522

Trieste, 479

Tripartite Pact, 414

Tripolitania, trusteeship of, 491

Truman, President, opens San Francisco Conference, 471; makes closing speech, 482–3; plan of, for developing backward countries, 518

Trusteeship, 479

Truter, Colonel, 130, 250

"Tsalta", 325

Tsumeb, 156

Tugela, Battle of the, 53–4, 57

Tunis, 427, 430, 448

Tunisia, fighting in, 426–7

Turkey, before First World War, 152; campaigns against, 153–4, 183; Smuts favours campaign in, 203; surrender of, 208

Tweedsmuir, Lord, 90

U-boat warfare, 153, 180, 198; African coasts vulnerable to, 150, 173, 421; "un-

limited", 182; Germany prepares for, 368; victory over, 451–2

Uitlanders, franchise rights for, 33, 45–7; grievances of, 41–2; mistrust idea of Union, 108

Ukraine, 473

Ulanga River, 167

Ulster, Smuts drafts King's speech to, 251

Ulugura Mountains, 170

Ulundi, Battle of, 10

Union, Act of, 117, 123, 311; entrenched clauses of, 342–3

Uniondale, 77

Unionist Party, 161, 248; and war issue, 158; merges with S. African Party, 249

United Nations Charter, 472–3, 477, 516; Preamble to, 472, 477–8; adoption of, 482–3; Smuts on, 484

United Nations Organisation, conception of, 425; and S. African Indian problem, 106, 497–8; and S. African native problem, 304; three Great Powers at head of, 442; Smuts on, 482, 492, 500, 504, 509; site for headquarters of, 489; and S.-W. African question, 498; talk of S. African withdrawal from, 500; disagreement in, 504

United Party, 377–8; results of elections for, 371; in wartime Cabinet, 383; loses election, 510–12; nine-point charter of, 521

United States Constitution of, 111, 113; federation in, 189–90; in First World War, 197, 207; and League of Nations, 219, 221–2, 358, 411; seeks sole right to Panama Canal, 220; and reparations, 223; war debts owing to, 247; British Commonwealth and, 251, 361–2, 411, 444; Smuts lectures in, 297–9; negro problem of, 304; S. Africa buys war material in, 383; helps Britain, 407, 413; need for full participation of, in War, 410; Lend-Lease Act of, 410, 413; exchanges destroyers for bases, 413–14; enters War, 418, 424–5; sends tanks to N. Africa, 417, 420; impatient for European landing, 422; bias of, towards Far East, 422, 450; slowly gets geared for war, 437–8; World Power of, 444–5, 517; supplies to Russia from, 452; Britain differs from, as to conduct of European fighting, 464–7; Smuts in, for San Francisco Conference, 470; seeks strategic bases, 479; gives in to Russia, 486; does not support S. Africa, 498–9

United States Air Force, 451

United States Army, in First World War, 200–1, 207–8; in North Africa, 426–7; in France, 464; European casualties of, 477

Universe, levels in evolution of, 319; relationship of life to, 319–21; holistic, 321–2

Upington, 137–8

Usambara Mountains, 166–8

Utrecht, 65

Vaal River, 68, 142

Van der Bijl, Dr. H. J., 382, 515

Van der Byl, Major Piet, 510

Van der Byl, Mrs. A. J., 260

Van Deventer, Sir Jacobus, in Cape sortie, 66–7, 70, 76–8; dispatch to, 87; in S.-W. African campaign, 157; in E. African campaign, 168, 170, 172–3

Van Rensburg, Dr. J. Hans, 129, 386, 516; Van Rensburg, Nicholaas, prophecy of, 136; surrender of, 145

Van Rensburg party on Great Trek, 522

Van Rhynsdorp, 66, 77–9

Van Riet Lowe, Mr., 336

Van Rooisvlei, 138

Van Ryneveld, General Sir Pierre, 206, 394; narrow escape of, 404, 463; reaches retiring age, 514

Van Zyl, Rt. Hon. G. Brand, 487

Vandenberg, Senator, 478–9

Vechtkop, 68

Venizelos, M., 152, 219

Ventersdorp, 100

Vereeniging, 65, 67; Conference at, 80–2

Versailles, Peace Conference at (see Peace Conference)

Versailles, Treaty of, 375; holds germ of next war, 153, 227; Smuts criticises terms of, 227; violates Fourteen Points, 229; signing of, 231, 234; and disarmament of Germany, 300–1

Vet River, 68

Veto, the, 468, 479, 481, 504

Victoria College, Stellenbosch, 15–16, 18–20

Victoria Falls, 339, 398

Victoria Nyanza, Lake, 168

Vienna, capture of, 469; Russia and, 476

Viljoen, Ben, 57

Villiers, Baron de (Sir Henry), 108–9, 111–112, 120

Vischrivier, 88

Volkstem, on Smuts as speaker, 133

Von Lettow Vorbeck, General, in E. Africa, 162, 165, 179; Smuts's tribute to, 173; dinner in honour of, 178; and post-War Germany, 346, 368

Voortrekker Monument at Pretoria, 522

Vrededorp, 126

Vredefort, 67

Vries, Bodewyn de, 7

Vries, Jan Christian, 6

Wakkerstroom, 267

Wales, South, Smuts prevents coal strikes in, 201–3

Walfish Bay, 156

Walton, Sir Edgar, on Smuts at National Convention, 112–15

War Cabinet, Smuts and, 184–7, 213, 422, 432; and Passchendaele plan, 198–9; and German secret weapon, 432–3

War Priorities Committee, 204

Warsaw, 393

Waschbank Mountains, 70

Washington, Smuts asked to address Senate and Congress in, 482–3

Washington Treaties (1922), 360–1

Waterberg, the, 63